SOMETHING ABOUT THE AUTHOR®

Something about
the Author *was named
an "Outstanding
Reference Source,"
the highest honor given
by the American
Library Association
Reference and Adult
Services Division.*

ISSN 0276-816X

SOMETHING ABOUT THE AUTHOR®

**Facts and Pictures about Authors
and Illustrators of Books for Young People**

volume 132

GALE®

Detroit • New York • San Diego • San Francisco • Cleveland • New Haven, Conn. • Waterville, Maine • London • Munich

THOMSON

GALE

Something about the Author, Volume 132

Project Editor
Scot Peacock

Editorial
Karen V. Abbott, Katy Balcer, Frank Castronova, Sara Constantakis, Anna Marie Dahn, Alana Joli Foster, Madeline Harris, Arlene M. Johnson, Michelle Kazensky, Julie Keppen, Jennifer Kilian, Joshua Kondek, Lisa Kumar, Marie Lazzari, Thomas McMahon, Jenai Mynatt, Judith L. Pyko, Mary Ruby, Anita Sundaresan, Maikue Vang, Denay L. Wilding, Thomas Wiloch

Research
Michelle Campbell, Nicodemus Ford, Sarah Genik, Barbara McNeil, Tamara C. Nott, Gary J. Oudersluys, Tracie A. Richardson, Cheryl L. Warnock

Permissions
Debra Freitas, Lori Hines

Imaging and Multimedia
Dean Dauphinais, Robert Duncan, Leitha Etheridge-Sims, Mary K. Grimes, Lezlie Light, Michael Logusz, Dan Newell, David G. Oblender, Christine O'Bryan, Kelly A. Quin, Luke Rademacher

Manufacturing
Stacy L. Melson

LIBRARY OF CONGRESS CATALOG CARD NUMBER 72-27107

ISBN 0-7876-5204-0
ISSN 0276-816X

Contents

Authors in Forthcoming Volumes

Below are some of the authors and illustrators that will be featured in upcoming volumes of *SATA*. These include new entries on the swiftly rising stars of the field, as well as completely revised and updated entries (indicated with *) on some of the most notable and best-loved creators of books for children.

*Cecil Bødker: An award-winning young adult and adult novelist, short story writer, and poet, Bødker is best known in the English-speaking world for her series of "Silas" books and *The Leopard.* Born in Denmark, she has received the Hans Christian Andersen Award.

Shana Corey: Corey, an editor at Random House, is the author of several books for young readers, including the popular "First Graders from Mars" series, as well as *You Forgot Your Skirt, Amelia Bloomer,* a send-up of the proper nineteenth-century world of heavily clothed women.

*Crescent Dragonwagon: The author of award-winning cookbooks, an acclaimed adult novel, and numerous books for children, Dragonwagon is a popular speaker and lecturer to both students and teachers alike. Among her most notable books for younger readers are *Half a Moon and One Whole Star, I Hate My Brother Harry,* and *Home Place.* Dragonwagon published *Sack of Potatoes* in 2002.

Elizabeth Gómez: Gómez is a Mexican painter who lives in San Francisco, California. Specializing in oil painting on a variety of surfaces, she focuses on animals, women, and personal history for thematic material. Gómez has illustrated two children's books by well-known Latino poets, Juan Felipe Herrera's bilingual story of his childhood, *The Upside Down Boy,* and Jorge Argueta's bilingual poem/memories of his youth in El Salvador and San Francisco, *A Movie in My Pillow.*

*Ann Grifalconi: Since the mid-1960s, Grifalconi has expanded children's literature by presenting realistic characters from other cultures. Her Caldecott Honor Book *The Village of Round and Square Houses* is just one of her works that tells of African village life and traditions. Grifalconi has also written about the Mexican and Mayan peoples and has been a pioneer in the portrayal of African American children, both with her own books and with her illustrations for others. In 2002 she published *The Village That Vanished,* a self-illustrated work.

David Lubar: Lubar is a former video-game designer and programmer who created Frogger and Frogger II for GameBoy. Now a full-time writer, his young adult novels are a blend of humor and horror that reviewers often recommend for reluctant readers. *Hidden Talents* was named an American Library Association Best Book for Young Adults.

Sophie Masson: Masson, who was born in Indonesia but lives in Australia, is a writer of fairy tales and novels for young adults that have earned critical acclaim for the depth of their historical detail. Amidst settings that range from medieval France to a modern-day drama club, Masson's characters all struggle with their self-identity and seek to forge closer ties with others. Her "Starmaker" series includes *Serafin, The First Day,* and *Malkin.*

*Katherine Paterson: A prolific, popular author who is considered among the most accomplished of contemporary writers for the young, Paterson creates fiction and nonfiction for children and young adults that reflect her personal background and Christian beliefs while successfully exploring universal subjects and themes. The winner of two Newbery Medals and two National Book Awards, among other prizes, Paterson has written several books that are considered classics of their genres. She is perhaps best known as the author of *Bridge to Terabithia,* the first of her Newbery winners.

C. D. Payne: Payne is the creator of the cult favorite "Nick Twisp" novels for teens, *Youth in Revolt* and *Revolting Youth.* Payne's reckless but brilliant teen hero moves from one fictional crisis to another, but always triumphs over his numerous adversaries in the end. The first book was self-published, and soon developed an enthusiastic following among teen and adult readers alike.

*Marjorie Weinman Sharmat: Sharmat writes humorous picture books, easy readers, and novels for children and young adults. She has published more than twenty titles in her popular "Nate the Great" series, some of them coauthored with various members of her family, including husband Mitchell and son Craig. *Nate the Great: San Francisco Detective* appeared in 2000.

*Jozef Wilkon: For more than thirty years Wilkon's art has graced books for both children and adults. In his native Poland and abroad he has won acclaim for his ability to evoke wonder in his illustrations, earning numerous awards throughout Europe and beyond. His work encompasses both straightforward narrative art and more symbolic approaches, and his media vary as well, including pastel, watercolor, gouache, and ink. In 2002 he published the self-illustrated work *Frau Droselmann.*

Introduction

Something about the Author (SATA) is an ongoing reference series that examines the lives and works of authors and illustrators of books for children. *SATA* includes not only well-known writers and artists but also less prominent individuals whose works are just coming to be recognized. This series is often the only readily available information source on emerging authors and illustrators. You'll find *SATA* informative and entertaining, whether you are a student, a librarian, an English teacher, a parent, or simply an adult who enjoys children's literature.

What's Inside SATA

SATA provides detailed information about authors and illustrators who span the full time range of children's literature, from early figures like John Newbery and L. Frank Baum to contemporary figures like Judy Blume and Richard Peck. Authors in the series represent primarily English-speaking countries, particularly the United States, Canada, and the United Kingdom. Also included, however, are authors from around the world whose works are available in English translation. The writings represented in *SATA* include those created intentionally for children and young adults as well as those written for a general audience and known to interest younger readers. These writings cover the entire spectrum of children's literature, including picture books, humor, folk and fairy tales, animal stories, mystery and adventure, science fiction and fantasy, historical fiction, poetry and nonsense verse, drama, biography, and nonfiction.

Obituaries are also included in *SATA* and are intended not only as death notices but also as concise overviews of people's lives and work. Additionally, each edition features newly revised and updated entries for a selection of *SATA* listees who remain of interest to today's readers and who have been active enough to require extensive revisions of their earlier biographies.

New Autobiography Feature

Beginning with Volume 103, *SATA* features two or more specially commissioned autobiographical essays in each volume. These unique essays, averaging about ten thousand words in length and illustrated with an abundance of personal photos, present an entertaining and informative first-person perspective on the lives and careers of prominent authors and illustrators profiled in *SATA*.

Two Convenient Indexes

In response to suggestions from librarians, *SATA* indexes no longer appear in every volume but are included in alternate (odd-numbered) volumes of the series, beginning with Volume 57.

SATA continues to include two indexes that cumulate with each alternate volume: the Illustrations Index, arranged by the name of the illustrator, gives the number of the volume and page where the illustrator's work appears in the current volume as well as all preceding volumes in the series; the Author Index gives the number of the volume in which a person's biographical sketch, autobiographical essay, or obituary appears in the current volume as well as all preceding volumes in the series.

These indexes also include references to authors and illustrators who appear in Gale's *Yesterday's Authors of Books for Children, Children's Literature Review,* and *Something about the Author Autobiography Series.*

Easy-to-Use Entry Format

Whether you're already familiar with the *SATA* series or just getting acquainted, you will want to be aware of the kind of information that an entry provides. In every *SATA* entry the editors attempt to give as complete a picture of the person's life and work as possible. A typical entry in *SATA* includes the following clearly labeled information sections:

- *PERSONAL:* date and place of birth and death, parents' names and occupations, name of spouse, date of marriage, names of children, educational institutions attended, degrees received, religious and political affiliations, hobbies and other interests.

- *ADDRESSES:* complete home, office, electronic mail, and agent addresses, whenever available.

- *CAREER:* name of employer, position, and dates for each career post; art exhibitions; military service; memberships and offices held in professional and civic organizations.

- *AWARDS, HONORS:* literary and professional awards received.

- *WRITINGS:* title-by-title chronological bibliography of books written and/or illustrated, listed by genre when known; lists of other notable publications, such as plays, screenplays, and periodical contributions.

- *ADAPTATIONS:* a list of films, television programs, plays, CD-ROMs, recordings, and other media presentations that have been adapted from the author's work.

- *WORK IN PROGRESS:* description of projects in progress.

- *SIDELIGHTS:* a biographical portrait of the author or illustrator's development, either directly from the biographee—and often written specifically for the *SATA* entry—or gathered from diaries, letters, interviews, or other published sources.

- *BIOGRAPHICAL AND CRITICAL SOURCES:* cites sources quoted in "Sidelights" along with references for further reading.

- *EXTENSIVE ILLUSTRATIONS:* photographs, movie stills, book illustrations, and other interesting visual materials supplement the text.

How a SATA Entry Is Compiled

A *SATA* entry progresses through a series of steps. If the biographee is living, the *SATA* editors try to secure information directly from him or her through a questionnaire. From the information that the biographee supplies, the editors prepare an entry, filling in any essential missing details with research and/or telephone interviews. If possible, the author or illustrator is sent a copy of the entry to check for accuracy and completeness.

If the biographee is deceased or cannot be reached by questionnaire, the *SATA* editors examine a wide variety of published sources to gather information for an entry. Biographical and bibliographic sources are consulted, as are book reviews, feature articles, published interviews, and material sometimes obtained from the biographee's family, publishers, agent, or other associates.

Entries that have not been verified by the biographees or their representatives are marked with an asterisk (*).

Contact the Editor

We encourage our readers to examine the entire *SATA* series. Please write and tell us if we can make *SATA* even more helpful to you. Give your comments and suggestions to the editor:

BY MAIL: Editor, *Something about the Author,* The Gale Group, 27500 Drake Rd., Farmington Hills, MI 48331-3535.

BY TELEPHONE: (800) 877-GALE

BY FAX: (248) 699-8054

Something about the Author Product Advisory Board

The editors of *Something about the Author* are dedicated to maintaining a high standard of excellence by publishing comprehensive, accurate, and highly readable entries on a wide array of writers for children and young adults. In addition to the quality of the content, the editors take pride in the graphic design of the series, which is intended to be orderly yet inviting, allowing readers to utilize the pages of *SATA* easily and with efficiency. Despite the longevity of the *SATA* print series, and the success of its format, we are mindful that the vitality of a literary reference product is dependent on its ability to serve its users over time. As literature, and attitudes about literature, constantly evolve, so do the reference needs of students, teachers, scholars, journalists, researchers, and book club members. To be certain that we continue to keep pace with the expectations of our customers, the editors of *SATA* listen carefully to their comments regarding the value, utility, and quality of the series. Librarians, who have firsthand knowledge of the needs of library users, are a valuable resource for us. The *Something about the Author* Product Advisory Board, made up of school, public, and academic librarians, is a forum to promote focused feedback about *SATA* on a regular basis. The five-member advisory board includes the following individuals, whom the editors wish to thank for sharing their expertise:

- **Eva M. Davis,** Teen Services Librarian, Plymouth District Library, Plymouth, Michigan

- **Joan B. Eisenberg,** Lower School Librarian, Milton Academy, Milton, Massachusetts

- **Francisca Goldsmith,** Teen Services Librarian, Berkeley Public Library, Berkeley, California

- **Harriet Hagenbruch,** Curriculum Materials Center/Education Librarian, Axinn Library, Hofstra University, Hempstead, New York

- **Monica F. Irlbacher,** Young Adult Librarian, Middletown Thrall Library, Middletown, New York

- **Robyn Lupa,** Head of Children's Services, Jefferson County Public Library, Lakewood, Colorado

- **Eric Norton,** Head of Children's Services, McMillan Memorial Library, Wisconsin Rapids, Wisconsin

- **Victor L. Schill,** Assistant Branch Librarian/Children's Librarian, Harris County Public Library/Fairbanks Branch, Houston, Texas

- **Caryn Sipos,** Community Librarian, Three Creeks Community Library, Vancouver, Washington

Acknowledgments

Grateful acknowledgment is made to the following publishers, authors, and artists whose works appear in this volume.

ANDERSON, LAURIE HALSE. Anderson, Laurie Halse, photograph. Chris Whitney/Doylestown, PA. Reproduced by permission./ Anderson, Laurie Halse. From a jacket of *Fever 1793*. Simon & Schuster, 2000. Jacket illustration copyright © 2000 by Lori Earley. Reproduced by permission.

APPLEBAUM, DIANA MUIR KARTER. Applebaum, Diana Muir Karter, photograph by Bachrach, Inc. Reproduced by permission./ McCurdy, Michael, illustrator. From an illustration in *Giants in the Land,* by Diana Appelbaum. Illustrations copyright © 1993 by Michael McCurdy. Houghton Mifflin Company, 1993. Reproduced by permission of Houghton Mifflin Company.

BASH, BARBARA. Bash, Barbara, 1995, photograph. Reproduced by permission./ Bash, Barbara, illustrator. From an illustration in her *In the Heart of the Village: The World of the Indian Banyan Tree.* Copyright © 1996 by Barbara Bash. Sierra Club Books for Children, 1996. Reproduced by permission of Sierra Club Books for Children.

BAWDEN, NINA (MARY MABEY). Hyman, Trina Schart, illustrator. From a jacket of *Granny the Pag,* by Nina Bawden. Clarion Books, 1996. Jacket illustration copyright © 1996 by Trina Schart Hyman. Reproduced by permission./ Kavanagh, George, photographer. From a cover of *Afternoon of a Good Woman,* by Nina Bawden. Copyright © Nina Bawden 1976. Virago Press, 1998. Reproduced by permission on Little Brown & Company (UK) Ltd./ Thompson, Ellen, illustrator. From a jacket of *Humbug,* by Nina Bawden. Text copyright © by Nina Bawden. Clarion Books, 1992. Reproduced by permission of Houghton Mifflin Company./ Bawden, Nina, photograph. Curtis Brown Ltd. Reproduced by permission.

BLEGVAD, ERIK. Blegvad, Erik, illustrator. From an illustration *The Gammage Cup,* by Carol Kendall. Odyssey/Harcourt Young Classic, Harcourt, Inc., 2000. Copyright © 1959 by Carol Kendall. Copyright renewed 1987 by Carol Kendall. Reproduced by permission of Harcourt, Inc. This material may not be reproduced in any form or by any means without the prior written permission of the publisher./ Blegvad, Erik, illustrator. From an illustration in *The Complete Book of Dragons,* by E. Nesbit. Hamish Hamilton, 1972. Illustrations © 1972 Erik Blegvad. All rights reserved. Reproduced by permission of Erik Blegvad./ Blegvad, Erik, illustrator. From an illustration in *Bed-Knob and Broomstick,* by Mary Norton. Odyssey/Harcourt Young Classic, Harcourt Brace & Company, 1990. Copyright © 1957 by Mary Norton; renewed 1985 by Mary Norton. Reproduced by permission of Harcourt, Inc. and the illustrator./ Blegvad, Erik, illustrator. From an illustration in *The Tenth Good Thing about Barney,* by Judith Viorst. Atheneum Books for Young Readers, 1971. Drawings copyright © 1971 by Erik Blegvad. Reproduced by permission of Atheneum Books for Young Readers, an imprint of Simon & Schuster Children's Publishing Division.

BRYAN, ASHLEY F. Bryan, Ashley F., illustrator. From an illustration in her *Ashley Bryan's ABC of African American Poetry.* Aladdin Paperbacks, 2001. Illustrations copyright © 1997 by Ashley Bryan. Reproduced by permission of Atheneum Books for Young Readers, an imprint of Simon & Schuster Children's Publishing Division.

CALVERT, PATRICIA. Calvert, Patricia, photograph. Reproduced by permission of Patricia Calvert.

CARR, JAN. Carr, Jan, photograph by Elizabeth Lehmann. Reproduced by permission./ Donohue, Dorothy, illustrator. From an illustration in *Dappled Apples,* by Jan Carr. Holiday House, 2001. Illustrations copyright © 2001 by Dorothy Donohue. Reproduced by permission of Holiday House, Inc.

CLEARY, BRIAN P. Cleary, Brian P., illustration. Reproduced by permission./ Prosmitsky, Jenya, illustrator. From a cover of *Hairy, Scary, Ordinary: What is an Adjective?,* by Brian P. Cleary. Carolrhoda Books, Inc., 2000. Copyright © 2000 by Carolrhoda Books, Inc. Reproduced by permission of the publisher.

CUNNINGHAM, JULIA (WOOLFOLK). Lobel, Anita, illustrator. From an illustration in *The Stable Rat and Other Christmas Poems,* by Julia Cunningham. Greenwillow Books, 2001. Illustrations copyright © 2001 by Anita Lobel. Used by permission of HarperCollins Publishers.

CURRIE, STEPHEN. William Cochrane/Impact Visuals, photograph. From a photograph in *Adoption,* by Stephen Currie. Lucent Books, 1997. Copyright © 1997 by Lucent Books, Inc. Reproduced by permission of the photographer.

CYRUS, KURT. Cyrus, Kurt, photograph. Reproduced by permission./ Cyrus, Kurt, illustrator. From an illustration in his *Tangle Town.* Farrar Straus Giroux, New York, 1997. Copyright © 1997 by Kurt Cyrus. Reproduced by permission of Farrar, Straus and Giroux, LLC.

DALKEY, KARA (MIA). Bober, Richard, illustrator. From a cover of *Bijapur: Blood of the Goddess,* by Kara Dalkey. Tor Books, 1997. Copyright © 1997 by Kara Dalkey. Reproduced by permission./ From a jacket of *Genpei,* by Kara Dalkey. Tor Hardcover, 2000. Jacket art courtesy of Art Resource. Reproduced by permission.

DERBY, SALLY. Derby, Sally, photograph. Burgess Photography. Reproduced by permission./ Swiatkowska, Gabi, illustrator. From an illustration in *Hannah's Bookmobile Christmas,* by Sally Derby. Henry Holt and Company, 2001. Illustrations copyright © 2001 by Gabi Swiatkowska. Reprinted by permission of Henry Holt and Company, LLC.

DODD, LYNLEY (STUART). Dodd, Lynley, illustrator. From an illustration in her *Hairy Maclary's Showbusiness.* Gareth Stevens Publishing, 2001. Original © 1991 by Lynley Dodd. Reproduced by permission of the publisher./ Dodd, Lynley, illustrator. From an illustration in her *Schnitzel von Drumm's Basketwork.* Gareth Stevens Publishing, 2001. Original © 1994 by Lynley Dodd. Reproduced by permission of the publisher./ Dodd, Lynley, illustrator. From an illustration in her *Slinky Malinki.* Gareth Stevens Publishing, 2001. Original © 1990 by Lynley Dodd. Reproduced by permission of the publisher.

DONALDSON, JULIA. Donaldson, Julia, photograph by Brian Logue. Reproduced by permission.

DUEY, KATHLEEN. Dowd, Jason, illustrator. From a cover of *Evie Peach: St. Louis, 1857,* (American Diaries Series), by Kathleen Duey. Aladdin Paperbacks, 1997. Cover illustration copyright © 1997 by Jason Dowd. Reproduced by permission of Aladdin Paperbacks./ Dowd, Jason, illustrator. From a cover of *Sarah Anne Hartford: Massachusetts, 1651* (American Diaries Series), by Kathleen Duey. Aladdin Paperbacks, 1996. Cover illustration copyright © 1996 by Jason Dowd. Reproduced by permission.

EHRLICH, AMY. Ehrlich, Amy, photograph. Reproduced by permission./ Angarola, Christina, photographer. From a cover of *When I Was Your Age, Volume One: Original Stories About Growing Up,* edited by Amy Ehrlich. Candlewick Press, 2001. Cover Photograph Copyright © 2001 Christina Angarola. Reproduced by permission of the publisher Candlewick Press, Inc., Cambridge, MA.

FACKLAM, MARGERY (METZ). Long, Sylvia, illustrator. From an illustration in *Bugs for Lunch,* by Margery Facklam. Charlesbridge, 1999. Text copyright © 1999 by Margery Facklam. Illustrations copyright © 1999 by Sylvia Long. Used with permission by Charlesbridge Publishing, Inc. All rights reserved./ Facklam, Paul, illustrator. From an illustration in *Creepy, Crawly, Caterpillars,* by Margery Facklam. Little, Brown and Company, 1996. Copyright © 1996 by Margery Facklam (Text); Copyright © 1996 by Paul Facklam. By permission of Little, Brown and Company, Inc. All rights reserved./ Male, Alan, illustrator. From an illustration in *Spiders and Their Web Sites,* by Margery Facklam. Little, Brown and Company, 1999. Copyright © 2001 by Margery Facklam (Text); Copyright © 2001 by Alan Male (Illustrations). By permission of Little, Brown and Company, Inc. All rights reserved.

FARLEY, WALTER (LORIMER). Rowe, John, illustrator. From a cover of *The Young Black Stallion,* by Walter Farley and Steven Farley. Random House, 2002. Cover art copyright © 2002 by John Rowe and Steven Farley, cover illustration by John Rowe. Reproduced by permission of Random House Children's Books, a division of Random House, Inc./ Rowe, John, illustrator. From a cover of *The Black Stallion Returns,* by Walter Farley. Random House, 2002. Cover art copyright © 2002 by John Rowe. Reproduced by permission of Random House Children's Books, a division of Random House, Inc./ Farley, Walter, photograph by Tim Farley. Reprinted by permission of International Creative Management, Inc./ Ward, Keith, illustrator. From an illustration in *The Black Stallion,* by Walter Farley. Random House, 1941. Copyright, 1941, renewed 1968, by Walter Farley. Used by permission of Random House Children's Books, a division of Random House, Inc.

FLEISHER, PAUL. Hunter, Jeff, photographer. From a photograph in *Coral Reef* (Webs of Life series), by Paul Fleisher. Benchmark Books, 1998. Photographs courtesy of The Image Bank/Jeff Hunter. Reproduced by permission of the publisher./ Saunders, David O., photographer. From a photograph in *Ice Cream Treats: The Inside Scoop,* by Paul Fleisher. Carolrhoda Books, Inc., 2001. Photographs copyright © 2001 by David O. Saunders. Reproduced by permission of the publisher.

FRENCH, FIONA. French, Fiona, illustrator. From an illustration in her *Little Inchkin.* Frances Lincoln, www.franceslincoln.com, 1994. Text and illustrations copyright © Fiona French 1994. Reproduced by permission of the publisher./ French, Fiona, illustration. From an illustration in her *Lord of the Animals: A Miwok Indian Creation Myth.* The Millbrook Press, 1997. Text and illustrations copyright © Fiona French, 1997. Reproduced by permission of the publisher./ French, Fiona, illustrator. From an illustration in her *Snow White in New York.* Oxford University Press, 1986. © Fiona French 1986. Used by permission of Oxford University Press, Inc./ French, Fiona, illustrator. From an illustration in *Pepi and the Secret Names,* by Jill Paton Walsh. Frances Lincoln, www.franceslincoln.com, 1994. Illustrations copyright © Fiona French 1994. Reproduced by permission.

GERTRIDGE, ALLISON. Gertridge, Allison, photograph. Reproduced by permission.

HASKINS, JAMES S. All photographs reproduced by permission of the author.

HAUSMAN, GERALD. Hausman, Gerald, photograph by Bobbe Besold. Reproduced by permission./ Baker, Leslie, illustrator. From an illustration in *Cats of Myth: Tales from around the World,* by Gerald and Loretta Hausman. Simon & Schuster Books for Young Readers, 2000. Illustrations copyright © 2000 by Leslie Baker. Reproduced by permission of Simon & Schuster Books for Young Readers, an imprint of Simon & Schuster Children's Publishing Division.

HEIDLER, DAVID S(TEPHEN). Heidler,David S., photograph by Joseph L. Twiggs, 2002. Reproduced by permission.

HOGAN, LINDA. Hogan, Linda, photograph by Gary Isaacs. From a jacket of her *Solar Storms.* NY: Scribner, 1995. © Gary Isaacs. Reproduced by permission./ Uelsmann, Jerry, photographer. Detail from "Small Woods Where I Met Myself," 1967 by Jerry Uelsmann, in *The Woman Who Watches Over the World: A Native Memoir,* by Linda Hogan. W. W. Norton & Company, 2001. Copyright © 2001 by Linda Hogan. Jacket photograph © Jerry Uelsmann. Reproduced by permission of W.W. Norton & Company, Inc. and the artist.

HOOVER, H(ELEN) M(ARY). Hoover, H. M., photograph. Reproduced by permission of H. M. Hoover.

HUBBELL, PATRICIA. DePalma, Mary Newell, illustrator. From an illustration in *Black Earth, Gold Sun,* by Patricia Hubbell. Marshall Cavendish, 2001. Illustrations copyright 2001 © Mary Newell DePalma. Reproduced by permission of the publisher./ Flavin, Teresa, illustrator. From an illustration in *City Kids,* by Patricia Hubbell. Marshall Cavendish, 2001. Illustrations copyright © 2001 by Teresa Flavin. Reproduced by permission of the publisher.

JOHNSON, PAUL BRETT. Johnson, Paul Brett, photograph. Reproduced by permission./ Johnson, Paul Brett, illustrator. From an illustration in his adaptation of *Fearless Jack.* Margaret K. McElderry Books, 2001. Copyright © 2001 by Paul Brett Johnson. Reproduced by permission of Margaret K. McElderry Books, an imprint of Simon & Schuster Children's Publishing Division.

JUSTER, NORTON. Juster, Norton, photograph by James Gipe photography. Reproduced by permission./ Illustration, "Woman Doing Wash," courtesy of the State Historical Society of Wisconsin. From a cover of *A Woman's Place: Yesterday's Women in Rural America,* by Norton Juster. Fulcrum Publishing, 1996. Reproduced by permission of the publisher./ Schmidt, George Paul, illustrator. From a jacket of *The Dot & the Line: A Romance in Lower Mathematics,* by Norton Juster. SeaStar Books, 1963. Copyright © 1963, 2001 by Norton Juster. Cupid illustration on jacket by George Paul Schmidt. Copyright © 1963, 2001 by Norton Juster. Used by permission of SeaStar Books, a division of North-South Books, Inc., New York./ Feiffer, Jules, illustrator. From an illustration in *The Phantom Tollbooth,* by Norton Juster. Bullseye Books, 1988. Illustrations by Jules Feiffer, copyright © 1961 by Jules Feiffer. Copyright renewed 1989 by Jules Feiffer, from *The Phantom Tollbooth* by Norton Juster, illustrated by Jules Feiffer. Used by permission of Random House Children's Books, a division of Random House, Inc., and the illustrator.

KEEFER, JANICE KULYK. Keefer, Janice Kulyk, photograph. Reproduced by permission.

KETCHUM, LIZA. Anaya, Stephen, photographer. From a photograph in *The Gold Rush,* by Liza Ketchum. Little Brown and Company, 1996. Copyright © by The West Project, Inc. Reproduced by permission./ Ketchum, Liza, photograph by John Guare. Reproduced by permission.

KNIGHT, HILARY. Knight, Hilary, illustrator. From an illustration in her *Where's Wallace?* Simon & Schuster Books for Young Readers, 2000. Copyright © 1964 by Hilary Knight. Reproduced by permission of Simon & Schuster Books for Young Readers, an imprint of Simon & Schuster Children's Publishing Division.

LATTANY, KRISTIN (EGGLESTON) HUNTER. McDaniel, Jerry, illustrator. From a jacket of *Lou in the Limelight,* by Kristin Hunter. Charles Scribner's Sons, 1981. Reproduced by permission of Charles Scribner's Sons, a division of Simon & Schuster, Inc./ Hunter, Kristin, photograph by John I. Lattany. Reproduced by permission of Kristin Hunter.

LAWRENCE, MICHAEL. Ingpen, Robert, illustrator. From an illustration in *The Poppykettle Papers,* by Michael Lawrence. Pavilion Books Limited, 1999. Text © Michael Lawrence 1999, Illustrations © Robert Ingpen 1999. Reproduced by permission of Pavilion Children's Books, a division of Chrysalis Books Plc., London.

LEROUX-HUGON, HÉLÈNE. Leroux-Hugon, Hélène, illustrator. From an illustration in her *I Can Draw Polar Animals.* Gareth Stevens Publishing, 2001. U.S. edition © 2001 by Gareth Stevens, Inc. Reproduced by permission of the publisher.

MAYER, MARIANNA. Craft, Kinuko Y., illustrator. From an illustration in *The Adventures of Tom Thumb,* by Marianna Mayer. SeaStar Books, 2001. Text copyright © 2001 by Marianna Mayer. Illustrations copyright © 2001 by Kinuko Y. Craft. Used by permission of SeaStar Books, a division of North-South Books Inc., New York.

SOMETHING ABOUT THE AUTHOR

ANDERSON, Laurie Halse 1961-

Personal

"Halse" rhymes with "waltz"; born October 23, 1961, in Potsdam, NY; daughter of Frank A., Jr. (a Methodist minister) and Joyce (in management; maiden name, Holcomb) Halse; married Gregory H. Anderson (a chief executive officer), June 19, 1983; children: Stephanie, Meredith. *Education:* Onandaga County Community College, A.A., 1981; Georgetown University, B.S.L.L., 1984. *Politics:* Independent. *Religion:* Quaker. *Hobbies and other interests:* Reading, running, skiing, hiking, basketball, history, travel, genealogy.

Addresses

Home—P.O. Box 3407, Maple Glen, PA 19002-8407. *E-mail*—laurie@voicenet.com.

Career

Author.

Member

Society of Children's Book Writers and Illustrators (organizer of fall conference in Philadelphia, PA, 1994-96).

Awards, Honors

"Pick of the Lists," American Booksellers Association, 1996, for *Ndito Runs; Turkey Pox* was on recommended reading lists of Kansas State Librarians, Nevada Department of Education, Top of Texas Literature Review Center; *Speak* was a finalist for the National Book

Laurie Halse Anderson

In Anderson's historical novel set in Philadelphia, a fourteen-year-old girl relates how her life is affected by the epidemic of yellow fever that took thousands of lives in the late eighteenth century. (Cover illustration by Lori Earley.)

Award and was named Michael L. Printz Award Honor Book.

Writings

Ndito Runs, illustrated by Anita Van der Merwe, Henry Holt (New York, NY), 1996.
Turkey Pox, illustrated by Dorothy Donohue, Albert Whitman & Co. (Morton Grove, IL), 1996.
No Time for Mother's Day, illustrated by Dorothy Donohue, Albert Whitman & Co. (Morton Grove, IL), 1999.
Speak, Farrar, Straus & Giroux (New York, NY), 1999.
Fever, 1793, Simon & Schuster (New York, NY), 2000.
Saudi Arabia, Carolrhoda Books (Minneapolis, MN), 2001.
The Big Cheese of Third Street, illustrated by David Gordon, Simon & Schuster (New York, NY), 2002.
Thank You, Sarah!!!: The Woman Who Saved Thanksgiving, illustrated by Matt Faulkner, Simon & Schuster (New York, NY), 2002.
Catalyst, Viking (New York, NY), 2002.

"WILD AT HEART" SERIES

Fight for Life, American Girl (Middleton, WI), 2000.
Homeless: Sunita, American Girl (Middleton, WI), 2000.
Trickster, American Girl (Middleton, WI), 2000.
Say Good-Bye, American Girl (Middleton, WI), 2001.
Storm Rescue, American Girl (Middleton, WI), 2001.
Teacher's Pet, American Girl (Middleton, WI), 2001.
Trapped, American Girl (Middleton, WI), 2001.
Fear of Falling, American Girl (Middleton, WI), 2001.
Time to Fly, American Girl (Middleton, WI), 2002.
Race to the Finish, American Girl (Middleton, WI), 2002.
Masks, American Girl (Middleton, WI), 2002.

Sidelights

Laurie Halse Anderson writes for children and young adults, in work ranging from lighthearted folktales such as *Ndito Runs,* to earnest morality tales for the publishers of the "American Girl" series, and taut dramas for older teens, such as *Speak* and the historical thriller *Fever 1793. Speak,* a first-person narrative written in the voice of a young rape victim, was a Michael L. Printz Award Honor Book the first year the prize was awarded. In her acceptance speech, which was printed in *Booklist,* Anderson spoke of her admiration for her adolescent audience: "I love teenagers because they are honest. I love teenagers because they are raw and passionate. They think in black and white and are willing to go to extremes to defend their beliefs. I love teenagers because they are artistic. They are risk-takers. They are shape-shifters, trying on new skins, new personalities, new dreams. I love teenagers because they challenge me, and because they frustrate me. They give me hope. They give me nightmares. They are our children, and they deserve the best books we can write."

Ndito Runs, Anderson's first book, follows a young Kenyan girl as she makes her lighthearted and cheerful journey from her home to her school. She leaves her village and enters the countryside, imagining herself to be any number of animals and birds indigenous to the African savanna. Hazel Rochman comments in *Booklist,* "The simple, poetic words and the vital ... paintings express Ndito's exhilaration and her connection with nature and with people." A reviewer for *Publishers Weekly* noted: "Both narrative and art paint an appealing portrait of an unusually vivacious heroine." In *School Library Journal,* Tom S. Hurlburt asserts that few multicultural titles share "this book's melding of illustration and text."

Anderson's *Turkey Pox* tells the humorous story of young Charity who, unbeknownst to everyone in her family, wakes up with chicken pox on Thanksgiving Day as they are all preparing to drive to Nana's house to celebrate the holiday. In the car on the way there, her chicken pox are discovered, and the family returns home amidst a swirling snowstorm. Disappointed at the thought of spending her first Thanksgiving without the presence of her beloved Nana, Charity is overjoyed when Nana, accompanied by a perfectly roasted turkey, does indeed arrive at their house, courtesy of four snowplow drivers to whom she has promised dinner in exchange for a ride through the snow. In addition, Nana has managed to "dress up" the turkey skin with numerous cherries to imitate Charity's affliction, hence the "turkey pox" of the title. Carolyn Phelan noted in *Booklist,* "Featuring a satisfying story and appealing illustrations, this picture book is just right for reading aloud to classes" during both the fall holiday season and spring chicken pox season. Janice Del Negro wrote in the *Bulletin of the Center for Children's Books* that the combination of illustrations and text creates "just the right note of jolly delirium."

Turkey Pox was followed by another lightly humorous depiction of a common problem in *No Time for Mother's Day.* In this story, Charity is puzzled by what to give her tremendously busy mother for Mother's Day until it dawns on her that the best gift of all would be to turn off all the clocks and machines in the house that keep her mother so busy. "There aren't too many books about Mother's Day, so this should be a welcome addition to holiday shelves," remarked Ilene Cooper in *Booklist.*

While these picture books were widely admired, Anderson's first young adult novel, *Speak,* found her nominated for two prestigious literary awards, the National Book Award, and the newly created Michael L. Printz Award, sponsored by *Booklist* and Young Adult Library Services Association. Anderson's daughters are teenagers, and she had been reading Mary Pipher's *Reviving Ophelia,* when a nightmare of a girl screaming awoke her. That voice became the narrator of *Speak,* a girl who had become nearly mute during her freshman year in high school in the face of her ostracism by the other students who are angry at her for calling 911 during a drinking party over the summer. Melinda can hardly speak to her peers or teachers, but her narrative is bursting with language, angry, sardonic, frightened, sad, and even funny, according to reviewers. "An uncannily funny book even as it plumbs the darkness, *Speak* will hold readers from first word to last," predicted a contributor to *Horn Book.* Other reviewers focused on Anderson's deadly accurate depiction of adolescent life. According to a *Publishers Weekly* reviewer, "In a stunning first novel, Anderson uses keen observations and vivid imagery to pull readers into the head of an isolated teenager."

In yet another departure for the author, *Fever 1793* is a historical young adult novel set during a yellow fever epidemic in what was then the capital of the United States, Philadelphia. Like *Speak,* *Fever 1793* is a first-person narrative of a fourteen-year-old girl living through a trauma. In the latter novel, Matilda narrates with growing horror as an ordinarily difficult existence running a coffeehouse with her widowed mother and grandfather becomes a nightmare when the town is struck by yellow fever, killing thousands in a matter of a few months. "Anderson has carefully researched this historical event and infuses her story with rich details of time and place," remarked Frances Bradburn in *Booklist.* Others similarly praised the author, including Kathleen Isaacs, who reviewed the book for *School Library Journal,* concluding, "Readers will be drawn in by the

characters and will emerge with a sharp and graphic picture of another world."

Anderson returned to the realm of lighted-hearted picture-book romps with *The Big Cheese of Third Street,* a charming story told from the perspective of Benny Antonelli, a very small kid in a neighborhood filled with tremendously large men, women, and older kids. Benny's ability to climb is often the only thing that saves him from good-humored torture by the older kids, until the day of the neighborhood block party. Benny's triumph in climbing a greased pole to capture the cheese at the top makes him a tiny hero that any kid can relate to. "Anderson's urban tall tale is a hoot, from her cheeky take on the woes of runt-hood to her plain use of exaggeration and sassy street talk," observed a contributor to *Publishers Weekly.*

Anderson has also written a series of books for the American Girl Company called "Wild at Heart." These novels for older elementary-school students broadcast a series of adventures surrounding a veterinary clinic for which the series is named, run by Maggie's grandmother and staffed by teenage volunteers. In the first installment, *Fight for Life: Maggie,* Maggie begins to suspect there is a puppy mill in the neighborhood when a litter of ten sick puppies are brought to the clinic. "Pet lovers will identify with the young characters as well as with their strong need to solve a real problem," remarked Janie Schomberg in *School Library Journal.* The second in the series, *Homeless: Sunita,* centers on a young girl's desire for a cat of her own, despite her parents' objections and a recent outbreak of rabies among wild cats in the area. Another book in the series, *Say Good-Bye,* adds a new character, Zoe, whose volunteer work at the Wild at Heart Clinic helps her learn how to housebreak her new puppy and teaches her about therapy-pets.

Anderson once told *SATA:* "I decided to become a writer in second grade. My teacher taught us how to write haiku. The giant light bulb clicked on over my head: 'Oh, my goodness! I can do this!' I hope every second grader learns how to write haiku.

"Despite evidence to the contrary, I believe the world has an abundance of goodness. Not all children get to see this, sadly. I would like to think my books serve up some goodness—with hot fudge, whipped cream, and a cherry on top.

"After [my teacher] got me writing poetry, I spent hours and hours and hours reading every book in my school library. The books took me everywhere—ripping through time barriers, across cultures, experiencing all the magic an elementary school library can hold.

"Becoming a children's author has been an incredible privilege. The thought that some kid is reading a book of mine in the library makes me feel like I can fly. I have the coolest job in the world."

Biographical and Critical Sources

PERIODICALS

Booklist, March 15, 1996, Hazel Rochman, review of *Ndito Runs,* p. 1268; September 1, 1996, Carolyn Phelan, review of *Turkey Pox,* p. 35; February 15, 1999, Ilene Cooper, review of *No Time for Mother's Day,* p. 1073; November 15, 1999, Stephanie Zvirin, review of *Speak,* p. 18; May 1, 2000, Lauren Peterson, review of *Fight for Life,* p. 1665; October 1, 2000, Frances Bradburn, review of *Fever 1793,* p. 332; November 15, 2000, Stephanie Zvirin, review of *Speak,* p. 632; January 1, 2001, Stephanie Zvirin, "The Printz Award Revisited," p. 932; March 15, 2001, Jean Hatfield, review of *Speak,* p. 1412; April 1, 2001, Stephanie Zvirin, review of *Fever 1793,* p. 1486, 1494; December 1, 2001, Ilene Cooper, review of *The Big Cheese of Third Street,* p. 644.

Bulletin of the Center for Children's Books, November, 1996, Janice Del Negro, review of *Turkey Pox,* pp. 89-90.

Children's Book Review Service, April, 1996, p. 97.

Horn Book, September, 1999, review of *Speak,* p. 605; September, 2000, Anita L. Burkam, review of *Fever 1793,* p. 562.

Horn Book Guide, fall, 1996, p. 246.

Journal of Adolescent and Adult Literacy, March, 2000, Sally Smith, review of *Speak,* p. 585.

New York Times Book Review, November 19, 2000, Constance Decker Thompson, review of *Fever 1793,* p. 45.

New York Times Upfront, November 13, 2000, review of *Fever 1793,* p. 22.

Publishers Weekly, March 18, 1996, review of *Ndito Runs,* pp. 68-69. September 13, 1999, review of *Speak,* p. 85; December 20, 1999, Jennifer M. Brown, "In Dreams Begin Possibilities," p. 24; July 31, 2000, review of *Fever 1793,* p. 96; July 16, 2001, John F. Baker, "Laurie Halse Anderson," p. 70; November 19, 2001, review of *The Big Cheese of Third Street,* p. 67.

School Library Journal, May, 1996, Tom S. Hurlburt, review of *Ndito Runs,* p. 84; October, 1996, p. 84; April, 1999, Roxanne Burg, review of *No Time for Mother's Day,* p. 85; October, 1999, Dina Sherman, review of *Speak,* p. 144; January, 2000, Claudia Moore, review of *Speak,* p. 76; March, 2000, "Author Turns Loss into Gain," p. 109; July, 2000, Janie Schomberg, review of *Fight for Life: Maggie,* p. 100; August, 2000, Kathleen Isaacs, review of *Fever 1793,* p. 177; December, 2000, Ronni Krasnow, review of *Homeless: Sunita,* p. 138; January, 2001, Carol Johnson Shedd, review of *Saudi Arabia,* p. 112; March, 2001, Tina Hudak, review of *Fever 1793,* p. 84; July, 2001, Jennifer Ralston, review of *Say Good-Bye,* p. 102; February, 2002, Genevoeve Gallagher, review of *The Big Cheese of Third Street,* p. 96.

OTHER

Laurie Halse Anderson Web Site, http://www.writerlady.com (December 11, 2001).*

APPELBAUM, Diana Muir Karter 1953- (Diana Muir)

Personal

Born November 9, 1953, in Fort Belvoir, VA; daughter of Peter (an engineer) and Elizabeth Carmen (a medical records librarian; maiden name, Whitman) Karter; married Paul Stuart Appelbaum (a psychiatrist), March 31, 1974; children: Binyamin Chaim, Yonatan Asher, Avigail Fruma. *Education:* Barnard College, A.B. (cum laude), 1975. *Politics:* Democrat. *Religion:* Jewish.

Addresses

Home—100 Berkshire Rd., Newton, MA 02460. *E-mail*—DianaMuir@aol.com.

Career

Writer. Public speaker; guest on radio programs, including *Voice of America* and National Public Radio's *Morning Edition* and *The Connection,* and on television programs for the History Channel.

Awards, Honors

Notable Book of the Year, American Library Association, and Top of the List (youth), *Booklist,* both 1994, both for *Giants in the Land;* Book of the Year finalist, Boston Author's Club, Best Books of 2000 citation, Vermont Book Professionals Association, both 2000, and Massachusetts Books Award, 2001, all for *Reflections in Bullough's Pond.*

Writings

Thanksgiving: An American Holiday, an American History, Facts on File (New York, NY), 1984.
The Glorious Fourth: An American Holiday, an American History, Facts on File (New York, NY), 1989.
Cocoa Ice (for children), illustrated by Holly Meade, Orchard Books (New York, NY), 1989.
Giants in the Land (for children), illustrated by Michael McCurdy, Houghton Mifflin (Boston, MA), 1993.
(Under name Diana Muir) *Reflections in Bullough's Pond: Economy and Ecosystem in New England,* University Press of New England (Hanover, NH), 2000.

Contributor of book reviews to the *Boston Globe* and the *Christian Science Monitor.*

Sidelights

Diana Muir Karter Appelbaum has written several works of history and books aimed at children. Under her given name, Diana Muir, she published the environmental chronicle *Reflections in Bullough's Pond: Economy and Ecosystem in New England.* It "seems a good name for a writer on environmental history," she said. Appelbaum's first book was *Thanksgiving: An American Holiday, an*

American History, of which she told *SATA:* "*Thanksgiving* was the first complete history of the holiday ever written. It overturned widely held misconceptions about where the holiday began (not in Plymouth, Massachusetts) and when it became a national holiday (several decades earlier and in a different manner than reported in most encyclopedias). Although the history of the Fourth of July traced in *The Glorious Fourth* does begin, as expected, in Philadelphia, Pennsylvania, in 1776, the book goes on to show that the celebration took some unexpected turns in the Federal and Progressive eras. Like *Thanksgiving, The Glorious Fourth* is the first full history of an important American holiday."

Appelbaum's books for children include *Giants in the Land,* about the trade in timber that formed a large part of colonial America's economy, and *Cocoa Ice,* which explains nineteenth-century trade between Maine and Santo Domingo through the eyes of two young girls. *Giants in the Land* notes how the huge white pines—200 feet tall or more—have disappeared, harvested in colonial New England to build British warships, but Appelbaum expresses optimism that new giants will replace them. Her writing style is "vigorous and robust" and her subject matter important, commented *Horn Book* reviewer Ellen Fader, while a *Publishers Weekly* critic praised Appelbaum's "wealth ... of well-presented facts." Both also praised Michael McCurdy's black-and-white illustrations of the towering trees. In *Cocoa Ice,* two girls learn about each other and their disparate cultures through trade. One is the niece of a Maine sea captain who takes ice south to Santo Domingo to exchange for cocoa beans; the other is a member of a Santo Domingo family that raises the crop. A *Kirkus Reviews* contributor described the book as "a tasty treat" with "marvelous images" by Holly Meade. *Booklist*'s Lauren Peterson remarked that "the first-person narrative is flawless, with each girl's fresh, authentic voice weaving a fascinating tale."

Reflections in Bullough's Pond, written under the name Diana Muir, details the environmental impact of New England's economic development since colonial times and uses as its motif a pond near the author's home in Newton, Massachusetts. New England, she says, has been pushed beyond its environmental boundaries: its soil has been worn out by over-farming, its streams have been dammed up to provide power for industry, and both land and water have been polluted by commerce's by-products. In the opinion of *Conservation Matters* reviewer Debra Simes, the book is "a rich romp through New England's history," providing "historic context and precedent for many of the crises New England (and the world) encounters today: habitat destruction, overexploitation of resources, industrial pollution of air, water, and soil." She continued, "Muir contends that New Englanders' particular problem-solving bent has repeatedly rescued the region from starvation and economic ruin. But she does not permit us to rest in the naive hope that this alone can save us from ourselves in a dramatically changed world." Simes reported that the author does not make unrealistic demands for a return to an agrarian past but instead calls for a future in which a common societal

Diana Muir Karter Appelbaum

recognition of the environment's importance supersedes the profit motive. Simes further praised Muir's use of Bullough's Pond "as touchstone for her connection to the historical material, and as local lens through which to sample the mutual impacts that ecosystem and humankind have weathered. She does it beautifully."

Jan Zita Grover, writing in the *Women's Review of Books,* commented on Muir's treatment of broad social issues interlaced with her own family history. "This intricate interweaving of seemingly unrelated human activities, ecosystem's responses, and human reactions to these responses, is the strength of *Bullough's Pond,*" noted Grover. Pointing to the vast scope of the book, reviewer Jane Knodell observed for *EH.NET Book Reviews:* "Its contribution is to weave disparate social and natural scientific literatures together into a well-written, interesting narrative. This is history made palpable and personal, written by one who has hiked New England's mountains and wandered along its beaches." In his review for the *Maine Sunday Telegram,* Joel Appel described *Reflections in Bullough's Pond* as "an engaging, continually surprising book, with the narrative momentum of compelling fiction and the historian's passion for getting it right." A *Publishers Weekly* critic had positive words as well, observing, "Mountains of research power this book, while Muir's direct yet conversational tone distinguishes it; the titular pond ... gives the book's lyrical bits a visual center, while her politics tint its prose a shade of green." When asked by interviewer Rebecca Brown of *RebeccasReads* where she found important clues in writing *Bullough's Pond,* the author replied: "The clues that make books of nonfiction exciting to read are all right there in the library waiting for a storyteller to come along and put then into the right canvas."

Appelbaum told *SATA:* "My family was in the habit of taking spare surnames that were hanging around on the family tree and giving them to innocent babies, so they named me Diana Muir Karter. The Muir came from some of my mother's ancestors who had come from Scotland and brought their name with them. Because I have a very nice first name, I think that I did rather well. After all, among my relatives are people whose *first* names are Machado, Hunter, Andrews, and Karter. Karter is still a baby. He is the son of my first cousin and is named for my father, who is a wonderful man.

"About 1970, Dad, who learned to be an engineer at West Point, noticed two things. The first was that the planet was in trouble because people were using

Giants in the Land, *Appelbaum's picture book about the colonial timber trade, tells the story of the now-extinct huge white pines harvested in New England to build British warships. (Illustrated by Michael McCurdy.)*

resources wastefully. The second was that my Mom and my sisters were spending weekend afternoons gathering up glass bottles, driving them to a huge metal bin near the Town Hall, and throwing them into the bin one at a time so that they would break into small pieces. Dad figured that there had to be a better way, so he invented one.

"He founded a recycling company that gathered up discarded paper, glass containers, and cans. Since so little recycling was being done when he founded his company, he also invented and patented a number of machines to do things like smash bottles into small pieces. Smashing one bottle is easy, but since glass has sharp edges, making a machine that can smash up millions of bottles is hard. The problem is that glass is so sharp the edges of the broken pieces will wear out most machines in a very short time. Even when the machines are made of hard steel.

"By the time my own children were growing up, Dad had a big company with recycling plants in many cities. When my children were small, they liked to go to one of Granddad's factories with him. Dad would climb into a forklift and put one of my children on his lap. Then he would let them operate the levers as the forklift drove up to a big pile of recycled material and lifted a pallet of cardboard boxes or a bale of shredded aluminum cans high into the air and loaded it onto a truck.

"I was the second in a family of four daughters. My oldest sister, Jean Gulliver, is the chairwoman of the State Board of Education in Maine. She has four children of her own, but she spends a lot of time figuring out ways to run better schools for children in Maine and other places. My book *Giants in the Land* is dedicated to Jean's youngest daughter, Jeanie.

"The third sister is an artist who paints very beautiful pictures. Some famous art galleries have hung her paintings on their walls. Her name is Patricia Whitman Karter. (Well, Whitman was just hanging there on the family tree, so Mom and Dad decided to put it to work.) Tricia wanted to be an artist and she wanted to run a business, so she studied at the Art Student's League and at Yale Business School. She is the founder and president of a company called Dancing Deer that makes the very best cookies in the whole world. I know that they are the best because Tricia's two children are cookie experts. Tricia drew the pictures of deer dancing on the packages.

"My youngest sister is called Liddy even though she was named Elizabeth. She did a lot of things when she was young that she doesn't want her son to know about. None of it was bad, just very dangerous. Like the summer she spent with a touring motorcycle stunt team. They were all French except Liddy, who was practicing her French and the country that they were touring was France. They would drive through town four motorcycles abreast. Three men would be standing on the shoulders of the four who were riding. Two men would stand on the shoulders of the three standing on the shoulders of the four who were riding. Liddy did a handstand on the shoulders of the top two. Mom and Dad thought she was in Paris practicing French verbs. She went to Barnard College and Yale Business School and after working on Wall Street came home to run the recycling company with Dad.

"Hmmm. Four daughters growing up in a New England town. Their father was off fighting a war when they were young. The oldest got married and had kids. The second was a bookworm. The third a talented artist. The name of the youngest, Elizabeth.

"One more thing about names. They can cause all sorts of trouble.

"I am married to a wonderful man. We met when we were both in college. He was at Columbia College, which was an all-boys school back then. I was at Barnard College, which is across the street and is an all-girls school. His name is Paul Appelbaum.

"When I started to write books I signed my name Diana Appelbaum. People had trouble spelling it. Everyone knows, after all, that apple is spelled A-P-P-L-E. It is very hard for people to remember to switch the e and the l. I was used to this, because I grew up with the name Karter, and everyone always wanted to spell it Carter. That, after all, is the way Carter is usually spelled. Being used to a problem, however, doesn't make the problem go away. Many indexes have my books listed in two places, some spelled el and some spelled le. That is why I decided to use the name my parents gave me.

"Diana Muir is easy to spell. And there is another advantage. I write about nature and people who like to read about nature like the name Muir because a hundred years ago there lived a wonderful writer named John Muir. He loved nature and he wrote about it so beautifully that he inspired Americans to set the Yosemite valley aside as a National Park. He also helped found a club for people who loved nature and hiking. The Sierra Club still leads the way as more and more Americans realize the importance of protecting our natural resources. A friend who admired John Muir's writing and the work that he had done in teaching Americans to see the importance of natural places set aside a beautiful valley just north of San Francisco in his honor. It is called Muir Woods and if you go there you can walk among giant redwood trees and even see young redwoods. Someday they will grow to be giant trees that our great-great-great-grandchildren will walk among."

Biographical and Critical Sources

PERIODICALS

Booklist, November 1, 1997, Lauren Peterson, review of *Cocoa Ice,* p. 466.
Conservation Matters, summer, 2000, Debra Simes, review of *Reflections in Bullough's Pond,* p. 34.
Horn Book, January-February, 1994, Ellen Fader, review of *Giants in the Land,* p. 83.
Kirkus Reviews, August 1, 1997, review of *Cocoa Ice.*
Maine Sunday Telegram, July 23, 2000, Joe Appel, "How One Pond's Ripples Rocked New England."
Publishers Weekly, August 2, 1993, review of *Giants in the Land,* p. 81; April 24, 2000, review of *Reflections in Bullough's Pond,* p. 77.
Women's Review of Books, January, 2001, Jan Zita Grover, "Laws of Nature."

OTHER

EH.NET Book Reviews, http://www2.eh.net/ (May, 2001), Jane Knodell, review of *Reflections in Bullough's Pond.*
RebeccasReads, http://rebeccasreads.com/ (October 1, 2000), Rebecca Brown, "Rebecca's eInterview with Diana Muir, Author of *Reflections in Bullough's Pond.*"

B

BASH, Barbara 1948-

Personal

Born October 20, 1948, in Barrington, IL; daughter of Philip and Flora Bash; married Steve Gorn (a musician), October 23, 1988; children: Wiley Gorn. *Ethnicity:* "White." *Education:* Attended University of Michigan and Antioch College. *Religion:* Buddhist. *Hobbies and other interests:* Illustrated journals.

Addresses

Home—72 Cherry Hill Rd., Accord, NY 12404; fax: 845-687-1116. *E-mail*—bash@ulster.net.

Career

Author and illustrator, 1972—. Taught book arts at Naropa University in Boulder, CO, 1980-90. Teacher of brush calligraphy and field sketching in workshops throughout the United States and Canada. Calligraphic performance art presented at theaters and conferences.

Awards, Honors

Reading Rainbow featured book, and Texas Bluebonnet Award Master List selection, both 1990, and Outstanding Science Trade Books for Children selection, National Science Teachers Association/Children's Book Council (NSTA/CBC), all for *Desert Giant: The World of the Saguaro Cactus;* John Burroughs List of Nature Books for Young Readers selection, and Outstanding Science Trade Books for Children selection, NSTA/CBC, both 1990, Texas Bluebonnet Award Master List selection, 1991, *Reading Rainbow* featured book, 1992, and Teachers' Choice selection, International Reading Association, all for *Urban Roosts: Where Birds Nest in the City;* Texas Bluebonnet Award Master List selection, 1993, for *Shadows of Night: The Hidden World of a Little Brown Bat* and *Ancient Ones: The World of the Old Growth Douglas Fir; Riverbank Review* Books of Distinction selection, 2001, and Outstanding Science

Barbara Bash

Trade Book for Children selection, NSTA/CBC, 2002, both for *Dig, Wait, Listen: A Desert Toad's Tale.*

Writings

SELF-ILLUSTRATED

Desert Giant: The World of the Saguaro Cactus, Sierra Club Books for Children (San Francisco, CA), 1989.

Tree of Life: The World of the African Baobab, Sierra Club Books for Children (San Francisco, CA), 1989.

Urban Roosts: Where Birds Nest in the City, Sierra Club Books for Children (San Francisco, CA), 1990.

Shadows of Night: The Hidden World of a Little Brown Bat, Sierra Club Books for Children (San Francisco, CA), 1993.

Ancient Ones: The World of the Old Growth Douglas Fir, Sierra Club Books for Children (San Francisco, CA), 1994.

In the Heart of the Village: The World of the Indian Banyan Tree, Sierra Club Books for Children (San Francisco, CA), 1996.

ILLUSTRATOR

Joan Stone, *A Letter to Myself to Water,* Press at Colorado College (Colorado Springs, CO), 1981.

Elizabeth Ring, *Tiger Lilies and Other Beastly Plants,* Walker & Co. (New York, NY), 1984.

Ron Hirschi, *Forest,* Bantam Books (New York, NY), 1991.

Ron Hirschi, *Ocean,* Bantam Books (New York, NY), 1992.

Ron Hirschi, *Desert,* Bantam Books (New York, NY), 1992.

Ron Hirschi, *Mountain,* Bantam Books (New York, NY), 1992.

Jonathan London, *Phantom of the Prairie: Year of the Black-Footed Ferret,* Sierra Club Books for Children (San Francisco, CA), 1998.

April Pulley Sayre, *Dig, Wait, Listen: A Desert Toad's Tale,* Greenwillow (New York, NY), 2001.

Lola M. Schaefer, *What's Up, What's Down?,* Greenwillow (New York, NY), 2002.

Sidelights

Barbara Bash is known for creating picture books on nature topics that capture the imagination of older and younger children alike. Simple texts explain the wonders of nature while meticulously detailed paintings capture the hearts and minds of readers. In her first book for youngsters, *Desert Giant: The World of the Saguaro Cactus,* Bash captures the life cycle of this Southwestern plant and its important role in the ecosystem of the desert, while *Tree of Life: The World of the African Baobab,* published in 1990, set the standard for Bash's later books. Here, Bash begins with the legend of how the baobab, a tree that can live a thousand years, came to be, and then focuses in on the wide variety of life that lives within its branches and flourishes in its shade. Then Bash describes the death of a baobab and depicts a new seedling springing to life in its shadow. "One of nature's great lessons is recreated dramatically in this stirring book," concluded a critic in *Publishers Weekly.*

In 1994, Bash published another book about a famous tree, the Douglas fir, a famed feature of the North American continent. In *Ancient Ones: The World of the Old-Growth Douglas Fir,* Bash shifts her focus from the old-growth forests of the Pacific Northwest to the creatures large and small for whom the tree is their natural habitat. Bash's illustrations make room for

Bash recounts an Indian legend about the creation of the banyan tree and offers a wealth of information on Indian village culture in her self-illustrated picture book. (From In the Heart of the Village.)

calligraphic insets highlighting various creatures, and the book ends, like *Tree of Life,* with an affirmation of the life cycle as the trees are felled and new ones planted. Deborah Abbott, who reviewed *Ancient Ones* for *Booklist,* remarked: "In Bash's stunning new book, the complex life of these trees becomes an ecology lesson wrapped in a miracle of natural wonder."

Bash turned to the city for her subject in *Urban Roosts: Where Birds Nest in the City.* In this book, the author focuses on the nesting habits of many of the birds that are commonly seen in urban environments. Here again the author was praised for infusing a natural history lesson with added interest through the clarity of her text and the drama of her illustrations. "Bash's accurately drawn pictures help to disseminate the information smoothly and will be remembered long after they are seen," contended a contributor to *Publishers Weekly.* This critic also remarked that the knowledge young readers gain from *Urban Roosts* may help boost the level of respect children are likely to show these creatures. A similar impetus is at the heart of Bash's *Shadows of the Night: The Hidden World of the Little Brown Bat.* In this book, Bash describes a year in the life of the most common type of bat and helps demystify the behavior and biology of these reclusive creatures. "Luminous watercolors and lively information ... present the world's only flying mammals in a sympathetic, even endearing light," remarked a contributor to _Publishers Weekly._

In _In the Heart of the Village: The World of the Indian Banyan Tree,_ Bash again places a tree of legendary proportions in the context of the creatures who depend upon it for their lives. As in _Tree of Life,_ Bash helps establish the setting of _In the Heart of the Village_ by recounting an Indian legend about the creation of the banyan. Her paintings, which show a banyan in a village in India from one sunrise to the next, emphasize the importance of the tree to both animal and human life. The wealth of information on Indian village culture is considered a welcome bonus to Bash's usual focus on the world of animals. Karen Morgan, writing in _Booklist,_ predicted reader appeal would span the grades as "the lively narrative makes it good for reading aloud" and there is enough detailed information about people and animals to capture the interest of older children.

Bash has also illustrated numerous books for others, including _Phantom of the Prairie,_ a fictional story in which a young black-footed ferret grows up on the prairie and eventually leaves her first home to make a residence of her own. _Booklist_ contributor Kay Weisman remarked that "[author Jonathan] London's vivid text and Bash's vibrant artwork convey much information about the life cycle and habits of this rarest of the North American mammals." April Pulley Sayre's _Dig, Wait, Listen: A Desert Toad's Tale,_ like Bash's own narratives, brings drama to a natural history lesson, this time on the life cycle of the spadefoot toad, who must wait for the rains to come before she can emerge from her hole in the ground, mate, and lay her eggs in a short-lived puddle, where they will hatch.

Bash told _SATA:_ "My books have taken me to many interesting places. It is fascinating to travel and explore in this way. It is essential that I capture the freshness of a place by sitting still and observing it and drawing it. Then something true and alive and personal can come through in my work."

Biographical and Critical Sources

PERIODICALS

Booklist, December 15, 1992, Carolyn Phelan, review of _Desert_ and _Mountain,_ p. 739; April 15, 1993, Janice Del Negro, review of _Shadows of the Night,_ p. 1507; September 15, 1994, Deborah Abbott, review of _Ancient Ones,_ p. 128; September 15, 1996, Karen Morgan, review of _In the Heart of the Village,_ p. 234; July, 1998, Kay Weisman, review of _Phantom of the Prairie,_ p. 1886.

Horn Book, March-April, 1989, Elizabeth S. Watson, review of _Desert Giant,_ p. 223; January-February, 1990, Ellen Fader, review of _Tree of Life,_ p. 85; January-February, 1991, Elizabeth S. Watson, review of _Urban Roosts,_ p. 81; July-August, 1993, Elizabeth S. Watson, review of _Shadows of the Night,_ p. 475; July, 2001, review of _Dig, Wait, Listen,_ p. 476.

New York Times Book Review, June 1, 1986, Susan Brownmiller, "What Makes the Crops Rejoice," p. 30; March 31, 1991, Nancy Cardozo, review of _Urban Roosts,_ p. 29.

Publishers Weekly, November 11, 1988, review of _Desert Giant,_ p. 56; January 12, 1990, review of _Tree of Life,_ p. 62; November 16, 1990, review of _Urban Roosts,_ p. 58; October 4, 1991, review of _Forest,_ p. 89; April 26, 1993, review of _Shadows of the Night,_ p. 81; July 18, 1994, review of _Ancient Ones,_ p. 146.

Reading Teacher, March, 1998, p. 504.

School Library Journal, March, 1985, Frances E. Millhouser, review of _Tiger Lilies,_ p. 170; December, 1988, George Gleason, review of _Desert Giant,_ p. 96; February, 1990, Susan Scheps, review of _Tree of Life,_ p. 80; November, 1990, Ruth S. Vose, review of _Urban Roosts,_ p. 121; November, 1991, Amy Nunley, review of _Forest,_ and _Ocean,_ p. 110; June, 1993, Diane Nunn, review of _Shadow of the Night,_ p. 94; October, 1994, Steve Matthews, review of _Ancient Ones,_ p. 108; November, 1996, Helen Rosenberg, review of _In the Heart of the Village,_ p. 96; August, 1998, Susan Oliver, review of _Phantom of the Prairie,_ p. 142; June, 2001, Ellen Heath, review of _Dig, Wait, Listen,_ p. 129.

Skipping Stones, March-April, 1997, Cecelia Martinez, review of _In the Heart of the Village,_ p. 5.

Utne Reader, September-October, 1989, Helen Cordes, review of _Desert Giant,_ p. 108.

OTHER

Barbara Bash Web Site, http://www.barbarabash.com (May 29, 2002).

*   *   *

BAWDEN, Nina (Mary Mabey) 1925- (Nina Mary Kark)

Personal

Born January 19, 1925, in London, England; daughter of Charles (a marine engineer) and Ellalaine Ursula May (a teacher; maiden name, Cushing) Mabey; married Harry Bawden, October, 1946 (died, 1954); married Austen Steven Kark (an executive for British Broadcasting Corp.), August 5, 1954; children: (prior marriage) Nicholas Bawden (deceased), Robert Humphrey Felix Bawden; (current marriage) Perdita Emily Helena Kark. _Education:_ Somerville College, Oxford, B.A., 1946, M.A., 1951; additional graduate study at Salzburg Seminar in American Studies, 1960. _Hobbies and other interests:_ Traveling, reading, garden croquet.

Addresses

Home—22 Noel Rd., London N1 8HA, England. _Agent_—Curtis Brown, Ltd., 575 Madison Ave., New York, NY 10022.

Career

Writer, 1952—. Assistant, Town and Country Planning Associates, 1946-47; Justice of the Peace, Surrey, England, 1968-76.

Member

PEN, Royal Society of Literature (fellow), Society of Women Writers and Journalists (president), Authors Lending and Copyright Society, Oriental Club, London Society of Authors (council).

Awards, Honors

Carnegie commendation, 1973, and Phoenix Award, the Children's Literature Association, 1993, for *Carrie's War; Guardian* Award for children's fiction, 1975, for *The Peppermint Pig; Yorkshire Post* Novel of the Year Award, 1977, for *Afternoon of a Good Woman;* Parents' Choice citation, 1982, and Edgar Allan Poe award nomination, 1983, both for *Kept in the Dark;* Parents' Choice citation, 1985, for *The Finding;* Booker Prize shortlist, 1987, for *Circles of Deceit;* Order of the British Empire, 1995, for lifetime literary achievement; honorary fellow, Somerville College, Oxford, 2002.

Writings

JUVENILE FICTION

The Secret Passage, Gollancz (London, England), 1963, reprinted, Penguin (New York, NY), 1979, published as *The House of Secrets,* Lippincott (Philadelphia, PA), 1964.
On the Run, Gollancz (London, England), 1964, published as *Three on the Run,* Lippincott (Philadelphia, PA), 1965.
The White Horse Gang, Lippincott (Philadelphia, PA), 1966.
The Witch's Daughter, Lippincott (Philadelphia, PA), 1966, reprinted, Chivers (Bath, England), 1988.
A Handful of Thieves, Lippincott (Philadelphia, PA), 1967.
The Runaway Summer, Lippincott (Philadelphia, PA), 1969.
Squib, Lippincott (Philadelphia, PA), 1971.
Carrie's War, Lippincott (Philadelphia, PA), 1973.
The Peppermint Pig, Lippincott (Philadelphia, PA), 1975.
Rebel on a Rock, Lippincott (Philadelphia, PA), 1978.
The Robbers, Lothrop (New York, NY), 1979.
(Adaptor) *William Tell,* illustrated by Pascale Allamand, Lothrop (New York, NY), 1981.
Kept in the Dark, Lothrop (New York, NY), 1982.
St. Francis of Assisi (nonfiction), Lothrop (New York, NY), 1983.
The Finding, Lothrop (New York, NY), 1985.
Princess Alice, Deutsch (London, England), 1985.
Henry, Lothrop (New York, NY), 1988, published as *Keeping Henry,* Gollancz (London, England), 1988.
The Outside Child, Lothrop (New York, NY), 1989.
Family Money, Gollancz (London, England), 1991.
Humbug, Chivers (Bath, England), 1992, Clarion (New York, NY), 1992.

Nina Bawden

The Real Plato Jones, Clarion (New York, NY), 1993, Hamish Hamilton (London, England), 1994.
In My Own Time: Almost an Autobiography, Virago (London, England), 1994.

ADULT NOVELS

Eyes of Green, Morrow (New York, NY), 1953, published as *Who Calls the Tune,* Collins (London, England), 1953.
The Odd Flamingo, Collins (London, England), 1954, reprinted, Chivers (Bath, England), 1977.
Change Here for Babylon, Collins (London, England), 1955.
The Solitary Child, Collins (London, England), 1956, Lancer (New York, NY), 1966.
Devil by the Sea, Collins (London, England), 1957, Lippincott (Philadelphia, PA), 1959, reprinted, Heineman Educational (London, England), 1984, abridged edition for children, Lippincott (Philadelphia, PA), 1976.
Glass Slippers Always Pinch, Lippincott (Philadelphia, PA), 1960, published as *Just Like a Lady,* Longmans, Green (London, England), 1960.
In Honour Bound, Longmans, Green (London, England), 1961.
Tortoise by Candlelight, Harper (New York, NY), 1963.
Under the Skin, Harper (New York, NY), 1964.
A Little Love, a Little Learning, Longmans, Green (London, England), 1965, Harper (New York, NY), 1966.

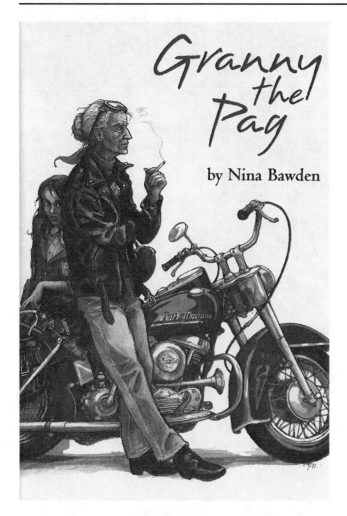

Granny the Pag
by Nina Bawden

Twelve-year-old Catriona lives with her grandmother, whose unconventional ways sometimes bother Catriona, but their mutual love becomes evident when they must fight the courts to stay together. (Cover illustration by Trina Schart Hyman.)

A Woman of My Age, Harper (New York, NY), 1967.
The Grain of Truth, Harper (New York, NY), 1968.
The Birds on the Trees, Longmans, Green (London, England), 1970, Harper (New York, NY), 1971.
Anna Apparent, Harper (New York, NY), 1972.
George beneath a Paper Moon, Harper (New York, NY), 1974.
Afternoon of a Good Woman, Harper (New York, NY), 1976.
Familiar Passions, Morrow (New York, NY), 1979.
Walking Naked, St. Martin's Press (New York, NY), 1981.
The Ice House, St. Martin's Press (New York, NY), 1983.
Circles of Deceit, St. Martin's Press (New York, NY), 1987.
Ruffian on the Stair, Little, Brown (Boston, MA), 2001.

OTHER

Contributor to *Evening Standard* and *Daily Telegraph* newspapers; contributor of essays and interviews to books and periodicals on children's literature.

Adaptations

Many of Bawden's children's stories have been adapted for television in Great Britain. A four-part adaptation of *Carrie's War* was shown on American Public Broadcasting in May, 1981; an adaptation of *The Finding* was broadcast in 1990 as part of the Public Broadcasting System's "Wonderworks" series. An adaptation of *The Witch's Daughter* was filmed by Scottish Television for Hallmark Entertainment in 1998; a four-part adaptation of *Family Money,* starring Claire Bloom, is planned as a BBC film, as are adaptations of *Peppermint Pig* and *Carrie's War.*

Work in Progress

Last Biscuit Day, a children's novel for Clarion.

Sidelights

"When someone takes time to count, Nina Bawden's body of work will be seen as the remarkable achievement it is," wrote Margaret Meek in *The School Librarian.* Bawden, a native of London, has written fiction of every sort—mysteries, gothic romances, and novels of manners for adults, as well as more than a dozen adventure-mystery works for children. She had been publishing for ten years before she wrote her first children's book, but in the last three decades her work for children and young adults has kept pace with her novels aimed at a mature audience. *Children's Book Review* contributor Margot Petts noted that in her children's books, Bawden "has an unerring ear and eye for the subtleties in relationships between children in a group—each one is a detailed portrait of a living, breathing human being, freckles an' all."

Bawden's books for young adults most commonly have realistic settings and plots drawn from daily life. Her characters may have vivid imaginations and indulge in fantasies, but often the world intrudes in ways that reveal life's unfairness and unpredictability. In *Children's Literature in Education,* Nicholas Tucker cited Bawden for books "both wise and immensely entertaining." Tucker added: "[Bawden's] characters are constantly made to recognize that most things don't work out easily 'like something in a book'.... If Nina Bawden's young characters get into trouble with the police, however noble their motives, there is no twinkle-eyed Inspector to bail them out and promise to come to tea next day. Instead, it's the real works: police station, worried parents and horrible embarrassment. When a crook is caught, it's usually a messy unheroic business, leaving you feeling sick in the stomach." Bawden's earliest children's work offered detailed, mystery-laden plots with moments of fast-paced excitement. Her more recent books highlight the personalities of the characters themselves, and how they relate to adults and other children.

Bawden was born in London and spent her earliest years in the suburbs of that city. Her father was a marine engineer who was often on a ship out at sea, but she and her younger brother enjoyed a conventional middle-class lifestyle with their mother. In *British Children's Authors,* Bawden stated that she began writing when she was quite young, completing a novel by the time she was eight years old. She also wrote plays for her toy theater "and an epic poem in blank verse about a beautiful orphan with curly golden hair—my own was straight and dark."

World War II intruded upon the household as it did amongst all Londoners. Bawden and her brother were among the hundreds of children who were tagged like suitcases and sent by rail to safer parts of the country. The two youngsters relocated first to a mining village in South Wales and then later moved to a more congenial farm in Shropshire. The circumstances of the evacuation forced the children to live with a variety of host families, some of whom offered very little hospitality.

Summers spent on the Shropshire farm were the favorite times for Bawden. She learned to drive a tractor and to care for farm animals. She even organized a group of Italian prisoners of war who were sent out to help with the hard labor in the fields. When she was seventeen she returned to London to finish school, even though the city was still under attack. She graduated from high school there and attended Somerville College, Oxford, earning a bachelor's degree in 1946 and a master's degree in 1951. She studied politics, economics, and philosophy.

After graduating from Oxford, the young woman married H. W. Bawden. The union was short but produced two sons. In 1954 she married Austen Kark, a controller at the British Broadcasting Corporation. By that time she had begun to publish novels under her first married name, Nina Bawden, and she retained the name professionally. *Dictionary of Literary Biography* essayist Gerda Seaman described Bawden's earliest fiction as "thrillers with a nice edge of menace." Works such as *Eyes of Green, The Odd Flamingo,* and *Change Here for Babylon* are almost standard thrillers, and *The Solitary Child* is a gothic romance. Bawden struck a change of pace with her 1957 novel *Devil by the Sea,* the first to feature children in important roles.

Devil by the Sea, which has since been adapted for a young adult audience, tells the story of Hilary, an imaginative youngster who becomes fascinated with a dim-witted derelict. As her interest in the man draws her closer to him, Hilary narrowly escapes becoming another victim of his murderous impulses. Seaman noted that this pivotal book introduced a theme that is present in much of Bawden's work for children, "that there is a world which is childhood's end, a world where 'other people are not to be relied upon ... promises can be broken; loyalty abandoned.'"

It was some six years after *Devil by the Sea* that Bawden made the decision to write a novel specifically for children. She accepted the challenge of her own growing children, who asked her to write something for them, and she soon discovered that she liked writing for young audiences very much. A number of works soon appeared

from her pen, including *The House of Secrets,* a mystery about a passage into a run-down cellar, and *The White Horse Gang,* a tale of three close friends in a wooded countryside. Bawden also drew notice for *Squib,* a story in which four children face real danger to discover the identity of a helpless street urchin.

The best known of Bawden's children's books are based most closely on her own experiences. *Carrie's War* tells the story of a brother and sister who are evacuated to Wales during the Second World War. The children are left in the care of grumpy Councillor Evans, whose rules are even more oppressive than his personality. Eventually Carrie and her brother learn to cope with and even to pity Mr. Evans, as Aidan Chambers noted in *Horn Book Magazine.* "By the end," Chambers wrote, "we've learned, as has Carrie, to understand, if not to feel affection for, the man. He could so easily have been a stock villain, the heavy of the piece. He becomes a person; and Carrie, he, and Nick develop three-dimensional relationships. Everyone has grown in the process—including the reader."

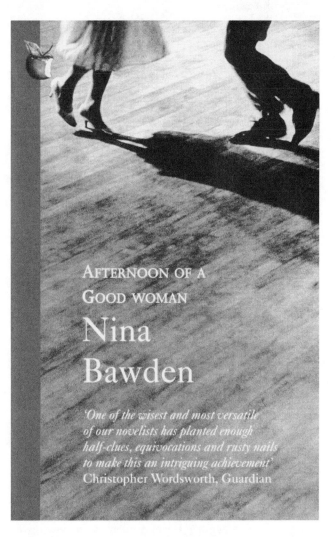

Penelope contemplates the cases before her as well as her own life and emotions on the day she has chosen to leave her husband. (Cover photo by George Kavanagh.)

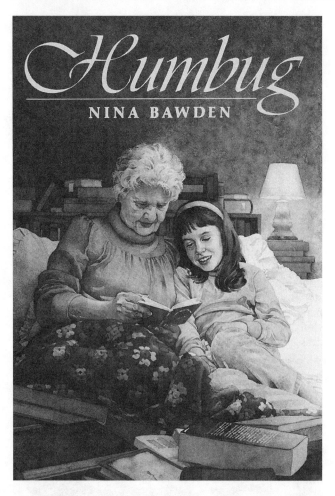

Cora finds it easier to deal with devious Angelica when Angelica's grandmother teaches Cora to recognize the girl's stories as nonsense. (Cover illustration by Ellen Thompson.)

Another Bawden favorite is her 1975 *Guardian* Award-winning novel, *The Peppermint Pig*. Once again the story focuses on uprooted children, suddenly made dependent upon relatives in a Norfolk country town. The children make a pet of Johnnie, a runt pig, but their affection for the animal cannot save its life during a time of ill fortune. *School Library Journal* contributor Jane Abramson called *The Peppermint Pig* "an uncommonly good family album whose portraits stand out in remarkably sharp focus."

Bawden's book *Family Money,* according to a reviewer in *Publishers Weekly,* "make(s) for a compelling read." Another reviewer in *Publishers Weekly* stated that Bawden has "struck the perfect balance between high-spirited storytelling and thoughtful content." Maeve Visser Knoth, a reviewer in *Horn Book Magazine,* called Bawden's *Humbug* "a satisfying novel about honesty and personal strength." Hazel Rochman, reviewing in *Booklist,* called Bawden's In *My Own Time: Almost an Autobiography* "a book especially for those who want to write themselves."

For some years now Bawden has been alternating between adult and juvenile fiction, turning out a novel a year. In *British Children's Authors,* Cornelia Jones and Olivia R. Way noted that the author feels that writing for children should be the same as writing for adults: "The books should present life honestly, with happiness and sadness, with excitement and discovery, but also with such negatives as poverty and loneliness. And so, she [writes], not with any age group in mind, but just to write an appealing story."

Bawden admits in the same publication that she actually enjoys writing for children more than writing for adults. "When boys and girls enjoy my books," she once commented, "it makes me want to write more. It's marvelous when they write and tell me they like my stories, and take the trouble to say what they like and why they like it. It's the most rewarding thing that can happen to a writer."

"I am still writing and hope to do so until death or senility prevents me," Bawden told SATA. "I know no other trade that makes more sense of life, or which makes such pleasurable use of all one's (by now quite long) experience."

Biographical and Critical Sources

BOOKS

Cambridge Guide to Literature in English, Cambridge University Press (New York, NY), 1995.
Children's Literature Review, Volume 2, Gale (Detroit, MI), 1976.
Dictionary of Literary Biography, Volume 14: *British Novelists since 1960,* Gale (Detroit, MI), 1983.
Drabble, Margaret, editor, *The Oxford Companion to English Literature,* 5th edition, Oxford University Press (New York, NY), 1998.
Jones, Cornelia and Olivia R. Way, *British Children's Authors,* American Library Association (Chicago, IL), 1976.
Tucker, Nicholas, "Getting Used to Things as They Are: Nina Bawden as a Children's Novelist," *Children's Literature in Education,* Number 13, 1974.

PERIODICALS

Booklist, December 1, 1995, Hazel Rochman, review of *In My Own Time: Almost an Autobiography,* p. 616.
Children's Book Review, September, 1971, Margot Petts, pp. 121-22.
Children's Literature in Education, fall, 1988.
Horn Book Magazine, June, 1974, Aidan Chambers, "Nina Bawden—Storyteller Argent, Children's Writer Proper," pp. 265-68; February, 1980; March-April, Maeve Visser Knoth, review of *Humbug,* p. 206.
Publishers Weekly, October 18, 1991, review of *Family Money,* p. 50; September 21, 1992, review of *Humbug,* p. 94.
School Librarian, September, 1973, Margaret Meek, pp. 259-60.
School Library Journal, February, 1975, Jane Abramson, p. 43.

OTHER

Nina Bawden's Home Page, http://www.ninabawden.net/ (April 2, 2002).

*   *   *

BILLINGSLEY, Franny

Personal

Born July 3, 1954; daughter of Patrick and Ruth Billingsley; married Richard Pettengill, June 18, 1988; children: Miranda, Nathaniel. *Education:* Tufts University, B.A. (summa cum laude), 1976; Boston University Law School, J.D. (cum laude), 1979.

Addresses

Home—5630 S. Kimbark Ave., Chicago, IL 60637. *E-mail*—rhpetten@midway.chicago.edu.

Career

Lawyer, 1979-83; 57th Street Books, Chicago, IL, children's bookseller, 1987-99; full-time writer and speaker, 1999—.

Awards, Honors

Best Book citation and "Sleeper: 100 Books Too Good to Miss," *School Library Journal,* one of the Top 10 First Novels for Youth selection, *Booklist,* and Anne Spencer Lindbergh Prize honor book, 1997-98, all for *Well Wished*; First Prize Winner for Fiction, Horn Book Award, *Boston Globe,* 2000, American Library Association (ALA) Notable Book, Editors' Choice, and one of Top 10 Fantasy Books for Youth selection, *Booklist,* Blue Ribbon Book, *Bulletin of the Center for Children's Books,* and Best Book citations, *School Library Journal* and *Publishers Weekly,* all for *The Folk Keeper.*

Writings

Well Wished, Atheneum (New York, NY), 1997.
The Folk Keeper, Atheneum (New York, NY), 1999.

Adaptations

The Folk Keeper is also available as an audiobook, narrated by Irish actress Marrian Tomas Griffin, from Listening Library.

Sidelights

Franny Billingsley began her adult life as a lawyer, a job that she held for five years. Then, in 1983, Billingsley took a trip to visit her sister in Barcelona, Spain. While she was there, she became "entranced by a lifestyle in which people did not make a lot of money yet lived richly and artfully," she recalled in an interview posted on the *Tab Reading Circle* Web site. Billingsley quit her job that year and moved to Barcelona with all of her favorite children's books, including *A Wrinkle in Time,*

Harriet the Spy, and *The Narnia Chronicles,* which were the furthest thing possible from the dry legal documents which she had been reading since law school. Billingsley intended to do nothing but read and eat tapas (small treats served on saucers placed on top of glasses of beer) in Spain, but while reading all of those books she had loved as a child, "I realized that this is where I truly belong, in the world of children's books.... And I rediscovered my passion for children's books, it was just a short step to deciding to try creating them myself," Billingsley commented in an interview with Cynthia Leitich Smith.

In 1986, Billingsley returned to the United States and took a job as the children's book-buyer at a large independent bookstore in Chicago. She stayed in this job for thirteen years, writing all the while. Her first few books were not very good, she now admits, but she learned a great deal about how to write from them. Billingsley eventually gravitated toward fantasy novels, and there she found her voice. Finally, fourteen years after Billingsley began writing, her children's fantasy novel *Well Wished* was published.

Well Wished was described as "a well-constructed and thought-provoking fantasy" by Anne Deifendeifer in a review for *Horn Book Magazine.* It is the tale of Nuria, the only child in the town of Bishop Mayne. The town contains a wishing well which will grant each person just one wish in their lifetime, but there is a catch: if there is any way that the well can twist a person's wish and make it have an unpleasant outcome, it will do so. The other children have presumably disappeared as a result of someone's wish having gone awry. Eleven-year-old Nuria, lonely and wishing for a friend, is delighted when grandfather uses his wish to bring the other children back. Only one child returns, however—the selfish, manipulative, wheelchair-bound Catty Winters. Still, Catty is eleven, and she and Nuria do become friends. Nuria, egged on by Catty, goes to the well and wishes that Catty had a body just like hers. Suddenly, the two girls switch bodies.

Billingsley received her inspiration for *Well Wished* in 1985. She had gone to a blood bank to donate plasma for a sick friend. While she was there, she met a young woman who was receiving a transfusion. This woman was so ill and weak that she could not even take the lid off of a jar of peanut butter. The two of them chatted, and Billingsley began to wonder what it would mean for an athletic person like herself to be trapped in a handicapped body like this woman's.

It took Billingsley years to figure out the magical mechanism which would result in the healthy girl winding up in the sick girl's body. She arrived at the idea of the wishing well from two directions: the nature of childhood friendships, where one child would sacrifice so much to keep a friend, and the way that Billingsley found stories to be more interesting when the character gets herself into trouble.

Deifendeifer commented, "Although the fantasy elements play a pivotal role in the plot, it is the keen character development that leaves the strongest impression." Susan Dove Lempke echoed this thought in a review for *Booklist,* praising Billingsley's "rich storytelling, vibrant and insightful characterization, and elegant writing style."

In *The Folk Keeper,* Billingsley draws on selkie folklore to create a fantasy with a strong Celtic flavor. Corinna Stonewall, so named because of her stubborn nature, is an orphan. She wants to be one of the Folk Keepers, the brave souls who protect others from the malevolent subterranean creatures called the Folk. The job of Folk Keeper is not open to women, so at fifteen Corinna disguises herself as a boy, changes her name to Corin, and secures a position in the town of Rhysbridge. She lives in a dark cellar, but she is content. It is easy there for her to hide her secrets, like the fact that her hair grows two inches a night. Corinna has one prized possession, her Folk Record, where she catalogues her life as a Folk Keeper. The story in *The Folk Keeper* is presented as entries from Corinna's Folk Record.

Then a mysterious, dying lord comes, sees through Corinna's disguise, and hires her to come protect his Northern Isles estate from the more dangerous Folk that inhabit the island of Cliffsend. The lord is good to Corin/Corinna, encouraging her to sit at the family table with himself and Lady Alicia. Corinna is uncomfortable with this at first, but she soon warms to the family, especially the Lady Alicia's son Finian. The romance grows, Corinna has terrifying adventures in the Folk's underground caverns, and she learns more about her true identity in the conclusion to this "evocative, unforgettable read," as it was termed by a *Publishers Weekly* contributor. Other critics also praised it: "The intricate plot, vibrant characters, dangerous intrigue, and fantastical elements combine into a truly remarkable novel steeped in atmosphere," noted *Horn Book Magazine* reviewer Anne St. John. *Booklist* contributor Sally Estes praised Billingsley's "immediate and compelling" storytelling, calling *The Folk Keeper* "a memorable story."

Billingsley quit her job at the bookstore around the time *The Folk Keeper* was published. She now writes children's books full time, working in the basement or in a playhouse in her backyard to get away from her children. "I don't need a space that triggers my imagination; in fact that might get in the way," Billingsley commented in an interview with Cynthia Leitich Smith. "Give me grime, give me damp, give me cold, and I'm happy. (And give me coffee.)"

Billingsley once stated, "I have to sit for a long time with my stories. I usually start out with the idea for the complication of the story (for example, in *Well Wished,* I began with the idea of two girls switching bodies), but I don't know how I am going to get my character into the trouble I envision for her, nor do I know how I will get her back out.

"I sometimes think of my process as being one of backing into knowledge: taking my plot idea and threading it into character, asking myself: What does my character want? Once I know what my character wants, that then loops back into the plot, because if my character wants something enough, she will do something to try to get it, and that generates narrative energy (plot). So, for example, I had given Nuria a history: she is an orphan who for most of her life has been shunted from one unfeeling relative to another. She has always been lonely. This knowledge led me to a discovery about her: she wants a friend more than anything else. And once I knew that, I could manipulate the circumstances to make her believe that she is in danger of losing her one friend unless she makes a wish on the Wishing Well. Nuria knows that the Wishing Well is dangerous and unpredictable, but because she is so desperate for a friend, she makes a wish anyway and this is what lands her in Catty's body.

"It takes me many years to back into this kind of knowledge, so that all the elements work together to become an organic whole. It must seem inevitable that my character would want what she wants. It must seem inevitable that my character would take the (perhaps foolish) course of action that she does to attain or keep what she wants. It must seem inevitable that that course of action would get her into the trouble I had contemplated for her ...

"When I first started *Well Wished,* there was no Wishing Well. When I first started *The Folk Keeper,* there were no Folk. So my process is one of writing draft after draft over the course of many years, each draft inching a little closer to the truth of who my character is and what she is going to do."

Biographical and Critical Sources

PERIODICALS

Booklist, June 1, 1997, Susan Dove Lempke, review of *Well Wished,* p. 1694; September 1, 1999, Sally Estes, review of *The Folk Keeper,* p. 126.

Horn Book Magazine, May-June, 1997, Anne Deifendeifer, review of *Well Wished,* p. 314; November, 1999, Anne St. John, review of *The Folk Keeper,* p. 734; January, 2001, Kristi Beavin, review of the audio version of *The Folk Keeper,* p. 120.

New York Times Book Review, January 16, 2000, Betsy Hearne, review of *The Folk Keeper,* p. 26.

Publishers Weekly, April 7, 1997, review of *Well Wished,* p. 92; October 18, 1999, review of *The Folk Keeper,* p. 83; September 11, 2000, review of the audio version of *The Folk Keeper,* p. 37.

School Library Journal, May, 1997, Lisa Dennis, review of *Well Wished,* p. 128.

OTHER

Cynthia Leitich Smith Children's Literature Resources, http://www.cynthialeitichsmith.com/ (April 7, 2001), interview with Franny Billingsley.

Franny Billingsley, http://www.frannybillingsley.com/ (October 19, 2001).

Tab Reading Circle, http://teacher.scholastic.com/ (October 19, 2001), "Meet Franny Billingsley."

*   *   *

BLEGVAD, Erik 1923-

Personal

Born March 3, 1923, in Copenhagen, Denmark; immigrated to France, 1947; immigrated to United States, 1951; immigrated to England, 1966; immigrated again to United States, 1986; son of Harald (a marine biologist for the Danish government) and Anna (a homemaker; maiden name, Claudi-Hansen) Blegvad; married Lenore Hochman (a painter and writer), September 12, 1950; children: Peter, Kristoffer. *Education:* Graduated from Copenhagen School of Arts and Crafts, 1944.

Addresses

Home and office—Mountain Spring Farm, P. O. Box 41, Wardsboro, VT 05355. *E-mail*—leblegvad@aol.com.

Career

Artist and illustrator. Employed in an advertising agency in Copenhagen, Denmark, during the end of World War II; freelance artist in London, 1947; freelance artist for book and magazine publishers in Paris, 1947-51; illustrator of children's books, 1951—; teacher of visual art, 1964-1965. *Exhibitions:* "Fifty Years of Illustration: Eric Blegvad," presented by Duncan of Jordanstone College of Art, Dundee, Scotland, 1991; Blegvad's works have also been featured in several exhibitions of the American Institute of Graphic Arts. *Military service:* Royal Danish Air Force, interpreter with the British forces in Germany, 1945-47.

Awards, Honors

American Library Association notable book, 1959, for *The Gammage Cup;* Children's Books of the Year, Child Study Association of America, 1972, for *The Tenth Good Thing about Barney,* 1973, for *The Narrow Passage,* 1974, for *Polly's Tiger,* and 1976, for *May I Visit?;* Children's Book Showcase Title, 1975, for *Mushroom Center Disaster* and 1976, for *The Winter Bear;* *New York Times* list of the ten best illustrated books of 1978 for *This Little Pig-a-Wig: And Other Rhymes about Pigs; Horn Book* honor list of books, 1979, for *Self-Portrait: Erik Blegvad.*

Writings

ILLUSTRATOR

E. Prunier, *Madame Prunier's Fiskekogebog,* Fonss Forlag (Copenhagen, Denmark), 1947.

Dore Ogrizek, *Les Pays Nordiques,* Editions Ode (Paris, France), 1950.

Thomas Franklin Galt, *Story of Peace and War,* Crowell (New York, NY), 1952.

Julie F. Batchelor and Claudia De Lys, *Superstitious: Here's Why!,* Harcourt (San Diego, CA), 1954.

Bob Brown, *The Complete Book of Cheese,* Random House (New York, NY), 1955.

Lee Kingman, *Village Band Mystery,* Doubleday (New York, NY), 1956.

Lillian Pohlman, *Myrtle Albertina's Secret,* Coward (New York, NY), 1956.

B. J. Chute, *Greenwillow,* Dutton (New York, NY), 1956.

Dan Wickenden, *Amazing Vacation,* Harcourt (San Diego, CA), 1956.

Edward Anthony, *Oddity Land,* Doubleday (New York, NY), 1957.

Mary Norton, *Bed-Knob and Broomstick,* Harcourt (San Diego, CA), 1957.

Jean Fritz, *Late Spring,* Coward-McCann (New York, NY), 1957.

(And translator) Hans Christian Andersen, *The Swineherd,* Harcourt (San Diego, CA), 1958.

Erik Blegvad's drawings capture the flavor of seventeenth-century England, where three children are given powers by a witch-in-training, who also provides them with a magic bed that transports them to a series of adventures. (From Bed-Knob and Broomstick, *written by Mary Norton.)*

Three banished Minnipins must rescue the others in their village when their ancient enemies, the Hairless Ones, threaten war in Carol Kendall's **The Gammage Cup,** *illustrated by Blegvad.*

Lee Kingman, *Flivver,* Doubleday (New York, NY), 1958.

Lillian Pohlman, *Myrtle Albertina's Song,* Coward (New York, NY), 1958.

B. J. Chute, *Journey to Christmas,* Dutton (New York, NY), 1958.

(And translator) Hans Christian Andersen, *The Emperor's New Clothes,* Harcourt (San Diego, CA), 1959.

Isabella Holt, *The Adventures of Rinaldo,* Little, Brown (Boston, MA), 1959.

Carol Kendall, *The Gammage Cup,* Harcourt (San Diego, CA), 1959.

Betty Miles, *Having a Friend,* Knopf (New York, NY), 1959.

Margaret Otto, *The Little Old Train,* Knopf (New York, NY), 1960.

Robert Paul Smith, *Jack Mack,* Coward-McCann (New York, NY), 1960.

Millicent Selsam, *Plenty of Fish,* Harper (New York, NY), 1960.

Seymour Reit, *Where's Willie?,* Artists and Writers Press (New York, NY), 1961.

Ronna Jaffe, *The Last of the Wizards,* Simon & Schuster (New York, NY), 1961.

Myra Cohn Livingston, *I'm Hiding,* Harcourt (New York, NY), 1961.

Marjorie Winslow, *Mud Pies and Other Recipes,* Macmillan (New York, NY), 1961.

Jane Langton, *The Diamond in the Window,* Harper (New York, NY), 1962.

Myra Cohn Livingston, *See What I Found,* Harcourt (San Diego, CA), 1962.

Miska Miles, *Dusty and the Fiddlers,* Little, Brown (Boston, MA), 1962.

Jean Stafford, *Elephi,* Farrar, Straus (New York, NY), 1962.

Leonard Wibberley, *The Ballad of the Pilgrim Cat,* Ives & Washbourne (New York, NY), 1962.

Margaret Rudkin, *The Pepperidge Farm Cook Book,* Atheneum (New York, NY), 1963.

Barbara Brenner, *The Five Pennies,* Knopf (New York, NY), 1963.

Felice Holman, *Elisabeth the Bird Watcher,* Macmillan (New York, NY), 1963.

Myra Cohn Livingston, *I'm Not Me,* Harcourt (San Diego, CA), 1963.

Richard Webber Jackson, *A Year Is a Window,* Doubleday (New York, NY), 1963.

Helen Taylor, *A Time to Recall,* Norton (New York, NY), 1963.

Miska Miles, *Pony in the Schoolhouse,* Little, Brown (Boston, MA), 1964.

Felice Holman, *Elisabeth the Treasure Hunter,* Macmillan (New York, NY), 1964.

Myra Cohn Livingston, *Happy Birthday!,* Harcourt (San Diego, CA), 1964.

William Allingham, *The Dirty Old Man,* Prentice-Hall (Englewood Cliffs, NJ), 1965.

Felice Holman, *Elisabeth and the Marsh Mystery,* Macmillan (New York, NY), 1966.

Myra Cohn Livingston, *I'm Waiting,* Harcourt (San Diego, CA), 1966.

Doris Orgel, *The Good-Byes of Magnus Marmalade,* Putnam (New York, NY), 1966.

Sally Clithero, editor, *Beginning-to-Read Poetry,* Follett (Chicago, IL), 1967.

Jane Langton, *The Swing in the Summer House,* Harper (New York, NY), 1967.

Doris Orgel, *Phoebe and the Prince,* Putnam (New York, NY), 1969.

Max Steele, *The Cat and the Coffee Drinkers,* Harper (New York, NY), 1969.

Monica Stirling, *The Cat from Nowhere,* Harcourt (New York, NY), 1969.

Janice Udry, *Emily's Autumn,* Albert Whitman (Chicago, IL), 1969.

E. Nesbit, *The Conscience Pudding,* Coward-McCann (New York, NY), 1970.

Margery Sharp, *Miss Bianca in the Orient,* Little, Brown (Boston, MA), 1970.

Alvin R. Tresselt, *Bonnie Bess: The Weathervane Horse,* Parents' Magazine Press (New York, NY), 1970.

Jane Langton, *The Astonishing Stereoscope,* Harper (New York, NY), 1971.

Judith Viorst, *The Tenth Good Thing about Barney,* Atheneum (New York, NY), 1971.

Margery Sharp, *Miss Bianca in the Antarctic,* Little, Brown (Boston, MA), 1971.

Roger Drury Wolcott, *The Finches' Fabulous Furnace,* Little, Brown (Boston, MA), 1971.

O. Henry, *The Gift of the Magi,* Hawthorn (New York, NY), 1971.

Margery Sharp, *Miss Bianca and the Bridesmaid,* Little, Brown (Boston, MA), 1972.

E. Nesbit, *The Complete Book of Dragons,* Macmillan (New York, NY), 1973.

Mark Taylor, *The Wind's Child,* Atheneum (New York, NY), 1973.

Oliver Butterworth, *The Narrow Passage,* Little, Brown (Boston, MA), 1973.

N. M. Bodecker, *The Mushroom Center Disaster,* Atheneum (New York, NY), 1974.

Ruth Craft, *The Winter Bear,* Collins (London, England), 1974, Atheneum (New York, NY), 1975.

Joan Phipson, *Polly's Tiger,* Dutton (New York, NY), 1974.

Jan Wahl, *The Five in the Forest,* Follett (Chicago, IL), 1974.

Jean O'Connell, *The Dollhouse Caper,* Crowell (New York, NY), 1976.

Charlotte Zolotow, *May I Visit?,* Harper (New York, NY), 1976.

Nancy Dingman Watson, *Blueberries Lavender,* Addison-Wesley (Reading, MA), 1977.

Jan Wahl, *The Pleasant Fieldmouse Storybook,* Prentice-Hall (Englewood Cliffs, NJ), 1977.

Jan Wahl, *Pleasant Fieldmouse's Valentine Trick,* Windmill (New York, NY), 1977.

(And reteller) *Burnie's Hill: A Traditional Rhyme,* Atheneum (New York, NY), 1977.

Charlotte Zolotow, *Someone New,* Harper (New York, NY), 1978.

Robert Louis Stevenson, *A Child's Garden of Verses,* Random House (New York, NY), 1978.

Gail Mack, *Yesterday's Snowman,* Pantheon (New York, NY), 1978.

Andrew Lang, *The Yellow Fairy Book,* Kestrel Books (London, England), 1979, Viking (New York, NY), 1980.

(And reteller) *The Three Little Pigs,* Atheneum (New York, NY), 1979.

Rare Treasures from Grimm: Fifteen Little-Known Tales, compiled and translated by Ralph Manheim, Doubleday (New York, NY), 1981.

Mary Stolz, *Cat Walk,* Harper (New York, NY), 1983.

Jan Wahl, *Peter and the Troll Baby,* Golden Press (New York, NY), 1984.

Jane L. Curry, *Little, Little Sister,* Macmillan (New York, NY), 1989.

Charlotte Zolotow, *I Like to Be Little,* Harper (New York, NY), 1990.

N. M. Bodecker, *Water Pennies* (poems), Margaret K. McElderry Books (New York, NY), 1991.

(And selector and translator) Hans Christian Andersen, *Twelve Tales: Hans Christian Andersen,* Margaret K. McElderry Books (New York, NY), 1994.

Elizabeth Spires, *With One White Wing: Puzzles in Poems and Pictures,* Margaret K. McElderry Books (New York, NY), 1995.

Marjorie Winslow, *Mud Pies and Other Recipes: A Cookbook for Dolls,* Walker (New York, NY), 1996.

N. M. Bodecker, *Hurry, Hurry, Mary Dear,* Margaret K. McElderry Books (New York, NY), 1998.

Elizabeth Spires, *Riddle Road: Puzzles in Poems and Pictures,* Margaret K. McElderry Books (New York, NY), 1999.

William Jay Smith, *Around My Room* (poems), Farrar, Straus (New York, NY), 2000.

Charlotte Zolotow, *The Seasons,* HarperCollins (New York, NY), 2001.

ILLUSTRATOR; WRITTEN BY WIFE, LENORE BLEGVAD

Mr. Jensen and Cat, Harcourt (San Diego, CA), 1965.
One Is for the Sun, Harcourt (San Diego, CA), 1968.
The Great Hamster Hunt, Harcourt (San Diego, CA), 1969.
Moon-Watch Summer, Harcourt (San Diego, CA), 1972.
Anna Banana and Me, Atheneum (New York, NY), 1985.
This Is Me, Random House (New York, NY), 1986.
Rainy Day Kate, Macmillan (New York, NY), 1987.
A Sound of Leaves, Margaret K. McElderry Books (New York, NY), 1995.
First Friends, HarperFestival (New York, NY), 2000.

ILLUSTRATOR; EDITED BY WIFE, LENORE BLEGVAD

Mittens for Kittens: And Other Nursery Rhymes about Cats, Atheneum (New York, NY), 1974.
Hark! Hark! The Dogs Do Bark: And Other Rhymes about Dogs, Atheneum (New York, NY), 1975.
This Little Pig-a-Wig: And Other Rhymes about Pigs, Atheneum (New York, NY), 1978.
The Parrot in the Garret: And Other Rhymes about Dwellings, Atheneum (New York, NY), 1982.

OTHER

Self-Portrait: Erik Blegvad, Addison-Wesley (Reading, MA), 1978.
Hans Christian Andersen: From an Artist's Point of View: A Lecture for International Children's Book Day, Children's Literature Center/Library of Congress (Washington, DC), 1988.

Blegvad captures the warmth of Judith Viorst's story about a family who pays tribute to their deceased pet cat. *(From* The Tenth Good Thing about Barney.*)*

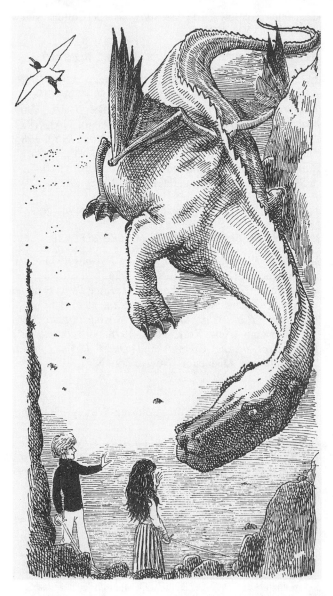

Blegvad illustrated The Complete Book of Dragons, *a collection of eight stories written by Edith Nesbit featuring outrageous and sometimes humorous plots involving battles with the imaginary beasts.*

Also illustrator of several works on fishing written by his father, Harald Blegvad. Contributor to periodicals in France, including *France Soir, Elle,* and *Femina,* and the United States, including *Esquire, Reader's Digest, Sports Illustrated, Life, American Heritage, McCall's, Saturday Evening Post,* and the *Woman's Day* serialization of Mary Norton's *The Borrowers* and *The Magic Bed Knob.*

Work in Progress

Illustrations for *Seagoing Clocks: The Story of Longitude,* by Louise Borden, Margaret K. McElderry Books (New York, NY).

Sidelights

Eric Blegvad is a distinguished artist who has illustrated over one hundred books for children. A Danish national, Blegvad has lived and worked in England, France, and the United States during his career, which spans almost six decades. His drawings can be found in several notable books, such as *The Emperor's New Clothes* by Hans Christian Andersen, *The Tenth Good Thing about Barney* by Judith Viorst, and *The Winter Bear* by Ruth Craft. He has also successfully collaborated with his wife, Lenore Blegvad, on numerous children's books, including *This Little Pig-a-Wig, Anna Banana and Me, The Sound of Leaves,* and *First Friends.* The recipient of several awards and honors, Blegvad is a talented artist whose drawings favorably compare to works by the famed illustrator of Winnie-the-Pooh: "Working in black and white line or tinted drawings, Erik Blegvad carries on a tradition we have associated with Ernest Shepard," according a *Illustrators of Children's Books, 1957-1966* contributor. "His decorations and illustrations on a small scale are very accessible to a child and provide the comfort of the known without ever sinking into the mannered or the banal."

Born on March 3, 1923, Blegvad spent his early years living in Copenhagen, Denmark, and traveling abroad. Visiting foreign countries greatly inspired the young artist. "When I was still a school boy I would go abroad with my family or sometimes by myself," Blegvad once recalled. "I suppose coming to places like Italy or London, where I saw things that I had never seen before, had an influence on me. I think the idea of taking a child outside his own environment opens his eyes to all sorts of things, especially if you come from a small bourgeois town like Copenhagen or from a flat country like Denmark. I was fascinated to see the mountains south of Munich, Germany, or the bright colors of London—like the red buses or the beautiful lettering on tube stations. These things had a visual impact that perhaps helped me decide to become an illustrator."

During these early years Blegvad was an avid reader. He began a lifelong interest in the works of Hans Christian Andersen, the nineteenth-century Danish author of such fairy tales as *The Princess and the Pea* and *The Ugly Duckling.* The young Blegvad also read newspapers and was thrilled by the illustrators whose drawings appeared in the Sunday paper. "The color supplements on Sunday were usually full of drawings by our best commercial artists. The term 'commercial artist' I may use a little bit loosely here, but these were people who made their living doing posters, book jackets, and book illustrations. They actually became our heroes. We looked for their drawings every Sunday."

Blegvad started drawing in childhood and received his formal training when he went to the Copenhagen School of Arts and Crafts from 1941 until 1944. At that time German troops occupied Denmark. "Studying art during the German occupation had a sort of hothouse effect," Blegvad once commented. "There was very little talk about politics at the school, and yet it was impossible not to be aware of what was going on. I think an awful lot of excuses for not having finished your homework came up because 'the war' and the Germans, 'the filthy Germans,' had prevented you from doing your work."

Although he did not excel in his studies, Blegvad learned some useful techniques in art school. "There was a rumor that the only reason I graduated was because I had been arrested by the Gestapo and that the school did not want to see somebody who had been arrested also fail his exams. I was not a very good student. But I did learn some valuable things. I really learned how to observe more clearly than I think people who did not have art training might. It wasn't as if I had been blind before, but art classes did open my eyes to a lot of things I might otherwise have just walked by."

Blegvad also made a lasting friendship in art school. "The friendship I enjoyed with N. M. Bodecker began with our first meeting in the art school in Copenhagen in February of 1941 and lasted until he died in Hancock, New Hampshire, in February of 1988. We shared a studio for a number of years in Westport, Connecticut, until my family and I moved to London in 1966. We collaborated on, among other projects, a series of soup labels for Pepperidge Farm. I ... illustrat[ed] his posthumous collection of poems, *Water Pennies*. It was a sobering experience, reminding me at every step how sublimely his own drawings complemented his wonderful poems."

When Germany was defeated in 1945, Blegvad signed up with the Royal Danish Air Force, hoping to realize a childhood dream of becoming a pilot. "I was always crazy about airplanes, completely mad about aviation." Instead of flying, however, Blegvad was assigned to serve as a translator with the British forces. Still, the assignment provided an opportunity for travel. "There was something about the occupation which had the effect of making you feel that you would never get out to see the world as you were meant to. So as soon as I saw an opportunity to join with the British forces, I volunteered for that and I came to Germany and worked for them. Towns like Hamburg and Hanover were completely ravaged, a dreadful part of the industrialized northwest of Germany. It was a pretty gruesome sight, but on the other hand we were so full of thoughts of revenge that I don't remember feeling particularly sorry for anybody."

After completing his military service in 1947, Blegvad moved to Paris to begin working as an illustrator. It was an important career move, though he initially had trouble adjusting to the city. "I remember hating Paris. I came during a very hot summer, and I couldn't speak a word of French. I couldn't understand what they were saying to me. I was very shocked that they didn't understand English, which was the first and only international tongue I had apart from German. I took it for granted that such an enlightened populace as the people of Paris would certainly have learned English at school, but, as many people have discovered, that was not the case.

"When I came to Paris the jobs that I managed to get were not very easy to land or very well paid to begin with. There were very few of them, so my life sort of fell into an extremely frugal, almost poverty-stricken routine. Then I landed a job with a very famous lady in Paris publishing, Madame Helene Lazareff, who had been in New York during the war with her family. She had been working for *Harper's Bazaar,* and she and her husband Pierre came back from New York when Paris was liberated. He became the editor of that enormous concern called Paris Presse, and she created a very famous ladies' weekly called *Elle*. When I showed her my drawings, she fell in love with them, and she gave me all the work I could handle. My fortune was actually made right there in Paris in April of 1948. The city is now my very favorite, perhaps because I speak and understand French."

While in Paris, Blegvad also met American painter Lenore Hochman, and the two were married in 1950. A year later they moved to America, where Blegvad began illustrating books for dozens of children's authors. Though he clearly enjoys working with various writers, some of his most pleasurable work has come from projects involving Lenore. He once described their working relationship: "Usually Lenore comes up with the idea in the beginning. She might say, 'let's see, you like to draw such and such a thing, I think I'll try and get something on that subject.' Her very first book was about Copenhagen. I remember that at the time I was homesick for Copenhagen, so it was nice to sit and draw those drawings. I also like to draw animals. So my wife came up with the idea of having these series of nursery rhymes, because she knew I liked to draw cats and dogs and pigs." First appearing in the mid-1970s, the series includes *Mittens for Kittens, Hark! Hark! The Dogs Do Bark, This Little Pig-a-Wig,* and *The Parrot in the Garret.*

Blegvad has continued to provide the illustrations for his wife's work as well as for the work of other authors, including American poets Elizabeth Spires and William Jay Smith. Together, Spires and Blegvad have produced two books of word puzzles for children, *With One White Wing* and *Riddle Road*. In each of the works, readers are challenged to find answers to the short lines of verse, each poem accompanied by Blegvad's watercolor artwork. Reviewing *With One White Wing* for *Booklist,* Carolyn Phelan noted that the artist's "imaginative watercolors illustrate the word puzzles with delicacy and charm," while in a review of *Riddle Road, Booklist* contributor Kay Weisman found that "Blegvad's charming watercolor illustrations provide plenty of suggestions for answers while leaving room for guesswork." In 2000, Blegvad worked with Smith to produce *Around My Room*. A collection of twenty-nine playful poems featuring a wide range of verse, *Around My Room* offers young children a variety of subjects, from limericks about a woman with a severe runny nose to a "silver-scaled Dragon with jaws flaming red." "Blegvad's watercolor-and-ink illustrations are in all instances charming, projecting a decidedly nostalgic flavor," wrote Lee Bock in a *School Library Journal* review.

Blegvad has also received special attention from critics for his work with fellow Danish countrymen Andersen and Bodecker. Translated and illustrated by Blegvad, *Twelve Tales: Hans Christian Andersen* features a dozen stories carefully selected by the artist, including popular favorites like "The Swineherd" and "The Emperor's New Clothes" and some lesser-known works like "The Sweethearts" and "What Father Does Is Always Right." Remarking on the collection for *Booklist,* Janice Del Negro commented that "it is Blegvad's selection of tales that makes this a strong addition to even the most complete Andersen collection." *Horn Book* critic Ann A. Flowers praised Blegvad's efforts, writing, "The illustrations, small and neat and delicately detailed, seem to contain the essence of Denmark and Andersen."

In 1998, Blegvad set to work illustrating a third book by Bodecker. In *Hurry, Hurry, Mary Dear,* the artist illustrates his late partner's poem about a woman who becomes frazzled trying to finish all of her husband's demands before cold weather sets in. As she hurries about, Mary's husband sits in a chair, telling her to "Hurry, hurry, Mary dear / fall is over, winter's here." In the end, however, Mary makes sure her displeasure is known as she brings her spouse his tea and donuts, though not in a manner he expects. "Blegvad wittily refreshes his late friend and collaborator's waggish poem about a hardworking, much put-upon wife and her hortatory husband," wrote a *Publishers Weekly* critic, "with this masterfully illustrated edition." According to *Booklist* critic GraceAnne A. DeCandido, the book's "verse and image work in tandem as easily as they must have when both men shared the same studio."

Over the years Blegvad has gained a reputation for producing richly detailed pen-and-ink drawings. Composed of carefully drawn lines, his pictures feature people and animals that are clearly defined without appearing stiff. While he also works with watercolors, Blegvad prefers pen and ink. "It's obvious that I feel most at home when I have a bottle of ink, a nib, a holder, and a rag to wipe the nib with," Blegvad once remarked. "Those are more or less the tools that I feel most at home with. I don't know why that should be. I suppose a pencil would be a very natural tool also, but I never fell in love with that. I think I smudge it too much. I like to see the illustration with my hand resting on the paper when I draw. I have friends who can draw from the shoulder or the elbow, but I'm used to drawing from the wrist, more or less. I don't have that lovely free-and-easy swing my wife has on her canvas. I can't do that. I more or less sit around and scratch my drawings with a movement from the wrist."

As he "scratches" out his drawings, Blegvad has a goal in mind: "It would be nice if my illustration could give a graphically satisfying pleasure to the person who is watching it. I hardly ever worry about whether it's a grown-up or child who has to see it. That doesn't seem to matter much to me. I'm a little worried about drawing simply for children and complicatedly for adults, as if children couldn't quite see or couldn't quite enjoy something that was a little sophisticated. I know it's

sometimes an argument between myself and editors. They're afraid I'm going to show something which might upset a child or frighten a child or puzzle too much. I don't think that's my own worry so much.

"I think the text should be the most important element and the picture should be the complement. I never became a real 'gung ho' picture book artist where there are just a few lines of text and this enormous picture in full color. I prefer the other imbalance, where the text is the dominating part and the drawing is just a suggestion of what you're reading. It also looks so nice on the page when there is a column of text and then the drawing."

With over one hundred books to his credit, Blegvad has covered a wide range of subjects. He likes diversity and is comfortable drawing almost anything. "I actually enjoy illustrating almost any subject you can imagine. It's a rich and varied world. I don't really have many preferences: I like drawing the sea and the ships as much as I like drawing the farm, the animals, the aircraft, the harbor, and the town. They all seem to me to be enjoyable subjects." Reflecting on his long career, Blegvad once commented, "I think it's the best possible life one could lead, and you don't have to just sit at home and do it. I didn't have to stay in Copenhagen. It must be one of the nicest jobs there is to be a commercial artist and to be a freelance illustrator. I can't really imagine anything nicer."

Biographical and Critical Sources

BOOKS

Carpenter, Humphrey, and Mari Prichard, *The Oxford Companion to Children's Literature,* Oxford University Press (New York, NY), 1984.
Childhood in Poetry, Gale (Detroit, MI), 1st edition, 1967, 3rd supplement, 1980.
Illustrator of Children's Books, 1946-1956, Horn Book (Boston, MA), 1958.
Illustrators of Children's Books, 1957-1966, Horn Book (Boston, MA), 1968.
Illustrators of Children's Books, 1967-1976, Horn Book (Boston, MA), 1978.
Silvey, Anita, editor, *Children's Books and Their Creators,* Houghton (Boston, MA), 1995.
St. James Guide to Children's Writers, 5th edition, St. James Press (Detroit, MI), 1999.
Smith, William Jay, *Around My Room,* Farrar, Straus (New York, NY), 2000.
Ward, Martha E., and Dorothy A. Marquardt, *Illustrators of Books for Young People,* 2nd edition, Scarecrow Press (Metuchen, NJ), 1975.

PERIODICALS

American Artist, September, 1961.
Booklist, October 1, 1994, Janice Del Negro, review of *Twelve Tales: Hans Christian Andersen,* p. 328; October 1, 1995, Carolyn Phelan, review of *With One White Wing: Puzzles in Poems and Pictures,* p. 325; May 1, 1996, Hazel Rochman, review of *A Sound of Leaves,* pp. 1505-1506; October 15, 1998, GraceAnne A. DeCandido, review of *Hurry, Hurry, Mary Dear,*

p. 424; July, 1999, Kay Weisman, review of *Riddle Road: Puzzles in Poems and Pictures,* p. 1949; February 1, 2000, Hazel Rochman, review of *Around My Room,* p. 1026; April 15, 2000, Hazel Rochman, review of *First Friends,* p. 1555.

Horn Book, November-December, 1994, Ann A. Flowers, review of *Twelve Tales: Hans Christian Andersen,* p. 729; September-October, 1996, Maeve Visser Knoth, review of *A Sound of Leaves,* p. 592; May, 1999, review of *Riddle Road,* p. 347; March, 2000, review of *Around My Room,* p. 207.

Publishers Weekly, July 11, 1994, review of *Twelve Tales,* p. 79; August 31, 1998, review of *Hurry, Hurry, Mary Dear,* p. 76; May 17, 1999, review of *Riddle Road,* p. 79; February 14, 2000, review of *Around My Room,* p. 196.

School Library Journal, April, 2000, Lee Bock, review of *Around My Room,* p. 126.

*   *   *

BROSTOFF, Anita 1931-

Personal

Born March 25, 1931, in Pittsburgh, PA; daughter of Leon (a pharmacist) and Gussie (a bookkeeper; maiden name, Weinberg) Keller; married Philip Brostoff (a physician), June 15, 1952; children: Leon, Richard, Lynn, Myra Brostoff Merritt. *Education:* University of Michigan, B.A., 1952; Carnegie-Mellon University, M.A., 1968, D.Arts, 1972.

Addresses

Home—1215 Murray Hill Ave., Pittsburgh, PA 15217. *E-mail*—abrostoff@worldnet.att.net.

Career

Carnegie-Mellon University, Pittsburgh, PA, assistant professor of English, 1972-75, assistant professor at Communication Skills Center, 1975-81; Brostoff Associates (communications consultants), Pittsburgh, PA, principal, 1981-94; writer, 1994—. University of Pittsburgh, lecturer and consultant to Graduate School of Business, 1983-86; Carnegie-Mellon University, instructor at Academy for Lifelong Learning, 1999—. Carnegie Museum of Art, docent, 1995—.

Member

American Society for Training and Development (chapter president, 1990).

Awards, Honors

Grant, National Endowment for the Humanities, 1979-81.

Writings

(Editor) *I Could Be Mute: The Life and Work of Gladys Schmitt,* Carnegie-Mellon University Press (Pittsburgh, PA), 1978.

Thinking through Writing, Carnegie-Mellon University Press (Pittsburgh, PA), 1981.

(Editor, with Sheila Chamovitz) *Flares of Memory: Stories of Childhood during the Holocaust,* Oxford University Press (New York, NY), 2001.

Biographical and Critical Sources

PERIODICALS

Antioch Review, spring, 1979, review of *I Could Be Mute: The Life and Work of Gladys Schmitt,* pp. 253-254.

Booklist, May 1, 1979, Edward Butscher, review of *I Could Be Mute,* p. 1340; May 15, 2001, George Cohen, review of *Flares of Memory: Stories of Childhood during the Holocaust,* p. 1727.

Library Journal, May 1, 2001, Jill Jaracz, review of *Flares of Memory,* p. 106.

*   *   *

BRYAN, Ashley F. 1923-

Personal

Born July 13, 1923, in New York, NY. *Education:* Earned degrees from Cooper Union Art School and Columbia University.

Addresses

Office—Department of Art, Dartmouth College, Hanover, NH 03755.

Career

Reteller and illustrator of books for children; professor emeritus of art and visual studies at Dartmouth College.

Awards, Honors

Coretta Scott King Book Award, 1980, for illustrating *Beat the Story-Drum, Pum-Pum,* 1986, for writing *Lion and the Ostrich Chicks and Other African Folk Tales,* and 1988, for illustrating *What a Morning! The Christmas Story in Black Spirituals;* Coretta Scott King Award, American Library Association, 1992, for *All Night, All Day: A Child's First Book of African-American Spirituals;* the Children's Room at the Mott Haven Library, the Bronx, New York, was named after Bryan, 2001.

Writings

RETELLER; SELF-ILLUSTRATED

The Ox of the Wonderful Horns and Other African Folktales, Atheneum (New York, NY), 1971.

The Adventures of Aku; or, How it Came about That We Shall Always See Okra the Cat Lying on a Velvet

Cushion while Okraman the Dog Sleeps among the Ashes, Atheneum (New York, NY), 1976.

The Dancing Granny, Macmillan (New York, NY), 1977.

Beat the Story-Drum, Pum-Pum (Nigerian folk tales), Atheneum (New York, NY), 1980.

The Cat's Drum, Atheneum (New York, NY), 1985.

Lion and the Ostrich Chicks and Other African Folk Tales, Atheneum (New York, NY), 1986.

All Night, All Day, Atheneum (New York, NY), 1988.

Sh-Ko and His Eight Wicked Brothers, Macmillan (New York, NY), 1988.

Turtle Knows Your Name, Macmillan (New York, NY), 1989.

ILLUSTRATOR

Rabindranath Tagore, *Moon, for What Do You Wait?* (poems), edited by Richard Lewis, Atheneum (New York, NY), 1967.

Mari Evans, *Jim Flying High* (juvenile), Doubleday (New York, NY), 1979.

Susan Cooper, *Jethro and the Jumbie* (juvenile), Atheneum (New York, NY), 1979.

John Langstaff, editor, *What a Morning! The Christmas Story in Black Spirituals,* Macmillan (New York, NY), 1987.

Black girl black girl
lips as curved as cherries
full as grape bunches
sweet as blackberries

DUDLEY RANDALL

Ashley F. Bryan selected twenty-six descriptive passages of verse for his self-illustrated alphabet book about African-Americans. (From Ashley Bryan's ABC of African-American Poetry.*)*

Sing to the Sun: Poems and Pictures, HarperCollins (New York, NY), 1992.

The Story of Lightning and Thunder, Atheneum, Maxwell Macmillan Canada (Toronto, Canada), 1993.

George David Weiss and Bob Thiele, *What a Wonderful World,* Atheneum (New York, NY), 1995.

Walter Dean Myers, *The Story of the Three Kingdoms,* HarperCollins (New York, NY), 1995.

Linda and Clay Goss, *It's Kwanzaa Time!,* Putnam (New York, NY), 1995.

Nikki Giovanni, *The Sun Is So Quiet,* Henry Holt (New York, NY), 1996.

Ashley Bryan's ABC of African-American Poetry, Atheneum (New York, NY), 1997.

Ashley Bryan's African Tales, Uh-Huh, Atheneum (New York, NY), 1998.

Langston Hughes, *Carol of the Brown King: Nativity Poems,* Atheneum (New York, NY), 1998.

The Night Has Ears: African Proverbs, Atheneum (New York, NY), 1999.

Brian Swann, *The House with No Door: African Riddle-Poems,* Harcourt (San Diego, CA), 1998.

Won-Ldy Paye and Margaret H. Lippert, *Why Leopard Has Spots: Dan Stories from Liberia,* Fulcrum Kids (Golden, CO), 1998.

(Introduction, with Andrea Davis Pinkney) *Jump Back, Honey: The Poems of Paul Laurence Dunbar,* Jump at the Sun/Hyperion Books for Children (New York, NY), 1999.

Nikki Grimes, *Aneesa Lee and the Weaver's Gift,* Lothrop (New York, NY), 1999.

Salting the Ocean: One Hundred Poems by Young Poets, Greenwillow Books (New York, NY), 2000.

OTHER

(Compiler) *Black American Spirituals,* Volume I: *Walk Together Children* (self-illustrated), Atheneum (New York, NY), 1974.

(Compiler and author of introduction) Paul Laurence Dunbar, *I Greet the Dawn: Poems,* Atheneum (New York, NY), 1978.

(Compiler) *Black American Spirituals,* Volume II: *I'm Going to Sing* (self-illustrated), Macmillan (New York, NY), 1982.

Adaptations

The Dancing Granny and Other African Tales, recorded by Bryan for Caedmon.

Work in Progress

Beautiful Blackbird, for Atheneum, 2003.

Sidelights

Ashley Bryan's own paintings and drawings grace the pages of his unique versions of traditional African and West Indian folktales and spirituals. "In my work as a black American artist," he commented in an interview with Sylvia and Kenneth Marantz in *Horn Book Magazine,* "it is the African root that nourishes whatever other world culture I may draw upon." Bryan has traveled to African countries such as Uganda and Kenya, but he has found that American libraries are a rich source of tribal tales. The multitalented Bryan is also known to audiences throughout the United States for his resonating poetry readings and lectures on black American poets.

Although Bryan grew up in rough sections of the Bronx, he embarked on a productive path early in life. "I learned from kindergarten that drawing and painting were the toughest assets I had to offer my community," Bryan stated in *Illustrators of Children's Books: 1967-76.* When an enterprising teacher introduced his class to book production, "I was author, illustrator, editor, publisher, and binder" of that first hand-stitched ABC book, recalled Bryan in a *Horn Book Magazine* interview. "Rave reviews" from the Bryan family encouraged him to generate countless original volumes.

Bryan continued to enjoy the support of family, friends, and teachers for his artistic abilities throughout his school years. This support, matched with the artist's internal drive and enthusiasm, led to higher studies at Cooper Union Art School. After serving in the army during World War II, Bryan returned to finish the program at Cooper Union and then went on to earn a degree in philosophy at Columbia University. While there, he also enrolled in a bookbinding course. Again finding himself in his element, Bryan generated thirty to forty bound books—about ten times the volume of his classmates.

When Bryan later opened a studio back in the Bronx, he was visited one day by Atheneum editor Jean Karl. At that time Bryan was in the process of illustrating his first professional book, *Fabliaux,* for Pantheon. The meeting with Karl was fortuitous: she sent Bryan a contract for drawings to accompany single-line poems by Indian poet Rabindranath Tagore, collected under the title *Moon, for What Do You Wait?* The artist told Sylvia and Kenneth Marantz what followed: "Later she asked if she could use some of my illustrations for a book of African tales. I said, 'You bet! But I don't like the way they are written.' She said, 'Tell them in your own way, Ashley.'" Bryan followed Karl's advice and continued to write and illustrate with her support, even after she went into semi-retirement. "As soon as I do one book, she is immediately encouraging me to do another," he added.

The first book resulting from this encouragement was a collection of five stories called *The Ox of the Wonderful Horns and Other African Folktales,* illustrated by Bryan in a distinctive painted style resembling woodcutting. *The Dancing Granny,* published in 1977, evolved from an Ashanti story collected in Antigua in the West Indies, the area from which Bryan's parents emigrated. In a *Horn Book Magazine* interview, Bryan described how he became inspired by a visit from his grandmother when she was in her seventies: "She picked up the latest dance steps from the great-grandchildren and outdanced them all! I drew upon that." Bryan used a brush painting

technique he borrowed from the Japanese to create a sense of movement in his illustrations.

In *The Cat's Purr,* which originated in the Antilles, Bryan unearthed a tale with an unexpected twist. When Cat inherits the miniature family drum, Rat *must* play it, despite Cat's wishes to the contrary. "Rat's trickery gives the story a nice bit of dramatic tension, and the notion of the tiny drum as the reason cats purr today will amuse young listeners or readers with its novelty," predicted Denise M. Wilms in *Booklist.*

During the 1800s, anthropologists and missionaries translated tribal stories into English, though they sought to preserve the languages more than the tales. Bryan begins with these materials and makes them his own, as he described in *Illustrators of Children's Books:* "I take the skeletal story motifs from the scholarly collections and use every resource of my background and experience to flesh them out and bring them alive." In all of his books, Bryan endeavors to impart the oral tradition of "texture and vitality and drama—the back and forth play of teller and audience of the oral setting," he explained to Sylvia and Kenneth Marantz. "I try things that will give a vitality of surface, a textural feeling, a possibility of vocal play to the prose of my stories. So I take risks in my books. I do a lot of things that people writing prose generally do not do: close rhythms, rhyme, onomatopoeia, alliteration, interior rhyme," he continued. Bryan recommends that stories and poetry be "read aloud, for the reader to understand the relationship between sound, spirit, and meaning," according to Alice K. Swinger in *Language Arts.* "Then, when the materials are read silently, the reader will receive more benefit because the sound and the spirit will already have been felt in the muscles and heard in the ears...."

Bryan has also found success with his collections of black American spirituals. For example, *Walk Together Children* "is as sweet and varied a collection of black spirituals as one could hope to find for children," wrote Virginia Hamilton in the *New York Times Book Review.* Bryan's interest in music reaches back to his childhood, when family and friends sang together on Sunday afternoons. Included among the twenty-four spirituals are the classics "Go Down Moses" and "Swing Low, Sweet Chariot." Bryan's accompanying black-and-white illustrations "surge with compassion and raw life," remarked Neil Millar in *Christian Science Monitor. I'm Going To Sing,* published in 1982, is the critically acclaimed companion volume to *Walk Together Children.*

But not all of Bryan's working hours are spent creating books, which he does primarily in the evenings. His days are devoted to painting in a studio on an island off the coast of Maine, which he made his permanent residence after he became professor emeritus at Dartmouth College. Since the 1940s Bryan had painted and exhibited his works on the island during the summer, with plans to live there year-round one day. In his interview with Sylvia and Kenneth Marantz, Bryan described his approach to painting: "I work with oils on canvas, outdoors, in the spirit of the impressionists. But I don't work from the essential feeling of light at a specific time; I work from a sense of rhythm." And while he used to prefer to depict scenes from the seashore, the artist has been fascinated by the garden and other areas around his home over the past decade or so. "I paint from changing patterns of color, as flowers bloom and fade, against the background of the fields stretching down to the ocean," revealed Bryan.

Bryan's award-winning *All Night, All Day* is his selection of twenty well-known spirituals, including full piano accompaniment and guitar chords. The music is brought to life with Bryan's "stylized watercolor paintings . . . [that] flow with the faith and hope of the songs they illustrate," according to *School Library Journal* contributor Susan Giffard. A critic in *Kirkus Reviews* described the artwork as "visual celebrations rather than literal illustrations, [which] merge the representational with the purely decorative." Other recent works by Bryan include *The Story of Lightning and Thunder,* a 1993 retelling of a West African tale in which Ma Sheep Thunder and her mischievous son Ram Lightning must flee Earth because of the trouble Ram causes, and *Ashley Bryan's ABC of African-American Poetry,* a 1997 children's book that presents a poem for each letter of the alphabet.

The dynamic artist began sharing his knowledge of painting and drawing as a teacher at Queens College in Brooklyn, but he was also able to reach younger children at various institutions in the New York City area, such as the Brooklyn Museum and Dalton School. Even though Bryan no longer teaches art at Dartmouth College, he still enriches people's lives through the use of another vehicle. He explained to Sylvia and Kenneth Marantz: "Through my programs in black culture I'm trying to push past the resistances and the stereotypes and open audiences to feelings that can change, or be included in, their lives. The same energies are still being called upon."

A man of many talents, Bryan continues to mesmerize audiences throughout the United States with poetry readings and storytelling sessions. Back in his studio on the island off the coast of Maine, he paints the changing forms in the garden and illustrates the compelling spirituals and tales he retells in a rhythmic written form. As Ethel L. Heins commented in *Horn Book Magazine,* "Ashley Bryan is a humane, articulate man who links ethnicity to universal culture."

Biographical and Critical Sources

BOOKS

Children's Literature Review, Volume 18, Gale (Detroit, MI), 1989.
Kingman, Lee, *Illustrators of Children's Books, 1967-76,* Horn Book (Boston, MA), 1978.
Silvey, Anita, *Children's Books and Their Creators,* Houghton (Boston, MA), 1995.

PERIODICALS

Booklist, April 15, 1985, Denise M. Wilms, "The Cat's Purr," p. 1189.
Christian Science Monitor, November 6, 1974, Neil Millar, "Songs of Lands and Seasons," p. 14.
Horn Book Magazine, March/April 1988, Sylvia and Kenneth Marantz, "Interview with Ashley Bryan," pp. 173-179; March/April, 1989.
Kirkus Reviews, April 15, 1991, review of *All Night, All Day,* p. 534.
Language Arts, March, 1984, Alice K. Swinger, "Profile: Ashley Bryan," pp. 305-311.
Ms., December, 1974.
New York Times Book Review, November 3, 1974, Virginia Hamilton, "Walk Together Children: Black American Spirituals," pp. 28-29; December, 1987.
Scientific American, December, 1980.
School Library Journal, May, 1991, Susan Giffard, review of *All Night, All Day,* p. 88.

OTHER

New York Public Library, http://www.nypl.org/ (August 9, 2001), "Landmark Mott Haven Library—the Oldest Public Library in the Bronx—Reopens after a $3.6 Million Renovation."

C

CALVERT, Patricia 1931-
(Peter J. Freeman)

Personal

Born July 22, 1931, in Great Falls, MT; daughter of Edgar C. (a railroad worker) and Helen P. (a children's wear buyer; maiden name, Freeman) Dunlap; married George J. Calvert (in insurance business), January 27, 1951; children: Brianne L. Calvert Elias, Dana J. Calvert Halbert. *Education:* Winona State University, B.A., 1976, graduate study, beginning 1976. *Politics:* Liberal Democrat. *Religion:* Unitarian-Universalist. *Avocational interests:* Reading, hiking, observing wildlife.

Addresses

Agent—c/o The Millbrook Press, Inc., 2 Old New Milford Rd., Brookfield, CT 06804.

Career

St. Mary's Hospital, Great Falls, MT, laboratory clerk, 1948-49; clerk typist at General Motors Acceptance Corp., 1950-51; Mayo Clinic, Rochester, MN, cardiac laboratory technician, 1961-64, enzyme laboratory technician, 1964-70, senior editorial assistant in section of publications, 1970—; instructor, Institute of Children's Literature, 1987—.

Member

American Medical Writers Association, Children's Reading Round Table, Society of Children's Book Writers, Society of Midland Authors.

Awards, Honors

Best book award from American Library Association, juvenile fiction award from Society of Midland Authors, and juvenile award from Friends of American Writers, all 1980, all for *The Snowbird;* award for outstanding achievement in the arts from Young Women's Christian

Patricia Calvert

Association (YWCA), 1981, for *The Snowbird;* Mark Twain Award nomination from Missouri Association of School Libraries, 1985, for *The Money Creek Mare;* Maude Hart Lovelace Award nomination, 1985, for *The Stone Pony; Yesterday's Daughter* was named a best book for young adults by the American Library Association, 1986; William Allan White Award, 1987, for

Hadder MacColl; When Morning Comes was named one of the "Best of 1990" by Society of School Librarians International, 1991; Christopher Award, The Christophers, 1997, for *Glennis, Before and After. Yesterday's Daughter* was a Junior Literary Guild selection.

Writings

NOVELS FOR YOUNG ADULTS

The Snowbird, Scribner's (New York, NY), 1980.
The Money Creek Mare, Scribner's (New York, NY), 1981.
The Stone Pony, Scribner's (New York, NY), 1982.
The Hour of the Wolf, Scribner's (New York, NY), 1983.
Hadder MacColl, Scribner's (New York, NY), 1985.
Yesterday's Daughter, Scribner's (New York, NY), 1986.
Stranger, You and I, Scribner's (New York, NY), 1987.
When Morning Comes, Macmillan (New York, NY), 1989.
Picking up the Pieces, Scribner's/Maxwell Macmillan International (New York, NY), 1993.
Bigger, Scribner's (New York, NY), 1994.
Writing to Richie, Scribner's (New York, NY), 1994.
Glennis, Before and After, Atheneum (New York, NY), 1996.
The American Frontier, Atheneum (New York, NY), 1997.
Sooner, Atheneum (New York, NY), 1998.
Michael, Wait for Me, Atheneum (New York, NY), 2000.
Daniel Boone, Marshall Cavendish (New York, NY), 2001.
Robert E. Peary, Marshall Cavendish (New York, NY), 2001.
Standoff at Standing Rock: The Story of Sitting Bull and James McLaughlin, Twenty-First Century Books (Brookfield, CT), 2001.

OTHER

(Editor) *The Communicator's Handbook: Techniques and Technology,* Maupin House Publishing (Gainesville, FL), 1990, fourth edition published as *The Communicator's Handbook: Tools, Techniques, and Technology,* 2000.

Contributor to *Developing Reading Efficiency,* fourth edition, edited by Lyle L. Miller, Burgess, 1980. Contributor, sometimes under the pseudonym Peter J. Freeman, of more than one hundred articles and stories to magazines, including *Highlights for Children, Grit, National Future Farmer, Friend, Junior Life,* and *Jack and Jill.*

Sidelights

Patricia Calvert was raised in rural Montana during the Great Depression. Her teenage parents, unable to find work, moved the family into an abandoned miner's shack in the country. "The cabin," Calvert once commented, "constructed nearly forty years before, was windowless; its puncheon floor had rotted away; rats and mice were its only inhabitants." Despite its rundown condition, the cabin was near creeks filled with trout and wild game was plentiful in the nearby countryside. The family was able to live off the land.

"The mountains that ringed the home where I grew up," Calvert recalled, "were known by such sonorous names as Thunder Mountain, Monument Peak, and Old Baldy; the brooks where I learned to fish were called Pilgrim Creek, Tenderfoot, Big Timber; the gold and silver mines that dotted the hillsides were labeled the Silver Bell, the Admiral Dewey, and the Gold Bug. It was a magic world for any child, one in which lodgepole pines grew like arrows toward a sky that seemed always blue. When I was older I had a sassy little horse named Redbird to ride, a collie named Bruno to keep me company, and a calico cat named Agamemnon to sleep at the foot of my bed."

Life in the country had drawbacks, too. "It was an isolated life," Calvert remembered, "and two of the few recreations available to me and to my brother (who was my only playmate) were story-telling and reading. It was our good fortune to have a mother who was a lively story-teller; she was black-haired and green-eyed and had been raised in an Irish family of ten children—and she never tired of telling us sad and funny (and often outrageous!) tales about her own childhood."

At the age of ten, Calvert knew that she wanted to be a writer when she grew up. Two novels especially influenced her decision: *Call It Courage* by Armstrong Sperry and *The White Stag* by Kate Seredy. "Those books," she recalled, "embraced things that were important to me: each dealt with themes of honor and courage; each took place in the out-of-doors; each was written in an artful, elegant manner."

It was only years later that she was able to begin writing the books she wanted. After her children had grown and left home, Calvert and her husband moved to the country, living on a small farm they named Foxwood. "We turned our acres into a wildlife preserve where deer, fox, and raccoon could wander where they wished," she explained. In addition, Calvert created a place for herself on the farm. "I converted an old chicken coop into a place to write," she related, "and when I did I returned to scenes from my childhood and to those half-forgotten tales told to me by my mother about her own childhood. I hoped that my first book, *The Snowbird,* would bring to young-adult readers some of the pleasure that came to me when I read *Call It Courage* and *The White Stag.* More than that, I hoped I could pass on to my readers my pet philosophy: that no matter how young one is, it is sometimes necessary to declare to the world *I am accountable.*"

Calvert is known for action-packed writings that often address serious issues such as death, the break up of families, and teenage pregnancy. This, combined with strong, realistic characters, has garnered the author a reputation as a prolific writer of well-crafted, fast-paced novels with themes that teens can relate to. In *Glennis, Before and After,* a twelve-year-old girl goes to live with relatives after her father is imprisoned for fraud and her mother suffers a nervous breakdown. Visits to the jail eventually reveal that, despite her hope and trust in her father, he is guilty. Glennis must learn to accept weakness in someone she loves rather than remain a prisoner of her own self-deception. "Glennis's phases of hope . . ., anger . . . and determination to regain some of her losses are vividly and sensitively portrayed," noted a reviewer in *Publishers Weekly.* "The story has some nice writing and wonderful images . . ., and Glennis is a strong female character with guts and ideas," Carol A. Edwards contended in *School Library Journal.*

Other recent publications by Calvert include *Picking up the Pieces* in which a girl comes to terms with an injury that has left her paralyzed, *Bigger,* an historical novel set during the American Civil War, and *Writing to Richie,* about a boy grieving over the death of his younger brother.

"I am everlastingly fascinated," Calvert once commented, "by that country from which we are all emigrants: the land of childhood—and that is the reason why my fiction is for (and about) children. When an acquaintance recently expressed to me the hope that, since I'd now had a couple of children's books published, I could write 'a real one' (that is, a novel for adults), I had to discourage him quickly. To write for and about children—and to write for and about the child in myself—is really all I intend to do."

Biographical and Critical Sources

BOOKS

Calvert, Patricia, essay in *Something about the Author Autobiography Series,* Volume 17, Gale (Detroit, MI), 1994.
Twentieth-Century Young Adult Writers, first edition, St. James (Detroit, MI), 1994.

PERIODICALS

Bulletin of the Center for Children's Books, November, 1985; December, 1986; December, 1987.
Publishers Weekly, July 29, 1996, review of *Glennis, Before and After,* p. 89.
School Library Journal, September, 1996, Carol A. Edwards, review of *Glennis, Before and After,* p. 201.*

*   *   *

CARR, Jan 1953-
(M. J. Carr)

Personal

Born September 10, 1953, in Syracuse, NY; daughter of James J. (a television account executive) and Janet (a homemaker) Carr; married Stan Baker (a writer and performer); children: Charlie C. *Education:* Cornell University, B.S., 1975; University of Cincinnati, M.Ed., 1978; attended Columbia University, 1981-83. *Hobbies and other interests:* Ballet, dance, theater.

Addresses

Home—New York, NY. *Agent*—c/o Holiday House, 425 Madison Ave., New York, NY 10017.

Jan Carr

Career

Writer and editor. Clinton Preschool Head Start, teacher, 1975-77; Arlitt Child Development Center, teacher, 1977-78; Children's Television Workshop, New York, NY, production assistant, 1979, associate editor/writer for *Sesame Street Parent's Newsletter,* 1980-83; Scholastic, Inc., New York, NY, associate editor, 1983-87.

Member

Authors Guild, National Writers Union.

Writings

(Editor with Eva Moore and Mary M. White) Beatrice S. De Regniers, selector, *Sing a Song of Popcorn: Every Child's Book of Poems,* Scholastic (New York, NY), 1988.
Be My Valentine, illustrated by Katy Bratun, Scholastic (New York, NY), 1992.
Beauty and the Beast, illustrated by Katy Bratun, Scholastic (New York, NY), 1992.
Harem Wish (for adults), Dutton (New York, NY), 1994
Dark Day, Light Night, illustrated by James Ransome, Hyperion (New York, NY), 1996.
(Adapter) *Disney's Toy Story: I Come in Peace,* Disney Press (New York, NY), 1996.

The Nature of the Beast, illustrated by G. Brian Karas, Tambourine Books (New York, NY), 1996.

Upside Down and Topsy-Turvy, illustrated by the Thompson Brothers, Disney Press (New York, NY), 1996.

(Adapter) *Walt Disney's Oliver & Company,* Disney Press (New York, NY), 1996.

(Adapter) *Doug's Secret Christmas,* (original script by Ken Scarborough), illustrated by Matthew C. Peters, Disney Press (New York, NY), 1997.

Hercules the Hero, illustrated by the Thompson Brothers, Disney Press (New York, NY), 1997.

Princess Anastasia, illustrated by the Thompson Brothers, HarperActive (New York, NY), 1997.

Frozen Noses, illustrated by Dorothy Donohue, Holiday House (New York, NY), 1999.

Swine Divine, illustrated by Robert Bender, Holiday House (New York, NY), 1999.

Big Truck and Little Truck, illustrated by Ivan Bates, Scholastic (New York, NY), 2000.

Dappled Apples, illustrated by Dorothy Donohue, Holiday House (New York, NY), 2001.

Splish, Splash, Spring, illustrated by Dorothy Donohue, Holiday House (New York, NY), 2001.

Sweet Hearts, illustrated by Dorothy Donohue, Holiday House (New York, NY), 2002.

Contributor to *Writer's Digest* and several arts publications, including *Playbill, Stagebill, TheaterWeek,* and *Variety.*

UNDER PSEUDONYM M. J. CARR

(Adapter) *Black Beauty* (novel by Anna Sewell), illustrated by John Speirs, Scholastic (New York, NY), 1994.

(Adapter) *The Baby-sitters Club* (from *The Baby-sitters Club* movie; based on the series by Ann M. Martin), Scholastic (New York, NY), 1995.

(Adapter) *The Little Princess,* (from the screenplay by Richard LaGravenese and Elizabeth Chandler; based on the book by Frances Hodgson Burnett), Scholastic (New York, NY), 1995.

You're Invited to Mary-Kate & Ashley's Ballet Party, Scholastic (New York, NY), 1998.

Author of children's books based on screenplays and classic novels under pseudonym M. J. Carr, including *Ariel the Spy* and *Arista's New Boyfriend* from "The Little Mermaid" series, *The Wizard of Oz,* and *The Little Princess,* and picture books based on children's characters, such as *Visit the Doctor* and *One Special Child* from the "Cabbage Patch Kids" series.

Sidelights

Jan Carr is the author of numerous books for young readers. Carr's original stories include *Dark Day, Light Night,* a 1996 title highly recommended by critics. Its story centers around a late-afternoon game of street ball and a little girl named Manda. Her playmate friend steals her ball as a joke, and Manda sulks off. She returns home, where her Aunt Ruby tries to console her. The adult recognizes Manda's dark mood and suggests that she make a list of things she likes in order to cheer herself. Manda says that there are none, but Aunt Ruby

gives up her own secret list, which lightens Manda's mood. Aunt Ruby says that this is how she pulls herself out of a "dark day." *Horn Book* reviewer Ellen Fader noted that "children who have been down in the dumps will quickly recognize themselves in this high-spirited picture book." Fader also liked James Ransome's images, which she described as "bursting with the exuberance of people enjoying life." Susan Dove Lempke, writing in *Booklist,* commended the way in which *Dark Day, Light Night* presented two strategies "to resolve angry feelings—listing favorite things and talking to a grown-up who loves you."

Carr has also written *The Nature of the Beast,* which features little Isabelle. She badly wants a pet, but has just one dollar to spend at the pet store. She is sold the "Beast" to take home, and with the encouragement of her researcher father, decides to make the Beast her science project. She keeps a minute record of all her strange creature's habits. The beast is large, furry, speaks French, likes to sleep in the chandelier, wears her father's ties, and generally causes havoc at home. A crisis mounts when the Beast becomes ill, but all ends well. *Horn Book*'s Elizabeth S. Watson predicted that Carr's young readers "will adore Beast and his relationship to Isabelle's family" and liked the way the text meshed with images from G. Brian Karas.

A trio of books that chronicle the seasons have also earned Carr enthusiastic reviews from librarians and teachers. These titles began in 1999 with *Frozen Noses,* in which three friends and a little gray puppy enjoy winter's charms. They also endure some of its more

Carr's picture book extols the special qualities of the autumn season in verse accompanied by cheerful paper-collage illustrations by Dorothy Donohue. (From Dappled Apples.*)*

negative aspects, such as the title occurrence and a chest cold. Yet there are also snowball games, a sleigh ride, and the warmth of a cup of hot chocolate once inside. The last page shows all asleep by a fireplace. Marta Segal, writing in *Booklist,* commended Carr for using some daring vocabulary for her intended readers: words such as "quiver, veer, and collide are folded so effortlessly into the rhyme," Segal stated, that she wondered why other books for young readers did not attempt to do so as well.

Carr's Rosie the pig, the star of *Swine Divine,* was directed at young readers with a keen sense of the absurd. Farmer Luke scrubs Rosie clean and takes her to Mr. Porkpie, the photographer. For a little while, Rosie enjoys modeling the different outfits, but balks when asked to wear a tutu. She flees back to the farm, and blissfully wallows in her favorite mud patch again. "Delightfully off-the-wall, the story has a raucous energy that will appeal to preschoolers," remarked *Booklist*'s Ilene Cooper.

The farm is also the locale for Carr's *Big Truck and Little Truck.* Big Fred and Little Fred Farley have many chores to do, and Big Truck is always a vital part of the day's work. He also teaches Little Truck how to help, and then Little Truck is left on his own one day when Big Truck visits the town mechanic for some maintenance. Little Truck winds up in a ditch, but remembers some words of advice from Big Truck in time to save himself. "When Big Truck returns, the two trucks share a joyful, proud reunion," noted *Booklist*'s Segal. *School Library Journal* reviewer Sally Bates Goodroe found that "There's lots here for truck lovers and any kids who need encouragement to try something on their own."

Carr's follow-up to *Frozen Noses* was *Splish, Splash, Spring.* Again, three youngsters and their dog romp through spring puddles, then joyfully shed their winter coats one sunny day. They roam about and observe telltale signs of the season, such as new flowers and baby robins. "The bouncy language, bright artwork, and nonstop action make this book a good choice for group sharing," asserted Anne Parker in *School Library Journal. Booklist*'s Shelley Townsend-Hudson stated that "Carr's bouncing rhymes are full of choice adjectives—sloppy and bloomy, swooping and snapping" and termed them a perfect match to Dorothy Donohue's almost tactile illustrations.

Fall and its treats were the subject of *Dappled Apples.* Carr's rhyming verse chronicles the sights, sounds, and pleasures of autumn, following the trio and their dog through an apple orchard and pumpkin patch. The jack-o'-lantern carving is paid homage as well: "Teeth are zigzag/Tail goes wigwag/Seeds are slimy/Scoop the goop." The children also romp through piles of leaves and celebrate Halloween together. *Booklist*'s Carolyn Phelan liked Carr's "playful, original way with words" and judged it a "spirited, staccato tribute to fall."

Carr once commented: "In some ways, I have always been a writer. Still, it has been a long, winding road for me to get to the point where I'm able to do the work I do today. My love of writing began when I was a child, with my love of reading. Each week, my mother would troop my brothers and me off to the neighborhood library, where we'd gather up a fresh stack of books. When I was too young to read them myself, my mother would read them to me. The books I read inspired me to try my own hand at writing. I wrote poems—some silly, some serious. I even wrote a long adventure story about a girl who got kidnaped and escaped her crude and clumsy kidnapers by outsmarting them!

"Though I continued to write while in school, when it was time for me to get a job, it never occurred to me to try to find one that was related to writing. I worked first as a teacher, then tried my hand at film editing (I was a disaster!), and after that I got a job working for a TV production company. Writing was what I did in my spare time. After work, I took classes and wrote (and rewrote!) my stories. Finally, I got a job in a publishing house, one that specialized in children's books. There, I learned all about the business of publishing—the stages of book production, the reasons a book might or might not be acquired, and how books are marketed.

"One day, I got the courage to go a step further—quit my job and write full-time. This could have been a foolhardy decision, as many writers, even ones who get published, do not make enough money to live on. But I was lucky enough, because of my experience in children's publishing, to get jobs writing books based on movies that were coming out. When I get these projects, the publishing house sends me a copy of the script of the movie, and my job is to put the script into story form. Often, the movies are taken from classic stories that already were books. I love working with these beautifully written stories, ones that I read and loved as a child.

"Still, my heart is in the stories that I make up myself, ones that are not based at all on anyone else's work, and I am happiest when I get one of my own stories published. I still use many of the story elements that I loved as a child. For instance, interesting language. I would much rather write, 'The rabbit nipped past her' than 'The rabbit ran past her.' To my ear, it's more fun to read, more colorful. Also, like the cunning little heroine who escaped her clumsy kidnapers, many of my stories are about girls. I like to write about girls who are plucky and scrappy. It expresses a plucky side of my own nature and feels light and freeing. In recent years, I've also been inspired to write stories for my young son. As he and I read together, I get a chance to see what sorts of stories he likes, what kinds of characters and scenes he responds to. When I'm writing, the key for me is to have fun. Otherwise the work gets heavy and leaden. If I'm interested in what I'm writing, there's a good chance that readers will find it interesting, too!"

Biographical and Critical Sources

BOOKS

Carr, Jan, *Dappled Apples,* illustrated by Dorothy Donohue, Holiday House (New York, NY), 2001.

PERIODICALS

Booklist, February 15, 1994, p. 1059; February 15, 1996, Susan Dove Lempke, review of *Dark Day, Light Night,* p. 1025; April 15, 1996, Stephanie Zvirin, review of *The Nature of the Beast,* p. 1445; March 1, 1999, Ilene Cooper, review of *Swine Divine,* p. 1218; September 15, 1999, Marta Segal, review of *Frozen Noses,* p. 266; November 15, 2000, Marta Segal, review of *Big Truck and Little Truck,* p. 646; April 1, 2001, Shelley Townsend-Hudson, review of *Splish, Splash, Spring,* p. 1477; October 1, 2001, Carolyn Phelan, review of *Dappled Apples,* p. 324.

Childhood Education, fall, 1999, Kevin McCloskey, review of *Swine Divine,* p. 44.

Horn Book, May-June, 1996, Ellen Fader, review of *Dark Day, Light Night,* p. 320; July-August, 1996, Elizabeth S. Watson, review of *The Nature of the Beast,* p. 445.

Kirkus Reviews, February 15, 1994, p. 158; March 1, 1999, review of *Swine Divine,* p. 373; August 15, 1999, review of *Frozen Noses,* p. 1308; August 15, 2001, review of *Dappled Apples,* p. 1208.

Publishers Weekly, January 31, 1994, p. 74; February 20, 1995, p. 203; March 8, 1999, review of *Swine Divine,* p. 68.

School Library Journal, September, 1999, Martha Topol, review of *Frozen Noses,* p. 178; November, 2000, Sally Bates Goodroe, review of *Big Truck and Little Truck,* p. 112; May, 2001, Anne Parker, review of *Splish, Splash, Spring,* p. 112; September, 2001, Shara Alpern, review of *Dappled Apples,* p. 184.

*　　*　　*

CARR, M. J.
See CARR, Jan

*　　*　　*

CLEARY, Brian P. 1959-

Personal

Born October 1, 1959, in Lakewood, OH; son of Michael J. (an international businessman) and Suzanne Cleary; children: Grace, Ellen, Emma. *Ethnicity:* "Irish-American." *Education:* John Carroll University, B.A., 1982. *Religion:* Roman Catholic.

Addresses

Home—16505 Southland Ave., Cleveland, OH 44111. *E-mail*—baberuth60@aol.com.

Career

Humor writer and freelance copywriter.

Awards, Honors

Children's Choice selection, International Reading Association/Children's Book Council, 1996, for *Give Me Bach My Schubert;* Benjamin Franklin Award for Best Juvenile/Young Adult Nonfiction, for *To Root, to Toot, to Parachute: What Is a Verb?,* 2002.

Writings

Jamaica Sandwich?, illustrated by Rick Dupre, Lerner (Minneapolis, MN), 1996.

It Looks a Lot Like Reindeer, illustrated by Rick Dupre, Lerner (Minneapolis, MN), 1996.

Give Me Bach My Schubert, illustrated by Rick Dupre, Lerner (Minneapolis, MN), 1996.

You Never Sausage Love, illustrated by Rick Dupre, Lerner (Minneapolis, MN), 1996.

A Mink, a Fink, a Skating Rink: What Is a Noun?, illustrated by Jenya Prosmitsky, Carolrhoda Books (Minneapolis, MN), 1999.

Hairy, Scary, Ordinary: What Is an Adjective?, illustrated by Jenya Prosmitsky, Carolrhoda Books (Minneapolis, MN), 2000.

To Root, to Toot, to Parachute: What Is a Verb?, illustrated by Jenya Prosmitsky, Carolrhoda Books (Minneapolis, MN), 2001.

Under, Over, by the Clover: What Is a Preposition?, illustrated by Brian Gable, Carolrhoda Books (Minneapolis, MN), 2002.

Nearly, Dearly, Insincerely: What Is an Adverb?, illustrated by Brian Gable, Carolrhoda Books (Minneapolis, MN), 2003.

Contributor of humor articles, essays, features, and cartoons to magazines.

Brian P. Cleary

Cartoon cats illustrate the meaning and significance of adjectives in Cleary's book that is full of exaggeration, wordplay, and nonsensical situations. (Cover illustration by Jenya Prosmitsky.)

Sidelights

Humorist Brian P. Cleary has filled his children's books with good clean fun. His picture books *Jamaica Sandwich?, It Looks a Lot Like Reindeer, Give Me Bach My Schubert,* and *You Never Sausage Love* rely heavily on pun-filled wordplay and simply intend to entertain. Yet some of Cleary's books have another purpose. He once told *SATA:* "I believe humor increases vocabulary, ignites curiosity and, therefore, teaches." Thus it is not surprising that he would create a series of books to explain in an entertaining way several fundamental parts of speech: nouns, verbs, adjectives, adverbs, and prepositions. For *A Mink, a Fink, a Skating Rink: What Is a Noun?,* Cleary created "humorous rhymes" that are combined with "silly illustrations," to quote Lisa Gangemi of *School Library Journal.* Using his "witty zeal," Cleary created "certainly one of the least serious grammar lessons imaginable," a *Publishers Weekly* contributor added. In *Hairy, Scary, Ordinary: What Is an Adjective?,* cartoon cats play among an array of adjectives, which *Booklist* reviewer Hazel Rochman predicted would "appeal to kids" for its exaggeration, wordplay, and nonsensical situations. Writing in *School Library Journal,* Adele Greenlee called the work a "lighthearted, multifaceted illustration of the importance of adjectives." And in keeping with the previous

volumes, through his *To Root, to Toot, to Parachute: What Is a Verb?,* Cleary reviewed the definition and use of verbs with the help of slapstick cartoon cats. Together, these rhymes and cartoons, according to Elaine Lesh Morgan of *School Library Journal,* "painlessly teach a grammar lesson."

Biographical and Critical Sources

PERIODICALS

Booklist, June 1, 2000, Hazel Rochman, review of *Hairy, Scary, Ordinary: What Is an Adjective?,* p. 1900; March 1, 2002, GraceAnne A. DeCandido, review of *Under, Over, By the Clover: What Is a Preposition?,* p. 1132.

Childhood Education, winter, 2000, Jorie Borden, review of *Hairy, Scary, Ordinary,* p. 107.

Horn Book Guide, spring, 1997, Peter D. Sieruta, reviews of *Give Me Bach My Schubert* and *You Never Sausage Love,* p. 23.

Kirkus Reviews, September 1, 1999, review of *A Mink, a Fink, a Skating Rink: What Is a Noun?,* p. 1424.

Publishers Weekly, February 26, 1996, review of *Jamaica Sandwich?,* p. 105; August 9, 1999, review of *A Mink, a Fink, a Skating Rink,* p. 352; February 26, 2001, "More Where That Came From," p. 88.

School Library Journal, June, 1996, Kathy Piehl, review of *Jamaica Sandwich?,* p. 120; June, 1996, Ellen M. Riordan, review of *It Looks a Lot Like Reindeer,* p. 120; December, 1996, Elizabeth Trotter, review of *Give Me Bach My Schubert,* p. 91; November, 1999, Lisa Gangemi, review of *A Mink, a Fink, a Skating Rink,* pp. 135-136; July, 2000, Adele Greenlee, review of *Hairy, Scary, Ordinary,* p. 92; July, 2001, Elaine Lesh Morgan, review of *To Root, to Toot, to Parachute: What Is a Verb?,* p. 92.

*   *   *

CUNNINGHAM, Julia (Woolfolk) 1916-

Personal

Born October 4, 1916, in Spokane, WA; daughter of John G. L. and Sue (Larabie) Cunningham. *Education:* Attended art school in Charlottesville, VA, and the Alliance Francaise Institut de Touraine, Tours, France.

Addresses

Home—333 Old Mill Road, Santa Barbara, CA 93310.

Career

Writer. Guaranty Trust Company, New York, NY, clerk, 1937-40; G. Schirmer, Inc. (music publishers), New York, NY, editorial coordinator, 1940-44; Dell Publishing Co., New York, NY, associate editor of *Screen Stories,* 1944-47; Air Reduction Company, New York, NY, secretary, 1947-49; Sherman Clay & Co., San Francisco, CA, assistant to the advertising manager,

1950-51; Metropolitan Museum of Art, New York, NY, saleswoman in book and art shop, 1953-56; Tecolote Book Shop, Santa Barbara, CA, assistant to owner, 1960-76.

Member

Authors Guild, Authors League of America.

Awards, Honors

First prize, *New York Herald Tribune* Children's Spring Book Festival, 1965, Southern California Council on Literature for Children and Young People Award, 1966, and Lewis Carroll Shelf Award, 1972, all for *Dorp Dead;* Outstanding Books of the Year citation, *New York Times,* 1970, for *Burnish Me Bright,* and 1973, for *The Treasure Is the Rose;* National Book Award finalist, 1973, for *The Treasure Is the Rose;* Christopher Award and Lewis Carroll Shelf Award, both 1978, both for *Come to the Edge;* Commonwealth Club of California Award and *Boston Globe* Honor Book citation, both 1980, both for *Flight of the Sparrow;* Southern California Council of Literature for Children and Young People Award, 1982, for body of work.

Writings

FICTION FOR CHILDREN

The Vision of Francois the Fox, illustrated by Nicholas Angelo, Houghton Mifflin (Boston, MA), 1960.
Dear Rat, illustrated by Walter Lorraine, Houghton Mifflin (Boston, MA), 1961.
Macaroon, illustrated by Evaline Ness, Pantheon (New York, NY), 1962.
Candle Tales, illustrated by Evaline Ness, Pantheon (New York, NY), 1964.
Viollet, illustrated by Alan Cober, Pantheon (New York, NY), 1966.
Onion Journey, illustrated by Lydia Cooley, Pantheon (New York, NY), 1967.
Burnish Me Bright, illustrated by Don Freeman, Pantheon (New York, NY), 1970.
Wings of the Morning, photographs by Katy Peake, Golden Gate (San Francisco, CA), 1971.
Far in the Day, illustrated by Don Freeman, Pantheon (New York, NY), 1972.
Maybe, a Mole, illustrated by Cyndy Szekeres, Pantheon (New York, NY), 1974.
Come to the Edge, Pantheon (New York, NY), 1977.
A Mouse Called Junction, illustrated by Michael Hague, Pantheon (New York, NY), 1980.
Flight of the Sparrow, Pantheon (New York, NY), 1980.
The Silent Voice, Dutton (New York, NY), 1981.
Wolf Roland, Pantheon (New York, NY), 1983.
Oaf, illustrated by Peter Sis, Knopf (New York, NY), 1986.
The Stable Rat and Other Christmas Poems, illustrated by Anita Lobel, Greenwillow (New York, NY), 2001.

FICTION FOR YOUNG ADULTS

Dorp Dead, illustrated by James Spanfeller, Pantheon (New York, NY), 1965.

The Treasure Is the Rose, illustrated by Judy Graese, Pantheon (New York, NY), 1973.
Tuppenny, Dutton (New York, NY), 1978.

Poems, short stories and a novella featured in *Cicada* magazine.

Sidelights

Julia Cunningham began to publish fiction for children at the age of forty-four, though she had been writing for most of her life. Now well into her third decade as a published author, she has won numerous prestigious awards for her work, most notably two *New York Times* Outstanding Book of the Year citations and the 1978 Christopher Award for *Come to the Edge.* Highly controversial in content, many of her books have nevertheless received praise for their sophisticated blend of fantasy and difficult, sometimes violent, reality. As Judith Crist commented in *Book Week,* "Here is one author who has recognized the sophistication of young readers geared to an age of television and film and shows that a book can be as hip and as exciting and far more memorable."

Cunningham's first memories are of growing up in New York City, where she and her two brothers turned city playgrounds into castles, beds into pirate ships, and old clothes into the regal robes of kings and queens. Although Cunningham remembered the fantasy life of her childhood fondly in her essay for *Something about the Author Autobiography Series* (*SAAS*), she also described the disappearance of her father when she was six years old as one of the defining points of her life. She was so distraught by his departure that by age nine she "gave up, and became so ill danger dwelled in the bottomless, drowning nightmares." Eventually she recovered, but admitted that she became a "pretender," learning "the rules that led to approval, acceptance, popularity and [using] them with success." Cunningham wrote: "Is this when so many of the characters in my books were fated to be orphans? I believe so, unconsciously and inevitably. One's characters are oneselves and no escape is possible."

Cunningham started writing at the age of eight or nine, she remembered in her autobiographical essay, crafting "three-page novels about nuns who fled their convents in order to live in a New York garret, poor but extremely happy, to fairy tales that, though I was of course unaware of this fact, dragged their seven-league boots through much-too-long winding roads, lined with too many dragons, princesses who were traditionally helpless, knights without fault, and very usual plots." At age twelve she sent out her first manuscript and, "The editor of the magazine wrote a letter, a serious rejection letter, saying I had talent.... I was very proud and this may well have set the mold of my goal to someday be published."

Cunningham would have a long wait to be published, however; she recalled building up "an edifice of rejection slips" as she waited for some publisher to

The Christmas story, told by observers both human and animal, is the focal point of Julia Cunningham's collection of elegant, powerful poems. (From The Stable Rat and Other Christmas Poems, *illustrated by Anita Lobel.)*

accept her manuscript. In the meantime she built up a well of experience from which much of her fiction is drawn. Following in her mother's footsteps, Cunningham traveled to France where she developed a fascination for the Middle Ages and the ancient cathedrals and monasteries. She recalled discovering that in "opening my mind to a living appreciation and application of what is so beautiful in the French language I gained a new appreciation of my own, a new and largely unconscious awareness of how to use English words to more effectively carpenter a story. I believe I arrived at a sense of essence, for this was when, after many years of rejections, I began to write well enough to publish." In fact her first published work was *The Vision of Francois the Fox,* the story of a crafty French fox who is awed by

the beautiful stained-glass windows of a cathedral. Many of her other stories are also set in her beloved France.

Cunningham is well known for her exploration of themes such as the meaning of life, value judgments, psychological isolation and spiritual freedom, themes that ordinarily receive little treatment in juvenile fiction. In a *Washington Post Book World* review of *Wolf Roland,* Michael Dirda suggested: "Adolescents, newly alert to questions of identity and morality, should enjoy following [the principal character] as he learns the proper value of friendship, personal integrity, simplicity, and kindness." Barbara Wersba, reviewing *The Treasure Is the Rose* for the *New York Times Book Review,* concluded that Cunningham's consummate achievement has been "to probe her characters to the point where we see the secret self that hides within all of them, waiting for someone to bring it forth."

Anita Moss, writing in *Twentieth-Century Children's Writers,* noted that "among Cunningham's most memorable creations are her anthropomorphic animal characters. Most often in her animal fables Cunningham reveals the power of love to bring forth the highest and best self." In many of the stories, the animals are outcasts, different from others in the way they think and feel; but by displaying love and affection, these characters are able to find friendship. In *Maybe, a Mole,* the title character is able to transform a worldly fox, who realizes that Maybe is "someone to be trusted, to be company, to be loved." With *The Vision of Francois the Fox,* Cunningham shows the power of love bringing out the best in a person, or in this case, a worldly fox. Francois is a pleasure-loving trickster, but when he enters a cathedral he is so awed by the stained-glass vision of a saint that he thereafter devotes his life to self-sacrifice, giving up his bad old ways. In *Macaroon* Cunningham focuses on a raccoon that likewise gives up his spoiled former persona after encountering a little girl who needs him. These tales show children who consider themselves outsiders, children much like Cunningham was herself, that they too can be loved for who they are, and that self-sacrifice is a noble end in itself.

Mystery and gothic elements also come into play in some of Cunningham's most popular works for children. *Dear Rat* features another anthropomorphic character, Andrew the Rat, a detective from Hampton, Wyoming, who wins the hand of a lovely princess rat in France by thwarting a jewel robbery from Chartres Cathedral. In *Viollet,* a thrush is a wonderful singer able to perform only when alone, even though he is spurred on by friends Warwick the fox and Oxford the hound. The singing bird and his friends manage to stop the murder of a kindly and music-loving count by his villainous foreman. *The Treasure Is the Rose* is a blend of gothic terror and medieval romance, set a thousand years ago. And in *Tuppeny,* a mysterious girl—something of a supernatural agent—comes into the lives of three families, each with its own secrets.

Cunningham's most famous and most controversial work is *Dorp Dead,* which has received numerous book awards. _Dorp Dead_ is the story of an orphan named Gilly who believes that he can live without love. This belief leads Gilly into the hands of the evil Master Kobalt, who represents "the regimentation and life-denying aspects of the technological world which values only the practical," wrote Moss. After a brush with death, Gilly escapes from Kobalt into a world that values life and love and the ability to be oneself. The story is intensely allegorical, and many critics felt that the book is too scary for its young adult audience. Crist, however, thought that Cunningham wrote in "frank, literate terms in the lingo of today's youngsters" and lauded her for not talking down to her readers.

In fact, Cunningham feels very close to the children for whom she writes. In her autobiographical essay, she remarked, "The children are believers in a very subtle sense and my quite frequent journeys to their schools, spring and autumn, are a kind of continuing reunion for me. I am neither higher nor lower than they. We think and feel on the same level." Wersba, in her review of _Come to the Edge_ in the _New York Times Book Review,_ commented that Cunningham is "able to write about childhood as though she had never left it." Cunningham once explained that she owes this faculty to her "second reality of the imagination. . . . It seems to me that one passes through a kind of gate into another country, into unfamiliar landscapes where one encounters all those characters that love, hate, torment and amuse. They take on their own vitality and I am only their interpreter. They speak and I record."

Biographical and Critical Sources

BOOKS

Cameron, Eleanor, _The Green and Burning Tree: On the Writing and Enjoyment of Children's Books,_ 4th edition, Atlantic-Little, Brown (Boston, MA), 1969.

Contemporary Literary Criticism, Volume 12, Gale (Detroit, MI), 1980.

Something about the Author Autobiography Series, Volume 2, Gale (Detroit, MI), 1986, pp. 51-65.

Egoff, Sheila, _Only Connect: Readings on Children's Literature,_ Oxford University Press (Don Mills, Ontario, Canada), 1969.

Huck, Charlotte S., and Doris Young Kuhn, _Children's Literature in the Elementary School,_ 2nd edition, Holt (New York, NY), 1968.

St. James Guide to Children's Writers, 5th edition, St. James Press (Detroit, MI), 1999.

PERIODICALS

Antiquarian Bookman, January 18, 1971.

Calendar, March-August, 1976.

Horn Book, June, 1966; June, 1972; February, 1974; August, 1980, p. 394.

New Statesman, June 4, 1971.

New York Times Book Review, April 25, 1965; November 6, 1966; May 24, 1970; November 4, Barbara Wersba, review of _The Treasure Is the Rose,_ 1973, p. 42; July 10, Barbara Wersba, review of _Come to the Edge,_ 1977, p. 21; September 14, 1980; February 8, 1981;

January 17, 1982, p. 30; May 16, 1982, p. 39; April 10, 1983, p. 39; April 6, 1986, p. 21.

Psychology Today, May, 1975.

Publishers Weekly, May 16, 1980, p. 212; October 16, 1981, p. 78; May 20, 1983, p. 223; June 10, 1983, p. 65; January 10, 1986, p. 84.

School Library Journal, May, 1980, p. 53; October, 1980, p. 14; January, 1982, p. 76; May, 1983, p. 80; April, 1986, p. 86.

Sunday Herald Tribune Book Week, May 9, 1965, Judith Crist, review of _Dorp Dead,_ p. 5.

Times Literary Supplement, November 30, 1967.

Washington Post Book World, May 8, 1983, Michael Dirda, review of _Wolf Roland,_ p. 15.

Writer, November, 1976.*

* * *

CURRIE, Stephen 1960-

Personal

Born September 29, 1960, in New York, NY; son of David Park (a law professor) and Barbara Suzanne (an Illinois state legislator; maiden name, Flynn) Currie; married Amity Elizabeth Smith (a teacher) July 3, 1983; children: Irene Elizabeth, Nicholas David. _Education:_ Williams College, B.A. (magna cum laude), 1982. _Hobbies and other interests:_ Swimming, singing, reading.

Addresses

Home—14 Oakwood Blvd., Poughkeepsie, NY 12603-4112. _Office_—Poughkeepsie Day School, 39 New Hackensack Rd., Poughkeepsie, NY 12603.

Career

Poughkeepsie Day School, Poughkeepsie, NY, teacher, 1982—. Korean Enrichment Program, language enrichment teacher, 1989-91; Duchess Community College, Saturday Enrichment Program teacher, 1986-89. Has cataloged and annotated maps for the Adriance Memorial Library, 1982-83; Hudson Valley Gilbert and Sullivan society, performer and member of board of directors, 1983-92; editorial referee for National Council of Teachers of Mathematics journals, 1993-94; served as counselor for art- and sports-related camps.

Member

National Association for the Education of Young Children, National Council of Teachers of Mathematics.

Writings

Music in the Civil War, Betterway Books (Cincinnati, OH), 1992.

Problem Play, Dale Seymour, 1993.

Problem Play Poster Set, Dale Seymour, 1994.

A Birthday-a-Day Easel, GoodYear Books (Cincinnati, OH), 1995.

The March of the Mill Children, Lerner Publications (Minneapolis, MN), 1995.

Adoption, Greenhaven Press (San Diego, CA), 1997.

We Have Marched Together: The Working Children's Crusade, Lerner Publications (Minneapolis, MN), 1997.

Issues in Sports, Greenhaven Press (San Diego, CA), 1998.

Life in a Wild West Show, Lucent Books (San Diego, CA), 1999.

The Olympic Games, Lucent Books (San Diego, CA), 1999.

Polynesians, Smart Apple Media (Mankato, MN), 1999.

Slavery, Greenhaven Press (San Diego, CA), 1999.

Life of a Slave on a Southern Plantation, Lucent Books (San Diego, CA), 2000.

Abortion, Greenhaven Press (San Diego, CA), 2000.

The Liberator: Voice of the Abolitionist Movement, Lucent Books (San Diego, CA), 2000.

Issues in Immigration, Lucent Books (San Diego, CA), 2000.

Pirates, Lucent Books (San Diego, CA), 2001.

Women Inventors, Lucent Books (San Diego, CA), 2001.

Thar She Blows: American Whaling in the Nineteenth Century, Lerner Publications (Minneapolis, MN), 2001.

(Editor) *The 1300's,* Greenhaven Press (San Diego, CA), 2001.

(Editor) *The 1500's,* Greenhaven Press (San Diego, CA), 2001.

Polar Explorers, Lucent Books (San Diego, CA), 2002.

The Salem Witch Trials, Kidhaven Press (San Diego, CA), 2002.

Life in the Trenches, Lucent Books (San Diego, CA), 2002.

Women of the Civil War, Lucent Books (San Diego, CA), 2003.

Terrorists and Terrorist Groups, Lucent Books (San Diego, CA), 2003.

Mia Hamm, Kidhaven Press (San Diego, CA), 2003.

Contributor to periodicals, including *Cobblestone, Cricket, Teaching K-8, Independent School, Civil War History, Chicago Tribune,* and *Baseball Hobby News;* author of mathematics materials for Curriculum Concepts, Inc.; consultant and author of teacher's guide for "Eleanor Roosevelt's Wallet," Franklin and Eleanor Roosevelt Library; author of juvenile series fiction.

Sidelights

Stephen Currie has been teaching history for many years and once told *SATA* that he "found that children in my class love to study history if it's presented as a story." Currie noted that it was this mixture of storytelling and fact that he aimed to convey in his nonfiction books on social history.

Among titles focusing on social history is *We Have Marched Together: The Working Children's Crusade,* a retelling of the history of child labor in the United States during the early-twentieth century. Currie uses the historic 1903 protest march, where thousands of children, led by labor activist Mother Jones, marched from Philadelphia to New York City in order to protest child labor practices in the country.

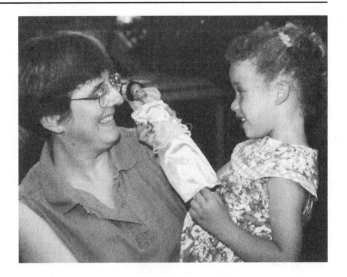

Adoption by Stephen Currie presents straightforward information on various issues, including interracial adoption and privacy concerns. (Photo by William Cochrane.)

Included among Currie's nonfiction works for children is *Problem Play,* a collection of mathematics problems organized to encourage problem-solving skills. A number of activities are included, such as puzzles, mazes, and maps, prompting Nancy W. McKirchy to note in *Arithmetic Teacher* that "*Problem Play* is an excellent resource that encourages primary-grade children to think logically."

Biographical and Critical Sources

PERIODICALS

Arithmetic Teacher, March, 1994, Nancy W. McKirchy, review of *Problem Play,* p. 424.

Booklist, May 1, 1997, Hazel Rochman, review of *We Have Marched Together: The Working Children's Crusade,* p. 1485; May 1, 1998, Chris Sherman, review of *Issues in Sports,* p. 1508; January 1, 2002, Randy Meyer, review of *Thar She Blows: American Whaling in the Nineteenth Century,* p. 834.

School Library Journal, September, 2000, Katie O' Dell, review of *Abortion,* p. 243; December, 2000, Diane S. Marton, review of *Issues in Immigration,* p. 157; July, 2001, Carrie Lynn Cooper, review of *Pirates,* p. 121; December, 2001. Carol Fazioli, review of *Women Inventors,* p. 157; April, 2002, Jessica Snow, review of *Thar She Blows,* p. 170.*

*　　　*　　　*

CYRUS, Kurt 1954-

Personal

Born August 17, 1954, in Redmond, OR; son of Warren H. and Joan Call Cyrus; partner of Linnea Lindberg. *Education:* Attended Oregon State University, 1974-76, and Art Center College of Design, 1978-80; Lane Community College, A.S. (respiratory therapy), 1985.

Hobbies and other interests: "Reforesting a twenty-acre tree farm."

Addresses

Home—Cottage Grove, OR. *Agent*—c/o Author Mail, Harcourt, 525 B. St., Ste. 1900, San Diego, CA 92101-4495. *E-mail*—kcyrus@efn.org.

Career

Sacred Heart General Hospital, Eugene, OR, respiratory therapist, 1984-94; author and illustrator of children's books, 1994—. SMART (Start Making A Reader Today) volunteer; Big Brother volunteer, 1998—.

Awards, Honors

Children's Choice Award, 1998, for *Tangle Town;* Best Children's Books of 1998 runner-up, *Time* magazine, for *Slow Train to Oxmox;* Christopher Award, 2000, for *The Mousery;* Pick of the Lists selection, American Booksellers Association, 2001, for *Oddhopper Opera; Sixteen Cows* was named a Junior Library Guild selection, 2002.

Writings

SELF-ILLUSTRATED

Tangle Town, Farrar, Straus & Giroux (New York, NY), 1997.
Slow Train to Oxmox, Farrar, Straus & Giroux (New York, NY), 1998.
Oddhopper Opera: A Bug's Garden of Verses, Harcourt (San Diego, CA), 2001.

ILLUSTRATOR

Judith Mathews, *There's Nothing to D-o-o-o!,* Harcourt (San Diego, CA), 1999.
Charlotte Pomerantz, *The Mousery,* Harcourt (San Diego, CA), 2000.
Eve Bunting, *The Bones of Fred McFee,* Harcourt (San Diego, CA), 2002.
Lisa Wheeler, *Sixteen Cows,* Harcourt (San Diego, CA), 2002.
Lisa Wheeler, *Avalanche Annie: A Not-So-Tall Tale,* Harcourt (San Diego, CA), 2003.

Work in Progress

Research on ocean life.

Sidelights

After working for a decade as a respiratory therapist, Kurt Cyrus quit his day job and made his debut as a picture book author and illustrator with *Tangle Town,* a place where everything is twisted up. When the mayor of Tangle Town cannot open his door because he is pushing when he should be pulling, it starts a chain reaction of misunderstandings, much like what happens when a group of children play the game "Telephone." It takes a practical girl searching for a lost cow to straighten out the confusion in Tangle Town. According

to *Horn Book Guide* reviewer Christine Heppermann, the illustrations, reminiscent of the artwork of William Joyce, are the high point of the book. Steven Engelfried, writing in *School Library Journal,* called the illustrations "lively" and the plot laden with "enough nonsense and wit to amuse most readers," an opinion borne out by its selection for a Children's Choice Award in 1998.

In *Slow Train to Oxmox,* Cyrus told the story of Edwin Blink, who accidentally boards the wrong train one morning on the way to work. Instead of the express, he is on a slow train to nowhere. He is accompanied by a host of strange characters in an atmosphere that a *Publishers Weekly* critic likened to the set of Jean Paul Sartre's existentialist play *No Exit.* In fact, the critic called the work an "atmospheric tour de force." As the ride progresses, these characters work to overcome some strange obstacles, yet they never reach a destination. In the opinion of Robin Tzannes, who reviewed *Slow Train to Oxmox* for the *New York Times Book Review,* Cyrus's drawings are "very fine" and "full of wit and clever detail." Tzannes judged that the "drawings alone make this book worthwhile."

Oddhopper Opera: A Bug's Garden of Verses, is just that—a book of verses about bugs. Cyrus illustrates a myriad of bugs through his poems and pictures. Dung beetles, flies, spiders, katydids, and many more are brought together in this book. A reviewer for *Publishers*

Kurt Cyrus

In Cyrus's tale of a hilariously mixed-up mess, a sensible farm girl untangles the jumbled residents of Tangle Town. (From Tangle Town, *written and illustrated by Cyrus.)*

Weekly noted, "bold, inventive artwork lends high spirits to Cyrus's down-and-dirty view of the garden." And *Kirkus Reviews* claims, "with no sacrifice of legibility,

the page design is inventive too, with poems and pictures ingeniously wrapped together."

Cyrus told *SATA:* "The chair I work in has wheels on it, so when I get tired of illustrating, I can roll myself across the room to the writing table for awhile. Usually the writing session is brief. Then I roll myself back to the drawing table. I think it's very important to have a well-organized work space that contains everything I need, but nothing else. I'm too easily distracted."

Biographical and Critical Sources

PERIODICALS

Booklist, August, 1998, GraceAnne A. DeCandido, review of *Slow Train to Oxmox,* p. 2013; June 1, 1999, John Peters, review of *There's Nothing to D-o-o-o!,* p. 1842; March 15, 2001, Stephanie Zvirin, review of *Oddhopper Opera: A Bug's Garden of Verse,* p. 1394.

Horn Book Guide, fall, 1997, Christine Heppermann, review of *Tangle Town,* p. 262.

Kirkus Reviews, March 1, 2001, review of *Oddhopper Opera: A Bug's Garden of Verses.*

New York Times Book Review, November 15, 1998, Robin Tzannes, "Little Engines That Could," p. 46.

Publishers Weekly, July 20, 1998, review of *Slow Train to Oxmox,* p. 218; June 7, 1999, review of *There's Nothing to D-o-o-o!,* p. 81; July 31, 2000, review of *The Mousery,* p. 94; April 23, 2001, review of *Oddhopper Opera,* p. 77; March 25, 2002, review of *Sixteen Cows,* p. 63.

School Library Journal, March, 1997, Steven Engelfried, review of *Tangle Town,* pp. 149-150; May, 2001, Margaret Bush, review of *Oddhopper Opera,* p. 140; April, 2002, Helen Foster James, review of *Sixteen Cows,* p. 128.

D

DALKEY, Kara (Mia) 1953-

Personal

Born 1953.

Addresses

Agent—c/o St. Martin's Press/Tor, 175 Fifth Ave., New York, NY 10010.

Career

Writer.

Writings

FANTASY NOVELS

The Curse of Sagamore, Ace (New York, NY), 1986.
The Nightingale, Ace (New York, NY), 1988.
Euryale, Ace (New York, NY), 1988.
The Sword of Sagamore, Ace (New York, NY), 1989.
Little Sister, Harcourt Brace (San Diego, CA), 1996.
Goa, Tor (New York, NY), 1996.
Bijapur, Tor (New York, NY), 1997.
Bhagavati, Tor (New York, NY), 1998.
The Heavenward Path, Harcourt Brace (San Diego, CA), 1998.
Genpei, Tor (New York, NY), 2001.

Contributor to the fantasy sequence *Liavek.*

Sidelights

Kara Dalkey is a fantasy writer who has set most of her novels in real locales during real historical periods. The result is a blend of history and fantasy that offers readers information on Indian and Japanese mythology and religion, as well as glimpses into the vastly different cultures of non-Western nations. Dalkey began her career as a short-story writer and then wrote a conventional fantasy sequence encompassing *The Curse of Sagamore* and *The Sword of Sagamore.* Even early in

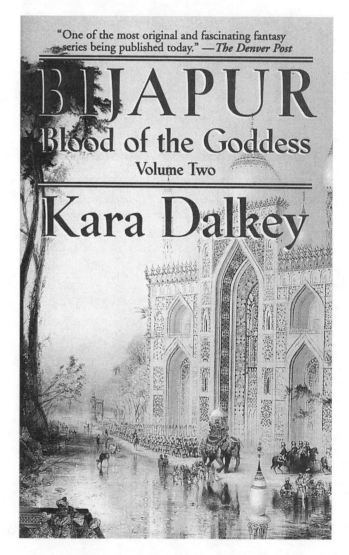

*The second volume of Kara Dalkey's "Blood of the Goddess" trilogy, set in sixteenth-century India, **Bijapur** follows English apothecary Thomas Chinnery who joins in the search for a legendary goddess. (Cover illustration by Richard Bober.)*

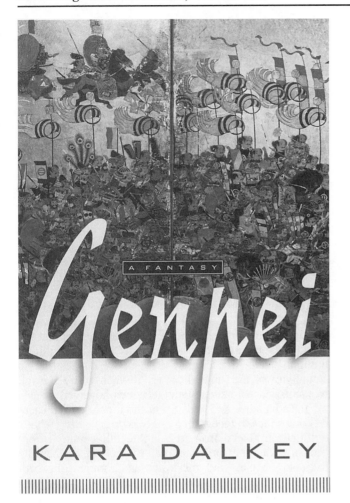

Based on the Tale of the Heike, *Dalkey's novel* Genpei *follows the battle between two clans in twelfth-century Japan, a rivalry which led the way for the rule of the first Shogun.*

her publishing history, however, she began to incorporate historical settings and myth into her books, as in *The Nightingale,* set in Japan but based on a Hans Christian Andersen fairy tale, and *Euryale,* a fresh take on the Roman myth of the Gorgon. According to a contributor to the *St. James Guide to Fantasy Writers,* "Kara Dalkey has proven herself capable of writing superior fantasy, both serious and humorous, and it is this flexibility that will probably ensure that her byline continues to find an audience, regardless of the direction her muse may next take her."

Dalkey "spins superior fantasy out of history and classic literature," noted Roland Green in *Booklist.* The author's more recent works include a trilogy set in Portugal and India, comprised of *Goa, Bijapur,* and *Bhagavati;* and another set in medieval Japan, comprised of *Little Sister, The Heavenward Path,* and *Genpei.* In the first trilogy, an herbalist named Thomas Chinnery runs afoul of the Portuguese Inquisition during his search for the Rasa Mahadevi, an Indian powder said to bring the dead back to life. In the second, sixteen-year-old Mitsuko and a helpful *tengu,* or spirit guide, contend with the demands of the underworld gods as they seek to restore the health

of Mitsuko's sister. In an online review of *Little Sister* and *Heavenward Path,* Laura Krentz declared that Dalkey's books "encourage some serious thought as they deal with spiritual and philosophical issues from a refreshingly different non-Western perspective." Green, in *Booklist,* suggested that Dalkey's novels are "richer and more fascinating" for those readers "seeking new and exotic settings for multivolume fantasies." And in a starred review of *Bhagavati,* a critic in *Publishers Weekly* concluded: "Rarely has research, religion and fine writing been blended into such a literate and lively elixir."

Biographical and Critical Sources

BOOKS

St. James Guide to Fantasy Writers, St. James Press (Detroit, MI), 1996.

PERIODICALS

Booklist, May 15, 1998, Roland Green, review of *Bhagavati,* p. 1600; June 1, 1998, Karen Morgan, review of *The Heavenward Path,* p. 1745; January 1, 2001, Roland Green, review of *Genpei,* p. 928.
Kirkus Reviews, December 1, 2000, review of *Genpei,* p. 1651.
Library Journal, June 15, 1998, Jackie Cassada, review of *Bhagavati,* p. 111; January 1, 2001, Jackie Cassada, review of *Genpei,* p. 163.
Publishers Weekly, April 28, 1997, review of *Bijapur,* p. 54; April 13, 1998, review of *Bhagavati,* p. 56.

OTHER

Two Books by Kara Dalkey, http://www.tc.umn.edu/~d-lena/ KaraDalkeyReviews.html/ (April 6, 2001), Laura Krentz, reviews of *Little Sister* and *Heavenward Path.**

*   *   *

DERBY, Sally 1934-

Personal

Born July 1, 1934, in Dayton, OH; daughter of Wallene (a chemist) and Hildred (a homemaker) Derby; married Karl S. Miller (a chemist), December, 1955; children: David, Michael, Steven, Philip, Matthew, Sarah. *Education:* Western College for Women, B.A. *Religion:* Episcopal. *Hobbies and other interests:* Children, books, walking.

Addresses

Home—770 Southmeadow Circle, Cincinnati, OH 45231.

Career

Writer and educator.

Sally Derby

Member

Society of Children's Book Writers and Illustrators, Authors' Guild.

Awards, Honors

Notable Books for Children selection, *Smithsonian* magazine, 2001, for *Hannah's Bookmobile Christmas.*

Writings

The Mouse Who Owned the Sun, illustrated by Friso Henstra, Four Winds (New York, NY), 1993.
Jacob and the Stranger, illustrated by Leonid Gore, Ticknor & Fields (New York, NY), 1994.
King Kenrick's Splinter, illustrated by Leonid Gore, Walker (New York, NY), 1994.
My Steps, illustrated by Adjoa Burrowes, Lee & Low (New York, NY), 1996.
Hannah's Bookmobile Christmas, pictures by Gabi Swiatkowska, Henry Holt (New York), 2001.
Taiko on a Windy Night, illustrated by Kate Kiesler, Henry Holt (New York, NY), 2001.

My Steps was published in Spanish as *Mi escalera* by Lee & Low (New York, NY), 1998.

Sidelights

With the publication of *The Mouse Who Owned the Sun,* Sally Derby realized a fifty-year-old dream. "In 1943," Derby once explained, "at the age of (almost) ten I decided that when I grew up I would write books for children. In 1993 my first book for children was published. . . . I've been walking on air ever since." What filled the fifty years in between was mostly children. "I grew up," Derby recalled, "went to college, married and then had six children and, a little later, at various times six foster children." Derby also worked as a substitute teacher and as a "laundry expert," answering consumers' laundry questions over an 800 number. "But all those years," she recalled, "whenever I could, I wrote. When I wasn't working or writing, I was reading. Finally I grew bold enough to send a manuscript to a publisher." Such was the beginning of *The Mouse Who Owned the Sun.*

A story for children ages five to eight, *The Mouse Who Owned the Sun* recounts the adventures of Mouse as he discovers the world. At one point Mouse muses that the world is even bigger than he thought: "It's a good thing I brought lunch." The cheeky little mouse fancies that he actually owns the sun and can tell it when to rise and set. Not satisfied with such static activities however, he sets off for adventure and ends up in the king's court. There he comes face to face with a huge, bewigged king who is outfitted in finery from the eighteenth century. Here Mouse trades the sun for a map of the forest where he lives so he can find his way back home. Elizabeth Hanson, writing in *School Library Journal,* dubbed the book a "charming tale." While noting that Derby's book illustrates "the many ways of seeing and interacting," Hanson concluded that "Readers are sure to smile at Mouse's special sense of place." A *Publishers Weekly* reviewer commented on Derby's "swift and sure" dialogue, but wondered about the emphasis and direction of the book. It was unclear to the reviewer whether the message of the tale was simply to poke fun at the naive and self-important Mouse, or if something deeper was intended: that Mouse finally found the real size and shape of his world and his place in it. The critic concluded that a "thin ending leaves the direction unresolved."

Derby's next title again targeted young readers with *Jacob and the Stranger,* a story about a boy named Jacob, who lives in Slavda. Honest and kind but rather lazy, Jacob only works when his pockets are empty, and then only at jobs that require little effort. One day a stranger leaves a rare plant for Jacob to tend and promises to pay the boy a florin a day for his troubles. Jacob, taking his task seriously, sets the plant in the sun and waters it dutifully, only to be rewarded by the strangest buds in the history of flora and fauna: each day a different variety of wild cat emerges from the buds—beginning with a panther—until Jacob's house is full of them. When the mysterious stranger—in reality a wizard—returns, he refuses to pay Jacob his money and the wild cats all swarm up into the wizard's clothing in order to leave with him. All but one, that is; a panther remains with Jacob and becomes the true friend the boy has always longed for. A *Kirkus Reviews* critic called the story "an intriguing, beautifully honed allegory," noting that both story and illustrations result in "an elegant piece of bookmaking." Anne Deifendeifer, writing in *Horn Book,* called *Jacob and the Stranger* "expertly paced," possessing "the magical quality of stories from the oral tradition." She concluded that "Derby reveals a depth of character rarely found in so brief a text."

In *King Kenrick's Splinter,* Derby tells the story of a king who attempts to ignore a painful splinter lodged in his toe, until he can stand it no longer, thus illuminating a child's dread of getting such splinters removed. Jumping out of bed on the morning of Hero's Day, King Kenrick gets a sliver in his big toe. The king is no different from anyone else in his aversion to pain and initially tries to hide the painful toe from his sadistic queen by wearing slippers. The queen is not fooled, however, and offers to remove the painful splinter, an offer the king hurriedly declines. Finally, however, King Kenrick realizes he must have the offending particle of wood removed if he is to lead the Hero's Day parade. Instead of the queen, King Kenrick opts for the cook's uncle, who is supposed to be an expert splinter remover. Teasing Uncle Archibald arrives with a bag full of tools, including an ice pick and a saw, "in case we don't get it out and have to amputate." But once finished with his teasing, Uncle Archibald removes the splinter painlessly. The king, however, gets revenge by ordering Archibald thrown into the dungeon. He is only kidding, though, and the two share a final laugh before the King sets off to lead the parade. A *Publishers Weekly* critic noted that the story is "subtly comforting," and that art work and story together display "a keen sense of humor." And a *Kirkus Reviews* writer concluded that the tale is amusing, "especially to anyone who has faced the unhappy tweezers."

Derby turned to a more commonplace setting for her next story, *My Steps,* which was illustrated by Adjoa Burrowes. A little girl lists all the fun she has playing on the steps of her apartment building, such as pretending its low walls are a horse's back for a journey, making a cave with a blanket, or simply enjoying time outside with her friends and neighbors. The book paces through the different seasons—from eating Popsicles on the stoop in the summer to clearing snow off the steps in the winter. Sandra Ray, writing in *Horn Book Guide,* called it a "thoughtful story" and liked the cut-paper collages from Burrowes, as did several other critics. *Booklist*'s Carolyn Phelan remarked that the setting would be a familiar one to most urban-dwelling youngsters, and those who were not "may end up wishing for a stoop of their own." Derby's book was also translated into Spanish and published as *Mi escalera* in 1998. A *Publishers Weekly* contributor called it a "joyous ... rendition" that retains much of the appeal that Derby's original English text possessed.

In *Taiko on a Windy Night,* with illustrations by Kate Kiesler, Derby's story follows the title feline on a jaunt through his neighborhood on an autumn evening. The work begins with a little girl on a porch, who lets her

Taiko out to play. He has several adventures under the light of the full moon: walking on a fence, playing with fallen leaves, visiting the neighbor beagle, and chasing a mouse before he relaxes near a bush for a grooming session. In the end, his owner reclaims him and he heads back into the warmth of home. *Booklist* critic John Peters commended "Derby's poetic text" which he felt struck the right note for illustrations by Kiesler and "this atmospheric nighttime excursion." Karen Scott, writing in *School Library Journal,* asserted that images and text combined to help readers "experience the feline's enjoyment of his freedom."

Derby's next story, *Hannah's Bookmobile Christmas,* recounted just that. A little girl named Hannah helps her librarian aunt on the local bookmobile, an old school bus, one Christmas Eve afternoon. The weather is worsening, however, and as the afternoon grows dark Aunt Mary is forced to negotiate the increasingly perilous roads. Snowfall eventually shuts down the road to Hannah's home, and so she and her aunt bunk in for the night on the comfortably furnished bookmobile bus. Illustrator Gabi Swiatkowska's images present the bookmobile as a charming and comfy wallpapered living room with bookshelves, and Hannah and her aunt

When a heavy snow falls on Christmas Eve, Mary and her young niece Hannah receive an unexpected treat— the chance to spend the night in a bookmobile. (From Hannah's Bookmobile Christmas, *written by Derby and illustrated by Gabi Swiatkowska.)*

settling in and reading their favorite holiday books to pass the time. They also enjoy many treats, for the bookmobile users they visited that day showered them with Christmastime goodies. A brief afterword by Derby discusses the history of the bookmobile in the United States. "The story is quiet and slow, but the situation is intriguing," wrote *Booklist* critic Gillian Engberg, who also noted that the story's sense of excitement came from the worsening weather. A reviewer for *School Library Journal* remarked that while the artwork was "appealing," the bus seemed "implausibly spacious"; a *Publishers Weekly* contributor liked the contrast between the warmth of the bus interior and the winter storm depicted through its windows, and commended the author for a "cozy holiday tale."

Derby intends to continue to build on her dream with more books for young readers. "For me, writing is a frustrating joy," she admitted. "It's what I want to do and enjoy doing but never do well enough to please myself. Having the leisure to write makes my life rich and satisfying."

Biographical and Critical Sources

BOOKS

Derby, Sally, *King Kenrick's Splinter,* illustrated by Leonid Gore, Walker (New York, NY), 1994.

PERIODICALS

Booklist, September 1, 1994, Ilene Cooper, review of *Jacob and the Stranger,* p. 40; October 15, 1996, Carolyn Phelan, review of *My Steps,* p. 432; May 15, 2001, John Peters, review of *Taiko on a Windy Night,* p. 1756; September 15, 2001, Gillian Engberg, review of *Hannah's Bookmobile Christmas,* p. 234.

Horn Book, September-October, 1994, Anne Deifendeifer, review of *Jacob and the Stranger,* p. 583.

Horn Book Guide, spring, 1997, Sandra Ray, review of *My Steps,* p. 24.

Kirkus Reviews, June 15, 1994, review of *Jacob and the Stranger,* p. 843; November 15, 1994, review of *King Kenrick's Splinter,* p. 1527.

New York Times Book Review, December 2, 2001, Heather Hepler, review of *Hannah's Bookmobile Christmas,* p. 83.

Publishers Weekly, September 20, 1993, review of *The Mouse Who Owned the Sun,* p. 71; October 31, 1994, review of *King Kenrick's Splinter,* p. 61; July, 1999, review of *Mi escalera,* p. 1958; September 24, 2001, review of *Hannah's Bookmobile Christmas,* p. 50.

School Library Journal, June, 2001, Karen Scott, review of *Taiko on a Windy Night,* p. 111; October, 2001, review of *Hannah's Bookmobile Christmas,* p. 64.

*   *   *

DODD, Lynley (Stuart) 1941-

Personal

Born July 5, 1941, in Rotorua, New Zealand; daughter of Matthew Fotheringhan (a forester) and Elizabeth Sinclair (a secretary; maiden name, Baxter) Weeks; married Anthony Robert Fletcher Dodd, January 2, 1965; children: Matthew Fletcher, Elizabeth Anne. *Education:* Elam School of Art, diploma, 1962; further study at Auckland Teachers College, 1962.

Addresses

Home and office—Edward Avenue, R.D. 3, Tauranga, New Zealand.

Career

Queen Margaret College, Wellington, New Zealand, art mistress, 1963-68; freelance author and illustrator, 1968—.

Member

PEN International.

Awards, Honors

Esther Glen Medal (with Eve Sutton), New Zealand Library Association, 1975, for *My Cat Likes to Hide in Boxes;* Choysa Bursary for Children's Writers, New Zealand Literary Fund and Quality Packers Ltd., 1978; New Zealand Book Award for Illustration, 1981, for *Druscilla;* New Zealand Children's Picture Book of the Year Award, 1984, for *Hairy Maclary from Donaldson's Dairy,* 1986, for *Hairy Maclary's Scattercat,* and 1988, for *Hairy Maclary's Caterwaul Caper;* AIM Children's Picture Book of the Year Award, third prize, 1990, for *Hairy Maclary's Rumpus at the Vet,* and 1991, for *Slinky Malinki;* New Zealand Commemorative Medal, 1990, in "recognition of services to New Zealand"; AIM Children's Picture Book of the Year Award, first prize, 1992, for *Hairy Maclary's Showbusiness;* Children's Choice Award, *New Zealand Post,* 2000, for *Hairy Maclary and Zachary Quack;* awarded the Distinguished Companion of the New Zealand Order of Merit, 2002, for "services to children's literature and book illustration."

Writings

FOR CHILDREN; SELF-ILLUSTRATED

(With Eve Sutton) *My Cat Likes to Hide in Boxes,* Hamilton (London, England), 1973, Era, 1984.

The Nickle Nackle Tree, Hamilton (London, England), 1976, Era, 1985.

Titimus Truim, Hamilton (London, England), 1979.

The Smallest Turtle, Mallinson Rendel (Wellington, New Zealand), 1982, Gareth Stevens (Milwaukee, WI), 1985, reprinted, 2000.

The Apple Tree, Mallinson Rendel (Wellington, New Zealand), 1982, Gareth Stevens (Milwaukee, WI), 1985.

Hairy Maclary from Donaldson's Dairy, Mallinson Rendel (Wellington, New Zealand), 1983, Gareth Stevens (Milwaukee, WI), 1985, reprinted, 2000.

Hairy Maclary's Bone, Mallinson Rendel (Wellington, New Zealand), 1984, Gareth Stevens (Milwaukee, WI), 1985, reprinted, 2001.

Hairy Maclary, Scattercat, Mallinson Rendel (Wellington, New Zealand), 1985, Gareth Stevens (Milwaukee, WI), 1988.

Wake up, Bear, Gareth Stevens (Milwaukee, WI), 1986, reprinted, 2001.

Hairy Maclary's Caterwaul Caper, Mallinson Rendel (Wellington, New Zealand), 1987, Gareth Stevens (Milwaukee, WI), 1989.

A Dragon in a Wagon, Mallinson Rendel (Wellington, New Zealand), 1988, Gareth Stevens (Milwaukee, WI), 1989.

Hairy Maclary's Rumpus at the Vet, Mallinson Rendel (Wellington, New Zealand), 1989, Gareth Stevens (Milwaukee, WI), 1990.

Slinky Malinki, Mallinson Rendel (Wellington, New Zealand), 1990, Gareth Stevens (Milwaukee, WI), 1991.

Find Me a Tiger, Mallinson Rendel (Wellington, New Zealand), 1991, Gareth Stevens (Milwaukee, WI), 1992.

Hairy Maclary's Showbusiness, Mallinson Rendel (Wellington, New Zealand), 1991, Gareth Stevens (Milwaukee, WI), 1992.

The Minister's Cat ABC, Mallinson Rendel (Wellington, New Zealand), 1992, Gareth Stevens (Milwaukee, WI), 1994.

Slinky Malinki, Open the Door, Mallinson Rendel (Wellington, New Zealand), 1993, Gareth Stevens (Milwaukee, WI), 1994.

Schnitzel von Krumm's Basketwork, Gareth Stevens (Milwaukee, WI), 1994.

Sniff-Snuff-Snap!, Mallinson Rendel (Wellington, New Zealand), 1995, Gareth Stevens (Milwaukee, WI), 2000.

Skinky Malinky Catflaps, Mallinson Rendel (Wellington, New Zealand), 1998, Gareth Stevens (Milwaukee, WI), 1999.

Hairy Maclary, Sit, Gareth Stevens (Milwaukee, WI), 1998.

Hairy Maclary and Zachary Quack, Gareth Stevens (Milwaukee, WI), 2000.

Hedgehog Howdedo, Mallinson Rendel (Wellington, New Zealand), 2000, Gareth Stevens (Milwaukee, WI), 2001.

Scarface Claw, Mallinson Rendel (Wellington, New Zealand), 2001.

Schnitzel von Krumm Forget-Me-Not, Gareth Stevens (Milwaukee, WI), 2001.

Schnitzel von Krumm, Dogs Never Climb Trees, Mallinson Rendel (Wellington, New Zealand), in press.

ILLUSTRATOR

Jillian Squire, *Pussyfoooting,* Millwood Press (Wellington, New Zealand), 1978.

Clarice England, *Druscilla,* Hodder & Stoughton (London, England), 1980.

Illustrator of several educational readers for Price Milburn, 1974-83.

Sidelights

Lynley Dodd is a New Zealand author and illustrator who has been widely praised for her books for children.

When the owners of dachshund Schnitzel von Krumm buy him a new basket, he turns up his nose at the change and goes off in search of a bed as cozy and comforting as his old one in Lynley Dodd's humorous picture book. (From Schnitzel von Krumm's Basketwork, *written and illustrated by Dodd.)*

Her illustrated stories for young children often feature animals, most often of the domesticated variety. In Dodd's popular "Hairy Maclary" books, a small, scruffy black terrier engages in adventures with a host of four-legged friends; terrorized by a maniacal tom cat named Scarface Claw in *Hairy Maclary, Scattercat,* he also turns into a bit of a terror himself when he organizes an insurrection at obedience school in the humorous *Hairy Maclary, Sit.* In addition to texts, Dodd brings to life Hairy and his many friends through illustrations characterized by *School Library Journal* contributor Susan Lissim as "attractive and simple enough for children to identify" the different animal characters.

Born in Rotorua, New Zealand, in 1941, Dodd was raised "in small, isolated forestry settlements," she once recalled to *SATA.* "There were few children in the neighborhood, but for those few there was unlimited space for play, and miles of pine trees in any direction provided plenty of scope for imagination." An artist from an early age, Dodd "always had pen and drawing paper ready," and eventually enrolled at the Elam School of Art, earning her diploma in 1962.

As a graduate of art school, Dodd first began working as an artist. "At the arrival of my first baby I took on work for a correspondence school," she explained, "illustrating fortnightly sets for seven- to nine-year-olds." Her career as an author began with Eve Sutton's suggestion that they collaborate on a children's book, *My Cat Likes to Hide in Boxes,* a picture book based on Dodd's family cat. It was through this collaboration that Dodd became fascinated with picture books, and with two small children to test out her story ideas, she decided to try writing her own, beginning with a counting book. 1976's self-illustrated *The Nickle Nackle Tree* was the result, a book that a reviewer in *Publishers Weekly* called "just the thing to lift the spirits in the bleak, lifeless winter months." In Dodd's story, the nickle nackle tree is burdened with various kinds and quantities of birds that perch on its branches, the variety and number of each species becoming the focus of counting exercises.

Several of Dodd's works focus on wild animals. In *Wake up, Bear,* a succession of animals are unable to waken the hibernating bear—until a bee comes along and reminds him of honey. *The Smallest Turtle* was praised by a critic in *Junior Bookshelf* as a "delightful story ... beautifully drawn." 1995's *Sniff-Snuff-Snap!* finds a crotchety warthog attempting to run other animals away from the local watering hole, until the task of chasing away first two animals, then three, then four, and so on, makes him give up his task. Noting that the warthog is "likeable," with both "an expressive face and a fallible nature," Francis Ball commented in *School Librarian* that *Sniff-Snuf-Snap!* would be a popular book among older preschoolers.

The lead character in Dodd's 1983 picture book is perhaps the most beloved she has created. Hairy Maclary is a small, black, scruffy terrier-type dog who inhabits a canine community that includes such friends as Hercules Morse, Mufflin McLay, Bitzer Maloney, Bottomley Potts, the dachshund Schnitzel von Krumm, and the dogs' arch enemy, the fierce tomcat Scarface Claw. *Hairy Maclary from Donaldson's Dairy* became the first in a series for which Dodd became well known around the world as well as in her native New Zealand. Collin Mills stated in a review in *Books for Keeps* that with the combination of Dodd's text and pictures, youngsters will learn a great deal "about sound, stress, intonation and the patterning of language."

The second book in the series, *Hairy Maclary's Bone,* begins happily enough with Butcher Stone bestowing his

Dodd's engaging canine protagonist invades a cat show, flusters the cats and their owners, and carries off the prize for "Scruffiest Cat of the Show." (From Hairy Maclary's Showbusiness, *written and illustrated by Dodd.*)

tastiest bone upon the grateful Hairy. But Hairy soon finds his bone the envy of all his canine friends. As they try to wrestle the bone from him, he leads them on an obstacle course through the neighborhood until the competition is eliminated one by one. In his next doggy adventure, *Hairy Maclary, Scattercat,* the black pup is out to terrorize all the cats in the neighborhood. Things are going well until Hairy meets up with Scarface Claw, a mangey tom-cat who turns the tables on Maclary and chases the dog home. In *Hairy Maclary's Caterwaul Caper,* the tough terrier and his friends save the day when Scarface gets stuck high up in a tree, their barking and yapping creating such a din that a nearby home-owner comes out to investigate and rescues the unfortu-nate feline. Phillis Wilson noted in a review for *Booklist* that Dodd's full-page illustrations capture "the particular personality of each dog" as well as "the humor of Scarface's wounded dignity."

Dodd's popular "Hairy Maclary" series continues with 1990's *Hairy Maclary's Rumpus at the Vet,* when the little dog gets nipped by a caged cockatoo at the vet's office and precipitates a riot in the waiting room. The canny canine is the cause of another rumpus—this time at a cat show—in *Hairy Maclary's Showbusiness,* where, after overturning chairs and flustering cats and owners alike, he eventually manages to carry off the prize for Scruffiest Cat of the Show. And *Hairy Maclary, Sit* finds the pooch bringing an abrupt end to a nightly dog obedience class.

Like Beatrix Potter, Dodd has been praised for creating animal characters with distinctly individual personali-ties, as well as for her ability to conjoin text and pictures. Two of Dodd's memorable creations from the Hairy Maclary series have gone on to become leading characters themselves. The dachshund is the star of *Schnitzel von Krumm's Basketwork* and *Schnitzel von Krumm Forget-Me-Not.* In the first book, Schnitzel has slept in the same basket all of his doggy years, and it is more than beginning to show its age. When his owners replace the basket with a stylish new one, Schnitzel turns up his nose at the change and goes off in search of a bed as cosy and comforting as his old one. *School Librarian* critic Carol Woolley praised the book as a "charming tale for any dog lover" and noted that its rhyme and rhythm "carry the story along swiftly." *Schnitzel von Krumm Forget-Me-Not* has the canine hero living a dog's worst nightmare when his owners leave for vacation without their beloved pet. Only concentrated wailing throughout the night will rouse his neighbor and get the dachshund reunited with his forgetful owners, in this 1996 picture book that contains "lively verses [that] speed the reader through the story," according to a *Junior Bookshelf* contributor.

The first feline of the Hairy Maclary cast to strike out on its own is the lithe black cat Slinky Malinki. In his self-titled picture-book debut, Slinky leads a secret life of crime until his loot is discovered and he reforms. *Slinky Malinki, Open the Door* finds him learning how to open all the doors and creates mayhem when he and a parrot are left alone in the house. A trip out to the garden wall precipitates a battle between Slinky and the scruffy Scarface Claw in *Slinky Malinki Catflaps,* which *Magpies* contributor Margaret Kedian praised for Dodd's "clever use" of words and "rhyming verse ... combined with paintings that take her reader far beyond the text."

Dodd's animal creations are by no means limited to Hairy Maclary and friends. Cats take the lead again in her 1992 book *The Minister's Cat ABC,* based on a traditional rhyming game. While some critics claimed the abstract adjectives used in the book are difficult concepts for young children to grasp, others, such as Trevor Dickinson, writing in *School Librarian,* saw the demands of the vocabulary as "easily overcome through the illustrations" which made the characteristics of each cat quite clear.

In *Find Me a Tiger,* one of Dodd's most artistically ambitious books, children have to look hard at her line and color drawings to find the cleverly camouflaged animals, while a four-line rhyming clue helps readers discover the hidden creatures. In a review in *Magpies,* Margaret Kelly praised the "wonderfully natural illustrations, evidence of Dodd's great knowledge of and ease with animals." Human beings do appear in Dodd's books as well, although the only one to take a leading role is Susie Fogg in *A Dragon in a Wagon.* On a walk with her dog, Sam, Susie imagines that he turns into various exciting creatures. It is not until Susie slips and falls that she appreciates the comfort of Sam being just a dog.

Dodd finds that "being able to plan the whole book from the outset [is] exciting and rewarding. The idea is roughed out first and fit into the format and length required. Then a 'dummy' is made, a complete miniature mock-up of the finished book. This gives the publisher a good indication of plan and serves as a working model for me when I come to do final illustrations." "Writing for children is an exacting business," Dodd also noted. "Beginning as an illustrator and only later trying my hand at writing text as well, I know only too well the truth of the saying:'The fewer the words, the harder the job.' It's exasperating to hear, from those who should know better, 'I'd like to try writing—I think I'll start with a children's book.' One hopes the results never reach the children!"

With the popularity of the "Hairy Maclary" books, Dodd finds herself responding to mail as often as she works on text and illustration. She participates in her country's writers-in-the-school program in order to keep in touch with the lives of her readers. "It's a two-way thing," the author/illustrator explained. "The children are able to put a face to the name on the books [while I get] feedback, plus the fun of sharing the books with large numbers of children, is stimulating and a spur to new ideas, as well as a way to keep myself on track." Dodd agrees that being a picture book author is, indeed, hard work, but it also is tremendously satisfying. "To travel halfway around the world and find a Glasgow audience of five-to seven-year-olds, muffled to the eyebrows against snow outside and draughts inside, happily chanting the results

Lithe black cat Slinky Malinki leads a secret life of thievery until his loot is discovered and he must change his ways. (From Slinky Malinki, *written and illustrated by Dodd.)*

of one's labours at a desk 12,000 miles away, is to reap the reward that makes it all worthwhile."

Biographical and Critical Sources

PERIODICALS

Booklist, December 1, 1988, Phillis Wilson, review of *Hairy Maclary's Caterwaul Caper,* p. 646.
Books for Keeps, January, 1986, Colin Mills, review of *Hairy Maclary from Donaldson's Dairy,* p. 13; November, 1993, p. 10; July, 1994, p. 6.
Horn Book Guide, fall, 1998, Carolyn Shute, review of *Hairy Maclary, Sit,* p. 290.
Junior Bookshelf, October, 1983, review of *The Smallest Turtle,* p. 206; October, 1996, review of *Schnitzel von Krumm Forget-Me-Not,* pp. 182-183.
Magpies, November, 1991, Margaret Kelly, review of *Find Me a Tiger,* p. 26; September, 1998, Margaret Kedian, review of *Slinky Malinki Catflaps,* p. 28.
Publishers Weekly, January 23, 1978, review of *The Nickle Nackle Tree,* p. 373.
School Librarian, February, 1992, p. 15; February, 1993, Trevor Dickinson, review of *The Minister's Cat ABC,* pp. 14-15; November, 1994, Carol Woolley, review of *Schnitzel von Krumm's Basketwork,* p. 145; February, 1996, Frances Ball, review of *Sniff-Snuff-Snap!,* p. 14.
School Library Journal, August, 1991, p. 144; February, 1992, p. 15; June, 1998, Heide Piehler, review of *Schnitzel von Krumm Forget-Me-Not,* p. 103; August, 1998, Susan Lissim, review of *Hairy Maclary, Sit,* p. 133.
Times Educational Supplement, July 29, 1988, p. 21; January 7, 1994, p. 33.

DONALDSON, Julia 1948-

Personal

Born September 16, 1948, in London, England; daughter of James (a geneticist) and Elizabeth (a secretary; maiden name, Ede) Shields; married Malcolm Donaldson (a pediatrician), September 30, 1972; children: Hamish, Alastair, Jesse. *Ethnicity:* "British." *Education:* Bristol University, degree in drama and French, 1970. *Politics:* "Labour voter." *Religion:* Agnostic. *Hobbies and other interests:* Piano, singing, walking, flowers, fungi.

Addresses

Home—2 Chapelton Ave., Glasgow G61 2RE, Scotland.

Career

Writer.

Awards, Honors

Smarties Prize, 1999, Blue Peter Book Award, 2000, and Experian Big Three Book Prize, 2000, all for *The Gruffalo;* Children's Book Award shortlist, Sheffield Children's Book Award shortlist, and Scottish Children's Book Award, all 2002, all for *Room on the Broom.*

Julia Donaldson

Writings

A Squash and a Squeeze, illustrated by Axel Scheffler, Methuen (London, England), McElderry (New York, NY), 1993.
Birthday Surprise (play), Ginn (Aylesbury, England), 1994.
Names and Games (play), Ginn (Aylesbury, England), 1995.
(Reteller) *Turtle Tug* (play), Ginn (Aylesbury, England), 1995.
(Reteller) *The Three Billy Goats Gruff* (play), Ginn (Aylesbury, England), 1995.
(Reteller) *The Boy Who Cried Wolf* (play), Ginn (Aylesbury, England), 1995.
(Reteller) *The Magic Twig* (play), Ginn (Aylesbury, England), 1995.
Space Girl Sue, illustrated by Clive Scruton, Ginn (Aylesbury, England), 1996.
(Reteller) *Town and Country Mouse,* illustrated by Nick Schon, Ginn (Aylesbury, England), 1996.
Mr. Snow, illustrated by Celia Canning, Ginn (Aylesbury, England), 1996.
(Reteller) *Counting Chickens,* illustrated by Jeffrey Reid, Ginn (Aylesbury, England), 1996.
The King's Porridge, Ginn (Aylesbury, England), 1996.
The Wonderful Smells (play), illustrated by Jan Nesbitt, Ginn (Aylesbury, England), 1997.
Top of the Mops (play), Ginn (Aylesbury, England), 1997.
The Brownie King, illustrated by John Eastwood, Heinemann (Oxford, England), 1998.
Books and Crooks (plays), Stanley Thornes (Cheltenham, England), 1998.
The False Tooth Fairy (plays), Ginn (Aylesbury, England), 1998.
Waiter! Waiter!, illustrated by Jim Kavanagh, Heinemann (Oxford, England), 1998.
All Gone!, illustrated by Alexa Rutherford, Ginn (Aylesbury, England), 1998.
The Gruffalo, illustrated by Axel Scheffler, Macmillan (London, England), Dial Books for Young Readers (New York, NY), 1999.
Steve's Sandwiches, Ginn (Aylesbury, England), 1999.
Clever Katya, Ginn (Aylesbury, England), 1999.
The Noises Next Door, Ginn (Aylesbury, England), 1999.
Monkey Puzzle, illustrated by Axel Scheffler, Macmillan (London, England), 2000.
(Reteller) *The Strange Dream,* illustrated by Thomas Sperling, Oxford University Press (Oxford, England), 2000.
Problem Page (play), illustrated by David Mostyn, Heinemann (Oxford, England), 2000.
The Boy Who Talked to Birds, illustrated by Suzanne Watts, Oxford University Press (Oxford, England), 2000.
One Piece Missing, Rigby Heinemann (Oxford, England), 2000.
Jumping Jack, Rigby Heinemann (Oxford, England), 2000.
The Giant Jumperee, Rigby Heinemann (Oxford, England), 2000.

Follow the Swallow, illustrated by Martin Ursell, Mammoth (London, England), 2000, Crabtree (New York, NY), 2002.

(Reteller) *The King's Ears,* illustrated by Lisa Berkshire, Oxford University Press (London, England), 2000.

The Monsters in the Cave, Ginn (Aylesbury, England), 2001.

Stop, Thief!, Ginn (Aylesbury, England), 2001.

Room on the Broom, illustrated by Axel Scheffler, Macmillan (London, England), Dial Books for Young Readers (New York, NY), 2001.

The Dinosaur's Diary, illustrated by Debbie Boon, Puffin (London, England), 2002.

Night Monkey, Day Monkey, illustrated by Lucy Richards, Egmont (London, England), 2002.

"TALES FROM ACORN WOOD" SERIES

Postman Bear, illustrated by Axel Scheffler, Campbell (London, England), 2000.

Fox's Socks, illustrated by Axel Scheffler, Campbell (London, England), 2000.

Hide and Seek Pig, illustrated by Axel Scheffler, Campbell (London, England), 2000.

Rabbit's Nap, illustrated by Axel Scheffler, Campbell (London, England), 2000.

OTHER

Also author of songs, scripts, and stories for BBC television and radio (mainly children's programs). Author of *Cat Whispers,* Rigby. Author of unpublished musicals, *King Grunt's Cake* and *Pirate on the Pier.* Contributor of poetry and plays to anthologies.

The Gruffalo has been published in over twenty languages and adapted into a board book, an oversized-format book, and a book with audio cassette.

Work in Progress

The Spiffied Giant in Town; picture books; plays; short novels.

Sidelights

When not performing her own material accompanied by her guitar-playing husband, British storyteller and songwriter Julia Donaldson writes material for other television and radio performers, including children's musicals. These creative activities led her to write picture books as well. "My book *A Squash and A Squeeze* started life as a song on a television programme," Donaldson told *SATA.* In *A Squash and a Squeeze* she retold the folk tale of an elderly woman who wishes for a larger house. In this "jolly version" of the story, to quote Liz Waterland of *Books for Keeps,* the elderly woman takes the advice of a wise man; she invites all of her farm animals into the house, and then after ousting them again, she concludes that her house is large enough after all.

Donaldson continued in the same humorous vein as *A Squash and a Squeeze* with *The Gruffalo* and *Room on the Broom,* both stories told in rhyming verse. The Gruffalo is an imaginary creature that a mouse invents to

rescue itself from other possible predators. The mouse escapes being eaten by a fox, an owl, and a snake, only to run across the very Gruffalo it has created. The work caught the attention of critics, including a *Publishers Weekly* contributor who found that Donaldson "manipulates the repetitive language and rhymes to good advantage." While a *Kirkus Reviews* critic was lukewarm about *The Gruffalo,* calling it a "fairly innocuous tale," others saw much to like with *Observer* contributor Sam Taylor describing it as "a modern classic." *Booklist* reviewer Stephanie Zvirin praised the story for its "bouncy, humorous text [that] flows smoothly," and Clive Barns of *Books for Keeps* called it "cleverly constructed."

With *Room on the Broom* Donaldson returned to the folktale format, this time telling the story of how helpful animals hitch a ride on the broomstick of a generous witch. A striped cat, spotted dog, green parrot, and frog each help the witch out of a jam and in return get a ride on what ends up being a very comfortable conveyance. According to a *Kirkus Reviews* critic, the "fluid rhyming and smooth rhythm work together." And while the "metrical rhyme and goofy suspense aren't groundbreaking," to quote a *Publishers Weekly* contributor, readers will "likely find it refreshing" to see a witch playing a new role. Pamela K. Bomboy, writing in *School Library Journal,* predicted that because *Room on a Broom* is "full of fun, and not at all scary," it would be a "surefire read-aloud hit."

Biographical and Critical Sources

PERIODICALS

Booklist, April 26, 1993, review of *A Squash and a Squeeze,* p. 78; July, 1999, Stephanie Zvirin, review of *The Gruffalo,* p. 1950; September 1, 2001, GraceAnne A. DeCandido, review of *Room on the Broom,* p. 120.

Books for Keeps, May, 1995, Liz Waterland, review of *A Squash and a Squeeze,* p. 8; May, 1999, Clive Barnes, review of *The Gruffalo,* p. 21.

Childhood Education, fall, 1999, Kelly Krawczyk, review of *The Gruffalo,* p. 44.

Children's Book Review Service, August, 1993, p. 158.

Horn Book Guide, fall, 1993, p. 325.

Kirkus Reviews, June 1, 1999, review of *The Gruffalo,* p. 882; August 1, 2001, review of *Room on the Broom,* p. 1121.

Los Angeles Times Book Review, May 2, 1993, p. 7.

Observer (London, England), April 4, 1999, Sam Taylor, "When you've been traumatized by a teddy, there's only one way out. . . ."

Publishers Weekly, April 26, 1993, p. 78; June 21, 1999, review of *The Gruffalo,* p. 67; September 10, 2001, review of *Room on the Broom,* p. 92.

School Library Journal, April, 1993, Nancy Seiner, review of *A Squash and a Squeeze,* pp. 95-96; August, 1999, Marianne Saccardi, review of *The Gruffalo,* pp. 132-133; September, 2001, Pamela K. Bomboy, review of *Room on the Broom,* p. 187.

Times (London, England), November, 1993, p. 45.

DUEY, Kathleen 1950-

Personal

Born October 8, 1950.

Addresses

Agent—c/o Publicity, Penguin/Putnam, 345 Hudson St., New York, NY 10014. *E-mail*—kathleen@kathleen-duey.com.

Career

Writer.

Member

Author's Guild.

Awards, Honors

Young Hoosier's Award nominee for *Train Wreck: Kansas, 1892;* Golden Duck Award for *Rex.*

Writings

"AMERICAN DIARIES" SERIES

Emma Eileen Grove: Mississippi, 1865, Aladdin (New York, NY), 1996.
Mary Alice Peale: Philadelphia, 1777, Aladdin (New York, NY), 1996.
Sarah Anne Hartford: Massachusetts, 1651, Aladdin (New York, NY), 1996.
Anisett Lundberg: California, 1851, Aladdin (New York, NY), 1996.
Willow Chase: Kansas Territory, 1847, Aladdin (New York, NY), 1997.
Ellen Elizabeth Hawkins: Mobeetie, Texas, 1886, Aladdin (New York, NY), 1997.
Evie Peach: St. Louis, 1857, Aladdin (New York, NY), 1997.
Alexia Ellery Finsdale: San Francisco, 1905, Aladdin (New York, NY), 1997.
Celou Sudden Shout: Idaho, 1826, Aladdin (New York, NY), 1998.
Summer MacCleary: Virginia, 1749, Aladdin (New York, NY), 1998.
Agnes May Gleason: Walsenberg, Colorado, 1933, Aladdin (New York, NY), 1998.
Amelina Carrett: Bayou Grand Coeur, Louisiana, 1863, Aladdin (New York, NY), 1999.
Josie Poe: Palouse, Washington, 1943, Aladdin (New York, NY), 1999.
Rosa Moreno: Hollywood, California, 1928, Aladdin (New York, NY), 1999.
Nell Dunne: Ellis Island, 1904, Aladdin (New York, NY), 2000.
Maddie Retta Lauren: Sandersville, Georgia, C.S.A, 1864, Aladdin (New York, NY), 2000.
Francesca Vigilucci: Washington, D.C., 1913, Aladdin (New York, NY), 2000.

Janey G. Blue: Pearl Harbor, 1941, Aladdin (New York, NY), 2001.
Zellie Blake: Massachusetts, 1836, Aladdin (New York, NY), 2002.

"SURVIVAL!" SERIES; WITH KAREN A. BALE

Earthquake, 1906, Aladdin (New York, NY), 1998.
Cave-In: St. Claire, Pennsylvania, 1859, Aladdin (New York, NY), 1998.
Stranded: Death Valley, 1850, Aladdin (New York, NY), 1998.
Flood: Mississippi, 1927, Aladdin (New York, NY), 1998.
Blizzard: Estes Park, Colorado, 1886, Aladdin (New York, NY), 1998.
Fire: Chicago, 1871, Aladdin (New York, NY), 1998.
Titanic: April 14, 1912, Aladdin (New York, NY), 1998.
Hurricane: Open Seas, 1844, Aladdin (New York, NY), 1999.
Train Wreck: Kansas, 1892, Aladdin (New York, NY), 1999.
Swamp: Bayou Teche, Louisiana, 1851, Aladdin (New York, NY), 1999.
Forest Fire: Hinckley, Minnesota, 1894, Aladdin (New York, NY), 1999.
Hurricane: New Bedford, Massachusetts, 1784, Aladdin (New York, NY), 1999.

"SPIRIT OF THE CIMARRON" SERIES

Esperanza, Penguin/Putnam (New York, NY), 2002.
Bonita, Penguin/Putnam (New York, NY), 2002.
Sierra, Penguin/Putnam (New York, NY), 2002.
Spirit: Stallion of the Cimarron (adapted from the motion picture) Penguin/Putnam (New York, NY), 2002.

"UNICORN'S SECRET" SERIES

Moonsilver, illustrated by Omar Rayyan, Aladdin (New York, NY), 2001.
The Silver Thread, Aladdin (New York, NY), 2001.
The Silver Bracelet, Aladdin (New York, NY), 2002.
Mountains of the Moon, illustrated by Omar Rayyan, Aladdin (New York, NY), 2002.
Beyond the Sunset, Aladdin (New York, NY), 2002.

OTHER

Double-Yuck Magic, Morrow/Avon (New York, NY), 1991.
Mr. Stumpguss Is a Third-Grader, Morrow/Avon (New York, NY), 1992.
The Third Grade's Skinny Pig, illustrated by Gioia Fiammenghi, Avon (New York, NY), 1993.
(With Karen A. Bale) *Three of Hearts,* Morrow/Avon (New York, NY), 1998.
San Francisco Earthquake, 1906, Pocket Books (New York, NY), 1999.
Louisiana Hurricane, 1860, Pocket Books (New York, NY), 2000.
Freaky Facts about Natural Disasters, Aladdin (New York, NY), 2000.
Nowhere to Run, Nowhere to Hide!, Smart Kids Publishing (Carlsbad, CA), 2000.
Stay Out of the Graveyard!, Smart Kids Publishing (Carlsbad, CA), 2000.

Bogeyman in the Basement!, Smart Kids Publishing (Carlsbad, CA), 2000.

Beware the Alien Invasion!, Smart Kids Publishing (Carlsbad, CA), 2000.

(With Mary Barnes) *Freaky Facts about Natural Disasters,* Aladdin (New York, NY), 2000.

(With Mary Barnes) *More Freaky Facts about Natural Disasters,* Aladdin (New York, NY), 2001.

(Editor) Robert Gould, *Rex* ("Time Soldiers" series), illustrated by Eugene Epstein, Big Guy Books (Encinitas, CA), 2001.

(Editor) Robert Gould, *Rex 2* ("Time Soldiers" series), illustrated by Eugene Epstein, Big Guy Books (Encinitas, CA), 2001.

Work in Progress

The Academy of Magic, a young adult fantasy trilogy and humorous historical fiction for grade school readers.

Sidelights

Kathleen Duey began her career as a children's book author in the early 1990s with such titles as *Mr. Stumpguss Is a Third-Grader* and *The Third Grade's Skinny Pig.* In 1996, she began a series for readers in grades four to six that presented American history in a fictional adventure format. These "Diary" books, all begin and end with a diary entry. Every "American Diaries" title is a single day. *Mary Alice Peale: Philadelphia, 1777,* chronicles the household dramas of its well-to-do title character, whose father is loyal to the English monarchy. Mary Alice's brother, meanwhile, has run off to fight with colonial independence forces. When he is injured, she secretly helps by hiding him in their barn, while the family's Philadelphia home is host to British soldiers.

In *Sarah Anne Hartford: Massachusetts, 1651,* Duey chronicles the fictional experience of a young girl in Salem, Massachusetts, during the harsh Puritan era. Sarah is distraught over her widowed father's impending marriage to the coldly righteous Mistress Goddard, and Sarah's diary entries—just two days apart—recount her tale of mischief and its consequences. On a cold winter Sunday, twelve-year-old Sarah and her friend Elizabeth disobey strict standards about Sabbath behavior, and play and laugh on the ice on their way home from church services. Caught, they are then "pilloried" as punishment, locked into stocks in the Salem town square. Cold and aching, Sarah begins to question the values of her community. "The story is exciting and the characters are sympathetic," wrote Connie Parker in *School Library Journal,* while *Booklist*'s Karen Hutt stated that the story "personalizes the social mores and everyday life of Puritan New England."

Duey won praise from critics for providing much interesting historical detail in her works, such as the fact that Puritans often brought their dogs to church to keep their feet warm. Similar insights are evident in *Anisett Lundberg: California, 1851,* a story about a young girl during the California Gold Rush. Anisett's father has

In Kathleen Duey's historical novel set in seventeenth-century Salem, Massachusetts, twelve-year-old Sarah pens diary entries in which she questions the strict standards of the Puritan era. (Cover illustration by Jason Dowd.)

died, and her mother earns a living cooking for the miners. Anisett and her brother help with the work, and one day, after delivering food by mule to the camps, Anisett is kidnaped by a bitter and desperate miner after he overhears her describing an unusual rock she has found. Susan F. Marcus, writing in *School Library Journal,* noted that the work portrays "the view of the gold-rush culture" and "highlights the courage of those who were part of it." Danger is also faced in *Willow Chase: Kansas Territory, 1847,* Duey's next title in the series. Willow is part of a wagon-train caravan full of settlers heading west across the Great Plains. Willow's mother gives one Native American man medicine for a sick child, and later, while crossing the swollen Platte River with her family, Willow is swept away. They assume she is dead and move on, but Willow is discovered by the Native American her mother had shown kindness to, and he gives the girl his horse with which she rejoins her family. *Booklist*'s Lauren Peterson termed it "a heartwarming family story with a likable protagonist."

A Texas cattle ranch is the setting for *Ellen Elizabeth Hawkins: Mobeetie, Texas, 1886.* Here, Duey's heroine writes of her desire to follow in her father's footsteps as a rancher, but is strongly discouraged from such talk because of her gender. That summer, however, a drought arrives, and with her father gone one day, Ellen's grandfather falls at their windmill; she must save him, fix the windmill blade, and drive their cattle, desperate for water, to the pastures. *School Library Journal* critic Sylvia V. Meisner called it a "satisfying story about a resourceful heroine" with "grit and determination to persevere against almost overwhelming odds."

Evie Peach: St. Louis, 1857 takes place before the American Civil War. The title character was once a slave, but their owner's last will and testament freed her and her father. They plan to buy her mother's freedom, save $750 to do so, and set out for the estate where she works. Irish neighbors plot revenge for a trick Evie has played on them. They steal Evie's mother's emancipation papers, and Evie's parents are arrested as runaway slaves. Evie is their only hope. *Booklist* writer Denia Hester liked this book's "good balance of warm, winning moments and well-plotted dramatic turns." *Alexia Ellery Finsdale: San Francisco, 1905,* another 1997 title from Duey in the series, recounts the story of a young girl whose mother has died. Alexia, living in a boarding house with her gambler father. Her landlady, a self-supporting seamstress, teaches her to sew. The promise of being able to fend for herself helps Alexia make the hardest decision of her life.

Celou Sudden Shout: Idaho, 1826 tells the story of a twelve-year-old girl whose father is a fur trapper of French origin. Her mother is Shoshone, but one day Celou's mother and brother are kidnaped by hostile Crow Indians when the father is away, and Celou must follow the raiding party in order to save them. Ann W. Moore, writing in *School Library Journal,* called it an "exciting adventure story [that] also conveys information about the Shoshone." *Summer MacCleary: Virginia, 1749,* another title from Duey in 1998, recounts the story of an indentured servant who has been accused by the daughter of the plantation owner of stealing a ring. Summer must clear her name and solve the mystery, and she possesses, as Janet Gillen wrote in *School Library Journal,* "redeeming qualities of strength and courage."

Duey's tales of young American girls facing danger and hardship span several decades and geographical places. *Agnes May Gleason: Walsenberg, Colorado, 1933* tells the story of a young girl whose family is on the verge of losing their dairy farm because of the Depression. Agnes's older brother has run away to find work elsewhere, and all must now work to keep the business afloat. When her father is injured, the Gleason parents travel to see a doctor, and Agnes and her siblings decide to bottle the milk and deliver it themselves one dawn. They have a hard time controlling the horses, but persevere and avoid disaster. Coop Renner, a *School Library Journal* writer, described this work as a "swiftly moving novel" with an "unusual setting and well-drawn minor characters."

Cajun country during the American Civil War era is the setting for *Amelina Carrett: Bayou Grand Coeur, Louisiana, 1863.* An orphan, Amelina lives with her war-profiteer uncle in a Cajun swamp community. After gunfire erupts, she discovers an injured Union Army soldier and helps him despite the Cajuns' strong sentiments against Northerners. Amelina even gives him her late father's clothes so that he may escape to safety. *School Library Journal* writer Gillen found this title from Duey "written with insight and sensitivity," and liked the interesting detail about "Cajun life in the Louisiana bayou"; Gillen also commended the protagonist's "courage and fortitude."

The glamorous world of early Hollywood is the setting of *Rosa Moreno: Hollywood, California, 1928.* Rosa's late father was a Mexican actor, and she and her mother are determined that Rosa will achieve stardom as well. She takes elocution lessons, visits a hair salon to achieve a set of curls similar to those of the most famous child

American Diaries

⇥ EVIE PEACH ⇤
ST. LOUIS, 1857

by Kathleen Duey

In pre-Civil War St. Louis, Evie and her father, both former slaves, face numerous dangers and challenges in their attempt to buy freedom for Evie's mother and establish a home for themselves. (Cover illustration by Jason Dowd.)

star of the era, Shirley Temple, and auditions frequently. When she meets a female film director, Rosa thinks she might like to direct, too. "Duey portrays Rosa's life vividly and realistically," noted *School Library Journal*'s Susan Knell, who also liked its glimpse into the rigors of child acting during this era.

The American immigrant experience was voiced by *Nell Dunne: Ellis Island, 1904,* Duey's 2000 title in the series. Nell sails from Ireland with her family, and as her diary recounts, the journey is hardly a luxurious one: the cabins for such passengers are cramped, and there are few facilities for washing. But Nell also tells of the magic she feels upon seeing her first views of New York City skyline. Duey, wrote *School Library Journal* critic Alison Grant, "captures the experience of thousands of immigrants seeking freedom and fortune" on the North American continent. The experiences of another immigrant group, the Japanese Americans, provide a subplot to *Janey G. Blue: Pearl Harbor, 1941.* Janey is from Kansas, but lives with her family near the Hawaii military base where her father works. She is curious about a shy quiet neighbor near her own age, Akiko Fujiwara. Janey and Akiko are thrown together in the confusion of the Japanese attack on Pearl Harbor's military installation. *School Library Journal*'s Elaine Lesh Morgan noted that "The mood of fear and uncertainty is well maintained, and information about the attack is neatly interwoven" into Janey's tale.

Duey is also the author of the "Survival" series with Karen A. Bale. These titles present young teens in heroic circumstances that test their courage amd their wits. Titles include, *Stranded: Death Valley, 1850* and *Flood: Mississippi, 1927.* She also writes fantasy, nonfiction, and unicorn stories for young readers growing into chapter books.

Biographical and Critical Sources

PERIODICALS

Booklist, May 15, 1996, Karen Hutt, review of *Sarah Anne Hartford: Massachusetts, 1651,* p. 1585; March 1, 1997, Lauren Peterson, review of *Willow Chase: Kansas Territory, 1847,* p. 1164; February 1, 1998, Carolyn Phelan, review of *Blizzard: Estes Park, Colorado, 1886* and *Earthquake,* p. 917; February 15,

1998, Denia Hester, review of *Evie Peach: St. Louis, 1857,* p. 1011; January 1, 2002, Susan Dove Lempke, review of *Moonsilver,* p. 856; March 1, 2002, Susan Dove Lempke, review of *The Silver Thread,* p. 1136.

Bulletin of the Center for Children's Books, May, 1996, Elizabeth Bush, review of *Sarah Anne Hartford,* pp. 297-298; April, 1998, Elizabeth Bush, review of *Earthquake,* p. 278.

Publishers Weekly, March 18, 1996, review of *Sarah Anne Hartford,* p. 70.

School Library Journal, June, 1996, Connie Parker, review of *Sarah Anne Hartford,* p. 120; December, 1996, Jane Gardner Connor, review of *Mary Alice Peale: Philadelphia, 1777,* p. 122, and Susan F. Marcus, review of *Anisett Lundberg: California, 1851,* p. 122; April, 1997, Rebecca O'Connell, review of *Willow Chase,* p. 137; August, 1997, Sylvia V. Meisner, review of *Ellen Elizabeth Hawkins: Mobeetie, Texas, 1886,* p. 157; March, 1998, Peggy Morgan, review of *Blizzard: Estes Park, Colorado,* p. 211, Robin L. Gibson, review of *Evie Peach,* p. 212, and Mary M. Hopf, review of *Earthquake,* p. 212; April, 1998, Denise Furgione, review of *Alexia Ellery Finsdale: San Francisco, 1905,* p. 131; June, 1998, Ann W. Moore, review of *Celou Sudden Shout: Idaho, 1826,* p. 143; September, 1998, Joan Zaleski, review of *Shipwreck: The Titanic* and *Fire: Chicago, 1871,* p. 200; December, 1998, Elaine Lesh Morgan, review of *Flood: Mississippi, 1927,* p. 121, and Janet Gillen, review of *Summer MacCleary: Virginia, 1749,* pp. 121-122; January, 1999, Coop Renner, review of *Agnes May Gleason: Walsenberg, Colorado, 1933,* p. 124; September, 1999, Janet Gillen, review of *Amelina Carrett: Bayou Grand Coeur, Louisiana, 1863,* p. 222; June, 2000, Susan Knell, review of *Rosa Moreno: Hollywood, California, 1928,* p. 143; October, 2000, Alison Grant, review of *Nell Dunne: Ellis Island, 1904,* p. 156; April, 2001, Betsy Barnett, review of *Francesca Vigilucci: Washington, D.C., 1913,* p. 139; October, 2001, Elaine Lesh Morgan, review of *Janey G. Blue: Pearl Harbor, 1941,* p. 154; December, 2001, Catherine Threadgill, review of *Moonsilver,* p. 99; April, 2002, Louise L. Sherman, review of *Sierra,* p. 146.

OTHER

Kathleen Duey Web Site, http://www.kathleenduey.com/ (May 25, 2002).

E

EHRLICH, Amy 1942-

Personal

Born July 24, 1942, in New York, NY; daughter of Max (a television writer and novelist) and Doris (Rubenstein) Ehrlich; married Henry Ingraham (a college professor), June 22, 1985; children: Joss. *Education:* Attended Bennington College, 1960-62 and 1963-65.

Addresses

Home—46 Stuart Ln., St. Johnsbury, VT 05819. *Office*—c/o Candlewick Press, 2067 Massachusetts Ave., Cambridge, MA 02140. *E-mail*—aehrlich@candlewick. com.

Career

Writer. Early jobs for short periods include teacher in day-care center, fabric colorist, and hospital receptionist. Freelance writer and editor for publishing companies; roving editor at *Family Circle* magazine; Delacorte Press, New York, NY, senior editor, 1977-78; Dial Books for Young Readers, New York, NY, senior editor, 1978-82, executive editor, 1982-84; Candlewick Press, Cambridge, MA, vice president, editor-in-chief, 1991-96, editor-at-large, 1996—. Vermont College, Montpelier, VT, instructor in writing for children in MFA program.

Member

Authors Guild, PEN.

Awards, Honors

New York Times Outstanding Book of the Year, 1972, *School Library Journal* Best Book of the Year, and American Library Association Children's Books of Exceptional Interest citations, 1972, all for *Zeek Silver Moon;* Editor's Choice, *Booklist,* Children's Choice, International Reading Association/Children's Book

Amy Ehrlich

Council (IRA/CBC), Children's Book of the Year, Child Study Association, and "Pick of the Lists" citation, American Booksellers Association (ABA), 1979, all for *Thumbelina;* Children's Choice citation, IRA/CBC, for *The Everyday Train;* "Pick of the Lists" citation, ABA, Kansas State Reading Circle selection, and Editor's Choice citation, *Booklist,* 1981, all for *Leo, Zack, and Emmie;* Children's Book of the Year citation, *Redbook,* 1987, for *The Wild Swans;* "Pick of the Lists" citation,

ABA, and Editor's Choice citation, *Booklist,* both for *The Snow Queen;* "Pick of the Lists" citation, ABA, Child Study Association Children's Book of the Year, and Kansas State Reading Circle selection, all for *Cinderella;* Young Adult Reviewer's Choice and Best of the Decade citations, *Booklist,* and Dorothy Canfield Fisher Award, 1990, all for *Where It Stops, Nobody Knows;* Editor's Choice citation, *Booklist,* 1993, for *Parents in the Pigpen, Pigs in the Tub.*

Writings

Zeek Silver Moon, illustrated by Robert Andrew Parker, Dial (New York, NY), 1972.

(Adapter) Dee Brown, *Wounded Knee: An Indian History of the AmericanWest* (from Brown's *Bury My Heart at Wounded Knee*), Holt (New York, NY), 1974.

The Everyday Train, illustrated by Martha Alexander, Dial (New York, NY), 1977.

(Reteller) Hans Christian Andersen, *Thumbelina,* illustrated by Susan Jeffers, Dial (New York, NY), 1979.

(Reteller) Hans Christian Andersen, *The Wild Swans,* illustrated by Susan Jeffers, Dial (New York, NY), 1981.

Leo, Zack, and Emmie, illustrated by Steven Kellogg, Dial (New York, NY), 1981.

(Reteller) Hans Christian Andersen, *The Snow Queen,* illustrated by Susan Jeffers, Dial (New York, NY), 1982.

(Adapter) *Annie* (storybook from John Huston's movie of the same title), Random House (New York, NY), 1982.

Annie Finds a Home, illustrated by Leonard Shortall, Random House (New York, NY), 1982.

Annie and the Kidnappers, Random House (New York, NY), 1982.

(Editor and adapter) *The Random House Book of Fairy Tales,* illustrated by Diane Goode, Random House (New York, NY), 1985.

(Adapter) *The Ewoks and the Lost Children* (storybook from the George Lucas television film), Random House (New York, NY), 1985.

(Adapter) *Bunnies All Day Long,* illustrated by Marie H. Henry, Dial (New York, NY), 1985.

(Adapter) *Bunnies and Their Grandma,* illustrated by Marie H. Henry, Dial (New York, NY), 1985.

(Adapter) *Bunnies on Their Own,* illustrated by Marie H. Henry, Dial (New York, NY), 1986.

(Adapter) *Bunnies at Christmastime,* illustrated by Marie H. Henry, Dial (New York, NY), 1986.

Leo, Zack, and Emmie Together Again, illustrated by Steven Kellogg, Dial (New York, NY), 1987.

Buck Buck the Chicken, illustrated by R. W. Alley, Random House (New York, NY), 1987.

Emma's New Pony, photographs by Richard Brown, Random House (New York, NY), 1988.

Where It Stops, Nobody Knows (young adult novel), Dial (New York, NY), 1988, published as *Joyride,* Candlewick Press (Cambridge, MA), 2001.

(Adapter) *Pome and Peel,* illustrated by Laszlo Gal, Dial (New York, NY), 1989.

The Story of Hanukkah, illustrated by Ori Sherman, Dial (New York, NY), 1989.

Part fiction and part memoir, Ehrlich's **When I Was Your Age** *is a compilation of stories about childhood penned by ten well-known writers for young people. (Cover photo by Christina Angarola.)*

(Adapter) Brothers Grimm, *Rapunzel,* illustrated by Kris Waldherr, Dial (New York, NY), 1989.

Lucy's Winter Tale, illustrated by Troy Howell, Dial (New York, NY), 1991.

The Dark Card (young adult novel), Viking (New York, NY), 1991.

Parents in the Pigpen, Pigs in the Tub, illustrated by Steven Kellogg, Dial (New York, NY), 1993.

Maggie and Silky and Joe, illustrated by Robert Blake, Viking (New York, NY), 1994.

(Editor) *When I Was Your Age: Original Stories about Growing Up,* Candlewick Press (Cambridge, MA), 1996.

Hurry up, Mickey, illustrated by Miki Yamamota, Candlewick Press (Cambridge, MA), 1996.

(Editor) *When I Was Your Age, Volume Two: Original Stories about Growing Up,* Candlewick Press (Cambridge, MA), 1999.

Kazam's Magic, illustrated by Barney Saltzberg, Candlewick Press (Cambridge, MA), 2001.

Bravo, Kazam!, illustrated by Barney Saltzberg, Candlewick Press (Cambridge, MA), 2001.

Rachel: The Story of Rachel Carson, illustrated by Wendell Minor, Harcourt (San Diego, CA), in press.

Work in Progress

The Girl Who Wanted to Dance, a picture book fantasy/fairy tale, for Candlewick Press, and *Willa: The Story of Willa Cather,* a picture book biography, for Harcourt.

Sidelights

The author of over thirty books, Amy Ehrlich is a writer and editor whose work for children encompasses both original picture books and critically acclaimed young adult novels. Her debut young adult novel, *Where It Stops, Nobody Knows,* was cited among *Booklist*'s "Best of the Decade," and was brought out in a new edition in 2001 as *Joyride.* Her second novel, *The Dark Card,* provides a complex psychological portrait of a teen on the edge. Additionally, Ehrlich's picture books and early readers—many of them topping the awards lists—are noted for their innovative story lines and language that challenges the reader. From her first book published in 1972, *Zeek Silver Moon,* it was apparent that Ehrlich would take a different slant on life and would explore themes that matter to young readers. Ehrlich has also retold a number of classic fairy tales such as Hans Christian Andersen's *Thumbelina* and the Grimm Brothers' *Rapunzel,* retellings noted for their innovative use of language and sympathetic characterizations.

"I always wanted to write, even from the time I was a young child," Ehrlich once noted in an interview for *SATA.* Such an ambition was natural, for Ehrlich was raised in a writer's household. Her father, Max Ehrlich, was a television writer and novelist. Though a distant father, deeply involved in his own work, he influenced his daughter to follow a writing life. "I did read some of his books," Ehrlich told *SATA,* "and I think in a way that had a big influence on me as a writer. He was always proud of my writing." As a young child, Ehrlich would make up a story at night in bed, continuing and building on the tale in her imagination each night. She was also a serious reader, absorbing everything from Laura Ingalls Wilder to Mary Poppins and Babar. The first adult novel she tackled was Betty Smith's *A Tree Grows in Brooklyn.* The wonder of books for her was that they "give the reader a very completely drawn alternate reality," as she told *SATA.* "I do really believe in the power of the story in books—not only in children's books, but also adult books."

Growing up in New York and Connecticut, Ehrlich did relatively well in school, but as she noted in *SATA,* she "always felt like a misfit. Inside I always felt different—alienated and out of step." A bright patch in this loneliness was the winning of an award for a short story in the ninth grade, the first time she ever felt special in a truly positive sense. When Ehrlich went to high school, her mother left the role of housewife and started what became a successful travel agency. As a junior in high school, Ehrlich wanted to leave public school, where she felt an outsider, and her parents sent her to a Quaker boarding school in Poughkeepsie, New York. "That was a very good experience because I was in an advanced English class in my senior year, and the teacher was very good," Ehrlich explained to *SATA.* Also, the entire atmosphere of the school, with its emphasis on academic and intellectual achievement, was a match for Ehrlich and prepared her for the rigors of a college education.

Ehrlich attended Bennington College from 1960 to 1962 and again from 1963 to 1965, but never quite finished. Throughout the 1960s and early 1970s, Ehrlich lived a roving life, taking jobs as a teacher in a day care center, as a fabric colorist, and as a receptionist. Eventually, she gravitated to freelance and part-time work in publishing, writing copy and working with children's books as an editorial assistant. During this time she would generally spend the summers on a farm in Vermont, then return to New York in the fall and find freelance work again.

"I had wanted to write a children's book for a long time and my boss encouraged me to write one," Ehrlich told *SATA.* "I was writing a lot of copy and she'd always say, 'Oh, your copy's so good—why don't you write a book?'" Ehrlich tried, but had trouble initially finding the right material. Then some friends of hers in California had a baby and Ehrlich wanted to send a little story as a present. "I sat down and started writing this thing. After I got to the second page I realized I was writing a book." The text for *Zeek Silver Moon* took a weekend of nonstop work to complete and was published exactly as written. The winner of the *New York Times* Outstanding Book of the Year award, among others, *Zeek Silver Moon* was representative of the manner in which parents were bringing up children at the time, tracing the everyday childhood events of the first five years of a boy's life.

Ehrlich then took a break from books, spending a year in Jamaica. Then in 1973, after returning to the United States, she had a son. "After my son was born," Ehrlich told *SATA,* "my view of life changed dramatically." Moving back to New York City, Ehrlich continued with her writing, adapting Dee Brown's *Bury My Heart at Wounded Knee* for young readers. Ehrlich's *Wounded Knee* was thus an overview of the conquest of the Indians of the American West by European settlers, ending with the carnage of Wounded Knee. A single parent, Ehrlich also took various editorial jobs, eventually ending up at Dial for six years. In 1977, she published *The Everyday Train,* a picture book story of a little girl who loves to watch the freight train pass her house each day. Ehrlich's 1979 retelling of the Hans Christian Andersen story, *Thumbelina,* also garnered a favorable response, as did her *Leo, Zack, and Emmie,* an easy-to-read title about how the new girl in Leo and Zack's class affects their friendship. There followed more retellings, based on both fairy tales and movies, as with Ehrlich's *Annie* books, based on the movie about Little Orphan Annie.

Much of Ehrlich's time, however, was devoted to the corporate world of publishing, and this executive life was not to her liking. Conventions and sales conferences were a strain, and when her sister became ill in Vermont, Ehrlich went to take care of her. She initially planned to be gone a matter of months; instead, she never returned. She began writing more and then met a man who eventually became her husband. More picture books and adaptations followed, including *Cinderella,* for which Ehrlich teamed up with the illustrator Susan Jeffers, with whom she had worked on several other adaptations. A *Publishers Weekly* reviewer commented that the pair's collaboration on *Cinderella* "surpasses them all." A *Bulletin of the Center for Children's Books* critic noted that "Ehrlich's simplified adaptation ... makes this edition particularly appropriate for reading aloud."

Reviewing Ehrlich's retelling of the Grimm fairy tale *Rapunzel, Horn Book* contributor Carolyn K. Jenks wrote that this is an "elegant, spare retelling" that is "more distanced from the reader, creating a feeling of mysterious beauty." Ehrlich also retold a Venetian fairy tale with her *Pome and Peel,* the story of Peel, who risks his life to save his brother Pome's bride from her father's curse. "Young readers will be entranced by this Venetian fairy tale, with its many classic ingredients," noted a *Publishers Weekly* critic, while Betsy Hearne of the *Bulletin of the Center for Children's Books* concluded that the "total effect is sophisticated enough to appeal beyond the older picture book crowd to romantic fairy tale readers." And with *The Random House Book of Fairy Tales,* Ehrlich acted as both editor and adapter.

Despite the favorable response to her retellings, Ehrlich began to leave adaptations behind, concentrating more and more on original picture books and young adult novels. Her subjects for picture books are wide-ranging, from the daily lives of second-graders, to the loss of a pet, to contemporary fairy tales, to the story of Hanukkah. Ehrlich returned to the world of Leo, Zack, and Emmie with her *Leo, Zack, and Emmie Together Again,* set during the winter amid a flurry of snowballs, valentines, and a bout of chicken pox. Lauralyn Persson, writing in *School Library Journal,* concluded that the "expert blend of picture and story makes this a book that will be a popular and worthwhile choice for the easy-reader shelves." Ehrlich teamed with illustrator Ori Sherman for *The Story of Hanukkah,* a "notable Hanukkah picture book that combines both cohesive storytelling and distinguished art," according to Betsy Hearne, writing in *Bulletin of the Center for Children's Books.* A *Kirkus Reviews* critic commented that the origin of the Festival of Lights is "retold in clear, well-cadenced, biblically formal language."

Ehrlich's rural Vermont life is also mirrored in much of her work, including the picture books *Lucy's Winter Tale, Parents in the Pigpen, Pigs in the Tub,* and *Maggie and Silky and Joe.* With *Lucy's Winter Tale,* Ehrlich created something of a modern fairy tale—the story of a farm girl named Lucy who performs with Ivan the juggler as he travels in search of his love, Martina. In the end, Lucy returns to her family, but will never forget the experience. "Ehrlich's poetic narrative puts her story in the special world of dream or allegory," noted a *Kirkus Reviews* commentator. Reviewing the work in *School*

Library Journal, Karen James referred to Ehrlich's "well-written text."

Parents in the Pigpen, Pigs in the Tub, described by a *Publishers Weekly* reviewer as "a barnyard switcheroo," tells of farm animals who get tired of their routine lives and decide to move into the house. The family, in turn, takes up residence in the barn, but eventually things return to normal when both groups get tired of the new arrangement. "Ehrlich and [illustrator Steven] Kellogg ... invest the naively accommodating family with a goofy cheerfulness that provides much of the book's humor," the *Publishers Weekly* writer added. Vanessa Elder, writing in *School Library Journal,* concluded that the book was "squeaky clean fun that's bound to get the children guffawing." And Maeve Visser Knoth, writing in *Horn Book,* felt that this "rollicking tale combines some of Ehrlich's best storytelling with Kellogg's hilarious illustrations [to form] ... an irresistible package." Knoth concluded that *Parents in the Pigpen* "is a delicious tall tale."

More somber in tone is *Maggie and Silky and Joe,* the story of a young farm boy who grows up with the family's cow dog, Maggie. When a stray puppy, Silky, comes to the farm, Maggie helps to train the younger dog. But Maggie grows old, and one day, taking refuge under the back porch during a thunder storm, she dies, and young Joe must learn to deal with loss. A *Publishers Weekly* reviewer called the book a "tender story of the death of a beloved pet," noting that it managed to avoid sentimentality by "letting honest facts speak for themselves." *Booklist*'s Hazel Rochman similarly asserted that "kids will feel Joe's sorrow, the physicality of his loss." Reviewing the same title in *School Library Journal,* Persson noted that Ehrlich "tells this 'boy loses dog' story with skilled restraint." Persson concluded, "All in all ... this is a title that anyone who has ever loved and lost an animal will appreciate."

Though she has written only two young adult novels, Ehrlich is perhaps better known for these than for her many picture books, retellings, and easy-readers. *Where It Stops, Nobody Knows* remains a popular title long after it was written, reissued in a new edition titled *Joyride,* while *The Dark Card* broke new ground in subject matter for YA novels. Inspired by a girl who was a classmate of her son, *Where It Stops, Nobody Knows* is the story of a young adolescent, Nina, and her mother, Joyce, who together move continually from place to place. There is a mystery surrounding these moves, for Nina can never let her friends know where she is going. Is it about the $16,000 that Joyce has hidden or perhaps stolen? Is Joyce her mother's real name? Clue is laid upon clue and, according to a *Kirkus Reviews* critic, "the narrative is taut enough to hold attention until its believable, unsentimental conclusion." Zena Sutherland, reviewing the novel in *Bulletin of the Center for Children's Books,* concluded that it was "trenchant and touching." Awards committees also responded favorably to the book, and *Where It Stops, Nobody Knows* earned several honorary citations.

With *The Dark Card,* Ehrlich again explores the life of a young girl in difficult circumstances. Trying to come to terms with her mother's death, seventeen-year-old Laura is lured into the glitzy world of Atlantic City's casinos. Dressing in her mother's clothes and jewelry, she assumes a new identity by night at the casinos, becoming involved with a slick gambler named Ari, who in one startling scene induces Laura to strip for him. Eventually Laura escapes from what becomes a dangerous situation for her, though as Robert Strang noted in *Bulletin of the Center for Children's Books,* her escape is "a relief rather than a victory." Strang added: "Laura's story is sad, but more significant, it's scary." A *Kirkus Reviews* critic commented that even "minor characters here are well drawn ... while relationships are deftly portrayed," and concluded that the book was a "well-structured cautionary tale ... that also thoughtfully explores the complicated feelings that can follow the loss of a flawed parent." And a contributor for *Publishers Weekly* felt *The Dark Card* was "as alluring and emotionally taut" as Ehrlich's first young adult novel. The same reviewer concluded, "[Ehrlich's] masterful control of language, ability to build suspense and keen psychological insights are sure to impress readers."

"Writing my two young adult novels meant a great deal to me," Ehrlich commented in *St. James Guide to Young Adult Writers.* "In them I wanted to tell truly gripping stories and to portray the pain and the searing discoveries of adolescence. This is a pivotal time in a human life and adults often flinch at remembering it. But I loved the intensity of recollection that came over me as I worked. The characters are made up and the stories of course are fiction, but I tried to tell the truth." In the same *St. James Guide* article, the contributing critic noted that in the characters of Nina and Laura, "Ehrlich presents portraits of adolescents on the edge of womanhood. Unlike characters in much other fiction ... these young women strive for individuality against profoundly confused and confusing circumstances .... Female readers will recognize themselves similarly engaged. Ehrlich offers them confirmation and release."

In 1990 Ehrlich returned to publishing as editor of Candlewick Press in Cambridge, Massachusetts, and for several years switched career focus from writing to editing. She stepped down from the position of vice president and editor-in-chief in 1996 to become editor-at-large, and since that time has concentrated once again on writing. In 1996 she edited *When I Was Your Age,* a compilation—part fiction and part memoir—of stories of childhood from ten well-known writers for young people. Included in the collection is a tale by Laurence Yep and his discovery that his father really did love him for himself, and Mary Pope Osborne's discussion of how she kept a deflated rubber ball given to her by her father before he went to the Korean War. Other writers featured are Susan Cooper, Avi, Nicholasa Mohr, Reeve Lindbergh, Walter Dean Myers, James Howe, Katherine Paterson, and Lia Block. Their stories, as well as Ehrlich's editing, earned praise from reviewers. *Booklist*'s Hazel Rochman noted that these ten stories "capture ... childhood experiences," and further praised

Ehrlich on her "fine introduction." Reviewing the collection in *Book Report,* Judith Beavers called it "superb," also noting that the underlying theme of all the tales "is that no matter the culture, no matter the era, growing up has never been easy." Nancy P. Reeder, writing in *School Library Journal,* called *When I Was Your Age* "a fascinating glimpse into a variety of times, places, plots, and people." "Fans of all ages will savor these perceptively chosen, affectingly disclosed episodes from the lives of favorite writers," concluded a reviewer for *Publishers Weekly.*

Ehrlich reprised this book idea with the 1999 *When I Was Your Age, Volume Two,* with contributions from Norma Fox Mazer, Jane Yolen, Joseph Bruchac, Rita Williams-Garcia, Paul Fleischman, Howard Norman, E. L. Konigsburg, Michael J. Rosen, Kyoko Mori, and Karen Hesse. "While the settings, themes and characters of these memoirs are as eclectic as their creators' individual writing styles, all express a poetic understanding and insight," wrote a contributor to *Publishers Weekly* in a review of this second volume of recollections. "Ehrlich's second anthology of short childhood memoirs is as good as the first," proclaimed *Booklist*'s Rochman, who concluded that this "will be a great read aloud to get YAs started on writing their own personal stories that speak to all of us." And reviewing this second volume in *School Library Journal,* Katie O'Dell noted, "It is the immediacy of the emotional experiences that drive the stories and make this collection well worth reading aloud in the classroom and library."

Ehrlich has also continued to write original picture books and easy readers. *Kazam's Magic* introduces young readers to a young magician whose magic tricks do not always turn out the way she wants. More tales about the youthful magician are served up in *Bravo, Kazam!,* a humorous easy reader. Ehrlich has also written picture book biographies about the environmentalist and biologist Rachel Carson, and the writer Willa Cather. "I hope," Ehrlich reported to *SATA,* "to write more novels too—very soon."

"I feel very strongly about the books that I'm writing and about the market in general," Ehrlich told *SATA.* "My books shouldn't preach or offer simple answers." Despite some criticism for the edgy situations depicted in her YA novels, Ehrlich feels that her first job as a writer is to provide a story. "I don't think kids have any trouble with any of it; I just think that some adults do." As she once remarked, books need to reach young readers. "Basically I do feel that the best book (at least for children) is the most readable and entertaining book. The writer's job as far as I am concerned is first and foremost to tell a good story about characters the readers will care about." And the editor in Ehrlich made her add: "Good editing is terribly important for writers. A good editor is as valuable as the financial terms of a contract or the promotion budget for a book—much *more* valuable, come to think about it."

Ehrlich continued to *SATA:* "I have always been split between writing and editing. Each feeds the other. A writer with whom I work just told me that one reason she appreciates my help with her stories is that I'm a writer too, and thus I understand a writer's vulnerability. But when I'm writing myself, the editorial voice is always there, asking me what I'm doing and what I mean to do.

"For me as a writer, the trick is to banish that editorial voice in the first draft so that I can stretch out and explore my own mental impulses and get to know my characters. Later on though, in revision after revision, the editorial voice is invaluable. A friend of mine who is a children's librarian and a serious student of children's literature recently entered a graduate writing program. She told me that it really changed the way she thinks about stories. She's learning to read now as a writer and not just a reader. 'What is the main thing you learned?' I asked her. Her answer came immediately, 'It's the idea of *intentionality*,' she said.

"What a great way to put it! Every paragraph, sentence, and word in a story is important and should have meaning. What is shown about the characters, how is the plot advanced? Is the language as clear as possible in communicating the writer's intention?

"Oh, and one other thing about writing—it's awfully hard work. There's just no getting around that. You need to be willing to put in the time and to enjoy the process for itself."

Biographical and Critical Sources

BOOKS

St. James Guide to Young Adult Writers, 2nd edition, St. James Press (Detroit, MI), 1999.
Twentieth-Century Young Adult Writers, edited by Laura Standley Berger, St. James Press (Detroit, MI), 1994, pp. 198-200.

PERIODICALS

Booklist, October 1, 1987, pp. 325-326; July, 1992, p. 1942; January 1, 1993, p. 818; September 15, 1993, p. 150; July, 1994, Hazel Rochman, review of *Maggie and Silky and Joe,* p. 1954; April 15, 1996, Hazel Rochman, review of *When I Was Your Age,* p. 1437; April 15, 1999, Hazel Rochman, review of *When I Was Your Age, Volume Two,* p. 1530; September 15, 1999, p. 254; May 1, 2001, p. 1610.
Book Report, September-October, 1996, Judith Beavers, review of *When I Was Your Age,* p. 45.
Bulletin of the Center for Children's Books, October, 1985, review of *Cinderella,* p. 35; January, 1989, Zena Sutherland, review of *Where It Stops, Nobody Knows,* p. 120; December, 1989, Betsy Hearne, review of *The Story of Hanukkah,* p. 82; September, 1990, Betsy Hearne, review of *Pome and Peel,* p. 6; April, 1991, Robert Strang, review of *The Dark Card,* pp. 190-191.
Christian Science Monitor, May 25, 1995, p. B1.
Horn Book, November-December, 1989, Carolyn K. Jenks, review of *Rapunzel,* p. 779; January, 1994, Maeve Visser Knoth, review of *Parents in the Pigpen, Pigs in the Tub,* p. 62.

Junior Bookshelf, June, 1986, pp. 103-104; December, 1989, pp. 291-292; December, 1991, pp. 272-273.
Kirkus Reviews, November 1, 1988, review of *Where It Stops, Nobody Knows,* p. 1603; July 15, 1989, review of *The Story of Hanukkah,* p. 1074; March 1, 1991, review of *The Dark Card,* p. 317; August 15, 1992, review of *Lucy's Winter Tale,* p. 1060.
New York Times Book Review, December 17, 1989, p. 29.
Publishers Weekly, September 27, 1985, review of *Cinderella,* p. 96; December 22, 1989, review of *Pome and Peel,* p. 56; February 22, 1991, review of *The Dark Card,* pp. 219-220; August 10, 1992, p. 70; August 16, 1993, review of *Parents in the Pigpen, Pigs in the Tub,* p. 102; July 25, 1994, review of *Maggie and Silky and Joe,* p. 55; March 4, 1996, review of *When I Was Your Age,* p. 66; February 22, 1999, review of *When I Was Your Age, Volume Two,* p. 96.
School Library Journal, October, 1987, Lauralyn Persson, review of *Leo, Zack, and Emmie Together Again,* pp. 110-111; July, 1990, p. 76; April, 1991, p. 141; September, 1992, Karen James, review of *Lucy's Winter Tale,* p. 202; October, 1993, Vanessa Elder, review of *Parents in the Pigpen, Pigs in the Tub,* p. 98; September, 1994, Lauralyn Persson, review of *Maggie and Silky and Joe,* p. 184; August, 1996, Nancy P. Reeder, review of *When I Was Your Age,* p. 152; July, 1999, Katie O'Dell, review of *When I Was Your Age, Volume Two,* p. 95.
Teen, February, 2002, Erin Zimring, review of *Joyride,* p. 107.

—Sketch by J. Sydney Jones

*   *   *

EUNSON, (John) Dale 1904-2002

OBITUARY NOTICE—See index for *SATA* sketch: Born August 15, 1904, in Neillsville, WI; died February 20, 2002, in Woodland Hills, CA. Screenwriter, magazine editor, and author. Eunson's writing career lasted for nearly sixty years and spanned several genres. His novels were generally based on people and events that were familiar to him. The children's novel *The Day They Gave Babies Away* was based on the story of his father, who as an orphaned child had fought his way through the snow of the Wisconsin countryside knocking on the doors of strangers, searching for homes for his siblings. He later adapted the novel as the screenplay *All Mine to Give.* As sole author or with his first wife, Katherine Albert Eunson, he penned several other screenplays. The team of Eunson and Eunson also wrote for television, including episodes of the popular series *Little House on the Prairie.* Eunson wrote for the stage as well; he was the coauthor of *Guest in the House,* later adapted as a screenplay featuring actors Ralph Bellamy and Anne Baxter, and *Loco,* which was adapted as the film *How to Marry a Millionaire.* Concurrently with his screenwriting career, Eunson spent almost twenty years at *Cosmopolitan* magazine, including five years as the fiction editor in the 1940s, and his own short stories appeared in many magazines.

OBITUARIES AND OTHER SOURCES:

PERIODICALS

Independent, March 16, 2002, obituary by Tom Vallance, p. 6.

Los Angeles Times, March 1, 2002, obituary by Myrna Oliver, p. B15.

New York Times, March 9, 2002, p. A14.

F

FACKLAM, Margery (Metz) 1927-

Personal

Born September 6, 1927, in Buffalo, NY; daughter of Eduard Frederick (a civil engineer) and Ruth (Schauss) Metz; married Howard F. Facklam, Jr. (a high school biology teacher), July 9, 1949; children: Thomas, David, John, Paul, Margaret Thomas. *Education:* University of Buffalo, B.A., 1947; State University of New York College—Buffalo, M.S., 1976. *Hobbies and other interests:* "Nature in general, animals in particular, traveling, and spending time with my ... wonderful grandchildren."

Addresses

Home—9690 Clarence Center Rd., Clarence Center, NY 14032.

Career

Erie County Department of Social Welfare, Buffalo, NY, caseworker, 1948; high school science teacher in Snyder, NY, 1949-50; Buffalo Museum of Science, Buffalo, NY, assistant administrator of education, 1970-74; Aquarium of Niagara Falls, Niagara Falls, NY, curator of education and public relations, 1974-77; Buffalo Zoo, Buffalo, NY, director of education, 1977-79; Institute of Children's Literature, Redding Ridge, CT, instructor, 1982-84; Vassar Summer Institute of Publishing, Poughkeepsie, NY, instructor, 1983—. Highlights Institute, Chautauqua, NY, staff member, 1987, 1990; Cape Cod Writers Workshop, Cape Cod, MA, teacher, 1992-95.

Member

Society of Children's Book Writers and Illustrators, Association of Professional Women Writers.

Awards, Honors

Booklist Children's Editor's Choice selection, 1986, for *Changes in the Wind: Earth's Shifting Climate;* Best Books for Teenagers selection, New York Public Library, 1988, for *Spare Parts for People;* Reading Magic Award, *Parenting* magazine, 1989, for *Do Not Disturb: The Mysteries of Hibernation and Sleep* and *Partners for Life: The Mysteries of Animal Symbiosis;* Recommended Books for Reluctant Young Adult Readers selection, *School Library Journal,* 1990, and Maud Hart Lovelace Award nomination, Youth Reading Project, 1992-93, both for *The Trouble with Mothers;* Best Books selection, *School Library Journal,* 1990, and William Allen White Award nomination, both for *And Then There Was One: The Mysteries of Animal Extinction;* Twenty-five Best Nonfiction Books selection, *Boston Globe,* 1992, for *Bees Dance and Whales Sing: The Mysteries of Animal Communication;* Best Books for the Teen Age selection, New York Public Library, 1993, for *Kid's World Almanac of Amazing Facts about Numbers, Math, and Money;* Best Books selection, *School Library Journal,* 1994, for *What Does the Crow Know?: The Mysteries of Animal Intelligence;* Notable Book selection, American Library Association, 1994, Pick of the Lists selection, American Booksellers Association, 1994, Texas Bluebonnet list, 1995-96, and Rhode Island State List, 1995-96, all for *The Big Bug Book.*

Frozen Snakes and Dinosaur Bones: Exploring a Natural History Museum, Wild Animals, Gentle Women, The Brain, Magnificent Mind Machine, Changes in the Wind: Earth's Shifting Climate, I Eat Dinner, Spare Parts for People, So Can I, Do Not Disturb, But Not Like Mine, Partners for Life, Plants—Extinction or Survival?, and *Bees Dance and Whales Sing* were named Outstanding Science Trade Books by the National Council of Science Teachers/Children's Book Council; *Frozen Snakes and Dinosaur Bones, Wild Animals, Gentle Women, Changes in the Wind, The Trouble with Mothers,* and *Who Harnessed the Horse?: The Story of Animal Domestication* were Junior Library Guild selections.

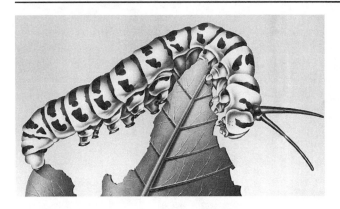

Beginning with an overview of the caterpillar's body and an explanation of the metamorphosis of the caterpillar to moth and butterfly, Facklam proceeds to introduce various caterpillar varieties. (From Creepy, Crawly Caterpillars, *illustrated by Paul Facklam.)*

Writings

Whistle for Danger, Rand McNally (Chicago, IL), 1962.

Behind These Doors: Science Museum Makers, Rand McNally (Chicago, IL), 1968.

(With Patricia Phibbs) *Corn Husk Crafts,* Sterling (New York, NY), 1973.

Frozen Snakes and Dinosaur Bones: Exploring a Natural History Museum, Harcourt (San Diego, CA), 1976.

Wild Animals, Gentle Women, illustrated by Paul Facklam, Harcourt (San Diego, CA), 1978.

(With Howard Facklam) *From Cell to Clone: The Story of Genetic Engineering,* illustrated by Paul Facklam, Harcourt (San Diego, CA), 1979.

(With Howard Facklam) *The Brain, Magnificent Mind Machine,* illustrated by Paul Facklam, Harcourt (San Diego, CA), 1982.

(With Howard Facklam) *Changes in the Wind: Earth's Shifting Climate,* illustrated by Paul Facklam, Harcourt (San Diego, CA), 1986.

But Not Like Mine (picture book), illustrated by Jeni Bassett, Harcourt (San Diego, CA), 1987.

I Eat Dinner (picture book), illustrated by Anita Riggio, Little, Brown (Boston, MA), 1987.

I Go to Sleep (picture book), illustrated by Anita Riggio, Little, Brown (Boston, MA), 1987.

So Can I (picture book), illustrated by Jeni Bassett, Harcourt (San Diego, CA), 1987.

Spare Parts for People, illustrated by Paul Facklam, Harcourt (San Diego, CA), 1987.

Do Not Disturb: The Mysteries of Hibernation and Sleep, illustrated by Pamela Johnson, Sierra Club Books (San Francisco, CA), 1989.

Partners for Life: The Mysteries of Animal Symbiosis, illustrated by Pamela Johnson, Sierra Club Books (San Francisco, CA), 1989.

The Trouble with Mothers (novel), Clarion (New York, NY), 1989.

Plants—Extinction or Survival?, Enslow Publishers (Hillside, NJ), 1990.

And Then There Was One: The Mysteries of Animal Extinction, illustrated by Pamela Johnson, Sierra Club Books (San Francisco, CA), 1990.

Avalanche! ("Nature's Disasters" series), Crestwood House (Mankato, MN), 1991.

Healing Drugs: The History of Pharmacology ("Science Sourcebooks" series), also published as *Pharmacology: The Good Drugs,* Facts on File (New York, NY), 1992.

I Go to Sleep, Boyds Mills Press (Honesdale, PA), 1992.

I Eat Dinner, Boyds Mills Press (Honesdale, PA), 1992.

Bees Dance and Whales Sing: The Mysteries of Animal Communication, illustrated by Pamela Johnson, Sierra Club Books (San Francisco, CA), 1992.

(With Margaret Thomas) *Kid's World Almanac of Amazing Facts about Numbers, Math, and Money,* Pharos Books, 1992.

Who Harnessed the Horse?: The Story of Animal Domestication, illustrated by Steven Parton, Little, Brown (Boston, MA), 1992.

The Big Bug Book, illustrated by Paul Facklam, Little, Brown (Boston, MA), 1994.

What Does the Crow Know?: The Mysteries of Animal Intelligence, illustrated by Pamela Johnson, Sierra Club Books (San Francisco, CA), 1994.

(Reviser) Frances N. Chrystie, *Pets: A Comprehensive Handbook for Kids,* Little, Brown (Boston, MA), 1995.

Only A Star, Eerdmans Publishing (Grand Rapids, MI), 1996.

Creepy, Crawly Caterpillars, illustrated by Paul Facklam, Little, Brown (Boston, MA), 1996.

Tracking Dinosaurs in the Gobi, Twenty-first Century Books (New York, NY), 1997.

Bugs for Lunch, illustrated by Sylvia Long, Charlesbridge (Watertown, MA), 1999.

Spiders and Their Web Sites, illustrated by Alan Male, Little, Brown (Boston, MA), 1999.

What's the Buzz?: The Secret Lives of Bees, Raintree Steck-Vaughn (Austin, TX), 2000.

(With Howard Facklam and Sean M. Grady) *Modern Medicines: The Discovery and Development of Healing Drugs,* Facts on File (New York, NY), 2003.

(With Alan Male) *Lizards: Weird and Wonderful,* Little, Brown (Boston, MA), 2003.

Crabs and Other Crusty Creatures, Little, Brown (Boston, MA), 2003.

"INVADER" SERIES

(With Howard Facklam) *Bacteria,* Twenty-first Century Books (New York, NY), 1994.

(With Howard Facklam) *Insects,* Twenty-first Century Books (New York, NY), 1994.

(With Howard Facklam) *Parasites,* Twenty-first Century Books (New York, NY), 1994.

(With Howard Facklam) *Viruses,* Twenty-first Century Books (New York, NY), 1994.

OTHER

Contributor to periodicals, including *Cobblestone, Cricket, Guideposts, Ranger Rick, Redbook,* and *Spider.* Some of Facklam's books have been translated into Japanese, Italian, Spanish, and French.

Sidelights

An award-winning author of over forty titles in the sciences, Margery Facklam blends hands-on animal knowledge with an easy and direct writing style to create both middle-grade readers and picture books. With a background in biology, Facklam has catered to the needs of children curious about science and scientists. Her first works of nonfiction allowed readers a behind-the-scenes view of natural history and gave them an introduction to the lives of women scientists. Facklam's later works have explored scientific puzzles involving global climate change, animal hibernation, extinction, intelligence, and communication, as well as the world of arthropods. Many critics have praised Facklam's work for its thorough research, clear organization, and the balanced representation of various debates, theories, and perspectives. Facklam's fascination with science is reflected in her texts.

When Facklam was a young girl growing up in Buffalo, New York, she did not know that she wanted to be a writer. She loved books, as she once explained to *SATA:* "One of the things I remember best is the weekly trip to the big Victorian downtown library every Friday evening to get our reading for the week. My mother and my aunts were avid readers and I caught the bug early." Facklam also loved science and avidly read about explorers like Roy Chapman Andrews, Osa Johnson, and Richard Halliburton. Facklam said that when she was in the third grade, she "wanted to be an explorer" and take long journeys. She "especially wanted to go down the Amazon River, see the Galapagos Islands, and go to the Gobi Desert, where the first dinosaur eggs were found [by Roy Chapman Andrews] in 1923."

In high school, Facklam worked every Saturday and after school at the Buffalo Zoo reptile house. There, Marlin Perkins, who hosted the television program about wildlife, *Wild Kingdom,* taught Facklam about snakes. As Facklam noted on *Eduplace.com,* "[Perkins] taught me more about snakes than any number of college courses ever could do." Later, she worked her "way through college by taking care of a colony of porcupines, a job that was to open interesting jobs" for her later. "I even know how to give a porcupine a bath," she noted on *Eduplace.com.* After receiving a B.A. in biology, Facklam married and, with her husband, Howard, had five children. She began to write when her "houseful of children settled in for naps." As she recalled, "At first, I wasn't very successful. I sold a few articles and a few funny poems. Then, with our last child and only daughter crawling under the table as I typed, I wrote my first book, *Whistle for Danger,* a fictionalized account of a summer I spent working at the zoo in a reptile house.

"Then I was hooked. I was a writer. Now I write about the things that fascinate me, mostly animals and nature. When our oldest son was starting college, I returned to work, first at a science museum and then at an aquarium and a zoo. Those jobs were motherlodes of material for new books. I met people and animals I could hardly wait to write about."

One of Facklam's first science books was *Frozen Snakes and Dinosaur Bones: Exploring a Natural History Museum.* According to Facklam, she wrote this book because she "was sure that children were missing the best part of the museum, behind the scenes where the exhibits are made, skeletons put together and animals mounted." Since the publication of *Frozen Snakes and Dinosaur Bones,* Facklam has concentrated her efforts on writing science books.

As she told a critic in *Junior Library Guild,* Facklam came up with the idea to create *Wild Animals, Gentle Women* after a teacher asked her to give a presentation to her class about women scientists. Finding too many women scientists to discuss, Facklam researched the lives of eleven "women from different backgrounds" and interests who work with animals. In *Wild Animals, Gentle Women,* Facklam describes the occupations of these women—observers, research scientists, animal trainers, and zoo workers—discusses the women's interest in the animals they work with, and even explains how the women trained for their jobs. Among these women are Heather Malcolm, Eugenie Clark, Leone Pippard, Belle Benchley, Jane Goodall, Birute Galdikas,

In rhyming text, Margery Facklam describes a host of critters that eat insects as part of their regular diet. (From Bugs for Lunch, *illustrated by Sylvia Long.*)

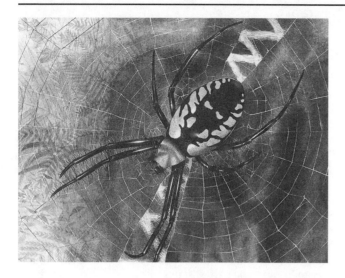

Facklam examines the webs spiders weave, comparing their design to that of Internet Web sites in their ability to draw visitors. (From Spiders and Their Web Sites, *illustrated by Alan Male.)*

and Dian Fossey. Finally, Facklam devotes a chapter to those looking forward to a career working with animals. She told the *Junior Library Guild* reviewer that she believes *Wild Animals, Gentle Women* will bring young people, and "especially girls," an understanding of the "variety of jobs available to 'animal lovers.'"

In *Partners for Life: The Mysteries of Animal Symbiosis* Facklam explains mutualism, commensalism, and parasitism, the three main types of symbiosis, and then describes symbiosis involving insects, sea creatures, birds, microscopic organisms, and parasites. While Frances E. Millhouser in *School Library Journal* noted that Facklam sometimes anthropomorphizes animals by ascribing "intent and purpose" to them, she observed that the author presents predators in a "non-judgmental way." Millhouser appreciated the "excellent" chapter on Darwin's survival of the fittest theory. A contributor for *People Weekly* felt that this "primer on symbiosis" is a "lively way to encourage budding scientists," while Margaret A. Bush concluded in *Horn Book* that *Partners for Life* is "exceptionally readable" and provides a "fine examination of its subject."

Facklam often works with her family. Several of her books have been written with her husband, Howard, a biology teacher. Their son, Paul, has illustrated many of her works. Facklam has also written a book with her daughter, Margaret Thomas, titled *Kid's World Almanac of Amazing Facts about Numbers, Math, and Money.* Another work, *Changes in the Wind: Earth's Shifting Climate,* was a family effort, with its text by the senior Facklams and diagrams by Paul. Facklam said in *Junior Library Guild* that her husband "was intrigued by the idea of writing a book about climate before I was." Nevertheless, as they researched their topic, their "enthusiasm gained momentum." Best of all, a call to the Duke University Marine Laboratory in North Carolina resulted in an exciting trip to the Galapagos Islands.

The result of the Facklams' research on climate, *Changes in the Wind,* discusses the effects of human activities and natural phenomena (like volcanic explosions and solar rhythms) on the Earth's climate and environment while asserting the interdependence of these effects. It also demonstrates how climate affects people, populations, and standards of living around the world: everyone on the planet may be affected by the greenhouse effect or a nuclear winter. Up-to-date scientific information and studies, computer-generated models, a glossary, and a bibliography are included. Despite the amount of technical information, the Facklams maintain what Allen Meyer in *School Library Journal* called a "conversational style." According to Meyer, this style "is used effectively to maintain interest and to explain difficult concepts."

The Facklams teamed up again to write *Spare Parts for People,* a book Denise L. Moll described in *School Library Journal* as a "fascinating look at some of the major advances in modern medicine in the field of bioengineering." The Facklams demonstrate how various specialists, including bioengineers, biochemists, and electronics technicians, have worked together with doctors to help those in need of body parts and organs, and how they have, in the process, made significant scientific discoveries. The Facklams discuss the development of artificial organs and body parts, organ transplants, and the possibilities of regenerating various body parts. As Zena Sutherland observed in the *Bulletin of the Center for Children's Books,* the case studies the Facklams provide are "exciting and dramatic."

Do Not Disturb: The Mysteries of Animal Hibernation and Sleep, as a *Kirkus Reviews* critic remarked, "is a fascinating look at the physical and chemical changes" animals undergo as they hibernate, estivate (hibernate in the summer), and sleep. Facklam discusses the three types of hibernation, which include deep and light sleep and daily dormancy, and the animals which demonstrate these types of sleep. The grizzly bear goes into a deep sleep during the winter, raccoons and skunks are "in-between hibernators," some reptiles estivate during dry spells, and bats and hummingbirds spend part of each day dormant to conserve energy. Eva Elisabeth Von Ancken, writing in *School Library Journal,* concluded that *Do Not Disturb* is an "excellent choice for curricular use and as leisure reading."

Leisure reading of a different sort is served up in Facklam's 1989 *The Trouble with Mothers,* a foray into the world of juvenile fiction. *The Trouble with Mothers* deals with the problem of censorship as well as a teenager's relationship with his mom. When eighth-grader Buzz Troy learns that his school-teaching mother's book, *The Passionate Pirate,* is the subject of a debate about censorship in his town, he suffers embarrassment and harassment. Troy cannot support his mother until he reads her book and discovers that it treats slavery in the United States. As Nancy Vasilakis wrote in *Horn Book,* "It is obvious" where Facklam's "sympathies lie and that she has little use" for those who promote censorship. On the other hand, Joyce Yen asserted in *Voice of Youth Advocates* that Facklam conveys "both sides" of the issue and that *The Trouble with Mothers* "will help" readers "understand" the issue of censorship.

Returning to her usual nonfiction beat, Facklam clarifies the meanings of evolution and extinction in *And Then There Was One: The Mysteries of Animal Extinction.* Presenting a discussion of extinction cycles throughout history, the author explains the human and non-human threats to animals and their habitats, and finally describes various attempts to revive endangered species. According to Margaret Bush in *School Library Journal, And Then There Was One* provides "thoughtful explanations" and a "well-crafted blend of information," as well as an "interesting narrative." Betsy Hearne judged in *Bulletin of the Center for Children's Books* that Facklam's book is "a tour de force in arguing for ecological balance."

Bees Dance and Whales Sing: The Mysteries of Animal Communication demonstrates that creatures communicate with their own kind and humans using body language, scents, voices, dances, pheromones, expressions, ultrasonic and infrasonic sounds, and even sign language. The communication methods of many animals and insects, including bats, beavers, cats, dogs, dolphins, fire ants, monkeys, and toadfish, are specified. As *School Library Journal* contributor Amy Nunley observed, *Bees Dance and Whales Sing* is "loaded with interesting facts" and includes the "latest scientific information." In addition, a critic remarked in *Publishers Weekly,* "Facklam's smooth, conversational style makes fact-reading easy."

Facklam attempts to answer the question of animal intelligence in *What Does the Crow Know?: The Mysteries of Animal Intelligence.* In addition to culling information from a number of studies while commenting on that research itself, Facklam provides stories about animals that have seemed to demonstrate different types of intelligence: parrots, dolphins, elephants, and chimpanzees. *School Library Journal* critic Karen M. Kearns appreciated Facklam's answer of the question, "which species is smartest?" with the statement, "Each animal is as smart as it needs to be" to "survive." While Hazel Rochman praised Facklam's ability to distinguish "trickery" from what is "proven" in her *Booklist* assessment, she lamented a lack of documentation. Yet for *Horn Book*'s Elizabeth S. Watson, *What Does the Crow Know?* is part of an "intriguing" series. Watson further remarked that Facklam "describes in fascinating detail" experiments to document animals' ability to learn and mimic humans.

In the thirteen chapters of *Who Harnessed the Horse?: The Story of Animal Domestication,* Facklam tells how various animals, from dogs and horses to ostriches and silkworms, were domesticated, and discusses the importance of these animals as companions, sources of food, and beasts of burden. In addition, Facklam relates how certain interactions between man and animals have resulted in the near-extinction of various species. As *Washington Post Book World* reviewer Michael Dirda observed, Facklam "laces her account" with "startling factoids." In Dirda's opinion, the book "will provide hours of educated diversion." Deborah Stevenson, however, noted for *Bulletin of the Center for Children's Books* that issues of animal rights or the inhumanity of some animal treatments are "not explored deeply or consistently."

Facklam is equally at home with picture books as she is with middle-grade nonfiction books. *But Not Like Mine* and *So Can I* were Facklam's first picture books. Facklam once explained that writing these books taught her "that the old truism is indeed true, 'Easy reading is hard writing.' I did a lot of revising on those books." *But Not Like Mine* and *So Can I* demonstrate the similarities and differences among human children and various animals. *But Not Like Mine* juxtaposes body parts like hands and feet, while *So Can I* compares capabilities like swimming, hopping, and hugging. In each book, double-page spreads feature an animal, and children are hidden under a flap. According to a reviewer in *Publishers Weekly,* the only "flaw" in these books occurs in *Not Like Mine,* where the text "emphasizes differences" and the illustrations "highlight similarities."

According to Roger Sutton, writing in *Bulletin of the Center for Children's Books, The Big Bug Book,* another of Facklam's picture books, "knows just how to seduce kids into some ... serious nature study." The first two pages are devoted to an introduction and general information about insects. Facklam's information about the behavior and reproduction of the largest insects in the world is neatly boxed on each page opposing one of Paul Facklam's large color illustrations. These illustrations feature exotic, enormous bugs like the wetapunga, tarantula hawk wasp, walking stick, Madagascar Hissing Cockroach, and dragonfly on household objects children know well—Tinkertoys, a model airplane, crayons, and alphabet blocks. *School Library Journal* contributor Karey Wehner found that the work was "concisely written and well organized," and that its "unique" illustrations made it "recreational reading par excellence." And reviewing the title in *Booklist,* Carolyn Phelan thought that the book with its "realistic, close-up views" would be "certain to intrigue young audiences."

More picture books have followed. *Creepy, Crawly Caterpillars,* with illustrations by Paul Facklam, presents "a cogent, particularly handsome guide to caterpillars," according to *Booklist*'s Phelan. The book employs the picture-book format while targeting readers in third to fifth grade. Beginning with an overview of the caterpillar body and an explanation of the metamorphosis of caterpillar to moth and butterfly, Facklam proceeds to introduce various individual caterpillar varieties, mostly from North America. Unique features and habits of each insect are examined in an "informative and readable" manner, according to Phelan, who also felt the book would be "great for backyard study or elementary research projects." Bush, reviewing the title in *Horn Book,* praised Facklam for her "lucid explanations with a nice flair for interesting bits of information."

Burns concluded that the caterpillar life cycle, "ever fascinating to children, is well served in this handsome introduction to a complex insect." And a contributor for *Kirkus Reviews* thought that this "splendid companion to *The Big Bug Book* will have budding entomologists poring over the pages." "There is not doubt you'll enjoy and learn from the great creepy-crawlers featured in this book," declared a contributor for *Children's Digest.* And with *Crabs and Crusty Creatures,* Facklam and her son do much the same service for the world of crustaceans as they did for caterpillars, describing thirteen of the varieties, including horseshoe, fiddler, soldier, and ghost crabs, among others.

In Facklam's next picture book, *Only a Star,* the author creates a unique blend of science and Christmas story in a prose poem which answers a child's questions about the first Christmas morning. When the child wants to know if there were any decorations, the father answers that there was only a star, and then begins to describe the events of that long ago time. As Facklam portrays the manger where Christ was born, she relies on her animal training to focus on the assortment of animals present and their activities. Writing in *School Library Journal,* Jane Marino dubbed the book a "treasure" to be shared "with a child you love." A reviewer for *Publishers Weekly* also commented on Facklam's science writing providing added strength to the story: "Science, nature and religion fit together nicely here, forming the framework for a respectful and deftly delivered story."

With *Bugs for Lunch* and *Spiders and Their Web Sites,* Facklam returns to the more familiar ground of insects in a picture-book format. Describing the former title, a contributor for *Publishers Weekly* noted that in "simple rhyming verse, Facklam offers a list of critters that regularly dine on insects." Such a list includes nuthatches, mice, and even a gecko. *Booklist*'s Kay Weisman noted that "Facklam's playful rhymed verses ... introduce young listeners to a variety of creatures that eat insects." Reviewing the same title in *School Library Journal,* Patricia Manning praised Facklam's "cheerful, rhyming text," concluding that "this is an attractive, high-interest book."

Spiders and Their Web Sites is also an "entertaining book," according to *Booklist*'s Connie Fletcher, which takes as its premise the idea that Web site designers are now doing what spiders managed to perfect millions of years ago: "lure visitors to complex communication centers," as Fletcher noted. Focusing on a dozen different spiders plus the daddy longlegs, Facklam examines the eggs they hatch and the webs they weave. Along the way she correlates this to modern web design, slipping in the interesting bit of information now and again, such as the fact that spider silk is stronger than any other natural fiber and was actually used in bombsights during the Second World War. She also manages to include some of the "satisfyingly gross" topics that kids seem to love, according to Fletcher. A *Horn Book* reviewer felt that Facklam's "sophisticated text presents facts effortlessly while remaining appealing throughout." Writing in *School Library Journal,* Karey

Wehner concluded that the book "has definite browser appeal."

With her *Tracking Dinosaurs in the Gobi,* Facklam returned to longer middle-grade nonfiction works and also to one of her early inspirations for studying animal behavior. The book is a "hard-to-put-down account," according to Cathryn A. Camper in *School Library Journal,* of the first American expedition to hunt for fossils in the Gobi Desert in the 1920s. As such, it is partially a biography of Roy Chapman Andrews, who led the expedition, and upon whom the fictional character of Indiana Jones was based. The book recounts the discoveries and adventures of this expedition. "Facklam's superb text keeps readers involved throughout," Camper further commented, concluding that this "superlative book ... captures the adventure of hunting for dinosaur bones." *Booklist*'s Helen Rosenberg similarly lauded Facklam's book, dubbing it a "lively account" and a "must for dinosaur and fossil enthusiasts as well as budding paleontologists." Reviewing the book in *Appraisal: Science Books for Young People,* a contributor wrote, "Young readers will be fascinated by the life of Andrews and the amount of knowledge he gained about dinosaurs, including his first discovery of a fossilized clutch of dinosaur eggs, and the now famous Velociraptor."

From dinosaurs, the versatile Facklam turns to bees with her year 2000 title, *What's the Buzz: The Secret Life of Bees.* But whatever the topic, Facklam brings the same enthusiasm in research and writing to the task. Facklam once told *SATA* that she loves her careers as a teacher and a writer, and that they are similar. "When you write, you teach, only you have a bigger classroom and you reach only the people who want to know what you have to tell them."

Writing has also allowed Facklam to visit the far away places she could only dream of as a child: The Gobi Desert and the Galapagos Islands. Facklam observed, "Although my dreams of becoming an explorer didn't come true, I am kind of [an] explorer in a small way as I research books." She further reflected, "Writing is hard work, but it is exciting, fun, exasperating, and the most wonderful job in the world."

Biographical and Critical Sources

BOOKS

Ward, Martha E., et al, *Authors of Books for Young People,* 3rd edition, Scarecrow Press (Metuchen, NJ), 1990.

PERIODICALS

Appraisal: Science Books for Young People, fall, 1998, review of *Tracking Dinosaurs in the Gobi,* pp. 10-11.
Booklist, June 8, 1992, p. 65; June 15, 1992, p. 1828; March 1, 1994, Hazel Rochman, review of *What Does the Crow Know?,* pp. 1256-1257; April 1, 1994, Carolyn Phelan, review of *The Big Bug Book,* p. 1440; January 1, 1995, p. 817; May 15, 1996, Carolyn Phelan, review of *Creepy, Crawly Caterpillars,* p. 1586; October 15, 1996, p. 426; February 1, 1998,

Helen Rosenberg, review of *Tracking Dinosaurs in the Gobi*, p. 914; February 1, 1999, Kay Weisman, review of *Bugs for Lunch*, p. 976; March 15, 2001, Connie Fletcher, review of *Spiders and Their Web Sites*, p. 1396.

Bulletin of the Center for Children's Books, October, 1987, Zena Sutherland, review of *Spare Parts for People*, p. 26; May, 1989, p. 221; September, 1990, Betsy Hearne, review of *And Then There Was One: The Mysteries of Animal Extinction*, p. 7; June, 1992, Deborah Stevenson, review of *Who Harnessed the Horse?*, pp. 258-259; March, 1994, Roger Sutton, review of *The Big Bug Book*, p. 220.

Children's Digest, July, 1999, review of *Creepy, Crawly Caterpillars*, p. 14.

Christian Science Monitor, March 30, 1995, p. B3.

Family Life, August, 2001, p. 168.

Horn Book, November, 1987, pp. 710-713; July-August, 1989, Nancy Vasilakis, review of *The Trouble with Mothers*, p. 481; September-October, 1989, Margaret A. Bush, review of *Partners for Life: The Mysteries of Animal Symbiosis*, p. 635; September-October, 1994, Elizabeth S. Watson, review of *What Does the Crow Know?*, p. 611; July-August, 1996, Margaret A. Bush, review of *Creepy, Crawly Caterpillars*, pp. 479-481; May-June, 2001, review of *Spiders and Their Web Sites*, p. 347.

Junior Library Guild, March, 1978, review of *Wild Animals, Gentle Women;* April-September, 1986, review of *Changes in the Wind: Earth's Shifting Climate.*

Kirkus Reviews, January 15, 1989, review of *Do Not Disturb: The Mysteries of Hibernation and Sleep*, p. 122; March 15, 1989, p. 462; March 1, 1996, review of *Creepy, Crawly Caterpillars*, p. 373.

New Yorker, November 27, 1989, p. 144.

New York Times Book Review, June 24, 1990, p. 28.

Publishers Weekly, April 8, 1988, review of *So Can I* and *But Not Like Mine*, p. 89; June 19, 1989, review of *Partners for Life*, p. 27; June 8, 1992, review of *Bees Dance and Whales Sing*, p. 65; September 30, 1996, review of *Only a Star*, pp. 89-90; January 11, 1999, review of *Bugs for Lunch*, p. 71.

School Library Journal, December, 1986, Allen Meyer, review of *Changes in the Wind*, p. 115; January, 1988, Denise L. Moll, review of *Spare Parts for People*, p. 91; February, 1988, pp. 59-60; March, 1989, Eva Elisabeth Von Ancken, review of *Do Not Disturb*, p. 190; September, 1989, Frances E. Millhouser, review of *Partners for Life*, p. 262; September, 1990, Margaret A. Bush, review of *And Then There Was One*, p. 240; August, 1992, Amy Nunley, review of *Bees Dance and Whales Sing*, p. 162; April, 1994, Karen M. Kearns, review of *What Does the Crow Know?: The Mysteries of Animal Intelligence*, p. 136; June, 1994, Karey Wehner, review of *The Big Bug Book*, p. 118; March, 1995, p. 229; May, 1996, p. 103; October, 1996, Jane Marino, review of *Only a Star*, p. 35; February, 1998, Cathryn A. Camper, review of *Tracking Dinosaurs in the Gobi*, p. 115; March, 1999, Patricia Manning, review of *Bugs for Lunch*, p. 192; August, 2001, Karey Wehner, review of *Spiders and Their Web Sites*, p. 168.

Voice of Youth Advocates, June, 1989, Joyce Yen, review of *The Trouble with Mothers*, p. 100.

Washington Post Book World, July 12, 1992, Michael Dirda, review of *Who Harnessed the Horse?: The Story of Animal Domestication*, pp. 8-9.

OTHER

Eduplace.com—Authors: Margery Facklam, http://www.twbookmark.com/ (February 22, 2002).

Meet Margery Facklam, http://www.eduplace.com/ (February 22, 2002).

*   *   *

FARLEY, Walter (Lorimer) 1915(?)-1989

Personal

Born June 26, 1915 (some sources say 1916, 1920, or 1922), in Syracuse, NY; died following a heart attack, October 16, 1989, in Sarasota, FL; son of Walter Patrick (a hotel manager) and Isabelle Louise (a homemaker; maiden name, Vermilyea) Farley; married Rosemary Lutz (a model for the John Robert Powers Agency), May 26, 1945; children: Pamela (deceased), Alice, Steven, Timothy. *Education:* Attended Columbia University School of Journalism. *Hobbies and other interests:* Raising, riding, and racing horses; traveling; sailing; jogging; reading; sports; pets.

Career

Writer, 1941-89, and breeder of Arabian horses, 1946-65. Copywriter (print and radio) for Batten, Barton, Durstine, and Osborn advertising agency, New York, NY, 1941. Consultant on and promoter of films *The Black Stallion* and *The Black Stallion Returns*, 1979 and 1983. *Military service:* U.S. Army, Fourth Armored Division, 1942-46; staff member of the army weekly *Yank.*

Awards, Honors

Young Readers Choice Award, Pacific Northwest Library Association, and Young Readers Choice Award, Montana State University, both 1944, for *The Black Stallion;* Young Readers Choice Awards, Pacific Northwest Library Association and Montana State University, and Boys Club of America Award, all 1948, for *The Black Stallion Returns.* Most of Farley's books were named Junior Literary Guild selections in their respective years of publication.

In 1964, Farley received a prize from a jury of young readers in France. The Walter Farley Literary Landmark was established in Venice, Florida, in 1989 by the Friends of the Venice Public Library.

Walter Farley

Writings

"BLACK STALLION" SERIES

The Black Stallion (also see below), illustrated by Keith Ward, Random House (New York, NY), 1941; new edition, 1982; Golden Anniversary edition, illustrated by Domenick D'Andrea, 1991; also published as *Walter Farley's The Black Stallion.*

The Black Stallion Returns (also see below), illustrated by Harold Eldridge, Random House (New York, NY), 1945.

Son of the Black Stallion (also see below), illustrated by Milton Menasco, Random House (New York, NY), 1947; 2nd edition with drawings by Hofbauer, Collins (London, England), 1950.

The Island Stallion, illustrated by K. Ward, Random House (New York, NY), 1948.

The Black Stallion and Satan (also see below), illustrated by M. Menasco, Random House (New York, NY), 1949.

The Blood Bay Colt, illustrated by M. Menasco, Random House (New York, NY), 1950, published as *The Black Stallion's Blood Bay Colt,* 1978.

The Island Stallion's Fury, illustrated by H. Eldridge, Random House (New York, NY), 1951.

The Black Stallion's Filly, illustrated by M. Menasco, Random House (New York, NY), 1952.

The Black Stallion Revolts, illustrated by H. Eldridge, Random House (New York, NY), 1953.

The Black Stallion's Sulky Colt, illustrated by H. Eldridge, Random House (New York, NY), 1954.

The Island Stallion Races, illustrated by H. Eldridge, Random House (New York, NY), 1955.

The Black Stallion's Courage, illustrated by Allen F. Brewer, Jr., Random House (New York, NY), 1956.

The Black Stallion Mystery (also see below), illustrated by Mal Singer, Random House (New York, NY), 1957.

The Horse-Tamer, illustrated by James Schucker, Random House (New York, NY), 1958.

The Black Stallion and Flame, illustrated by H. Eldridge, Random House (New York, NY), 1960.

The Black Stallion Challenged!, illustrated by Angie Draper, Random House (New York, NY), 1964, published in England as *The Black Stallion's Challenge,* Hodder and Stoughton (London, England), 1983.

The Black Stallion's Ghost, illustrated by Angie Draper, Random House (New York, NY), 1969.

The Black Stallion and the Girl, illustrated by Angie Draper, Random House (New York, NY), 1971.

Walter Farley's Black Stallion Books (omnibus; includes *The Black Stallion, The Black Stallion Returns, The Black Stallion and Satan,* and *The Black Stallion Mystery*), Random House (New York, NY), 1979.

The Black Stallion Legend, Random House (New York, NY), 1983.

(With son, Steven Farley) *The Young Black Stallion,* Random House (New York, NY), 1989.

The Black Stallion Books (omnibus; includes *The Black Stallion, The Black Stallion Returns,* and *Son of the Black Stallion*), Random House (New York, NY), 1992.

"LITTLE BLACK" SERIES; EASY READERS

Little Black, a Pony, illustrated by James Schucker, Random House (New York, NY), 1961.

Little Black Goes to the Circus, illustrated by James Schucker, Random House (New York, NY), 1963.

The Little Black Pony Races, illustrated by James Schucker, Random House (New York, NY), 1968.

EASY READERS AND PICTURE BOOKS

(With Josette Frank) *Big Black Horse* (adaptation of *The Black Stallion*), illustrated by P. K. Jackson, Random House (New York, NY), 1953, 2nd edition, with illustrations by James Schucker, Publicity Products (New York, NY), 1955.

The Horse That Swam Away, illustrated by Leo Summers, Random House (New York, NY), 1965.

The Black Stallion Picture Book, illustrated with photographs from the motion picture, Random House (New York, NY), 1979.

The Black Stallion Returns: A Storybook Based on the Movie, edited by Stephanie Spinner, Random House (New York, NY), 1983.

The Black Stallion: An Easy-to-Read Adaptation, illustrated by Sandy Rabinowitz, Random House (New York, NY), 1986.

The Black Stallion Beginner Book, Random House (New York, NY), 1987.

FICTION

Larry and the Undersea Raider, illustrated by P. R. Jackson, Random House (New York, NY), 1942.

Man o' War (fictionalized biography), illustrated by Angie Draper, Random House (New York, NY), 1962.

The Great Dane, Thor, illustrated by Joseph Cellini, Random House (New York, NY), 1966.

OTHER

How to Stay Out of Trouble with Your Horse: Some Basic Safety Rules to Help You Enjoy Riding (nonfiction), photographs by Tim Farley, Doubleday (Garden City, NY), 1981.

Contributor to *Yank* magazine, U.S. Army. Farley's works have been translated into twenty-one languages. His papers are housed in the Butler Library, Columbia University. A permanent exhibit of memorabilia related to the "Black Stallion" series is located at the Walter Farley Literary Landmark, Venice, FL.

Adaptations

The Black Stallion and *The Black Stallion Returns* were released as motion pictures by United Artists in 1979 and 1983, respectively; both films were produced by Francis Ford Coppola. *The Black Stallion* was directed by Carroll Reed with a script by Melissa Mathieson, Jeanne Rosenberg, and David D. Witliff. *The Black Stallion Returns* was directed by Robert Dalva with additional production by Fred Ross and Tom Sternberg. *The Black Stallion* was released on video in 1984 and on DVD in 1998 by United Artists. *The Black Stallion Returns* was released on video in 1995 and on DVD in 2002 by MGM. *The Black Stallion* and *The Black Stallion Returns* have been issued as sound recordings, including a reading of the first book produced by Recorded Books, 1995. *The Black Stallion* and *The Black Stallion Returns* were adapted as comic strip albums by Robert Genin (text) and Michel Faure (illustrations); initially published in France, they were released by Random House in 1983 and 1984, respectively. *The Adventures of the Black Stallion,* a cable television series, aired on The Family Channel, 1990-93. Several of the episodes were released on video by GoodTimes Home Video and Alliance. *The Young Black Stallion* is scheduled to be released as a motion picture by Walt Disney Pictures in 2002.

Sidelights

A popular, prolific American writer of fiction and nonfiction for children and young adults, Walter Farley is considered a major contributor to juvenile literature as well as a prominent author of animal stories. He is best known as the creator of the "Black Stallion" series, twenty-one tales that feature a magnificent, half-wild Arabian horse and his offspring, the colts Satan and Bonfire and the fillies Black Minx and Black Sand, as well as Flame, a red stallion who becomes associated with "the Black," as the main character is called. The series, which has been a favorite of young readers for over sixty years and has sold over a hundred million

copies, also features teenage protagonists Alec Ramsey and Steve Duncan, boys who form loving bonds with the creatures, tame them, and race them to victory in events such as the Kentucky Derby; Alec is aided in the training of the Black by Henry Dailey, a retired jockey.

Setting his works on American horse farms, stables, and race courses as well as in international locales like the Middle East, Spain, and South America, Farley created exciting, fast-paced adventures that place both the human and animal characters in desperate situations, such as being separated after plane crashes. The protagonists also must surmount various personal obstacles, often related to dealing with the animal natures of the horses, in order to win races. Initially, Farley wrote plots that were straightforward in nature. However, as the series continued, the author deepened his characterizations—for example, Alex has an emotional breakdown after the loss of his friend Pam, who is killed in an auto accident—and added supernatural and mystical elements to his stories. Farley underscores his "Black Stallion" books with a wealth of authentic information about horses: their personalities, their care, their training, and the events in which they compete.

In the first of Farley's immensely popular books, the Black Stallion, a magnificent, half-wild Arabian horse, is rescued by Alec Ramsey, the devoted teenage boy who lovingly tames and races him. (From The Black Stallion, *illustrated by Keith Ward.)*

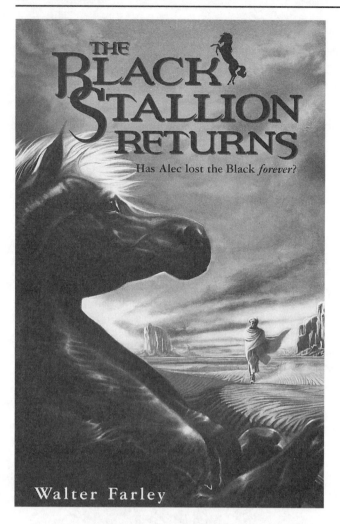

Alec Ramsey loses the Black Stallion to an Arabian sheik who is the rightful owner of the horse, and the heartbroken boy sets off, determined to buy the horse he loves so dearly. (Cover illustration by John Rowe.)

In addition to his "Black Stallion" series, Farley created books for younger children, including three easy readers about Little Black, a pony who saves his young master's life. The author also wrote a fictionalized biography of the famous horse Man o' War, who won twenty of the twenty-one races in which he competed; a story featuring a boy, his father, and the man's Great Dane; a novel about two teens, one American and one Hawaiian, who uncover a plot by the Japanese to sink U.S. ships off Hawaii; and an informational book on horse ownership.

Farley's stories characteristically revolve around the love of a boy for an animal and his ability to gain its trust through kindness and sensitivity. The works also address such themes as courage, independence, responsibility, hard work, friendship, and the appropriate treatment of animals. As a writer, Farley began his career by favoring simple sentences in subject/predicate order that use a number of exclamation points; he also tended to concentrate on action rather than on character. As he developed his style, the author added more complex sentences and fleshed out his characterizations. According to some observers, it is this latter aspect that

separates the "Black Stallion" books from series such as "Nancy Drew" and the "Hardy Boys." Although each book in the "Black Stallion" series is linked by story and character, it can stand alone.

Although he is criticized for his early writing style as well as for the improbability of some of his plots, the omniscient point of view that occasionally described the thoughts of his horses, and the stereotyped portrayals of some of his female and ethnic characters, Farley is usually commended as an author whose works reflect his knowledge of his subject as well as his understanding of young people and what appeals to them. A writer in *St. James Guide to Young Adult Writers* called Farley "the master of the horse story," while Richard Brunner of *Christian Science Monitor* noted, "In the field of publishing, where 'phenomenal' authors appear with the regularity of the spring lilacs and the autumn asters (and disappear just as regularly), Walter Farley is a genuine phenomenon." Writing in *Children's Books and Their Creators*, Elizabeth Hurd stated that Farley "has become one of the most respected authors of books for young readers because he consistently provides his audience with stories that maintain their sense of adventure while remaining true to the development of characters introduced over the course of many books.... Farley's particular skill lies in the fact that his stories in no way feel churned out as do so many other contemporary writers.... Alec and the Black Stallion and their counterparts Steve Duncan and Flame ... remain interesting, vital characters in each book." Hurd concluded that devoted horse fans "will continue to cheer as the Black and Alec thunder down the homestretch for many years to come."

Farley's books are informed by his genuine affection for horses as well as his personal life and travels. Born in Syracuse, New York, to Walter Patrick Farley, a hotel manager of Irish and French Canadian descent, and Isabelle Louise Vermilyea Farley, a homemaker of English and Dutch descent, Farley was enamored of horses since he was a small boy. He once told *Something about the Author* (*SATA*), "My great love was, and still is, horses. I wanted a pony as much as any boy or girl could possibly want anything—but I never owned one." He wrote that he made life miserable for his parents because he could not understand why they would not let him keep a horse in the garage and let it graze on the family lawn. The Farleys lived in a section of Syracuse that was called Tipperary Hill because of its large Irish population. Every year, their parents would take Walter and his brother Bill to the New York State Fair to see the races. Farley's father also took him to see the great racehorse Man o' War at Faraway Farm in Kentucky. During the summer, the Farley boys would visit their aunt, who lived on Oneida Lake near a farm. In the foreword to the Golden Anniversary edition of *The Black Stallion*, Bill Farley wrote that Walter "was up on the farm horses at every opportunity."

As a third grader, Farley wrote a composition, a story about a big black horse, perhaps in response to a family legend about one of their relatives, a soldier who shot a

German officer during World War I in order to steal the man's beautiful black stallion. Forced to abandon the horse in a London train station, the soldier never saw the animal again. Bill Farley recalled that most of his brother's compositions were horse stories, usually accompanied by a drawing of a horse in black crayon. Young Walter entered every contest that had a horse or a pony for a prize, but never won. In order to pacify him, his parents gave Farley every book on horses that they could find—both fiction and technical books on breeding, training, and horse anatomy. Farley decided that he wanted to become either a jockey, a veterinarian, or a breeder of horses. However, his career choice was about to change.

When he was eleven, Farley began to write stories about horses with titles like "The Winged Horse," "My Black Horse," "Red Stallion," and "The Pony." When he was twelve, the fledgling author became acquainted with his Uncle Bill, who had moved to Syracuse from the West Coast with a stable of show horses and jumpers. Farley told *SATA,* "I was deliriously happy. I was at the stables every chance I could get." Farley often would skip school and hitchhike to see his uncle at his riding stables; at night, he would sleep in the hay. Bill Farley recalled, "Uncle Bill was an excellent horseman, teacher, and trainer of show horses and their young riders (mostly young ladies, an added attraction for Walter)."

Quoted in the Golden Anniversary edition of *The Black Stallion,* Farley commented that his uncle "wasn't the most successful trainer of racehorses, and in a way I profited by it. He switched from runners to jumpers to show horses to trotters and pacers, then back to runners again. Consequently, I received a good background in different kinds of horse training and the people associated with each." Bill Farley noted that his brother "had three major interests while growing up; school was not one of them. They were horses, running, and girls, not always in that order." The boys' father, who was once a catcher in semipro baseball, encouraged them in sports and bought them the best equipment that he could afford. Both boys became finalists in a tennis championship in Syracuse. Walter also became an accomplished speed skater. While attending Porter Junior High School, he entered the Syracuse Junior Olympics, an annual citywide competition, and won the championship in his age group.

Farley began his high school career at Syracuse Central High School, where he made the track team. In 1933, he moved to New York City, where his father became manager of the bars and grill rooms of the Hotel Roosevelt. Farley decided to enroll at Erasmus Hall High School in Brooklyn because of their exceptional track team. At Erasmus Hall, he became a member of the mile relay team, which won the city championship. Farley enjoyed living in New York City for all of the opportunities that it afforded, especially concerning sports. He told Lee Bennett Hopkins in *More Books by More People* that he "was able to play tennis, ride, run, and ice skate most of the year. And there were plenty of horses." Farley enjoyed going to the race tracks at Belmont, Jamaica, and Aqueduct Parks where, he told Hopkins, "I spent many, many days." Later, he moved to Flushing, where several of his friends had horses stabled in lots. "And it was there," he told Hopkins, "I set the locale for *The Black Stallion* as I rode on trails through Kissena Park and along the Long Island Expressway."

Farley kept extensive notes of his experiences with horses that he witnessed, shared, or dreamed about; he would adhere to this practice all of his life. While at Erasmus Hall, Farley continued writing his own horse stories. He told Hopkins, "I enjoyed writing as much as I did reading or participating in sports or anything else. I enjoyed writing stories on the typewriter, any kind of story at all, at the ages of fourteen, fifteen, and sixteen. I read a great deal, but there were few books about horses—at least only a couple that I knew of. There was Anna Sewell's *Black Beauty* and Will James' *Smoky, the Cow Horse,* but these were not enough to satisfy me. I honestly thought, even at that age, about the thousands of horse lovers like me who wanted more books about horses. I became absorbed in *The Black Stallion* by becoming Alec, of course, a boy from New York City

Farley and his son Steven cowrote this prequel to **The Black Stallion,** *which relates the adventures of the Black's early life in the mountains of Arabia. (Cover illustration by John Rowe.)*

who brought a horse like The Black to my Flushing barn. I remember well devoting two and three nights a week writing it."

Due to his accomplishments in track at Erasmus Hall, Farley received an athletic scholarship to Mercersburg Academy in Mercersburg, Pennsylvania. According to Bill Farley, "Mercersburg turned him around academically through the encouragement and interest of his teachers, especially the faculty advisor for the school newspaper. Walter became a reporter for the newspaper and an 'A' student." The faculty advisor, David F. Chapman, taught English and was in charge of the *Mercersburg News.* While at Mercersburg, Farley kept on working on his story about the Black Stallion. After graduating with honors from Mercersburg in 1935, he returned to New York City and worked as a messenger at an advertising agency while teaching himself to become a copywriter. He then wrote ad copy for print and radio at the agency. In the foreword to the Golden Anniversary edition of *The Black Stallion,* Farley's wife Rosemary noted, "He enjoyed writing advertising slogans, but his heart was in his book and the freedom of being a creative writer."

Farley entered the School of Journalism at Columbia University, attending at night. He took a course on writing for children taught by Mabel L. Robinson, a professor who also wrote books for boys and girls. Robinson told Farley that he should be writing horse stories for young people and invited him to join her advanced workshop. Farley remembered her tutelage as "very tough." *The Black Stallion* was completed in Robinson's class. One evening, Robinson's editor Louise Bonino, a woman who worked for Random House publishers, visited the class and heard *The Black Stallion* being discussed. She bought the book in 1940 and issued it the next year.

In *The Black Stallion,* seventeen-year-old Alec Ramsey is coming home to New York on the tramp steamer *Drake* after spending the summer with his uncle in India; also aboard the ship is a fierce, unmanageable black stallion. When the *Drake* sinks, Alec frees the Black, and the horse swims with the boy to safety on a deserted island off the Spanish coast; the two are the only survivors of the wreck. Alec and the Black must depend on each other for survival. They develop a mutual trust, and Alec creates a secret language of touches, whispers, and whistles that enables him to communicate successfully with the animal and tame his savage ways. After he and the Black are rescued by a southbound freighter and taken to New York, Alec meets with his friend Henry Dailey, who helps him to train the Black by night (without the knowledge of Alec's parents). Finally, Alec rides the Black to victory in a match race against two national champions.

At the time of its publication, Marguerite Nahigian of *Library Journal* wrote of *The Black Stallion,* "The secret and careful training which the Black received, the breath-taking excitement of the nocturnal tryouts at the track, the final dramatic victory in the race, all add up to a virile action thriller." Margery Fisher of *Growing Point* called *The Black Stallion* "an adventure story whose outsize plot is curbed by a firm attention to the relationship between the hero, Alec Ramsey ... and the stallion." Writing about Farley in *Chronicle of the Horse,* John Strassburger commented that *The Black Stallion* "is quite a remarkable book for one so young. The research is excellent, the characterizations strong, and the descriptions vivid." The novel is recognized as a classic of its genre. Farley's son Steven, writing in the Golden Anniversary edition of *The Black Stallion,* concluded that the Black is "a horse who became a symbol of the unconquerable, wild side of nature for millions of readers."

Young readers discovered *The Black Stallion* and made it their own. Farley and Random House received a deluge of mail asking for more stories about Alec and the Black. After *The Black Stallion* was published, Farley left the ad agency and went on a year-long trip with the advance payment that he had received for his novel. He once wrote that when he learned that boys and girls liked the story of the Black, he was inspired to leave the agency and travel in order to find material for books to come. He went to a dude ranch in Wyoming, then to Mexico, and then to the West Coast, where he visited the only Arabian horse farms in the United States at that time. Farley then went to Hawaii, where he developed the idea for *Larry and the Undersea Raider,* a book that features a Japanese submarine in U.S. waters near Hawaii. At first, Random House rejected the story, but they reconsidered quickly after the events at Pearl Harbor. Farley also took a tramp steamer to Tahiti. He returned to New York City before going to Bogota, Colombia, to write. According to Rosemary Farley, these trips "set a pattern of traveling for business and pleasure that lasted his whole life."

During World War II, Farley was in the U.S. Army in the Fourth Armored Division; he also served as a reporter for *Yank,* the weekly magazine produced by the army. While stationed in Alaska, Farley and author Dashiell Hammett, who was also a reporter, accompanied long-range bombing missions into northern Japan. During the long winter and on plane flights, Farley completed the second novel in his series, *The Black Stallion Returns.* In 1944, Farley was reassigned to New York City, where he met Rosemary Lutz, a model for the John Robert Powers Modeling Agency who had a degree in political science from the University of Pittsburgh. The couple got married the next year; they had four children: Pam, Alice, Steve, and Tim. Although he was advised by his editor, Louise Bonino, not to consider writing for children as a profession, Farley decided to devote himself to creating books for the young. For the next forty years, Farley would create new installments of his series, often at the rate of one per year. After writing the third volume in the series, *Son of the Black Stallion,* Farley bought a farm near Boyertown, Pennsylvania, where he could breed and raise his own horses, both Arabians and Standards (trotters and pacers).

Throughout his series, Farley involves Alec and the Black in thrilling adventures, some of which revolve around the separation of boy and horse, while introducing the stallion's heirs. The Black is claimed by his original owner, an Arabian sheik who sends Alec the horse's first-born colt, Satan, as a gift. At his death, the sheik's daughter bequeaths the Black to Alec. Satan, who initially is as dangerous as the Black had been, meets his father and fights with him; the two race for their lives when they are put into the path of a raging forest fire. Alec becomes a successful trainer on his father's New York horse farm, and races the Black, Satan, Bonfire (a sulky colt that wins the Hambletonian Stakes), and Black Minx (a spoiled filly that becomes a Kentucky Derby champion). After Alec retires the Black, he brings him back to race in order to win money to replace his barn, which has been destroyed by fire. The Black and Alec also go traveling and encounter mystery and intrigue as well as some surprising turns of event: for example, in *The Black Stallion Revolts,* Alec gets amnesia after he and the Black survive a plane crash. The boy thinks that he has committed murder, and spends months running from the police. At the end of the story, Alec regains his memory and is reunited with the Black at an Arizona ranch. Throughout the series, Alec must make tough decisions, such as whether to go to college. He develops business sense in his chosen field of racing, and must rely on survival skills in his adventures with the Black.

In 1948, Farley introduced his readers to Steve Duncan and Flame in *The Island Stallion.* The story describes how Steve and his friend Pitch, an archeologist, visit Azul Island, a fictitious place in the Caribbean that was used as a base by the Spanish Conquistadors. The pair discover an uncharted valley, where they find a herd of beautiful horses led by Flame, a red stallion that has haunted Steve's imagination since childhood; the idea for Flame came to Farley while being anaesthetized for an ear operation. At first, Flame is unapproachable, but the horse begins to trust Steve after he saves him from a horrible death. Steve and Pitch also uncover a treasure of Spanish gold. Although Steve must leave Flame on the island, he vows to return. In *The Island Stallion Races,* Steve takes Flame from Azul Island to Cuba to enter the famed International Race. Like the Black, Flame is an independent stallion with a tendency to attack other horses, but Steve treats him with great care. Aiding Steve are two extraterrestrials that are visiting Earth. At the end of the story, Flame wins the race and is transported secretly back to Azul Island.

Flame meets the Black Stallion in *The Black Stallion and Flame.* The Black, who drifts to the island after being separated from Alec in a plane crash, and Flame vie for leadership of the herd, but they band together to kill a vampire bat before the Black is reunited with Alec. In *The Black Stallion Challenged,* Steve contacts Alec and explains that he wants to race Flame, who has already won a race in Cuba, in the United States. Steve needs to raise the money to buy Azul Island, so he asks Alec to help him train the horse. Both the Black and Flame enter the race, which ends in a photo finish between the two horses. The judges decide that the Black has won by a nose. However, since Steve has won all of the money that he needs to buy Azul Island, he decides not to race again.

In 1968, Farley's oldest daughter Pam, a junior in college, was killed in an auto accident in the Austrian Alps. In 1971, her father produced a tribute to Pam: *The Black Stallion and the Girl.* This work, the first of the series in which a woman plays a leading role, addresses the issue of sexism. Alec hires Pam Athena, a bright, idealistic, and free-spirited girl, as a trainer. However, he has a hard time persuading his partners to retain Pam's services—trainer Henry Dailey even threatens to quit if she stays in what has traditionally been a male-dominated sport. Alec also must convince his partners to let Pam ride the Black after he is suspended as a jockey. Drawn to each other by their mutual love of horses, Alec and Pam fall in love. When he asks her to marry him, Pam realizes that, though she loves Alec, she cannot stay with him. Alec is settled in his world of horse racing, and she needs to explore the world. However, Pam believes that she will return to Alec eventually.

Twelve years after the publication of this novel, Farley produced *The Black Stallion Legend.* In this work, which is often considered his best, Alec suffers a nervous breakdown after he reads about the death of Pam Athena, who has perished in an auto accident in the Alps. Alec takes the Black and flees to the southwestern United States. There, he wanders, exhausted, until he meets a Native American shepherd boy, who tells him about a legend in which a rider on a black horse will appear to lead his people to safety at the time of great natural disasters; at that time, floods and earthquakes were taking place throughout the United States. Alec and the Black lead the tribe to safety, and Alec releases the Black to run with a herd of wild horses. Through his experience, Alec has learned about faith and courage. In addition, he has discovered the wisdom in Pam's advice to him, which is to ride for the joy of it, not for the money it brings.

Farley's last book, *The Young Black Stallion,* is a prequel to the first volume of the series. Written in collaboration with his son Steven, the novel was published in 1989, the year of Walter Farley's death. The narrative describes the Black's early life in the mountains of Arabia. Bred to strengthen the bloodlines of the herd of his owner, Sheik Abu Ishak, the Black (originally named Shetan) is thought to be the unearthly son of the legendary "Stallion of the Midnight Sky." Stolen by the sheik's enemies and angered by the cruelty he encounters, Shetan escapes from his pasture and joins a herd of ibex; soon he is scaling rocks and dueling young rams to their deaths. Befriended by Rashid, a young Bedouin, the stallion travels to the desert and encounters dangers while attempting unsuccessfully to elude the horse traders who want to capture him. The Black ends up on the tramp steamer *Drake,* where he meets Alec Ramsey. At the end of the story, the Farleys disclose that the story is actually a vision that Alec has had while recovering from the events of *The Black Stallion Legend.*

Calling the series "wonderfully improbable," a reviewer in *Publishers Weekly* said, "Although this prequel never quite matches the sparkle of the earlier works, it certainly should answer several questions about the Black's beginnings. Even the book's rather cloying mystical streak is unlikely to disturb the loyal followers of the legendary stallion." Writing in *School Library Journal,* Charlene Strickland noted, "Some coincidences mar the plot's believability, but readers will enjoy the story's twists and exciting scenes. The last chapters rehash the truck racing scenes from *Raiders of the Lost Ark,* but readers will be driven to complete the story." After noting an inconsistency (a real-life stallion, Ziyadeh, sired the Black, as documented in *The Black Stallion Mystery*), Strickland concluded, "Anxious fans will savor the story nonetheless." Denise M. Wilms of *Booklist* claimed, "the Black is as compelling a figure as ever, and there will be a ready-made audience for this book. Not first-rate, but certainly a worthwhile part of Farley's extensive chronicle." After the publication of *The Black Stallion Legend,* Steven Farley continued the series with his own "Black Stallion" volumes.

In assessing the "Black Stallion" series, John Strassburger of *Chronicle of the Horse* stated that Farley's books "are more than just an ordinary collection of stories about a boy and his horse growing up together in America. Carried in these scores of pages are strong moral themes, messages to children about life.... Some three generations of children have now experienced the Black Stallion because the books are healthy and enjoyable reading for children. They stir the imagination, they evoke emotion, they teach children to care and to dream." Elizabeth Hurd, writing *in Children's Books and Their Creators,* commented that fans introduced to the Black Stallion "are meeting one of the most enduring and popular animal characters ever created," while Martha Bacon, writing about the Black in *Atlantic Monthly,* said that in "his artless horsey way he seems to me to carry on the satisfactory tradition of Black Beauty."

Writing in *Twentieth-Century Children's Writers,* Rebecca J. Lukens noted, "The strongest feature of Farley's stories is the successful involvement of the reader in admiration for the horses, his true subject: whatever the plot, the horse is the focus. Alec Ramsey may be the protagonist, but life to Alec is the Black.... The Black Stallion and his offspring remain alive, more memorable than plots or people." Richard Brunner of the *Christian Science Monitor* added, "Today's children starting the series may not realize they are reading a 'modern classic,' but they are as enthusiastic as their parents or grandparents were when they embarked on this adventure." Margery Fisher of *Growing Point* concluded, "The energy of the Black Stallion books and their strong subject-matter have kept them in print since the 1940's and should guarantee them a further extension of published life."

The "Black Stallion" series, much of which has never been out of print, has consistently prompted tie-ins, promotions, and adaptations. In 1949, the first Black Stallion Club was founded in Kentucky. The club consisted of boys and girls who were interested in horses and horsemanship, and it fostered neighborhood clubs and activities throughout the country. Farley designed a button for the club that was in demand for many years. Before the publication of *The Black Stallion's Filly* in 1952, Farley and Random House sponsored a contest to choose a name for a filly sired by the Black. More than 50,000 children submitted names in order to win the prize: a purebred Arabian foal. Black Minx was the name chosen in the contest. The "Black Stallion" series also prompted several adaptations as well as two comic book albums and several coloring and activity books. In 1979, United Artists released *The Black Stallion,* a film produced by Francis Ford Coppola (the director of *The Godfather,* among other movies), directed by Carroll Reed, and scripted in part by Melissa Mathieson, who also wrote Steven Spielberg's film *E.T.* This live-action version of Farley's book was a critical and a popular success. It also won three Academy Awards, including ones for Best Actor in a Supporting Role (Mickey Rooney), Film Editing (Robert Dalva), and Sound Editing (Alan R. Spiet). In 1983, United Artists released the film adaptation of *The Black Stallion Returns,* which was directed by Robert Dalva, the film editor from the previous film; though considered not quite as successful as its predecessor, the film is still regarded as a worthy successor. Farley consulted on both films and did promotion for them.

The Family Channel premiered a cable television program based on Farley's books called *The Adventures of the Black Stallion;* filmed in Canada, France, and New Zealand, it ran from 1990-93. In 1999, the Black Stallion Literacy Project (BSLP) was formed by photographer Tim Farley, Walter Farley's youngest son, who now is the director of the Black Stallion, Inc., and Mark Miller, the owner of the Arabian Nights Equitheater, a theater in Kissimmee, Florida, that features horses as its stars. A nonprofit organization dedicated to getting children to read, the BSLP uses the "Little Black" and "Black Stallion" books to entice children in the first and fourth grades to read. For each book that they complete, children can meet real horses at locations around the country. The "Black Stallion" books also have inspired a number of Web sites, many of them tributes to the Black and its creator.

Farley's interest in children was an active one. Besides his involvement in children's reading programs, such as the Black Stallion Club, he made frequent appearances at schools, libraries, and book fairs. In addition to their farm in Pennsylvania and apartment in New York City, Walter and Rosemary Farley kept a beach house in Venice, Florida. In 1962, they organized a group that formed the Friends of the Library of the Venice Area to establish a free public library there. The library opened in 1965 and became a success. On January 29, 1989, the Friends of the Library dedicated the Walter Farley Literary Landmark, which includes a permanent exhibit of materials related to *The Black Stallion.* Rosemary Lutz Farley said of her husband, "Through history, there have always been people who have a special bond with horses. Walter Farley was one of that special breed.... For ... forty-five years I lived with the man and his horse, the Black. Although we had real live horses and ponies, the center of his life was that paper horse galloping through his studio or wherever he had a typewriter in front of him." Bill Farley said of his brother, "Walter's life was a love affair with the horse."

Walter Farley told Lee Bennett Hopkins in *More Books by More People,* "I have no occupation other than writing. The only income I've ever had has come from writing books. I do raise horses and Arabians occasionally and sell them, but there's really little money in it. Writing for me is fun. All my books are completely different from one another, otherwise I could never have stayed with the same characters who are used as springboards into whatever it is I want to write about. Kids know how different my books are; most adults don't." He continued, "Kids are so apt to think something that is fun and comes easy to them is not important. I was no different. When I go to book fairs, I always make a point of encouraging kids to develop the talent that comes easy and naturally. You ought to pursue your hobby—not become a lawyer so you can spend your spare time pursuing your hobby. If you can't make a living water skiing, then take up something related to it—sell the equipment or edit a magazine about it." Farley saved all of the hundreds of thousands of letters that he received, storing them in his tack room above horses and stalls. "How different," he inquired, "are kids in their love for horses now than they were in the 1940s? I think little. Many kids would rather ride on the back of a horse at twenty to twenty-five miles per hour than pilot a spaceship to the moon!" Quoted in the Golden Anniversary edition of *The Black Stallion,* Farley concluded, "I believe half the trouble in the world comes from people asking "What have I achieved?" rather than "What have I enjoyed?" I've been writing about a subject I love as long as I can remember—horses and the people associated with them, anyplace, anywhere, anytime. I couldn't be happier knowing that young people are reading my books. But even more important to me is that I've enjoyed so much the writing of them."

Biographical and Critical Sources

BOOKS

Almanac of Famous People, 6th edition, Gale (Detroit, MI), 1998.

Farley, Rosemary, and Steven, Walter, and Dr. William Farley, "Walter Farley and the Birth of 'The Black Stallion': The Family Remembers," *The Black Stallion: Golden Anniversary Edition,* Random House (New York, NY), 1991.

Farley, Walter, *How to Stay Out of Trouble with Your Horse: Some Basic Safety Rules to Help You Enjoy Riding,* Doubleday (New York, NY), 1981.

Farley, Walter, interview with Lee Bennett Hopkins, *More Books by More People: Interviews with Sixty-Five Authors of Books for Children,* edited by Hopkins, Citation Press, 1974.

Hurd, Elizabeth, "Walter Farley," *Children's Books and Their Creators,* edited by Anita Silvey, Houghton Mifflin (Boston, MA), 1995.

Junior Book of Authors, edited by Stanley J. Kunitz and Howard Haycraft, 2nd edition, Wilson (New York, NY), 1951.

Legends in Their Own Time, Prentice Hall General Reference (New York, NY), 1994.

Lukens, Rebecca J., "Walter Farley," *Twentieth-Century Children's Writers,* 3rd edition, St. James Press (Detroit, MI), 1989.

Sadler, Philip A., "Walter Farley," *Dictionary of Literary Biography,* Volume 22: *American Writers for Children, 1900-1960,* Gale (Detroit, MI), 1983.

St. James Guide to Young Adult Writers, 2nd edition, St. James Press (Detroit, MI), 1999.

PERIODICALS

Atlantic Monthly, December, 1969, Martha Bacon, "Tantrums and Unicorns," p. 150.

Booklist, February 15, 1990, Denise Wilms, review of *The Young Black Stallion,* p. 1162.

Christian Science Monitor, February 1, 1971, Richard Brunner, "In a Field of Seasonal Authors, a Perennial Phenomenon."

Chronicle of the Horse, November 13, 1987, John Strassburger, essay on Walter Farley.

Growing Point, November, 1978, Margery Fisher, "A Bundle of Old Favourites," pp. 3406-3407.

Library Journal, November 1, 1941, Marguerite Nahigian, review of *The Black Stallion,* p. 953.

Publishers Weekly, November 10, 1989, review of *The Young Black Stallion,* p. 61.

School Library Journal, December, 1989, Charlene Strickland, review of *The Young Black Stallion,* p. 100.

Wilson Library Bulletin, February, 1949, Earle F. Walbridge, "Walter Farley," p. 412.

OTHER

Big Movie Zone—Coming Attractions, http://www.bigmoviezone.com/ (March 24, 2002).

Black Stallion Fan Club, http://www.blackstallionfanclub.com/ (March 24, 2002).

Black Stallion Literacy Project, http://www.bslp.org/ (March 24, 2002).

Black Stallion's Unofficial Home Page, http://www.oceanbay.com/The Black/ (March 24, 2002).

Black Stallion Tribute: The Unofficial 'The Black Stallion' Fan Site, http://www.theblackstallion.net/ (March 24, 2002).

Farm Goods for Kids, http://www.farmgoodsforkids.com/ (March 24, 2002).

Greenville Public Library: Juvenile Books Author of the Month—Walter Farley, http://www.yourlibrary.ws/ (March 24, 2002).

Horse Industry Alliance (HIA): Online, http://www.horseindustryalliance.com/ (March 24, 2002).

Official Black Stallion Website, http://www.theblackstallion.com/ (March 24, 2002).

Venice Public Library: Walter Farley Literary Landmark, http://www.venice-florida.com/ (March 24, 2002).*

—*Sketch by Gerard J. Senick*

*   *   *

FENNER, Carol (Elizabeth) 1929-2002

OBITUARY NOTICE—See index for *SATA* sketch: Born September 30, 1929, in Almond, NY; died of cancer, February 16, 2002, in Battle Creek, MI. Author and illustrator. Fenner wrote nearly a dozen children's books, beginning in 1963 with *Tigers in the Cellar,* which she also illustrated. Over the next thirty-five years she earned several literary awards for her work, including a Newbery Honor Book award from the American Library Association in 1996 for *Yolanda's Genius.* Fenner's topics varied widely, depending on the interests or issues that engaged her attention at the time. *Gorilla, Gorilla,* a Christopher Medal winner and Library of Congress "book of the year" in 1973, relates the true story of a lonely gorilla who lived in a Tokyo zoo. *Randall's Wall,* on the other hand, is a fictional tale about a young boy who hides from the neglect and poverty of his real world behind an imaginary wall. *Yolanda's Genius* is a similar story of isolation about a young girl with issues of self esteem. Fenner's other books include *The Skates of Uncle Richard, Saving Amelia Earhart,* and *The King of Dragons.* She also wrote short stories for magazines such as *Cricket.*

OBITUARIES AND OTHER SOURCES:

BOOKS

Something about the Author Autobiography Series, Volume 24, Gale (Detroit, MI), 1997, pp. 105-126.

PERIODICALS

Los Angeles Times, February 22, 2202, p. B13.
Washington Post, February 22, 2002, p. B8.

*   *   *

FLEISHER, Paul 1948-

Personal

Born June 23, 1948, in Bel Air, MD; son of Joseph H. (a biochemist) and Tresa (a sanitarian) Fleisher; married Debra Sims (an educator), July 12, 1975. *Education:* Brandeis University, B.A. (cum laude), 1970; Virginia Commonwealth University, M.Ed., 1975. *Politics:* "Progressive." *Hobbies and other interests:* "Long time involvement in peace and justice activities, nuclear disarmament activist, gardening, fishing, reading."

Addresses

Home—2781 Beowulf Ct., Richmond, VA 23231.

Career

Teacher in Providence, RI, 1970-72, at Petersburg Public Schools, Petersburg, VA, 1975-76, and Williamsburg Public Schools, Williamsburg, VA, 1976-78; Richmond Public Schools, Richmond, VA, teacher in Programs for the Gifted, 1978—. Virginia Commonwealth University, instructor, 1981-86; Johns Hopkins University, Center for Talented Youth, adjunct member of faculty, 1989-90; instructor in adult continuing studies, University of Richmond, 1998; leader of computer literacy workshops. Richmond Nuclear Freeze Campaign, coordinator, 1985-90; Richmond Peace Education Center, member of board of directors, 1992—, treasurer, 1994.

Member

Women's International League for Peace and Freedom, National Education Association, Sierra Club, Chesapeake Bay Foundation, Virginia Writer's Club, Virginia Education Association, Richmond Education Association (former member of board of directors); Richmond Peace Education Center.

Awards, Honors

Parent's Choice Award, 1985, for *Perplexing Puzzles* (computer software); Peace and International Relations Award, Virginia Education Association, 1988; Media and Methods Awards Portfolio winner, for *Let's Talk about . . . Responsibility;* National Educational Film and Video Festival honorable mention, and Media and Methods Awards Portfolio honorable mention, both for *I Blew It: Learning from Our Failures;* National Parenting Seal of Approval, for *The Master Violinmaker;* Thomas Jefferson Medal for outstanding contributions to national science education, Virginia Museum of Natural History, 1999.

Writings

Secrets of the Universe: Discovering the Universal Laws of Science, illustrated by Patricia A. Keeler, Atheneum (New York, NY), 1987.
Understanding the Vocabulary of the Nuclear Arms Race, Dillon (Minneapolis, MN), 1988.
Write Now!, Good Apple (Carthage, IL), 1989.
Tanglers, Synergetics (Parkersburg, WV), 1991.
(With Patricia A. Keeler) *Looking Inside: Machines and Constructions,* illustrated by Patricia A. Keeler, Atheneum (New York, NY), 1991.
Changing Our World: A Handbook for Young Activists, Zephyr Press (Somerville, MA), 1993.
The Master Violinmaker, photographs by David Saunders, Houghton (Boston, MA), 1993.
Ecology A to Z, Dillon Press (New York, NY), 1994.
Our Oceans: Experiments and Activities in Marine Science, illustrated by Patricia A. Keeler, Millbrook Press (Brookfield, CT), 1995.
Life Cycles of a Dozen Diverse Creatures, Millbrook Press (Brookfield, CT), 1996.

Brain Food: Games That Teach Kids to Think, Zephyr Press (Somerville, MA), 1997.

Tanglers Too, Synergetics (Parkersburg, WV), 1998.

Coral Reef, Benchmark Books (New York, NY), 1998.

Mountain Stream, Benchmark Books (New York, NY), 1998.

Oak Tree, illustrated by Jean Cassels, Benchmark Books (New York, NY), 1998.

Saguaro Cactus, illustrated by Jean Cassels, Benchmark Books (New York, NY), 1998.

Tide Pool, illustrated by Jean Cassels, Benchmark Books (New York, NY), 1998.

Salt Marsh, illustrated by Jean Cassels, Benchmark Books (New York, NY), 1999.

Pond, Benchmark Books (New York, NY), 1999.

Alpine Meadow, Benchmark Books (New York, NY), 1999.

Ants, Benchmark Books/Marshall Cavendish (New York, NY), 2001.

Gorillas, Benchmark Books (Tarrytown, NY), 2001.

Ice Cream Treats: The Inside Scoop, photographs by David Saunders, Carolrhoda Books (Minneapolis, MN), 2001.

Liquids and Gases: Principles of Fluid Mechanics, Lerner Publications (Minneapolis, MN), 2002.

Matter and Energy: Principles of Matter and Thermodynamics, Lerner Publications (Minneapolis, MN), 2002.

Objects in Motion: Principles of Classical Mechanics, Lerner Publications (Minneapolis, MN), 2002.

Relativity and Quantum Mechanics: Principles of Modern Physics, Lerner Publications (Minneapolis, MN), 2002.

Waves: Principles of Light, Electricity, and Magnetism, Lerner Publications (Minneapolis, MN), 2002.

Creator of computer software, including *Analogies Tutorial,* 1983, *Advanced Analogies,* 1984, *The Chemical Elements,* 1984, *Famous Scientists,* 1984, *Perplexing Puzzles,* 1985, and *College Prep Analogies,* 1985, all produced by Hartley Courseware. Author of scripts for videotapes, including *Let's Talk About . . . Responsibility,* 1987, and *I Blew It: Learning from Our Failures,* 1988, both from Sunburst Communication. Contributor to periodicals, including *Instructor, Farmstead, Ms., Mother Earth News, Metropolitan Woman, Style Weekly, Classroom Computer Learning,* and *Technology and Learning.* Editor, *REALworld* and *Actionline,* 1980-85, Virginia Educators for Peace newsletter, 1982-86, and National Education Association's Peace Caucus News, 1987-88; *Virginia Forum,* member of editorial board, 1990-94, vice chair, 1993-94.

Sidelights

As an educator, writer, and activist, Paul Fleisher attempts to provide young people with the knowledge they need to make intelligent decisions. Many of his works use everyday objects and simple, fun-to-do experiments to demonstrate basic science concepts and theories. His first book, *Secrets of the Universe: Discovering the Universal Laws of Science,* explains more than twenty principles of physics and discusses how they were discovered by scientists from Archimedes to Heisenberg. Topics covered include planetary

One of Paul Fleisher's well-received books on habitats, **Coral Reef** *discusses the underwater phenomenon, the creatures that live in and near it, and its importance to the environment. (Photo by Jeff Hunter.)*

motion, Newton's laws of motion, gravity, the behavior of gases, and quantum mechanics. Experiments and projects that facilitate the understanding of these principles, as well as a bibliography and appendix, are included. Margaret Chatham of *School Library Journal* stated that "in clear prose and workaday format, Fleisher builds a solid framework of basic principles."

Understanding the Vocabulary of the Nuclear Arms Race discusses a more controversial topic than Fleisher's first book, and one that the author feels strongly about—nuclear proliferation. In a dictionary format, the book presents and explains the terms that people encounter in spoken and written discussions of nuclear warfare. Jonathan Betz-Zall of *School Library Journal* noted that "a scrupulously objective viewpoint" is maintained throughout the work. Various sections of *Understanding the Vocabulary of the Nuclear Arms Race* describe physics concepts, types of bombs and missiles, and important politicians and scientists, all organized alphabetically. *Booklist*'s Carolyn Phelan remarked that this "good, basic book" would be helpful for young people and "could be useful to adults as well."

Looking Inside: Machines and Constructions, written by Fleisher and Patricia A. Keeler, "reveals the hows and whats of things you never even realized you wanted to know," wrote Elizabeth Ward in the *Washington Post Book World.* As each of the seventeen objects discussed here are presented whole on the right-hand page of the spread, readers must turn the page to "look inside." A door lock, a toilet, a piano, the Statue of Liberty, and even a coin-operated telephone are featured. "Unfortunately," observed *School Library Journal* contributor Kathleen Riley, the "text neither stands alone nor communicates much about how things work."

The Master Violinmaker provides the inside story of just one object—the violin. This book allows readers to witness the making of fine violins from the selection of the wood to the varnishing of the final product. Violinmaker John Larrimore's skills, tools, and love for his work are pictured in photographs by David Saunders and described in Fleisher's text. The work is "readable, understandable, and precise," commented Elizabeth S. Watson in *Horn Book,* and Joanne Schott of *Quill and Quire* noted that it "holds the reader's attention almost as an adventure story would."

In addition to his growing body of writing, Fleisher has created award-winning computer software for children, including the popular *Perplexing Puzzles.* He has also written several well-received books on habitats and ecology. *Ecology A to Z,* published in 1994, gives

Everything from the history of ice cream to its modern production is covered in Fleisher's instructive **Ice Cream Treats: The Inside Scoop.** *(Photos by David Saunders.)*

encyclopedic coverage to ecological and environmental terms and defines them in easy-to-understand explanations. *Our Oceans: Experiments and Activities in Marine Science* and *Tide Pool* introduce youngsters to sea life and marine environmental concerns. The first title explains the chemistry of salt water, presents recent geological discoveries about the ocean floor, and discusses the effect of ocean currents on weather patterns. *Oak Tree* tracks the life of one tree and in doing so illustrates the complex ecological structure of a deciduous forest. There are many plants and animals that live in and around the oak tree, and even its demise gives life to new forms. *Booklist*'s Phelan reviewed *Tide Pool* and *Oak Tree,* and found that each book delivers "both basic information and intriguing details in a straightforward way."

Along the same lines, Fleisher wrote *Saguaro Cactus,* about the behemoth structures of the Sonoran desert in the southwest United States, and *Coral Reef,* which discusses this underwater phenomenon, the creatures that live in and near it, as well as its importance to the environment. Fleisher continued this "Web of Life" series for Benchmark Books with the titles *Pond, Salt Marsh, Alpine Meadow* and *Mountain Stream.* Each describes a different type of biome, or community of living organisms in a single ecological environment. A year in the life of each is tracked, with illustrative photographs. *Alpine Meadow* focuses on a mountain environment in Montana, where despite harsh conditions several types of plant life thrive. *Mountain Stream* follows the seasons in an Appalachian stream and points out such streams' significance to human life in the area. *Salt Marsh* concentrates on the Chesapeake Bay region, and how its changing tides affect plant and animal life there on a day to day basis. Fleisher investigates a shallow pool in New York state for *Pond,* and his text describes life forms both apparent and visible only with a microscope. A reviewer for *Appraisal* critiqued all four titles and asserted, "This series is the best reference series that I have seen for readers of this age level."

Fleisher also wrote *Life Cycles of a Dozen Diverse Creatures,* which gives step-by-step life histories of animals as varied as a jellyfish, a bullfrog, an emperor penguin, and an opossum. "Lucid and expressive, the writing describes how each species grows into different forms and how it produces its kind," wrote Phelan in *Booklist.* Fleisher visited a special factory with photographer David O. Saunders for *Ice Cream Treats: The Inside Scoop.* The pages provide a history of the dessert and describe how it is made. Carolyn Jenks, writing in *School Library Journal,* called it "an appealing and instructive book."

In 2002, Fleisher authored five titles for Lerner Publications' "Secrets of the Universe" series. *Matter and Energy: Principles of Matter and Thermodynamics* discusses the concept of a natural law and explains why energy cannot be eliminated, but instead only changes form. "Complex concepts are made accessible through the use of simple language, clear diagrams, and interesting real-life examples," wrote *Booklist*'s Heather Hepler of this title. Other works in the series include *Objects in Motion: Principles of Classical Mechanics* and *Waves: Principles of Light, Electricity, and Magnetism.*

Biographical and Critical Sources

PERIODICALS

Appraisal: Science Books for Young People, fall, 1994, p. 23; spring, 1999, review of *Salt Marsh, Pond, Alpine Meadow,* and *Mountain Stream,* p. 56.

Booklist, March 15, 1988, Carolyn Phelan, review of *Understanding the Vocabulary of the Nuclear Arms Race,* p. 1257; January 1, 1996, Hazel Rochman, review of *Our Oceans,* p. 804; December 1, 1996, Carolyn Phelan, review of *Life Cycles of a Dozen Diverse Creatures,* p. 659; February 15, 1998, Carolyn Phelan, review of *Oak Tree* and *Tide Pool,* p. 1002; January 1, 2001, Gillian Engberg, review of *Gorillas,* p. 944; August, 2001, Heather Hepler, review of *Matter and Energy: Principles of Matter and Thermo-dynamics,* p. 2104.

Horn Book, November-December, 1993, Elizabeth S. Watson, review of *The Master Violinmaker,* p. 754.

Horn Book Guide, spring, 1997, Kelly A. Ault, review of *Life Cycles of a Dozen Diverse Creatures,* p. 117; spring, 1998, Kitty Flynn, review of *Tide Pool, Saguaro Cactus,* and *Coral Reef,* p. 125; fall, 1999, Melinda Greenblatt, review of *Mountain Stream, Salt Marsh, Pond,* and *Alpine Meadow,* p. 339.

Kirkus Reviews, April 15, 1987, p. 636; August 15, 1993, p. 1073.

Los Angeles Times Book Review, May 26, 1991, p. 7.

Quill and Quire, January, 1994, Joanne Schott, review of *The Master Violinmaker,* p. 39.

School Library Journal, June-July, 1987, Margaret Chatham, review of *Secrets of the Universe: Discovering the Universal Laws of Science,* p. 105; April, 1988, Jonathan Betz-Zall, review of *Understanding the Vocabulary of the Nuclear Arms Race,* p. 116; June, 1991, Kathleen Riley, review of *Looking Inside: Machines and Constructions,* p. 116; November, 1993, p. 114; March, 1996, Frances E. Millhouser, review of *Our Oceans,* p. 207; April, 1998, Frances E. Millhouser, review of *Coral Reef* and *Tide Pool,* p. 115; July, 2001, Carolyn Jenks, review of *Ice Cream Treats,* p. 123.

Voice of Youth Advocates, June, 1987, p. 96.

Washington Post Book World, March 10, 1991, Elizabeth Ward, review of *Looking Inside: Machines and Constructions,* p. 8.

OTHER

Paul Fleisher Web Site, http://www.richmond.infi.net/~pfleishe/ (June 3, 2002).

*   *   *

FREEMAN, Peter J.
See CALVERT, Patricia

FRENCH, Fiona 1944-

Personal

Born June 27, 1944, in Bath, Somerset, England; daughter of Robert Douglas (an engineer) and Mary G. (Black) French. *Education:* Croydon College of Art, Surrey, N.D.D., 1966. *Avocational interests:* Collecting "blue and white" china and old editions of children's books.

Addresses

Home—The Deepings, The Street, Little Birmingham, Norfolk NR11 7AG, England. *Office*—c/o Frances Lincoln Ltd., 4 Torriano Mews, Torriano Ave., London NW5 2RZ, England. *Agent*—Pat White, Rogers, Coleridge & White, 20 Powis Mews, London W11 1JN, England.

Career

Long Grove Psychiatric Hospital, Epsom, Surrey, children's art therapy teacher, 1967-69; assistant to the painter Bridget Riley, 1967-72; Wimbledon School of Art, design teacher, 1970-71; Leicester and Brighton

Filled with entrancing art-deco illustrations, Fiona French's rendition of Snow White *is set in glittering Jazz-Age New York. (From* Snow White in New York, *written and illustrated by French.)*

In ancient Egypt, Pepi's father is commissioned to decorate the prince's tomb, and young readers can use hieroglyphic symbols to decipher the meaning of the pictures he paints. (From Pepi and the Secret Names, *written by Jill Paton Walsh and illustrated by French.)*

polytechnics, design teacher, 1973-74; freelance illustrator, 1974—.

Awards, Honors

Children's Book Showcase award, 1973, for *Blue Bird;* Kate Greenaway commended book, British Library Association, 1973, for *King Tree;* Kate Greenaway Medal, 1987, for *Snow White in New York.*

Writings

SELF-ILLUSTRATED; FOR CHILDREN

Jack of Hearts, Harcourt (San Diego, CA), 1970.
Huni, Oxford University Press (Oxford, England), 1971.
The Blue Bird, Walck (New York, NY), 1972.
King Tree, Walck (New York, NY), 1973.
City of Gold, Walck (New York, NY), 1974.
Aio the Rainmaker, Oxford University Press (Oxford, England), 1975, (New York, NY), 1978.
Matteo, Oxford University Press (Oxford, England), 1976, (New York, NY), 1978.
Hunt the Thimble, Oxford University Press (Oxford, England), 1978.

The Princess and the Musician, Evans Brothers (London, England), 1981.
(Reteller) *John Barleycorn,* Abelard-Schuman (New York, NY), 1982.
Future Story, Oxford University Press (Oxford, England), 1983, Peter Bedrick (New York, NY), 1984.
Maid of the Wood, Oxford University Press (Oxford, England), 1985.
Snow White in New York, Oxford University Press (Oxford, England), 1986, (New York, NY), 1987.
The Song of the Nightingale, Blackie (London, England), 1987.
(Reteller) *Cinderella,* Oxford University Press (Oxford, England), 1987, (New York, NY), 1988.
Rise & Shine, Little, Brown (Boston, MA), 1989, published as *Rise, Shine!,* Methuen (London, England), 1989.
The Magic Vase, Oxford University Press (Oxford, England), 1991.
Anancy and Mr. Dry-Bone, Little, Brown (Boston, MA), 1991.
King of Another Country, Oxford University Press (New York, NY), 1993.
(Reteller) *Little Inchkin,* Dial (New York, NY), 1994.
Nikos the Fisherman, Oxford University Press (New York, NY), 1996.
Lord of the Animals: A Miwok Indian Creation Myth, Millbrook Press (Brookfield, CT), 1997.
(Reteller) *Jamil's Clever Cat: A Folk Tale from Bengal,* Star Bright, 1999.
(Editor) *Bethlehem: With Words from the Authorized Version of the King James Bible,* HarperCollins (New York, NY), 2001.
(Editor) *Easter: With Words from the Authorized Version of the King James Bible,* HarperCollins (New York, NY), 2001.

ILLUSTRATOR

Margaret Mayo, *The Book of Magical Birds,* Kaye & Ward (London, England), 1977.
(With Joanna Troughton) Richard Blythe, *Fabulous Beasts,* Macdonald Educational (London, England), 1977.
(With Kim Blundell and George Thompson) Carol Crowther, *Clowns and Clowning,* Macdonald Educational (London, England), 1978.
Oscar Wilde, *The Star Child,* abridged by Jennifer Westwood, Evans Brothers (London, England), 1979.
Mary de Morgan, *The Necklace of Princess Florimonde,* 1980.
Josephine Karavasil, *Hidden Animals: Investigator's Notebook,* Dinosaur, 1982.
Jennifer Westwood, *Fat Cat,* Abelard-Schuman (New York, NY), 1984.
Jennifer Westwood, *Going to Squintum's: A Foxy Folktale,* Blackie (London, England), 1985.
Jill Paton Walsh, *Pepi and the Secret Names,* Lothrop (New York, NY), 1994.
Walter Dean Myers, *The Dragon Takes a Wife,* Scholastic (New York, NY), 1995.
Joyce Dunbar, *The Glass Garden,* F. Lincoln (London, England), 1999.

ADULT BOOKS

Un-Fairy Tales, privately printed, 1966.

Sidelights

Fiona French is an English author and illustrator who has won a number of awards for her children's books. Her books, she once commented, have "details in the pictures which might hold [children's] . . . attention even if they cannot read, but are being 'read to.'" Titles such as *Snow White in the Wood, The Song of the Nightingale,* and *The Magic Vase* are strongly evocative of myths and fairy tales, and feature "not only authentic detail but an almost tangible atmosphere," according to a *St. James Guide to Children's Writers* essayist, who also praised her for her "gloriously rich illustrative style" illustrations that colorfully reflect the period and culture of books by other authors. Commenting on French's illustrations for her own 1994 picture book *Little Inchkin,* a *Publishers Weekly* contributor wrote that the author/illustrator's "complex designs . . . are dazzling without being overwhelming, opulent but never cluttered. The combination of elegant compositions and lush colors lends unusual depth."

French was born in Bath, England, on June 27, 1944, but much of her childhood was spent in Devon and Surrey. She was raised in an English convent school while her family lived for much of that time in the Middle East. French herself visited Lebanon and Iran for a short time, gaining new images for her later pictures. While growing up, French's interests included art, history, geography, and literature. She attended art school from 1961 to 1966, receiving a diploma in painting and lithography, and taught at several art colleges and technical schools, as well as assisting painter Bridget Riley.

In 1970 French started writing and illustrating her own books. She once remarked, "when I begin a story it is at first only a vague idea." After thinking about it until the idea grows, she then does a lot of research, and finally creates the pictures. The themes in French's works are varied. Her first book, *Jack of Hearts,* is based on playing cards; the four Kings—hearts, diamonds, clubs, and spades—celebrate at the birthday feast of the Jack of Hearts. *King Tree* has "Orange Tree," planted in a French garden much like the one at Versailles, taking nominations for King of the Trees, while all the other trees make extravagant election promises.

In another vein, *City of Gold* tells of the fight between good and evil as two brothers journey on easy and hard roads and struggle with the Devil. In *Blue Bird,* which won a Children's Book Showcase award, French writes of a Chinese girl seeking a cure for her pet bird's loss of voice. *Snow White in New York,* also an award winner, retells the familiar story within a 1920s setting and replaces the seven dwarves with seven jazz musicians. *Future Story,* with a space age theme, shows the influence of space photography, while *Little Inchkin* takes readers to early Japan as it recounts the adventures of a tiny warrior who seeks fortune and fame and becomes a heroic samurai. Reviewing this adaptation of a traditional tale, *Booklist* contributor Carolyn Phelan praised the illustrations in particular, noting that they possess "a dramatic flair that children will appreciate."

Many of the books French illustrates for other authors feature birds and animals. In these and her own books, the illustrations, with their vivid colors and outstanding design, add much to the story. In creating the art for Jill Paton Walsh's *Pepi and the Secret Names,* she researched Egyptian hieroglyphics and traditional designs to create "boldly colored illustrations" that augment Walsh's tale of a young boy who helps his father decorate the tomb of Prince Dhutmose and "echo both the style and content of Egyptian funereal decorations." French lives in Norfolk, England, and continues to write and illustrate her own works. *Bethlehem,* which contains the biblical version of the Nativity story, features artwork designed to resemble stained glass. "Majestic and memorable," exclaimed a *Publishers Weekly* contributor, adding that French's illustrations prompt "the eye to linger" over their many intricate details.

In the tradition of the legend of Tom Thumb, the Japanese story **Little Inchkin** *relates the tale of a tiny warrior with great bravery. (Retold and illustrated by French.)*

Coyote, creator of the world, must settle the disputes over the characteristics he should give to the Lord of the Animals in this Miwok Indian creation myth, retold and illustrated by French. (From Lord of the Animals.*)*

Biographical and Critical Sources

BOOKS

St. James Guide to Children's Writers, 5th edition, St. James Press (New York, NY), 1999.

PERIODICALS

Booklist, June 1, 1993, Janice Del Negro, review of *King of Another Country,* p. 1856; June 1, 1994, Carolyn Phelan, review of *Little Inchkin,* p. 1824; October 15, 2001, Carolyn Phelan, review of *Bethlehem,* p. 398.

English Journal, December, 1992, Trish Tripepi, review of *Snow White in New York,* p. 79; June 1, 1997, Karen Hutt, review of *Lord of the Animals,* p. 1708.

Horn Book, January-February, 1992, Lolly Robinson, review of *Anancy and Mr. Dry Bone,* p. 57.

New York Times Book Review, October 22, 1989, p. 55.

Publishers Weekly, March 24, 1989, p. 67; November 30, 1990, p. 71; February 15, 1993, review of *King of Another Country,* p. 238; May 16, 1994, review of Little Inchkin,* p. 63; March 13, 1995, review of *Pepi and the Secret Names,* p. 69; March 17, 1997, review of *Lord of the Animals,* p. 83; September 24, 2001, review of *Bethlehem,* p. 51.

School Library Journal, July, 1989, p. 64; March, 1990, p. 153; April, 1992, Joan McGrath, review of *The Magic Vase,* p. 91; April, 1993, Marilyn Iarusso, review of *King of Another Country,* p. 96; July, 1994, John Philbrook, review of *Little Inchkin,* p. 94; March, 1995, Cheri Estes, review of *The Dragon Takes a Wife,* p. 185; April, 1995, Cathryn A. Camper, review of *Pepi and the Secret Names,* p. 119; September, 1997, Susan M. Moore, review of *Lord of the Animals,* p. 202; March, 2000, Susan Hepler, review of *Jamil's Clever Cat,* p. 224; October, 2001, review of *Bethlehem,* p. 65.

Times Educational Supplement, June 9, 1989, p. B10; November 7, 1990, p. R4.

G–H

GERTRIDGE, Allison 1967-

Personal

Born December 11, 1967, in Lindsay, Ontario, Canada; daughter of John Fraser (a minister) and Jean (a homemaker; maiden name, McKee) Gertridge; married Wally Krysciak (a creative director), June 28, 1997; children: Christopher, Madeleine. *Education:* Attended University of Waterloo and Wilfrid Laurier University. *Religion:* United Church. *Hobbies and other interests:* Design, cooking.

Addresses

Agent—c/o Scholastic Canada Ltd., 175 Hillmount Rd., Markham, Ontario L6C 1Z7, Canada. *E-mail*—allison. gertridge@rogers.com.

Career

Scholastic Canada Ltd., Markham, Canada, editor, 1989-93; writer, 1993—.

Member

Canadian Society of Children's Authors, Illustrators, and Performers.

Writings

Animals by Alphabet, Scholastic Canada (Markham, Canada), 1991.
Skating Superstars, Scholastic Canada (Markham, Canada), 1994, revised edition, Firefly Books, 1996.
Meet Canadian Authors and Illustrators, Scholastic Canada (Markham, Canada), 1994.
Skating Superstars II, Scholastic Canada (Markham, Canada), 1997.
Trim a Tree, Scholastic Canada (Markham, Canada), 2000.
Meet Canadian Authors and Illustrators II, Scholastic Canada (Markham, Canada), 2001.*

Allison Gertridge

HALL, Katy
See McMULLAN, Kate (Hall)

*   *   *

HAMILTON, Virginia (Esther) 1936-2002

OBITUARY NOTICE—See index for *SATA* sketch: Born March 12, 1936, in Yellow Springs, OH; died of breast cancer, February 19, 2002, in Dayton, OH. Author. Hamilton wrote more than thirty children's books that covered many genres, from mysteries, science fiction, and mainstream fiction to biographies and collections of folk tales. What critics and readers alike appreciated in her fiction was that her characters were African-American children living in a mainstream world. Her focus was less on African-American issues and more on the universal issues that affect all young people. She gave children a multitude of characters through which they could see themselves and their lives. Hamilton was the first African-American author to receive the prestigious Newbery Award for her novel *M. C. Higgins, the Great,* which also received a National Book Award in 1975. She won an Edgar Allan Poe Award from the Mystery Writers of America for *The House of Dies Drear.* The American Library Association honored Hamilton with many awards, including several Coretta Scott King Awards and the Laura Ingalls Wilder Medal for lifetime achievement in 1995. In the same year she became the first children's author to receive the coveted "genius grant" of the John D. and Catherine T. MacArthur Foundation. Hamilton combined her successful career as a novelist with her interest in black oral tradition, folk tales, and history in several nonfiction works. *Many Thousands Gone: African Americans from Slavery to Freedom* celebrates the lives of the famous and the unknown with equal respect. Her folktale collections include *The People Could Fly: American Black Folktales* and *Her Stories: African American Folktales, Fairy Tales, and True Tales.* In the year of her death she published *Time Pieces,* a work that has been described as a semi-autobiographical novel.

OBITUARIES AND OTHER SOURCES:

BOOKS

Mikkelsen, Nina, *Virginia Hamilton,* Twayne (New York, NY), 1994.
Wheeler, Jill C., *Virginia Hamilton,* ABDO and Daughters (Minneapolis, MN), 1997.

PERIODICALS

Chicago Tribune, February 21, 2002, p. 2-8.
Los Angeles Times, February 23, 2002, obituary by Maria Elena Fernandez, p. B16.
New York Times, February 20, 2002, obituary by Margalit Fox, p. A21.
Washington Post, February 22, 2002, p. B8.

HASKINS, James S. 1941-
(Jim Haskins)

Personal

Born September 19, 1941, in Demopolis, AL; son of Henry (a contractor) and Julia (a homemaker; maiden name, Brown) Haskins. *Education:* Georgetown University, B.A., 1960; Alabama State University, B.S., 1962; University of New Mexico, M.A., 1963; graduate study at New School for Social Research, 1965-67, and Queens College of the City University of New York, 1967-68.

Addresses

Home—325 West End Ave., Apt. 7D, New York, NY 10023. *Office*—Department of English, University of Florida, Gainesville, FL 32611. *E-mail*—jshnyc@aol.com.

Career

Smith Barney & Co., New York, NY, stock trader, 1963-65; New York City Board of Education, New York, NY, teacher, 1966-68; New School for Social Research, New York, NY, visiting lecturer, 1970-72; Staten Island Community College of the City University of New York, Staten Island, NY, associate professor, 1970-77; University of Florida, Gainesville, FL, professor of English, 1977—. New York *Daily News,* reporter, 1963-64. Elisabeth Irwin High School, visiting lecturer, 1971-73; Indiana University/Purdue University—Indianapolis, IN, visiting professor, 1973-76; College of New Rochelle, visiting professor, 1977. Union Mutual Life, Health and Accident Insurance, director, 1970-73. Member of board of advisors, Psi Systems, 1971-72; member of board of directors, Speedwell Services for Children, 1974-76. Member of Manhattan Community Board No. 9, 1972-73, academic council for the State University of New York, 1972-74, New York Urban League Manhattan Advisory Board, 1973-75, and National Education Advisory Committee and vice-director of Southeast Region of Statue of Liberty—Ellis Island Foundation, 1986. Consultant to Education Development Center, 1975—, Department of Health, Education and Welfare, 1977-79, National Research Council, 1979-80, and Grolier, Inc., 1979-82, to HarperCollins Publishers on multicultural English readings text, 1992—, and to Virginia State University on its library holdings, 1992—. Member of National Education Advisory Committee, Commission on the Bicentennial of the Constitution; consulting curator for the Smithsonian Institution Traveling Exhibition Services (SITES) exhibition, *The Jazz Age in Paris,* 1994—; board of advisors, *Cobblestone Magazine,* 1994—; board of advisors, *Footsteps: African-American History for Kids,* 2000—.

Member

National Book Critics Circle, Authors League of America, Authors Guild, 100 Black Men, Phi Beta Kappa, Kappa Alpha Psi.

Awards, Honors

Notable children's book in the field of social studies citations from *Social Education,* 1971, for *Revolutionaries: Agents of Change,* from *Social Studies,* 1972, for *Resistance: Profiles in Nonviolence* and *Profiles in Black Power,* and 1973, for *A Piece of the Power: Four Black Mayors,* from National Council for the Social Studies—Children's Book Council book review committee, 1975, for *Fighting Shirley Chisholm,* and 1976, for *The Creoles of Color of New Orleans* and *The Picture Life of Malcolm X,* and from Children's Book Council, 1978, for *The Life and Death of Martin Luther King, Jr.;* World Book Year Book literature for children citation, 1973, for *From Lew Alcindor to Kareem Abdul Jabbar;* Books of the Year citations, Child Study Association of America, 1974, for *Adam Clayton Powell: Portrait of a Marching Black* and *Street Gangs: Yesterday and Today;* Books for Brotherhood bibliography citation, National Council of Christians and Jews book review committee, 1975, for *Adam Clayton Powell;* Spur Award finalist, Western Writers of America, 1975, for *The Creoles of Color of New Orleans;* Coretta Scott King Award, and children's choice citation, Children's Book Council, both 1977, both for *The Story of Stevie Wonder;* Carter G. Woodson Outstanding Merit Award, National Council for the Social Studies, 1980, for *James Van DerZee: The Picture Takin' Man;* Deems Taylor Award, American Society of Composers, Authors and Publishers, 1980, for *Scott Joplin: The Man Who Made Ragtime;* Ambassador of Honor Book, English-Speaking Union Books-Across-the-Sea, 1983, for *Bricktop;* Coretta Scott King honorable mention, 1984, for *Lena Horne;* best book for young adults citation, American Library Association (ALA), 1987, and Carter G. Woodson Award, 1988, both for *Black Music in America: A History through Its People;* Alabama Library Association best juvenile work citation, 1987, for "Count Your Way" series; Coretta Scott King honor book, 1991, for *Black Dance in America: A History through Its People;* Parents Choice picture book award, 1992, and Hungry Mind YA nonfiction award, 1993, for *Rosa Parks: My Story;* Carter G. Woodson Award, 1994, for *The March on Washington; Washington Post*/Children's Book Guild award, 1994, for body of work in nonfiction for young people; Coretta Scott King honor book for text, 1997, for *The Harlem Renaissance* and 1998, for *Bayard Rustin: Behind the Scenes of the Civil Rights Movement;* Carter G. Woodson merit books, 1998, for *I Am Rosa Parks* and *Bayard Rustin.* "Bicentennial Reading, Viewing, Listening for Young Americans" selections, ALA and National Endowment for the Humanities, for *Street Gangs: Yesterday and Today, Ralph Bunche: A Most Reluctant Hero,* and *A Piece of the Power: Four Black Mayors;* certificate of appreciation, Joseph P. Kennedy Foundation, for work with Special Olympics.

Writings

FOR CHILDREN

Resistance: Profiles in Nonviolence, Doubleday (New York, NY), 1970.

The War and the Protest: Vietnam, Doubleday (New York, NY), 1970.

Revolutionaries: Agents of Change, Lippincott (Philadelphia, PA), 1971.

Religions, Lippincott (Philadelphia, PA), 1971, revised edition as *Religions of the World,* Hippocrene (New York, NY), 1991.

Witchcraft, Mysticism and Magic in the Black World, Doubleday (New York, NY), 1974.

Street Gangs: Yesterday and Today, Hastings House (New York, NY), 1974.

Jobs in Business and Office, Lothrop (New York, NY), 1974.

The Creoles of Color of New Orleans, Crowell (New York, NY), 1975.

The Consumer Movement, F. Watts (New York, NY), 1975.

Who Are the Handicapped?, Doubleday (New York, NY), 1978.

(With J. M. Stifle) *The Quiet Revolution: The Struggle for the Rights of Disabled Americans,* Crowell (New York, NY), 1979.

The New Americans: Vietnamese Boat People, Enslow (Hillside, NJ), 1980.

The New Americans: Cuban Boat People, Enslow (Hillside, NJ), 1982.

The Guardian Angels, Enslow (Hillside, NJ), 1983.

(With David A. Walker) *Double Dutch,* Enslow (Hillside, NJ), 1986.

(With Kathleen Benson) *The Sixties Reader,* Viking (New York, NY), 1988.

India under Indira and Rajiv Gandhi, Enslow (Hillside, NJ), 1989.

Ella Fitzgerald: A Life through Jazz, New English Library (England), 1991.

(With Rosa Parks) *Rosa Parks: My Story,* Dial (New York, NY), 1992.

The Methodist Church, Hippocrene (New York, NY), 1992.

The March on Washington, introduction by James Farmer, HarperCollins (New York, NY), 1993.

(Reteller) *The Headless Haunt and Other African-American Ghost Stories,* illustrated by Ben Otera, HarperCollins (New York, NY), 1994.

(With Joann Biondi) *From Afar to Zulu: A Dictionary of African Cultures,* Walker (New York, NY), 1995.

The Freedom Rides: Journey for Justice, Hyperion Books for Children (New York, NY), 1995.

Distinguished African American Political and Governmental Leaders, Oryx Press (Phoenix, AZ), 1999.

(With Kathleen Benson) *Bound for America: The Forced Migration of Africans to the New World,* illustrated by Floyd Cooper, Lothrop (New York, NY), 1999.

One Nation under a Groove: Rap Music and Its Roots, Jump at the Sun/Hyperion Books for Children (New York, NY), 2000.

(With Kathleen Benson) *Out of the Darkness: The Story of Blacks Moving North, 1890-1940,* Benchmark Books, 2000.

(Coauthor) *Building a New Land,* HarperCollins (New York, NY), 2001.

History of Rap, Hyperion (New York, NY), in press.

History of Reggae, Hyperion (New York, NY), in press.

BIOGRAPHIES FOR CHILDREN

From Lew Alcindor to Kareem Abdul Jabbar, Lothrop (New York, NY), 1972.

A Piece of the Power: Four Black Mayors, Dial (New York, NY), 1972.

Profiles in Black Power, Doubleday (New York, NY), 1972.

Deep Like the Rivers: A Biography of Langston Hughes, 1902-1967, Holt (New York, NY), 1973.

Ralph Bunche: A Most Reluctant Hero, Hawthorne (New York, NY), 1974.

Adam Clayton Powell: Portrait of a Marching Black, Dial (New York, NY), 1974.

Babe Ruth and Hank Aaron: The Home Run Kings, Lothrop (New York, NY), 1974.

Fighting Shirley Chisholm, Dial (New York, NY), 1975.

The Picture Life of Malcolm X, F. Watts (New York, NY), 1975.

Dr. J: A Biography of Julius Irving, Doubleday (New York, NY), 1975.

Pele: A Biography, Doubleday (New York, NY), 1976.

The Story of Stevie Wonder, Doubleday (New York, NY), 1976.

Always Movin' On: The Life of Langston Hughes, F. Watts (New York, NY), 1976, revised edition, Africa World Press (Trenton, NJ), 1992.

Barbara Jordan, Dial (New York, NY), 1977.

The Life and Death of Martin Luther King, Jr., Lothrop (New York, NY), 1977.

George McGinnis: Basketball Superstar, Hastings House (New York, NY), 1978.

Bob McAdoo: Superstar, Lothrop (New York, NY), 1978.

James Van DerZee: The Picture Takin' Man, illustrated by James Van DerZee, Dodd (New York, NY), 1979.

Andrew Young: Man with a Mission, Lothrop (New York, NY), 1979.

I'm Gonna Make You Love Me: The Story of Diana Ross, Dial (New York, NY), 1980.

"Magic": A Biography of Earvin Johnson, (Hillside, NJ), 1981.

Katherine Dunham, Coward-McCann (New York, NY), 1982.

Sugar Ray Leonard, Lothrop (New York, NY), 1982.

(With J. M. Stifle) *Donna Summer: An Unauthorized Biography,* Little, Brown (Boston, MA), 1983.

Lena Horne, Coward, McCann, 1983.

(With Kathleen Benson) *Space Challenger: The Story of Guion Bluford, an Authorized Biography,* Carolrhoda (Minneapolis, MN), 1984.

About Michael Jackson, Enslow (Hillside, NJ), 1985.

Diana Ross: Star Supreme, Viking (New York, NY), 1985.

Leaders of the Middle East, Enslow (Hillside, NJ), 1985.

Corazon Aquino: Leader of the Philippines, Enslow (Hillside, NJ), 1988.

The Magic Johnson Story, Enslow (Hillside, NJ), 1988.

Shirley Temple Black: From Actress to Ambassador, illustrated by Donna Ruff, Puffin Books (New York, NY), 1988.

Bill Cosby: America's Most Famous Father, Walker (New York, NY), 1988.

Sports Great Magic Johnson, Enslow (Hillside, NJ), 1989, revised and expanded edition, 1992.

(With Helen Crothers) *Scatman: An Authorized Biography of Scatman Crothers,* Morrow (New York, NY), 1991.

Christopher Columbus: Admiral of the Ocean Sea, Scholastic (New York, NY), 1991.

Thurgood Marshall: A Life for Justice, Holt (New York, NY), 1992.

Colin Powell: A Biography, Scholastic (New York, NY), 1992.

I Am Somebody! A Biography of Jesse Jackson, Enslow (Hillside, NJ), 1992.

The Scottsboro Boys, Holt (New York, NY), 1994.

The First Black Governor, Pinckney Benton Stewart Pinchback, Africa World Press (Trenton, NJ), 1996.

Bayard Rustin: Behind the Scenes of the Civil Rights Movement, Hyperion Books for Children (New York, NY), 1997.

Spike Lee: By Any Means Necessary, Walker (New York, NY), 1997.

(With Rosa Parks) *I Am Rosa Parks,* pictures by Wil Clay, Dial Books for Young Readers (New York, NY), 1997.

Jesse Jackson: Civil Rights Activist, Enslow (Hillside, NJ), 2000.

Toni Morrison: The Magic of Words, Millbrook Press (Brookfield, CT), 2000.

Champion: A Biography of Muhammad Ali, Walker (New York, NY), 2002.

NONFICTION FOR CHILDREN; UNDER NAME JIM HASKINS

Jokes from Black Folks, Doubleday (New York, NY), 1973.

Your Rights, Past and Present: A Guide for Young People, Hawthorne (New York, NY), 1975.

Teen-Age Alcoholism, Hawthorne (New York, NY), 1976.

The Long Struggle: The Story of American Labor, Westminster (Philadelphia, PA), 1976.

Real Estate Careers, F. Watts (New York, NY), 1978.

Gambling—Who Really Wins, F. Watts (New York, NY), 1978.

(With Pat Connolly) *The Child Abuse Help Book,* Addison Wesley (Reading, MA), 1981.

Werewolves, Lothrop (New York, NY), 1982.

(Editor) *The Filipino Nation,* three volumes, Grolier (Danbury, CT), 1982.

Break Dancing, Lerner (Minneapolis, MN), 1985.

The Statue of Liberty: America's Proud Lady, Lerner (Minneapolis, MN), 1986.

Outward Dreams: Black Inventors and Their Inventions, Walker (New York, NY), 1991.

I Have a Dream: The Life and Words of Martin Luther King, Millbrook Press (Brookfield, CT), 1992.

The Day Martin Luther King, Jr. Was Shot: A Photo History of the Civil Rights Movement, Scholastic (New York, NY), 1992.

Amazing Grace: The Story behind the Song, Millbrook Press (Brookfield, CT), 1992.

Against All Opposition: Black Explorers in America, Walker (New York, NY), 1992.

One More River to Cross: The Story of Twelve Black Americans, Scholastic (New York, NY), 1992.

Get On Board: The Story of the Underground Railroad, Scholastic (New York, NY), 1993.

Black Eagles: African Americans in Aviation, Scholastic (New York, NY), 1995.

The Day They Fired on Fort Sumter, Scholastic (New York, NY), 1995.

Louis Farrakhan and the Nation of Islam, Walker (New York, NY), 1996.

The Harlem Renaissance, Millbrook Press (Brookfield, CT), 1996.

Power to the People: The Rise and Fall of the Black Panther Party, Simon and Schuster Books for Young Readers (New York, NY), 1997.

Separate, But Not Equal: The Dream and the Struggle, Scholastic (New York, NY), 1997.

(Reteller) *Moaning Bones: African-American Ghost Stories,* illustrated by Felicia Marshall, Lothrop (New York, NY), 1998.

Black, Blue, and Grey: African Americans in the Civil War, Simon and Schuster (New York, NY), 1998.

(Editor) Otha Richard Sullivan, *African American Inventors,* Wiley (New York, NY), 1998.

African American Military Heroes, Wiley (New York, NY), 1998.

African American Entrepreneurs, Wiley (New York, NY), 1998.

(Editor) Clinton Cox, *African American Healers,* Wiley (New York, NY), 1999.

The Exodusters, Millbrook Press (Brookfield, CT), 1999.

Blacks in Colonial America, Lothrop (New York, NY), 1999.

The Geography of Hope: Black Exodus from the South after Reconstruction, Millbrook Press (Brookfield, CT), 1999.

(With Kathleen Benson) *Carter G. Woodson: The Man Who Put "Black" in American History,* Millbrook Press (Brookfield, CT), 2000.

(Editor) Clinton Cox, *African American Teachers,* Wiley (New York, NY), 2000.

(Editor) Brenda Wilkinson, *African American Women Writers,* Wiley (New York, NY), 2000.

(Editor) Eleanora E. Tate, *African American Musicians,* Wiley (New York, NY), 2000.

(Editor) Otha Richard Sullivan, *African American Women Scientists & Inventors,* Wiley (New York, NY), 2001.

(With Kathleen Benson) *Conjure Times: Black Magicians in America,* Walker (New York, NY), 2001.

(With Kathleen Benson) *Building a New Land: African Amercans in Colonial America,* HarperCollins (New York, NY), 2001.

(With Kathleen Benson) *Following Freedom's Star: The Story of the Underground Railroad,* Marshall Cavendish (London, England), 2001.

One Love, One Heart: A Story of Reggae, Hyperion (New York, NY), 2001.

"COUNT YOUR WAY" SERIES; UNDER NAME JIM HASKINS

Count Your Way through China, illustrated by Martin Skoro, Carolrhoda (Minneapolis, MN), 1987.

Count Your Way through Japan, Carolrhoda (Minneapolis, MN), 1987.

Count Your Way through Russia, Carolrhoda (Minneapolis, MN), 1987.

Count Your Way through the Arab World, illustrated by Martin Skoro, Carolrhoda (Minneapolis, MN), 1987.

Count Your Way through Mexico, illustrated by Helen Byers, Carolrhoda (Minneapolis, MN), 1989.

Count Your Way through Canada, illustrated by Steve Michaels, Carolrhoda (Minneapolis, MN), 1989.

Count Your Way through Africa, illustrated by Barbara Knutson, Carolrhoda (Minneapolis, MN), 1989.

Count Your Way through Korea, illustrated by Dennis Hockerman, Carolrhoda (Minneapolis, MN), 1989.

Count Your Way through Israel, illustrated by Rick Hanson, Carolrhoda (Minneapolis, MN), 1990.

Count Your Way through India, illustrated by Liz Brenner Dodson, Carolrhoda (Minneapolis, MN), 1990.

Count Your Way through Italy, illustrated by Beth Wright, Carolrhoda (Minneapolis, MN), 1990.

Count Your Way through Germany, illustrated by Helen Byers, Carolrhoda (Minneapolis, MN), 1990.

(With Kathleen Benson) *Count Your Way through Greece,* illustrated by Janice Lee Porter, Carolrhoda (Minneapolis, MN), 1996.

(With Kathleen Benson) *Count Your Way through France,* illustrated by Andrea Shine, Carolrhoda (Minneapolis, MN), 1996.

(With Kathleen Benson) *Count Your Way through Ireland,* illustrated by Beth Wright, Carolrhoda (Minneapolis, MN), 1996.

(With Kathleen Benson) *Count Your Way through Brazil,* illustrated by Liz Brenner Dodson, Carolrhoda (Minneapolis, MN), 1996.

"A HISTORY THROUGH ITS PEOPLE" SERIES; UNDER NAME JIM HASKINS

Black Theater in America: A History through Its People, Crowell (New York, NY), 1982.

Black Music in America: A History through Its People, Harper & Row (New York, NY), 1987.

Black Dance in America: A History through Its People, Harper & Row (New York, NY), 1990.

NONFICTION; UNDER NAME JIM HASKINS

Diary of a Harlem School Teacher, Grove (New York, NY), 1969, 2nd edition, Stein & Day (Briarcliff Manor, NY), 1979.

(Editor) *Black Manifesto for Education,* Morrow (New York, NY), 1973.

(With Hugh F. Butts) *The Psychology of Black Language,* Barnes & Noble (New York, NY), 1973, enlarged edition, Hippocrene (New York, NY), 1993.

Snow Sculpture and Ice Carving, Macmillan (New York, NY), 1974.

The Cotton Club, Random House (New York, NY), 1977, revised edition, Hippocrene (New York, NY), 1994.

(With Kathleen Benson and Ellen Inkelis) *The Great American Crazies,* Condor Publishing (Ashland, MA), 1977.

Voodoo and Hoodoo: Their Tradition and Craft as Revealed by Actual Practitioners, Stein & Day (Briarcliff Manor, NY), 1978.

(With Kathleen Benson) *The Stevie Wonder Scrapbook,* Grosset and Dunlap (New York, NY), 1978.

Richard Pryor, a Man and His Madness: A Biography, Beaufort Books (New York, NY), 1984.

Queen of the Blues: A Biography of Dinah Washington, Morrow (New York, NY), 1987.

NONFICTION; UNDER NAME JAMES HASKINS

Pinckney Benton Stewart Pinchback: A Biography, Macmillan (New York, NY), 1973.

A New Kind of Joy: The Story of the Special Olympics, Doubleday (New York, NY), 1976.

(With Kathleen Benson) *Scott Joplin: The Man Who Made Ragtime,* Doubleday (New York, NY), 1978.

(With Kathleen Benson) *Lena: A Personal and Professional Biography of Lena Horne,* Stein & Day (Briarcliff Manor, NY), 1983.

(With Bricktop) *Bricktop,* Atheneum (New York, NY), 1983.

(With Kathleen Benson) *Nat King Cole,* Stein and Day (Briarcliff Manor, NY), 1984, updated and revised edition, Scarborough House, 1990.

(With Kathleen Benson) *Aretha: A Personal and Professional Biography of Aretha Franklin,* Stein & Day (Briarcliff Manor, NY), 1986.

Mabel Mercer: A Life, Atheneum (New York, NY), 1988.

Winnie Mandela: Life of Struggle, Putnam (New York, NY), 1988.

(With N. R. Mitgang) *Mr. Bojangles: The Biography of Bill Robinson,* Morrow (New York, NY), 1988.

(With Lionel Hampton) *Hamp: An Autobiography* (with discography), Warner Books (New York, NY), 1989, revised edition, Amistad Press (New York, NY), 1993.

(With Joann Biondi) *Hippocrene U.S.A. Guide to the Historic Black South: Historical Sites, Cultural Centers, and Musical Happenings of the African-American South,* Hippocrene (New York, NY), 1993.

(With Joann Biondi) *Hippocrene U.S.A. Guide to Black New York,* Hippocrene (New York, NY), 1994.

(With Kathleen Benson) *African Beginnings,* illustrated by Floyd Cooper, Lothrop (New York, NY), 1995.

(With Hal Jackson) *The House That Jack Built: My Life Story as a Trailblazer in Broadcasting and Entertainment,* HarperCollins (New York, NY), 2001.

Keeping the Faith: African-American Sermons of Liberation, Welcome Rain (New York, NY), 2001.

General editor of Hippocrene's "Great Religions of the World" series, Hippocrene's "African Language Concise Dictionaries," and with Jack Salzman, of *African-American Culture and History: A Student's Guide.*

Contributor to books, including *Children and Books,* 4th edition, 1976; *Understanding Human Behavior in Health and Illness* by Emily Mumford, Williams and Wilkins, 1977; *New York Kid's Catalog,* Doubleday, 1979; *Notable American Women Supplement,* Radcliffe College, 1979; *Clearings in the Thicket: An Alabama Humanities Reader,* by Jerry Brown, 1985; and *Author in the Kitchen.*

Contributor of articles and reviews to periodicals, including *American Visions, Now, Arizona English Bulletin, Rolling Stone, Children's Book Review Service, Western Journal of Black Studies, Elementary English, Amsterdam News, New York Times Book Review, Afro-Hawaii News,* and *Gainesville Sun.*

Adaptations

Diary of a Harlem Schoolteacher has been recorded by Recordings for the Blind; *The Cotton Club* inspired the 1984 film of the same name, produced by Orion.

Sidelights

Teacher, lecturer, and author James S. Haskins has written biographies and histories that cover a wide range of subjects. Many of Haskins's works, especially his biographies of luminaries such as Magic Johnson and Shirley Chisholm and his histories of events such as the Civil Rights movement, are written specifically for young people.

Haskins's first book grew out of his experiences teaching a Special Education class at Public School 92 in New York City. A social worker gave him a diary and suggested that he write down his thoughts about teaching disadvantaged students. Ronald Gross of the *New York Times Book Review* called *Diary of a Harlem Schoolteacher* "plain, concrete, unemotional, and unliterary ... The book is like a weapon—cold, blunt, painful." The success of *Diary* impressed numerous publishers who approached Haskins about writing a series of books for young people. Haskins commented: "I knew exactly the kind of books I wanted to do—books about current events and books about important black people so that students could understand the larger world around them through books written on a level that they could understand."

Haskins's writings about black culture include *Black Theater in America* and the award-winning *Black Music in America,* which traced musical roots from slave times through spirituals, ragtime, blues, jazz, gospel and soul. Jeffrey Cooper, writing in *Kliatt,* announced that "It's difficult to imagine the library that could not find a place in its shelves for this clear and concise history of African-American music." The story of African-American contributions to the world of dance was also documented in *Black Dance in America.*

Haskins also continues to give expression to the full gamut of black achievement, both in the U.S. and around the world. The story of an apartheid activist was chronicled in *Winnie Mandela: Life of Struggle,* a book, *Kirkus Reviews* concluded, that "readers won't forget." Important figures in the Civil Rights movement such as

Rosa Parks and Martin Luther King, Jr., have been profiled more than once by Haskins. *The Day Martin Luther King, Jr. Was Shot* uses that attention-grabbing title to present "a photo history of the African American struggle from the time of slavery through today," according to Hazel Rochman in *Booklist*. The life of the first African American Supreme Court Justice was presented in *Thurgood Marshall: A Life for Justice*. *Booklist*'s Karen Hutt concluded that the "historical, social, and political perspective Haskins incorporates makes the work an illuminating, in-depth portrait of a courageous leader as well as an excellent resource for study of the civil rights movement."

Haskins has also written a score of books centered on pivotal historical times and issues. *The March on Washington* recounts that momentous occasion in 1963 when a quarter million people marched from the Washington Monument to the Lincoln Memorial in support of racial equality and, according to *Horn Book*'s Ellen Fader, "Haskins provides a lucid, in-depth, and moving study" of the march and the work that led up to it. Cultural history was at the heart of *The Harlem Renaissance*, Haskins's re-creation of the flowering of black music, dance, theater, and literature that took place between 1916 and 1940. In *Power to the People*, Haskins turned to the rise and fall of the Black Panther Party, the radical 1960s political organization, in a book that is a "unique source of information on an important period of our history," according to *School Library Journal* reviewer Jonathan Betz-Zall. Haskins has also focussed on the hidden history of African Americans and their contributions to society. In *Black, Blue, and Grey* he examines the participation of African American soldiers in the American Civil War, a book marked by "diligent research and intelligent writing," according to *Kirkus Reviews*. And in *African American Entrepreneurs* and *African American Military Heroes*, Haskins carries his black history lessons even further.

Haskins has spent a career setting the historical record straight about the achievements of African Americans. In doing so, he has also attempted to give a balanced and fair picture of the lives and times he is chronicling. While Haskins often uses his writing ability to support the causes he believes in, such as the renovations of the Statue of Liberty and Ellis Island, he continues to write about African-American culture with recent efforts such as *One Nation under a Groove: Rap Music and Its Roots*, which Gillian Engberg described in *Booklist*: "In engaging, sophisticated language, veteran writer Haskins draws clear, well-researched connections between artists and movements, bolstered by plenty of quotes from performers and the press that give sufficient attention to female rappers."

Haskins told *SATA*: "I grew up in the 1940s and 1950s in Demopolis, Alabama. My segregated school was provided outdated, cast-off textbooks that mentioned African Americans only as slaves. The school library was poorly equipped, and I was barred from visiting the town's public library. My mother obtained volumes of an encyclopedia as a premium at the grocery store, and a white woman with whom she was friendly borrowed books from the library on my behalf. Books were thus of great value to me from an early age.

"I favored nonfiction almost from the beginning. In part, that was because of my limited opportunities for reading. It was largely due, however, to my parents' and teachers' keen interest in the goings-on in the outside world and to the fact that, in the segregated Deep South in those days, truth was indeed often 'stranger than fiction.'

"After attending college, I became a teacher myself. The era was the 1960s, when the political and social upheaval of the times was also 'stranger than fiction.' I felt that my students should have opportunities to read books on their level about the civil rights movement, the black power movement, the anti-war movement, and other issues. After my first book, *Diary of a Harlem Schoolteacher*, I shared my feelings with an editor at Doubleday and Co. whom I had met, and soon I was approached by Doubleday to write three informational books: *Resistance: Profiles in Nonviolence, The War and the Protest: Vietnam*, and *Profiles in Black Power*. Since then, I have written and published many informational books for young readers, including biographies of important blacks in America, both historical and contemporary. I wanted young people—especially young African Americans—to be able to read about role models for themselves. I have also written biographies of African Americans for the adult trade audience.

"As a writer, I have not been limited—nor have I confined myself—to African-American subject matter. Two of those first three informational books had a much broader purview. International affairs have always interested me, and a number of my books have reflected that curiosity. Biographies of the Gandhis of India, of Corazon Aquino of the Philippines, and a collective biography of the leaders of the Middle East are among the books for younger readers that provide information about other cultures through the numbers one to ten in various languages.

"Although I am aware, during the writing process, that I am addressing a particular audience—e.g., young people or adults—my approach is very much that of telling a story to myself. I write books about people and subjects that intrigue me, and hope to inspire similar interest in my readers."

Biographical and Critical Sources

BOOKS

Brown, Jerry, *Clearings in the Thicket: An Alabama Humanities Reader*, Mercer University Press, 1985.
Children's Literature Review, Volume 3, Gale (Detroit, MI), 1978.
In Black and White, 3rd edition, Gale (Detroit, MI), 1985.

Schomburg Center Guide to Black Literature, from the Eighteenth Century to the Present, Gale (Detroit, MI), 1996.

St. James Guide to Young Adult Writers, 2nd edition, St. James Press (Detroit, MI) 1999.

Twentieth-Century Young Adult Writers, St. James Press (Detroit, MI), 1994.

PERIODICALS

American Visions, December-January, 1995, p. 36.

Booklist, September 15, 1974, p. 100; January 1, 1977, p. 666; July 15, 1979, p. 1618; February 1, 1982, Linda S. Callaghan, review of *"Magic": A Biography of Earvin Johnson,* pp. 709-710; January 15, 1983, p. 676; September 1, 1984, p. 65; January 15, 1992, Ilene Cooper, review of *Amazing Grace: The Story behind the Song,* p. 115; February, 1992, Hazel Rochman, review of *The Day Martin Luther King, Jr. Was Shot: A Photo History of the Civil Rights Movement,* p. 1024; July, 1992, Karen Hutt, review of *Thurgood Marshall: A Life for Justice,* p. 1939; May 15, 1993, p. 1691; January 1, 1995, p. 818; September 1, 1996, p. 116; February 15, 1997, p. 1020; March 15, 1997, p. 1233; May 1, 1997, p. 1488; February 15, 1998, p. 995; February 15, 1999, p. 1068; February 15, 2001, Gillian Engberg, review of *One Nation under Groove: Rap Music and Its Roots,* p. 165.

Bulletin of the Center for Children's Books, January, 1975, p. 78; September, 1983, p. 9; November, 1985; June, 1988, p. 205; July, 1988, p. 229; July, 1996, p. 375; May, 1997, p. 323; April, 1998, p. 281.

Chicago Tribune Book World, April 13, 1986.

Christian Science Monitor, March 12, 1970, p. 9; February 21, 1990, p. 13.

Horn Book, July-August, 1993, Ellen Fader, review of *The March on Washington,* pp. 477-478.

Interracial Books for Children Bulletin, Volume 7, No. 5, 1976, pp. 12-13.

Kirkus Reviews, June 1, 1972, p. 631; May 1, 1974, p. 492; June 15, 1979, p. 692; August 1, 1979, p. 862; November 1, 1984, p. 1036; April 15, 1988, review of *Winnie Mandela: Life of Struggle,* p. 618; June 1, 1988, review of *Bill Cosby: American's Most Favorite Father,* pp. 827-828; December 1, 1997, review of *Black, Blue, and Grey: African Americans in the Civil War,* pp. 1775-1776; January 15, 1998, pp. 111, 112; April 15, 1998, p. 618; June 1, 1998, pp. 827-828; December 1, 1998, p. 1733.

Kliatt, May, 1993, Jeffry Cooper, review of *Black Music in America: A History through Its People,* p. 36.

Los Angeles Times Book Review, July 24, 1983, p. 8; March 11, 1984, p. 9; January 20, 1985, p. 6; July 17, 1988, p. 10; February 23, 1992, p. 10.

New York Times Book Review, December 6, 1970, Ronald Gross, review of *Diary of a Harlem Schoolteacher;* February 8, 1970; May 7, 1972; May 5, 1974; August 4, 1974; November 20, 1977; September 23, 1979; October 7, 1979; January 20, 1980; March 4, 1984; May 17, 1987; September 13, 1987; February 16, 1997, p. 25.

Publishers Weekly, July 20, 1992, review of *Thurgood Marshall: A Life for Justice,* p. 252; December 8, 1997, p. 74; February 2, 1998, p. 92.

School Library Journal, November, 1980, Diane Haas, review of *I'm Gonna Make You Love Me: The Story of Diana Ross,* p. 86; August, 1992, Jeanette Lambert, review of *I Am Somebody!: The Biography of Jesse Jackson,* pp. 181-182; March, 1997, Jonathan Betz-Zall, review of *Power to the People: The Rise and Fall of the Black Panther Party,* p. 201; January, 1999, p. 142.

Skipping Stones, November, 1998, p. 32; April 2001, Tim Wadham, review of *One Nation under a Groove: Rap Music and Its Roots,* p. 160.

Times Literary Supplement, May 24, 1985.

Tribune Books (Chicago), February 14, 1993, p. 5.

Voice Literary Supplement, October, 1988, p. 5.

Voice of Youth Advocates, April, 1984, review of *Lena Horne,* pp. 46-47; February, 1986, p. 40; August, 1988, p. 146; April, 1989, p. 58; June, 1992, p. 125; August, 1992, p. 188; December, 1992, pp. 300-301; August, 1993, p. 177; October, 1994, p. 230; February, 1995, p. 358; June, 1995, p. 132; August, 1995, p. 182; August, 1996, p. 150; December, 1996, p. 288; August, 1997, p. 202; October, 1997, p. 264; February, 1998, p. 402.

Washington Post Book World, November 10, 1974, p. 8; September 11, 1977, p. E6; February 5, 1978, p. G4; August 17, 1983; December 9, 1984, p. 15; January 16, 1985; May 10, 1987; May 13, 1990, p. 17; September 1, 1991, p. 13.

OTHER

James S. Haskins Web site, http://www.web.clas.ful.edu/users/jhaskins/ (October 7, 2001).

*   *   *

HASKINS, Jim
See HASKINS, James S.

*   *   *

Autobiography Feature

Jim Haskins

I remember the first time I saw that: "Jim Haskins, 1941—." It was on the copyright page of my first book, *Diary of a Harlem Schoolteacher*. It's standard procedure in books to put on that page an author's name and date—or dates, if he or she is dead. This information is called "Library of Congress Cataloging in Publication Data" and I am sure it is necessary, but it felt kind of funny to see my name followed by that one date and a "—" after it, as if the information was somehow incomplete. It would have looked a lot neater with a second date at the end, but of course that would have meant I was dead and wouldn't be writing any more books. Since that first book, I've written around sixty more, and so I've gotten used to seeing that strange "1941—" on copyright pages and in *Who's Who* and those kinds of books where you can look up people. But I still think it looks unfinished, and sometimes when I talk to certain librarians I get the feeling that they feel the same way—it would be neater if that second date was there. Nothing personal, of course. They are "fact people," and so am I.

I have always liked true stories better than made-up ones. Every single one of my books is nonfiction and I have no desire whatsoever to write fiction, although I admire the people who write fiction well. It has always seemed to me that truth is not just "stranger than fiction," but also more interesting. Also, it seems to me that the more you know about the real world the better off you are, and since there is so much in the real world to learn about, you are better off concentrating on fact rather than fiction.

I think I probably got this attitude because I am black and was born in the South at a time when southern black people did not have many rights. The real world was a hard place to live in, and in order to survive in it at all you had to pay very careful attention to it. There were no black hospitals, for example, and white hospitals had inadequate areas for blacks. So, I was born at home. The state of Alabama wasn't too interested in recording the births of black babies, so I didn't have a birth certificate until I was considerably older and found I needed it for such things as Social Security numbers and passports. (That may have been the first time I really began to appreciate historical documents.)

I was born into a society in which blacks were in deep trouble if they forgot about the real world. For if they daydreamed and were caught off-guard, they could pay dearly. We knew we had to lower our eyes or cross over to the other side of the street if we encountered a white person. We knew we had to enter a white store through the back way. We knew we could not go to the nearest drinking fountain if we were thirsty; we had to look for the one with the sign that said "Colored." My cousin Susie went skipping by the white school one day and got beaten up because the white kids said she was too close to their grass.

My point in mentioning these things is to show that when I was growing up, it was very important to pay attention to the real world. That was how we survived. And I was taught at a very young age that it was my own fault if I did not pay attention. My family did not blame all their

Jim Haskins, 2001

"The one and only photograph in existence of me before the age of eighteen"

troubles on the white folks; they simply accepted the fact that in Demopolis, Alabama, the white folks had the power.

We lived in an all-black neighborhood. There were several all-black areas in town, and ours was the most "middle class" because it contained one of the major black churches and the black elementary and high schools. A good proportion of the people owned their own homes and land and worked hard to keep them. Everyone knew everybody else's business, and everyone talked about everybody else's business endlessly. And what business it was! I have a feeling that one reason why I believe that truth is stranger than fiction is that the real stories of the people in my family and in my neighborhood were far more interesting than the made-up stories in books.

One of my uncles (my mother's brother) was personal valet to General George Patton in World War II. After he got out of the army, he never wore anything but his uniform in public, and that included his army pistol. To the white folks, this behavior was so crazy that they left him alone and allowed him to brandish his pistol whenever he felt like it.

Quite a few people in the neighborhood resorted to selling bootleg liquor when times were hard. Sometimes my relatives were among them. Bootleg liquor is made in illegal stills in out-of-the-way places; it is also called

"moonshine" because the safest time to make it is at night. I had another uncle who used to regularly swim a wide creek with large bottles of this "moonshine" slung over his shoulders.

My aunt Cindy was the greatest storyteller who ever lived. The stories she told to the grown-ups were not for children's ears, and I remember that when Aunt Cindy started in with these stories my grandma Hattie would start to spit snuff on me. This was Grandma Hattie's signal for me to leave. For us children, Aunt Cindy had a special kind of story, which can only be described as the most fascinating hodgepodge of classic fairy tales: "Well, now, the Three Little Pigs commenced to crying 'We're late, we're late, for a very important date,' and they slid down the rabbit's hole and who should they meet but the Red Queen, and she was powerful angry. 'Who's that sleeping in my bed?' she wanted to know. 'It's Hansel and Gretel,' said the Three Little Pigs. 'The Wicked Stepmother doesn't want them in the gingerbread house.'" While Aunt Cindy's stories made absolutely no sense, especially after we were old enough to read the real stories, there was something fascinating about the way she combined them. In an odd way, Aunt Cindy's versions probably taught us to think about the versions we had read in the story-books and to recognize the parts of them that also made no sense.

Aunt Cindy's stories taught me that things are not always as they seem. But I came to understand that truth in a variety of other ways as well. When I say that I was taught to pay attention to the real world, I do not mean to suggest that it was a simple, straightforward world. Far from it. I learned that there were all sorts of goings-on under the surface of the real world, or things that might be going on. These were mystical, magical things that were called hoodoo. The belief in such things can be traced way back to West Africa, where the slaves came from. I was a child nearly a century after slavery ended, but the beliefs had survived. My family were relatively well educated and possessed a healthy skepticism about hoodoo. Nevertheless, they had a certain respect for this ancient art, and for those who practiced it. In other words, to be on the safe side, we children were to be very respectful of the local hoodoo practitioners. We were not to go near their houses, or to make fun of them or aggravate them in any way, for things happened to people who displeased them. I recall that there was a man in the neighborhood who threw a brick at a dog that belonged to the local male hoodoo doctor. Within a week, that man began gagging and vomiting. Though taken to a hospital, he grew progressively weaker and finally died. Disbelievers said it was mere coincidence; the old people rocked in their chairs and smiled knowingly.

I was warned not to eat anything at the homes of known practitioners or at the homes of people who visited them. Much conjuring was accomplished by the use of food. At birth, I was given a Christian name and a middle name. I was also given a "basket name." It was much more powerful than a nickname, for in southern black tradition it symbolized, in a very real way, me, as a person. It could be used for good or ill. Used for good, it somehow protected me. Used for ill, it could harm me. Needless to say, it was not a name to be shared with very many other people.

And then there were the superstitions. If you have your hair cut outside, remember to gather up all the cuttings. Otherwise, the birds will make a nest of it and you will get headaches. If your nose itches, someone is talking about you. If you drop a fork, a woman will visit. If you drop a knife, your next visitor will be a man. Eat rice and black-eyed peas on New Year's Eve, and you will have good luck in the coming year. My family didn't really believe in these things. But they were traditions, handed down from generation to generation, and there was something comforting about that. They are like other superstitions that have survived: If you break a mirror, you will have seven years bad luck. Never walk under a ladder. Never let a black cat cross your path.

My parents didn't have any problem teaching me these superstitions while at the same time insisting that I listen to the news on the radio and read the daily newspapers as soon as I was able. What was really happening and what might happen were equal parts of my world. They would sit out on the front porch in the evening and discuss the Korean conflict, the latest hoodoo victim, and the current neighborhood scandal all in the same conversation. And Grandma Hattie would spit snuff on me whenever the topic of conversation was too "adult."

Unlike the other children, who were more likely to be off playing, I liked to listen to the grownups. I was like a sponge, soaking up information. I was small for my age and not very athletic, and I was more interested in grown-up talk and books than children's games. I learned to read early, and my mother encouraged my love of reading as best she could. There was not a lot of money for books, and the Demopolis Public Library was off-limits to blacks. Some of my earliest reading material was the *World Book Encyclopedia.* A local supermarket had a special offer—buy a certain dollar amount of groceries, and get a volume of the encyclopedia. My mother got an entire set that way, and while other neighborhood kids were out playing, I sat under the kitchen table (where I was out of the way) and read the encyclopedia. My mother did washing for a white woman in town, and when she told the white woman how much I loved to read, the woman began going to the library and taking out books for me. Every time my mother brought a load of freshly laundered clothes to the woman, she would return with a stack of books for me. In this way, I got to read about King Arthur and knights and princesses. I enjoyed these stories, but since my first major reading was the encyclopedia, this is probably another reason why I prefer nonfiction.

In 1979, I returned to Demopolis and at the invitation of the Demopolis Public Library paid a visit to that institution. As I entered the building, I noticed one of my young cousins sitting at one of the reading tables with her boyfriend (who now plays for the New York Giants football team) and marveled at how things had changed. At the main desk, I autographed copies of my books for the librarian who had asked me to visit. "When I was a child, I couldn't come to this library," I remarked. She flushed and murmured, "I wasn't here then." I left it at that.

I attended a segregated school; my classmates and teachers were all black. We did not have up-to-date textbooks, or sports equipment, or many musical instruments. But we had teachers who regarded teaching as far more than just a job—it was a calling. Back then, few blacks could hope to be in professions like law or medicine.

Teaching was the highest profession to which they could aspire. They were highly respected in the black community, and they earned that respect by caring about their students as if it was their mission in life to educate us. When they traveled, they brought back books for us, shared their experiences with us, tried to give us a sense of the larger world. They did independent research on subjects they believed were important to us. One such subject was black history. It was not on the official curriculum of the Demopolis Public Schools. In fact, if my teachers had followed the official curriculum, I would have grown up thinking that blacks had never done anything in the history of the world except be slaves. But they taught us that there had been many important black heroes in history. Not only did we learn about the lives of famous blacks like Booker T. Washington and W.E.B. DuBois, Duke Ellington and Marian Anderson, but most of the time their portraits stared down at us from the walls of the halls and classrooms. These were removed on the occasions when the white superintendent of schools came to visit. The teachers in my school also got together and sponsored oratorical contests and talent shows, held bake sales to pay for sports equipment and musical instruments. They were not paid to do this. They did it out of love.

When I returned to Demopolis in 1979, I also attended a school reunion and had a chance to visit, for the first time in many years, a number of my early teachers. Mrs. Aligee Black was retired by that time, but she still had, prominently displayed in her living-room, photograph albums containing hundreds of school pictures of the students she'd

"High-school graduation photo, about 1958"

Jim Haskins at P.S. 92 in Harlem, New York, late sixties

taught. In one album—one of the *older* ones—was a picture of me in second grade. To those whose families took a lot of photographs, this might not seem particularly memorable, but my family did not take many pictures. The photograph that Mrs. Aligee Black so carefully preserved is the one and only photograph in existence of me before the age of about eighteen.

I also visited Mr. and Mrs. Wallace. When I was going to school, she was Miss Hall. She also noticed how much I liked to read, and lent me books from her own library. Nearly every week she drove to Selma, about an hour away, to visit her mother. Often she took me because she wanted me to know that there was a larger world outside Demopolis. She knew that a young boy couldn't ride a whole hour in a car without needing something to eat. She also knew that there were few places between Demopolis and Selma where black people could stop—to eat or to do anything else. So, she would pack sandwiches, and about halfway into the trip we would pull up at a roadside rest area and have a picnic. Prince Wallace, to whom she was married by the time I returned to Demopolis in 1979, had been the musician (a guitarist) who had taught me to play the ukelele. I remember spending many afternoons with Mr. Prince, as we called him, trading comic books and music talk. He persuaded my parents to buy me my first

secondhand trumpet, which I still have. I practiced on the roof of our house while the other kids played football.

And then there was Mr. Bell, who not only taught mathematics at the high school but also ran the local convenience store, was treasurer of the church, did all the printing for the black community, and prepared the income-tax returns for the entire neighborhood. Mr. Bell never called me anything but Haskins and never did just one thing at a time, which may be how I learned some of my early entrepreneurial skills, like realizing that my family had one of the first televisions around and charging the neighborhood kids two cents (or a candy bar, or a bag of peanuts, if they had no money) to come in and watch.

It was partly because of the devotion of these teachers that when I moved to Boston with my mother I did not suffer from my "Southern schooling." In fact, in Boston, I gained admittance to one of the special, academic high schools. Boston Latin School was an old, old school with a tradition of academic excellence. There were very few blacks in it. While going to school with mostly white kids was an adjustment for me, it was not as difficult as it could have been. I was able to keep up academically. And my parents and relatives and neighbors had instilled in me the idea that I was just as good as anybody else, so I did not feel inferior because I was black.

When I graduated from high school, there was no question that I would go to college. My family wanted me to do so, and I'd had just enough experience doing things like picking cotton to know that I was not cut out for manual labor. (You have to pick cotton early in the morning when it is glistening with dew to understand how heavy it can be. I did this about three times before I began to develop mysterious ailments around cotton-picking time.) I chose to return to Alabama and attend the all-black Alabama State College in Montgomery. I missed "home," and the comfort of being with people who were like me. Also, there were some exciting things happening in Montgomery that I wanted to be part of. The Civil Rights Movement had started in Montgomery.

It had started a few years earlier in protest over the segregated conditions on the city buses. One day a black woman named Rosa Parks had decided that she was too tired to give up her seat to a white man, as she was supposed to do, and had been arrested for her "crime." In response, blacks in Montgomery had decided to boycott the city buses until they had won the right to sit anywhere they wanted to, and until the bus company agreed to hire some black drivers. The Montgomery Bus Boycott had been successful not just in winning those demands but in uniting black people in the city. They had formed the Montgomery Improvement Association and a young Baptist preacher named Martin Luther King, Jr., had been chosen as its leader. The Montgomery Improvement Association hoped to win other rights for black people—the right to eat at downtown restaurants, to drink at public drinking fountains, etc.

Not long after I arrived at Alabama State, I sought out Martin Luther King, Jr., and asked how I could help the Montgomery Improvement Association. Soon, I was putting leaflets under doors in the dormitories at Alabama State and stuffing envelopes and doing other fairly innocent tasks. But Alabama State was very conservative. The college depended heavily on contributions from important whites and appropriations from the all-white State Legislature, and the administration frowned on student activism, fearing that if Alabama State students got involved in the Civil Rights Movement, the important contributions from the white folks would stop. In a student body of several hundred, only nineteen of us were willing to become active in the Movement. The college administration called us "out-of-state rabblerousers," and in some cases that was true. I was now from Boston, though I had been born and brought up in Alabama. Bernard Lee was from Virginia. Floyd Coleman and Marzel Watts were from Ohio. We all sort of hung around together. But Trenholm Hope was from Selma, and several of the others were from Alabama. Still, it was easier for the administration to classify us all as "outside agitators" when we made the unforgivable mistake of going over to the black Regal Cafe on High Street to eat with some white and black Freedom Riders who had risked their lives trying to integrate interstate buses and had made it alive to Montgomery.

The man who ran the Regal Cafe was a postal worker whose son, Scottie, attended Alabama State and had volunteered the Regal Cafe as a place where the Freedom Riders could eat together without fear of being beaten up. About nineteen of us went to eat with the Freedom Riders at the Regal Cafe. In the group, there were perhaps thirty blacks and four whites, but that was too much integration for the Montgomery Police. They arrested the whites and told us Alabama State students to go back to the campus. When we got back to the campus, we told other students what had happened, and they got angry and spontaneously we started to march downtown. There, we got arrested. I had never been arrested before, and my family was very upset. But they were not angry at me. They were angry at a system under which I would be arrested for marching to downtown Montgomery, Alabama. That's when they were radicalized and began offering their home to Civil Rights workers, black and white, who passed through Demopolis. More than twenty years later, they still get letters and telephone calls, as I do, from people, white and black, who were young and activist back then and who remember how brave and how hospitable my family were to them when they needed a good, home-cooked meal and a safe place to sleep.

I was to be arrested several more times in the course of my work in the Civil Rights Movement, but that first arrest is the most memorable. Not only was it my first brush with "the law," it resulted in my expulsion from Alabama State. I enrolled next at Georgetown University in Washington, D.C., and completed my first undergraduate degree there. But I felt I had unfinished business in Montgomery and I later returned not only to be arrested several more times but also to complete a second undergraduate degree at Alabama State. By that time, public opinion had changed to favor the Civil Rights Movement, and the college administration was rather proud to have an "out-of-state rabble-rouser" return to the fold.

So there I was, young, gifted, and black, with two degrees, and I had no idea at all what I wanted to do with my life. It is hard to explain, but there was a certain comfort in the old, segregated world of few opportunities. You didn't have many choices. I happened along when the range of choices was opening up, and I wasn't at all sure which way to go. So, I decided to get another degree, which really meant that I wanted at least another year to decide what I was going to do. I went to the University of New Mexico this time, and earned a graduate degree. By then my family was beginning to ask just when I was going to get a job.

I went to New York. I worked at the *New York Recorder,* a black newspaper in Brooklyn, for the New York City Department of Welfare, and for the *New York Daily News* in Manhattan before I got a job for an old and venerable brokerage house on Wall Street that had decided to recruit a few promising young blacks. This job on Wall Street was part of what the Civil Rights Movement had been all about—it was one of those opportunities that had opened up for blacks, and I was enjoying the benefits of all the marching and beatings and arrests that had brought it about. But *I,* Jim Haskins, human being, wasn't happy.

I loved New York, and I made several lasting friendships at the brokerage house, but I was not the "Wall Street type." I was more the "Village type," and I spent my evenings in Greenwich Village with singers and painters and poets, many of whom are now famous. I liked them but I did not want to be like them. I wasn't sure what I wanted to be. And then, gradually, it dawned on me that what I wanted to be was like the people who had made the strongest impression on me—and those people were teachers. I applied for a job with the New York City Board of Education. My first job was traveling among several schools teaching music. Eventually, I got a job teaching a Special Education class at Public School 92 in Harlem. My students had a variety of mental handicaps, but the most basic was a lack of stimulation and awareness of the outside world. They came from poor families and broken homes, and there wasn't much I could do about that. But I could try to bring some of the outside world to them. I started bringing newspapers to school and talking about current events. I tried to teach them by allowing them to experience what I was trying to teach, and so it made sense

Teaching at New School for Social Research, New York City, early seventies

As teacher at State University College, New Paltz, New York, early seventies

to me that when we were talking about sound I should bring in a few pots and pans and a couple of sticks for drumming. That got me into trouble with the principal. In fact, I was in trouble quite a lot at P.S. 92. I also took my students on too many field trips, but it seemed to me that they ought to see what a museum was and to know something about how grass grows and what makes the leaves of trees turn red and yellow and brown in the fall. I often departed from the established lesson plan and preferred to have my students try to read newspapers rather than the standard "Dick and Jane" texts. I would like to have gotten for them books about current events written for young readers, but such books were not available.

While I could not do much about their home lives, I worried about my students constantly and wondered what kind of future awaited them. With friends, I talked incessantly about "my kids," and probably bored most of them. But a social worker at P.S. 92 named Fran Morrill understood how I felt. One day she gave me a diary and suggested that I write down my thoughts about my students and teaching disadvantaged children in Harlem. *Diary of a Harlem Schoolteacher* was the result. It was published in 1969 by Grove Press, an independent company that had a reputation for publishing controversial books. I doubt if a major publishing company would have touched it.

But, once I was a "published author," major publishing companies actually approached me about writing books for young people. I knew exactly the kinds of books I wanted to do—books about current events and books about

important black people so that students could understand the larger world around them through books written on a level that they could understand. My first book for young people was called *Resistance: Profiles in Nonviolence*. It tried to put into perspective the nonviolent Civil Rights Movement of the time by showing that throughout history there have been nonviolent warriors for change, among them Patrick Henry and Henry David Thoreau and Kemal Atatürk—not just Martin Luther King, Jr. My next two books for young people were *Profiles in Black Power* and *The War and the Protest: Vietnam*. Both also talked about what was happening in the country and in the world at the time—the Black Power Movement and the war in Vietnam—and tried to place these events in historical perspective.

I then started doing biographies of important black people—living black people, not just dead ones. It seemed to me that young people ought to have some living black heroes to read about, and because of the gains made by black people, there were more living black heroes to write about. In the beginning, I wrote about important blacks in politics and international affairs—Adam Clayton Powell and Ralph Bunche, Shirley Chisholm and Barbara Jordan. I deliberately stayed away from sports biographies, because it seemed to me that young blacks should have other role models besides successful athletes. But when Hank Aaron's home-run total started creeping up on Babe Ruth's record, and too many people seemed to be taking sides as to who was the better hitter, and the better man, I could not resist doing *Babe Ruth and Hank Aaron: The Home Run Kings*. What I tried to show in that book was that both men were great hitters and great athletes, and people ought to celebrate them both.

I got more "fan mail" from children who had read that book than I had gotten for all the other books put together. That saddened me a bit, but eventually I realized that it doesn't matter so much *what* kids read as it does *that* they read. You can use new words and put sentences together properly just as easily when you are writing about a sports hero as when you are writing about a politician. The same goes for show-business stars like Stevie Wonder. I've written quite a few books about those kinds of heroes. Whoever I write about, I try very hard to make that person seem like a real person, with troubles as well as triumphs, and it pleases me that, more often than not, when a young person writes to me about a book, he or she mentions the grit along with the glitter. They are inspired as much by hardships overcome as by victories won. To inspire young people to overcome the obstacles that confront them is, next to simply inspiring them to read, my purpose in writing these books.

Around 1973, I also began writing adult biographies of important blacks, and to date I've written quite a few. I've also written books for adults that are not biographies. One of them, believe it or not, was *Snow Sculpture and Ice Carving*. I was interested in the beautiful sculptures that people make out of snow and ice, and so I wrote a book about them. An advertising agency in New York that represented a hand-cream product decided that it would be great to advertise how nice that hand cream was for hands that got frostbitten in the course of making snowmen, and one cold winter day I found myself out in Central Park making a snowman for the television cameras. I don't know if the hand-cream company sold more bottles of cream because of that ad, but I got a whole case of hand cream as payment.

I also wrote an adult book called *Voodoo and Hoodoo*. The stories of hoodoo men and women had always fascinated me as a child, and the book is mostly about how those beliefs have survived among black people for hundreds and hundreds of years. Right in the beginning of the book I said that I did not practice these occult arts and was simply interested in the history and survival of the beliefs. But after that book was published I started getting letters from people who had somehow decided that I could help them by working magic for them. Fortunately, they only had the publisher's address, so none of the letters came to me directly. One woman sent me a picture of her husband, a piece of his undershirt, and two dollars. I think she wanted me to get rid of him for her. I wasn't sure how to respond. I couldn't very well return the picture and the piece of undershirt. What if her husband opened my letter? So, I kept the picture and the piece of undershirt. But I sent back the two dollars with a note (no return address on either the stationery or the envelope!) that just said I was very sorry I couldn't help her, and good luck. In some ways, I regret writing that particular book, because the letters I have received have been mostly from people with troubles, and it is very hard to tell them that I cannot help them.

Another adult book I wrote was about the Cotton Club, a very famous nightclub in Harlem in the 1920s and 1930s where almost all the patrons were white and all the entertainers were black. This was the inspiration for the movie of the same title, though the movie was not at all like the book. I got to visit the movie set and meet the actors and actresses. I even got a director's chair with my name on it, though I had nothing really to do with the movie.

Still, the majority of my books have been, and probably will continue to be, for young people. I spend a good percentage of my time with them, teaching.

Since 1970, I have taught adolescent literature and writing nonfiction on the college level. There is a little more freedom to teach the way you want to in college. I have taught in New York City (the New School for Social Research and Staten Island Community College), in upstate New York (Manhattanville College and the State University of New York at New Paltz) as well as at Indiana University-Purdue University in Indianapolis. In fact, for a couple of years I was teaching in New York City (days) and in upstate New York (evenings) *and* in Indiana (weekends and summers) all during the same time! Looking back, I'm not quite sure how I managed it and lived to tell about it. Since 1977, I've been teaching in one place, the University of Florida at Gainesville, and commuting to New York, which isn't an easy schedule either.

A couple of years ago, I read a brief biographical sketch of myself in an encyclopedic work; it said that since 1975 I have been devoting full time to writing. I think it would be very nice to do that, but it is very hard to make a living by writing the kinds of books I write. In fact, most writers of books have other jobs. My other job is teaching. Writing is a sideline. Sometimes I think it would be nice to do just one thing, but I would probably be bored in no time

and looking for additional things to do.

I like the combination of teaching and writing. There is nothing more exciting than to see a young person's eyes light up in recognition or understanding. Former students of mine are working with the Peace Corps in Africa, doing videos in Hollywood, working in television in New York, making music in Philadelphia. One has published a novel for young people. Quite a few are still writing and calling after ten or more years. They are friends now, and interesting ones.

I meet a lot of fascinating people in both my lines of work. One of the nice things about writing books, especially about people who are still alive, is that you get to meet them. To write *The Story of Stevie Wonder* I went to Los Angeles and spent a couple of days with him. It was strange to be up and out in the middle of the night, but because Stevie is blind he doesn't have the same idea of night and day as sighted people. If he's hungry at 2:00 a.m., then he wants to go out and get a pizza, which is probably why he chooses to live in big cities where you *can* get a pizza at 2:00 a.m. And he made music all the time and everywhere, beating on a table with a fork or making rhythms with his feet on steps.

While researching my biography of basketball star Bob McAdoo, I got to know his mother, who was a basketball star when she was in high school and who had a wonderful collection of family photographs that she let me borrow.

My favorite subject was Bricktop, who was born Ada Beatrice Queen Victoria Louise Virginia Smith. I helped her write her autobiography a few years ago. When I was growing up, my parents used to read about her in the black newspapers, for she was very famous in Europe where she

With author Harry Crews, University of Florida at Gainesville, 1977

Haskins with interviewees for Now *magazine: Yusef Lateef, musician, and Nikki Giovanni, poet, 1977*

operated nightclubs where kings and princes and famous movie stars went. (At that time, most educated black people kept up with the news about those few blacks who were successful. In fact, my family talked about Bricktop as if she were a relative.) By the time I met her, she was over eighty, but still just as fascinating. I am proud to have helped her write her life story before she died.

I also write articles for magazines, and for a time in 1977-78 I was doing a lot of interviews of famous people for a magazine called *Now* that is no longer published. I had a good time while it lasted. I interviewed all sorts of interesting people, including the writer Rosa Guy, the poet Nikki Giovanni, the photographer Francesco Scavullo, the fashion designer Scott Barrie, and Arthur Mitchell, the founder of the Dance Theater of Harlem.

Almost everyone you will ever meet turns out to be an interesting person, though the vast majority will never have a book, or even an article, written about them. I like having the opportunity to meet them and to hear their stories. In fact, one of the nice things about being a writer is that you get a chance to do research on all sorts of interesting people and events and pretend that it's work!

Most of my books and articles are about black subjects—black history, black people. Partly, that's be-

cause I remember being a child and not having many books about black people to read. I want children today, black and white, to be able to find books about black people and black history in case they want to read them. Partly, too, that's because even today there is a certain segregation in the publishing industry—white authors can write about black subjects, but black authors are rarely allowed to write about white subjects. There are a lot of "white subjects" that interest me, but I've learned from experience that a proposal to write a book about one will usually be politely declined.

I encounter racism in other areas of life as well. At every college where I've taught, I've come across students who have never before had a black teacher and who have been either afraid of me or hostile toward me. In the South, I still find that some people look at my sports jacket and tie and decide that I must be a preacher. Even in New York City, not too many years ago, I arrived at an expensive restaurant and was mistaken for a member of the band. Sometimes, after a newspaper has done an article about me and mentioned where I live, I get telephone calls from people who call me "Nigger" and want to know how I dare write a book or teach at a college, or wear a suit and tie even when I am not going to a funeral. But I don't let that kind of thing bother me. I have seen great changes in racial attitudes in my lifetime, especially in the South.

In 1983 I was invited to return to Alabama to participate in an Alabama History and Heritage Festival. I gave a speech at Auburn University, which is practically all white, and another one in Demopolis, my hometown. The man who invited me to be part of the festival was Bert Hitchcock, chairman of the English Department at Auburn University, and also a native of Demopolis. In fact, his father was superintendent of the Demopolis Public Schools when I was in school there (and the man whose visits to the black school occasioned the quick removal of the portraits of famous blacks from the walls). Bert is about my age, but of course when we were children we never met each other, for he was white and I was black. Nor had I ever met the other natives of Demopolis who gave speeches there. They were all white. In 1983 we went to dinner together at a white restaurant in Demopolis. Turns out that another of my fellow speakers lives in New York, too, and we have had dinner together there as well.

I was offered fine hospitality by the whites in Demopolis in 1983, and having been brought up well I sent thank-you notes to everyone who extended that hospitality. But I was not "over grateful," if you know what I mean. Seems to me that I always should have been able to go to the public library and to eat in whatever restaurant I chose. I was brought up to feel that the failings of society were not my failings. There was never any question in my mind that I was an American. And so when I read about the campaign to raise funds to restore the Statue of Liberty, I offered to help refurbish the monument I had often visited, and I felt good about being an American when I did. I ended up being on the National Education Advisory Committee and vice-director of the Southeast Region of the Statue of Liberty-Ellis Island Foundation. I wrote articles for various newspapers and magazines about why I believe that Lady Liberty's torch shines for black Americans, too. This was another way that I found I could use my writing abilities in support of what I believe in.

In the future, I have no doubt that I will find still other ways. And when, some day, the missing second date after that "1941—" gets filled in, I will know that I not only have done something worthwhile in the years between, but also that I have had a good time doing it.

POSTSCRIPT

Jim Haskins contributed the following update to *SATA* in 2002:

It has been some fifteen years since I wrote the first autobiographical article for *Something about the Author*. After reading it over, I wish I could rewrite it. I wouldn't change the facts, but I would make some different word choices and elaborate on several of the points I made back then. I believe I have become a better writer over the last

At the History and Heritage Festival in Demopolis, Alabama, with fellow "Demopolites," 1983. From left: Alan Koch, Haskins, Bert Hitchcock, Raymond Waites, and Bill Cobb

Statue of Liberty-Ellis Island Foundation Southeast Region meeting, Atlanta, Georgia, 1985

fifteen years; moreover, my perspective on some things has changed, perhaps because I am older.

Much has not changed. I am still teaching in the department of English at the University of Florida and commuting between Gainesville, FL, and New York City. I am still writing books and have written, edited, or co-authored about 125 by now. Continuing the trend established earlier in my writing career, I write biographies and informational books, primarily for the young adult audience but also for the adult trade audience and for young readers.

My most memorable experience writing for young audiences was working with Mrs. Rosa Parks on two versions of her autobiography for young people—one for the upper elementary-junior high group and the other a picture book for the early elementary ages. I was invited to undertake this project by Phyllis Fogelman, then editor-in-chief at the Dial Press, which had published some of my earlier books.

This was in the late 1980s, and I remember how nervous I was when I went to Mrs. Parks's home in Detroit for my first meeting with this living icon of the civil rights movement. Mrs. Parks quickly put me at ease, however. Noticing a loose button on my sports jacket, the "mother of the movement," who also happened to be a former seamstress, proceeded to take out needle and thread and tighten it for me!

Mrs. Parks and I spent many hours reliving those days in Montgomery, AL, in the middle 1950s when her simple, courageous act of refusing to give up her bus seat to white passengers sparked a year-long boycott of the city buses and eventually led to the direct-action civil rights movement. Over the years, the myth had arisen that she had refused to get up from her bus seat because she was tired; she wanted to make clear that, as she put it, "the only tired I was, was tired of giving in."

During the years when that myth had grown, Mrs. Parks had lived in relative obscurity. Forced to leave Montgomery in the late 1950s because of white backlash against her—death threats to her family and her and her husband Raymond's inability to find work—she and her husband had moved to Detroit, MI. There, she had worked for many years in the office of Michigan Congressman John Conyers. Quiet and unassuming, she had never sought the limelight. In fact, many people were surprised to learn that she was still alive. Fortunately, by the time I met her, she was beginning to receive the honor she deserved. She was constantly traveling around the country to accept awards and to be otherwise celebrated for her crucial role in American history. She used her new-found public platform to raise funds for the organization she had formed to help young African Americans, the Rosa and Raymond Parks Institute for Self-Development.

Among the biographies for the adult trade audience on which I have worked during the past fifteen years was *Mr. Bojangles: The Biography of Bill Robinson*. My co-author was N.R. Mitgang, who had spent much of his life collecting print material and taped interviews on the great African-American tap dancer. Published in both the United States and Great Britain, the book was made into a film for the cable channel *Showtime*. The great contemporary tap dancer Gregory Hines produced and starred in it. At this writing, efforts are in progress to adapt my young adult biography of the late Congresswoman Barbara Jordan for a television movie.

My work with Bricktop, whose autobiography I co-authored, led to my participation in a fascinating project: an exhibition entitled *The Jazz Age in Paris, 1914-1940* created by the Smithsonian Institution Traveling Exhibition Service (SITES). As consulting curator, I had the opportunity to travel to Europe in search of objects and documents for the exhibition and to work with a group of scholars to tell the story of the growth of jazz in Europe between the two world wars. I learned a great deal about museum practices and especially about the challenges of telling a story visually rather than simply putting "a book on a wall." The exhibition premiered at the Smithsonian in 1997 and then went on to a variety of cities across the country for three years, after which three smaller versions continued to tour for several more years.

Coincidentally, in 1994 while I was traveling with some frequency to Washington, D.C., to work on the exhibition, I was presented the *Washington Post*/Children's Book Guild award for my body of work in nonfiction for young people. It is the highest tribute I have received. Some of my books have won important prizes in the field of children's books, the Coretta Scott King Award and the Carter G. Woodson Award among them. But this was for my work in its entirety, and I was deeply honored to receive that kind of recognition.

Not long afterward, I was approached by Howard Gotlieb, curator of the Department of Special Collections at Boston University. Dr. Gotlieb had focused on collecting popular culture of the twentieth century and had acquired Groucho Marx's jokes, Ella Fitzgerald's sheet music, and Bette Davis's film and personal memorabilia. Among the writers whose papers were in the BU collection was George Bernard Shaw. I was gratified to be asked but procrastinated for several years—during which Dr. Gotlieb sent a number of follow-up letters and Christmas cards—before accepting his invitation. In part, my reluctance was practical: over one hundred books' worth of research notes, manuscripts, galley proofs, and correspondence is a lot of material. I had it stored in cartons in the basement of my New York City apartment building and in file cabinets in both New York and Gainesville. Organizing it for shipment to Boston was quite a job, even though Dr. Gotlieb sent two helpers. About two-thirds of that material now resides at Boston University. I was loath to give up the correspondence, especially since I have been fairly successful in acquiring the rights to my books when they go out of print and then reselling them.

Moreover, the act of giving up the raw material of one's life's work, added to the acceptance of an award for that work, does tend to signal a looming end.

Looking back upon my life and writing career, I realize how many changes I have witnessed. The greatest change, of course, is in the legal rights of African Americans. Racism is hardly history—witness the recent cases of racial murder and racial profiling in various parts of the country. But the difference between the American society into which I was born and that in which I live and work today is astonishing.

I have also seen many changes in the publishing industry—not progress so much as the back-and-forth swinging of a market pendulum. Sometimes collective biographies for young people are "in"; sometimes they are "out." Series of books will be popular in one decade, unpopular in the next. Publishing follows fashions, just as do other areas of human endeavor. Currently, fiction, with its potential for media and merchandizing tie-ins, seems to be greatly preferable to publishers than nonfiction and informational books. As a nonfiction writer, I find that somewhat frustrating. Although I have watched the publishing pendulum swing back and forth, I still cannot predict the timing of its movement one way or the other. It is serendipitous, as was my becoming a writer of books.

I became a writer at a time when the publishing industry was scrambling to find African-American authors and when the government was earmarking special funds to libraries to purchase books by and about blacks. Being both a teacher and a published writer, I was naturally in demand. In retrospect, I am quite amazed that two of my first three books for young people were not about exclusively black subjects. Only *Profiles in Black Power* was about blacks. *Profiles in Nonviolence* spanned a spectrum of ethnicities, and *The War and the Protest: Vietnam,* was largely about a movement by white Americans. Although the publishing world was segregated then—as a rule whites could write about blacks but blacks could not write about whites—I was able to step "out of the box," as it were, from the beginning. Had my purpose been to further break down racial barriers, I would have focused more on white subject matter. But I was really interested in black history and culture—and in the activities of whites only as context for those of blacks in the historical continuum.

Currently, I serve as Books Editor and write occasional articles for both the venerable *Opportunity* magazine, published in New York City by the National Urban League, and for *FlaVour,* a new magazine for African Americans published in Florida. I have recently completed a biography of Cecil F. Poole (1914-1997), the first black federal judge in California, and edited a collection of sermons by African-American ministers. There are dozens of people and topics about which I would like to write. I plan to continue contributing to the general knowledge about African Americans as long as I am able.

HAUSMAN, Gerald 1945-
(Gerry Hausman)

Personal

Born October 13, 1945, in Baltimore, MD; son of Sidney (an engineer) and Dorothy (Little) Hausman; married Lorry Wright, June, 1968; children: Mariah Fox, Hannah. *Education:* New Mexico Highlands University, B.A., 1968. *Hobbies and other interests:* Reading, swimming, storytelling, qigong.

Addresses

Home—12699 Cristi Way, Bokeelia, FL 33922. *E-mail*—ghausman@compuserve.com.

Career

Poetry teacher in Lenox, MA, 1969-72; Bookstore Press, Lenox, MA, editor, 1972-77; Sunstone Press, Santa Fe, NM, vice-president, 1979-83; Santa Fe Preparatory School, Santa Fe, NM, teacher of English, 1983-87. Poet-in-residence in public schools, 1970-76, and at Central Connecticut State College, 1973. Blue Harbour

Gerald Hausman

Creative Writing School, Port Maria, Jamaica, cofounder, 1986-93.

Member

Poets and Writers, Authors Guild, Society of Children's Book Writers and Illustrators.

Awards, Honors

Union College poetry prize, 1965, for *Quebec Poems;* Gerald Hausman Scholarship awarded in author's name to two Native American high-school students at Santa Fe Preparatory School, 1985; Aesop Accolade Award, American Folklore Society (Children's Section), 1995, for *Duppy Talk: West Indian Tales of Mystery and Magic;* Notable Social Studies Book for Young People, Children's Book Council/National Council for the Social Studies, 1996, and 1999, for *Doctor Bird: Three Lookin' Up Tales from Jamaica;* Pick of the Lists selection, American Booksellers Association, 1999, for *Dogs of Myth: Tales from around the World;* Bank Street College of Education Best Book selection, 2000, for *Tom Cringle: Battle on the High Seas* and *Cats of Myth: Tales from around the World.*

Writings

(With David Kherdian) *Eight Poems,* Giligia, 1968.
(Editor) *Shivurrus Plant of Mopant and Other Children's Poems,* Giligia, 1968.

New Marlboro Stage, Giligia, 1969, 2nd edition, Bookstore Press (Lenox, MA), 1971.
Circle Meadow, Bookstore Press (Lenox, MA), 1972.
The Boy with the Sun Tree Bow, Berkshire Traveller Press (Stockbridge, MA), 1973.
Beth: The Little Girl of Pine Knoll, Bookstore Press (Lenox, MA), 1974.
Sitting on the Blue-Eyed Bear, Lawrence Hill (Westport, CT), 1975.
(Under name Gerry Hausman with wife, Lorry Hausman) *The Pancake Book,* Persea Books (New York, NY), 1976.
(Under name Gerry Hausman with Lorry Hausman) *The Yogurt Book,* Persea Books (New York, NY), 1977.
The Day the White Whales Came to Bangor, Cobblesmith, 1977.
Night Herding Song, Copper Canyon Press (Port Townsend, WA), 1979.
No Witness, Stackpole (Harrisburg, PA), 1980.
Runners, Sunstone Press (Santa Fe, NM), 1984.
Meditations with Animals: A Native American Bestiary, Bear & Co. (Santa Fe, NM), 1986.
Meditations with the Navajo: Prayers, Songs, and Stories of Healing and Harmony, Bear & Co. (Santa Fe, NM), 1988.
Turtle Dream, Mariposa (Santa Fe, NM), 1989.
Stargazer, Lotus Press (Santa Fe, NM), 1989.
Ghost Walk, Mariposa (Santa Fe, NM), 1991.
Turtle Island Alphabet, St. Martin's (New York, NY), 1992.
Coyote Walks on Two Legs, Philomel (New York, NY), 1993.
Eagle Boy, illustrated by Cara and Barry Moser, HarperCollins (New York, NY), 1993.
Turtle Island Alphabet for Young Readers, HarperCollins (New York, NY), 1993.
(Reteller) *The Gift of the Gila Monster: Navajo Ceremonial Tales,* Simon & Schuster (New York, NY), 1993.
(Reteller) *Duppy Talk: West Indian Tales of Mystery and Magic,* Simon & Schuster (New York, NY), 1994.
(Coauthor) *Wilderness,* Forge (New York, NY), 1994.
(Editor) *Prayer to the Great Mystery: The Uncollected Writings and Photography of Edward S. Curtis,* St. Martin's Press (New York, NY), 1995.
Doctor Moledinky's Castle: A Hometown Tale, Simon & Schuster (New York, NY), 1995.
(Collector and reteller) *How Chipmunk Got Tiny Feet: Native American Animal Origin Stories,* HarperCollins (New York, NY), 1995.
(Coauthor) *African-American Alphabet: A Celebration of African-American and West Indian Culture, Custom, Myth, and Symbol,* St. Martin's Press (New York, NY), 1996.
Night Flight, Philomel Books (New York, NY), 1996.
(Editor) *The Kebra Nagast: The Lost Bible of Rastafarian Wisdom and Faith from Ethiopia and Jamaica,* St. Martin's Press (New York, NY), 1997.
(Coauthor) *The Mythology of Dogs: Canine Legend and Lore through the Ages,* St. Martin's Press (New York, NY), 1997.
Doctor Bird: Three Lookin' Up Tales from Jamaica, illustrated by Ashley Wolff, Philomel Books (New York, NY), 1998.

(Coauthor with Loretta Hausman) *The Mythology of Cats: Feline Legend and Lore through the Ages,* St. Martin's Press (New York, NY), 1998.

(Reteller) *The Story of Blue Elk,* illustrated by Kristina Rodanas, Clarion Books (New York, NY), 1998.

The Coyote Bead, Hampton Roads (Charlottesville, VA), 1999.

(Coauthor with Loretta Hausman) *Dogs of Myth: Tales from around the World,* illustrated by Barry Moser, Simon & Schuster (New York, NY), 1999.

(Coauthor) *Cats of Myth: Tales from around the World,* illustrated by Leslie Baker, Simon & Schuster (New York, NY), 2000.

Tom Cringle: Battle on the High Seas, illustrated by Tad Hills, Simon & Schuster (New York, NY), 2000.

(Coauthor with Uton Hinds) *The Jacob Ladder,* Orchard Books (New York, NY), 2001.

Tom Cringle: The Pirate and the Patriot, Simon & Schuster (New York, NY), 2001.

(Coauthor with Loretta Hausman) *The Metaphysical Cat: Tales of Cats and Their Humans,* Hampton Roads (Charlottesville, VA), 2001.

(Coeditor with Cedella Marley) *The Boy from Nine Miles: The Early Life of Bob Marley,* illustrated by Mariah Fox, Hampton Roads (Charlottesville, VA), 2002.

(Coauthor with Loretta Hausman) *The Mythology of Horses: Horse Legend and Lore throughout the Ages,* Three Rivers Press (New York, NY), 2003.

Contributor to *Poets in the Schools,* edited by Kathleen Meagher, Connecticut Commission on the Arts, 1973. Contributor to anthologies, including *Contemporaries: 28 New American Poets,* Viking (New York, NY); *Desert Review Anthology,* Desert Review Press; *Poetry Here and Now,* edited by David Kherdian, Morrow (New York, NY); *Tales from the Great Turtle,* edited by Piers Anthony and Richard Gilliam, Tor (New York, NY), 1994; *Warriors of Blood and Dream,* edited by Roger Zelazny, Avon (New York, NY), 1995; *Wheel of Fortune,* edited by Roger Zelazny, Avon (New York, NY), 1995; *The Gift of Tongues: Twenty-five Years of Poetry,* edited by Sam Hammill, Copper Canyon Press (Port Townsend, WA), 1996; *Lord of the Fantastic: Stories in Honor of Roger Zelazny,* edited by Martin H. Greenberg, Avon (New York, NY), 1998; and *Urban Nature: Poems about Wildlife in the City,* edited by Laure-Anne Bosselaar, Milkweed Editions (Minneapolis, MN), 2000. Some of Hausman's work has been recorded on audiotapes and released by Lotus Press (Santa Fe, NM), including "Navajo Nights," 1987, "Stargazer," 1989, "Native American Animal Stories," 1990, and "Ghost Walk," 1991.

Sidelights

Gerald Hausman writes books for young readers that mine Navajo and Caribbean lore. In *Duppy Talk: West Indian Tales of Mystery and Magic,* Hausman presents tales centering around the "Duppy," a West Indian term for a soul who has not yet settled peacefully in the spirit world and continues to haunt the living. The Duppy ghost has links to indigenous African religions, which came to the Caribbean region with African slaves.

Hausman also served as editor of *The Kebra Nagast: The Lost Bible of Rastafarian Wisdom and Faith from Ethiopia and Jamaica.* "Kebra Nagast," as he explains in the preface, means "the glory of the Kings." The Rastafarian religion rests on the belief that King Solomon had Ethiopian children, whose descendants brought oral traditions to the Caribbean world many centuries later. Rastafarian ideas were popularized in the mid-twentieth century by reggae music, particularly the songs of the late Bob Marley. *The Kebra Nagast* explains Rastafarian ideas, and Hausman provides examples of some parallel passages to this belief system that can be found in the Christian Bible.

Hausman is also the author of another adaptation of a West Indian folktale, *Doctor Bird: Three Lookin' Up Tales from Jamaica.* The "doctor" is a figure allegedly native to the north coast of Jamaica, a top hat-wearing streamer-tailed hummingbird who helps other animals. He gives guidance to a little homeless mouse, who finds shelter and nourishment in the trees, and helps a kleptomaniac mongoose realize that stealing is wrong. "Rather than write in dialect, Hausman lightly evokes oral cadences with a few scattered words or turns of phrase," noted *Booklist*'s John Peters.

Cats of Myth, *cowritten by Hausman and his wife, Loretta, incorporates nine stories collected from different countries and includes an afterword discussing each of the breeds depicted. (Illustrated by Leslie Baker.)*

Hausman wrote *The Jacob Ladder,* another story of Jamaica, with coauthor Uton Hinds. Based on Hinds's childhood, the work is set in the 1960s and narrated by a boy named Tall T. He reveals his troubled home life, with a father who gambles, drinks, and eventually abandons the family for a neighbor woman. Tall T's mother gathers her children and tells them: "Brothers and sisters stick together. They don't wash away like gully water." Because the narrator cannot afford the uniform required to attend school, he spends his days at the local library, where a kindly librarian teaches him how to read. When his father dangles a chance to participate in a local festival in one of its coveted musician spots, Tall T is tempted by the offer. The biblical story of Jacob's ladder is like the cliff that Tall T climbs in order to think about what he should do. *School Library Journal* reviewer Ellen Vevier found *The Jacob Ladder* "A compelling and vibrant book that will give young readers a real look into the Jamaica behind the postcard and cruise-ship images." Hazel Rochman, writing in *Booklist,* termed it "a harsh story of poverty and betrayal. It's also about family love and faith."

Navajo lore and stories from other indigenous nations of the American Southwest continue to fascinate Hausman and provide inspiration for some of his books. He adapted different variants of one tale for *The Story of Blue Elk.* A baby is born in a Pueblo community on the same day that a giant elk casts a shadow over the village. This means that the infant, named Blue Elk, will be mute for life. During his childhood, however, the boy is able to communicate with his namesake, who appears to him in animal form. When that animal dies, it falls next to a cedar tree, and its antlers merge with the cedar wood. The mute Blue Elk, now a grown man, uses that wood to carve a special flute. He then plays it to communicate with a woman whom he has loved from afar for many years. *School Library Journal*'s Judith Gloyer, reviewing the book, commended Hausman's "beautiful, vivid language," and called it "a lyrical tale from a gifted and experienced storyteller."

Hausman also used Navajo history in writing *The Coyote Bead.* The story is set in 1864, as Dineh, a young Tobachischin, is orphaned when his parents are slain by federal government troops. The backdrop of the story is the Long Walk, a tragic chapter in Navajo history that was taking place during this time. It involved the enforced migration of the Navajo to Fort Sumner, New Mexico. Dineh hides from troops with his grandfather, a medicine man, and also from a treacherous Ute named Two Face. Dineh's grandfather is slain by one of Two Face's arrows, a death which he had prophesied for himself, and Dineh saves the prized medicine bag and forges on alone. He comes across a Ute massacre, and is shot at by Mary, a young woman who was adopted by a sympathetic white family. Her adoptive parents were also victims of Two Face. "Interestingly, the [Long Walk]'s heroes and villains aren't divided along racial lines," noted a critic writing for *Hungry Mind Review.* The writer also liked the way that Hausman depicted Navajo culture, noting that "cooking and eating, rituals, [and] interpreting nature ... are astutely and painstak-

ingly relayed, making the reader's transport back in time an effortless and worthwhile journey."

In the late 1990s, Hausman and his wife, Loretta Hausman, began writing paeans to two of the most popular domesticated animals in the world. *The Mythology of Dogs: Canine Legend and Lore through the Ages* is a collection of seventy folk tales, facts, and true stories, arranged in alphabetical order by breed. *The Mythology of Cats: Feline Legend and Lore through the Ages* is arranged along similar lines. In the latter volume, the Hausmans debunk the popular association of cats with negative spiritual forces. Both Buddha and Muhammad enjoyed feline companionship, they note, and in other cultures and other points in time, cats have been revered as harbingers of good luck and good harvests, or as healers and guides. *Library Journal*'s Florence Scarinci called the work "an entertaining compilation."

Hausman and his wife gathered more folktales for *Dogs of Myth: Tales from around the World.* The stories here are divided into categories, including the trickster dog, the enchanted hound, or the guardian animal. One from Africa recounts how a clever dog stole fire and brought it to his human friend, but it meant that he forever lost the ability to bark. The Hausmans also present a Celtic legend of a miniature bloodhound, "King Herla's Hound," as well as a Norse tale that explains why the Rottweiler's growl sounds like thunder. Others borrow from Japanese and Inuit culture. A *Publishers Weekly* reviewer praised the work, noting that the authors' "storytelling flows in an unbroken, lyrical stream, right from the poetic introduction."

Cats of Myth: Tales from around the World, published in 2000, follows the same format. Here the Hausmans present an East Indian tale that explains how the cat was domesticated, recount a Japanese martial-arts fable about a temple cat and a rat, and write an afterword that discusses each of the breeds depicted. *Booklist*'s Ilene Cooper extolled *Cats of Myth* as "a treat for cat lovers [and] for readers who enjoy a good folktale." Hausman and his wife have also written *The Metaphysical Cat: Tales of Cats and Their Humans,* and *The Mythology of Horses: Horse Legend and Lore throughout the Ages.* Reviewing *The Metaphysical Cat,* a *Publishers Weekly* critic said, "anyone believing that cats live in another dimension will relish" this book.

In 2000, Hausman authored a solo work for young readers that drew upon eighteenth- and nineteenth-century English literature for its inspiration. *Tom Cringle: Battle on the High Seas* recounts in fictional diary form the adventures of a thirteen-year-old English boy who goes to sea—not an uncommon experience in his day and age. Tom serves on board the *Bream,* a guard vessel in Caribbean waters during the War of 1812, as a midshipman. Hausman based his work on two actual accounts, one from a Scottish planter in Jamaica who had entered the Royal British Navy at a similar age. It was an era when the flogging of sailors as a disciplinary measure was still legal.

Tom Cringle's direst hardships on board the *Bream,* however, initially involve adjusting to life at sea, for he and his best friend, a boy his own age, are frequently nauseous. Tom finds his niche as an "eagle eye," who can spot an unfriendly ship far off on the horizon. "The wind ever since noon has been blowing heavy squalls," the book reads. "One of these gusts is so violent, it buries our cannons in white surf. The sea's rolling us heavily, side to side. I see the last of the sun, red and raw, slumping behind a hillock of bloodstained clouds. And true enough, we're not the only spectators of this gloomy splendor. At some distance I spy a long warship, a frigate. She's tossing, too, rolling in the trough just like we are."

Piracy is a great danger in this part of the world, but so are tropical storms. One wrecks the *Bream,* and just Tom and two others, plus his dog Sneezer, survive. They are picked up by a pirate ship and manage to bribe its captain into delivering them to a British naval base in the area; they offer the gold buttons of their uniform as payment. Tom views the captain, a fierce Scot named Obediah Glasgow, with some fear, but the two forge an unlikely friendship, and Tom and his companions are delivered to safety. *School Library Journal* critic William McLoughlin liked the first third of the book, which he felt was "brimming with colorful descriptions of life aboard the *Bream,* where Tom experiences drudgery, disease, thrilling naval battles, and the death of a companion."

Hausman wrote a sequel, *Tom Cringle: The Pirate and the Patriot,* that finds Tom a year older and promoted to first lieutenant. He is still in the Caribbean, on the lookout for pirates, and this time his ship survives a storm. They then surprise a pirate ship and board it by force. It carries slaves, taken from a plantation called Cinnamon Hill, and Tom is assigned to take them back there. The mission presents a moral quandary for him, for he believes slavery is wrong. In the end, after all experience several adventures, Tom is relieved when the Royal Navy agrees to take the slaves as new conscripts. *School Library Journal*'s Patricia B. McGee faulted *The Pirate and the Patriot* for what she felt was a pat solution to the slavery issue in the plot—"since Royal Navy life at this time was brutal"—but she also found merits in Hausman's book as well, noting that its "lively plotting, picturesque language, and colorful setting make this an exciting tale." Writing in *Booklist,* Roger Leslie praised the author for "his epistolary format and *Treasure Island*-like dialogue."

Biographical and Critical Sources

PERIODICALS

Booklist, December 1, 1995, Janice Del Negro, review of *Doctor Moledinky's Castle: A Hometown Tale,* p. 618; February 1, 1996, Carolyn Phelan, review of *Eagle Boy,* p. 934; February 15, 1996, Brad Hooper, review of *African-American Alphabet,* p. 985; March 1, 1996, Hazel Rochman, review of *Night Flight,* p. 1174; October 1, 1997, Mike Tribby, review of *The Kebra Nagast,* p. 284; May 15, 1998, Ilene Cooper, review of

The Story of Blue Elk, p. 1628; June 1, 1998, John Peters, review of *Doctor Bird,* p. 1754; November 1, 1999, Michael Cart, review of *Dogs of Myth: Tales from around the World,* p. 520; November 1, 2000, Carolyn Phelan, review of *Tom Cringle: Battle on the High Seas,* p. 526; December 15, 2000, Ilene Cooper, review of *Cats of Myth: Tales from around the World,* p. 813; May 1, 2001, Hazel Rochman, review of *The Jacob Ladder,* p. 1678; September 15, 2001, Roger Leslie, review of *Tom Cringle: The Pirate and The Patriot,* p. 222.

Boys' Life, July, 2001, review of *Tom Cringle: Battle on the High Seas,* p. 32.

Horn Book Guide, fall, 1998, Pam McCuen, review of *Doctor Bird,* and Debbie A. Reese, review of *The Story of Blue Elk,* p. 364.

Hungry Mind Review, winter, 1999, review of *The Coyote Bead,* p. 50.

Kirkus Reviews, November 1, 1997, review of *Dogs of Myth,* p. 1742.

Library Journal, October 1, 1997, L. Kriz, review of *The Kebra Nagast,* p. 88; July, 1998, Florence Scarinci, review of *The Mythology of Cats: Feline Legend and Lore through the Ages,* p. 121;

Publishers Weekly, December 18, 1995, review of *Eagle Boy,* p. 54; May 11, 1998, review of *Doctor Bird,* p. 67; November 8, 1999, review of *Dogs of Myth,* p. 68; September 3, 2001, review of *The Metaphysical Cat,* p. 82.

School Library Journal, August, 1998, Judith Gloyer, review of *The Story of Blue Elk,* pp. 150-151; March, 2000, Cheri Estes, review of *Dogs of Myth,* p. 254; November, 2000, William McLoughlin, review of *Tom Cringle: Battle on the High Seas,* p. 154; December, 2000, Nancy Call, review of *Cats of Myth,* p. 133; April, 2001, Ellen Vevier, review of *The Jacob Ladder,* p. 140; October, 2001, Patricia B. McGee, review of *Tom Cringle: The Pirate and the Patriot,* p. 160.

Tribune Books (Chicago, IL), February 9, 1997, Robert Rodi, review of *The Mythology of Dogs: Canine Legend and Lore through the Ages,* pp. 1, 11.

OTHER

Gerald Hausman Web Site, http://www.geraldhausman. com (June 3, 2002).

*   *   *

HAUSMAN, Gerry
See HAUSMAN, Gerald

*   *   *

HEIDLER, David S(tephen) 1955-

Personal

Born April 4, 1955, in Atlanta, GA; son of C. D., Jr. and Jane (Autry) Heidler; married Jeanne Twiggs (a historian and educator), June 13, 1981; *Ethnicity:* "White." *Education:* Auburn University, Ph.D., 1985. *Religion:*

David S. Heidler

Protestant. *Hobbies and other interests:* Sailing, music, hiking, reading.

Addresses

Agent—c/o Author Mail, ABC-CLIO, 130 Cremona Dr., Santa Barbara, CA 93117. *E-mail*—dsheidler@ msn.com.

Career

Salisbury State University, Salisbury, MD, assistant professor of history, 1984-93; University of Southern Colorado, Pueblo, CO, visiting professor of history, 1994-99.

Member

American Historical Association, Organization of American Historians, Society of Historians of the Early Republic, Southern Historical Association.

Awards, Honors

Best Reference Source, *Library Journal,* 2000, Editor's Choice, *Booklist,* 2000, Independent Publisher Book Award, 2001, Outstanding Reference Source, RUSA/ ALA, 2001, and Dartmouth Medal Honorable Mention, 2001, all for *Encyclopedia of the American Civil War.*

Writings

Pulling the Temple Down: The Fire-Eaters and the Destruction of the Union, Stackpole (Harrisburg, PA), 1994.

(With wife, Jeanne T. Heidler) *Old Hickory's War: Andrew Jackson and the Quest for Empire,* Stackpole (Harrisburg, PA), 1996.

(Editor, with wife, Jeanne T. Heidler) *Encyclopedia of the War of 1812,* ABC-CLIO (Santa Barbara, CA), 1997.

(Consulting editor, with wife, Jeanne T. Heidler) Mark Crawford, *Encyclopedia of the Mexican-American War,* ABC-CLIO (Santa Barbara, CA), 1999.

(Editor, with wife, Jeanne T. Heidler) *Encyclopedia of the American Civil War: A Political, Social, and Military History,* ABC-CLIO (Santa Barbara, CA), 2000.

(With wife, Jeanne T. Heidler) *The War of 1812,* Greenwood Press (Westport, CT), 2002.

Work in Progress

(With wife, Jeanne T. Heidler) *Manifest Destiny,* for Greenwood Press (Westport, CT); editor (with wife, Jeanne T. Heidler) *Encyclopedia of the American Civil War,* for Norton (New York, NY).

Sidelights

David S. Heidler and his wife, Jeanne T. Heidler, both history professors, have teamed up on a number of historical studies and reference works. In *Old Hickory's War: Andrew Jackson and the Quest for Empire*, they discussed the complexities of General Andrew Jackson's defeat of the Creek and Seminole tribes of Native Americans and the acquisition of Spanish-controlled territory in Florida. The couple also edited *Encyclopedia of the War of 1812* and the award-winning *Encyclopedia of the American Civil War: A Political, Social, and Military History. Encyclopedia of the War of 1812,* which Samuel J. Watson of *Journal of Southern History* described as the "first comprehensive reference work on the war," contains 500 essays, numerous illustrations, several dozen maps, and a lengthy bibliography. Watson determined that the more than seventy essay contributors are well matched to their articles and the articles in his area of expertise are "accurate and up to date." Other critics praised the work as well. In *Library Journal* Stephen G. Weisner called the encyclopedia an "excellent reference work," as did Marsha S. Holden of *School*

Library Journal, who called it an "excellent and important source for all libraries." Although *Booklist* reviewer Mary Ellen Quinn noted that the "work is not free of factual errors," she called it a "treasure trove of information on this watershed in U.S. history." Likewise, Watson noticed what he considered a few problems of organization and comprehensiveness in the chronology, glossary, bibliography, and index; yet he decided that the positives outweigh any flaws. Writing in *Choice,* J. R. Burch concluded that *Encyclopedia of the War of 1812* is a "thorough and factual examination" of the conflict that "fills a significant void in the reference literature." Watson summed up, the "*Encyclopedia of the War of 1812* is the only resource of the kind to treat this conflict. It will serve to delight scholars for many years to come."

The number of books on the market about the American Civil War period attests to the popularity of this subject. In their five-volume *Encyclopedia of the American Civil War* the Heidlers and 350 contributors wrote over 1,600 articles on a wide variety of aspects of the time period, including military engagements, military life in general, and the effects of the war on politics, government, technology, commerce, and domestic life. *Encyclopedia of the American Civil War* earned critical acclaim and a handful of awards. Enthusiasts of the work included Starr E. Smith of *School Library Journal,* who declared that this work is an "all-together excellent resource for research or general browsing interest." A *Booklist* reviewer commented on the primary source materials, calling them "an invaluable enhancement to the set," and praised the index as "detailed and comprehensive." *Encyclopedia of the American Civil War,* the *Booklist* critic concluded, "is the most comprehensive reference work written about its topic, providing both the novice and the expert an opportunity to expand their knowledge."

Biographical and Critical Sources

PERIODICALS

Booklist, April, 1998, Mary Ellen Quinn, review of *Encyclopedia of the War of 1812,* pp. 1346-1347; January 1, 2001, review of *Encyclopedia of the American Civil War: A Political, Social, and Military History,* p. 1006; September 1, 2001, Mary Ellen Quinn, review of *Encyclopedia of the American Civil War,* p. 146.

Choice, May, 1998, J. R. Burch, Jr., review of *Encyclopedia of the War of 1812,* p. 1520.

Civil War History, September, 1995, Robert E. May, review of *Pulling the Temple Down: The Fire-Eaters and the Destruction of the Union,* pp. 264-266.

Journal of American History, September, 1995, Carl R. Osthaus, review of *Pulling the Temple Down,* pp. 732-733; June, 1999, Lawrence Frederick Kohl, review of *Old Hickory's War: Andrew Jackson and the Quest for Empire,* pp. 234-235.

Journal of Military History, October, 2001, Mark Grimsley, review of *Encyclopedia of the American Civil War,* pp. 1096-1097.

Journal of Southern History, February, 1996, Eric H. Walther, review of *Pulling the Temple Down,* p. 142; August, 1997, Samuel J. Watson, review of *Old Hickory's War,* pp. 649-650; November, 2001, Samuel J. Watson, review of *Encyclopedia of the War of 1812,* pp. 840-842.

Journal of the Early Republic, fall, 1997, Frank Lawrence Owsley, Jr., review of *Old Hickory's War,* pp. 544-545; winter, 1998, David Curtis Skaggs, review of *Encyclopedia of the War of 1812,* pp. 731-733.

Library Journal, March 1, 1998, Stephen G. Weisner, review of *Encyclopedia of the War of 1812,* p. 80.

Presidential Studies Quarterly, summer, 1996, Russ Braley, review of *Old Hickory's War,* pp. 893-894.

Publishers Weekly, February 12, 1996, review of *Old Hickory's War,* p. 66.

School Library Journal, May, 1998, Marsha S. Holden, review of *Encyclopedia of the War of 1812,* p. 168; May, 2001, Starr E. Smith, review of *Encyclopedia of the American Civil War,* p. 87.

*   *   *

HEIDLER, Jeanne T. 1956-

Personal

Born January 20, 1956, in Atlanta, GA; daughter of Joseph L. and Sarah (Daniel) Twiggs; married David S. Heidler (a historian and educator), June 13, 1981. *Ethnicity:* "White." *Education:* Auburn University, Ph.D., 1988. *Religion:* Protestant. *Hobbies and other interests:* Gardening, cooking, hiking, reading.

Addresses

Office—Department of History, United States Air Force Academy, Colorado Springs, CO 80840. *Agent*—c/o Author Mail, ABC-CLIO, 130 Cremona Dr., Santa Barbara, CA 93117. *E-mail*—jtheidler@msn.com.

Career

Salisbury State University, Salisbury, MD, professor, 1985-93; United States Air Force Academy, Colorado Springs, CO, professor of history, 1993—.

Awards, Honors

Best Reference Source, *Library Journal,* 2000, Editor's Choice, *Booklist,* 2000, Independent Publisher Book Award, 2001, Outstanding Reference Source, RUSA/ALA, 2001, and Dartmouth Medal Honorable Mention, 2001, all for *Encyclopedia of the American Civil War.*

Writings

(With husband, David S. Heidler) *Old Hickory's War: Andrew Jackson and the Quest for Empire,* Stackpole (Harrisburg, PA), 1996.

(Editor, with husband, David S. Heidler) *Encyclopedia of the War of 1812,* ABC-CLIO (Santa Barbara, CA), 1997.

(Consulting editor, with husband, David S. Heidler) Mark Crawford, *Encyclopedia of the Mexican-American War,* ABC-CLIO (Santa Barbara, CA), 1999.

(Editor, with husband, David S. Heidler) *Encyclopedia of the American Civil War: A Political, Social, and Military History,* ABC-CLIO (Santa Barbara, CA), 2000.

(With husband, David S. Heidler) *The War of 1812,* Greenwood Press (Westport, CT), 2002.

Work in Progress

(With husband, David S. Heidler) *Manifest Destiny,* for Greenwood Press (Westport, CT); editor (with husband, David S. Heidler) *Encyclopedia of the American Civil War,* for Norton (New York, NY).

Sidelights

See HEIDLER, David S. entry above.

*   *   *

HOGAN, Linda 1947-

Personal

Born July 16, 1947, in Denver, CO; daughter of Charles and Cleona (Bower) Henderson; children: Tanya Park, Sandra. *Ethnicity:* Chickasaw Native. *Education:* University of Colorado, M.A. (creative writing), 1978. *Religion:* "Traditional indigenous."

Addresses

Agent—Beth Vesel, 55 Fifth Ave., 15th Floor, New York, NY 10003.

Career

Retired professor; writer and poet.

Member

Authors Guild; Writers Guild.

Awards, Honors

American Book Award; Five Civilized Nations Play-writing award; fellowships from the Guggenheim and Lannan foundations and the National Endowment for the Arts; *Mean Spirit* was a finalist for the Pulitzer Prize in fiction, 1991; Oklahoma Book Award; Lifetime Achievement Award from Native Writers Circle, Colorado Book Awards.

Writings

Calling Myself Home, Greenfield Review Press (Greenfield Center, NY), 1978.

Eclipse (poems), American Indian Studies Center—University of California (Los Angeles, CA), 1983.

Seeing through the Sun, University of Massachusetts Press (Amherst, MA), 1985.

(Editor with Carol Bruchac and Judith McDaniel) *The Stories We Hold Secret,* Greenfield Review Press (Greenfield Center, NY), 1986.

Savings: Poems, Coffee House Press (Minneapolis, MN), 1988.

Mean Spirit: A Novel, Atheneum (New York, NY), 1990.

Red Clay, Greenfield Review Press (Greenfield Center, NY), 1992.

The Book of Medicines: Poems, Coffee House Press (Minneapolis, MN), 1993.

Dwellings: A Spiritual History of the Living World, W. W. Norton (New York, NY), 1995.

Solar Storms: A Novel, Scribner (New York, NY), 1995.

Power, W. W. Norton (New York, NY), 1998.

(Editor with Deena Metzger and Brenda Peterson) *Intimate Nature: The Bond between Women and Animals,* Fawcett Columbine (New York, NY), 1998.

The Woman Who Watches Over the World: A Native Memoir, W. W. Norton (New York, NY), 2001.

(With Brenda Peterson) *Sightings: The Gray Whale's Mysterious Journey,* National Geographic Society (Washington, DC), 2002.

(Editor with Brenda Peterson) *The Sweet Breathing of Plants: Women Writing on the Green World,* North Point Press (New York, NY), 2001.

Contributor to *Uncommon Waters: Women Write about Fishing.*

Work in Progress

A volume of poetry, *Light,* and a novel, *Devil Fish;* researching the Vietnam War.

Sidelights

Author and poet Linda Hogan, a Chickasaw Indian, has written a number of works, both fiction and nonfiction, that are heavily influenced by Native American philosophy and indigenous knowledge. One of her novels, *Mean Spirit,* was nominated for a Pulitzer Prize in fiction in 1991. That particular work was set in 1920s Oklahoma, as its Native American population was displaced by an oil rush. Other books from Hogan include a 1995 novel *Solar Storms,* which presents a coming-of-age tale alongside an historic look at an indigenous nation and their contemporary struggles. Critic Bettina Berch discussed Hogan's testimonials to the Native American political struggle in her works in an article for *Belles Lettres.* "Hogan makes you realize that they haven't been about property rights or legal jurisdictions or money as much as a struggle between two very different world views."

Born in Colorado in 1947, Hogan earned a graduate degree in creative writing from the University of Colorado in 1978. That same year, her first book, *Calling Myself Home,* was published. This collection of poems drew heavily upon Chickasaw Indian themes, those tribes which once lived in the Southeastern part of the United States. Many of the selections pay homage to the turtle, an important animal to some of the indigenous nations who once lived in the area. A turtle, as Hogan's verse illustrates, was considered a powerful creature, one who lived in two worlds, land and water, and is both hard and soft in its physical constitution. Other poems reflect profound longings. "Hogan is concerned with the home one physically inhabits and the home one holds in the imagination, and home is shown to be a spiritual process of growing connection to place rather than a static location," wrote *American Indian Quarterly* reviewer Craig Womack of her work. Womack also commended one selection in *Calling Myself Home,* "Celebration: Birth of a Colt," as "perhaps one of the most ecstatic poems in the English language."

Other volumes of poetry followed, and Hogan wrote her first novel, *Mean Spirit,* in 1990. Its plot is set in Oklahoma in the early 1920s, a place that was once known as Indian Territory, for the U.S. federal government had encouraged hundreds of thousands of Native Americans in the Southeast to resettle there; those that did not comply were forcibly removed in the 1830s. The subsequent discovery of oil in Oklahoma complicated matters further. Hogan's novel centers around two families of Osage, the nation of Plains Indians who lived in Oklahoma prior to the migration period. One matriarch, Grace Blanket, owns valuable land, and her slaying rouses the interest of a federal law enforcement official who is of Native heritage. This agent, Stace Red Hawk, begins to suspect an official cover-up. Cynthia Ogorek, writing for *Booklist,* called *Mean Spirit* "a slow-moving but intense story that makes a lasting impression." The novel also elicited a positive review from Sybil Steinberg in *Publishers Weekly.* "Hogan . . . mines a rich vein of Indian customs and rituals," Steinberg wrote, claiming the author's characters are "[brought] to life with quick, spare phrases."

Hogan also earned an enthusiastic critical response for her 1993 volume of poetry, *The Book of Medicines,* a finalist for the National Book Critics Award. Again, the verse draws upon Native traditions and Hogan's Chickasaw-shaped values. Environmental concerns and the need to respect the Earth are the themes throughout. At some moments, a feminist perspective shapes ideas. One work in particular presents a history of the word "red"—connecting the red of clay soil to life-giving human blood. Robert L. Berner, reviewing *The Book of Medicines* for *World Literature Today,* found it rife with "startling images that capture the naked power of the natural world: a mountain lion frightened by the wild human animal it confronts, a fetal whale floating on a block of ice, a crow and wolf scavenging the body of a fallen moose." A *Publishers Weekly* reviewer also liked the way in which Hogan "imbues simple things like crows, salt and bamboo with grace and dignity." The critic concluded that with this volume of poetry, "Hogan has come into her own as an artist."

Hogan's second novel, *Solar Storms,* recounts a hope-filled tale of a disfigured teenager, Angel Jensen. At the age of seventeen, the adopted Angel has little knowledge of who she is but learns she comes from a place called

Linda Hogan

Adam's Rib, an island in the waters that separate Minnesota and Canada. She journeys there to learn more about herself and discovers that her scarred face was the result of an act of abuse by her mother, Hannah—a victim of abuse herself—who then abandoned her. Angel's great-grandmother, Agnes Iron, tells her that local lore narrates Hannah's story differently: Angel's mother supposedly became a cannibal and gave herself to the spirit of ice and winter; the spirit then took revenge on the infant Angel and bit her face.

Angel also comes to know her great-great-grandmother, DoraRouge, who came from a more northerly territory known as the land of Fat Eaters. It is believed Hannah now lives there, and since DoraRouge wants to return there to die, the women in *Solar Storms* set off on a long trek. Along the way Angel is told much about her people's history, from the days when beavers were plentiful and were a staple of their economy to the onslaught of European fur traders, who decimated the beaver population. The indigenous people starved, and sometimes children were removed by the government and sent to boarding schools. A more current threat now looms: a planned hydroelectric dam will forever flood ancestral hunting grounds. "Hogan's finely tuned descriptions of the land and its spiritual significance draw a parallel between the ravages suffered by the environment and those suffered by" Hannah, wrote a contributor to *Publishers Weekly. Booklist* critic Donna Seaman also wrote effusively of *Solar Storms,* remarking that "Hogan—magnetic, ardent, and sagacious—has created a universe within these pages that readers won't want to leave."

Another novel from Hogan, *Power,* also featured a teenage protagonist struggling to come to terms with her heritage and deciding on her future path. The novel is set in Florida among a dwindling indigenous nation, the Taiga. Omishto Eaton is sixteen, the child of a white father and a mother who denies her Taiga heritage. She is adopted by an eccentric relative, Aunt Ama, and when a hurricane comes, the two women track a wounded deer into the forest and use it to bait a panther. To the Taiga, the panther is a sacred animal, and it has been designated an endangered species by the Florida wildlife officials. Ama kills the weakened, ailing panther, which incites a furor in the Taiga community and criminal proceedings by the government against her as well. Omishto is in the center of the drama, for all interested parties plague her with the question: why did Ama kill it? Seaman, writing in *Booklist,* found the author of *Power* "absolutely

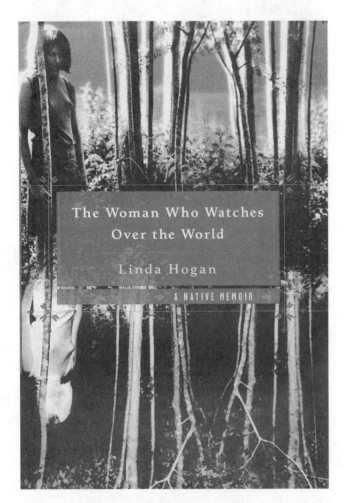

Hogan weaves stories of legendary Native Americans into her memoir, an emotional account of her suffering and her victory over her afflictions. (Cover photo by Jerry Uelsmann.)

magnificent in one radiantly dramatic scene after another." *Book World*'s Lese Funderburg found the novel "a love letter to the world through one girl's struggle to find her place in it." Funderburg also stated that "Hogan's narrator is so gifted in marrying simple language to complex thought that her internal detours become more important than outside events."

Hogan tells her own story in *The Woman Who Watches Over the World: A Native Memoir.* She recounts her childhood as the daughter of an alcoholic father and mother who suffered from depression. At the age of twelve, she became involved with an adult man and developed a severe drinking problem as she entered adulthood. She healed herself by learning more about her Native American heritage, and throughout her own recollections, Hogan interweaves tales of Native figures who were inspirational to her, such as Lozen, a healer who served as military advisor to Apache leader Geronimo.

The Woman Who Watches Over the World reveals some trying experiences that Hogan has survived in adulthood as well: she and her husband adopted two Native American girls and learned later that they had been severely abused. She was diagnosed with a neuromuscular disease called fibromyalgia, and a serious head injury gave her amnesia. "Hogan's memories spill out in waves of layered associations: from fire to pain, from 'phantom pain' to 'phantom worlds,' from glaciers to dreams," noted a reviewer for *Publishers Weekly,* who termed it a work "deep and full of grace." Seaman, writing in *Booklist,* commended it as an "indelible narrative [that] ultimately celebrates love, the 'mighty force' that enables even the most harrowed not only to endure but to grow."

Hogan is also the coauthor of *Sightings: The Gray Whale's Mysterious Journey* and with Brenda Peterson also edited *The Sweet Breathing of Plants: Women Writing on the Green World.*

Hogan told *SATA:* "I write to say what can't be said in ordinary language. My work rises out of the American earth and water. It is rooted in traditional indigenous traditions and I try to open this world into the pages of a book.

"My novels are based on factual history, though fictionalized. Their focus and impetus more toward healing ourselves, our land, our spiritual lives. I am excited that I have an opportunity to follow the migration of whales and, also, to look to how whaling was/is involved in ceremonial life, that there is a 'relationship.' In fact, this word typifies my writings—all of it—and my life. But, also, I love to write. Daily. With almost self-indulgence that I earn my living doing what I most like.

"Poetry is my first choice. It is mysterious in its origins, even to the writer. It is a voice, if whole, of pure being.

"I never thought of myself as a writer. I never wanted to be one. I wanted to be a veterinarian or a biologist and look at the secrets of life. Yet as a writer, I've been able to do this. I live with a Horse Rescue horse and a wild mustang, I've worked with eagles, hawks, owls, even once a fawn, and I'm a serious gardener. I love my work and I love this world."

Biographical and Critical Sources

BOOKS

Contemporary Women Poets, St. James Press (Detroit, MI), 1998.

PERIODICALS

American Indian Quarterly, winter, 1993, Craig Womack, review of *Red Clay,* p. 102; summer, 1998, Joe Staples, review of *Solar Storms,* p. 397.

Belles Lettres, January, 1996, Bettina Berch, review of *Solar Storms,* p. 13.

Bloomsbury Review, May, 1988, Marc Weber, review of *Calling Myself Home,* p. 29;

Booklist, December 1, 1985, Joseph Parisi, review of *Seeing through the Sun,* p. 525; June 1, 1988, Mary Patricia Monaghan, review of *Savings,* p. 1638; October 1, 1990, Cynthia Ogorek, review of *Mean Spirit,* p. 255; August, 1995, Donna Seaman, review of *Dwellings,* p. 1914; September 15, 1995, Donna Seaman, review of *Solar Storms,* p. 142; May 1, 1998, Donna Seaman, review of *Power,* p. 1501; February 1, 2001, Donna Seaman, review of *The Sweet Breathing of Plants,* p. 1031; May 15, 2001, Donna Seaman, review of *Woman Who Watches Over the World,* p. 1723;

Book World, August 16, 1998, Lese Funderburg, review of *Power,* p. 4.

Choice, February, 1996, B. Hans, review of *Solar Storms,* p. 950.

Kirkus Reviews, December 15, 2000, review of *The Sweet Breathing of Plants,* p. 1741.

Kliatt, November, 1999, Penelope Power, review of *Intimate Nature,* p. 43.

Library Journal, December 15, 1979, Susan Shafarzek, review of *Calling Myself Home,* p. 2626; November 1, 1989, Richard Churchill, review of *Mean Spirit,* p. 125; March 1, 1992, Louis McKee, review of *Red Clay,* p. 91; July, 1993, Ellen Kaufman, review of *The Book of Medicines,* p. 84; September 15, 1995, Faye A. Chadwell, review of *Solar Storms,* p. 92; January, 1998, Joan S. Elbers, review of *Intimate Nature,* p. 132; January, 2001, Sue O'Brien, review of *The Sweet Breathing of Plants,* p. 150; June 1, 2001, Sue Samson, review of *Woman Who Watches Over the World,* p. 174.

Publishers Weekly, August 3, 1990, Sybil Steinberg, review of *Mean Spirit,* p. 63; May 3, 1993, review of *The Book of Medicines,* p. 299; June 26, 1995, review of *Dwellings,* p. 101; August 28, 1995, review of *Solar Storms,* p. 104; April 20, 1998, review of *Power,* p. 48; December 1, 1997, review of *Intimate Nature,* p. 42; April 20, 1998, review of *Power,* p. 48; January 1, 2001, review of *The Sweet Breathing of Plants,*

p. 81; May 21, 2001, review of *Woman Who Watches Over the World,* p. 92.

Wilson Library Bulletin, April, 1995, Maureen Delaney-Lehman, review of *The Book of Medicines,* p. 47.

Women's Review of Books, February, 1996, Heid E. Erdrich, review of *Dwellings* and *Solar Storms,* pp. 11-12.

World Literature Today, summer, 1986, Robert L. Berner, review of *Seeing through the Sun,* pp. 506-507; autumn, 1989, Robert L. Berner, review of *Savings,* p. 723; spring, 1994, Robert L. Berner, review of *The Book of Medicines,* pp. 407-408; fall, 1996, Robert L. Berner, review of *Solar Storms,* p. 1007.

*   *   *

HOLLAND, Isabelle (Christian) 1920-2002
(Francesca Hunt)

OBITUARY NOTICE—See index for *SATA* sketch: Born June 16, 1920, in Basel, Switzerland; died February 9, 2002, in New York, NY. Copywriter, publicist, and novelist. Holland wrote more than forty novels. About half of them were for children or young adults, and it is for these works that she is chiefly remembered. Holland was often cited for the authenticity of her teenage characters and the realism reflected in her fictional worlds. Her topics were the serious issues that affect young people's lives, and they were often controversial. *Cecily* is the story of an overweight and wretchedly unhappy girl at a boarding school where the most popular students were the attractive, athletic, and congenial ones; it was originally marketed as an adult novel because the "young adult" genre had not yet come into common use. *Amanda's Choice* relates the story of an emotionally neglected girl who misbehaves to attract her father's attention. *The Man without a Face* is about a similarly marginalized boy, who turns to his tutor for solace and healing; the implication of a homosexual relationship alarmed some adult readers and critics, but led others to praise Holland for confronting real-life issues; the novel was later adapted as a film starring Mel Gibson. In books like these, Holland sent a message that misery need not be permanent, that problems can be solved, and young people can triumph over their troubles. She was nominated for a National Book Award for another realistic look at young adult life, *Of Love and Death and Other Journeys,* and received the Ott Award of the Church and Synagogue Library Association for the *Abbie's God Book.* Holland also penned more than twenty novels for adult readers. Early in her career she had worked as an advertising copywriter and a publicity director for New York City publishers. Some of her work appeared under the pseudonym Francesca Hunt.

OBITUARIES AND OTHER SOURCES:

PERIODICALS

New York Times, March 9, 2002, p. A14; March 14, 2002, p. A2.

HOOVER, H(elen) M(ary) 1935-

Personal

Born April 5, 1935, in Stark County, OH; daughter of Edward Lehr (a teacher) and Sadie (a teacher; maiden name, Schandel) Hoover. *Education:* Attended Mount Union College and Los Angeles County School of Nursing. *Religion:* Protestant.

Addresses

Home—9405 Ulysses Ct., Burke, VA 22015.

Career

Writer.

Member

Smithsonian Institution, Washington, DC, Children's Book Guild.

Awards, Honors

Child Study Association of America Children's Book of the Year, and American Library Association (ALA) Best Books for Young Adults designation, both 1974, both for *The Lion's Cub;* ALA Best Books for Young Adults designation, 1981, Ohioana Award, 1982, and ALA Best of the Best 100 Books of the Past 25 Years designation, 1994, all for *Another Heaven, Another Earth;* Central Missouri State College Award for outstanding contribution to children's literature, 1984; Parents Choice Honor Award, 1987, for *Orvis;* ALA Best Books for Young Adults designation, Enoch Pratt Library "Youth to Youth Books List" designation, and Parents Choice Honor Award, all 1988, and Library of Congress best books for children designation, and *Social Education* notable children's trade book designation, both 1989, all for *The Dawn Palace;* Parents Choice Gold Medal, 1995, for *The Winds of Mars.*

Writings

Children of Morrow, Four Winds Press (New York, NY), 1973.

The Lion's Cub, Four Winds Press (New York, NY), 1974.

Treasures of Morrow, Four Winds Press (New York, NY), 1976.

The Delikon, Viking (New York, NY), 1977.

The Rains of Eridan, Viking (New York, NY), 1977.

The Lost Star, Viking (New York, NY), 1979.

The Return to Earth, Viking (New York, NY), 1980.

This Time of Darkness, Viking (New York, NY), 1980.

Another Heaven, Another Earth, Viking (New York, NY), 1981, reprinted, 2002.

The Bell Tree, Viking (New York, NY), 1982.

The Shepherd Moon: A Novel of the Future, Viking (New York, NY), 1984.

(Contributor) Aileen Pace Nilsen and Kenneth L. Donelson, editors, *Literature for Today's Young Adults* (textbook), Scott, Foresman (Reading, MA), 1985.

(With Janice Antczak) *Science Fiction: The Mythos of a New Romance,* Neal-Schuman (New York, NY), 1985.

(Contributor) *Innocence and Experience: Essays and Conversations on Children's Literature* (textbook), Lothrop (New York, NY), 1987.

Orvis, Viking (New York, NY), 1987, reprinted, 2002.

Anatomy of Wonder: A Critical Guide to Science Fiction, Bowker (New York, NY), 1987.

The Dawn Palace: The Story of Medea, Dutton (New York, NY), 1988.

Away Is a Strange Place to Be, Dutton (New York, NY), 1990.

Only Child, Dutton (New York, NY), 1992.

The Winds of Mars, Dutton (New York, NY), 1995.

The Whole Truth—and Other Myths: Retelling Ancient Tales, National Gallery of Art (Washington, DC), 1996.

(Contributor) Sandy Asher, editor, *But That's Another Story: Famous Authors Introduce Popular Genres,* Wallace & Co. (New York, NY), 1996.

(Contributor) *The Big Book for Our Planet,* Dutton (New York, NY), 2000.

Contributor to *Language Arts, Children's Literature Association Quarterly,* and *Top of the News.* Author's work included in the Kerlan Collection, University of Minnesota.

H. M. Hoover

Sidelights

A respected writer of fantasy and science fiction for young adults, H. M. Hoover is the author of such novels as *The Lost Star, This Time of Darkness,* and *The Dawn Palace: The Story of Medea.* Praising Hoover for creating interesting, believable female protagonists with unique qualities, an essayist for *St. James Guide to Science-Fiction Writers* noted, "In Hoover's fiction we find provocative images of scientific concepts and a liberating experience for the human spirit."

In her novel *This Time of Darkness,* two children in an underground community are shunned due to their ability to read, and make their escape to a new life where their skills will be valued. Published in 1995, *The Winds of Mars* focuses on Annalyn, a teen whose position as the daughter of Mars' president puts her in danger after a civil war erupts. Mind-transfer computer implants, android parents, and political intrigue combine to make *The Winds of Mars* "a fast-paced SF adventure" characterized by "quirky, well-thought-out details" and a "distinctive setting," according to a *Publishers Weekly* reviewer. *The Shepherd Moon* finds thirteen-year-old Merry attempting to counter the efforts of an alien plotting to take over planet Earth. Through her growing reliance on her grandfather's help, Merry comes to terms with her relationship with her parents while she also proves victorious against her extraterrestrial enemy. Citing the underlying message of *The Shepherd Moon* as "an exploration of the uses of power and privilege and the consequences of overcrowding on Earth," a *St. James Guide to Young Adult Writers* contributor maintained that this focus is found in many of Hoover's novels for young readers.

Hoover expressed her thoughts on writing in this genre in *Horn Book:* "Writing science fiction is far easier than writing historical fiction. The author isn't limited to what really happened or is supposed, by reputable authority, to have happened. You can make up your own world, your own self-authenticated details, and so long as you stay true to yourself, no one can contradict you. It is the 'staying true to yourself' part that may give you problems—that and the telling detail that serves to fix the science or character or relationship in the mind. I am never sure if the detail will have the same weight for the reader as it does for me."

Born in 1935, Hoover was raised in the Midwest, and took to science fiction at an early age. "My parents were both amateur naturalists," she explained in *Language Arts.* "They could identify most plants, birds, and animals." The family's library reflected this interest in science and natural history, and provided inspiration to the future writer. "I began writing the sort of stories I write for the simple reason that they are the type of stories I liked best when I was a child," the author added.

Hoover includes "hard" science in her science fiction, and avoids technical jargon due to the fact that it quickly goes out of style. "When one writes about an alien

world," she explained in *St. James Guide to Science-Fiction Writers,* ". . . . [the reader] must be told how and why it functions, and the telling must have consistency or all is lost. It must also be part of the story and not an inventory of facts. As a child I resented authors who ignored known facts (or facts they established within their fantasy) to make their plots work. I suspect them at first of ignorance and later, of contempt for their readers. It is still done and I still have those suspicions."

Biographical and Critical Sources

BOOKS

Gallo, Donald R., editor, *Speaking for Ourselves: Autobiographical Sketches by Notable Authors of Books for Young Adults,* National Council of Teachers of English, 1990.

St. James Guide to Science-Fiction Writers, 4th edition, St. James Press (Detroit, MI), 1996.

St. James Guide to Young Adult Writers, 2nd edition, St. James Press (Detroit, MI), 1999.

Something about the Author Autobiography Series, Volume 8, Gale (Detroit, MI), 1989.

PERIODICALS

Booklist, May 15, 1992, Karen Hutt, review of *Only Child,* p. 1682; August, 1995, Carolyn Phelan, review of *The Winds of Mars,* p. 1940.

Book Report, September-October, 1995, Jo Clarke, review of *The Winds of Mars,* p. 1940.

Horn Book, September-October, 1988, pp. 591-592.

Language Arts, April, 1980; September, 1982.

Publishers Weekly, April 6, 1992, review of *Only Child,* p. 66; June 26, 1995, review of *The Winds of Mars,* p. 107.

School Library Journal, July, 1992, Lucinda Snyder Whitehurst, review of *Only Child,* p. 73; April, 1995, review of *The Dawn Palace,* p. 36; August, 1995, Susan L. Rogers, review of *The Winds of Mars,* p. 140.

Top of the News, fall, 1982.

*　　　　*　　　　*

HUBBELL, Patricia 1928-

Personal

Born July 10, 1928, in Bridgeport, CT; daughter of Franklin H. (a watershed manager) and Helen Osborn Hubbell (a housewife; maiden name, Osborn); married Harold Hornstein (a newspaper editor), March 10, 1954; children: Jeffrey, Deborah. *Education:* University of Connecticut, B.S., 1950. *Politics:* Independent. *Religion:* Unitarian Universalist. *Hobbies and other interests:* Painting, crafts, gardening, reading, horses.

Addresses

Home—90 Norton Rd., Easton, CT 06612. *E-mail*—PatHubbell@kidspoet.com.

A series of richly metaphorical poems celebrating the garden, Patricia Hubbell's **Black Earth, Gold Sun** *is written from the perspective of both people and plants, with watercolor illustrations by Mary Newell DePalma.*

Career

Newtown Bee, Newtown, CT, reporter, 1950-51; *Westport Town Crier,* Westport, CT, reporter, 1951-54; *Bridgeport Sunday Post,* Bridgeport, CT, horse and dog columnist, 1958-68; freelance writer specializing in gardening and nature, 1968-88.

Member

Authors Guild.

Awards, Honors

Nick, Jr. Magazine Best Books of the Year list, Oppenheim Toy Group Gold Medal, Bank Street College Best Books of the Year list all for *Bouncing Time. Parents Magazine* Best Books of the Year list, American Booksellers Association Kids' Pick of the Lists for *Wrapping Paper Romp.* Bank Street College Best Books of the Year, 1999, Parenting Magazine Reading Magic Award, 1999, both for *Sidewalk Trip. A Grass Green Gallop* was a finalist for the Sequoyah Oklahoma Children's Book Award.

Writings

The Apple Vendor's Fair, Atheneum (New York, NY), 1963.
8 a.m. Shadows, Atheneum (New York, NY), 1965.

Catch Me a Wind, Atheneum (New York, NY), 1968.
The Tigers Brought Pink Lemonade (poems), illustrations by Ju-Hong Chen, Atheneum (New York, NY), 1988.
A Grass Green Gallop: Poems, illustrations by Ronald Himler, Atheneum (New York, NY), 1990.
(With Bethany Roberts) *Camel Caravan,* illustrations by Cheryl Munro Taylor, Tambourine (New York, NY), 1996.
(With Bethany Roberts) *Eleven Elephants Going Up!,* illustrations by Minh Uong, Whispering Coyote Press (Boston, MA), 1996.
Boo!: Halloween Poems and Limericks, illustrations by Jeff Spackman, Marshall Cavendish (New York, NY), 1998.
Pots and Pans, illustrations by Diane de Groat, HarperFestival (New York, NY), 1998.
Wrapping Paper Romp, illustrations by Jennifer Plecas, HarperFestival (New York, NY), 1998.
Earthmates: Poems, illustrations by Jean Cassels, Marshall Cavendish (New York, NY), 1999.
Pig Picnic, illustrations by Nadine Bernard Westcott, Golden Books (New York, NY), 1999.
Sidewalk Trip, illustrations by Mari Takabayashi, HarperFestival (New York, NY), 1999.
Bouncing Time, illustrations by Melissa Sweet, HarperCollins (New York, NY), 2000.
Black Earth, Gold Sun: Poems, illustrations by Mary Newell DePalma, Marshall Cavendish (New York, NY), 2001.
City Kids: Poems, illustrations by Teresa Flavin, Marshall Cavendish (New York, NY), 2001.
Sea, Sand, Me!, illustrations by Lisa Campbell Ernst, HarperCollins (New York, NY), 2001.
Pig Parade, illustrations by Nadine Bernard Westcott, Golden Books (New York, NY), 2002.
Rabbit Moon, illustrations by Wendy Watson, Marshall Cavendish (New York, NY), 2002.
Black All Around, illustrations by Don Tate, Lee & Low (New York, NY), 2003.

Work in Progress

Picture Books.

Sidelights

Patricia Hubbell writes children's books and poetry. She once told *SATA* that her work reflects the delight she feels when "playing with words, thoughts and dreams" as well as the pleasure she derives from her "surroundings." She related that although she had worked as a journalist and reporter for many years, she first began writing books when she was at home with her children, often using the kitchen table as her office while they played on the floor. Hubbell writes mostly rhyming verse, short poems that are often accompanied by illustrations. For example, *The Tigers Brought Pink Lemonade* is a set of twenty-one poems, accompanied by graphic illustrations that combine with the collection to create a "picture book," noted Betsy Hearne in the *Bulletin for the Center of Children's Books.*

Pots and Pans, a story about a toddler emptying out kitchen cupboards to accompanying rhymes and sounds was another one of Hubbell's rhyming picture books, "skillfully epitomizing the boundless inquisitiveness of toddlers" in a "lively impromptu performance," noted a *Kirkus Reviews* critic. Hubbell's rhymes and de Groat's accompanying illustrations make *Pots and Pans* a "fine candidate for a lap-sit story," said John Peters in *School Library Journal.* Another toddler is the focus of Hubbell's *Wrapping Paper Romp,* in which a series of rhyming couplets describes the child's antics as he tears apart a brightly-wrapped present. Carolyn Phelan, writing in *Booklist,* described this story as a "book that young children will enjoy opening again and again."

Critics have noted the realistic quality of Hubbell's writing, especially when she is recreating the world of young children. Although the characters in Hubbell's writing have no names and she mentions no specific places, critics have consistently remarked on the concrete nature of Hubbell's writing and her ability to present the child's viewpoint. In *Sidewalk Trip,* the tale of a little girl and her mother's trip to the ice-cream truck, Hubbell's writing and the accompanying illustrations are "almost jet-propelled by enthusiasm," said a critic in *Kirkus Reviews.* In *Earthmates,* Hubbell focuses

Hubbell's energetic poems about childhood days living and playing in the city also touch on troubling subjects such as homelessness and crime. (From City Kids, *illustrated by Teresa Flavin.)*

on animals, writing thirty-five poems about various creatures, including minnows, deer, elephants, and even barnacles. Barbara Chatton of *School Library Journal* was especially appreciative of the realistic illustrations as well as vivid images invoked by Hubbell's writing, characterizing the work as a "lovely collection." And Hazel Rochman, writing in *Booklist,* noted that "the rhythm and sound of the very short lines reinforce the sense of the wild, astonishing creatures." In *Bouncing Time,* Hubbell tells the story of a baby's trip to the zoo with her mother. The "vibrant" illustrations and "playfulness of the text" make this book a "romp to read any time of day," said Marta Segal in a *Booklist* review. Again, Hubbell was praised for the powerfully realistic portrayal of the events in her book, with a *Publishers Weekly* critic writing that the "mom and child almost seem to dance—and readers will want to join in" this "slice of pure pleasure."

The tone of Hubbell's *City Kids* is slightly different from her earlier works, this time focusing on children playing in the city. Although the poems focus on the fun they are having, the book is tinged with sadness, mentioning the mugging of a friend's grandmother. Once again, although there is no specific city or even neighborhood mentioned, Hubbell writes a "concrete poem" from the "child's viewpoint," said Hazel Rochman in *Booklist.*

In *Black Earth, Gold Sun* Hubbell "describes, discovers, and celebrates" the garden in a series of poems that are written in a "contemplative mood," according to Nina Lindsay in *School Library Journal.* The metaphors are rich and the poems are written in the voices of "children, adults, and even plants" said *Booklist*'s Gillian Engberg, noting that the "sophisticated language" and comparisons evoked by Hubbell are "powerful and exciting."

Hubbell told *SATA,* "I think the reason I began to love poetry so much is because my mother and grandmother read a great deal of poetry to me when I was very young. The wonderful word-pictures and rhythms got into my head at an early age—and never left. I began writing poems myself when I was in the third grade. Sometimes, I would write them out on the cardboard pieces that came with shirts returned from the laundry and draw pictures around the edges.

"One of the first poems I remember doing was about a fox that I saw in the meadow across from our house. He was leaping in the sun and his coat was shining gold and red. He looked like a dancer! Many years later, that same fox put in an appearance in a poem that was published in my first book, *The Apple Vendor's Fair.* He was still dancing, but now I knew that what he was really doing was going after a mouse, the poem was titled, "Prey Ballet."

"I think writing poems is a lot like gardening. When you garden you choose a plant, set it in place, move it if it's not doing well, weed out unwanted plants, tend it carefully and try for something beautiful. When you write poetry you do the same thing—only with words!"

Biographical and Critical Sources

PERIODICALS

Booklist, December 1, 1998, Carolyn Phelan, review of *Wrapping Paper Romp,* p. 670; September 15, 1999, Kathy Broderick, review of *Sidewalk Trip,* p. 268; March 15, 2000, Hazel Rochman, review of *Earthmates: Poems,* p. 383; April 1, 2000, Marta Segal, review of *Bouncing Time,* p. 469; March 1, 2001, Hazel Rochman, review of *City Kids,* p. 1283; May 1, 2001, Carolyn Phelan, review of *Sea, Sand, Me!,* p. 1694; September 15, 2001, Gillian Engberg, review of *Black Earth, Gold Sun,* p. 220.

Bulletin of the Center for Children's Books, January, 1989, Betsy Hearne, review of *The Tigers Brought Pink Lemonade,* p. 124.

Children's Book Review Service, October, 1998, review of *Boo! Halloween Poems and Limericks,* p. 15.

Horn Book Guide, fall, 1999, Sheila M. Geraty, review of *Sidewalk Trip,* p. 234.

Kirkus Reviews, June 1, 1998, review of *Pots and Pans,* p. 812; June 1, 1999, review of *Sidewalk Trip,* p. 883.

Publishers Weekly, May 8, 2000, review of *Bouncing Time,* p. 220.

School Library Journal, fall, 1989, Nancy A. Gifford, review of *The Tigers Brought Pink Lemonade,* p. 78; June, 1998, John Peters, review of *Pots and Pans,* p. 109; September, 1998, Judith Constantinides, review of *Boo! Halloween Poems and Limericks,* p. 192; February, 1999, Blair Christolon, review of *Wrapping Paper Romp,* p. 84; March, 2000, Barbara Chatton, review of *Earthmates: Poems,* p. 226; July, 2000, Janet M. Bair, review of *Bouncing Time,* p. 80; July, 2001, Alicia Eames, review of *City Kids,* p. 94; August, 2001, Genevieve Ceraldi, review of *Sea, Sand, Me!,* p. 154; November, 2001, Nina Lindsay, review of *Black Earth, Gold Sun,* p. 146.

OTHER

Patricia Hubbell Web Site, http://www.kidsport.com (May 31, 2002).

*   *   *

HUNT, Francesca
See HOLLAND, Isabelle (Christian)

*   *   *

HUNTER, Kristin
See LATTANY, Kristin (Eggleston) Hunter

J

JOHNSON, Paul Brett 1947-

Personal

Born May 19, 1947, in Mousie, KY; son of Paul and Harriet (Slone) Johnson. *Hobbies and other interests:* Travel.

Addresses

Home—444 Fayette Park, Lexington, KY 40508. *E-mail*—paulbrett@aol.com.

Career

Freelance artist and writer, 1974—.

Member

Society of Children's Book Writers and Illustrators.

Awards, Honors

School Library Journal best book award, 1993, for *The Cow Who Wouldn't Come Down,* and 1996 for *Lost;* 100 Notable Books for Reading and Sharing, New York Public Library, 1993, for *The Cow Who Wouldn't Come Down,* 1999, for *Old Dry Frye,* and 2001, for *Fearless Jack;* Kentucky Bluegrass Award, 1995, for *The Cow Who Wouldn't Come Down,* and 1999, for *A Perfect Pork Stew;* Notable Book Award, *Smithsonian* magazine, 1997, for *Farmers' Market;* Children's Choice selection, International Reading Association/Children's Book Council, 2000, for *The Pig Who Ran a Red Light;* California Young Readers Medal, 2000, for *Lost.*

Writings

SELF-ILLUSTRATED

The Cow Who Wouldn't Come Down, Orchard (New York, NY), 1993.
Frank Fister's Hidden Talent, Orchard (New York, NY), 1993.

Paul Brett Johnson

(Coauthor) Celeste Lewis, *Lost,* Orchard (New York, NY), 1996.
Farmers' Market, Orchard (New York, NY), 1997.
A Perfect Pork Stew, Orchard (New York, NY), 1998.
Old Dry Frye: A Deliciously Funny Tall Tale, Scholastic (New York, NY), 1999.
The Pig Who Ran a Red Light, Orchard (New York, NY), 1999.

Bearhide and Crow, Holiday House (New York, NY), 2000.

Mr. Persnickety and Cat Lady, Orchard (New York, NY), 2000.

(Adapter) *Fearless Jack,* McElderry (New York, NY), 2001.

The Goose Who Went Off in a Huff, Orchard (New York, NY), 2001.

Jack Outwits the Giants, McElderry (New York, NY), 2002.

ILLUSTRATOR

Margaret Hodges, reteller, *Saint Patrick and the Peddler,* Orchard (New York, NY), 1993.

Megan McDonald, *Insects Are My Life,* Orchard (New York, NY), 1995.

Tres Symour, *Too Quiet for These Old Bones,* Orchard (New York, NY), 1997.

George Ella Lyon, *A Traveling Cat,* Orchard (New York, NY), 1998.

James Still, *An Appalachian Mother Goose,* University Press of Kentucky (Lexington, KY), 1998.

Megan McDonald, *Bedbugs,* Orchard (New York, NY), 1999.

Megan McDonald, *Reptiles Are My Life,* Orchard (New York, NY), 2001.

Kathi Appelt, *The Best Kind of Gift,* HarperCollins (New York, NY), 2003.

Work in Progress

Little Bunny Foo Foo, publication expected in 2004.

Sidelights

Paul Brett Johnson writes and illustrates whimsical picture books for young readers that draw upon his fascination with the folklore of his native Kentucky. Born in 1947, Johnson grew up in the town of Mousie, a place which "lies in the heart of the Appalachian mountain chain," as he explained in a biography published on the *Visiting Authors* Web site. "Here I grew up alongside coal trains, annual hog killings, Sunday dinners on the ground, and a whole lot of whittling and spitting. I often spent long summer days with my grandfather, helping him tend to his honeybees and listening to his doubtful tales."

Johnson was interested in art at an early age, and even enjoyed private lessons. As a young man, he studied art at the University of Kentucky, and often dreamed of writing a children's book. His occasional attempts, sent off to publishers, met with rejection but Johnson eventually set his mind to the task and began researching the field in earnest. He read books about children's publishing, read children's books himself, and sent away for catalogs from publishers to study their offerings. His next try, *The Cow Who Wouldn't Come Down,* was a hit with critics and readers alike when it was published in 1993. The title character is Gertrude, an irrepressible bovine on Miss Rosemary's farm who can fly and even play the piano. Other children's books, including Marga-

ret Hodges' *Saint Patrick and the Peddler* and the self-illustrated *Frank Fister's Hidden Talent,* soon followed.

Over the next few years, Johnson was offered jobs illustrating the work of other authors. These projects included *Lost,* a book coauthored with Celeste Lewis. The story centers around a little girl and her pet beagle, Flag. Flag disappears on a family camping trip in Arizona's Tonto National Forest. A search party is formed, notices are posted, false leads are pursued, and finally the little girl's father tells her that they must give up. She is heartbroken, but then a prospector finds an emaciated Flag and a happy ending results. Johnson's illustrations tell two narratives: one is from the little girl's viewpoint, depicting the worried search efforts, while the other page shows Flag off by himself, chasing rabbits, having dog adventures, but then growing thinner and howling at the moon in loneliness. A *Publishers Weekly* contributor noted that this "juxtaposition creates almost unbearable tension," but praised the story's "cathartic ending that, like the rest of this dramatic story, rings true in its fullness of feeling."

Johnson also illustrated Tres Symour's *Too Quiet for These Old Bones,* about four children banished to a day at their grandmother's house. They dread the experience, believing they will have to be quiet, but are surprised to learn that their granny craves a bit of noise and excitement. "Johnson uses earth-tone acrylics framed in a clean white border to suggest a cozy house with patterned wallpaper," noted a reviewer for *Publishers Weekly.* Another lost pet is the subject of the images Johnson created for George Ella Lyon's *A Traveling Cat.* A little girl recounts the story of finding her cat at the drive-in theater. She takes it home and names her Bouvie, short for Boulevard. Bouvie has kittens, but then floods come to the area, and the cat disappears. The little girl is sad, but realizes that her cat was a roamer when she found her. Her mother remarks that Bouvie might have found another family, to which the narrator responds that she would tell them, if she could, "'Don't expect to keep her. She's a traveling cat.'" One of Bouvie's kittens stays behind at the little girl's house. *Booklist's* Carolyn Phelan commended the story as "a quiet picture book with a rural American setting." A contributor to *Publishers Weekly* praised the "deeply brooding illustrations" that Johnson created for the tale, including one of the little girl and her neighbors looking for the community's lost pets. They stand near a rickety bridge and "swollen water reveals the grief-stricken narrator standing alone near a cluster of worried neighbors," the reviewer noted.

The sixth book that Johnson wrote and illustrated for young readers was *A Perfect Pork Stew.* The story centers around two stock characters from Russian folklore, the fearsome witch Baba Yaga and Ivan the Fool. In his version, the little boy Ivan takes his wheelbarrow full of dirt past Baba Yaga's house on a day that has started off badly for the witch. The witch has misplaced her eyeglasses, and without them she believes she spies a pig in Ivan's wheelbarrow. She tricks Ivan into giving it to her, trading it for a supposed "magic" turnip, and then tries to make perfect pork stew from her treasure. When Baba Yaga samples the broth from the cooking pot, she says it tastes like dirt. Ivan suggests adding the turnip, trading it for Baba Yaga's "magic cabbage." The cabbage eventually goes into the pot as well, but Baba Yaga suffers a stomachache from her concoction, and Ivan escapes unscathed. "The humor is reinforced through Johnson's comic illustrations," remarked Denise Anton Wright, writing in *School Library Journal.* "Johnson's tale entertains," noted a *Kirkus Reviews* contributor, who liked the "fuzzy pastel drawings [that] keep the wart-nosed witch from being too scary."

Food also plays a central role in Johnson's next work, *Old Dry Frye: A Deliciously Funny Tall Tale.* The story takes place in Troublesome Creek, where the preacher, Old Dry Frye, loves fried chicken to the point of gluttony. One evening he dines with a local family who are serving his favorite meal and chokes on a chicken bone. The family hides his body, but someone finds it and hides it again. In the end, Old Dry Frye is said to wander the hills around Troublesome Creek, looking for another fried chicken dinner. "The tall-tale mood emanates from Johnson's scenes of Appalachia and the exaggerated expressions of its inhabitants," remarked a *Publishers Weekly* contributor, while *Booklist* reviewer

Based on Richard Chase's 1943 retelling of an Appalachian folktale, **Fearless Jack** *tells the story of a boy who earns a reward after defeating several wild varmints. (Illustrated by Johnson.)*

Marta Segal liked the way both images and text "respectfully show the humor and silliness of the rural community and the story without being condescending."

Miss Rosemary's farm and Gertrude the cow made a return appearance for Johnson's 1999 book, *The Pig Who Ran a Red Light.* In this story, George the pig imitates everything Gertrude does, even attempting to drive. He is stopped by the sheriff for the traffic violation of the title and is cautioned that "it's a known fact pigs don't drive." Still, George keeps trying to copy Gertrude, and Miss Rosemary has a talk with him. "Just because Gertrude is a silly nincompoop, doesn't mean you have to be one too," she tells him. Finally Miss Rosemary enlists Gertrude's help: the special bovine begins acting like pig, which seems to set George straight. In the end Magnolia, Miss Rosemary's goose, starts to oink. "Johnson's animated illustrations are wonderfully expressive and filled with zany animal antics," declared *Booklist*'s Lauren Peterson. *School Library Journal* critic Barbara Elleman found that "the characters' well-executed expressions and postures bring life to this affable tale," and a *Publishers Weekly* reviewer predicted that Gertrude's behavior "will likely strike a chord of recognition for those who live in the shadow of accomplished older siblings."

Johnson began drawing more heavily on Appalachian lore for his works, as evidenced by *Bearhide and Crow.* Part of the story comes from a bit of Appalachian lore that holds that a crow can be taught to speak. Amos, a young farmer, likes to trade things with friends and neighbors. One day he gives away the blue-ribbon gourds belonging to his wife in an unwise trade with the scheming Sam Hankins. In return, Amos gets an old bearskin which Sam claims has magical powers. After scaring his wife by wearing the rug, Amos overhears a pair of robbers discussing the gold they have hidden in Sam's rain barrel. Amos then concocts a ruse, telling Sam that a crow has told him about the stash of gold, and then wheedles Sam into a trade involving the bearskin and the crow in return for the gold. "Johnson's bright, earth-toned illustrations capture the locale and humor of the story," stated *Booklist*'s Catherine Andronik. A *Publishers Weekly* contributor liked the way the figures "wear their personalities on their faces; Amos has a smooth, unpretentious grin, while both Sam and his spotted hound dog sneer with greed."

A more universal situation is the reason behind the conflict between neighbors in Johnson's *Mr. Persnickety and Cat Lady.* The Cat Lady has thirty-seven cats at her house, and Mr. Persnickety wants them gone. He tries various means, including turning the water hose on them, playing a recording of dozens of barking dogs, and even calling the Humane Society. When the animal investigators come to Cat Lady's house, they give her an award instead. Fed up, Cat Lady plants some mice in Mr. Persnickety's house, which then quickly multiply in number. Some even make a nest in his teddy bear, prompting *School Library Journal*'s Meghan R. Malone to note that "the look on the man's face at this indignity is worth the price of the book."

Magnolia returns in Johnson's *The Goose Who Went Off in a Huff.* Magnolia longs to be a mother and makes various attempts to become a parent to something. She steals George's rubber ducky, tries to hatch Easter eggs, and at one point Gertrude and George both try to disguise themselves as little goslings to soothe Magnolia's frustrated feelings. Miss Rosemary tells Magnolia that her time will come, but Magnolia's feelings are hurt, and she stalks off. Miss Rosemary searches for her next day, even checking to see if she joined the traveling circus. But she finds the sad Magnolia in a shed, coaxing her out when the circus leaves behind a baby elephant who needs a parent. *School Library Journal*'s Rosalyn Pierini called the book "a read-aloud full of personality. This gem is destined to be a storytime favorite," while *Booklist* writer Connie Fletcher commended the way "Johnson makes his heroine look huffy and haughty and put-upon."

Johnson has been especially indebted to his grandfather's tall tales and the stories culled from a children's book, *The Jack Tales.* These Appalachian-based stories were collected by folklorist Richard Chase and published in 1943. Johnson adapted one of these stories for *Fearless Jack.* Loosely based on the "Jack and the Varmints" story, itself a variant of the Grimm Brothers' *The Brave Little Tailor,* this story features a boastful youngster who must leave his impoverished home to find work. On his way, he slaps some yellow jackets that have buzzed him and then writes "Fearless Jack Killed Ten at a Whack" on his cap. This attracts the attention of the sheriff of a ghost town that has been overrun with wild varmints, and the sheriff offers a large monetary reward to Jack if he can rid the town of the pests. By sheer luck, Jack manages to trap a wild boar, a grizzly bear, and even a unicorn. Shelley Townsend-Hudson, writing in *Booklist,* observed that "Johnson's colorful, comical, sturdy pictures are just as energetic as the story," while *School Library Journal* writer Wendy Lukehart commended the "impressionistic layering of strokes and dabs of color, a style that infuses each scene with vitality and warmth." A *Horn Book* contributor commended both text and images, describing the latter as "sweeping landscapes whose spare detail is a fine foil for the humorous characterizations and the delicious perils that ensue."

Biographical and Critical Sources

BOOKS

Johnson, Paul Brett, *The Pig Who Ran a Red Light,* Orchard (New York, NY), 1999.
Lyon, George Ella, *A Traveling Cat,* Orchard (New York, NY), 1998.

PERIODICALS

Booklist, May 1, 1994, Julie Corsaro, review of *Frank Fister's Hidden Talent,* p. 1608; March 1, 1995, Stephanie Zvirin, review of *Insects Are My Life,* p. 1249; April 1, 1996, Carolyn Phelan, review of *Lost,* p. 1372; March 15, 1997, Kay Weisman, review of *Farmers' Market,* p. 1247; November 15, 1997, Lauren Peterson, review of *Too Quiet for These Old Bones,* p. 567; March 15, 1998, Diane Janoff, review of *A Perfect Pork Stew,* p. 1249; November 15, 1998, Carolyn Phelan, review of *A Traveling Cat,* p. 596; March 1, 1999, GraceAnne A. DeCandido, review of *An Appalachian Mother Goose,* p. 1218; May 1, 1999, Lauren Peterson, review of *The Pig Who Ran a Red Light,* p. 1599; December 1, 1999, Marta Segal, review of *Old Dry Frye: A Deliciously Funny Tall Tale,* p. 707; April 1, 2000, Catherine Andronik, review of *Bearhide and Crow,* p. 1469; May 15, 2001, Connie Fletcher, review of *The Goose Who Went Off in a Huff,* p. 1758; July, 2001, Shelley Townsend-Hudson, review of *Fearless Jack,* p. 2014.
Bulletin of the Center for Children's Books, March, 1996, Roger Sutton, review of *Lost,* p. 231; April, 1997, Pat Mathews, review of *Farmers' Market,* p. 286.
Horn Book, May-June, 1993, Ann A. Flowers, review of *The Cow Who Wouldn't Come Down,* p. 319; March-April, 1995, Margaret A. Bush, review of *Insects Are My Life,* p. 185; September, 2001, review of *Fearless Jack,* p. 602.
Kirkus Reviews, January 1, 1998, review of *A Perfect Pork Stew,* p. 57; January 15, 1999, review of *The Pig Who Ran a Red Light,* p. 146; August 1, 1999, review of *Old Dry Frye,* p. 1228.
Publishers Weekly, March 29, 1993, review of *The Cow Who Wouldn't Come Down,* p. 53; August 23, 1993, review of *Saint Patrick and the Peddler,* p. 70; December 20, 1993, review of *Frank Fister's Hidden Talent,* p. 71; January 16, 1995, review of *Insects Are My Life,* p. 454; March 11, 1996, review of *Lost,* p. 63; August 11, 1997, review of *Too Quiet for These Old Bones,* p. 401; February 23, 1998, review of *A Perfect Pork Stew,* p. 76; July 27, 1998, review of *A Traveling Cat,* p. 76; March 29, 1999, review of *The Pig Who Ran a Red Light,* p. 103; October 11, 1999, review of *Old Dry Frye,* p. 76; February 28, 2000, review of *Bearhide and Crow,* p. 79; April 23, 2001, review of *The Goose Who Went Off in a Huff,* p. 76; May 28, 2001, review of *Fearless Jack,* p. 87.
School Library Journal, April, 1996, Ruth Semrow, review of *Lost,* p. 112; June, 1997, Judith Gloyner, review of *Farmers' Market,* p. 94; April, 1998, Denise Anton Wright, review of *A Perfect Pork Stew,* p. 100; March, 1999, Barbara Elleman, review of *The Pig Who Ran a Red Light,* p. 177; September, 1999, Maryann H. Owen, review of *Old Dry Frye,* p. 214; May, 2000, Margaret Bush, review of *Bearhide and Crow,* p. 146; November, 2000, Meghan R. Malone, review of *Mr. Persnickety and Cat Lady,* p. 125; July, 2001, Rosalyn Pierini, review of *The Goose Who Went Off in a Huff,* p. 83; July, 2001, Wendy Lukehart, review of *Fearless Jack,* p. 95.

OTHER

Visiting Authors, http://www.visitingauthors.com (December 9, 2001), biography of Paul Brett Johnson.

JUSTER, Norton 1929-

Personal

Born June 2, 1929, in Brooklyn, NY; son of Samuel H. (an architect) and Minnie (Silberman) Juster; married Jeanne Ray (a graphic designer), August 15, 1964; children: Emily. *Education:* University of Pennsylvania, B. of Arch., 1952; University of Liverpool, graduate study, 1952-53. *Avocational interests:* gardening, bicycling, reading.

Addresses

Home—259 Lincoln Ave., Amherst, MA 01002. *Agent*—Sterling Lord Literistic, 1 Madison Ave., New York, NY 10010.

Career

Juster & Gugliotta, New York, NY, architect, 1960-68; Pratt Institute, Brooklyn, NY, professor of environmental design, 1960-70; Juster-Pope-Frazier Associates, Shelburne Falls, MA, architect, 1969—; Hampshire College, Amherst, MA, professor of design, 1970-1992, Emeritus Professor of Design, 1992—. *Military service:* U.S. Naval Reserve, Civil Engineer Corps, active duty, 1954-57.

Awards, Honors

Fulbright fellowship, 1952-53; Ford Foundation grant, 1960-61; National Academy of Arts and Sciences award for outstanding achievement, 1968-69; Guggenheim fellowship, 1970-71; George G. Stone Center for Children's Books Seventh Recognition of Merit, 1971.

Writings

FOR CHILDREN

The Phantom Tollbooth, illustrated by Jules Feiffer, Random House (New York, NY), 1961.
The Dot and the Line: A Romance in Lower Mathematics, Random House (New York, NY), 1963, reprinted, 1977.
Alberic the Wise, illustrated by Domenico Gnoli, Pantheon (New York, NY), 1965.
Otter Nonsense, Philomel (New York, NY), 1982.
As: A Surfeit of Similes, illustrated by David Small, Morrow (New York, NY), 1989.

FOR ADULTS

Stark Naked, Random House (New York, NY), 1970.
So Sweet to Labor: Rural Women in America, 1865-1895, Viking (New York, NY), 1979, new edition published as *A Woman's Place: Yesterday's Women in Rural America,* Fulcrum Publishing (Golden, CO), 1996.

Adaptations

The Dot and the Line was produced as an animated short film by Metro-Goldwyn-Mayer (MGM) in 1965; *The*

Norton Juster

Phantom Tollbooth was produced as an animated full-length feature film by MGM in 1970, and as an opera for OperaDelaware in 1995.

Sidelights

Norton Juster is a practicing architect, a talented wordsmith, and a popular writer of juvenile books. His story *The Phantom Tollbooth* made the *New York Times* list of best-selling books for children in 1962, and in 1966 was included in that paper's list of the fifty best children's books of the previous five years. Diane Manuel commented in the *New York Times Book Review* that "this is a book that could help sell youngsters on the devilish delights of well-turned phrases."

Juster was born on June 2, 1929, in Brooklyn, New York. There he attended Public School #99 and James Madison High School before studying architecture at the University of Pennsylvania. In 1952 he won a Fulbright fellowship, which took him to England, where he studied city planning at the University of Liverpool.

From 1954 to 1957 Juster served in the United States Navy; his assignments included legal officer, personnel officer, and education officer in the Civil Engineering

Juster's classic story The Phantom Tollbooth *follows bored Milo who finds a magic tollbooth in his bedroom and through it embarks on a quest to the Mountains of Ignorance to rescue twin Princesses Rhyme and Reason. (Illustrated by Jules Feiffer.)*

Corps, helping to build airfields in Morocco and Newfoundland. Following his military service he worked as an architect. In 1959, he began writing stories as a form of relaxation, but soon was hooked.

Juster is best known for *The Phantom Tollbooth,* which has been compared to *Alice in Wonderland* as well as been called "a modern day *Pilgrim's Progress*" in *Who's Who in Children's Literature.* In this tale, the Tollbooth appears mysteriously in the room of a bored schoolboy named Milo. Milo drives his pedal car past the Tollbooth into a fantasy world, the Kingdom of Wisdom, where all is not well. The brothers Azaz, king of the word-oriented Dictionopolis, and Mathemagician, king of the numbers-oriented Digitopolis, are allegories for subjects Milo has studied in school. The brothers were once able to get along well together, with the intercession of their sisters Rhyme and Reason. But when the sisters once could not decide whether words or numbers were the most important, they found themselves banished to a Castle in the Air. Like Dorothy in *The Wizard of Oz,* Milo enlists the aid of a cast of humorous and allegorical characters as he sets off on his quest to free the princesses. With the help of the "Official Which," Tock, the very literal clock, and the bug named Humbug, Milo rescues the Princesses Rhyme and Reason from the Mountains of Ignorance and brings meaning back to words and numbers. Reviewing a 1996 edition of the book, Carol A. Burdbridge stated in *Book Report* that it "has become a modern classic." Burdbridge further mentioned that the book "has delighted young and old with Juster's humorous writing style and his wonderful play on

words." A contributor for *St. James Guide to Young Adult Writers* noted that *The Phantom Tollbooth* "has proven to be timeless." The same contributor further explained: "This fantasy novel presents a rare combination of a convincing, well-rounded secondary world with a rollicking use of wordplay that proves both entertaining and provocative."

Juster is also the author of *The Dot and the Line: A Romance in Lower Mathematics,* about a sensible straight line falling in love with a frivolous dot and trying to woo her away from her current beau, a lazy squiggle. Reviewing a 2001 reprint of that popular title, a writer for *Publishers Weekly* called the tale "poignant yet humorous," and promised that "much merriment will be had by all before the hero gets his girl." His *Alberic the Wise and Other Journeys* is a group of three stories reminiscent of fairy tales; it was chosen by the American Institute of Graphic Arts as one of the ten children's books to appear in their "Fifty Books of the Year" show in 1966. A fable on the nature of wisdom and success, *Alberic the Wise* tells of a wisdom-seeking simple country youth and his adventures in discovering knowledge. A reviewer for *Publishers Weekly* felt the tale was "overlong" for a picture book, but praised Juster's "compelling prose, elevated without being lofty," which "will draw in advanced readers." "Ultimately," wrote the same contributor, "this multi-faceted and sophisticated tale about art, wisdom and life itself may find its most appreciative audience with adults." Juster's other books include *Otter Nonsense,* published in 1982, and *As: A*

In this work, geometric figures are the subject of an unusual love story. Cover illustration by George Paul Schmidt.

"A beautiful testament to the ongoing American search for freedom."
—*Ken Burns*

A Woman's Place

Yesterday's Women in Rural America

NORTON JUSTER

Drawing on information gleaned from articles, letters, and poems of the era between the Civil War and the turn of the century, Juster's **A Woman's Place** *traces the duality between the battle for women's rights and the still-sanctified view of the homemaker and mother.*

Surfeit of Similes, which *School Library Journal* reviewer Michael Cart called "as clever as paint!"

Through his well-received books for young readers, Juster has developed a reputation as a "talented and ingenious" wordsmith, Cart noted.

In addition to his books for young readers, Juster has also written two adult titles, including *So Sweet to Labor: Rural Women in American 1865-1895.* An Emeritus Professor of Design at Hampshire College in Amherst, Massachusetts, Juster is also an architect at his firm, Juster-Pope-Frazier Associates, work which takes much of his creative energy.

Biographical and Critical Sources

BOOKS

Beacham's Guide to Literature for Young Adults, Volume 5, Beacham Publishing (Osprey, FL), 1991, pp. 2471-2476.
St. James Guide to Fantasy Writers, St. James Press (Detroit, MI), 1996.
St. James Guide to Young Adult Writers, 2nd edition, St. James Press (Detroit, MI), 1999.
Twentieth-Century Children's Writers, 3rd edition, St. James Press (Detroit, MI), 1989.
Twentieth-Century Young Adult Writers, 1st edition, St. James Press (Detroit, MI), 1994.
Who's Who in Children's Literature, Schocken Books (New York, NY), 1968.

PERIODICALS

Atlantic Monthly, December, 1961, p. 120.
Booklist, January 15, 1993, p. 908.
Book Report, September-October, 1996, Carol A. Burdbridge, review of *The Phantom Tollbooth,* p. 39.
Chicago Tribune, December 17, 1961, p. 7.
Commonweal, November 10, 1961, p. 186.
Horn Book, September-October, 1989, pp. 638-639; March-April, 1993, p. 231.
Language Arts, September, 1989, p. 566.
Library Journal, January 15, 1962, p. 332.
Los Angeles Times Book Review, March 26, 1989, p. 8; February 14, 2001, p. E2.
Nation, September 8, 1979, pp. 187-188.
New Statesman, December 21, 1962, p. 907.
New Yorker, November 18, 1961, pp. 222-224; December 4, 1965, p. 236; September 24, 1979, pp. 162-163.
New York Herald Tribune, November 12, 1961, p. 14.
New York Review of Books, December 9, 1965, p. 38.
New York Times Book Review, November 12, 1961, p. 35; November 14, 1982, p. 43; Diane Manuel, review of *As: A Surfeit of Similes,* October 22, 1989, p. 35.
Opera News, July, 1995, p. 50.
Publishers Weekly, April 28, 1989, p. 75; November 30, 1992, review of *Alberic the Wise,* p. 55; January 8, 2001, "Great Comebacks," p. 69.
Saturday Review, January 20, 1962, p. 27; January 22, 1966, p. 45.
School Library Journal, November, 1983, p. 55; April, 1989, Michael Cart, review of *As: A Surfeit of Similes,* pp. 112-113; November, 1994, p. 98.
Spectator, November 9, 1962, p. 732.
Time, December 15, 1961, p. 89; March 22, 1971.
Times Literary Supplement, November 23, 1962, p. 892; November 24, 1966, p. 1089.
Washington Post Book World, February 3, 1980, p. 10; May 14, 1989, p. 15; January 10, 1993, p. 11.*

K

KARK, Nina Mary
See BAWDEN, Nina (Mary Mabey)

*   *   *

KEEFER, Janice Kulyk 1952-

Personal

Born June 2, 1952, in Toronto, Ontario, Canada; daughter of Joseph (a dentist) and Natalie (a designer) Kulyk; married Michael Keefer (a university professor); children: Thomas, Christopher. *Education:* University of Toronto, B.A. (with honors); University of Sussex, M.A., D.Phil.

Addresses

Office—"Slapsie," University of Guelph, Guelph, Ontario N1G 2W1, Canada. *Agent*—Dean Cooke, Livingston-Cooke Agency, 457A Danforth Ave., Toronto, Ontario M4K 1P1, Canada. *E-mail*—jkeefer@uoguelph.ca.

Career

Writer. University of Guelph, Guelph, Canada, professor.

Awards, Honors

Fiction winner, CBC Radio Literary Competition, for "Mrs. Putnam at the Planetarium," and "The Wind"; National Magazine Award for poetry, for "The Fields"; Malahat Long Poem Prize, for "Isle of Demons"; Governor General's Award for non-fiction shortlist, for *Under Eastern Eyes;* Governor General's Award for fiction shortlist, for *The Green Library.*

Writings

The Paris-Napoli Express, Oberon (Ottawa, Canada), 1986.

White of Lesser Angels, Ragweed Press (Charlottetown, Canada), 1986.
Transfigurations, Ragweed Press (Charlottetown, Canada), 1987.
Under Eastern Eyes: A Critical Reading of Canadian Maritime Fiction, University of Toronto Press (Toronto, Canada), 1987.
Constellations, Random House (Toronto, Canada), 1988.
Reading Mavis Gallant, Oxford University Press (Toronto, Canada), 1989.
Travelling Ladies, Random House (Toronto, Canada), Morrow (New York, NY), 1991.

Janice Kulyk Keefer

Rest Harrow, HarperCollins (Toronto, Canada), 1992.

The Green Library (novel), HarperCollins (Toronto, Canada), 1996.

(Editor, with Danielle Schaub and Richard E. Sherwin) *Precarious Present/Promising Future?: Ethnicity and Identities in Canadian Literature,* Magnes Press (Jerusalem, Israel), 1996.

Marrying the Sea, Brick (London, Canada), 1998.

(Editor, with Solomea Pavlychko) *Two Lands, New Visions: Stories from Canada and Ukraine,* Coteau Books (Regina, Canada), 1998.

Honey and Ashes: A Story of Family (memoir), HarperCollins (Toronto, Canada), 1998.

Anna's Goat (for children), illustrated by Janet Wilson, Orca Book Publishers (Victoria, Canada), 2001.

Author of short stories "Mrs. Putnam at the Planetarium" and "The Wind," and poems "The Fields" and "Isle of Demons." Contributor of short stories and poetry to anthologies, including *More Stories by Canadian Women,* Oxford University Press, 1987; *Poetry by Canadian Women,* Oxford University Press, 1989; *Canadian Short Stories,* Oxford University Press, 1991; *Without a Guide: Canadian Women's Travel Adventures,* McFarlane, Walter & Ross, 1994; *The New Oxford Book of Canadian Short Stories in English,* Oxford University Press, 1995; and *Writing Away and Writing Home: PEN Canada Anthologies,* McClelland & Stewart, 1997. Contributor of articles and reviews to magazines and journals, including *University of Toronto Quarterly, Studies in Canadian Literature, Dalhouse Review, Canadian Literature, Books in Canada, British Journal of Canadian Studies,* and *International Journal of Canadian Studies.*

Sidelights

Janice Kulyk Keefer told *SATA:* "*Anna's Goat* is my first book for children, and the experience of writing and editing in this genre was one of the most challenging and rewarding of my writing life. I have published novels, short stories, and poetry—all 'for grownups'—but I've never before collaborated on a book with a close friend (the illustrator Janet Wilson) about the life of a mutually and equally close friend—the Anna of the title!

"*Anna's Goat* grew out of a dear friend's childhood stories about war and dislocation, and out of the impact of traumatic world events. I was profoundly moved by seeing television and newspaper photos of child refugees during the recent war in Kosovo. My friend Anna's life has been one of initial hardship, danger, and loss; through the love of her parents and the generous heart of the wartime community in which she first found herself, she was able not only to survive, but to nourish her imagination and spirit. Anna's childhood story has a particularly crucial resonance in the torn, uncertain world we are all a part of today; I would like to think that children disturbed by images and stories of the painful lives of other children around the ever-shrinking globe could find in *Anna's Goat* possibilities of love, hope, and healing.

"My interest in dislocation and the remaking of immigrant lives stems from the fact that my family members were lucky enough to escape from Poland to Canada just before World War II, a story I explore in a recent memoir, *Honey and Ashes: A Story of Family,* and in fictionalized form in the novel *The Green Library.*"

Biographical and Critical Sources

PERIODICALS

Booklist, March 15, 2001, Helen Rosenberg, review of *Anna's Goat,* p. 1404.

Publishers Weekly, December 18, 2000, review of *Anna's Goat,* p. 77.

School Library Journal, May, 2001, Sheilah Kosco, review of *Anna's Goat,* p. 126.

OTHER

University of Guelph, http://www.uoguelph.ca/ (June 2, 2002).*

*   *   *

KETCHUM, Liza 1946-
(Liza Ketchum Murrow)

Personal

Born June 17, 1946, in Albany, NY; daughter of Richard M. (a writer and historian) and Barbara (a sheep farmer and conservationist) Ketchum; married John H. Straus (a pediatrician), March 25, 1996; children: Derek Murrow, Ethan Murrow. *Education:* Sarah Lawrence College, B.A., 1968; Antioch Graduate School of Education, M.Ed., 1971. *Hobbies and other interests:* Music, canoeing, traveling, gardening, environmental conservation.

Addresses

Home and office—7 Arthur Terrace, Watertown, MA 02472. *Agent*—Virginia Knowlton, Curtis Brown, Ltd., 10 Astor Pl., New York, NY 10003. *E-mail*—lizaketchum@earthlink.net.

Career

Writer and teacher. Meetinghouse School, Marlboro, VT, founder and director, 1973-78; participant in the Vermont Council of the Arts Artist in Education Program, 1988-91; faculty member at Antioch Graduate School of Education, Emerson College, Simmons College, and Vermont College; teacher, Cape Cod Writers' Conference; leader of writing workshops and seminars. Water testing volunteer, Charles River Watershed Association; South Vermont AIDS Project Buddy.

Member

Authors Guild, Society for Children's Book Writers and Illustrators, Teachers and Writers Collaborative, PEN New England Children's Book Caucus, Vermont Nature Conservancy (past board member); Massachusetts Au-

Liza Ketchum

dubon Society, Massachusetts Trustee of Reservations, Massachusetts Climate Action Network, Watertown Citizens for Environmental Safety.

Awards, Honors

Virginia Jefferson Cup Honor Book, Virginia Library Association, 1988, Dorothy Canfield Fisher Award List (Vermont), and Iowa Teen Award List, all for *West against the Wind;* Best Book for Young Adults selection, American Library Association (ALA), 1990, and Mark Twain Award list (Missouri), 1991-92, both for *Fire in the Heart;* Mark Twain Award list (Missouri), and Sequoyah Award list (Oklahoma), both 1993-94, and Colorado State Book Award list, 1995, all for *The Ghost of Lost Island;* Best Books for the Reluctant Reader selection, ALA, 1994, Sequoyah Award (Oklahoma), 1995, and "Project 21" Book selection, 1996, all for *Twelve Days in August;* Pick of the List selection, American Booksellers Association, 1996, and Notable Trade Book in the Field of Social Studies, National Council for the Social Studies/Children's Book Council, 1997, both for *The Gold Rush;* Lambda Award nomination, "Project 21" Book selection, 1998, and Books for the Teen Age selection, New York Public Library, 1998, all for *Blue Coyote;* Best Books for Young Adults selection, ALA, 2001, for *Into a New Country: Eight Remarkable Women of the West;* Sequoyah Award List

(Oklahoma), and Children's Crown Award, both 2002, both for *Orphan Journey Home.*

Writings

MIDDLE-GRADE NOVELS

(As Liza Ketchum Murrow) *Dancing on the Table,* illustrated by Ron Himler, Holiday House (New York, NY), 1990.
(As Liza Ketchum Murrow) *The Ghost of Lost Island,* Holiday House (New York, NY), 1991.
(As Liza Ketchum Murrow) *Allergic to My Family,* Holiday House (New York, NY), 1992.
Orphan Journey Home (first published in serial form), illustrated by C. B. Mordan, Avon Books (New York, NY), 2000.

YOUNG ADULT NOVELS

(As Liza Ketchum Murrow) *West against the Wind,* Holiday House (New York, NY), 1987.
(As Liza Ketchum Murrow) *Fire in the Heart* (companion book to *West against the Wind*), Holiday House (New York, NY), 1989.
(As Liza Ketchum Murrow) *Twelve Days in August,* (sequel to *Fire in the Heart*), Holiday House (New York, NY), 1993.
Blue Coyote, Simon & Schuster (New York, NY), 1997.

OTHER

(With Casey Murrow) *Children Come First: The Inspired Work of English Primary Schools,* American Heritage Press (New York, NY), 1971.
(As Liza Ketchum Murrow) *Good-Bye, Sammy* (picture book), illustrated by Gail Owens, Holiday House (New York, NY), 1989.
(As Liza Ketchum Murrow) *Lolly Cochran, Veterinarian* ("Women Scientists" series), photographs by Marsha Schwarz, Teachers' Laboratory (Brattleboro, VT), 1989.
(As Liza Ketchum Murrow) *Susan Humphris, Geologist* ("Women Scientists" series), Teachers' Laboratory (Brattleboro, VT), 1989.
The Gold Rush (companion volume to the PBS television series "The West"), introduction by Ken Burns, Geoffrey C. Ward, and Stephen Ives, Little, Brown (Boston, MA), 1996.
Into a New Country: Eight Remarkable Women of the West, Little, Brown (Boston, MA), 2000.

Contributor to periodicals, including *Society of Children's Book Writers and Illustrators Bulletin, Country Journal, New England Gardener, Teachers and Writers Collaborative,* and *Scholastic Storyworks.* Contributor of essay, "Starting with Characters," to *Old Faithful: Eighteen Writers Present Their Favorite Writing Assignments,* Teachers and Writers Collaborative (New York, NY), 1995, and short story, "Sables Mouvant," to *On the Edge,* edited by Lois Duncan, Simon & Schuster (New York, NY), 2000.

Work in Progress

A historical novel for young readers, "based on an ancestor who was a Paced midwife and healer in Vermont in the late-eighteenth century"; a picture book "about my Middle Eastern neighborhood just outside Boston, Massachusetts."

Sidelights

Liza Ketchum once told *SATA* that she has been writing stories ever since she was a young girl, often writing in her room at night, after she was in bed and supposed to be asleep. Her abiding interest in writing and the encouragement of her parents, coupled with her own experiences as an educator working with young children, are what led Ketchum to begin writing books in earnest, beginning with her first young adult work, *West against the Wind.*

This novel tells the story of Abigail and her family's trek across the country to California in 1850. Ketchum uses the tale to describe the dangers and monotony of the trip through Abigail's eyes. Ketchum's next book for young adults, *Fire in the Heart,* focuses once again on a young girl. This time, fourteen-year-old Molly O'Connor is searching for a connection between the death of her mother ten years ago and her ancestors, including Abby

from *West against the Wind.* Another novel set in the nineteenth century by Ketchum is *Orphan Journey Home,* the story of Jesse and her older brother, Moses, as they struggle to protect their younger siblings on their journey back to Kentucky after their parents die of an illness in southern Illinois. Writing in *School Library Journal,* Catherine T. Quattlebaum noted that although the action of the book is often "cruel," the narrative makes a "riveting adventure" as Jesse makes her way home to her grandmother's house. According to the author, *"Orphan Journey Home* reached millions of readers through publication in 120 newspapers nationwide."

Other young adult works by Ketchum include *Twelve Days in August,* a story for older teens that deals with the prejudice often faced by homosexuals. The focus of this tale is Alex Beekman, a young soccer player who struggles to find a place for himself after he moves into a new town. At the same time, Alex is also trying to establish his sexual identity. Alex's story is continued in a sequel to *Twelve Days in August,* titled *Blue Coyote.* In this book, Alex has become a star soccer player and has moved to Los Angeles, where he is in search of his lost friend, Tito. The work was nominated for a Lambda Literary Award. Reviewing *Blue Coyote* for *School*

Published as one of three companion volumes to the documentary **The West** *by Ken Burns, Stephen Ives, and Geoffrey C. Ward,* **The Gold Rush** *offers young readers the story of the bold individuals who struck out in search of riches in the mid-nineteenth century.*

Library Journal, Claudia Morrow called it a "solid addition" to the collection of other coming-out fiction.

In addition to her young adult books, Ketchum has also written nonfiction books, including *Into a New Country: Eight Remarkable Women of the West.* A collection of biographies focusing on women who challenged the norms of their times, the book includes vignettes on women such as Susan Magoffin, Lotta Crabtree, and Bethenia Owens-Adair. All the women featured in the book were either born in or traveled to the American West during the nineteenth century, and Carol Fazioli noted in *School Library Journal* that Ketchum's research efforts are evident in "the depth of characterization." Another nonfiction title by Ketchum is *The Gold Rush,* a book based on the PBS television series "The West" and written as a juvenile companion to the television show. Reviewing the work for *School Library Journal,* George Gleason called the work "a real achievement ... sure to inform, entertain, and invite further investigation."

Biographical and Critical Sources

PERIODICALS

Booklist, August, 1996, Hazel Rochman, review of *The Gold Rush,* p. 1897; June 1, 1997, Hazel Rochman, review of *Blue Coyote,* p. 1685; June 1, 2000, Hazel Rochman, review of *Orphan Journey Home,* p. 1894; January 1, 2001, Hazel Rochman, review of *Into a New Country: Eight Remarkable Women of the West,* p. 935.

Horn Book, September-October, 1993, Patty Campbell, review of *Twelve Days in August,* p. 571.

Horn Book Guide, fall, 1997, Peter D. Sieruta, review of *Blue Coyote,* p. 314.

Lambda Book Report, September-October, 1993, Nancy Garden, review of *Twelve Days in August,* p. 18.

Publishers Weekly, March 8, 1991, review of *The Ghost of Lost Island,* p. 74; March 16, 1992, review of *Allergic to My Family,* p. 80; May 10, 1993, review of *Twelve Days in August,* p. 73; September 2, 1996, review of *The Gold Rush,* p. 132-133.

School Library Journal, October, 1996, George Gleason, review of *The Gold Rush,* p. 156; May, 1997, Claudia Morrow, review of *Blue Coyote,* pp. 134-135; August, 2000, Catherine T. Quattlebaum, review of *Orphan Journey Home,* p. 182; September, 2000, Leda Schubert, "Breakfast Serials," pp. 38-39; December, 2000, Carol Fazioli, review of *Into a New Country: Eight Remarkable Women of the West,* p. 162.

OTHER

Liza Ketchum Web Site, http://www.lizaketchum.com (May 29, 2002).

*   *   *

KNIGHT, Hilary 1926-

Personal

Born November 1, 1926, in Hempstead, Long Island, NY; son of Clayton (an artist and writer) and Katharine (an artist and writer; maiden name, Sturges) Knight. *Education:* Attended Art Students League, New York, NY.

Addresses

Home—300 East 51st St., New York, NY 10022.

Career

Artist, illustrator, designer, and writer. Began art career after his drawings were published in *House and Garden* and *Mademoiselle.* Has designed theater posters for numerous Broadway plays, including *Sugar Babies, Half a Sixpence, Irene,* and *Mike.* Contributing artist for *Vanity Fair* magazine. Artwork has been included in the seventh annual exhibition of "The Original Art: Celebrating the Fine Art of Children's Book Illustration," at the Major Eagle Gallery. *Military service:* U. S. Navy, 1944-46.

Writings

SELF-ILLUSTRATED

ABC, Golden Press (New York, NY), 1961.

(Reteller) *Hilary Knight's "Mother Goose,"* Golden Press (New York, NY), 1962.

Angels and Berries and Candy Canes (also see below), Harper (New York, NY), 1963.

A Christmas Stocking Story (also see below), Harper (New York, NY), 1963.

A Firefly in a Fir Tree (also see below), Harper (New York, NY), 1963.

(With Clement Clarke Moore) *Christmas Nutshell Library* (contains Knight's *Angels and Berries and Candy Canes, A Christmas Stocking Story, A Firefly in a Fir Tree,* and Moore's *The Night before Christmas*), Harper (New York, NY), 1963.

Where's Wallace?, Harper (New York, NY), 1964, new edition, 2000.

Sylvia, the Sloth: A Round-About Story, Harper (New York, NY), 1969.

The Circus Is Coming, Golden Press (New York, NY), 1978.

(Reteller) *Hilary Knight's "Cinderella,"* Random House (New York, NY), 1978, new edition, 2001.

(Reteller) *Hilary Knight's "The Owl and the Pussy-Cat"* (based on poem by Edward Lear), Macmillan (New York, NY), 1983, revised edition, 2001.

(Reteller) *Hilary Knight's "The Twelve Days of Christmas,"* Macmillan (New York, NY), 1987.

"ELOISE" BOOKS; ILLUSTRATOR

Kay Thompson, *Eloise: A Book for Precocious Grown Ups,* Simon & Schuster (New York, NY), 1955, expanded edition published as *Kay Thompson's Eloise: The Absolutely Essential Edition* (with new material by Marie Brenner), 1999.

Kay Thompson, *Eloise in Paris,* Simon & Schuster (New York, NY), 1957, new edition, 1999.

Kay Thompson, *Eloise at Christmas Time,* Random House (New York, NY), 1958, new edition, Simon & Schuster (New York, NY), 1999.

Wallace the orangutan escapes from the zoo whenever he can and ends up hidden somewhere in each of the panoramas featured in **Where's Wallace?,** *Knight's self-illustrated picture book for sharp-eyed young readers.*

Kay Thompson, *Eloise in Moscow,* Simon & Schuster (New York, NY), 1959, fortieth anniversary edition published as *Kay Thompson's Eloise in Moscow,* 2000.

Kay Thompson, *Eloise's Guide to Life: How to Eat, Dress, Travel, Behave & Stay Six Forever* (excerpts from the four previous Eloise books, with six new illustrations), Simon & Schuster (New York, NY), 2000.

ILLUSTRATOR

Patrick Gordon Campbell, *Short Trot with a Cultured Mind through Some Experiences of a Humorous Nature,* Simon & Schuster (New York, NY), 1955.

Jan Henry, *Tiger's Chance,* Harcourt (New York, NY), 1957.

Betty MacDonald, *Mrs. Piggle-Wiggle,* Lippincott (Philadelphia, PA), 1957.

Betty MacDonald, *Hello, Mrs. Piggle-Wiggle,* Lippincott (Philadelphia, PA), 1957.

Betty MacDonald, *Mrs. Piggle-Wiggle's Magic,* Lippincott (Philadelphia, PA), 1957.

Jeremy Gury, *Wonderful World of Aunt Tuddy,* Random House (New York, NY), 1958.

Dorothea W. Blair, *Roger: A Most Unusual Rabbit,* Lippincott (Philadelphia, PA), 1958.

Peg Bracken, *The I Hate to Cook Book,* Harcourt (New York, NY), 1960, expanded edition published as *The Compleat I Hate to Cook Book,* Harcourt (San Diego, CA), 1986.

Evelyn Gendel, *Tortoise and Turtle,* Simon & Schuster (New York, NY), 1960.

Cecil Maiden, *Beginning with Mrs. McBee,* Vanguard (New York, NY), 1960.

Cecil Maiden, *Speaking of Mrs. McCluskie,* Vanguard (New York, NY), 1962.

Margaret Stone Zilboorg, *Jeremiah Octopus,* Golden Press (New York, NY), 1962.

Peg Bracken, *The I Hate to Housekeep Book,* Harcourt (New York, NY), 1962.

Marie Le Prince de Beaumont, *Beauty and the Beast,* translated from the French by Richard Howard, Macmillan (New York, NY), 1963, new edition, Simon & Schuster (New York, NY), 1990.

Evelyn Gendel, *Tortoise and Turtle Abroad,* Simon & Schuster (New York, NY), 1963.

Clement Clarke Moore, *The Night before Christmas,* Harper (New York, NY), 1963.

Charles Dickens, *Captain Boldheart* [and] *The Magic Fishbone,* Macmillan (New York, NY), 1964.

Peg Bracken, *I Try to Behave Myself: Peg Bracken's Etiquette Book,* Harcourt (New York, NY), 1994.

Ogden Nash, *The Animal Garden: A Story,* M. Evans (New York, NY), 1965.

Charlotte Zolotow, *When I Have a Little Girl* (also see below), Harper (New York, NY), 1965.

Charlotte Zolotow, *When I Have a Son,* Harper (New York, NY), 1967, combined edition published as *When I Have a Little Girl; When I Have a Little Boy,* Callaway (New York, NY), 2000.

Judith Viorst, *Sunday Morning: A Story,* Harper (New York, NY), 1968, new edition, Atheneum (New York, NY), 1992.

Margaret Fishback, *A Child's Book of Natural History* (poems), Platt & Munk (New York, NY), 1969.

Patricia M. Scarry, *The Jeremy Mouse Book: Stories,* American Heritage Press (New York, NY), 1969.

Nathaniel Benchley, *Feldman Fieldmouse: A Fable,* Harper (New York, NY), 1971.

Duncan Emrich, compiler, *The Book Wishes and Wishmaking,* American Heritage Press (New York, NY), 1971.

Janice Udry, *Angie,* Harper (New York, NY), 1971.

Adelaide Holl, *Most-of-the-Time Maxie: A Story,* Xerox Family Education Services (Stamford, CT), 1974.

Robert Kraus, *I'm a Monkey,* Windmill Books (New York, NY), 1975.

Marilyn Sachs, *Matt's Mitt,* Doubleday (Garden City, NY), 1975.

Steven Kroll, *That Makes Me Mad!,* Pantheon (New York, NY), 1976.

Lucille Ogle and Tina Thoburn, *The Golden Picture Dictionary,* Golden Press (New York, NY), 1976.

Robert Kraus, *The Good Mousekeeper,* Windmill Books (New York, NY), 1977.

Jay Williams, *Pettifur: A Story,* Four Winds Press (New York, NY), 1977.

(With others) Norma Farber, *Six Impossible Things before Breakfast,* Addison-Wesley (Reading, MA), 1977.

Night Light Calendar 1977, Windmill Books (New York, NY), 1977.

Alice Bach, *Warren Weasel's Worse Than Measles,* Harper (New York, NY), 1980.

Val Schaffner, *Algonquin Cat: A Story,* Delacorte Press (New York, NY), 1980, new edition, Wings Books (New York, NY), 1995.

Stephanie Calmenson, compiler, *Never Take a Pig to Lunch; and Other Funny Poems about Animals,* Doubleday (Garden City, NY), 1982.

Robert Kraus, *Screamy Mimi,* Simon & Schuster (New York, NY), 1983.

Ellen Weiss, *Telephone Time: A First Book of Telephone Do's and Don'ts,* Random House (New York, NY), 1986.

Natalie Standiford, *The Best Little Monkeys in the World,* Random House (New York, NY), 1987.

Lee Bennett Hopkins, editor, *Side by Side: Poems to Read Together,* Simon & Schuster (New York, NY), 1988.

Narcissa G. Chamberlain, *The Omelette Book,* David R. Godine (New York, NY), 1990.

Lee Bennett Hopkins, compiler, *Happy Birthday: Poems,* Simon & Schuster (New York, NY), 1991.

Nancy Robinson, *Ten Tall Soldiers,* Holt (New York, NY), 1991.

Contributor to periodicals, including *Mademoiselle, House and Garden, Gourmet, McCall's, Woman's Home Companion,* and *Vanity Fair.*

Adaptations

Eloise motion picture and merchandising rights were purchased by the Itsy Bitsy Entertainment Company, June, 1999, with plans to develop both a motion picture and prime-time television series.

Sidelights

Hilary Knight is a well-respected author and multitalented illustrator with a worldwide reputation for creating unique and delightful characters in both words and pictures. Reviewers, such as a critic for *Bulletin of the Center of Children's Books,* have called his creations "ebullient and imaginative."

Very prolific and hardworking, Knight has written and illustrated nine books for children, illustrated nearly sixty other books for both children and adults, breathed new life into a number of classic folktales with his illustrations, and designed theater posters promoting several very popular Broadway plays.

Although he has illustrated books written by such famous children's authors as Betty MacDonald, Charlotte Zolotow, and Judith Viorst, Knight is probably most identified as the illustrator of Kay Thompson's enormously popular *Eloise* books. A longtime favorite character of children and adolescents, Eloise is a feisty six-year-old girl who lives in one of New York City's classic hotels, The Plaza, with her English nanny, her dog, Weenie, and her turtle, Skipperdee. In Thompson's original book, *Eloise,* and her three follow-up stories, *Eloise in Paris, Eloise at Christmas Time,* and *Eloise in Moscow,* Knight has charmed readers with Eloise's delightful antics and funny adventures.

In a *McCall's* interview with Cynthia Lindsay, Kay Thompson discussed her search for an illustrator for her idea of *Eloise* and shared her first impression of Knight: "A Princetonian young man, shy, gentle and soft-spoken, came in. He seemed terribly impressed with me, which naturally impressed me terribly with him. I noticed his hands, which were slim and artistic, and thought that was a step in the right direction. So I wrote twelve lines on a piece of paper and handed it to him. 'I'm going to write this book,' I said. 'I'll leave this with you. If you're interested, get in touch with me.' Then I spoke a few words of Eloisiana and left."

Thompson continued: "That Christmas I received a card from Knight. It was an interesting, beautifully executed and highly stylized picture of an angel and Santa Claus, streaking through the sky on a Christmas tree. On the end of the tree, grinning a lovely grin, her wild hair standing on end, was Eloise. It was immediate recognition on my part. There she was. In person. I knew at once Hilary Knight had to illustrate the book."

In a review of *Eloise,* a writer for *Books of Wonder News* noted: "Knight's two-color drawings bring Eloise to life better than words alone ever could. You and your favorite youngster can follow her high-speed travels up and down the elevator ... through formal dining rooms ... across the lobby ... up the stars—zigzagging merrily across the page as she goes."

Reviewers and readers have wondered for years who was Knight's inspiration for his vision of Thompson's Eloise. While many people guessed a number of famous children, including the late Judy Garland's now famous daughter Liza Minnelli, Knight remarked to Edith Newhall of *New York* that his inspiration for the character was really a family acquaintance. "Her look— her little face—was based on a friend of my parents," Knight told Edith Newhall, "a friendly woman named Eloise Davison who was a food writer for the *Herald Tribune.* She was in her fifties when I knew her, so I imagined what she looked like as a little girl."

Knight and Thompson's Eloise character is so solidly linked with The Plaza Hotel that Knight was Plaza manager Ivana Trump's obvious choice to design a day care-type suite in the hotel where guests could leave their children. Demonstrating his versatility, Knight also created children's menus sprinkled with drawings of Eloise for the Plaza restaurants.

In 1999, nearly a year after Thompson's death and forty years since Eloise made her debut, Simon & Schuster gave the mischievous imp a new lease on life, publishing new editions of all the books in the series, some thirty-five years after Thompson had taken most of them off the market.

Insisting that "she's still six, no matter what," Knight marked Eloise's anniversary with an exhibition of forty years of his art at the Giraffics Gallery in East Hampton, Long Island, drawing on his work for Eloise and others of his more than sixty books. Titled "A Family of Artists," the exhibition ran from July to August, 1999, and also included selections from the work of his mother, Katharine Sturges (a fashion and book illustrator who was strongly influenced by Japanese art), his father, Clayton Knight (a World War I pilot and illustrator who concentrated on aviation subjects), and his late brother, Clayton Knight, Jr.

Commenting on the Eloise "revival" in a recent interview for the *New Yorker,* Knight declared, "Kay and I were like parents to Eloise. We decided that we'd never make her older than six, and that we'd always keep the parents in the background.... And I guess my job now is to continue what Kay might have thought she was doing when she pulled the books in the first place—to protect Eloise."

A critic's-eye view of Hilary Knight from almost forty years ago still rings true of the artist today. The "special world of Hilary Knight," wrote Joan Hess Michel in *American Artist,* is "busy, bright, and full of zest for living. His keen intelligence and perception of the warmth and humor in the world of human beings and animals give his work a special and unique flavor."

Biographical and Critical Sources

BOOKS

Kingman, Lee and others, compilers, *Illustrators of Children's Books, 1957-1966,* Horn Book (Boston, MA), 1968.

PERIODICALS

American Artist, March, 1963, Joan Hess Michel, "The Whimsical Illustrations of Hilary Knight."
Booklist, November 15, 1999, Ilene Cooper, review of *Eloise at Christmas,* p. 638; August, 2001, Shelle Rosenfeld, review of *Hilary Knight's "The Owl and the Pussy-Cat,"* p. 2124; August, 2001, Ilene Cooper, review of *Hilary Knight's "Cinderella,"* p. 2130.
Books of Wonder News, November, 1988, review of *Eloise.*

Bulletin of the Center for Children's Books, April, 1984, review of *Hilary Knight's "The Owl and the Pussy-Cat."*
McCall's, January, 1975, Cynthia Lindsay, "*McCall's* Visits Kay Thompson."
New York, January 16, 1989, Edith Newhall, "Hilary of the Plaza," p. 22.
New Yorker, May 31, 1999, Lauren MacIntyre, "Eloise's Other Parent Gets His Due."
New York Herald, November 12, 1961.
New York Newsday, July 15, 1999, Blake Greene, "Drawing on the Past: *Eloise* Illustrator Discovers Character Is Still in Demand."
New York Times Book Review, November 12, 1961.
Publishers Weekly, May 14, 2001, review of *Hilary Knight's The Owl and the Pussy-Cat,* p. 80.
Saturday Review, October 17, 1964.

OTHER

BookPage, http://bookpage.com/9905bp/hilary_knight.html/ (May, 1999), "Meet the Illustrator: Hilary Knight."
Children's Literature, http://www.childrenslit.com/f_knight/ (October 8, 2001), "A Conversation with Hilary Knight."
Eloise Web Site, http://www.gti.net/iksrog/eloise/hilary_knight/ (October 8, 2001), extensive information about the character and her creators.*

*   *   *

KOVACS, Deborah 1954-

Personal

Born October 2, 1954, in Chicago, IL; daughter of Stanton H. Kovacs (a sales manager) and Judith Genesen (a library association director); adoptive father, Louis Genesen (a business executive); married Nicholas Sullivan; children: Sarah J., Lucy. *Education:* Middlebury College, B.A. (cum laude), 1975. *Politics:* "Eternal optimist."

Addresses

Home—25 Jordan Rd., South Dartmouth, MA 02748.

Career

Children's Television Workshop, New York, NY, 1975-80, began as toy, game, and record developer for *Sesame Street,* became editor of *Sesame Street* magazine; Scholastic, New York, NY, 1980-85, began as magazine editor, became founder and creative director of software division; freelance writer for book, magazine, and computer software publishers, including National Audubon Society, Scholastic, Grosset & Dunlap, Western Publishing, Jim Henson Productions, and Children's Television Workshop; children's book author. Woods Hole Oceanographic Institution, editor of *Ocean Explorer,* 1991-95. Co-founder, Editor in Chief, Turnstone Publishing Group, 1996-2001; vice president of Publishing and Education Center, Walden Media, Boston, MA, 2001—.

Awards, Honors

"Communicating with Children" Award, American Institute of Graphic Arts (AIGA), for *Sesame Street* magazine, 1980; EdPress Award for Best News Story, 1981; National Science Teachers Association/Children's Book Council Outstanding Science Trade Books for Children; American Bookseller's Association "Pick of the List," and Best Science Books for Children, 1997; American Association for the Advancement of Science for *Beneath Blue Waters: Meetings with Remarkable Deep-Sea Creatures;* Best Science Books for Children, 1998, American Association for the Advancement of Science for *The Very First Things to Know about Bears.*

Writings

Frazzle's Fantastic Day, Children's Television Workshop/Western Publishing (Racine, WI), 1980.

(Editor) *Country Cat,* illustrated by Marlies Merk Najaka, McGraw-Hill (New York, NY), 1980.

(Editor) *The Baby Strawberry Book of Baby Farm Animals,* illustrated by Barbara Pickett, McGraw-Hill (New York, NY), 1980.

(Editor) *The Baby Strawberry Book of Pets,* illustrated by Barbara Pickett, McGraw-Hill (New York, NY), 1980.

When Is Saturday?, illustrated by Richard Brown, Children's Television Workshop/Western Publishing (Racine, WI), 1981.

Battle of the Bands, illustrated by Tom Tierney, Western Publishing (Racine, WI), 1987.

A Day Underwater, Scholastic (New York, NY), 1987.

The Hottest Group in Town, illustrated by Tom Tierney, Western Publishing (Racine, WI), 1987.

Moondreamers: The Evening Song, illustrated by Gene Biggs, Western Publishing (Racine, WI), 1988.

Woody's First Dictionary, illustrated by Eve Rose, Grosset & Dunlap (New York, NY), 1988.

(With James Preller) *Meet the Authors and Illustrators: Sixty Creators of Favorite Children's Books Talk about Their Work,* Scholastic (New York, NY), Volume 1, 1991, Volume 2, 1993.

Disney's Chip 'n Dale Rescue Rangers: The Big Cheese Caper, illustrated by Darrell Baker, Western Publishing (Racine, WI), 1991.

The Tooth Fairy Book, illustrated by Laura Lydecker, Running Press (Philadelphia, PA), 1992.

(Adaptor) Muriel Pépin, *Little Bear's New Friend,* illustrated by Marcelle Geneste, Reader's Digest Kids (Pleasantville, NY), 1992.

(Adaptor) Ariane Chottin, *A Home for Little Turtle,* illustrated by Pascale Wirth, Reader's Digest Kids (Pleasantville, NY), 1992.

Brewster's Courage, illustrated by Joe Mathieu, Simon & Schuster (New York, NY), 1992.

Ernie's Neighborhood, illustrated by Joe Ewers, Children's Television Workshop/Western Publishing (Racine, WI), 1993.

Moonlight on the River, illustrated by William Shattuck, Viking (New York, NY), 1993.

All about Dolphins, Third Story Books (Bridgeport, CT), 1994.

All about Whales!, Third Story Books (Bridgeport, CT), 1994.

(With Kate Madin) *Beneath Blue Waters: Meetings with Remarkable Deep-Sea Creatures,* photographs by Larry Madin, Viking (New York, NY), 1996.

Very First Things to Know about Bears, illustrated by Richard Cowdrey, Workman (New York, NY), 1997.

Dive to the Deep Ocean: Voyages of Exploration and Discovery, Raintree Steck-Vaughn (Austin, TX), 2000.

Noises in the Night: The Habits of Bats, Raintree Steck-Vaughn (Austin, TX), 2001.

Off to Sea: An Inside Look at a Research Cruise, Raintree Steck-Vaughn (Austin, TX), 2000.

Also author of computer-based interactive fiction stories for the *Audubon Wildlife Adventure* computer software series published by National Audubon Society; for the "Microzine" series, published by Scholastic; and, with Patricia Relf, *Snooper Troops 2: The Disappearing Dolphin,* for Tom Snyder Productions, published by Spinnaker Software.

Sidelights

Children's book author Deborah Kovacs has penned a number of well-received nonfiction books about the sea. In *Dive to the Deep Ocean: Voyages of Exploration and Discovery,* Kovacs shares with readers how scientists have investigated the great depths of the sea, beginning with early attempts at submersible vessels and continuing on to modern methods of scanning the ocean floor. As she details the development of modern research equipment, the author also spends time discussing the various discoveries scientists have made through the years using different technological advances. Also included are numerous photographs, maps, and diagrams, features that earned praise from critics. Calling the work "a lively look" at the history of ocean research, *School Library Journal* reviewer Frances E. Millhouser recommended *Dive to the Deep Ocean* as "great reading for those interested in ocean work."

In *Off to Sea: An Inside Look at a Research Cruise,* Kovacs explains to young readers all of the operations surrounding an ocean research trip. The author discusses the role each member of the research crew plays while on a daylong expedition. In covering the assignments of crew members, Kovacs explains the equipment the scientists use in researching a thermal vent on the bottom of the ocean as well as what constitutes a successful mission. Reviewing *Off to Sea* in *Booklist,* Shelle Rosenfeld found "the lively, present-tense narrative ... engaging and easy to follow," while *School Library Journal* contributor Frances E. Millhouser called the book "a lively look at oceanography."

Kovacs once told *SATA:* "From the ages of seven to nine, I spent most of my waking hours making tiny figures out of a putty called 'Hold-it' and then inventing scenarios for the little creations to act out. I never thought that the stories I made up would have any life beyond the moment. Enter the author Sydney Taylor (of the *All-of-a-Kind* family books) who materialized in my elementary school library on a winter day in 1964. In her presence and by her example I found a form for my heart's desire. Someday, somehow, I hoped I would become a writer too.

"I stumbled through adolescence and college and arrived at *Sesame Street* in its early days. There I spent the better part of five years perched on a series of just-out-of-the-way stools from where I could watch great and inspired artists at work as they invented puppets (I remember seeing the first Miss Piggy as pieces of a pattern on the worktable of a gifted designer) and brought them to life (the gymnastics that the puppeteers had to go through to make some of the classic *Sesame Street* bits was unbelievable). It was a very creative, exciting time.

"After ten years in New York City, I moved with my family to a beautiful and remote seaside spot. The sudden isolation after years of city living was a shock, and then, finally, an inspiration. In the solitude of our surroundings, I found my voice and have enjoyed giving it expression.

"Several of my books were the result of collaborations with friends. *Brewster's Courage* was born over lunch with my old friend Joe Mathieu. At the beginning of the lunch, he said, 'We should do a book together.' I agreed, because in our *Sesame Street* days we had collaborated happily on a lot of projects, and we both share a love of the music and culture of Southwest Louisiana. As we ate pizza, Joe told me about a trip he had recently taken there. He described the backwoods dance halls he had visited, and a boat ride he took in a swamp. He told me an exciting story about a bike ride on a twenty-mile road with no turnoffs where he was chased by a pack of hungry dogs.

"He paused, and asked, 'What should our book be about?' I knew instantly. 'It should be about your trip to Louisiana, but different,' I said. I sorted out the elements: a bicycle, a dog-chase, Cajun dance halls, the fact that Joe likes to draw animals. What animal fits on a bicycle? A ferret (or better yet, a rare, endangered black-footed ferret, like the ones I learned about when I worked for Audubon). Wait a minute—black-footed ferrets are found *only* in South Dakota. What would it be like if one showed up in a Louisiana swamp? How did I feel when I moved to Massachusetts? Not too great, until I convinced everyone around me that I meant to stay. . . .

"Then and there, I told the story of *Brewster's Courage* to Joe (who, I remember with satisfaction, was amazed). After that, putting the story down on paper was a matter of happy mechanics, characters springing into my imagination just about fully rendered. I even found some 'Hold-it' at a nearby art supply store, and shaped it as I wrote. Since then, I have been convinced that fiction-writing is more than anything the process of receiving gifts from the cosmos, or from life's experiences and observations, internalizing them, altering them alchemically, and retransmitting them.

"*Moonlight on the River* was created as a tribute to a beautiful tidal river, to the mystery of a childhood adventure, and to the work of a talented artist who has depicted the river in all its moods for many years. Bill Shattuck and I are friends and neighbors. His studio looks out on the Slocum River, and he has often made paintings and drawings of it. He and his family spend a lot of time on the river, boating, fishing, and swimming. I live a half mile from the river, and often swim in it, riding the tide in and out as bluefish nip my toes, and loons and great blue herons skid to graceful landings in the water beside me.

"We created the book to capture a moment and turn it into a timeless memory. We began with the story of a nighttime journey made dangerous by a sudden storm. As the story passed back and forth between us, crucial elements were added. Bill placed the character of Joshua Slocum in the book, and introduced the tree with the initials J. S. and the date 1894. As the story progressed, a number of other elements came into play: was Slocum only in the character Will's imagination? If he wasn't real, who carved the initials in the tree? I realized that the boys in the story would grow and change, perhaps always remembering their night on the river, but the river itself would go on rising and falling with the tide, seemingly unchanged. Whether the story really happened or not is unimportant. That it *could* have happened, at any time, to any children, is the point."

Biographical and Critical Sources

PERIODICALS

Booklist, May 1, 1993, Hazel Rochman, review of *Moonlight on the River,* p. 1604; December 1, 1996, Hazel Rochman, review of *Beneath Blue Waters: Meetings with Remarkable Deep-Sea Creatures,* p. 659; October 15, 1999, Hazel Rochman, review of *Dive to the Deep Ocean: Voyages of Exploration and Discovery,* p. 428; March 1, 2000, Shelle Rosenfeld, review of *Off to Sea: An Inside Look at a Research Cruise,* p. 1239.

Kirkus Reviews, June 15, 1992, p. 780.

Publishers Weekly, May 31, 1993, review of *Moonlight on the River,* p. 53.

School Library Journal, September, 1992, Elaine E. Knight, review of *Brewster's Courage,* p. 254; August, 1993, Shirley Wilton, review of *Moonlight on the River,* p. 146; January, 1997, Frances E. Millhouser, review of *Beneath Blue Waters,* p. 128; April, 2000, Frances E. Millhouser, review of *Dive to the Deep Ocean,* p. 151; April, 2000, Frances E. Millhouser, review of *Off to Sea,* p. 151.

L

LATTANY, Kristin (Eggleston) Hunter 1931-
(Kristin Hunter, Kristin Lattany)

Personal

Born September 12, 1931, in Philadelphia, PA; daughter of George Lorenzo (a principal and U.S. Army colonel) and Mabel (a pharmacist and teacher; maiden name, Manigault) Eggleston; married Joseph Hunter (a journalist), 1952 (divorced, 1962); married John I. Lattany, June 22, 1968. *Education:* University of Pennsylvania, B.S. (education), 1951.

Addresses

Agent—Jane Pystel Literary Management, One Union Square West, New York, NY 10003.

Career

Writer. Columnist and feature writer for Philadelphia, PA, edition of *Pittsburgh Courier,* 1946-52; copywriter for Lavenson Bureau of Advertising, Philadelphia, 1952-59, and Werman & Schorr, Inc., Philadelphia, 1962-63; research assistant, University of Pennsylvania, 1961-62; City of Philadelphia, information officer, 1963-64, 1965-66; University of Pennsylvania, Philadelphia, lecturer in English, 1972-79, adjunct associate professor of English, 1981-83, senior lecturer in English, 1983-95. Writer-in-residence, Emory University, 1979.

Awards, Honors

Fund for the Republic Prize, 1955, for television documentary, *Minority of One;* John Hay Whitney fellowship, 1959-60; Philadelphia Athenaeum Award, 1964; National Council on Interracial Books for Children award, 1968, Mass Media Brotherhood Award from National Conference of Christians and Jews, 1969, and Lewis Carroll Shelf Award, 1971, all for *The Soul Brothers and Sister Lou;* Sigma Delta Chi reporting award, 1968; Spring Book Festival Award, 1973,

Kristin Hunter Lattany

Christopher Award, and National Book Award finalist, both 1974, all for *Guests in the Promised Land;* Drexel Children's Literature Citation, 1981; New Jersey State Council on the Arts prose fellowship, 1981-82, 1985-86; Pennsylvania State Council on the Arts literature fellowship, 1983-84; Moonstone Black Writing Celebration Lifetime Achievement Award, 1996.

Writings

YOUNG ADULT NOVELS; UNDER NAME KRISTIN HUNTER

The Soul Brothers and Sister Lou, Scribner (New York, NY), 1968.
Boss Cat, illustrated by Harold Franklin, Scribner (New York, NY), 1971.
The Pool Table War, Houghton (Boston, MA), 1972.
Uncle Daniel and the Raccoon, Houghton (Boston, MA), 1972.

Guests in the Promised Land (story collection), Scribner (New York, NY), 1973.

Lou in the Limelight, Scribner (New York, NY), 1981.

UNDER NAME KRISTIN HUNTER, UNLESS OTHERWISE NOTED

Minority of One (documentary), Columbia Broadcasting System, 1956.

God Bless the Child, Scribner (New York, NY), 1964, Howard University Press (Washington, DC), 1986.

The Double Edge (play), first produced in Philadelphia, PA, 1965.

The Landlord, Scribner (New York, NY), 1966.

The Survivors, Scribner (New York, NY), 1975.

The Lakestown Rebellion, Scribner (New York, NY), 1978.

Kinfolks, Ballantine (New York, NY), 1996.

(Under the name Kristin Lattany) *Do unto Others,* One World (New York, NY), 2000.

(Contributor) Langston Hughes, editor, *The Best Short Stories by Negro Writers,* Little, Brown (Boston, MA), 1967. Contributor to *Nation, Essence, Black World,* and other periodicals.

Adaptations

The Landlord (motion picture), United Artists, 1970.

Sidelights

Kristin Hunter Lattany has produced a series of novels and a collection of short stories that explore the experiences of modern black teenagers. Her works are variations on the theme of growing up black—and often poor—in America, a country still struggling with racism and inequality. While Lattany's adult novels are often grim or darkly humorous, her books for teens offer a more optimistic picture. The author told *Publishers Weekly:* "I have tried to show some of the positive values existing in the so-called ghetto—the closeness and warmth of family life, the willingness to extend help to strangers in trouble,... the natural acceptance of life's problems and joys—and there is a great deal of joy in the ghetto—and the strong tradition of religious faith. All of these attitudes have combined to create the quality called 'soul.'"

In *Black World,* Huel D. Perkins called Lattany "an excellent storyteller [who] does it with such an economy of words that she makes the form seem easy. But more important, she uses her terse style to speak to younger children and teenagers of limited attention spans with a directness and freshness which makes her a joy to read." Perkins added that Lattany "never fails to drive home the thesis that humanity is the only consideration that matters in this topsy-turvy world—a deep abiding concern for one's fellowman and ultimately the human condition."

Lattany did not grow up in the ghetto, but rather in a middle-class neighborhood near Camden, New Jersey. Her father was a school principal and her mother was a teacher who was reluctantly forced into early retirement

In this sequel to **The Soul Brothers and Sister Lou,** *the band members struggle with drug problems and a greedy manager. (Cover illustration by Jerry McDaniel.)*

when Lattany was born. The youngster grew up in an extended family, including her stern father and the "tigresses"—her mother, her grandmother, and two aunts, one of whom lived with her parents. "I never got to finish a sentence around these loud, vocal women, while my father's stern silences were even more intimidating than their speech," Lattany once recalled.

Lattany was an only child who discovered her two passions, reading and swimming, early. By four she was reading adult books smuggled from her parents' library. In an interview with Jean W. Ross, she said: "I really cannot say when I *didn't* want to be a writer. It probably started shortly after I became a reader, which was when I was four. I found books very exciting, and it was my biggest ambition to produce something myself that would be in books."

An only child, Lattany always felt that she had somehow ruined her mother's life. "In that place and that time (New Jersey in the 1930s and 1940s), women with children were forbidden by law to teach ...," the author once noted. "My mother was unable to teach because of me. She never explained it to me that clearly, however. Instead she spoke often and vehemently, if vaguely, of the 'sacrifices' she had made (for me, I thought), and at least once said that I had ruined her life. I reacted, of course, with mingled guilt and resentment, coupled with the determination never to have a child."

Both of Lattany's parents pushed her to become a teacher herself, so she enrolled at the University of Pennsylvania in nearby Philadelphia as an education major. She finished the degree but lasted only four months in a classroom. She simply wasn't suited for the work, and she knew without doubt that she wanted to be a writer.

In fact, she had been writing a column for the Philadelphia edition of the *Pittsburgh Courier* since her early teens, and that experience brought her into contact with other black writers and journalists in Philadelphia. As a young woman, she herself moved to Philadelphia—to a neighborhood dominated by a busy avenue called South Street—and set about achieving her real goals. Throughout the 1950s and early 1960s she held a series of jobs as an advertising copywriter, and she even worked for the city of Philadelphia as an information officer. Somehow she found the time and energy to write fiction in her spare time, and by 1964 she had finished and published her first novel, *God Bless the Child.*

Both *God Bless the Child* and Lattany's next novel, *The Landlord,* are adult novels with mature themes. Both are set in a community similar to the one Lattany encountered on South Street. The idea of writing for children came to Lattany when she heard an *a cappella* singing group practicing through long summer evenings in her neighborhood. Her imagination brought to life Louretta Hawkins, a fourteen-year-old growing up poor but proud in a big city.

The Soul Brothers and Sister Lou—perhaps Lattany's best-known book—appeared in 1968. Louretta, better known as Sister Lou, persuades her brother to let a group meet and rehearse in his printing shop. Not surprisingly, some of Lou's friends are militant, anti-white extremists. Others have different philosophies, however, and Lou must choose the path that feels right to her. When white policemen harass the gang and kill one of its members in an unprovoked attack, Lou leans toward militancy. Then she discovers that she is not a hater, and that more can be achieved by positive forces than negative ones. At story's end, she and her friends are offered a recording contract on the basis of the eulogy they sing for their slain friend at his funeral.

The Soul Brothers and Sister Lou won a number of important awards, including the Lewis Carroll Shelf Award. It was cited as a novel that could serve to introduce young white readers to the black culture, with all its joys and frustrations. Lattany once commented that the work brought her more children than she ever could have had by natural means—"thousands ... who have formed intense personal bonds with my characters, and then with me through their letters. This responsive audience, the fans and the critics alike, is one of the greatest rewards I have gained from writing for children."

So many of her fans asked for further news of Lou that Lattany wrote *Lou in the Limelight,* a no-holds-barred portrait of the teens as exploited and abused singing stars. As Lou and her friends cross the country to perform, they fall prey to drug use and gambling and are taken advantage of by a dishonest manager. The group is finally saved by the aunt of their murdered comrade, who brings them back to cleaner habits and a sane lifestyle.

Lattany received further awards for her short story collection *Guests in the Promised Land.* Once again realistic in both setting and character, the stories explore the special problems of black adolescents as they try to make their way in a white-dominated world. The work was a finalist for the National Book Award and won a Christopher Award. *Horn Book* reviewer Paul Heins found the stories "superb" for their depiction of black experience "as well as for their art." The critic added that the pieces "present various facets of lives that have been warped by a frustrating racial milieu and—at the same time—have gone beyond it into universal humanity."

Lattany's work for adults explores many of the same themes as her juvenile fiction. After a fifteen-year hiatus from publishing novels, Lattany returned to the longer fictional form with her 1996 *Kinfolks,* the story of Cherry and Patrice, two former political radicals in the 1960s who have maintained a lifelong friendship. In their forties, the two women have weathered storms from their days in the Black Panther party to single-parenting, and now their kids are in love and about to marry. "The impending marriage sends the mothers on a mission to untangle some family skeletons," wrote Lillian Lewis in a *Booklist* review of the novel. These searches turn up the surprising fact that both children have the same father, a poet with little regard for life's conventions. Cherry's and Patrice's children adjust themselves to the fact that they are half-siblings, but the mothers go on a mission to save other children from the same mistake, searching out former lovers of the poet. "[Lattany] has woven an incredible story about the complexities and frailties of love and relationships," concluded Lewis. A contributor for *Publishers Weekly* found Patrice and Cherry to be "some of [Lattany's] most mature creations," further noting that the author uses these characters "to demonstrate that true kinship resides in the heart rather than in the bloodline."

In the year 2000 novel, *Do unto Others,* Lattany deals with the gap between Africans and African Americans, at the same time acknowledging linkages between the two cultures. Zena is an African American struggling with her own ancestry, while at the same time taking in a young, homeless Nigerian woman, Ifa. The owner-operator of a beauty salon, Zena is proud of her African heritage, promoting African culture to her customers. She is a survivor, having worked her way up the economic ladder from cleaning lady to small business owner, but when she takes in the homeless African, cultures clash and received knowledge is challenged. Rebecca A. Stuhr, reviewing *Do unto Others* in *Library Journal,* felt that "the reader is in for both education and entertainment" in Zena's tale.

Lattany lives with her second husband, John Lattany, in the home she grew up in. Through the marriage she has a number of stepchildren and grandchildren, not to mention a far-flung family of nephews, nieces, cousins, and friends who help to enliven her environment. The author once noted: "I have said, even recently, that I must be in a dreadful rut because I live in the house I grew up in, and teach at the same university I attended.... But at some unconscious level, I knew that a life of exile was not for me. And so I am still here, still experiencing life and still writing about it, which may mean that the faithful guardian angel who sits on my shoulder has deliberately kept me close to home. And I see that the rut may be a reason for gratitude and even celebration, not complaining and self-criticism, and that it may not even be a rut at all."

Biographical and Critical Sources

BOOKS

Authors and Artists for Young Adults, Volume 21, Gale (Detroit, MI), 1997.
Beacham's Guide to Literature for Young Adults, Volume 3, Beacham Publishing (Osprey, FL), 1990, pp. 1258-1264.
Children's Literature Review, Volume 3, Gale (Detroit, MI), 1978.
Contemporary Literary Criticism, Volume 35, Gale (Detroit, MI), 1985.
Dictionary of Literary Biography, Volume 33: *Afro-American Fiction Writers after 1955,* Gale (Detroit, MI), 1984.
Something about the Author Autobiography Series, Volume 10, Gale (Detroit, MI), 1990, pp. 119-133.
St. James Guide to Young Adult Writers, 2nd edition, St. James Press (Detroit, MI), 1999.
Tate, Claudia, *Black Women Writers at Work,* Crossroad Publishing, 1983.
Varlejs, Jana, editor, *Young Adult Literature in the Seventies: A Selection of Readings,* Scarecrow Press (Metuchen, NJ), 1978.

PERIODICALS

Black World, September, 1974, Huel D. Perkins.
Booklist, October 15, 1996, Lillian Lewis, review of *Kinfolks,* p. 405.
English Journal, March, 1977.
Horn Book, August, 1973, Paul Heins, review of *Guests in the Promised Land,* p. 386.
Library Journal, January, 2000, Rebecca A. Stuhr, review of *Do unto Others,* p. 160.
Publishers Weekly, October 19, 1968, Kristin Lattany, "'The Soul Brothers': Background of a Juvenile," p. 37; September 30, 1996, review of *Kinfolks,* p. 60; November 29, 1999, p. 54; December 13, 1999, p. 44.
School Library Journal, November, 1981.

LATTANY, Kristin
See LATTANY, Kristin (Eggleston) Hunter

*   *   *

LAWRENCE, Michael 1943–

Personal

Born 1943, in Huntingdonshire, England; children: Max; one daughter.

Addresses

Agent—c/o Author Mail, Dutton Children's Books, 345 Hudson St., New York, NY 10014-3657. *E-mail*—mail@wordybug.com.

Career

Writer. Also worked as a freelance photographer for various publications, including the *Financial Times,* and for advertising agencies, pop music managements, and others. Worked variously as a graphic designer, antiques dealer, painter, sculptor, kibbutz worker, farmhand, copywriter, photographic printer, and press officer for a traveling circus.

Awards, Honors

Poltergoose was shortlisted for the Blue Peter Best Book to Read Aloud Award, 2000; *The Killer Underpants* was named Stockton Children's Book of the Year, 2001.

Writings

When the Snow Falls (novel), Anderson Press, 1995.
Finella Minella, illustrations by Louise Armour-Chelu, Dolphin (London, England), 1998.
Baby Loves, illustrated by Adrian Reynolds, DK Publishing (New York, NY), 1998.
(With Robert Ingpen) *The Poppykettle Papers,* illustrated by Robert Ingpen, Pavilion (London, England), 1999.
The Caterpillar That Roared, illustrations by Alison Bartlett, DK Publishing (New York, NY), 2000.
Baby Loves Hugs and Kisses, illustrated by Adrian Reynolds, DK Publishing (New York, NY), 2000.
Baby Loves Visiting, illustrated by Adrian Reynolds, DK Publishing (New York, NY), 2002.
Young Dracula, illustrated by Chris Mould, Barrington Stoke, 2002.
Baby Loves Visiting, illustrated by Adrian Reynolds, DK Publishing (New York, NY), 2002.

Also author of *Milking the Novelty,* a personal memoir; *Nudes and Victims* (poetry collection), 1993; and educational textbooks. Contributor to juvenile anthologies, including three stories to *Read Me a Story, Please,* compiled by Wendy Cooling, illustrations by Penny Dann, 1999; and five stories to *The Animals' Bedtime Storybook,* compiled by Wendy Cooling, illustrations by

A band of explorers embark on a mythical quest to a new land at the World's Edge and discover adventure and frightening perils in Michael Lawrence's rousing story, illustrated by Robert Ingpen. (From The Poppykettle Papers.)

Penny Dann, 2000. Adapted *Dr. Jekyll and Mr. Hyde, A Christmas Carol,* and *Great Expectations* for juvenile readers.

"JIGGY McCUE" SERIES

The Poltergoose, Orchard Books (London, England), 1999, Dutton Children's Books (New York, NY), 2002.
The Killer Underpants, Orchard Books (London, England), 2000, Dutton Children's Books (New York, NY), 2002.
The Toilet of Doom, Orchard Books (London, England), 2001, Dutton Children's Books (New York, NY), 2002.
Maggot Pie, Orchard Books (London, England), 2002.

Work in Progress

The Aldous Lexicon, a "trilogy about alternative realities for young adults and adults with young minds"; two novels for adults.

Sidelights

Michael Lawrence was a freelance photographer for many years before he began writing children's books in the mid-1990s. Since then, he has published many stories and books for young children, including his "Jiggy McCue" series, as well as several others. Lawrence's work is characterized by humor, and his *Finella Minella,* a story about seven-year-old Finella and her life, is no different. Reviewing the work for *School Librarian,* Ruth France said that she would recommend the "pleasant" book to all readers. Other books by Lawrence include *The Poppykettle Papers,* a story about two boys who discover a box full of stories about a tiny people called the Hairy Peruvians. The book recounts the adventures of five of these tiny people as they set out on an adventure at the behest of their god, El Nino.

Lawrence once commented: "I am easily bored, which is probably why I have taken up so many different lines of work in the past. Now that I'm writing full-time, I try and make each book very different from others I've written (unless part of a series, like the "Jiggy McCue" novels). I rarely write about subjects that don't interest me, which is why I turn down all offers to do books or stories about sport. My latest project, *The Aldous Lexicon,* is possibly the most exciting thing I've done or will do. Not only is it full of ideas, twists, and surprises, but it is set in the actual house (a large riverside mansion) in which I was born, so it is very personal."

Biographical and Critical Sources

PERIODICALS

Booklist, January 1, 2002, Todd Morning, review of *The Poltergoose,* p. 858.

Kirkus Reviews, December 15, 2001, review of *The Poltergoose,* p. 1760.

Publishers Weekly, March 29, 1999, review of *Baby Loves,* p. 106.

School Librarian, summer, 1999, Ruth France, review of *Finella Minella,* p. 75.

School Library Journal, March, 2000, Barbara Buckley, review of *The Poppykettle Papers,* p. 240; September, 2000, Bina Williams, review of *The Caterpillar That Roared,* p. 203; December, 2000, Shanla Brookshire, review of *Baby Loves* and *Baby Hugs and Kisses,* p. 113; March, 2002, Elaine E. Knight, review of *The Poltergoose,* p. 232.

*   *   *

LEROUX-HUGON, Hélène 1955-

Personal

Born October 20, 1955, in Angers, France; daughter of Pierre (an architect) and Lucie (Jacqueminot) Barriol; married Emmanuel Leroux (a physician), 1978; children: Siegfried, Edgar, Esther. *Education:* École nationale supérieure des beaux arts, diploma, 1979. *Religion:* Roman Catholic.

Addresses

Home—12 rue des Martyrs, 44100 Nantes, France. *E-mail*—helene.lerouxhugon@caramail.com.

Career

Illustrator and author of children's books, 1983—. Madeleine (private art school), Angers, France, teacher, 1978-86; Lycée St. Pierre la Joliverie, Nantes, France, art teacher, 1999—; Ravensburger (publisher), graphic artist and design director, 2000—; *Artkids* (children's art magazine), production supervisor, 2001—.

Writings

SELF-ILLUSTRATED; IN FRENCH

Petits ateliers au fil des saisons, Fleurus (Paris, France), 1993.

Gouache: jeux et décors peints, Dessain & Tolra (Paris, France), 1994.

In her book featuring polar animals, Hélène Leroux-Hugon introduces children to the rudiments of drawing by observing, practicing, and working in a step-by-step fashion. (From I Can Draw Polar Animals, *written and illustrated by Leroux-Hugon.)*

Fleurs fruits et couronnes, Dessain & Tolra (Paris, France), 1994.

Masques en papiers pour jouer, Dessain & Tolra (Paris, France), 1996.

Collages, Dessain & Tolra (Paris, France), 1996.

Pochoirs: premiers pas, Dessain & Tolra (Paris, France), 1997.

Vite on se déguise, Fleurus (Paris, France), 1997.

Douces mousses, Bordas (Paris, France), 1997.

Ma ferme pâte à modeler, Fleurus (Paris, France), 1998.

(With Natasha Seret) *Déguisements pour tous,* Fleurus (Paris, France), 1998.

"J'AIME DESSINER" SERIES; PUBLISHED IN ENGLISH AS "I CAN DRAW ANIMALS" SERIES

J'aime dessiner les animaux d'Afrique, Bordas (Paris, France), 1997.

J'aime dessiner les animaux de nos régions, Bordas (Paris, France), 1997.

J'aime dessiner les animaux du froid, Dessain & Tolra (Paris, France), 1999, translation by Valerie J. Weber published as *I Can Draw Polar Animals,* Gareth Stevens (Milwaukee, WI), 2001.

J'aime dessiner les animaux de la forêt, Bordas (Paris, France), 1998, translation by Valerie J. Weber published as *I Can Draw Forest Animals,* Gareth Stevens (Milwaukee, WI), 2001.

J'aime dessiner les animaux sauvage, Dessain & Tolra (Paris, France), 1998, translation by Valerie J. Weber published as *I Can Draw Wild Animals,* Gareth Stevens (Milwaukee, WI), 2001.

J'aime dessiner les animaux de la campagne, Bordas (Paris, France), translation by Valerie J. Weber published as *I Can Draw Country Animals,* Gareth Stevens (Milwaukee, WI), 2001.

OTHER

(Illustrator) Ann Rocard, *Je commence à compter,* Hachette (Paris, France), 1989.

Contributor to *Pâques,* Fleurus (Paris, France), 2000.

Sidelights

In addition to creating her own art, French artist and educator Hélène Leroux-Hugon has shared her passion for creating art with children. She has taught art at several schools in France and produced *Artkids,* a children's art magazine. Moreover, she has written and illustrated more than a dozen instructive books for children. Of these how-to titles, several of the "I Can Draw Animals" series has been translated into English. In such titles as *I Can Draw Country Animals* and *I Can Draw Polar Animals,* she introduces children to the rudiments of drawing, beginning with observing, practicing, and working in a step-by-step fashion. The "polar animals" book includes polar bears, seals, and walruses, while the "country animals" book includes deer, wild boar, fox, badger, and marten, and the "wild animals" volume includes hippopotamuses, crocodiles, and elephants. The difficulty of the drawings increases as each book progresses. Each drawing is enhanced with a short text about the animal portrayed. Although *School Library Journal* reviewer Carolyn Janssen expressed reservations that the intended independently reading audience would find *I Can Draw Country Animals* and *I Can Draw Forest Animals* "too babyish," Augusta R. Malvagno praised the works in her review of *I Can Draw Polar Animals* for *School Library Journal.* She described the titles as "well designed with a clean, appealing layout" and predicted that they would be "popular."

Leroux-Hugon told *SATA:* "I studied in the Beaux Arts, a school of fine arts and design, and I am fascinated by the relationship between creation, teaching, and the inspiration of great contemporary artists. Most of my job entails researching and creating in my workshop. I am interested in the impact of shapes and colors on people's minds. My work comes in large canvases and colorful sculptures. I get most of my inspiration from nature. I am a great admirer of the earliest forms of expression, such as primitive totems, as well as of contemporary artists.

"I teach design, color, volume, and the history of art, which enables me to share my passion and to help my students in their personal projects. I have written and edited about twenty art books for children and I supervise the production of an art magazine for children, *Artkids,* to give them basic knowledge and enthusiasm for drawing, painting, and the history of art through activities, learning about great artists, such as Picasso, Calder, Miro, Tinguely, or Niki de Saint Phalle, etc."

Biographical and Critical Sources

PERIODICALS

School Library Journal, May, 2001, Carolyn Janssen, reviews of *I Can Draw Forest Animals* and *I Can Draw Country Animals,* p. 144; September, 2001, Augusta R. Malvagno, review of *I Can Draw Polar Animals.**

M

MAYER, Marianna 1945-

Personal

Born November 8, 1945, in Queens, NY; married Mercer Mayer (an author and illustrator; divorced). *Education:* Attended the Art Students League.

Addresses

Home—Route 67, Roxbury, CT 06783.

Career

Author and illustrator. Also worked as a commercial artist at an advertising agency, and as a copywriter.

Awards, Honors

Brooklyn Art Books for Children citation, 1973, for *A Boy, a Dog, a Frog, and a Friend;* Michigan Young Readers award, 1982, for *Beauty and the Beast;* Colorado Children's Book Award, 1984, and Washington Children's Choice, 1986, both for *The Unicorn and the Lake; Aladdin and the Enchanted Lamp* was exhibited at Bologna International Children's Book Fair, 1985.

Writings

The Unicorn and the Lake, illustrated by Michael Hague, Dial (New York, NY), 1982.
Alley Oop!, illustrated by Gerald McDermott, Holt (New York, NY), 1985.
The Brambleberrys Animal Book of Colors, illustrated by Gerald McDermott, Bell Books (Honesdale, PA), 1987.
The Unicorn Alphabet, illustrated by Michael Hague, Dial (New York, NY), 1989.
Marcel the Pastry Chef, illustrated by Gerald McDermott, Bantam (New York, NY), 1991.
Marcel at War, illustrated by Gerald McDermott, Bantam (New York, NY), 1991.

The Brambleberrys Animal Alphabet, illustrated by Gerald McDermott, Boyds Mills Press (Honesdale, PA), 1991.
The Brambleberrys Animal Book of Shapes, illustrated by Gerald McDermott, Boyds Mills Press (Honesdale, PA), 1991.
The Brambleberrys Animal Book of Counting, illustrated by Gerald McDermott, Bell Books (Honesdale, PA), 1991.
The Mother Goose Cookbook: Rhymes and Recipes for the Very Young, illustrated by Carol Schwartz, Morrow (New York, NY), 1998.
Young Mary of Nazareth, Morrow (New York, NY), 1998.
Young Jesus of Nazareth, Morrow (New York, NY), 1999.
The Twelve Apostles: Their Lives and Acts, Penguin/Putnam (New York, NY), 2000.
The Real Santa Claus, Penguin/Putnam (New York, NY), 2001.
Seeing Jesus in His Own Words, Phyllis Fogelman Books (New York, NY), 2002.
Remembering the Prophets of Sacred Scripture, Phyllis Fogelman Books (New York, NY), 2003.

WITH MERCER MAYER

Mine (self-illustrated), Simon & Schuster (New York, NY), 1970.
A Boy, a Dog, a Frog, and a Friend, illustrated by Mercer Mayer, Dial (New York, NY), 1971.
Me and My Flying Machine, illustrated by Mercer Mayer, Parents' Magazine Press (New York, NY), 1971.
One Frog Too Many, illustrated by Mercer Mayer, Dial (New York, NY), 1975.

RETELLER

Marie Leprince de Beaumont, *Beauty and the Beast,* illustrated by Mercer Mayer, Four Winds (New York, NY), 1978, SeaStar Books (New York, NY), 2001.
Carlo Collodi, *Pinocchio,* illustrated by Gerald McDermott, Four Winds (New York, NY), 1981.
My First Book of Nursery Tales: Five Favorite Bedtime Tales, illustrated by William Joyce, Random House (New York, NY), 1983.
The Black Horse, illustrated by Katie Thamer, Dial (New York, NY), 1984.

Heroic Tom Thumb faces many challenges and menacing opponents, including the giant Gembo, in Mayer's retelling of a family classic. (From The Adventures of Tom Thumb, *illustrated by Kinuko Y. Craft.)*

Aladdin and the Enchanted Lamp, illustrated by Gerald McDermott, Macmillan (New York, NY), 1985.

The Sorcerer's Apprentice, illustrated by Allen Atkinson, Little Simon (New York, NY), 1986, illustrated by David Wiesner, Bantam (New York, NY), 1989.

Thumbelina, illustrated by John O'Brien, Simon & Schuster (New York, NY), 1986.

The Little Jewel Box, illustrated by Margaret Tomes, Dial (New York, NY), 1986.

Hans Christian Andersen, *The Ugly Duckling,* illustrated by Thomas Locker, Macmillan (New York, NY), 1987.

Iduna and the Magic Apples, illustrated by Laszlo Gal, Macmillan (New York, NY), 1988.

The Prince and the Princess: A Bohemian Fairy Tale, illustrated by Jacqueline Rogers, Bantam (New York, NY), 1989.

The Twelve Dancing Princesses, illustrated by Kinuko Y. Craft, Morrow (New York, NY), 1989.

The Golden Swan: An East Indian Tale of Love from the Mahabharata, illustrated by Robert Sauber, Bantam (New York, NY), 1990.

Noble-Hearted Kate: A Celtic Tale, illustrated by Winslow Pels, Bantam (New York, NY), 1990.

The Spirit of the Blue Light, illustrated by Laszlo Gal, Macmillan (New York, NY), 1990.

Rapunzel, illustrated by Sheila Beckett, Western Publishing (Racine, WI), 1991.

Baba Yaga and Vasilisa the Brave, illustrated by Kinuko Y. Craft, Morrow (New York, NY), 1994.

Turandot, illustrated by Winslow Pels, Morrow (New York, NY), 1994.

Iron John, illustrated by Winslow Pels, Morrow (New York, NY), 1998.

Pegasus, illustrated by K. Y. Craft, Morrow (New York, NY), 1998.

The Prince and the Pauper, illustrated by Gary A. Lippincott, Dial (New York, NY), 1999.

Women Warriors: Myths and Legends of Heroic Women, illustrated by Julek Heller, Morrow (New York, NY), 1999.

The Adventures of Tom Thumb, illustrated by Kinuko Y. Craft, SeaStar Books (New York, NY), 2001.

Parsifal: The Legend of the Grail, illustrated by Thomas Canty, Phyllis Fogelman Books (New York, NY), 2002.

Perseus, illustrated by Joel Spector, Phyllis Fogelman Books (New York, NY), 2002.

Sidelights

Marianna Mayer has written many children's books, but it is as a reteller of familiar fairy tales and folktales that she is perhaps best known. Keeping the original elements of the tales intact, Mayer adds her own interpretation to the familiar stories and characters, making them her own, often resulting in an old tale with a new twist. In addition to retelling stories and writing children's books on her own, Mayer has also collaborated on several juvenile works with her former husband and children's author and illustrator, Mercer Mayer.

Among Mayer's best-known works as a reteller is *Beauty and the Beast,* in which she portrays the Beast as a lion without a mane, whose true identity is revealed to all (except Beauty) in a series of dream sequences. Ruth M. McConnell praised Mayer's "magical account" in *School Library Journal,* calling it a "lushly romantic picture book."

Mayer examines an Irish folktale in her 1984 work *The Black Horse.* The adventure begins when Tim, an Irish prince who has lost his fortune, acquires a black horse that speaks to him. The horse asks for Tim's trust, which he receives, and proceeds to dive into the sea to face the evil Sea King who is after the Princess of the Mountains. Through the course of many trials and challenges, Tim and the black horse defeat the Sea King, after which the horse is released from a spell and transformed back into Tim's brother. Mayer's version of *The Black Horse* "exudes the magic that spellbound audiences of famous storytellers," maintained a *Publishers Weekly* contributor. Kay McPherson pointed out in *School Library Journal* that "Mayer has taken what was ... a sketchy folktale and fleshed it out, while retaining the richness of a folktale."

Mayer continued retelling other fairy and folktales through the 1980s, including *The Little Jewel Box* in 1986, *Iduna and the Magic Apples* in 1988, and *The Prince and the Princess: A Bohemian Fairy Tale* in 1989. In the 1990s she began retelling stories for the "Timeless Tales" series, first with *The Golden Swan: An East Indian Tale of Love from the Mahabharata* and *Noble-Hearted Kate: A Celtic Tale.* The first is based on the Hindu myth concerning King Nala and his lover Damayanti, who are brought together by the help of a golden swan. Separated by the goddess Kali, who is jealous of their happiness, the two lovers are united in the end because of Damayanti's love and patience. Tales from the country of Scotland are combined in the story of *Noble-Hearted Kate,* who goes in search of a cure for her stepsister Meghan, who is under a witch's spell. Their adventures bring the two sisters in contact with the tree of knowledge, as well as the fairy realm, which Kate fights to free from the enchantment of a knight. In her review of *The Golden Swan* for the *Bulletin of the Center for Children's Books,* Betsy Hearne related: "Mayer has undertaken a formidable challenge, and her re-creation of the romance elements is effective." And Hearne stated in her review of *Noble-Hearted Kate* that "Mayer's style attains stretches of poetic simplicity," and she concludes that the story "is a romanticized telling that will hook readers."

In 1994, Mayer based a retelling of the Cinderella tale on a Russian version of the story in *Baba Yaga and Vasilisa the Brave.* The story begins with the death of Vasilisa's father and the resulting abuse she receives from her stepmother and stepsisters. Her only consolation is a magical doll made for her by her mother before her death. When she is sent by her stepmother to the house of Baba Yaga the witch to fetch a magic light, Vasilisa becomes the witch's servant and must now complete a series of tasks to get her freedom. With the help of her magic doll, Vasilisa gains her freedom and also destroys her stepmother and stepsisters. Alone once again, she is sent to live with an old woman who teaches Vasilisa to spin and weave. A new cloth she creates with this new skill catches the eye of the tsar, who asks for her hand in marriage. *School Library Journal* reviewer Denise Anton asserted that Mayer's "engaging text" sets this version of the tale apart from others, adding that "Mayer's graceful prose conveys both the wonder and power of the tale."

China is the setting for Mayer's 1995 effort *Turandot,* a tale of the Princess Turandot and her search for a suitor. Although there are several versions of this tale, Mayer follows a version dramatized by playwright Carlo Gozzi in the late nineteenth century, and was praised by Margaret A. Chang in *School Library Journal* for writing a "sentimental ... love story." The tale of Iron Hans is the basis for Mayer's *Iron John,* but she modernizes the original tale greatly, including an awareness of both environmental issues and even feminism. Writing in *Kirkus Reviews,* a critic noted that although the "message of the peaceable kingdom is not subtle, ... it is worthy." Other famous tales retold by Mayer

include *The Prince and the Pauper, The Adventures of Tom Thumb, The Ugly Duckling,* and many more.

In addition to her retellings of stories from the past, Mayer has also written several picture books of her own, including *Alley Oop!, Marcel the Pastry Chef,* and others. One of her more recent efforts, *The Mother Goose Cookbook: Rhymes and Recipes for the Very Young,* presents a collection of fourteen nursery rhymes, each presented with an accompanying recipe, and Carolyn Jenks of *School Library Journal* called it an "enjoyable addition to the genre." She is also author of several books on religious figures, including Jesus, who is featured in *Young Jesus of Nazareth,* and St. Nick, who is featured in *The Real Santa Claus.* In the latter work, a biography of St. Nicholas, Mayer includes the famous poem "A Visit from St. Nicholas" as well as a collection of interesting facts concerning the origin of the legend of Santa Claus. Reviewing the work for *Booklist,* Carolyn Phelan praised *The Real Santa Claus* as "a well written and beautifully illustrated book." Other biographical works by Mayer include *The Twelve Apostles: Their Lives and Acts.*

Biographical and Critical Sources

PERIODICALS

Booklist, October 1, 2001, Carolyn Phelan, review of *The Real Santa Claus,* p. 332; October 15, 2001, Grace-Anne A. DeCandido, review of *The Adventures of Tom Thumb,* p. 398.

Bulletin of the Center for Children's Books, February, 1991, Betsy Hearne, review of *The Golden Swan,* p. 154; March, 1991, Betsy Hearne, review of *Noble-Hearted Kate,* p. 171.

Horn Book Guide, fall, 1998, Gail Hedge, review of *The Mother Goose Cookbook: Rhymes and Recipes for the Very Young,* p. 395.

Kirkus Reviews, November 1, 1999, review of *Iron John,* p. 1746.

Publishers Weekly, September 28, 1984, review of *The Black Horse,* p. 112; November 15, 1999, review of *The Prince and the Pauper,* pp. 66-67; July 24, 2000, review of *The Twelve Apostles: Their Lives and Acts,* p. 91.

School Library Journal, December, 1978, Ruth M. McConnell, review of *Beauty and the Beast,* p. 46; January, 1985, Kay McPherson, review of *The Black Horse,* p. 78; July, 1994, Denise Anton, review of *Baba Yaga and Vasilisa the Brave,* p. 112; October, 1995, Margaret A. Chang, review of *Turandot,* p. 149; April, 1998, Carolyn Jenks, review of *The Mother Goose Cookbook: Rhymes and Recipes for the Very Young,* p. 120; October, 2001, review of *The Real Santa Claus,* p. 67; December, 2001, Jeanne Clancy Watkins, review of *The Adventures of Tom Thumb,* p. 124.*

McGOVERN, Ann 1930-

Personal

Born May 25, 1930, in New York, NY; daughter of Arthur (a bacteriologist) and Kate (a teacher; maiden name, Malatsky) Weinberger; married Martin L. Scheiner (an engineer), June 6, 1970 (died, January 1, 1992); children: (previous marriage) Peter McGovern; adopted children: Charles, Ann, Jim. *Education:* Attended University of New Mexico. *Hobbies and other interests:* Travel, photography, scuba diving, collage art, cinema.

Addresses

Home—New York, NY. *Agent*—Lisa Voges, Kirchoff/ Wohlberg, 866 United Nations Plaza, New York, NY 10017. *E-mail*—McGovernAnn@aol.com.

Career

Scholastic Book Services, New York, NY, associate editor of Arrow Book Club, 1958-65, editor and founder of See Saw Book Club, 1965-67. Full-time writer, 1967—. Lecturer to educational and conservation groups; poet and collage artist. Goddard Riverside Community Center, New York, NY, board member.

Member

International PEN, International Food, Wine and Travel Writers, American Society of Journalists and Authors, Authors League of America, Authors Guild, Society of Children's Book Writers, Writers Union, Society of Women Geographers, Explorers Club (fellow), Players Club, National Arts Club.

Awards, Honors

Scholastic Book Services' Lucky Book Club Four-Leaf Clover award, 1972; named author of the year by Lucky Book Club, 1974; National Science Teachers Association Outstanding Science Trade Book awards, 1976, for *Sharks,* 1977, for *Shark Lady: True Adventures of Eugenie Clark,* 1984, for *Night Dive,* and 1992, for *Swimming with Sea Lions and Other Adventures in the Galapagos Islands;* Arkansas Traveler Award, 1979; Earthworm Award, for *Little Whale;* honorable metion, Cuffie Award for Best Treatment of a Social Issue, *Publishers Weekly,* for *Lady in the Box;* Horn Book award, for *Scram, Kid!;* Editor's Choice, *Booklist,* for *Night Dive;* List of Recommended Books, American Humane Society, for *Little Wolf;* Notable Children's Book in the Field of Social Studies citation, for *Half a Kingdom;* International Biographical Roll of Honor, for distinguished service to education and the writing professions. A children's room in the New York Public Library was named after McGovern, 2001.

Ann McGovern

Writings

FICTION

Annie Oakley and the Rustlers, Simon & Schuster (New York, NY), 1955.

Roy Rogers and the Mountain Lion, illustrated by Mel Crawford, Simon & Schuster (New York, NY), 1955.

(Reteller) *Aesop's Fables,* Scholastic (New York, NY), 1963.

Who Has a Secret?, illustrated by Nola Langner, Houghton Mifflin (Boston MA), 1964.

Zoo, Where Are You?, illustrated by Ezra Jack Keats, Harper (New York, NY), 1964.

Too Much Noise, illustrated by Simms Taback, Houghton Mifflin (Boston, MA), 1967, reprinted, Trumpet, 1992.

Stone Soup, Scholastic (New York, NY), 1968, new edition, illustrated by Winslow Pinney Pels, 1986.

Robin Hood of Sherwood Forest, illustrated by Arnold Spilka, Crowell (New York, NY), 1968.

Black Is Beautiful (poetry), illustrated by Hope Wurmfeld, Four Winds Press (New York, NY), 1969.

Hee-Haw (adapted from a fable by Aesop), illustrated by Eric von Schmidt, Houghton Mifflin (Boston, MA), 1969.

Squeals and Squiggles and Ghostly Giggles, illustrated by Jeffrey Higginbottom, Four Winds Press (New York, NY), 1973.

Scram, Kid!, illustrated by Nola Langner, Viking (New York, NY), 1974.

Half a Kingdom: An Icelandic Folktale, illustrated by Nola Langner, F. Warne (New York, NY), 1977.

Feeling Mad, Feeling Sad, Feeling Bad, Feeling Glad (poetry), illustrated by Hope Wurmfeld, Magic Circle (New York, NY), 1977.

Mr. Skinner's Skinny House, illustrated by Mort Gerberg, Four Winds Press (New York, NY), 1980.

Nicholas Bentley Stoningpot III, illustrated by Tomie de Paola, Holiday House (New York, NY), 1982.

Eggs on Your Nose, illustrated by Maxie Chambliss, Macmillan (New York, NY), 1987.

Drop Everything, It's D.E.A.R. Time!, illustrated by Anna DiVito, Scholastic (New York, NY), 1993.

Happy Silly Birthday to Me, illustrated by Sue Dreamer, Scholastic (New York, NY), 1994.

The Lady in the Box, illustrated by Marni Backer, Turtle Books (New York, NY), 1997.

NONFICTION

Dog Stamps, illustrated by Edwin Megargee, Simon & Schuster (New York, NY), 1955.

The Complete Book of Cats, Arco (New York, NY), 1959.

Zoo Pals—Big Cats, Great Apes: A Look at Zoo Life, Scholastic/Ridge Press (New York, NY), 1960.

Why It's a Holiday, Random House (New York, NY), 1960.

The Story of Christopher Columbus, illustrated by Joe Lasker, Random House (New York, NY), 1962, reprinted, Scholastic (New York, NY), 1992.

The Question and Answer Book about the Human Body, Random House (New York, NY), 1965.

Little Wolf, illustrated by Nola Langner, Abelard-Schuman (New York, NY), 1965.

The Pilgrims' First Thanksgiving, Scholastic (New York, NY), 1973, new edition, illustrated by Elroz Freem, 1993.

Sharks, illustrated by Murray Tinkelman, Four Winds Press (New York, NY), 1976, revised edition published as *Questions and Answers about Sharks,* illustrated by Pam Johnson, Scholastic (New York, NY), 1995.

The Underwater World of the Coral Reef, Four Winds Press (New York, NY), 1976.

Little Whale, illustrated by John Hamberger, Four Winds Press (New York, NY), 1979.

Great Gorillas, illustrated by Mamoru Funai, Scholastic (New York, NY), 1980.

Elephant Baby: The Story of Little Tembo, illustrated by Fred Brenner, Scholastic (New York, NY), 1982.

Night Dive, illustrated by James B. and Martin Scheiner, Macmillan (New York, NY), 1984.

Down Under, Down Under: Diving Adventures on the Great Barrier Reef, illustrated by James B. and Martin Scheiner, Macmillan (New York, NY), 1989.

(With Eugenie Clark) *The Desert beneath the Sea,* illustrated by Craig Phillips, Scholastic (New York, NY), 1991.

Swimming with Sea Lions and Other Adventures in the Galapagos Islands, illustrated with photographs by the author, Scholastic (New York, NY), 1992.

Playing with the Penguins and Other Adventures in Antarctica, illustrated with photographs by the author

and Colin Monteath, Scholastic (New York, NY), 1994.

BIOGRAPHY

Runaway Slave: The Story of Harriet Tubman, illustrated by R. M. Powers, Four Winds Press (New York, NY), 1965, published as *Wanted Dead or Alive: The Story of Harriet Tubman,* Scholastic (New York, NY), 1977.

The Defenders: Osceola, Tecumseh, Cochise, Scholastic (New York, NY), 1970.

The Secret Soldier: The Story of Deborah Sampson, illustrated by Ann Grifalconi, Four Winds Press (New York, NY), 1975.

Shark Lady: True Adventures of Eugenie Clark, illustrated by Ruth Chew, Four Winds Press (New York, NY), 1978.

Adventures of the Shark Lady: Eugenie Clark around the World, Scholastic (New York, NY), 1998.

"IF YOU LIVED..." SERIES

If You Lived in Colonial Times, illustrated by Brinton Turkle, Four Winds Press (New York, NY), 1964, new edition, illustrated by June Otani, Scholastic (New York, NY), 1992.

If You Grew up with Abraham Lincoln, illustrated by Brinton Turkle, Four Winds Press (New York, NY), 1966, new edition, illustrated by George Ulrich, Scholastic (New York, NY), 1992.

If You Sailed on the Mayflower, illustrated by J. B. Handlesman, Four Winds Press (New York, NY), 1969, new edition, illustrated by Anna DiVito, Scholastic (New York, NY), 1991.

If You Lived with the Circus, illustrated by Ati Forberg, Four Winds Press (New York, NY), 1971.

If You Lived with the Sioux Indians, illustrated by Bob Levering, Four Winds Press (New York, NY), 1974, new edition, illustrated by Jean Drew, Scholastic (New York, NY), 1992.

McGovern has written a picture-book biography of the great woman who led three-hundred slaves to freedom via the Underground Railroad. (Cover illustration by Brian Pinkney.)

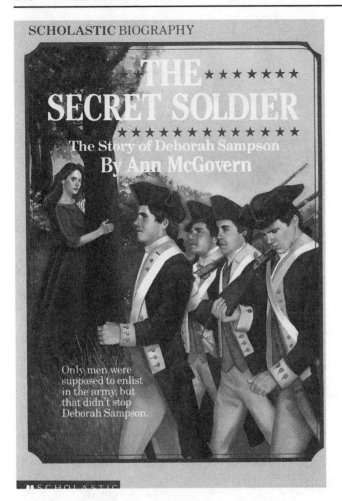

SCHOLASTIC BIOGRAPHY

THE ★ ★ ★ ★ ★ ★ ★
SECRET SOLDIER
★ ★ ★ ★ ★ ★ ★ ★ ★ ★ ★ ★ ★
The Story of Deborah Sampson
By Ann McGovern

Only men were
supposed to enlist
in the army, but
that didn't stop
Deborah Sampson.

SCHOLASTIC

McGovern's biography relates the story of the daring young woman who disguised herself as a man and enlisted in the army during the Revolutionary War. (Cover illustration by Katherine Thompson.)

If You Lived 100 Years Ago, illustrated by Anna DiVito, Scholastic (New York, NY), 1999.

If You Lived in the Days of the Knights, illustrated by Dan Andreasen, Scholastic (New York, NY), 2001.

Also author of several "Little Golden Books" during the 1950s, and author of a screenplay, *The Princess and the Pea,* 1965.

EDITOR

Treasury of Christmas Stories, Scholastic (New York, NY), 1960, new edition, illustrated by David Lockhart, Galahad Books (New York, NY), 1974.

Arrow Book of Poetry, Scholastic (New York, NY), 1965.

Shakespearean Sallies, Sullies, and Slanders: Insults for All Occasions, illustrated by James and Ruth McCrea, Crowell (New York, NY), 1969.

Voices from Within: The Poetry of Women in Prison, Magic Circle (New York, NY), 1975.

Contributor to *Newsday, WomenSports, Lears, New Choices,* and *Saturday Review.* Publisher and editor, *The Privileged Traveller* (magazine), 1985-87. Reviewer of children's books, *New York Times,* 1960-66.

Work in Progress

Dear Mom, Guess What?, a picture book, and poetry for adults.

Sidelights

Ann McGovern, states a biographical release from Scholastic Books, "is excited. She's excited about the world: the world of history, science, and fables—even the world under the sea. Her enthusiasm is the foundation for each word she writes." In a career spanning more than forty years and covering more than fifty volumes, she has opened new worlds to young readers. McGovern once wrote, "Looking backward (and forward) at my books, I realize that they reflect my life in three ways: 1) ideas I strongly believe in; 2) desire for knowledge (I never finished college); and 3) exciting personal experiences." McGovern has visited all seven continents, seen seven total eclipses, attended a Sultan's birthday party in Malaysia, watched orangutans in Borneo, ridden on an elephant to photograph tigers in India, viewed the huge Komodo dragons in Indonesia, stood on the spot of the North Pole and was among the first Americans ever to scuba dive in China.

"I began writing when I was eight years old," McGovern stated, "because I couldn't speak. A severe childhood stutter kept me from expressing myself verbally, and so I turned my feelings and thoughts to writing and reading." She spent many hours in her local public library, and many others in a tree in Central Park, writing poems and stories. Years later, divorced and faced with the prospect of raising a son on an editor's salary, she turned to writing as a means of earning additional income, and found fulfillment as well. "I can hardly believe," she exclaimed, "that the sad, shy, stuttering child I once was grew up to become a happy adult with fifty books published."

McGovern's books range from biography to science to folklore. The author explained, "In *Wanted Dead or Alive: The Story of Harriet Tubman,* I chose a woman in history whom black and white girls could admire. I like to write books about heroines for today's society. Unfortunately, there are still too few. Another biography, *The Secret Soldier: The Story of Deborah Sampson,* is a suspenseful true story about a young woman who fought in the Revolutionary War, not so much out of patriotism as from a yearning for the adventure denied her because of her sex and poverty.

Sharks led to McGovern's fifth biography, *Shark Lady: True Adventures of Eugenie Clark.* Clark, McGovern writes, is a good friend, and the two of them have dived together in the Red Sea, China, Indonesia and the Caribbean. Their joint interest in the tiny creatures who live in the sandy bottom beneath the sea inspired *Desert beneath the Sea,* and McGovern has written another biography, *Adventures of the Shark Lady: Eugenie Clark around the World,* which continues the story of this extraordinary scientist.

"Shark Lady: True Adventures of Eugenie Clark combines my love and deep concern for the underwater world and my admiration for this dedicated scientist, whose work has led to such amazing discoveries as sharks found 'sleeping' in underwater caves beneath the sea," explained McGovern. Expedition photographs taken by the author's late husband, Martin Scheiner, and son Jim Scheiner have been used to illustrate *Night Dive* and other books by McGovern on underwater life.

Besides sharks and other creatures who live in the sea, McGovern cares deeply about the future of other fragile places of the world and its inhabitants. Her travels have deepened her concerns and have resulted in such books as *Little Whale, Great Gorillas,* and *Elephant Baby.* Later books, written in the form of a child's journal, take readers to such places as the Galapagos Islands in *Swimming with Sea Lions,* and to Antarctica in *Playing with Penguins,* both of which are illustrated with her own photographs. She has plans for many such books and in writing them she hopes to heighten both geographical and environmental awareness.

In addition to biographies, nature books, and histories, McGovern writes picture books, composes poetry, adapts folk tales and has recently been writing novels. As for her poetry, McGovern states that she always strives to write verse that is "meaningful to children." For many years, she also conducted a poetry-writing workshop for long-term prisoners in Bedford Hills, NY, which eventually led to the compilation of *Voices from Within.*

For *Night Dive,* McGovern made dozens of dives in inky darkness. Two trips to Australia led to *Down Under, Down Under: Diving Adventures on the Great Barrier Reef.* She has also received inspiration from her grandchildren for picture books such as *Eggs on Your Nose.* "My granddaughter Sharon told me about her reading time in school, called D.E.A.R. Time (Drop Everything and Read)," McGovern told *Something about the Author.* "I learned that many of the schools where I lectured also had a period of silent reading. And so *Drop Everything, It's D.E.A.R. Time* was born. When I took Christopher, age two, for his first elevator ride to view his newly-born brother in the hospital, he said, 'I want my birthday in an elevator!' That was the inspiration for *Happy Silly Birthday to Me."* After McGovern became acquainted with a homeless man who lived out of a box near her Manhattan apartment, the idea for *The Lady in the Box* began to take shape. "I notice a lot of parents with children walk away [from the homeless] to avoid any contact and questions," McGovern said in a *People Weekly* interview. Inspired "to put a human face on the homeless," the author hopes adults can "encourage children's natural compassion by helping at a soup kitchen, donating a coat."

In 1992 McGovern lost her long-time companion in scuba diving, sailing, and photography around the world when her husband, Martin Scheiner, died. She still travels widely, frequently with her family that numbers eleven people plus "four granddogs and three grand-cats." McGovern also continues to lecture to students around the world and across the United States about the many experiences that have led to her different books. "Sometimes," she wrote, "when I look at a sad, shy face in the audience, I see the lonely child I once was and I hope that maybe my words can have some influence on a life. Making a difference in children's lives is why I plan to write till I'm ninety!"

In 2001, at the reopening of New York City's newly renovated Muhlenberg Branch Library, to which McGovern was a major contributor, the author remarked, "Books can be an escape hatch from a troubled childhood, a window to a world of possibilities, a meeting of inspiring heroes and heroines, surprising soul mates that change a life, and spur creativity; they were all these for me and more."

Biographical and Critical Sources

BOOKS

Children's Literature Review, Volume 50, Gale (Detroit, MI), 1998.

Scientist Eugenie Clark, who has traveled worldwide to study sharks, is the subject of McGovern's biography for young readers. (From Shark Lady, *illustrated by Ruth Chew.)*

Something about the Author Autobiography Series, Volume 17, Gale (Detroit, MI), 1994.

Wyatt, Flora R., and others, editors, *Popular Nonfiction Authors for Children,* Libraries Unlimited (Englewood, CO), 1998.

PERIODICALS

Booklist, September 1, 1997, review of *The Lady in the Box,* p. 138.

Horn Book, March-April, 1993, review of *Nicholas Bentley Stoningpot III,* p. 230.

People Weekly, February 2, 1998, Lan N. Nguyen, "A Book Finds a Home" (Talking with Ann McGovern), p. 33.

Publishers Weekly, September 8, 1997, review of *The Lady in the Box,* p. 75.

Scholastic Books Publicity Release, c. 1991, biographical profile, "About Ann McGovern."

OTHER

Ann McGovern Web site, http://www.annmcgovern.com/ (November 15, 2001).

Scholastic, http://www.teacher.scholastic.com/ (November 15, 2001), author's biography and booklist.

A Talk with Ann McGovern (video recording), Tom Podell Productions (Scarborough, NY), 1991.

*   *   *

McMULLAN, Kate (Hall) 1947-
(Katy Hall)

Personal

Born January 16, 1947, in St. Louis, MO; daughter of Lee Aker (a physician) and Kathryn (a teacher and flight attendant; maiden name, Huey) Hall; married James Burroughs McMullan (an illustrator), June 9, 1979; children: Leigh Fenwick. *Education:* University of Tulsa, B.S., 1969; Ohio State University, M.A., 1972. *Hobbies and other interests:* Gardening, birding, reading.

Addresses

Home and office—18 Bluff Point Rd., Sag Harbor, NY 11963. *Agent*—Holly McGhee, Pippin Properties, 155 E. 38th St., Ste. 2H, New York, NY 10016. *E-mail*—KateMcMullan@aol.com.

Career

Teacher at public schools in Los Angeles, CA, 1969-71; U.S. Department of Defense, Washington, DC, schoolteacher in Hahn, West Germany, 1972-75; Harcourt, Brace, Jovanovich, Inc., New York, NY, editor, 1976-78; writer, 1978—; New York University School of Continuing Education, New York, NY, lecturer in "Writing for Children," 1989—.

Member

Authors Guild, PEN, Society of Children's Book Writers and Illustrators.

Awards, Honors

Honor Award from New York Academy of Sciences, 1980, for *Magic in the Movies;* Mark Twain List of Excellent Books (Missouri), 1989, and Bluebonnet List of Excellent Books (Texas), 1989, both for *The Great Ideas of Lila Fenwick;* Children's Book Award List (West Virginia), 1989-90, for *Great Advice from Lila Fenwick;* Intellectual Freedom Award honorable mention, New York Library Association, 1993; Pick of the List, *American Bookseller,* and one of the Ten Best Picture Books of 1993, *New York Times,* both for *Nutcracker Noel;* CRABbery honor, 1993, for *The Great Eggspectations of Lila Fenwick;* Ten Best Picture Books of 1995 selection, *New York Times,* 1995 Picture Book Award, Parents' Choice, Reading Magic Award, *Parenting,* 1995, all for *Hey, Pipsqueak!*

Writings

The Mystery of the Missing Mummy, Scholastic (New York, NY), 1984.

(Adapter) Robert Louis Stevenson, *Dr. Jekyll and Mr. Hyde,* Random House (New York, NY), 1984.

The Great Ideas of Lila Fenwick, Dial (New York, NY), 1986.

(Adapter) Gaston Leroux, *Phantom of the Opera,* Random House (New York, NY), 1989.

Dinosaur Hunters, Random House (New York, NY), 1989.

Great Advice from Lila Fenwick, Dial (New York, NY), 1989.

Good Night, Stella, Penguin/Putnam Books for Young Readers (New York, NY), 1990.

The Story of Harriet Tubman, Penguin/Putnam Books for Young Readers (New York, NY), 1990.

The Great Eggspectations of Lila Fenwick, Farrar, Straus, (New York, NY), 1991.

Under the Mummy's Spell, Farrar, Straus, (New York, NY), 1991.

(With Jim McMullan) *The Noisy Giants' Tea Party,* HarperCollins (New York, NY), 1992.

The Biggest Mouth in Baseball, Grosset & Dunlap (New York, NY), 1993.

Nutcracker Noel, Demco (Madison, WI), 1993.

Hey, Pipsqueak!, illustrated by Jim McMullan, HarperCollins (New York, NY), 1995.

The Story of Bill Clinton and Al Gore, Gareth Stevens (Milwaukee, WI), 1996.

Muppet Treasure Island, Penguin/Putnam Books for Young Readers (New York, NY), 1996.

Noel the First, illustrated by Jim McMullan, HarperCollins/ Michael di Capua (New York, NY), 1996.

The Mummy's Gold, Penguin/Putnam Books for Young Readers (New York, NY), 1996.

If You Were My Bunny, illustrated by David McPhail, Scholastic (New York, NY), 1996.

Dragon Slayer's Academy: The New Kid at School, Putnam/Grosset (New York, NY), 1997.

Harriet Tubman, Gareth Stevens (Milwaukee, WI), 1997.

No No, Jo!, HarperCollins (New York, NY), 1998.

Class Trip to the Cave of Doom, Grosset & Dunlap (New York, NY), 1998.

Countdown to the Year 1000, Grosset & Dunlap (New York, NY), 1999.

Papa's Song, illustrated by Jim McMullan, Farrar (New York, NY), 2000.

As Far as I Can See: Meg's Diary, St. Louis to the Kansas Territory, 1856, Scholastic (New York, NY), 2001.

Supercat, illustrated by Pascal Lemaitre, Workman (New York, NY), 2002.

I Stink!, illustrated by Jim McMullan, HarperCollins (New York, NY), 2002.

I'm Mighty, illustrated by Jim McMullan, Joanna Cotler Books (New York, NY), 2003.

Nubby Bear, illustrated by Stan Herman, Random House (New York, NY), 2003.

Nubby Bunny, illustrated by Stan Herman, Random House (New York, NY), 2003.

Nubby Cat, illustrated by Stan Herman, Random House (New York, NY), 2003.

Nubby Puppy, illustrated by Stan Herman, Random House (New York, NY), 2003.

Pearl and Wagner: Two Good Friends, illustrated by R. W. Alley, Dial (New York, NY), 2003.

Rock-a-Baby Band, illustrated by Janie Bynum, Little Brown (Boston, MA), 2003.

Editor of *Early Bird,* 1982.

"MYTH O' MANIA" SERIES

Phone Home, Persephone!, illustrated by David LaFleur, Hyperion Books for Children (New York, NY), 2002.

Have a Hot Time, Hades!, illustrated by David LaFleur, Hyperion Books for Children (New York, NY), 2002.

Say Cheese, Medusa!, illustrated by David LaFleur, Hyperion Books for Children (New York, NY), 2002.

Nice Shot, Cupid!, illustrated by David LaFleur, Hyperion Books for Children (New York, NY), 2002.

Stop That Bull, Theseus!, illustrated by David LaFleur, Hyperion Books for Children (New York, NY), 2003.

"FLUFFY" SERIES

Fluffy Goes to School, illustrated by Mavis Smith, Turtleback Books (Madison, WI), 1997.

Fluffy's Happy Halloween, illustrated by Mavis Smith, Scholastic (New York, NY), 1998.

Fluffy Saves Christmas, illustrated by Mavis Smith, Turtleback Books (Madison, WI), 1998.

Fluffy and the Fire Fighters, illustrated by Mavis Smith, Scholastic (New York, NY), 1999.

Fluffy Meets the Dinosaurs, illustrated by Mavis Smith, Scholastic (New York, NY), 2000.

Fluffy's 100th Day of School, illustrated by Mavis Smith, Turtleback Books (Madison, WI), 2000.

Fluffy Meets the Tooth Fairy, illustrated by Mavis Smith, Scholastic (New York, NY), 2000.

Fluffy's Valentine's Day, illustrated by Mavis Smith, Scholastic (New York, NY), 2000.

Kate McMullan

Fluffy's School Bus Adventure, illustrated by Mavis Smith, Scholastic (New York, NY), 2000.

Fluffy's Thanksgiving, illustrated by Mavis Smith, Scholastic (New York, NY), 2000.

Fluffy's Funny Field Trip, illustrated by Mavis Smith, Scholastic (New York, NY), 2001.

Fluffy's New Garden, illustrated by Mavis Smith, Scholastic (New York, NY), 2001.

Fluffy, the Secret Santa, illustrated by Mavis Smith, Scholastic (New York, NY), 2001.

Fluffy Goes Apple Picking, illustrated by Mavis Smith, Scholastic (New York, NY), 2001.

Fluffy's Trick-or-Treat, illustrated by Mavis Smith, Scholastic (New York, NY), 2001.

Fluffy's Spring Vacation, illustrated by Mavis Smith, Scholastic (New York, NY), 2001.

Fluffy Meets the Groundhog, illustrated by Mavis Smith, Scholastic (New York, NY), 2001.

Fluffy Learns to Swim, illustrated by Mavis Smith, Scholastic (New York, NY), 2002.

Fluffy Goes to Washington, illustrated by Mavis Smith, Scholastic (New York, NY), 2002.

Fluffy's Lucky Day, illustrated by Mavis Smith, Scholastic (New York, NY), 2002.

Fluffy and the Snow Pig, illustrated by Mavis Smith, Scholastic (New York, NY), 2003.

Fluffy Plants a Jelly Bean, illustrated by Mavis Smith, Scholastic (New York, NY), 2003.

UNDER NAME KATY HALL

Nothing But Soup, Follett (Chicago, IL), 1976.

(With Lisa Eisenberg) *Chicken Jokes and Puzzles,* Scholastic (New York, NY), 1977.

(With Jane O'Connor) *Magic in the Movies: The Story of Special Effects,* Doubleday (New York, NY), 1980.

(With Lisa Eisenberg) *A Gallery of Monsters,* Random House (New York, NY), 1980.

(With Lisa Eisenberg) *Pig Jokes and Puzzles,* Scholastic (New York, NY), 1983.

(With Lisa Eisenberg) *Fishy Riddles,* Dial (New York, NY), 1983.

(With Lisa Eisenberg) *101 Bug Jokes,* Scholastic (New York, NY), 1984.

Garfield: Jokes, Riddles, and Other Silly Stuff, Random House (New York, NY), 1984.

Garfield: The Big Fat Book of Jokes and Riddles, Random House (New York, NY), 1984.

(With Lisa Eisenberg) *Buggy Riddles,* Dial (New York, NY), 1986.

(With Lisa Eisenberg) *Grizzly Riddles,* Dial (New York, NY), 1987.

(With Lisa Eisenberg) *101 Back to School Jokes,* Scholastic (New York, NY), 1987.

(With Lisa Eisenberg) *Mummy Riddles,* illustrated by Nicole Rubel, Dial (New York, NY), 1997.

(With Lisa Eisenberg) *Olive You! And Other Valentine Knock-Knock Jokes You'll A-Door,* illustrated by Stephen Carpenter, HarperFestival (New York, NY), 1997.

(With Lisa Eisenberg) *Bunny Riddles,* illustrated by Nicole Rubel, Dial (New York, NY), 1997.

(With Lisa Eisenberg) *Chicky Riddles,* illustrated by Thor Wickstrom, Dial (New York, NY), 1997.

(With Lisa Eisenberg) *Easter Yolks: Eggs-Cellent Riddles to Crack You Up,* illustrated by R. W. Alley, Harper-Festival (New York, NY), 1997.

(With Lisa Eisenberg) *Hearty Har Har: Valentine Riddles You'll Love,* illustrated by R. W. Alley, HarperFestival (New York, NY), 1997.

(With Lisa Eisenberg) *Puppy Riddles,* illustrated by Thor Wickstrom, Dial (New York, NY), 1998.

(With Lisa Eisenberg) *Creepy Riddles,* illustrated by S. D. Schindler, Dial (New York, NY), 1998.

Really, Really Bad Sports Jokes, illustrated by Rick Stromoski, Candlewick Press (Cambridge, MA), 1998.

Really, Really, Really Bad Jokes, illustrated by Mike Lester, Candlewick Press (Cambridge, MA), 1999.

(With Lisa Eisenberg) *Kitty Riddles,* illustrated by R. W. Alley, Dial (New York, NY), 2000.

(With Lisa Eisenberg) *Jingle Jokes: Christmas Riddles to Deck the Ha Ha Halls,* illustrated by Stephen Carpenter, HarperFestival (New York, NY), 2000.

(With Lisa Eisenberg) *Turkey Ticklers: And Other A-Maize-Ingly Corny Thanksgiving Knock-Knock Jokes,* illustrated by Stephen Carpenter, HarperFestival (New York, NY), 2000.

(With Lisa Eisenberg) *Boo Who? And Other Wicked Halloween Knock-Knock Jokes,* illustrated by Stephen Carpenter, HarperFestival (New York, NY), 2000.

(With Lisa Eisenberg) *Easter Crack-Ups: Knock-Knock Jokes Funny Side-Up,* illustrated by Stephen Carpenter, HarperFestival (New York, NY), 2000.

(With Lisa Eisenberg) *Ribbit Riddles,* illustrated by Robert Bender, Dial (New York, NY), 2001.

McMullan's collection of lullabies depicts several animal mothers who coo a goodnight song to their babies, with the lyrics changed to fit each species. *(From* If You Were My Bunny, *illustrated by David McPhail.)*

(With Lisa Eisenberg) *Hanukkah Ha-Has: Knock-Knock Jokes That Are a Latke Fun,* illustrated by Stephen Carpenter, HarperFestival (New York, NY), 2001.

(With Lisa Eisenberg) *Summer Camp Crack-Ups: And Lot S'More Knock-Knock Jokes to Write Home About,* illustrated by Stephen Carpenter, HarperCollins (New York, NY), 2001.

(With Lisa Eisenberg) *Turkey Riddles,* illustrated by Kristin Bora, Dial (New York, NY), 2002.

(With Lisa Eisenberg) *Dino Riddles,* illustrated by Nicole Rubel, Dial (New York, NY), 2002.

Back-to-School Belly Busters, illustrated by Stephen Carpenter, HarperFestival (New York, NY), 2002.

Sidelights

During the late 1990s Kate McMullan authored dozens of titles for young readers, including numerous joke books with Lisa Eisenberg under the name Katy Hall. She has also written a lullaby collection, *If You Were My Bunny,* with illustrations by David McPhail. Here, several different little animals are depicted with their mothers. The mother bear, cat, rabbit, duck, and dog each coo a good-night song to their charges, with the lyrics changed to befit each species. A review from Amy E. Brandt in the *Bulletin of the Center for Children's Books* noted that its "coziness will appeal to those not-quite-drowsy youngsters who plead for one more song." A critic for *Kirkus Reviews* noted that *If You Were My Bunny* "serves as a missing link between board books and ... picture books."

McMullan has worked with her husband, Jim, on several titles. These include *The Noisy Giants' Tea Party* and *Nutcracker Noel,* the latter title centering upon a little girl and her dedication to ballet. Both books grew out of experiences with their own daughter—*The Noisy Giants' Tea Party* was a tale they invented to explain the loud noises emanating from the garbage trucks in the street below their New York City apartment. Their daughter also loved ballet, and in *Nutcracker Noel* the little girl is initially dejected about being chosen to play a tree in an annual holiday production of the classic children's ballet. Noel's ballet saga continues in *Noel the First,* and in this story she is thrilled when Madame orders her to move to first place, an honored position, at the barre. But a new dancer joins the class, and usurps Noel's spot; another, even better new student arrives, and the other two dancers battle it out, with Noel observing. In the end, Noel dances with her heart, which pleases Madame. The other two, Regina and Anne Marie, are initially depicted by Jim McMullan's drawings as graceful and snooty, but descend into hard nosed, ungainly figures as their competition grows fiercer. "For all the exaggeration, there is plenty of truth to this tale—not just for prima ballerinas," noted a *Publishers Weekly* reviewer. Carol Schene, writing for *School Library Journal,* forecasted that "young readers will identify with Noel and the dilemma of wanting to be first."

McMullan has also penned a comic fantasy tale, *Dragon Slayer: The New Kid at School.* The story centers on humble Wiglaf of Pinwick, ill-treated by his boorish family. A traveling minstrel tells his fortune, which leads Wiglaf to the Dragon Academy. He brings his pet pig, Daisy, along. At the school, Wiglaf realizes that his aversion to gore makes him a poor candidate for a Dragon Slayer degree, unlike his zealous new friend, Eric. The pair are sent off on their first mission to slay the dragon Gorzil, and the situation seems dire until Wiglaf finds that the dragon's secret weakness is for knock-knock jokes—for Wiglaf has long list of them in his memory. "Wiglaf is a hero without spilling a single drop of blood," wrote *School Library Journal* critic Virginia Golodetz, while *Booklist*'s John Peters remarked that "McMullan creates an appealing, unwarlike protagonist, with the inner stuff to cope with situations both daffy and dangerous."

McMullan continues to write for the very youngest readership. In *Papa's Song,* published in 2000, Baby Bear does not want to fall asleep, though his family is exhausted. His mother and grandparents each try, with no luck, and finally Baby Bear's father takes him for boat ride. The soothing sounds of the water—the frogs croaking, otters splashing, and waves lapping—result in the desired effect. When Papa Bear returns home with the sleeping Baby, he simply tells the others, "I knew the right song." Writing in *School Library Journal,* Maryann H. Owen called it "A bedtime story almost guaranteed to provide sweet dreams"; a contributor to *Publishers Weekly* also commended this "appealing bedtime story, at once gentle and wry, in which father knows best."

McMullan once commented: "Many of my warmest memories of childhood are of my mother reading aloud to me. As a sixth-grade teacher in the early 1970s, I rediscovered the pleasure of children's books—this time as a reader—and left teaching to study children's literature at Ohio State University. After graduating with a master's degree, I went back to teaching, reading aloud—and writing.

"As a quick glance at my book titles will indicate, humor has been a large part of my writing, especially the work I do with my partner, Lisa Eisenberg. We very much enjoy visiting schools and swapping riddles with first, second, and third graders. Our series of easy-to-read riddle books is popular with kids, as well as librarians and teachers, because the controlled vocabulary makes the books accessible to beginning readers, and the punch lines provide good motivation for reading. . . .

"I have begun writing middle-grade novels based on my childhood experiences in the Midwest and my years as a teacher. The books deal with issues that many ten- and eleven-year-olds have to deal with, such as up-and-down friendships and the pleasures and pains of growing up. I find that, in writing these books, I am drawn back to the books I encountered when I was in fifth or sixth grade—*A Tale of Two Cities* or *The Adventures of Tom Sawyer*—and I enjoy weaving aspects of these books into my own stories. I believe that the pleasure I have derived from reading good books has been my main motivation for wanting to write them myself."

Biographical and Critical Sources

PERIODICALS

Booklist, May 1, 1996, Ilene Cooper, review of *If You Were My Bunny,* p. 1512; January 1, 1997, Susan Dove Lempke, review of *Noel the First,* p. 870; December 1, 1997, John Peters, review of *Dragon Slayer's Academy: The New Kid at School,* p. 637; February 15, 2000, Ellen Mandel, review of *Papa's Song,* p. 1118.

Bulletin of the Center for Children's Books, July, 1996, Amy E. Brandt, review of *If You Were My Bunny,* pp. 379-380.

Horn Book, July-August, 1996, Hanna B. Zeiger, review of *If You Were My Bunny,* p. 451; May, 1998, Maeve Visser Knoth, review of *No No, Jo!,* p. 275; March, 2000, review of *Papa's Song,* p. 189.

Kirkus Reviews, January 1, 1996, review of *If You Were My Bunny,* p. 71.

Publishers Weekly, October 7, 1996, review of *Noel the First,* p. 73; October 6, 1997, review of *Dragon Slayer's Academy: The New Kid at School,* p. 84; April 10, 2000, review of *Papa's Song,* p. 97; February 18, 2002, review of *I Stink!,* p. 95.

School Library Journal, December, 1996, Carol Schene, review of *Noel the First,* p. 100; May, 1998, Virginia Golodetz, review of *Dragon Slayer's Academy: The New Kid at School,* p. 120, and DeAnn Tabuchi, review of *No No, Jo!,* p. 121; May, 2000, Maryann H. Owen, review of *Papa's Song,* p. 149; May, 2002, Rita Soltan, review of *As Far as I Can See: Meg's Diary, St. Louis to the Kansas Territory, 1856,* p. 193.

Tribune Books (Chicago, IL), March 10, 1996, Mary Harris Veeder, review of *Hey, Pipsqueak!,* p. 7.

OTHER

Kate McMullan Web Site, http://www.katemcmullan.com (June 7, 2002).

*　　*　　*

MONTGOMERY, Sy 1958-

Personal

Born February 7, 1958, in Frankfurt, Germany; daughter of Austin James (a U.S. Army general) and Willa Zane (Brown) Montgomery; married Howard Mansfield (a writer), September, 1987. *Education:* Syracuse University, dual B.A.s (French and psychology; magazine journalism), 1979. *Politics:* "Town meeting." *Religion:* Christian. *Avocational interests:* "I have an eleven-year-old, 750-pound pig."

Addresses

Agent—Sarah Jane Freymann, 59 West 71st St., #9B, New York, NY 10023.

Career

Freelance journalist; associate, Center for Tropical Ecology & Conservation, Antioch New England Graduate School, Keene, NH. Has lectured on conservation topics at the Smithsonian Institution, American Museum of Natural History, California Academy of Sciences, and other schools, universities, and conservation organizations.

Member

Society of Women Geographers, New England Environmental Educators.

Awards, Honors

Ray Bruner science writing fellow, American Public Health Association, 1982; Best New Nonfiction, New England Writers and Publishers Project, and finalist, *Los Angeles Times* science book award, both 1991, both for *Walking with the Great Apes;* Chris Award for Best Science Documentary, Columbus Film Festival, 1998, for *Mother Bear Man; Bulletin of the Center for Children's Books'* Blue Ribbon Prize, 1999, International Reading Association Award for Excellence in Children's Books on Science, 2000, Orbis Pictus Honor Book by the National Council of Teachers of English, 2000, John Burrough List of Nature Books for Young Readers, Texas Bluebonnet Award nominee, Texas Library Association, all for *The Snake Scientist;* Thomas Cook Travel Book Award nomination, 2001, for *Journey of the Pink Dolphins: An Amazon Quest;* Oppenheim Toy Portfolio Gold Award, 2002, for *The Man-Eating Tigers of Sundarbans.*

Writings

Walking with the Great Apes: Jane Goodall, Dian Fossey, Birute Galdikas, Houghton Mifflin (Boston, MA), 1991.

Nature's Everyday Mysteries: A Field Guide to the World in Your Backyard (essays), foreword by Roger Tory Peterson, illustrated by Rodica Prato, Chapters (Shelburne, VT), 1993, also published as *The Curious Naturalist: Nature's Everyday Mysteries,* Down East Books (Camden, ME), 2000.

Spell of the Tiger: The Man-Eaters of Sundarbans, Houghton Mifflin (Boston, MA), 1995.

Seasons of the Wild: A Year of Nature's Magic and Mysteries (essays), foreword by Elizabeth Marshall Thomas, illustrated by Rodica Prato, Chapters (Shelburne, VT), 1995.

The Snake Scientist (juvenile), photographs by Nic Bishop, Houghton Mifflin (Boston, MA), 1999.

Journey of the Pink Dolphins: An Amazon Quest, Simon & Schuster (New York, NY), 2000.

The Man-Eating Tigers of Sundarbans (juvenile), photographs by Eleanor Briggs, Houghton Mifflin (Boston, MA), 2001.

Encantado: Pink Dolphin of the Amazon, illustrated by Dianne Taylor-Snow, Houghton Mifflin (Boston, MA), 2002.

Search for the Golden Moon Bear: Science and Adventure in Pursuit of a New Species (adult), Simon & Schuster (New York, NY), 2002.

Contributor to journals, including *International Wildlife, GEO, Nature, Animals, Orion,* and *Ranger Rick,* and to *Encyclopedia Britannica.* Contributor to *The Nature of Nature: New Essays by America's Finest Writers on Nature,* Harcourt Brace, 1994. Author of monthly column for the *Boston Globe,* radio commentaries on nature for National Public Radio's *Living on Earth* program, and scripts for *National Geographic Explorer* television programs, including the documentaries *Spell of the Tiger* (1996) and *Mother Bear Man* (1999).

Adaptations

A sound recording of *The Snake Scientist* was produced by Magnetix Corporation, 2000.

Work in Progress

Two children's books; one adult book.

Sidelights

Sy Montgomery's writings about the natural world extend from the ordinary to the exotic, from the common firefly of many North American backyards to the elusive man-eating tigers of Borneo. In her first book, *Walking with the Great Apes,* the author profiles three famous women primatologists, Englishwoman Jane Goodall, American Dian Fossey, and Canadian Birute Galdikas, each of whom was fundamentally transformed by her years of research and living among apes, Montgomery argues. "This is an exciting book," attested the *Booklist* reviewer, Sally Estes, who was attracted to the author's characterization of her subjects' pursuit of the apes as a kind of vision quest not easily articulated in scientific language. Genevieve Stuttaford in *Publishers Weekly* referred to this aspect of Montgomery's book as "the intriguing view of these scientists as pioneers of a particularly female way of scientific knowing." Estes dubbed *Walking with the Great Apes* "a splendid, well-written account ... that will draw in readers unfamiliar with the research projects [of Goodall, Fossey, and Galdikas] as well as those who have been following them through the years."

In *Nature's Everyday Mysteries,* a collection of Montgomery's columns from the *Boston Globe,* the author provides many little-known facts about the natural world all around us. "For readers who know little about the natural world, [Montgomery's] writing will entertain and inform in equal proportions," averred Jon Kartman in *Booklist.*

For her third book, *Spell of the Tiger,* Montgomery returned to the realm of the exotic. She traveled to the Bay of Bengal, home to the world's largest mangrove swamp, and to the only population of tigers that seeks out human beings as prey rather than shying away from mankind, as most tigers do. "I avoided being eaten by my study subjects," Montgomery reported, "while living in a mud hut among the most deadly man-eaters in the world." The people of the Sundarbans worship the tiger as a god even as hundreds of them every year are hunted and killed by the animals they call Daksin Ray. "Montgomery writes lyrically of an alien land where outlines blur, tree roots reach for the sky, cyclones claim whole villages, and chanted mantras keep tigers from becoming angry," observed a critic for *Kirkus Reviews.* Other reviewers, like a critic writing in *Publishers Weekly,* similarly focused on the author's "vivid picture of the coastal forest and its people." *Booklist* reviewer Donna Seaman noted that Montgomery appeared to "absorb the unique and surprisingly cosmic dynamic of the delta" as she pursued her elusive subject; she concluded: "After all, there can be no revelation more humbling than the recognition that we, like other animals, are meat."

Montgomery wrote and narrated the script for a TV documentary based on her work with the tigers for a *National Geographic Explorer* program that first aired in 1996 to a worldwide audience. For National Geographic, she also developed and wrote the Chris Award-winning documentary *Mother Bear Man,* which aired in April, 1999. "The film profiles the lives of three orphaned bear cubs," she explained, "and their unlikely mother—Ben Kilham, a friend of mine who raised these babies like a mother bear would: by spending nine hours a day roaming the woods with them. The film chronicles Ben's extraordinarily intimate observations of these normally shy animals as they grow into some of the largest carnivores in North America."

While Montgomery's first books were written for the general reader, her award-winning *The Snake Scientist* was specifically written for a younger audience. The strength of this work, according to Ruth S. Vose in her appraisal for *School Library Journal,* is that it exhibits "the excitement of science in action." Montgomery's text centers on a zoologist who studies the red-sided garter snake in Canada, while the book's sidebars include information about aspects of the species that continue to mystify scientists and hints on how to visit snake dens. Montgomery's "lively text" makes this an "outstanding" science book for young people, Vose averred.

Montgomery once commented: "I write for both adults and children in order to help us remember our duty to the earth. Children are a particularly important audience for they have an intuitive connection with plants and animals I hope to help honor and foster in my work. If our kind is to avert the poisonings and extinctions now in progress, today's children will do it.

"To research my books and articles, I have been chased by an angry silverback gorilla in Zaire and bitten by a vampire bat in Costa Rica. I have spent a week working in a pit with 18,000 snakes in Manitoba. I have been deftly undressed by an orangutan in Borneo, hunted by a tiger in India, and—for my upcoming book, *At the Meeting of the Waters*—swum with piranhas, eels, and dolphins in the Amazon.

"*Journey of the Pink Dolphins: An Amazon Quest* is the true story of my quest to follow an enigmatic, little-studied species of freshwater dolphin into the heart of the Amazon. My research required four separate expeditions, each a journey not only into some of the world's greatest jungles, but also a trip back into time, and a foray into a mythical, enchanted world where people say the dolphins can turn into people and seduce both men and women to live with them in a beautiful city beneath the water.

Montgomery's recent books have focused for the most part on a younger audience. They include *The Man-Eating Tigers of Sundarbans* and *Encantado: Pink Dolphin of the Amazon,* which features illustrations by Dianne Taylor-Snow to help introduce the freshwater dolphins called *Encantados* (enchanted) to juvenile readers. A contributor to Kirkus Reviews commented that in *Encantado,* Montgomery "writes with a contagious sense of wonder." Ilene Cooper, writing for *Booklist,* noted that *The Man-Eating Tigers of Sundarbans* has "clearly been written with young people in mind." Set in the Sundarbans Tiger Reserve, the book details tiger behavior and offers views of the tiger from both scientists and villagers. "It immediately captures attention with fresh, engaging writing that turns a scientific study into a page-turning mystery," wrote Cooper.

Biographical and Critical Sources

PERIODICALS

Booklist, March 15, 1991, Sally Estes, review of *Walking with the Great Apes,* p. 1441; April 1, 1993, Jon Kartman, review of *Nature's Everyday Mysteries,* April 1, 1993, p. 1395; January 15, 1995, Donna Seaman, review of *Spell of the Tiger,* p. 878; February 15, 1999, Stephanie Zvirin, review of *The Snake Scientist,* p. 1064; February 15, 2000, Donna Seaman, review of *Journey of the Pink Dolphins: An Amazon Quest,* p. 1064; March 1, 2001, Ilene Cooper, review of *The Man-Eating Tigers of Sundarbans,* p. 1277.

Choice, March, 2001, A. Ewert, review of *The Curious Naturalist: Nature's Everyday Mysteries,* p. 1295.

Horn Book, July, 1999, Diana Lutz, review of *The Snake Scientist,* p. 485; March, 2001, review of *The Man-Eating Tigers of Sundarbans,* p. 232.

Kirkus Reviews, December 1, 1994, review of *Spell of the Tiger,* p. 1596; March 15, 2002, review of *Encantado: Pink Dolphin of the Amazon.*

Library Journal, February 15, 2000, Nancy J. Moeckel, review of *Journey of the Pink Dolphins,* p. 193.

Publishers Weekly, January 11, 1991, Genevieve Stuttaford, review of *Walking with the Great Apes,* p. 85; January 9, 1995, review of *Spell of the Tiger,* p. 53; February 21, 2000, review of *Journey of the Pink Dolphins,* p. 79.

School Library Journal, May, 1999, Ruth S. Vose, review of *The Snake Scientist,* p. 140; March, 2001, Margaret Bush, review of *The Man-Eating Tigers of Sundarbans,* p. 274.

OTHER

Paula Gordon Show, http://www.paulagordon.com/shows/montgomery/ (January 15, 2001), "Spirit of Adventure" (includes audio excerpts from the show).

*   *   *

Autobiography Feature

Sy Montgomery

On an April day in 1997, my life was hanging by a thread.

Or it seemed like a thread. High above a tea-colored tributary of the Amazon, I was actually suspended by a rope, tied to the top of a machimango tree in the Peruvian rainforest. Seven stories below me, people were fishing for piranhas. But as I climbed, I tried not to look down. If I did, I was afraid I'd never make it to the top.

This wasn't the first time I'd found myself in an odd position while working on a book. Researching books, articles, and documentaries, I sometimes get myself in a fix. I've been chased by an angry silverback gorilla in Africa and been bitten by bats in Costa Rica. I've had to pull leaches off my skin after slogging through swamps after orangutans in Borneo. I've been attacked by biting ants on three continents. In order to find and watch the animals I write about, I've skied over hills after bears and ridden elephants through jungles to find tigers. So maybe it shouldn't have seemed strange to be hanging by a rope up a tree in the Amazon—except for one thing. I was up there looking for dolphins.

I was researching a book on the Amazon's pink dolphins. That sounds crazy enough. Whoever heard of a pink dolphin? And what's more, who ever heard of a dolphin who lives not in the ocean, but in a rainforest river? But pink dolphins are real, and they really do live in the Amazon. I'd learned a little bit about them at a conference on marine mammals I attended in Florida. I was so enchanted with the creatures that I decided to write a book about them. The problem was, pink dolphins are often very hard to see.

This I had discovered several weeks before I found myself up that tree. I'd come to the Amazon to try to learn more about these fascinating creatures, and had already visited them in Brazil and Peru. When I traveled by canoe, they often came near my boat. I could spot them, all right— but only for a second or two, and got only a glimpse each time.

Unlike the marine dolphins you've probably seen performing in aquariums or on whale watches in the ocean, the pink river dolphins of the Amazon don't leap high out of the water. They behave and look very different from the dolphins you see performing in aquariums, or like Flipper on T.V. For instance, they don't have a tall fin on the back. When I was trying to study them for my new book, I was often very frustrated, because they swim low in the water. Also, much of the Amazon's waters are dark—not clear

Sy Montgomery

like in an aquarium—so I could only see a small piece of the dolphin each time.

By the time I got to the Tamshiyacu-Tahuayo Community Reserve in Peru, I'd already tried everything I could think of to see them better. I tried watching them from a canoe. For hours, I sat in the hot sun with binoculars. I might see the top of a dolphin's shiny pink head—then it would dive and disappear. Or I might hear one blow air out of the blowhole—CHAA!—and turn around and see nothing but a trail of bubbles. Sometimes I might get a glimpse of someone's tail or someone's back—but that was all. Sometimes I'd hear a pink dolphin blow to the side of my canoe, and seconds later, see a tail flip on the other side. Was it the same dolphin—or a different one? I couldn't even tell how many dolphins I was watching! How was I going to write my book if I couldn't even see the thing I was writing about? I was getting worried.

Maybe, I thought, I could see them better if I actually got in the water and swam with them. One day I dove overboard into the dark water. I opened my eyes beneath the water and tried to see. It was black as night. In fact, I couldn't even see my own feet—but someone else could: I had a bandaid on the bottom of my foot that day and, all of a sudden, felt it ripped off—by some unseen creature in the black water. (Could it be a piranha? An electric eel? Or perhaps a mischievous pink dolphin?)

I had a lovely swim in the cool, dark water that hot day, but still couldn't see the dolphins. That's why now I was climbing that tree. My idea was this: maybe if I changed my perspective, I could see down beneath those dark waters. Maybe from the top of a tall tree, I would get a better vantage point, and maybe I could watch the dolphins swimming beneath me.

So, up I climbed. The rope was attached to the sort of gear mountain climbers use to scale peaks. Leather loops grip you around the thighs and across the pelvis, and there's a sort of noose in which you put your foot. You step into the noose like climbing a stair, and straightening that leg, push yourself up along the rope, using the strong muscles in the legs instead of the relatively weak muscles in the arms.

"My parents, Brigadier General A.J. Montgomery and Willa Zane Brown Montgomery"

At first I was so nervous I shook with fear. I had never done anything like this before. But after a few minutes, I found myself mesmerized by the wonders around me. I found there was actually a forest *in* the trees! Up I climbed, past a rhododendron bush much like those around a house where my family had lived in Virginia—but this was growing on the branches. Up I climbed, alongside a giant philodendron vine with leaves as big as the paddles we used in our canoes. Up I climbed, past birds' nests, wasps' nests, termite nests. Butterflies and parrots flew beneath me. Up near the very top, where the rope was tied, I found a plant like a pineapple known as a bromiliad growing on a branch. Its leaves formed an overlapping bowl which had caught rainwater. And inside this miniature lake the size of a teacup, I found a whole little world teeming with life: mosquito larvae squiggled in the water. A tiny frog clung to the leaves. Other plants—they looked like tiny lily pads— were growing on the water inside this plant. In fact, scientists have catalogued five hundred plant and animal species that can live just in the water of a bromiliad's bowl.

I was astonished and thrilled. I had discovered a whole world up in that tree. Then I looked down, into the water. I couldn't see the dolphins at all. The water was just too dark.

I hadn't accomplished my original objective. But I hadn't failed, either. Instead, my journey up that tree provided me the opportunity to discover something new and important—something I never would have even known to look for.

Trying to see something new—and trying to find new ways of seeing. Both are part of what I do as I research and write about the natural world. Both efforts usually bring surprises. When you're exploring the unexplored, when you're trying to solve nature's mysteries, you have to be prepared for unexpected answers—and be ready to accept unexpected blessings.

This is something the natural world has shown me again and again, ever since I was a little girl.

When I was in grade school, we had to fill out questionnaires about what we wanted to do when we grew up. I was born in 1958, and grew up at a time when boys and girls were expected to enter different professions. So the form had separate columns; the girls' choices listed things like "mother," "housewife," "teacher," "nurse" and for the exotically inclined, "airline stewardess." The boys' side had stuff like "airline pilot," "doctor," and "fireman." Neither column offered anything like "climbing up Amazon rainforest trees in search of dolphins." Nobody suggested a career that involved being hunted by a swimming tiger in India, or searching for an unknown golden bear in Cambodia's forests, or bathing in a swamp in Borneo while orangutans drink your shampoo and eat your bath soap.

But this is the sort of stuff I get to do in my work as an author, writing books and articles and scripts for adults and children. I feel like the luckiest person in the world.

And apparently, I am. On a recent trip to northern Thailand researching yet another book, one called *Search for the Golden Moon Bear,* I was talking with a sort of witchdoctor or shaman of a tribe called the Black Lahu. He looked at my wrists and gasped as if he saw something really wonderful. What was so special about my wrists? The Black Lahu read the patterns of blue veins of your wrists like a palm reader sees your future in the lines on your hand. And he said mine were the luckiest wrists he had ever seen!

I don't know if fortune-tellers can really see the future. But I can tell you this for sure: I really have been very lucky. But not, perhaps, in the way you would expect.

I've never won the lottery. I've never found buried treasure. In fact, I've gotten into enough trouble for a lifetime, even though, at forty-four as I write this for you, I'm only halfway through: I contracted a mosquito-born disease called dengue fever in Borneo, which can kill you. I was held up by a guy with a gun in Africa. I've been mighty near getting kidnapped twice in two different countries. (But see how lucky I am: I'm still here!)

My astonishing good fortune is that, even when I run into trouble, I am doing exactly what I love most and have made it my living.

I've also been blessed by some really good teachers. Some were my teachers in school: I still remember the day I met my first-grade teacher, Miss Benvenuti. On the first day of class she told us that Benvenuti comes from the world for "welcome" in Italian, "and that," she said, "is what I want to extend to you." I had a wonderful biology teacher in junior high school named Mr. Profit. One day he brought in a live bat for us to see, and we peered at it in a box—I thought it was so perfect, so tiny, so wonderful—and he had us dissect a crawfish and glue all its parts to a piece of cardboard. I still have it at my mother's house in Alexandria, Virginia. And in college, I had some wonderful professors. In college, too, I met my husband, Howard Mansfield, also an author, who has taught me more than any other writer.

I've found many of my best teachers outside of school. Some were people far younger than me—the girls who used to live next door to my husband and me in New Hampshire, Kate and Jane Cabot, who taught me how to write books for kids just by showing me what they liked to read. Some of my teachers have been shamans in foreign lands where the people live in mud huts; fishermen and women in the Amazon and in India and Bangladesh, who told me stories that sounded impossible—but which turned out to be true. Some of my teachers were scientists. Some were dancers. Some were dolphins. Others were orangutans, chimpanzees, and gorillas. One was a Scottish terrier named Molly and one was a 750-pound pig named Christopher Hogwood. I'd like to introduce a few of them to you in the pages that follow.

While I was growing up, my father was my hero. I even got in trouble in Sunday school once for saying I loved him more than God. He was a hero in World War II, and had survived three years of torture and captivity at the hands of the Japanese. I loved looking at all the ribbons on his Army uniform signifying the medals he had earned. He had won the Purple Heart many times, once after being shot in the head—but most of his medals were for bravery in saving other people. As a child I used to lie awake at night wondering if I could muster such courage and strength as he had during the war. He taught me this is possible only if you believe in something larger than, and more important

"Molly, with Sy—both pups, 1966"

than yourself—and that often, it is just as important to think as to fight, and that sometimes the most important thing is simply to endure. (This later came in handy when I was trying to stay still watching gorillas while I was being bitten by safari ants!)

My father never talked about the war, though, not even when I was grown up. When I was little, he would read to me. We loved *Alice in Wonderland,* with its wonderful talking animals and delightful rhymes. He would often recite from this and Lewis Carroll's other books and poetry from memory. He would make up stories, too, about gnomes and elves and princesses. We used to pretend we were in a circus, and that he was a trained gorilla and I was an acrobat. He would walk an imaginary tightrope over a pit of poisonous snakes while I sat on his shoulders. Of course, even if our tightrope had been real, and beneath us venomous reptiles, I would not have been afraid, because my father would never let me down, whether in human form or gorilla.

My mother, too, was an extraordinary person. She had been a pilot back in the days when very few women flew. She also knew how to hunt. She had shot squirrels and possums to eat growing up in the tiny, rural town of Lexa, Arkansas, the only daughter of an ice man and a postmistress. (Although I gave up eating meat many years ago, I still admire the ability to hunt; it makes my mother seem more like a tiger.) My mother was an excellent student, and although her family wasn't wealthy, she had gone to college—again, at a time when few women did so. Upon graduation she landed a job working at the FBI, which was how she met my father, who was at the time working at the Pentagon.

By the time I was born, my parents were stationed in Frankfurt, Germany. Although I don't remember it, when I was a toddler, my parents took me to the Frankfurt Zoo and discovered I was strangely drawn to the hippos, into whose enclosure I nearly wandered during a split second they took their eyes off me. Alas, I never learned German, since we moved to the United States before I was two. But long before I started school, I was already studying French. My father seemed to be able to pick up nearly any language almost instantly, and it was fun to be able to speak to him in French because it was like a secret code to us. At night, before going to sleep, if my father was home, I would reach up into the sky and pretend to grab the moon and the stars and put them in his pocket.

Just before I started first grade, my father got his stars for real. He was promoted to Brigadier General. The silver eagles he wore on the shoulders of his uniform as a colonel used to scratch my arms up when he would come home and I would hug him. I attended the parade at the Brooklyn Army Terminal in his honor. I hoped the stars would be easier to hug.

My father's promotion put him in command of the Brooklyn Army Terminal and military traffic management for the east coast of the United States as well as several areas overseas. He traveled a lot in those days, and would come home with wonderful gifts in his suitcase: soft, striped Bursa towels and sequined shoes with turned-up toes from Turkey; silk kimonos and little bamboo cricket cages from Japan. He never held any anger against the Japanese people from his years as a prisoner, even though he had testified in the War Crimes trials to some of the atrocities he had seen.

One day he was sent overseas in a big hurry. He came home the day before leaving very sick with fever. He had just gotten a whole lot of shots to protect against the diseases that were rampant in the jungles of Vietnam. Normally, you get these shots spaced weeks apart; many years later, I would take similar vaccines before I would

"Home: the tent where I lived in Australia"

travel to Laos, Thailand, and Cambodia writing a new book. But he had to get them all at once because the Army was in a rush. I didn't know it at the time, but they were sending him to Vietnam to try to figure out how to bomb the Ho Chi Minh trail; as it turned out, this couldn't be done. When he came back in a few weeks, the most important news he had to offer me was he didn't see any monkeys in the jungle, which was very disappointing to both of us. He loved animals as much as I did.

While my father went bravely off to war, my mother faced terrors at home. One of her worst fears was that my pet lizard would get out. This had happened several times before, when I was in school and my father wasn't home to catch it. I also had turtles and fish, including, at one time, seahorses (the male seahorse incubates the eggs in a pouch on his stomach; I watched as they seemed to squirt out of his belly), and a green parakeet named Jerry who used to sit on my finger. My best friend and one of my best teachers ever was our dog, a Scottish terrier named Molly. In the manner of all Scottish terriers, Molly was fearless, despite her size. Her jaws were strong enough to crunch bones. She could see in the dark. She could smell and hear things people could not. I wanted to be like her. I imagined what it would be like if I could live somewhere in the woods with her and learn dog secrets. But from her more than anyone else, I learned to imagine what the world might be like to a non-human creature.

Molly had been given to us as a puppy by friends of my parents who bred Scottish terriers; people I loved so much I called them Aunt Grace and Uncle Clyde, even though we weren't related at all. In fact, I had few relatives. No brothers or sisters. My mother had, like me, been an only child. Her father, and my father's mother and brother, had all died before I was born. My mother's mother, one of the sweetest, strongest, and most patient people I have ever met, used to visit us for several weeks once a year. I only remember meeting my father's father once, but we were still close because we wrote each other long letters.

I always loved to write—letters to my grandfather and grandmother, stories I would illustrate with clumsy drawings, and even, for a time, a daily newspaper circulated only in our house. I don't remember playing with other children—ever. In family photo albums, my parents have pictures of me with other kids, but clearly this didn't impress me much. I preferred the company of animals.

I admired even the smallest insect more than I admired other kids my age, because animals can do things we could not. Molly, of course, could see, smell and hear things no human could. My Jerry could fly. My lizards could re-grow their tails. Even earthworms amazed me, because they could literally eat their way through the soil. Crickets could sing by fiddling their legs against their wings. Lightning bugs could glow in the dark.

All of these creatures were more than just playmates; they were teachers. They taught me how to watch and to listen, allowing me to broaden the focus of my interests beyond my own species, and take in a bigger world. What did the world feel like to an earthworm, a bee, a turtle? I would watch all of these creatures for hours, transfixed. I haunted the local libraries for books about animals. Sometimes I would write reports on them—not for school, just for fun. And at night, before I would go to bed, I would

Howard Mansfield and Sy Montgomery on their wedding day, 1987

often close the door and pace around my room for hours, just thinking about these things.

My parents must have worried about me. Once, when I was very young, I was sent home from school for biting a boy. He had richly deserved it, in my opinion; he had pulled the legs off a Daddy Long Legs. (I often looked to Molly for moral guidance; I simply did what she would have done if equally annoyed.) My father had once brought home from his travels a real stuffed baby alligator, which I adored, and I had horrified my mother when I took the baby dolls she gave me to play with and ejected them from their pram, tore off their clothes, and used them to dress the stuffed alligator.

I really didn't care much about playing with other children when there were animals to watch instead. Until, that is, I met Ann Wolicki.

Before I began junior high school, my father retired from the Army and took a new job with the shipping industry. We moved to Alexandria, Virginia. This was the first place we had lived that actually had a real woods nearby that I could explore. And Ann, our backyard neighbor, a girl my age, showed me The Creek.

Although it was just a few blocks away, The Creek was the wildest place I had ever seen. I had known nothing like it on the Army base or in suburban New Jersey. You could walk for half an afternoon and not see a house, or another person. You could find fish and frogs. Usually Ann and I could find box turtles. We sometimes took these home and would build spacious outdoor pens for them. At The Creek we found most of the creatures for the insect collection Mr. Profit had us create for biology class. (During this project, my poor mother would shriek when she'd find all sorts of insects in the freezer, which was how we killed them before mounting them with pins in a cigar

box.) Though Ann and I also liked to bike and watch our turtles at home, we also enjoyed time in the tree fort her father had built in her backyard. But The Creek was our favorite place. It was magic.

It was then that I probably began to imagine the life that I lead now, exploring the living, leafy, wild world and writing about it.

We moved again only three years later. I was devastated to have to leave Ann and The Creek. I found solace mostly in the local church, which became the center of my social life: Bible Study, Methodist Youth Fellowship, and choir. With my friend Herbie, I founded a church newspaper, *Maranatha.* (Herbie is a minister today; Ann became a veterinarian.) And I wrote for the high school paper, the *Hi's Eye.* I took my first journalism classes in high school, with a spectacular, tall teacher, Mr. Clarkson. He was also the track coach, and was given to feats of athleticism: sometimes he would leap off a desk to illustrate a point. This, for me, became the measure of a successful story: it should be so exciting to read that it would make Mr. Clarkson want to jump off a desk.

Thanks to Mr. Clarkson, I decided to study journalism in college. I chose Syracuse University because of its journalism school. But there were so many fascinating courses in college I eventually declared not just one, but three majors: Magazine Journalism, French Language and Literature, and Psychology. I wanted to declare a fourth, Biology, but the school wouldn't let me. I took as many biology courses as I could nonetheless, where I got to dissect a fetal pig, a shark, and a cat. I now feel bad those animals died for my education, but at the time, I was filled with wonder of getting to see what was inside thir beautiful bodies. I suppose this is also what attracted me to psychology: in theory, it allowed me to see what was inside people's heads, which had always seemed a mystery to me. (Why would anyone pull the legs off a Daddy Long Legs?)

College is great because it allows you to experiment at being many things. I got to be a playwright: I wrote and directed a two-hour musical comedy for a sort of school club called Traditions Commission. I got to be a teacher: I taught a French conversation class for credit. I got to be an athlete, of sorts: I completed three, three-day dance marathons to raise money for muscular dystrophy—endurance was something I could do. And I got to be a journalist: I wrote for the daily college newspaper, *The Daily Orange.* In fact I later became an editor of the paper. I was hired for the job by the man I would later marry, Howard Mansfield, a dual major in American Studies and Magazine Journalism, and the paper's managing editor. He was and is the most interesting person I have ever met. He was always full of ideas, and it seemed everything he saw was inspiration for his writing.

One of the many things Howard taught me was that if you are going to write about things that matter, you are bound to make people mad. If you think something is wrong, and after researching it carefully you see it really IS wrong, you *have* to point it out. In our junior year at college, Howard and I were co-editors of the paper's

Visiting Gorillas in Rwanda, Africa, 1986

editorial or opinion section. Our university had plans to give the Empress of Iran a big award for being a good humanitarian. We weren't so sure it was a good idea. At the time, the Empress' husband, the Shah of Iran, was accused by many reputable international organizations of torturing political prisoners. We did a lot of research on this, and decided it was true. But during the time we were researching our editorial against giving the award to the Empress, we would come in to our office and find groups of Iranian students waiting for us there. One day it would be a pro-Shah group. The next day it would be an anti-Shah group. Each group wanted us to give them the names of the people in the other group. (Why? So they could beat them up? We wouldn't do it.) And we eventually wrote an editorial that convinced our school not to give the wife of a despot an award for good deeds. Some of the Iranian students told us we should be careful after writing that editorial, and that if we ever visited Iran we would be killed! But it was a good thing we wrote it, because only days after the award would have been given, the Iranian people, angry at their rulers' cruelty, rose up and overthrew the Shah.

Working on the daily paper not only showed me not to fear criticism, but also how to listen and learn from it. When you have a daily deadline to meet, there is little room to nurse hurt feelings because someone criticizes your story; you just go back and rewrite it until it's good enough to print. One day one of the other editors brought Howard a story to approve before it would go into the paper. As Howard read it, he saw it was so badly written it would have to be redone from scratch. Without a word, he picked up a lighter and torched the pages. The editor had a new, much better story ready in two hours.

When we graduated from college, Howard began to write a book, and I took a job with a newspaper. At first I worked for the *Buffalo Evening News,* covering business. Within a few months, though, I was offered a job at a smaller newspaper for less pay, which I eagerly accepted. I didn't want to write about business; I wanted to write about biology and the environment. The newspaper I now joined wasn't offering me a job writing about that, either. But at the *Courier-News* in Bridgewater, NJ, I would be working in the state with more scientists per capita than any other. New Jersey also was the center of the nation's chemical and pharmaceutical industries, with many interesting environmental stories to cover. At this smaller paper, I would probably have more freedom.

At first, I covered nine towns in the rural county of Hunterdon. This meant writing about a lot of boring meetings, at which people make decisions about sewerage. But I got to do some great stories, too. One was a two-part investigation of why a Getty oil pipeline had broken and poisoned a pristine trout stream running through two of my towns. I went to Washington, D.C. (at my own expense, staying with my parents) and looked up Getty Oil Company's maintenance records at The Petroleum Institute for the pipeline. In the story, I showed the trout stream had been poisoned because a rich corporation hadn't bothered to maintain its own property in order to save its stockholders money.

So, some people were mad at me again—but I also won an award for the story, and more awards for stories like it. I was promoted to medical and science writer/

general assignment. I wrote about the unusually high incidence of cancer in New Jersey, including the deaths from a lung cancer called asbestosis at an asbestos manufacturer, Johns Manville. I wrote a series about paralyzing football injuries among high school and college players, showing that, among other things, helmet designs contributed to breaking young men's necks for the sake of a game. I worked fourteen hours a day, six days a week. Meanwhile, Howard was working about the same hours on his book. We took Sundays off. Sometimes we were so tired all we could do was lie around and read the *New York Times*.

After five years on the paper, my parents decided it was time for me to take a special vacation. I had always wanted to go to Australia, because of its strange, pouched mammals like kangaroos and koalas. My father said he would finance a trip. But where on this giant continent would I go? What would I do? I began to research my options and discovered an organization called Earthwatch. This nonprofit outfit matches regular people like me who are willing to pay for the opportunity to volunteer helping scientists work on projects around the world. I volunteered for a project called Drought Refugia in South Australia, working with Dr. Pamela Parker. Part of the year, Pam worked at the Brookfield Zoo in Chicago; but she also

worked in South Australia, studying the habitat of the rare and endangered southern hairy-nosed wombat.

Wombats, like koalas and kangaroos, are pouched mammals known as marsupials. They look sort of like giant groundhogs, and live in holes which they dig with powerful claws out of the rock-hard soil of the South Australian outback. You seldom see them except when they're sunning themselves on the mounds of their warrens. So how could you study them? For two weeks, with the other handful of volunteers, I lived in a tent and assisted Pam taking measurements of the wombat's systems of holes and tunnels, cataloging the plant life, and learning from the edges of the animals' lives. One important way of learning how many wombats there are is by looking for their pellet-like feces, or scats. We learned to tell wombat scat from kangaroo scat (wombats' are bigger). We could tell which wombat warrens had residents by looking for these scats, and for the marks their teeth made on the plants growing nearby. At night, while we ate by the campfire, Pam would give us lectures about the animals that lived in the area: the spine-covered, egg-laying echidnas, with their tongues shaped like long ribbons for eating ants; the red and gray kangaroos; the colorful rainbow lorikeets that chattered in the scrubby eucalypts above our heads; the pink and gray cockatoos known as galahs, who look like flying sunsets as their flocks bank and turn overhead.

Montgomery with a Siberian tiger

I fell in love with this astonishing landscape, and the animals there. Seeing my enthusiasm for field work, Pamela made me an offer I couldn't refuse: if I wanted to continue studying Australian animals, she couldn't pay me a salary, cover my airfare, or fund my insurance—but if I wanted to come back, to study anything I wanted, she would give me free food for as long as I wished, and I could camp for as long as I wanted at her study site at Blanchetown Conservation Park.

I quit my job and moved to a tent in the outback.

At first I didn't know what I would study. My first few days I helped out a graduate student with her study of plants. One day, when I was alone, lopping off plants with a small knife and stuffing them into paper bags to bring back to her at camp, I suddenly looked up and saw, twenty-five yards away, three birds, each nearly as tall as a man, staring at me. They were emus.

Emus are ancient, ostrichlike birds, with eight-foot stumps for wings, haystack-colored bodies, long black necks topped with periscope heads, and legs on which they can run at forty miles per hour and strong enough to sever fencing wire with a single kick. I couldn't believe they had come this close to me. While I stayed motionless, they peered at me, as if curious. Then they strolled away, unafraid. I realized I was sweating in the forty-degree cold. I couldn't have been more astonished if angels had come down from Heaven to look at me. And I knew what I would study.

For six months, I followed them whenever I saw them, recording their every movement on a checksheet I created, noting the time they walked, sat, ran, drank, grazed. I learned to recognize which bird was which, giving each a name. After a few weeks, I found I could locate them daily. I never knew their sex—this is impossible to know by appearance alone. But I knew that, though no longer tiny, striped chicks, these birds were young. They lacked the turquoise patch on the neck of mature emus. They always traveled together, which suggested they were siblings who had hatched from the same clutch of large, greenish black eggs, which are incubated by the father.

During this time, I often thought about a scientist I had long admired, Jane Goodall. Before I could read, I had seen pictures of her in National Geographic magazine, a slender blonde in a ponytail, squatting in the dirt and holding her hand out to a wild chimpanzee, who was stretching his hand out to hers. No scientist had ever been able to do this before. I modeled my study on hers. Like me, she had no formal scientific training when she began her study. But she had good eyes, and a good understanding of how to approach animals. That's why she was able to study them at close range, when all the other scientists before her had only gotten glimpses of chimpanzees running away into the trees. I remember how she got the apes used to her presence among them: she wore the same thing every day. So did I: jeans, the shirt I'd slept in, my father's old green Army jacket, and a red bandana. Jane approached the chimps only to the point where they felt comfortable, never chasing them. So did I with the emus. I never wanted them to feel I was sneaking up on them, or stealing from them, not even glimpses. Their presence was a gift I accepted on their terms.

Soon I could approach them within five feet—close enough to see the veins on the leaves they were eating,

Montgomery with Namita (left) in the village of James-pur in Sundarbans, West Bengal, India, 1996

close enough to enjoy the glowing the reddish-mahogany irises of their eyes, close enough to hear the sound of their beaks combing their feathers as they preened. I discovered they were very smart, and also had a sense of humor.

One day I saw the three approach the park ranger's dog. She was on a chain, and barking ferociously at the interlopers. But the birds were completely calm. They knew exactly how long the chain was! They approached within a foot of the frenzied dog—and then leapt in the air, kicking their legs, flinging their necks—and the dog went wild. Then they ran off to a safe distance, flopped onto the ground, and preened themselves—apparently well-satisfied with the success of their prank.

For six months, I simply recorded what they did all day—what they ate, how they played, where they traveled. There were no major scientific breakthroughs to report. But from them, I learned something very important. Ours was a friendship, and a kind of trust, unlike any other I had known. Unlike my treasured pets, the emus didn't have to tolerate me. They were not living in my home; I was living in theirs. They could get away from me any time they wished. Not only could they run away from me if they wanted; they could have attacked me; and in fact, emus sometimes do, when threatened, and they can kill you with a swift kick from their strong, clawed feet. But they didn't. Even though the emus, being birds, were more closely related to dinosaurs than to people, they favored me with a gift I would cherish forever: the gift of allowing me into their lives *on their terms.*

When I had to return to the United States six months later, my life had changed. For one thing, I realized that after living in a tent, spending all day each day walking outside, and having no boss to answer to, I would hate working in an office. I simply couldn't put on stupid panty hose and high heels and a suit and work in a cubicle all day. I decided to write on my own, as Howard had been doing ever since we graduated from Syracuse University in 1979.

In New Hampshire, a state full of forests and wetlands, I began writing for different magazines and newspapers. On my way back from Australia, I had stopped in New Zealand, in order to visit the windswept, cliffside home of the world's heaviest insect—a handsome, maple-syrup-colored cricket-like species known as the giant weta who weighs three times as much as a mouse. I wrote a story about the insect for *International Wildlife* magazine. Every week, I mailed in a science column to my old newspaper, the *Courier-News*. I wrote for the *Boston Globe*'s science section about endangered insects, and for *Animals* magazine about backyard toxins. Each story seemed to lead to another. *International Wildlife* liked my giant weta story enough that I convinced them to let me go back to New Zealand to write about some of the other fascinating animals there, including a flightless, endangered parrot called the kakapo. It had nearly gone extinct, not because people hunted it, but because the young birds were eaten by weasels and cats—animals that Europeans had brought to New Zealand, predators the kakapo had never evolved to avoid. But people also helped the kakapo. Realizing the amazing parrot was nearly gone, people moved them to cat- and weasel-free areas, and also set up special nests so they could breed in captivity and later be released to the wild. This was the sort of story I loved to write most: stories that show how people have, even without intending to, upset the natural balance of the world—and the ways we have learned to make amends for our blunders.

After five years of writing stories for magazines and newspapers, I longed to write something longer and more in-depth: a book. A book is a big project. Could I do it? I was lucky once again, to have a husband and friends who told me I could. About this time, I met a very special person, who would become one of my best friends, even though she is thirty years older than me. Her name is Elizabeth Marshall Thomas, and when she was my age, she had written her first book: *The Harmless People*. It was the story of her family's extraordinary expedition to Namibia, to contact the hunter-gathering people of the desert, the Bushmen. She'd next written another wonderful book about African people, *Warrior-Herdsmen*. She had then had two children and not written any more books for two decades. But recently she had traveled to Africa again. Now she was, like me, facing a whole new challenge. Now she was trying to write fiction. Her novel (which eventually became the best-selling *Reindeer Moon*) was about halfway done when I met her. Liz helped show me that you can *always* start something new. And even when your confidence in yourself might fail, you can keep yourself going by confidence in your project—in the message you want to convey—in the thing that is bigger and more important than yourself.

I wanted my first book to be about people's relationships with animals. Most people know animals in only one of two ways: we take animals into our homes as pets. We take them into our bodies as foods. Most people never really get to know wild animals on the animals' terms, as I had done with the emus. But Jane Goodall had, with her chimps. As a result, she came to see the animals in an entirely new way. To the researchers before her, the chimps

With kangaroos in Australia, 1983

were just study subjects. They never called chimps by names. They just numbered them, like rocks. Jane, though, saw each as an individual. She didn't just study them—she considered them her friends and her teachers. Jane's unusual approach inspired other studies modeled on her own. After she went into the field, another woman, Dian Fossey, had begun a long-term study of mountain gorillas in Rwanda. And after Dian, a third woman, Birute Galdikas, had begun to study orangutans in Borneo. This seemed a logical place for me to start. My first book would honor three of my heroines. They had a lot in common: all three were women, and all three were sent into the field by the same man: Louis Leakey, a scientist famous for finding the first fossils of early human ancestors in Africa. He had sent these women to study apes because apes are humans' closest living relatives: chimps are so biologically similar to us that blood transfusions between chimps and people are possible. And all three had devoted their lives—not just a few months—to their study animals. Other people, all of them men, had tried to study these animals before. But Jane, Dian, and Birute were the first to study apes for such a long time, and in such detail.

Their studies resulted in astonishing new findings. Jane Goodall discovered that chimpanzees use tools, like sticks to fish out termites to eat or crushed leaves to sop up water to drink. Before her work, people thought humans were the only creatures to use tools. Dian Fossey discovered that gorillas weren't frightening, violent creatures, but gentle vegetarians who live in devoted family groups: a noble silver-backed adult male and his several females and their children. And Birute Galdikas found that orangutans are extremely intelligent. Among other things, they have incredible memories, keeping track of hundreds of trees in the vast forest, remembering where they are and when they fruit.

Why had these women made these important discoveries, when the people who tried before them had failed? How was their approach different? And why had they decided to stay so long with the animals they studied, when everyone else had given up after only a few months?

I spent three years finding out the answers. I read everything I could find about the three women and about Louis Leakey. I watched films of the women working which had aired on National Geographic T.V. specials and other shows. I interviewed people who knew the women. I interviewed other scientists who had studied the great apes. I also interviewed Jane Goodall twice—once in the United States, and once in her home in England. I met and interviewed her son, Grub, and her mother, Vanne. Dian Fossey had been murdered by the time I wrote the book, but I traveled to Rwanda and Zaire where she had worked and met the gorillas she had studied. To get to the gorillas, you sometimes have to walk for hours on little paths along the forested slopes of the Virunga Volcanoes, up to 10,000 feet where the air starts to get thin and hard to breathe. You have to plow through patches of stinging nettles, which hurt your skin. There are safari ants, which bite so hard sometimes you have to pinch their heads off and then pry away their jaws to remove them. It was a long, hard hike to get to the gorillas the day I saw them, with a small group of people who had hired a guide to take us there. But actually walking in Dian's footsteps, I learned many things. First, I began to understand just how hard a life she had chosen. And second, the minute I saw the gorillas, I knew that it was worth it.

For my research, I also went to Kenya. There I interviewed scientists who had known Dian and Jane. Louis Leakey had died in 1972, but his family still lives there, and I interviewed one of his sons. I also traveled to the Gombe Stream Reserve in Tanzania where Jane Goodall still works whenever she can. There, on the sunny lake shore and in the forest, I met many of the chimps I had read about. I recognized some of them the same way you recognize a movie star from a photograph: at once I knew Fifi, because I had seen pictures of her ever since she was an infant. Now Fifi had a little baby of her own.

I went to Borneo, too, and got to work with Birute Galdikas. Earthwatch had a project there, and I joined the volunteers as they helped learn about wild orangutans' lives. Before dawn, with a native Dayak guide, we would slog through leech-filled swamps to find the tree in which

"Our pig, Christopher Hogwood, with our neighbor, one of his many fans"

an orangutan had made a nest the night before. Beneath it, we'd sling up hammocks between two trees, to rest and get away from the leeches. We'd listen as gibbons whooped their elastic, alien-sounding songs as the sun rose. We'd hear the buzz of insects whose calls were loud as chain saws. Finally the orangutan would wake up, move from the nest, and begin to swing between the branches of trees along toward a good fruit tree. We'd struggle to follow below—plagued by mosquitoes and flies, trying to keep up without falling into the swamp, trying not to touch any of the trees (which sometimes have spines or toxic sap or fire ants) but above all, trying not to lose the orangutan. At the end of the day, after the orangutan had nested, we'd walk all the way back, sometimes in the dark, completely exhausted. Again, I came to appreciate how hard Birute had worked—and how much she had to love her study animals to do so.

The result of my research, *Walking with the Great Apes: Jane Goodall, Dian Fossey and Birute Galdikas,* was published in 1991. My father never got to see it; he died in 1990 after a fight with cancer just as I was finishing the last pages of the book. I read him some of the book, especially the closing words of the acknowledgements, the part where the author thanks those who helped them in their research: ". . . finally I would like to thank my father . . . in whose intrepid footsteps I falteringly follow."

I was with him when he died. He had shown me how to live, and he also showed me how to die. Now I am not afraid.

One book lead to another, and another. Having written about women scientists and their studies of humans' closest relatives, I wanted to next examine a different kind of relationship between people and animals. Jane, Dian and Birute had loved the apes they studied, and worked very hard to keep them safe from poachers, loggers, and illegal animal dealers in their forest homes. But what about animals who are less loveable, less like people, than chimps, gorillas and orangutans? I wanted next to write about animals who seemed more difficult to understand, and even more difficult to love: predators.

Humans have long warred with predators. In New England, one of the first things the settlers did was kill off all the wolves and the mountain lions. The same is the case around the world. People fear predators, and we compete with them. We want their prey for ourselves. Predators also need a lot of land on which to hunt—and people want that same land to build houses, farms, factories, and cities. That is why predators of all kinds are in danger of extinction around the world—and why I chose a predator as the subject of my next book.

I chose what I considered the mightiest and most beautiful predator of all: the tiger. No other cat can grow so big. A tiger can weigh three hundred pounds more than a big male lion. No other cat is so strikingly gorgeous: the tiger's striped coat glows as if aflame. I went to the wonderful library at Harvard's Museum of Comparative Zoology to read more about tigers, hoping to find a particular place which offered a tiger story around which to frame my book.

All day I read, rapt, about tigers all over the world: the biggest subspecies of tiger, the Siberian, who stalks prey in

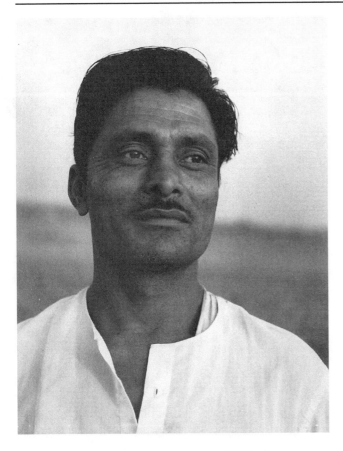

Girindra, Sy's boatman and friend

the snows of Russia, the Indo-Chinese tiger, who hunts in the jungles of Southeast Asia. I discovered that there were five different subspecies of tiger, in fact—and that not long ago there had been eight. Three kinds of tiger had gone extinct since the turn of the century. That made writing my book even more urgent, as all the remaining tigers were endangered, too. They're shot because people fear them. They're being crowded out of their habitat as people convert wild places to towns. They're killed for their spectacular coat. They are also being murdered so people can eat parts of their bodies in soups and potions they think will make them strong like tigers. Some articles I read suggested tigers might be extinct in the wild during my own lifetime. I had no time to waste.

Then I came upon an article that suggested the very sort of mystery I wanted to explore. It described a forest that seemed like no other: stretching for 10,000 square kilometers along the Bay of Bengal between India and Bangladesh, the Sundarbans mangrove swamp is a forest drowned by sea. Tides flush the rivers, flood the trees, then drain away. The animals here drink water tinged with salt. And the tigers here are unlike any others. Some five hundred of them inhabit the mangrove forest—the only tigers to live in such a habitat. And they are unusual in other ways, as well: they swim out after your boat and eat you!

Though tigers elsewhere seldom bother people, here tigers kill some three hundred people a year. Why? But there was an even deeper mystery to explore. Even though

elsewhere tigers are hunted to near extinction, here the people don't hurt the tigers—they worship them instead.

To investigate these two mysteries, I embarked on my journey into Sundarbans. The trip would extend to four separate expeditions in two different countries. It would result in two books (one for adults, one for kids), a National Geographic Explorer T.V. documentary, and friendships with one special family that would last a lifetime.

The first trip was almost a complete disaster. At first, it seemed everything was going well. Unlike my trip to Africa, I wasn't going to India and Bangladesh alone, but in the company of a wonderful friend, Dianne Taylor-Snow. I had met Dianne in Borneo, while I was working on *Walking with the Great Apes.* She had been working with Birute Galdikas, helping her to care for the orphaned baby orangutans who were constantly being brought to the study center. Dianne had many talents; she had worked in the past as a zookeeper, a model, an airline stewardess, and a clothing designer. She was also a talented photographer, and eager to accompany me to India to take pictures for my new book. First, we were going to Bangladesh, and next to India, where we would meet the Indian wildlife biologist who had authored the article I read back in the Harvard Library, Dr. Kalyan Chakrabarty. He had generously offered to act as our guide and translator in Sundarbans, and would also take care of arranging for us to travel on a speed boat.

But as soon as we got to India, everything fell apart. On the plane ride over, a filling fell out of my tooth, leaving a painful hole. We arrived in Calcutta in darkness (there was a power failure) and had to locate our luggage at the airport by flashlight. The next day we found to our dismay that Dr. Chakrabarty had just taken a new job—and now he wouldn't be able to accompany us to Sundarbans after all. Dianne and I were heading into a tiger reserve full of man-eaters with no speedboat, no translator, and no guide.

And things only got worse from there.

Civil unrest rocked the Indian subcontinent when Muslims and Hindus began to fight over an ancient temple both religions claimed as theirs. Protesters on both sides attacked people in trains, on busses, and in the streets. Martial law was declared. No movement between cities and towns was allowed. We couldn't leave the tiger reserve.

With the little Bengali I had picked up from language tapes, I was able to hire a boatman to take us through the reserve's waterways. Girindra Nath Mridha had lived here all his adult life. He had made his boat by hand. One of his uncles, he told me, had been killed by a tiger—and he saw it happen. He knew everything, it seemed, that I needed to know. But we could hardly speak. He knew just a little more English than I knew Bengali!

For two weeks, every day we would take Girindra's boat down the twisting waterways of Sundarbans, hoping to see a tiger. Though we found their footprints everywhere, we only saw a tiger once—it was swimming across the river right in front of us! But it seemed to vanish in an instant, melting into the forest once it reached the other side. (Dianne got a picture of that tiger—but more disaster awaited us. When we finally did get out of Sundarbans, Dianne had to store her exposed film in her checked baggage at the airport to avoid exposing it to the Calcutta airport's unreliable X-ray machine. When she arrived home in Fresno, California, all her baggage had been stolen. It was never retrieved.)

Those two weeks in Sundarbans, every day, every hour, Girindra and I struggled to speak to each other. We were both so frustrated! There was so much he wanted to tell me, and so much I wanted to ask. We simply didn't have the words. We were from very different worlds: Girindra from a world where everything is made by hand, mostly from mud and reeds; I had flown in on an airplane—a vehicle Girindra had only seen in the sky. He wondered aloud whether airplanes might have tennis courts on board. Girindra was Hindu, believing that humans live many different lives, and that God has many faces, including tigers and many-armed goddesses; I was Christian. But during those two weeks, we formed a deep and lasting bond. Later, when I was able to secure a translator, he told me he thought I was once his sister in a former life. He and his wife, Namita, and their eight children adopted me into the family, calling me Pishima, which means "father's sister." And as it turned out, my friendship with Girindra was the key that unlocked the mystery to Sundarbans.

On my later trips to Sundarbans, my friendship with Girindra and his family eventually allowed me to talk freely with everyone in his village—not as a researcher, but as a family friend. The people told me astonishing stories. At first they were unbelievable! "The tiger can fly through the air," people said. "Yes, and the tiger can become invisible!" they would insist. How could that be? But I was sure the people weren't lying. So instead of arguing—telling them their stories were impossible—I just listened. And soon enough, I learned their stories were true.

A tiger CAN become invisible—its striped coat allows the cat to blend so perfectly with its environment you can't see it even if it's right in front of you. A tiger CAN fly—it can leap for over twenty feet through the air. Girindra and his friends taught me many natural history facts about tigers, but much more than that, too. They taught me how to listen for truth, even when it comes in stories that at first seem impossible—and how to look for wisdom in places that at first seem humble and poor.

Had Dr. Chakrabarty been able to escort Dianne and me as originally planned, I still would have written a book—but not these books! Again, I was lucky, because a disaster turned out to be a blessing in disguise.

As always, researching this book lad me to the next one. In Sundarbans, I had glimpsed strange, pinkish dolphins who lived in the brown rivers by the sea. These were among the five species of little-known river dolphins in the world. Though I had only caught a few glimpses, the image of those dolphins stayed with me—and when I went to a marine mammal conference in Florida years later, I understood why. There I met a man who studied pink river dolphins in the Amazon, and he told me legends about these dolphins that claim they have magical powers. No wonder I couldn't forget them! And thus was born yet another book.

My friend Dianne accompanied me to take photos on three of the expeditions I made researching that book. This time the airlines didn't lose her luggage! Dianne's photos appear in *Journey of the Pink Dolphins,* and she took all the pictures in the children's book, *Encantado: Pink Dolphin of the Amazon.* Even though she is afraid of heights, she

Dianne Taylor-Snow, the author's photographer and friend on Lake Charro in Peru, 1997

climbed up that machimango tree after I did. In the books, you can see a picture of the view down, with our canoe below looking tiny in the dark Amazon water.

The dolphins of the Amazon led me to bears in Southeast Asia. On my second research expedition to the Amazon, I met a scientist who had traveled all over the world, Dr. Gary Galbreath. One night, as we were out in a canoe looking for the Amazonian crocodiles called caimans, he told me about something really strange he had seen in China. It was a bear with a golden coat, unlike any he had ever seen. It was such a strange bear he had even wondered if it might be an unknown, new species! But that was eleven years ago, and he had never had the chance to return to China and see if there were other bears like that one. A year later, though, through a strange coincidence, I was able to help Gary begin to solve the mystery of the golden moon bear.

In the little town where my husband and I live, a friend's birthday party provided the occasion for an unusual meeting. Another friend brought as a guest to the party the deputy director of the Cambodian wildlife protection office, whose name was Sun Hean. Sun Hean felt lonely and awkward at the party. He didn't know anyone, but I was eager to talk to him. We talked about Cambodia's tigers. Then we talked about bears. Had he ever seen or heard of a bear in Cambodia that wasn't black? Sun Hean looked astonished at my question. Just recently he had received a photograph of a very unusual bear with a golden coat! He didn't know what it was. Had I ever heard of such a thing?

Indeed I had. Even though the part of China where Gary had seen his golden bear was one thousand kilometers away from Sun Hean's home in Cambodia, I suspected they might be the same kind of bear—and possibly a new species no one had documented before. I got Sun Hean together with Gary. The three of us began to plan a new expedition . . . and I another book.

These are just some of the true stories I have been lucky enough to report in my books. I've also written documentary film and radio scripts. I write magazine and newspaper articles. I work from home, a 120-year-old farmhouse here in New Hampshire which I share with my husband, Howard, our border collie, Tess, our sixteen laying hens, a lovebird (she had a mate but ate his head off) and our 750-pound, twelve-year-old pig, Christopher Hogwood. Once Howard thanked Christopher Hogwood in the acknowledgements of a book for teaching him about "the appetites of this world." Born a runt among a litter of a dozen piglets (they're all bacon now) he lies basking in the summer sunshine and accepts slops brought to him from friends' refrigerators and the local cafe. He has taught us another lesson, one the Bible puts as "the meek shall inherit the earth."

I love travel and I love writing at home. And I love working freelance, instead of writing for just one newspaper or just one magazine. I want my words to reach many different people—children and adults, book-lovers and radio listeners. Americans and people in other countries see the documentaries I write on TV around the world and read my books in translation (so far my books have been translated into Japanese, Korean, and German). For I am carrying an urgent message, at a critical turning point in human history. All my writing tells the same story in a different way: We need to cherish all the life forms on this earth. We need to learn from the dolphins and tigers and apes. We need the life-giving oxygen of the world's forests. We need the nourishing waters of the rivers and seas. We need to the wisdom of all the world's people. And yet, largely because of greed, we are allowing human overpopulation, pollution and poaching to wipe out wild lives and wild places.

When we forget our connections to the larger, wilder world, we can literally lose sight of our place in the universe. In one of Howard's books, *The Same Ax, Twice: Restoration and Renewal in a Throw-Away Age,* he writes about the human desire to restore, repair and renew old houses, favorite landscapes, and even antique machinery. We need those connections to our past. He points out that today, for the first time in human history, we have allowed even the night skies to be so polluted with artificial lights, that most of us can't even see the Milky Way.

But some of us remember our ancient connection to the animals, plants, landscapes, and skies that make up the rich

Montgomery in the office where she writes, with cockatiel, Octavio

planet that nurtures us all. In the Amazon I met shamans who believe that everything has a spirit, even the rivers. They believe we can learn from these spirits. They show us which plants can be made into healing medicines, for instance. The shamans say that dolphins have much to teach us, too—and I found that was true for sure! In India, Girindra and his village understand that tigers are so important that even though they sometimes kill people, it's essential that people learn to live with them rather than wiping them out. Jane Goodall, Dian Fossey, and Birute Galdikas, too, realized how much we can learn from our fellow apes. These scientists have spent most of their careers learning from the animals they studied, and they are still making new discoveries.

The snake scientist about whom I wrote my first book for kids, Dr. Bob Mason, says that by studying snakes, we might even discover how to send astronauts to Mars! But as he points out, learning about the creatures who share our world satisfies an even deeper human need than the thirst for knowledge. Without the beauty, surprise, and sheer fun these creatures offer us, Bob told me, "life would be diminished in a very real sense."

Happily, there's a lot we all can do to protect and preserve the natural world. In the back of all of my books, I list organizations you can join, places you can visit, books you can read, questions you can ponder. We can all do things to help: Join a forest, town or beach clean-up. Raise money for an environmental group. Start a recycling program in your school. We can also change our daily lives in ways that reduce the stress that humans put on the natural world. We can buy fuel-efficient cars (instead of wasteful, dangerous SUVs!). We can have smaller families. We can vote for politicians who will enact laws to combat pollution and protect wild land in our country and others. Children can't vote, but you can write letters to the editor at the local paper—and your letter will count even more if they know you're a child—so include your age when you sign your letter.

The more you learn, the more ideas you'll come up with for ways to help. And that is my hope in all my writing: that the teachers I meet on my travels—shamans and scientists, dolphins and dancers, apes and ants—can inspire us to remember and rebuild the connections by which we know the wholeness of the world.

MUIR, Diana
See APPELBAUM, Diana Muir Karter

*   *   *

MURPHY, Patricia J. 1963-

Personal

Born April 9, 1963, in Chicago, IL; daughter of Donald J. (in medical surgical supplies) and Joanne O. (in Irish tourism and travel, and a philanthropist; maiden name, Ebbeson) Murphy. *Education:* Northern Illinois University, B.A. (journalism), 1985; National Louis University, M.A.T., 1990.

Addresses

Home—Northbrook, IL 60062.

Career

Pattycake Productions, writer and photographer, 1985—; Chicago Cubs, Chicago, IL, marketing assistant, 1985-86; Davidson Marketing Group, Chicago, IL, copywriter, 1986-87; Pritchett Elementary, Buffalo Grove, IL, teacher, 1990-91; Everett Elementary, Lake Forest, IL, teacher.

Member

Society of Children's Book Writers and Illustrators, Goldstar Families, Make-a-Wish Foundation, St. Jude's Children's Hospital, Raggedy Ann Club.

Writings

FOR CHILDREN

Everything You Need to Know about Staying in the Hospital, Rosen Publishing (New York, NY), 2001.
Canada Day ("Rookie Read about Holidays" series), Children's Press (New York, NY), 2002.
Election Day ("Rookie Read about Holidays" series), Children's Press (New York, NY), 2002.
My Body (in English and Spanish), Me and Mí Publishing (Wheaton, IL), 2002.
Everybody Works (in English and Spanish), Me and Mí Publishing (Wheaton, IL), 2002.
Denmark ("Countries of the World" series), Bridgestone Books (Mankato, MN), 2003.
Tanzania ("Countries of the World" series), Bridgestone Books (Mankato, MN), 2003.
I Need You ("Rookie Reader Fiction" series) Grolier Publishing (Danbury, CT), 2003.

Contributor to children's magazines, including *Appleseeds, Current Health, U.S. Kids, Guideposts, Owl,* and *Odyssey.*

Patricia J. Murphy

"ROOKIE READ ABOUT SCIENCE" SERIES

Around and Around, Children's Press (New York, NY), 2002.

Back and Forth, Children's Press (New York, NY), 2002.

Push and Pull, Children's Press (New York, NY), 2002.

Up and Down, Children's Press (New York, NY), 2002.

"LET'S SEE LIBRARY: OUR NATION" SERIES

The Presidency, Compass Point Books (Minneapolis, MN), 2001.

Our National Holidays, Compass Point Books (Minneapolis, MN), 2002.

The U.S. Supreme Court, Compass Point Books (Minneapolis, MN), 2002.

Voting and Elections, Compass Point Books (Minneapolis, MN), 2002.

The U.S. Congress, Compass Point Books (Minneapolis, MN), 2002.

"TRUE BOOK" SERIES

Hearing, Children's Press (New York, NY), 2003.

Sight, Children's Press (New York, NY), 2003.

Smell, Children's Press (New York, NY), 2003.

Taste, Children's Press (New York, NY), 2003.

Touch, Children's Press (New York, NY), 2003.

"LIBRARY OF WHY" SERIES

Why Are the North and South Poles So Cold? Powerkids Press (New York, NY), 2003.

Why Do Some Animals Hibernate?, Powerkids Press (New York, NY), 2003.

Why Does the Moon Change Its Shape?, Powerkids Press (New York, NY), 2003.

Why Is the Earth Round?, Powerkids Press (New York, NY), 2003.

Why Is the Sun So Hot?, Powerkids Press (New York, NY), 2003.

Why Do Snakes and Other Animals Shed Their Skins?, Powerkids Press (New York, NY), 2003.

Work in Progress

Children's books and poetry; adult magazine stories and communications.

Sidelights

Patricia J. Murphy told *SATA:* "As long as I could either hold a book or a pencil, I loved to read, write, and share what I learned. As I grew older (and taller), I realized the power of words—how they can heal, inspire, build bridges, and touch hearts and souls. This is why I write.

"Whether I am writing something for big people (adults) or smaller ones (pre-K to sixth grade), I try to picture the faces of the people who will be reading what I write. This reminds me of the great privilege and responsibility that I have being a writer. I am very grateful to be able to do what I do. And, I take it very seriously.

"I am not sure which stage of writing I enjoy the most. Writing is a lot like life. Beginnings can be fun and scary at the same time. Then, middles ... they can be filled with unexpected adventure and surprises—and a lot of mess and hard work. And, the ends—they are filled with exhilaration, excitement, some sadness, and the realization that something's over. But, then it is back to the beginning again!

"I often tell aspiring writers to 'read, read, read, read and then write, write, write, write.' My mother taught me to love to read and write. I believe that this love (and my continued reading and writing) have rubbed off on to me and made me the writer I am today. (Thanks, Mom!)

"If writers have their hearts set on writing for children, I share with them one of my trade secrets. What is it? Well ... it is to NEVER grow up. That's it. Because then, when you're writing for children, you are always writing for kids around your own age! Don't believe me? Ask me how old I am. That would be nine. I think I will always be nine. Nine is a great age. Don't you think?"

*   *   *

MURROW, Liza Ketchum
See KETCHUM, Liza

O

OAKES, Elizabeth H. 1964-

Personal

Born April 12, 1964, in Radford, VA; daughter of Robert L. (a banker) and Jeraldine Hines (a secretary; maiden name, Kellison) Oakes; children: Colter Lee Wilson, Ella Brooks Wilson. *Education:* Northwestern University, B.S.; Eastern Washington University, M.F.A.

Addresses

Home—301 Burlington Ave., Missoula, MT 59801.

Career

Writer.

Writings

Encyclopedia of World Scientists, Facts on File (New York, NY), 2000.

International Encyclopedia of Women Scientists, Facts on File (New York, NY), 2001.

A to Z Biographical Dictionary of Chemists, Facts on File (New York, NY), 2002.

A to Z Biographical Dictionary of STS Scientists and Inventors, Facts on File (New York, NY), 2002.

Social Science Resources in an Electronic Age, Oryx Press, 2002.

Multicultural Resources in the Electronic Age, Oryx Press, 2003.

Sidelights

Elizabeth H. Oakes is a writer of reference books whose works have been applauded for providing valuable information in very accessible formats. Oakes has authored a one-volume resource, *Encyclopedia of World Scientists,* a work that provides information on nearly five hundred scientists, including both contemporary and historical figures. The entries, arranged alphabetically,

are comprised of biographical data such as birth and death dates (where applicable), area of expertise, and a one-page essay summarizing family background, education, and life's work. An index on the field of study allows users to locate all the biochemists, for example, included in the volume. Other indexes include country of major activity, year of birth, and a general index. There is also a chronology that allows users to see overlapping careers and the relation between scientific discoveries over time.

About half the entries in *Encyclopedia of World Scientists* include a portrait of the scientist, and a similar number of entries are dedicated to women and minority-group scientists. The result, according to Erica Lilly in *Reference and User Services Quarterly,* "is a very readable volume of almost five hundred concise and informative biographies." The one-volume format, which requires that the book cannot pretend to be all-inclusive, as a contributor to *Booklist* noted, also makes the work "convenient" to use and "an affordable choice for most school and public libraries," this reviewer concluded.

Biographical and Critical Sources

PERIODICALS

Booklist, August, 2001, review of *Encyclopedia of World Scientists,* p. 2169.

Choice, May, 2001, R. J. Havlik, review of *Encyclopedia of World Scientists,* p. 1606.

Reference and User Services Quarterly, summer, 2001, Erica Lilly, review of *Encyclopedia of World Scientists,* p. 383.*

*   *   *

ORMEROD, Jan(ette Louise) 1946-

Personal

Born September 23, 1946, in Bunbury, Western Australia; daughter of Jack and Thelma (Harvey) Hendry;

married Paul Ormerod (an information scientist), January 21, 1971 (divorced, 1991); children: Sophie, Laura. *Education:* Western Australian Institute of Technology, associateship (graphic design), 1966, (art teaching), 1973; Claremont Teachers College, teacher's certificate, 1967.

Addresses

Home—Cambridge, England. *Agent*—Laura Cecil, 17 Alwyne Villas, London N1 2HG, England.

Career

Author and illustrator of children's books. Western Australian Education Department, Bunbury, art teacher, 1968-72; Mt. Lawley College of Advanced Education, Perth, Western Australia, lecturer in art education, 1973-75; Western Australian Institute of Technology, Perth, part-time lecturer in drawing and basic design, 1976-79.

Member

Society of Authors.

Awards, Honors

Kate Greenaway Medal commendations, 1982, for *Sunshine,* and 1986, for *Happy Christmas, Gemma;* Mother Goose Award, and Australian Picture Book of the Year Award, Australian Children's Book Council, both 1982, both for *Sunshine;* notable book citations, American Library Association (ALA), 1981, for *Sunshine,* 1982, for *Moonlight,* 1985, for *Dad's Back, Messy Baby, Sleeping,* and *Reading,* 1986, for *The Story of Chicken Licken,* and 1987, for *Bend and Stretch, Making Friends, Mom's Home,* and *This Little Nose.*

Writings

SELF-ILLUSTRATED; FOR CHILDREN

Sunshine, Lothrop (New York, NY), 1981.
Moonlight, Lothrop (New York, NY), 1982.
Be Brave, Billy, Dent (London, England), 1983.
101 Things to Do with a Baby, Lothrop (New York, NY), 1984.
(Reteller) *The Story of Chicken Licken,* Walker (London, England), 1985, Lothrop (New York, NY), 1986.
Young Joe, Lothrop (New York, NY), 1986.
Silly Goose, Lothrop (New York, NY), 1986.
Our Ollie, Lothrop (New York, NY), 1986.
Just Like Me, Lothrop (New York, NY), 1986.
Gemma's First Christmas, Lothrop (New York, NY), 1987.
The Saucepan Game, Lothrop (New York, NY), 1989.
Kitten Day, Lothrop (New York, NY), 1989.
(Reteller, with David Lloyd) *The Frog Prince,* Lothrop (New York, NY), 1990.
When We Went to the Zoo, Lothrop (New York, NY), 1991.
Come Back, Kittens, Lothrop (New York, NY), 1992.
Come Back, Puppies, Lothrop (New York, NY), 1992.
Joe Can Count, Mulberry Books (New York, NY), 1993.
Midnight Pillow Fight, Candlewick Press (Cambridge, MA), 1993.

Jan Ormerod

Emily Dances: A Novelty Action Book, Tupelo Books (New York, NY), 1999.
Ben Goes Swimming: A Novelty Action Book, HarperCollins (New York, NY), 1999.
Miss Mouse's Day, Lothrop (New York, NY), 2000.
Miss Mouse Takes Off, HarperCollins (New York, NY), 2001.

"JAN ORMEROD BABY BOOK" SERIES; SELF-ILLUSTRATED

Sleeping, Lothrop (New York, NY), 1985.
Reading, Lothrop (New York, NY), 1985.
Dad's Back, Lothrop (New York, NY), 1985.
Messy Baby, Lothrop (New York, NY), 1985.
Jan Ormerod's Baby Books, Lothrop (New York, NY), 1986.
Jan Ormerod's Little Ones, Lothrop (New York, NY), 1987.

"JAN ORMEROD NEW BABY BOOK" SERIES; SELF-ILLUSTRATED

Bend and Stretch, Lothrop (New York, NY), 1987.
Making Friends, Lothrop (New York, NY), 1987.
This Little Nose, Lothrop (New York, NY), 1987.
Mom's Home, Lothrop (New York, NY), 1987.
Jan Ormerod's To Baby with Love, Lothrop (New York, NY), 1994.
Rock-a-Baby, Dutton (New York, NY), 1998.

ILLUSTRATOR

Jan Mark, *Hairs in the Palm of the Hand,* Kestrel (Harmondsworth, England), 1981.
Margaret Mahy, *The Chewing-gum Rescue and Other Stories,* Dent (London, England), 1982.

Pat Thompson, compiler, *Rhymes around the Day*, Lothrop (New York, NY), 1983.

Karin Lorentzen, *Lanky Longlegs*, translated by Joan Tate, Atheneum (New York, NY), 1983.

Sarah Hayes, *Happy Christmas, Gemma*, Lothrop (New York, NY), 1986.

James M. Barrie, *Peter Pan*, Viking (New York, NY), 1987.

Sarah Hayes, *Eat up, Gemma*, Lothrop (New York, NY), 1988.

Sarah Hayes, *Stamp Your Feet*, Lothrop (New York, NY), 1988.

Vivian French, *One Ballerina Two*, Lothrop (New York, NY), 1991.

The Magic Skateboard, Candlewick Press (Cambridge, MA), 1992.

Father Christmas and the Donkey, Viking (New York, NY), 1993.

Helen E. Buckley, *Grandfather and I*, Lothrop (New York, NY), 1994.

Grandmother and I, Lothrop (New York, NY), 1994.

Cloud Nine, Clarion (New York, NY), 1995.

Sky Dancer, Lothrop (New York, NY), 1996.

(And author) *Ms. McDonald Has a Class*, Clarion (New York, NY), 1996.

Mary Hoffman (reteller), *A Twist in the Tail: Animal Stories from Around the World*, Holt (New York, NY), 1998.

(And author) *Who's Whose?*, Lothrop (New York, NY), 1998.

Where Did Josie Go?, Lothrop (New York, NY), 1999.

(And author) *Miss Mouse Takes Off*, HarperCollins (New York, NY), 2001.

Robie H. Harris, *Goodbye Mousie*, Margaret K. McElderry (New York, NY), 2001.

Sidelights

Australian-born author and illustrator Jan Ormerod has established herself as a sensitive and skillful creator of children's picture books. Often wordless or of minimal text, Ormerod's works are characterized by detailed watercolor illustrations that frequently depict warm domestic scenes. When assessing her work, reviewers have pointed to Ormerod's ability to render everyday events with both insight and gentle humor, a quality that makes her books appealing to both children and their parents. Her work has also been popular with critics; in a *Washington Post Book World* article, Michael Dirda judged Ormerod to be "a contemporary master of the board book."

Ormerod's family life inspired her successful career in children's literature. Her husband, Paul, worked as a children's librarian at the time the couple's first child, Sophie, was born. Sophie's interest in the books her father brought home for her encouraged Ormerod, then an art teacher, to begin creating picture books of her own. Confident of realizing some success in this venture, Ormerod and her husband decided to quit their jobs and move from Australia to London, England, home of a number of publishing companies. Ormerod drew on her training in graphic design to create a portfolio and submitted her illustrations to various London publishing houses. Her efforts resulted in the publication of *Sunshine* in 1981.

In *Sunshine* Ormerod's colorful, naturalistic illustrations depict a little girl's morning routine. Using cartoon-like panels to separate scenes from one another, Ormerod wordlessly presents the little girl (modeled after her daughter, Sophie) waking up, prodding her lethargic parents out of bed, getting dressed, eating breakfast, and going to school. Scenes such as the father distractedly allowing the breakfast toast to burn as he reads the newspaper provide comic relief. The companion book to *Sunshine, Moonlight* uses the same format to describe the end of the little girl's day: she eats dinner, takes a bath, listens to a story, and eventually goes to bed. Despite the absence of words in both books, Michele Landsberg stated in *Reading for the Love of It: Best Books for Young Readers,* that "the drama of nuance and character are fully present." In *Books for Your Children* Margaret Carter described Ormerod's illustrations as "gentle, tolerant, tender, observant and shrewd," and in *Growing Point,* Margery Fisher declared, "Domestic truth is achieved by pictures alone in *Moonlight,* and with complete success."

Many of Ormerod's later books also focus on small slices of day-to-day family life. In *Be Brave, Billy,* for

In her gentle illustrations, Ormerod has captured the warmth of Helen E. Buckley's **Grandfather and I,** *the story of the love between a grandfather and his grandchild.*

instance, a little boy comes to terms with everyday anxieties, and in *101 Things to Do with a Baby* a young girl discovers a variety of activities that can be done with her new sibling. Reviewers praised these titles, assessing that Ormerod sensitively depicts the fears, jealousies, and triumphs of young children. Her illustrations in *101 Things to Do with a Baby* were deemed "magnificent" by Joe McGinniss in the *New York Times Book Review,* who also noted that the pictures evoke "both the tenderness and tumult with which each day in a two-sibling household is filled."

Ormerod's two series of books for very young children also revolve around the home and family ties. The "Jan Ormerod Baby Book" series—highlighting a father and infant's affectionate relationship—includes *Reading, Sleeping, Messy Baby,* and *Dad's Back.* In *Reading* and *Sleeping* the baby attempts to become the center of the father's attention. Father cleans house in *Messy Baby,* while the child follows behind and undoes his handiwork. And in *Dad's Back,* the father's return from an errand gives the child an opportunity to play with his keys, gloves, and scarf. Robert Wool, writing in the *New York Times Book Review,* noted that Ormerod effectively brought the father and baby's relationship to life "with a novelist's eye for detail and a painter's grasp of nuance." The reviewer added that Ormerod's "marvelous, soft, figurative drawings [make] you smile with recognition."

The 1987 "Jan Ormerod New Baby Book" series also focuses on a family relationship—this time between a pregnant mother and her infant—and includes *Bend and Stretch, Making Friends, Mom's Home,* and *This Little Nose.* In these books Mom exercises with baby underfoot, makes a doll for baby, and brings home a shopping bag full of items for the child to explore. Critics judged that this series reflects Ormerod's familiarity with and understanding of parents and infants. In a *Horn Book* review Karen Jameyson declared that in "Ormerod's hands the most ordinary chunks of everyday life are given vivid shape and substance."

In a departure from her typical home settings, Ormerod uses minimal text and bright illustration panels to describe a family outing in *When We Went to the Zoo.* The reader follows two children and their father as they visit creatures such as gibbons, pelicans, elephants, otters, toucans, and orangutans. Near the zoo's exit the family notices a pair of sparrows building a nest and decides that "in the end we liked that best, spying the sparrows and their nest." Observant readers will have noticed the sparrows earlier, as they are present in the illustrations throughout the family's tour. Critics commented that drawing attention to the sparrows in a zoo of exotic animals reflects Ormerod's ability bring charm to the commonplace.

Ormerod collaborated with David Lloyd in the retelling of the classic fairy tale *The Frog Prince,* which Ormerod illustrated using double-page spreads and decorative borders. In Ormerod's and Lloyd's version, a princess loses her ball in a pond and promises a frog her love if he finds it for her. Once the frog retrieves the ball,

however, the princess takes it and runs home, hoping the frog will forget her promise. But the persistent frog follows her, and the princess is forced to keep her promise by letting the frog sit on her lap, eat with her, and sleep on her pillow. After sleeping on her pillow for three nights, the frog transforms into a prince and, "as in all the best deep, dark, and royal stories," the narrator states, "they lived happily ever after."

In addition to her own work, Ormerod has illustrated a number of books by children's authors, including *Hairs in the Palm of the Hand,* by Jan Mark, *Peter Pan,* by James M. Barrie, and *One Ballerina Two,* by Vivian French. According to Michael Patrick Hearn writing in the *New York Times Book Review,* Ormerod "is a keen observer of the intimate details of childhood.... She can make the mundane beautiful with her extraordinary figure studies.... She can take the simplest subject ... and weave it into an engrossing picture book."

Mary M. Burns, a reviewer in *Horn Book,* noted that the illustrations in *A Twist in the Tail: Animal Stories from Around the World* by Mary Hoffman "provide opportunities to extend the text without interrupting the pace." Commenting on Ormerod's own book *Miss Mouse Takes Off,* Carolyn Phelan in *Booklist* stated, "bright washes of color give the scenes a cheerful look." Joy Fleishhacker, reviewing in *School Library Journal,* noted that Ormerod's illustrations in *Goodbye Mousie* by Robie H. Harris include "pleasing buff-colored backgrounds" and that the "black-pencil line and watercolor washes echo the emotional nuances" of the book. A reviewer in *Publishers Weekly* commented about *Goodbye Mousie,* the story of a child's first experience with the death of a pet, that "the artist's fluid pencil lines

The story of Ms. MacDonald's class, that visits a farm and then gives a spirited performance, is written to the tune of the popular song about Old MacDonald and his barnyard animals. (From Ms. MacDonald Has a Class, *written and illustrated by Ormerod.*

Narrated by stuffed animal Miss Mouse, Ormerod's self-illustrated picture book reflects the playful activities of a toddler and her favorite toy. (From Miss Mouse's Day.*)*

underscore the vulnerability of the boy and the poignancy of his story."

Biographical and Critical Sources

BOOKS

Children's Literature Review, Volume 20, Gale (Detroit, MI), 1990.

Landsberg, Michele, *Reading for the Love of It: Best Books for Young Readers,* Prentice Hall, 1987.

Ormerod, Jan, *When We Went to the Zoo,* Lothrop (New York, NY), 1991.

Ormerod, Jan, and David Lloyd, retellers, *The Frog Prince,* Lothrop (New York, NY), 1990.

PERIODICALS

Booklist, June 1, 2001, Carolyn Phelan, review of *Miss Mouse Takes Off,* p. 1894.

Books for Your Children, autumn-winter, 1983, Margaret Carter, "Cover Artist—Jan Ormerod," p. 7.

Growing Point, July, 1982, Margery Fisher, review of *Moonlight,* p. 3917.

Horn Book, March-April, 1988, Karen Jameyson, review of *Bend and Stretch,* p. 193; September, 1990, p. 611; May, 1991, p. 319; November, 1998, Mary M. Burns, review of *A Twist in the Tail: Animal Stories from Around the World,* p. 746.

New York Times Book Review, November, 11, 1984, Joe McGinniss, "How to Survive a Sibling," p. 48; March 24, 1985, Robert Wool, reviews of *Messy Baby, Reading, Dad's Back,* and *Sleeping,* p. 35; August 19, 1990, Michael Patrick Hearn, review of *The Frog Prince,* p. 29.

Publishers Weekly, July 30, 2001, review of *Goodbye Mousie,* p. 83.

School Library Journal, September, 1989, p. 230; September, 2001, Joy Fleishhacker, review of *Goodbye Mousie,* p. 190.

Washington Post Book World, June 8, 1986, Michael Dirda, "Books for Beach Bag and Knapsack," p. 10.*

P

PARKER, Nancy Winslow 1930-

Personal

Born October 18, 1930, in Maplewood, NJ; daughter of Winslow Aurelius (a textile executive) and Beatrice McCelland (Gaunt) Parker. *Education:* Mills College, B.A., 1952; attended Art Students League, 1956-57, and School of Visual Arts, 1966-67. *Avocational interests:* Carpentry, tennis, gardening, geneology.

Addresses

Home—51 East 74th St., Apt. 3R, New York, NY 10021. *E-mail*—nwparker52@aol.com.

Career

National Broadcasting Company (NBC), New York City, sales promoter, 1956-60; New York Soccer Club, New York City, sports promoter, 1961-63; Radio Corporation of America (RCA), New York City, sales promoter, 1964-67; Appleton-Century-Crofts (publishers), New York City, art director, 1968-70; Holt, Rinehart & Winston (publishers), New York City, graphic designer, 1970-72; freelance writer and illustrator, 1972—.

Member

Authors Guild, Mills College Club of New York, Mantoloking Yacht Club.

Awards, Honors

Junior Literary Guild selections, 1974, for *Oh, A-Hunting We Will Go!,* 1977, for *Love from Uncle Clyde,* 1978, for *The President's Cabinet,* 1978, for *No Bath Tonight,* and 1980, for *Poofy Loves Company;* Jane Tinkham Broughton fellowship in writing for children, Bread Loaf Writers Conference, 1975; notable children's book in the field of social studies, 1975, for *Warm as Wool, Cool as Cotton: The Story of Natural Fibers,* and

Told from the perspective of Geraldine the goat, **The Goat in the Rug,** *relates the process of creating a Navajo rug, while Nancy Winslow Parker's illustrations depict the creative teamwork between the goat and her friend Glenmae. (Written by Charles L. Blood and Martin Link.)*

1976, for *The Goat in the Rug; The Goat in the Rug* was cited as best of the season in children's books, *Saturday Review,* 1976; Book-of-the-Month Club selection, 1976, for *Willy Bear;* year's best children's book citation, *Philadelphia Inquirer,* Christopher Award, and exhibited at American Institute of Graphic Arts Children's Book Show, all 1976, all for *Willy Bear;* School Library *Journal's* best books of spring, named to New York Public Library list of children's books, both 1980, both for *Poofy Loves Company;* Christopher Award, named one of the ten best illustrated books by *New York Times,* and exhibited at American Institute of Graphic Arts Children's Book Show, all 1981, for *My Mom Travels a Lot;* New York Academy of Science honorable mention, 1981, Sequoyah Children's Book Award, Oklahoma Library Association, 1983-84, Alabama Library Association Children's Choice, 1985, all for *The President's Car;* named to New York Public Library list of children's books, 1983, for *The Christmas Camel,* 1985, for *The United Nations from A to Z; Paul Revere's Ride* was included in Library of Congress' Books for Children, No. 2, 1986, *Bugs* was included in Library of Congress' Books for Children, No. 4, 1988; Association of Booksellers for Children Choice, 1988, for *Bugs.*

Writings

SELF-ILLUSTRATED CHILDREN'S BOOKS

The Man with the Take-Apart Head, Dodd, 1974.
The Party at the Old Farm, Atheneum (New York, NY), 1975.
Mrs. Wilson Wanders Off, Dodd, 1976.
Love from Uncle Clyde, Dodd, 1977.
The Crocodile under Louis Finneberg's Bed, Dodd, 1978.
The President's Cabinet (nonfiction), Parents Magazine Press, 1978, revised as *The President's Cabinet and How It Grew,* introduction by Dean Rusk, HarperCollins (New York, NY), 1991.
The Ordeal of Byron B. Blackbear, Dodd, 1979.
Puddums, the Cathcarts' Orange Cat, Atheneum (New York, NY), 1980.
Poofy Loves Company, Dodd, 1980.
The Spotted Dog, Dodd, 1980.
The President's Car (nonfiction), introduction by Betty Ford, Crowell, 1981.
Cooper, the McNallys' Big Black Dog, Dodd, 1981.
Love from Aunt Betty, Dodd, 1983.
The Christmas Camel, Dodd, 1983.
The United Nations from A to Z, Dodd, 1985.
(With Joan R. Wright) *Bugs,* Greenwillow (New York, NY), 1987.
(With Joan R. Wright) *Frogs, Toads, Lizards and Salamanders,* Greenwillow (New York, NY), 1990.
Working Frog, Greenwillow (New York, NY), 1992.
Money, Money, Money: The Meaning of the Art & Symbols on United States Currency, HarperCollins (New York, NY), 1995.
Locks, Crocs, and Skeeters: The Story of the Panama Canal, Greenwillow (New York, NY), 1996.
Land Ho! 50 Glorious Years in the Age of Exploration with 12 Important Explorers, HarperCollins (New York, NY), 2001.

ILLUSTRATOR

John Langstaff, *Oh, A-Hunting We Will Go!* (songbook), Atheneum (New York, NY), 1974.
Carter Hauck, *Warm as Wool, Cool as Cotton: The Story of Natural Fibers,* Seabury, 1975.
Charles L. Blood and Martin Link, *The Goat in the Rug,* Parents Magazine Press, 1976.
Mildred Kantrowitz, *Willy Bear,* Parents Magazine Press, 1976.

John Langstaff, *Sweetly Sings the Donkey* (songbook), Atheneum (New York, NY), 1976.
Ann Lawler, *The Substitute,* Parents Magazine Press, 1977.
John Langstaff, *Hot Cross Buns and Other Old Street Cries* (songbook), Atheneum (New York, NY), 1978.
Jane Yolen, *No Bath Tonight,* Crowell, 1978.
Caroline Feller Bauer, *My Mom Travels a Lot,* Warne, 1981.
Henry Wadsworth Longfellow, *Paul Revere's Ride,* Greenwillow (New York, NY), 1985.
Eve Rice, *Aren't You Coming Too?,* Greenwillow (New York, NY), 1988.
Rachel Field, *General Store,* Greenwillow (New York, NY), 1988.
Eve Rice, *Peter's Pockets,* Greenwillow (New York, NY), 1989.
Shirley Nietzel, *The Jacket I Wear in the Snow,* Greenwillow (New York, NY), 1989.
Eve Rice, *At Grammy's House,* Greenwillow (New York, NY), 1990.
Ginger Foglesong Guy, *Black Crow, Black Crow,* Greenwillow (New York, NY), 1990.
Patricia Lillie, *When the Rooster Crowed,* Greenwillow (New York, NY), 1991.
John Greenleaf Whittier, *Barbara Fritchie,* Greenwillow (New York, NY), 1991.
Shirley Nietzel, *The Dress I'll Wear to the Party,* Greenwillow (New York, NY), 1992.
T. B. Read, *Sheridan's Ride,* Greenwillow (New York, NY), 1993.
Charlotte Pomerantz, *Here Comes Henny,* Greenwillow (New York, NY), 1994.
Shirley Nietzel, *The Bag I'm Taking to Grandma's,* Greenwillow (New York, NY), 1995.
We're Making Breakfast for Mother, Greenwillow (New York, NY), 1997.
The House I'll Build for the Wrens, Greenwillow (New York, NY), 1997.
I'm Taking a Trip on My Train, Greenwillow (New York, NY), 1999.
Shirley Nietzel, *I'm Not Feeling Well Today,* Greenwillow (New York, NY), 2001.
Shirley Nietzel, *Our Class Took a Trip to the Zoo,* Greenwillow (New York, NY), 2002.

Adaptations

Bugs was a "Reading Rainbow" selection; *My Mom Travels a Lot* was adapted into a filmstrip by Live Oak; *The Ordeal of Byron B. Blackbear* was made into a film.

Sidelights

Nancy Winslow Parker is an award-winning children's book author and illustrator. Parker insists that her illustrations and stories have one characteristic in common: they are all done in the spirit of fun. Critiquing a representative group of Parker's works, Dulcy Brainard, writing in *Publishers Weekly,* remarked, "The books are marked by a fresh simplicity and an observant, ironic sense of humor that is particularly apparent in the unexpected ways her pictures expand on the text."

Parker was born in Maplewood, New Jersey, in 1930. Her favorite reading material was *National Geographic,* a magazine of which her family had an extensive collection. Although Parker had dreamed of being an artist since childhood, her family did not think it was a legitimate or profitable career and instead urged her to get a mainstream job. "I cannot remember when I have not been interested in children's literature. As a writer, [I find] the field has limited potential for fantasy and the joy of creation. As an illustrator, [I believe] the opportunity to let yourself go in wild interpretation is an artist's dream come true," Parker once said. After college, she moved to New York City, working for a magazine and as a secretary, although she continued her artwork on the side. Eventually, however, she went to the School of Visual Arts and soon found work as an art director and book designer. Parker tried to work as a freelance illustrator, but realized that she would have to illustrate *and* write stories before being noticed by publishers. After she took this approach, she realized immediate success. In an interview with Brainard in *Publishers Weekly,* Parker commented, "My first story was *The Man with the Take-Apart Head.* It's one of my favorites, and as good as any I've written."

Parker often finds inspiration for her books in real-life situations. Her 1980 work *Poofy Loves Company* was based on an actual incident in which her overly friendly dog ambushed a visiting youngster, messing up her clothes and stealing her cookie. In a *Junior Literary Guild* review of *Poofy Loves Company,* the author recalled that the story "took about fifteen minutes to write, the whole thing coming at once in a delicious outburst of creativity." Praising Parker's re-creation of this event, the critic remarked that the book contained "hilarious four-color pictures."

As shown by *Poofy Loves Company,* animals, especially dogs, are Parker's favorite subjects. Sometimes she includes more exotic animals in her books and is forced to conduct extensive research to ensure the accuracy of her drawings and facts. *Love from Uncle Clyde* is the story of a boy named Charlie who receives an unusual Christmas present—a three-thousand-pound hippopotamus from Africa. These same characters reappear in *The Christmas Camel.* In this book Charlie receives a camel from eccentric Uncle Clyde and labors over the woolly animal's care. However this beast is magical and whisks Charlie to Bethlehem on Christmas Eve for an extraordinary experience.

Parker also illustrates works written by other authors. Two of the books she has illustrated, *Willy Bear,* by Mildred Kantrowitz, and *My Mom Travels a Lot,* by Caroline Feller Bauer, earned the prestigious Christopher Award. Both of these works focus on children handling new and somewhat scary situations. In *Willy Bear* a youngster uses his teddy bear to act out his fear of going to school, and in *My Mom Travels a Lot,* a young girl examines the positive and negative aspects of her mother's hectic business career. In each instance, Parker's drawings were credited by reviewers as com-plementing the text, thus helping to produce superior picture books.

Although Parker has achieved success with fiction for children, she has also delved into the field of nonfiction in her writing and illustrating career. For instance, her 1987 work, *Bugs,* written with Joan R. Wright, examines the physical structure and habitats of several types of insects. Patti Hagan, writing in the *New York Times Book Review* about *Bugs,* remarked that "the color illustrations, with precise anatomical tags, are a fine tool for introducing children" to the creatures portrayed in the book.

Parker once said, "Since my last entry I have had the enormous pleasure of writing and illustrating a book about explorers—the ones who came to North America in 1492 and worked their way across the continent, explorer by explorer, finally sailing up the California coast from New Spain. There are maps for each of the twelve explorers with tiny little trees, boats, sea monsters, caves, bays, oceans—all there to show the terra incognito the explorers faced. Helping me do all this is Ruby, a black cat with green eyes. She was adopted at the Humane Society of New York, from a selection of over forty cats in all colors and ages.

"Art is an extension of my life."

Biographical and Critical Sources

PERIODICALS

Booklist, May 1, 1991, p. 1710; June 15, 1992, p. 1851.
Junior Literary Guild, March, 1980, review of *Poofy Loves Company,* p. 8.
Kirkus Reviews, April 1, 1992, p. 470.
Library Talk, November, 1991, p. 28.
New York Times Book Review, February 7, 1988, Patti Hagan, review of *Bugs,* p. 29.
Publishers Weekly, February 22, 1985, Dulcy Brainard, interview with Nancy Winslow Parker, pp. 161-162.
Quill & Quire, July, 1992, p. 50.
Reading Teacher, September, 1993, p. 51.
School Library Journal, July, 1991, p. 84; August, 1992, p. 146.

*   *   *

POTTER, (Helen) Beatrix 1866-1943

Personal

Born July 28, 1866, in Bolton Gardens, Kensington, England; died December 22, 1943, in Sawrey, England; daughter of Rupert (a non-practicing barrister and an amateur photographer) and Helen (Leech) Potter; married William Heelis (a lawyer), 1913. *Education:* Tutored at home by governesses; primarily a self-taught artist except for a brief period of private lessons.

Beatrix Potter

Career

Author and illustrator of books for children. Also worked as a farmer of Herdwick sheep in the Lake District following her marriage; became first woman president of the Herdwick Sheepbreeder's Association, 1930. Was an active conservationist.

Writings

SELF-ILLUSTRATED CHILDREN'S BOOKS

The Tale of Peter Rabbit, privately printed, 1901, Warne (London, England), 1902.

The Tailor of Gloucester, privately printed, 1902, Warne (London, England), 1903.

The Tale of Squirrel Nutkin, Warne (London, England), 1903.

The Tale of Benjamin Bunny, Warne (London, England), 1904.

The Tale of Two Bad Mice, Warne (London, England), 1904.

The Tale of Mrs. Tiggy-Winkle, Warne (London, England), 1905.

The Pie and the Patty-Pan, Warne (London, England), 1905, published as *The Tale of the Pie and the Patty-Pan,* Warne (London, England), 1930.

The Tale of Mr. Jeremy Fisher, Warne (London, England), 1930.

The Story of a Fierce Bad Rabbit, Warne (London, England), 1906.

The Story of Miss Moppet, Warne (London, England), 1906.

The Tale of Tom Kitten, Warne (London, England), 1907.

The Tale of Jemima Puddle-Duck, Warne (London, England), 1908.

The Roly-Poly Pudding, Warne (London, England), 1908, published as *The Tale of Samuel Whiskers; or, The Roly-Poly Pudding,* Warne (London, England), 1926.

The Tale of the Flopsy Bunnies, Warne (London, England), 1909.

Ginger and Pickles, Warne (London, England), 1909.

The Tale of Mrs. Tittlemouse, Warne (London, England), 1910.

Peter Rabbit's Painting Book, Warne (London, England), 1911.

The Tale of Timmy Tiptoes, Warne (London, England), 1911.

The Tale of Mr. Tod, Warne (London, England), 1912.

The Tale of Pigling Bland, Warne (London, England), 1913.

Tom Kitten's Painting Book, Warne (London, England), 1917.

The Tale of Johnny Town-Mouse, Warne (London, England), 1918.

Jemima Puddle-Duck's Painting Book, Warne (London, England), 1925.

Peter Rabbit's Almanac for 1929, Warne (London, England), 1928.

The Fairy Caravan, privately printed, 1929, McKay (Philadelphia, PA), 1929.

The Tale of Little Pig Robinson, McKay (Philadelphia, PA), 1930.

Wag-by-Wall, Horn Book (Boston, MA), 1944.

Yours Affectionately, Peter Rabbit: Miniature Letters by Beatrix Potter, edited by Anne Emerson, Warne (New York, NY), 1983.

The Complete Tales of Peter Rabbit: And Other Favorite Stories, Courage Books (Philadelphia, PA), 2001.

VERSE

Appley Dapply's Nursery Rhymes, Warne (London, England), 1917.

Cecily Parsley's Nursery Rhymes, Warne (London, England), 1922.

Beatrix Potter's Nursery Rhyme Book, Warne (New York, NY), 1984.

FOR ADULTS

The Art of Beatrix Potter: Direct Reproductions of Beatrix Potter's Preliminary Studies and Finished Drawings, Also Examples of Her Original Manuscript, edited by Leslie Linder and W. A. Herring, Warne (London, England), 1955, revised edition, 1972.

The Journal of Beatrix Potter from 1881 to 1897, transcribed from her code writing by Leslie Linder, Warne (London, England), 1966.

Letters to Children, Harvard College Library Department of Printing and Graphic Arts (Cambridge, MA), 1967.

Beatrix Potter's Birthday Book, edited by Enid Linder, Warne (New York, NY), 1974.

Dear Ivy, Dear June: Letters from Beatrix Potter, edited by Margaret Crawford Maloney, Other Press, 1977.

Beatrix Potter's Americans: Selected Letters, edited by Jane Crowell Morse, Horn Book (Boston, MA), 1981.

ILLUSTRATOR

F. E. Weatherley, *A Happy Pair,* c. 1893.
Comical Customers, c. 1894.
W. P. K. Findlay, *Wayside and Woodland Fungi,* 1967.

Also illustrator of Joel Chandler Harris's *Tales of Uncle Remus,* and Lewis Carroll's *Alice in Wonderland.*

OTHER

Sister Anne, illustrated by Katharine Sturges, McKay (Philadelphia, PA), 1932.
The Tale of the Faithful Dove, illustrated by Marie Angel, Warne (London, England), 1955, Warne (New York, NY), 1956.
The Tale of Tuppenny, illustrated by Marie Angel, Warne (New York, NY), 1973.

Collections of Potter's works are housed in the Leslie Linder Bequest at the National Book League, London, England, and at the Free Library, Philadelphia, PA.

Adaptations

Filmstrips: Peter Rabbit, Curriculum Films, 1946, revised version, Curriculum Materials Corp., 1957, other filmstrips by Stillfilm, 1949, Museum Extension Service, 1965, and Educational Projections Corp., 1968; *The Tale of Benjamin Bunny,* Weston Woods, 1967; *The Tale of Mr. Jeremy Fisher,* Weston Woods, 1967; *The Tale of Peter Rabbit,* Weston Woods, 1967; *The Tale of Tom Kitten,* Weston Woods, 1967; *The Tale of Two Bad Mice,* Weston Woods, 1967. Other filmstrip adaptations include: *Four Tales of Beatrix Potter* (four filmstrips with cassettes and teacher's guide), United Learning; and *Treasury of Animal Stories, Parts I and II,* (four filmstrips, four records or cassettes), read by Frances Sternhagen, Miller-Brody Productions.

Screenplays: Peter Rabbit and the Tales of Beatrix Potter (movie), Metro-Goldwyn-Mayer, 1971; *Tales of Beatrix Potter* (video; six stories and eight nursery rhymes), Children's Video Library, 1986; *The Tale of Mr. Jeremy Fisher and The Tale of Peter Rabbit* (video), Sony Video Software Company, 1988; also a television production aired as *Beatrix Potter: A Private World.* In 1993 the Family Channel aired a six-part series based on Potter's children's tales.

Recordings: The Tale of Peter Rabbit and Other Stories (record), Caedmon (New York, NY), 1970; *The Tale of the Flopsy Bunnies and Five Other Beatrix Potter Stories* (record or cassette), read by Claire Bloom, Caedmon (New York, NY), 1973; *The Peter Rabbit Books or The Tales of Beatrix Potter,* read by Eleanor Quirk, Warne (New York, NY), c. 1973; *Beatrix Potter Nursery Rhymes and Tales* (record or cassette), read by Claire Bloom, Caedmon (New York, NY), 1974; *The Pie and the Patty-Pan,* Caedmon (New York, NY), 1974; *The Tailor of Gloucester and Other Stories* (record or cassette), read by Claire Bloom, Caedmon (New York, NY), 1974; *The Tale of Little Pig Robinson* (record or cassette), read by Claire Bloom, Caedmon (New York, NY), 1974; *The Tale of Squirrel Nutkin and Other Tales* (record or cassette), read by Claire Bloom, Caedmon (New York, NY), 1974; *The Sly Old Cat and Other Stories,* Caedmon (New York, NY), 1976; *The Tale of the Faithful Dove,* Caedmon (New York, NY), 1976; *The Tale of Tuppenny from The Fairy Caravan and Other Stories,* Caedmon (New York, NY), 1976; *The World of Animal Stories by Beatrix Potter* (four cassettes, forty books; or one cassette, ten books), Spoken Arts (New Rochelle, NY), 1976; *Peter Rabbit* (cassette and paperback text), Spoken Arts (New Rochelle, NY), 1986; *The Tale of Benjamin Bunny* (cassette with paperback book), Warner Juvenile Books (New York, NY), 1988; *The Tale of Jemima Puddle-Duck* (cassette with paperback book), Warner Juvenile Books (New York, NY), 1988; *The Tale of Mr. Tod and The Tale of Timmy Tiptoes* (one cassette), Caedmon (New York, NY), 1988; *The Tale of Peter Rabbit* (cassette with paperback book), Warner Juvenile Books (New York, NY), 1988; *The Tale of Tom Kitten* (cassette with paperback book), Warner Juvenile Books (New York, NY), 1988.

Other works adapted into recordings include: *Peter Rabbit and His Friends—The Favorite Tales of Beatrix Potter* (record or cassette), read by Elinor Basescu, Miller-Brody Productions; *Peter Rabbit & Tales of Beatrix Potter,* Angel Records; *The Tale of Peter Rabbit*

Potter's self-illustrated classic **The Tale of Peter Rabbit** *is the story of a naughty bunny who disobeys his mother, goes into Mr. McGregor's garden, and suffers for his defiance.*

(cassette only), Scholastic; *The Tale of Peter Rabbit and Other Stories* (six cassettes with teacher's guide), read by Claire Bloom, Caedmon; *Treasury of Animal Stories, Volume I,* read by Frances Sternhagen, Spoken Arts; and *Treasury of Animal Stories, Volume II,* read by Frances Sternhagen, Spoken Arts.

Sidelights

English author and illustrator Beatrix Potter was a beloved children's storyteller and artist. Her classic, enduring series featuring woodland animals began with the publication of *The Tale of Peter Rabbit* in 1901 and continued over the next two decades as she produced over twenty self-illustrated "tales" that have entertained young and old readers for nearly a century. Her menagerie of little animals, including rabbits, squirrels, hedgehogs, and mice were unique in that the author depicted them as animals possessing animal qualities rather than animals possessing human qualities. Indeed, humans played a small role in Potter's works, primarily because she was unable to draw them as accurately as she drew the animals with which she was so familiar. The series was also significant because Potter used adult language to convey her ideas and was not afraid to portray realistic events in her stories. Potter wrote and illustrated a handful of books for children later in life, but the creative burst that dominated her early work was not to be equaled.

Potter was born on July 28, 1866, and was raised in Victorian England. The first child of wealthy parents (both Rupert and Helen Potter had inherited fortunes earned in the cotton trade), young Potter wanted for nothing except companionship. Her father was a non-practicing lawyer who was extremely knowledgeable about art; he would later help develop his daughter's interest in the subject by exposing her early and often to gardens and museums. Except for these outings, the Potters kept their daughter secluded in the third-floor nursery of the family home in Bolton Gardens, London, leaving her care and education to nurses and governesses. They allowed Potter to keep small pets, including tame rabbits, mice, and a family of snails. From the time she was very small Potter displayed a natural curiosity, innate intelligence, and strong sense of independence that would serve her all her life.

When she was six years old, Potter's younger brother Bertram was born. He provided the friendship she desperately needed and shared her interests in drawing and studying nature and wildlife. The two were scientific in their approach, often bringing home dead creatures to skin in order to reveal the bone structure, once even boiling and dissecting the remains of a fox. The family traditionally summered in the Scottish highlands and in the Lake District of northern England, which allowed Potter and Bertram months of roaming the countryside, carefully observing nature, and honing their skills as budding artists. When he was old enough, Bertram was sent away to boarding school, thus leaving Potter alone again. Because of the prolonged periods of isolation, she

When it seems a tailor is too ill to finish his work for the mayor, a group of mice the tailor has saved help him in secret. (From The Tailor of Gloucester, *written and illustrated by Potter.)*

grew up very shy and uncomfortable around adults, but always had a natural affinity for children.

Between the ages of twelve and seventeen, Potter took private art instruction from two different teachers, earning an art student's certificate from the Science and Art Department of the Committee of Council on Education—the only certificate of education she ever received. Other than these brief lessons, she was self-taught. Writing in her journal about her first instructor, a Miss Cameron, Potter observed, "I have great reason to be grateful to her, though we were not on particularly good terms for the last good while. I have learnt from her freehand, model, geometry, perspective and a little water-colour flower painting. Painting is an awkward thing to teach except the details of the medium. If you and your master are determined to look at nature and art in two different directions you are sure to stick."

Potter's journal, kept between the ages of fifteen and thirty, revealed another aspect of her personality; it was written in a secret code or "cypher" writing that took years to break and translate following her death. Writing in a script so small that it could not be read without a magnifying glass, Potter religiously recorded her thoughts about everything from politics to family history, thus supplying scholars with information about a period in her life that was otherwise unaccounted for. The fact that Potter felt the need to hide these often bland comments as well as the very existence of the journal is an example of her inbred solitude. In 1966, on the centenary of Potter's birth, *The Journal of Beatrix Potter* was published.

About the time she was twenty, Potter began drawing hundreds of microscopically detailed pictures of fungi that she hoped would be used in a textbook. Though she was encouraged by her uncle, Sir Henry Roscoe, a chemist who was interested in botany, Potter's drawings were not considered publishable because she was an untrained scientist. However, her paper, "The Germination of the Spores of Agaricineae," was presented to the distinguished Linnean Society of London in 1897. Her drawings were eventually published posthumously in 1967 in *Wayside and Woodland Fungi*. Potter's first published illustrations were of rabbits and other animals for F. E. Weatherley's *A Happy Pair,* a book of children's verse published around 1893.

It was in an 1893 letter to Noel Moore, the son of one of Potter's former governesses, that *The Tale of Peter Rabbit* was born. She had corresponded with the child—sick with scarlet fever—all summer and began the now famous missive, complete with black-and-white drawings, "I don't know what to write you, so I shall tell you the story about four little rabbits, whose names were Flopsy, Mopsy, Cottontail, and Peter. . . ." Seven years later Potter decided the story would make a good children's book, and, after enlarging it, submitted it to several local publishers, including Frederick Warne & Co., all of whom rejected it. Not easily discouraged, she used her savings to have it privately printed and was pleased that the 250 copies sold swiftly. In 1902 Warne reconsidered and agreed to publish the little book (5 3/4" x 4 1/4" to fit small hands, with facing pages of text and illustration) if Potter would provide colored illustrations, which she did. At age thirty-six, still living with her parents, Potter became a successful children's writer.

Potter wrote and illustrated twenty more books—several of which also had their beginnings in letters to children—at a rate of two per year, including *The Tailor of Gloucester* (also initially privately printed and generally considered her best book), *The Tale of Squirrel Nutkin, The Tale of Mrs. Tiggy-Winkle, The Tale of Jemima Puddle-Duck,* and *The Tale of Mr. Tod.* Potter revised her work endlessly, often making minute changes in the text or drawings of a particular book in between editions. Her signature watercolor illustrations were painted in subtle, muted shades of green, grey, brown, and pastels that perfectly complemented the stories. Many of the scenes in Potter's books were based on actual places and things in her life.

Potter continued to produce books in this format—though at a slower pace—until 1918, including such favorites as *Appley Dapply's Nursery Rhymes* and *The Tale of Johnny Town-Mouse.* Writing in *Horn Book* in 1941, Bertha Mahony Miller summarized Potter's contribution to children's literature: "These books are genuine classics because they have been written out of an environment known and loved, and to which they are

After engaging in boisterous play, Tom and his siblings are dressed in their Sunday best by their mother, but Tom bursts the buttons on his fancy suit from eating too many pork pies. (From The Tale of Tom Kitten, *written and illustrated by Potter.)*

true. They live for children because they are of those things which have given their author and illustrator infinite joy. . . . For nearly forty years Beatrix Potter's little books have been providing youngest children with volumes charming on three counts—story, drawings and style of book."

The proceeds from the sales of her books brought Potter financial independence, enabling her to buy Hill Top Farm and Castle Farm in Sawrey, England, and, ultimately, several thousand acres of surrounding farmland. Potter continued to live with her parents (renting her property at very generous terms to caretakers) until the age of forty-seven when she disregarded their wishes and married William Heelis, a solicitor who had been instrumental in acquiring the Hill Top land. Earlier, Potter had been engaged to marry Norman Warne of the Warne publishing family—also against her parents' wishes—but his sudden and tragic death from leukemia prevented the union.

By the time Potter became Mrs. Heelis the focus of her life had changed from writing to farming; she devoted herself to breeding Herdwick sheep and in 1930 became the first woman president of the Herdwick Sheepbreeder's Association—an honor she prized. The few books published in her later years were primarily based on ideas conceived in the early part of her life and were not considered critical successes. *The Fairy Caravan* is notable in that it is more autobiographical than her previous works, but, wrote Marcus Crouch in *Three Bodley Head Monographs,* "It is nevertheless a sad book, as every work of fading genius must be sad." Indeed, Potter herself recognized its weaknesses and only allowed a limited printing in the United States and England. The last book Potter wrote and illustrated was *The Tale of Little Pig Robinson,* published in 1930. Her *Wag-by-Wall* was published in 1944 to satisfy requests for a new book from American friends with whom she regularly corresponded at *Horn Book.* Potter's last published work was *The Tale of the Faithful Dove,* written in 1907, but not published until 1956; it contained illustrations by Marie Angel.

Potter died in 1943 in her home in Sawrey at the age of 77, "as she had lived, as simply as possible, conscious of what she was doing, without fuss or regret," wrote her biographer, Margaret Lane, in *The Tale of Beatrix Potter.* Her home and property were willed to the National Trust for preservation. The modest little

Duchess tries to politely fool her friend Ribby but ends up fooling herself in this charming tale of two pies, two ovens, and a very lovely tea party. (From The Tale of the Pie and the Patty-Pan, *written and illustrated by Potter.)*

woman spawned a vast marketing empire whose diversity and breadth even she could not have imagined. Many of her books have never been out of print and have been translated into a dozen languages, selling hundreds of thousands of copies worldwide. And a thriving business of related products is still going strong, ranging from cassettes and videotapes to calendars and candies based on her endearing creations. As well, many writers and illustrators of children's books credit Potter for influencing their work.

In 2002, Peter Rabbit turned 100. To note the milestone, Frederick Warne, the publisher of the Beatrix Potter books, began a year-long celebration, and the National Museum of Natural History in Washington, D.C. hosted an exhibition of Potter's works, including original illustrations.

Potter will be remembered for the complex person she was: conservationist, naturalist, scientist, artist. In an article for *Illustrators of Children's Books: 1957-1966,* Rumer Godden wrote of her: "Simplicity, modesty, truth, balance: these are the qualities to be found in Beatrix Potter and, overriding all of them, love."

Biographical and Critical Sources

BOOKS

Aldis, Dorothy, *Nothing Is Impossible: The Story of Beatrix Potter,* Atheneum (New York, NY), 1969.

Bingham, Jane M., editor, *Writers for Children,* Scribner (New York, NY), 1988.

Children's Literature Review, Volume 19, Gale (Detroit, MI), 1990.

Kingman, Lee, Joanna Foster, and Ruth Giles Lontoft, compilers, *Illustrators of Children's Books, 1957-1966,* Horn Book (Boston, MA), 1968, pp. 54-64.

Lane, Margaret, *The Tale of Beatrix Potter: A Biography,* Warne (London, England), 1946, revised edition, 1968.

Linder, Leslie, *A History of the Writings of Beatrix Potter,* Warne (London, England), 1971.

Potter, Beatrix, *The Journal of Beatrix Potter from 1881-1897,* transcribed from her code writing by Leslie Linder, Warne (London, England), 1966.

Smaridge, Norah, *Famous Author-Illustrators for Young People,* Dodd (New York, NY), 1973.

Three Bodley Head Monographs, Walck, 1961, revised edition, Bodley Head (London, England), 1969, pp. 162-224.

PERIODICALS

Dallas Morning News, January 30, 2002, Jean Nash Johnson, "Peter Rabbit Is 100 This Year."

Elementary English, March, 1968.

Horn Book, May-June, 1941, Bertha Mahony, "Beatrix Potter and Her Nursery Classics," pp. 230-238; December, 1946.

Publishers Weekly, July 11, 1966.*

R–S

RUBIN, Susan Goldman 1939-

Personal

Born March 14, 1939, in New York, NY; daughter of Abraham (a manufacturing jeweler) and Julia (a home-maker; maiden name, Berlin) Moldof; married Hubert M. Goldman (a physician), June, 1959 (divorced, 1976); married Michael B. Rubin (a real estate broker), December 30, 1978; children: (first marriage) Katie Goldman Kolpas, John, Peter; (second marriage) Andrew. *Education:* Oberlin College, B.A. (with honors), 1959; graduate study at the University of California—Los Angeles, 1961-62, attended extension program, 1980-91. *Politics:* Democrat. *Religion:* Jewish. *Hobbies and other interests:* Jogging, cooking, life drawing, going to movies and theater.

Addresses

Home—6330 Sycamore Meadows Dr., Malibu, CA 90265. *Agent*—Andrea Brown, P.O. Box 429, El Granada, CA 94018-0429.

Career

Children's book writer and illustrator, 1975—; freelance writer of educational filmstrips, 1975-78. California State University Department of Continuing Education, Northridge, CA, instructor, 1977-86; University of California Extension School Writer's Program, Los Angeles, CA, instructor, 1986—. Designers West, Los Angeles, CA, editorial assistant, 1991-92.

Member

Society for Children's Book Writers and Illustrators, PEN, Authors Guild, Authors League of America, Southern California Council on Literature for Children and Young People.

Awards, Honors

National Endowment for the Humanities Travel to Collections grant, 1993, for research on a juvenile biography of Frank Lloyd Wright; International Reading

Susan Goldman Rubin depicts dedicated and fearless photojournalist Margaret Bourke-White, who captured some of the most memorable images of the twentieth century, many during her term as chief photographer for Life *magazine. (From* Margaret Bourke-White: Her Pictures Were Her Life.*)*

Association Young Adults' Choice, 1995, for *Emily Good as Gold.*

Writings

(And illustrator) *Grandma Is Somebody Special,* Albert Whitman (Morton Grove, IL), 1976.

(And illustrator) *Cousins Are Special,* Albert Whitman (Morton Grove, IL), 1978.

(And illustrator) *Grandpa and Me Together,* Albert Whitman (Morton Grove, IL), 1980.

Walk with Danger (young adult mystery), Silhouette Books (New York, NY), 1986.

The Black Orchid (young adult mystery), Crosswinds, 1988.

Emily Good as Gold (middle-grade novel), Browndeer/Harcourt (San Diego, CA), 1993.

The Rainbow Fields, illustrated by Heather Preston, Enchante Publishing, 1993.

Frank Lloyd Wright (biography; "First Impressions" series), Abrams (New York, NY), 1994.

Emily in Love, Browndeer/Harcourt (San Diego, CA), 1996.

Margaret Burke-White (biography; "First Impressions" series), Abrams (New York, NY), 1996.

The Whiz Kids Plugged In, illustrated by Doug Cushman, Scholastic (New York, NY), 1997.

The Whiz Kids Take Off!, illustrated by Doug Cushman, Scholastic (New York, NY), 1997.

Toilets, Toasters, and Telephones: The How and Why of Everyday Objects, illustrated by Elsa Warnick, Harcourt (San Diego, CA), 1998.

Margaret Bourke-White: Her Pictures Were Her Life, photographs by Margaret Bourke-White, Abrams (New York, NY), 1999.

Fireflies in the Dark: The Story of Friedl Dicker-Brandeis and the Children of Terezin, Holiday House (New York, NY), 2000.

The Yellow House: Vincent van Gogh and Paul Gauguin Side by Side, illustrated by Joseph A. Smith, Abrams (New York, NY), 2001.

There Goes the Neighborhood: Ten Buildings People Loved to Hate, Holiday House (New York, NY), 2001.

Steven Spielberg: Crazy for Movies, Abrams (New York, NY), 2001.

Edgar Degas: The Painter of Dancers, Abrams (New York, NY), 2002.

Also author of educational filmstrips for McGraw-Hill, BFA, and Pied Piper Productions; author of a story published in *Highlights for Children. Walk with Danger* was published in Italy, 1987, and France, 1990; *The Black Orchid* was published in Spain and France, both 1988.

Sidelights

Susan Goldman Rubin is the author of a number of acclaimed nonfiction works for younger readers. Her subjects have ranged from nineteenth-century Dutch painter Vincent van Gogh to moviemaker Steven Spielberg, but she has also written some well-received novels for teens. Rubin once commented: "I dreamt of becoming an artist and illustrating children's books. However, when I moved to California as a young wife and mother, I couldn't easily go back to New York to show my portfolio and try to get illustrating assignments. So I began writing my own stories to give myself something to illustrate. When I sent my picture book dummies to editors, I found, to my great surprise, that they were as interested in my writing as my artwork. With their rejection letters came suggestions for revisions, and I started taking writing classes at UCLA Extension to learn my craft. I published my first story in *Highlights for Children.*

"A few years later I finally published my first picture book, *Grandma Is Somebody Special,* which I also illustrated. More books about my family followed. My two young adult novels, *Walk with Danger* and *The Black Orchid,* both mysteries, grew from incidents I read about in the newspaper. My biography of Frank Lloyd Wright stemmed from my desire to introduce young readers to architecture as an art form, and to acquaint them with the life and career of one of the most innovative architects of the twentieth century.

"*Emily Good as Gold* developed from an educational filmstrip that I made with my husband. We researched and photographed at a special school for handicapped children in Los Angeles, and I was deeply moved by the students I met. I felt that our filmstrip would only scratch the surface in terms of changing people's negative attitudes toward those who are disabled. I thought a middle grade novel featuring a heroine who is mentally retarded would be more effective."

Rubin received letters from readers telling her how much they liked *Emily Good as Gold,* and now viewed their developmentally disabled classmates with more compassion and tolerance. In 1997, Rubin penned a sequel, *Emily in Love,* that follows the teen's experiences at a regular high school. Determined to date a non-learning disabled student, Emily unwisely takes advice from her friend and classmate Molly, who appeared in the first book. The two host a party with the goal of wooing a boy named Hunt, on whom Emily has developed a crush. The party has a disastrous outcome, and Emily realizes that she has lied to her family and even her best friend in her single-minded pursuit of Hunt. In the end, Hunt makes amends for hurt feelings, and Emily finds out who her true allies are. "This book succeeds in showing how alike Emily is to most fourteen-year-old girls," remarked *Voice of Youth Advocates* reviewer Melissa Thacker, while Stephanie Zvirin, writing in *Booklist,* felt that the book's theme would resonate with all readers. "There's a universal message here as Rubin clearly shows the effects of prejudice on self-esteem," Zvirin wrote.

Toilets, Toasters, and Telephones: The How and Why of Everyday Objects was Rubin's look at the industrial design history of some common household items. She recounted the development of vacuum cleaners, a stove, and even the bathtub, and explains how they caught on with consumers. She also takes some detours by mentioning some failed designs, like the idea of revolving shelves for refrigerators. "The text is solid, serious, and backed by an impressive bibliography," opined *Booklist* critic Randy Meyer.

Rubin has also penned some biographies of famous names in the arts. Her *Frank Lloyd Wright* won kudos in 1994, and she followed it with another book for the esteemed New York City art-book publisher, Abrams, five years later titled *Margaret Bourke-White: Her Pictures Were Her Life.* Bourke-White, as Rubin explains, was one of the first woman photojournalists, and the capturer of some of most memorable images of the twentieth century. One of *Life* magazine's "Founding Four" photographers, Bourke-White was dedicated and fearless, and often took great risks to get her picture. She spent time on the battlefields of World War II, and her photographs of the skeletal survivors of Nazi Germany's recently liberated concentration camps were indelible. As Rubin notes, Bourke-White's mother voiced some anti-Semitic views, but the photographer later learned that she herself was part Jewish on her father's side.

Rubin's story of Bourke-White and her career is enhanced by the inclusion of fifty-six of some of her greatest images. "Rubin does a brilliant job of bringing in personal elements that resonate with real emotion," noted *Booklist* critic Roger Leslie, terming *Margaret Bourke-White* "by far one of the best biographies of the year." A contributor to *Publishers Weekly* predicted that "Rubin's understated, seemingly effortless narrative will" help readers realize "that many of the images they take for granted today had their roots in the work of this daring pioneer."

Rubin's next book was *Fireflies in the Dark: The Story of Friedl Dicker-Brandeis and the Children of Terezin.* This biography revealed the life of the woman who was responsible for a cache of 5,000 drawings and poems done by the children of one World War II-era concentration camp, Terezin, in Czechoslovakia. The art was discovered after the war's end in suitcases that had been hidden in the attic of one of Terezin's barracks buildings. Friedl Dicker-Brandeis, as Rubin's biography explains, was an art therapist in Prague before she was deported to Terezin. She managed to take her art supplies with her and began giving secret art classes to some of the 15,000 children who passed through there. Only a hundred would survive to adulthood, and Dicker-Brandeis herself died at the Auschwitz camp in Poland. The drawings, many of them reproduced in Rubin's book, show tragic glimpses into the minds of children who were longing for their parents and a lost world: some show the landscapes of their home villages, one depicts a family sitting down for a Seder meal during the Passover holiday, and still others depict the horrors of life at Terezin. Rubin interviewed some of the survivors and recounts their stories as well as that of Dicker-Brandeis. *School Library Journal*'s Patricia Manning called it a keen addition to the literature of the Holocaust as well as "elegant in appearance, devastating in content, almost overwhelming in its quiet intensity." Other reviewers offered similar praise. "There's no sensation-

Rubin's biography presents Steven Spielberg's life through recollections of his friends and family and centers on his early preoccupation with storytelling and filmmaking. (From Steven Spielberg: Crazy for Movies.*)*

alism here," declared *Booklist*'s Hazel Rochman. "Everything is distanced, but the sense of loss is overwhelming."

Rubin tackled an unusual theme for her next art biography, *The Yellow House: Vincent van Gogh and Paul Gauguin Side by Side.* Her book recounts a two-month period in late 1888 when French painter Paul Gauguin stayed at van Gogh's farmhouse in the south of France. During the time, despite a growing contention between the pair, each painted several works. As Rubin explains, the two artists had vastly different temperaments and work habits: Gauguin was a slow, deliberate painter who often made many preliminary drawings of his subject before committing paint to canvas. Van Gogh, by contrast, was an exuberant, emotional painter who sometimes squeezed the paint from the tube right onto his brush. The men quarreled much, which led to Gauguin's eventual departure and an increasingly frail state of mental health for his host. Rubin's book shows the works the artists painted during this time, and its publication coincided with an exhibition of them at the Art Institute of Chicago titled "Studio of the South." A reviewer for *Publishers Weekly* found that Rubin's "incisive, accessible analysis of some of the paintings created during their time together accompanies crisp reproductions of their work."

Budding cultural critics were the target audience for Rubin's next work, *There Goes the Neighborhood: Ten Buildings People Loved to Hate,* published in 2001. She recounts the harsh critical and public reception of some of the world's most famous structures, from the Washington Monument in America's capital city to Paris's Eiffel Tower. She also discusses Frank Lloyd Wright's daring design for New York City's Solomon R. Guggenheim Museum, as well as another controversial museum by two 1970s architects, the Centre Pompidou in Paris. These and the other edifices in Rubin's list were initially vilified by architecture critics, public officials, and the general public, but their uniqueness eventually caused them to become accepted landmarks. "This volume may well inspire readers to examine buildings ... in new ways and bolster their courage to think differently," stated a *Publishers Weekly* reviewer. *Booklist* critic Gillian Engberg also liked *There Goes the Neighborhood*. "Written in simple, engaging language that never condescends," Engberg stated, "the stories reveal how architects identified and solved aesthetic and engineering problems, and include fascinating" details about the history of each building, its neighborhood, and the visionary architects who designed them.

When Rubin wanted to write a biography of filmmaker Steven Spielberg, she knew that the man behind *E. T.* and *Schindler's List* was infamously uncooperative when it came time to such projects. She also knew, however, that Spielberg's mother owned a kosher restaurant called "The Milky Way," and so visited it to ask her first. She also brought along some of her published books. Leah Adler initially said no to Rubin, but while Rubin and a friend were eating, Spielberg's mother came to the table and told her, "'I like you. I like your books,'" as Rubin told *Publishers Weekly,* and agreed to help. The result was *Steven Spielberg: Crazy for Movies,* published in 2001, which presents his life through comments from some of the most incisive critics of all: his family and friends. Many of the recollections hint at Spielberg's fascination with filmmaking, using an 8-millimeter camera, and storytelling at an early age, and family photographs add depth to this personal biography. Spielberg also explains how many of his films grew out of incidents of his childhood, or particular fears he harbored then. As he notes, *Poltergeist*—a 1982 film which starred a young Drew Barrymore—had its roots in Spielberg's torment of his younger sisters. "Fans of film will revel in this behind-the-scenes look at Spielberg's childhood, movies and the choices that led to his stellar career," stated a *Publishers Weekly* reviewer.

Rubin is also the author of *Edgar Degas: The Painter of Dancers,* published by Abrams in 2002.

Biographical and Critical Sources

PERIODICALS

Booklist, November 1, 1993, Stephanie Zvirin, review of *Emily Good as Gold,* p. 514; January 1, 1995, Hazel Rochman, review of *Frank Lloyd Wright,* p. 812; May 15, 1997, Stephanie Zvirin, review of *Emily in Love,* pp. 1573-1574; November 1, 1998, Randy Meyer, review of *Toilets, Toasters and Telephones: The How and Why of Everyday Objects,* p. 488; November 1, 1999, Roger Leslie, review of *Margaret Bourke-White: Her Pictures Were Her Life,* p. 526; January 1, 2000, review of *Margaret Bourke-White,* p. 820; March 1, 2000, Stephanie Zvirin, review of *Margaret Bourke-White,* p. 1249; July, 2000, Hazel Rochman, review of *Fireflies in the Dark: The Story of Friedl Dicker-Brandeis and the Children of Terezin,* p. 2023; December 15, 2000, Gillian Engberg, review of *Fireflies in the Dark,* p. 811; August, 2001, Gillian Engberg, review of *There Goes the Neighborhood: Ten Buildings People Loved to Hate,* p. 2105; November 15, 2001, Gillian Engberg, review of *The Yellow House: Vincent van Gogh and Paul Gauguin Side by Side,* pp. 578-579; December 1, 2001, Randy Meyer, review of *Steven Spielberg: Crazy for Movies,* p. 641.

Book Report, September-October, 1995, Melinda Bronte, "First Impressions: *Frank Lloyd Wright,*" p. 47.

Horn Book, March, 1999, Mary M. Burns, review of *Toilets, Toasters and Telephones,* p. 229; January, 2000, review of *Margaret Bourke-White,* p. 102; September, 2000, review of *Fireflies in the Dark,* p. 599.

Kirkus Reviews, November 1, 1999, review of *Margaret Bourke-White,* p. 1748; September 15, 2001, review of *The Yellow House,* p. 1366; October 15, 2001, review of *Steven Spielberg,* p. 1492.

New York Times Book Review, January 20, 2002, review of *Stephen Spielberg,* p. 14.

Publishers Weekly, October 25, 1993, review of *Emily Good as Gold,* p. 64; November 8, 1999, review of *Margaret Bourke-White,* p. 70; June 5, 2000, "A Lasting Legacy," p. 96; July 9, 2001, review of *There Goes the Neighborhood,* p. 69; August 13, 2001, "A.I.—Active Imagination?," p. 174; September 3, 2001, review of *The Yellow House,* p. 87; November 12, 2001, review of *Steven Spielberg,* pp. 60-61.

School Library Journal, October, 1993, Cindy Darling Codell, review of *Emily Good as Gold,* pp. 152-153; January, 1995, Jeanette Larson, review of *Frank Lloyd Wright,* p. 143; May, 1997, Renee Steinberg, review of *Emily in Love,* p. 139; November 1, 1998, Ann G. Brouse, review of *Toilets, Toasters, and Telephones,* p. 142; December, 1999, Carol Fazioli, review of *Margaret Bourke-White,* pp. 159-160; August, 2000, Patricia Manning, review of *Fireflies in the Dark,* p. 206; September, 2001, Mary Ann Carcich, review of *There Goes the Neighborhood,* p. 254; December, 2001, Shauna Yusko, review of *Steven Spielberg,* p. 171; January, 2002, Robin L. Gibson, review of *The Yellow House,* p. 124; March, 2002, Kathleen Baxter, "Castles in the Air," p. 49.

Voice of Youth Advocates, June, 1997, Melissa Thacker, review of *Emily in Love,* p. 113.*

*　　*　　*

SÁNCHEZ-SILVA, José Maria 1911-

Personal

Born November 11, 1911, in Madrid, Spain; son of Lorenzo (a journalist) and Adoracion (a poet; maiden name, Garcia-Morales) Sánchez-Silva; married María del Carmen Delgado, 1933; children: six. *Education:* Attended El Dabate, Madrid.

Addresses

Agent—c/o Ediciones Anaya SA, Juan Ignacio, Luca de Tena 15, Madrid 28027, Spain.

Career

Author. Worked previously as a reporter, editor-in-chief, and assistant director for *Arriba,* Madrid, Spain, during the late 1930s and early 1940s, and as editor of *Revista de las Artes y los Oficios,* beginning in 1946.

Member

General Society of Spanish Authors (appointed to council, 1963).

Awards, Honors

Francisco de Sales Prize, 1942; National Prize for Literature (Spain), 1944, 1957; National Prize for Journalism (Spain), 1945; Mariano de Cavia Prize, 1947; Rodriguez Santamaria Prize, 1948; Grand Cross of the Order of Cisneros (Spain), 1959; Virgen del Carmen Prize, 1960; award for special services from the government of Peru, 1962; Hans Christian Andersen highly commended author, 1966; Hans Christian Andersen Award, 1968; Grand Cross of the Order of Alphonso X (Spain), 1968.

Writings

IN ENGLISH TRANSLATION

Marcelino Pan y Vino: Cuento de Padres a Hijos, illustrated by Lorenzo Goñi [Madrid, Spain], 1953, translation by Angela Britton published as *Marcelino: A Story from Parents to Children,* Newman Press (Westminster, MD), 1955, translation by John Paul Debicki published as *The Miracle of Marcelino,* Scepter (Chicago, IL), 1963.

Adios, Josefina!, illustrated by Lorenzo Goñi, Alameda (Madrid, Spain), 1962, translation by Michael Herron published as *The Boy and the Whale,* illustrated by Margery Gill, McGraw-Hill (New York, NY), 1964.

Un Gran Pequeno, Editorial Marfil (Alcoy, Spain), 1967, translation by Michael Herron published as *Ladis and the Ant,* illustrated by David Knight, McGraw-Hill (New York, NY), 1969.

El Segundo Verano de Ladis, Editorial Marfil (Alcoy, Spain), 1968, translation by Isabel Quigly published as *Second Summer with Ladis,* illustrated by David Knight, Bodley Head (London, England), 1969.

UNTRANSLATED WORKS

El Hombre y la Bufanda (short stories; title means "The Man and the Neckcloth"), 1934.

Un Palato en Londres: La Vuelta al Mundo y Otros Viajes (title means "A Country Boy in London: The Return to Earth and Other Journeys"), Editoria Nacional (Madrid, Spain), 1952.

Adelaida y Otros Asuntos Personales (title means "Adelaida and Other Personal Affairs"), illustrated by Lorenzo Goñi, Editoria Nacional (Madrid, Spain), 1953.

Historias de Mi Calle (title means "Stories of My Street"), [Madrid, Spain], 1954.

Quince o Veinte Sombras (title means "Fifteen or Twenty Shadows"), Ediciones CID (Madrid, Spain), 1955.

Fabula de la Burrita Non (title means "Fable of the Little Donkey Odd"), illustrated by Lorenzo Goñi, Ediciones CID (Madrid, Spain), 1956.

El Hereje: Cuento para Mayores (title means "The Heretic: Tales to Elders"), illustrated by Alvaro Delgado, A. Aguado (Madrid, Spain), 1956.

Tres Novelas y Pico (title means "Three Odd Stories"), A. Aguado (Madrid, Spain), 1958.

Cuentos de Navidad (title means "Christmas Stories"), illustrated by Jose Francisco Aguirre, Editorial Magisterio Espanol (Madrid, Spain), 1960.

San Martin de Porres (title means "Saint Martin of Porres"), Secretariado Martin de Porres (Palencia, Spain), 1962.

Colasin, Colason, Editoria Nacional (Madrid, Spain), 1963.

Pesinoe y Gente de Tierra, [Madrid, Spain], 1964.

Cartas a un Nino Sobre Francisco Franco, [Madrid, Spain], 1966.

Tres Animales Son (title means "Three Animal Sounds"), Doncel (Madrid, Spain), 1967.

Adan y el Senor Dios (title means "Adam and the Lord"), illustrated by Lorenzo Goñi, Escelicer (Madrid, Spain), 1969.

(With Luis de Diego) *Luiso,* illustrated by Lorenzo Goñi, Doncel (Madrid, Spain), 1969.

(With José Luis Saénz de Heredia) *Franco . . . Ese Hombre (1892-1965)* (title means "Franco . . . That Man [1892-1965]"), Difusión Librera (Madrid, Spain), 1975.

Historias Menores de Marcelino Pan y Vino (title means "Short Stories of Marcelino Pan y Vino"), illustrated by Lorenzo Goñi, Doncel (Madrid, Spain), 1975.

Artículos Periododísticos (title means "Journalistic Articles"), Fundación Central Hispano (Madrid, Spain), 1996.

Cuentos Adultos (title means "Adult Stories"), Fundación Central Hispano (Madrid, Spain), 1996.

Relatos Infantiles y Juveniles (title means "Stories for Children and Youth"), Fundación Central Hispano (Madrid, Spain), 1996.

Cuentos Cristíanos (title means "Christian Stories"), Planeta (Barcelona, Spain), 1998.

Also author of *Aventura en Cielo* (title means "Adventures in Heaven"); *El Espejo Habitado* (title means "The Lived-in Mirror"); and *Historias Menores* (title means "Little Stories"). Scriptwriter for motion picture *Ronda Espanola,* 1952.

Sidelights

One of the most renowned Spanish children's writers whose works have been translated into English, José Maria Sánchez-Silva is known in the United States as the author of *Marcelino: A Story from Parents to Children, The Boy and the Whale, Ladis and the Ant,* and *Second Summer with Ladis,* all books that were first published in his native language. Sánchez-Silva's children's books have won praise for their poetic fusion of the magical and the real in themes centering on family, religion, and death through portrayals of relationships between children and animals. The Spanish version of *Marcelino,* titled *Marcelino Pan y Vino: Cuento de Padres a Hijos,* likened to Antoine de Saint-Exupery's

The Little Prince, has often been used as a textbook to introduce students to Spanish. Sánchez-Silva "is the greatest Spanish contemporary writer for children both as regards the quality and the quantity of his work," maintained a *Bookbird* contributor.

Sánchez-Silva was born in Madrid to literary parents: his father, Lorenzo, was a journalist, and his mother, Adoracion, wrote poetry. By the time Sánchez-Silva reached the age of ten he fell on hard times: his mother died and his father vanished, leaving him to provide for himself. He went to live with his godmother and worked in a series of odd jobs, including as a drugstore errand boy, a hotel kitchen worker, and a tailor's helper. Sánchez-Silva was then placed in an orphanage when his godmother immigrated to Mexico, and in 1926 he began attending school in Madrid. Training in stenography and typing landed him a job in Madrid's city hall after he left school. In 1932 he won a scholarship to El Dabate, a school of journalism, after distinguishing himself in a class he attended there, and soon thereafter he began to work as a journalist. The following year, 1933, Sánchez-Silva married María del Carmen Delgado, the daughter of a judge, and over the course of their marriage the couple has had six children.

Sánchez-Silva's first book, *El Hombre y la Bufanda,* a collection of short stories for adults, appeared in 1934, shortly after he and his wife returned from a trip to France, Cuba, Mexico, and the United States. He then settled into newspaper work, except for a short period when he worked as a salesman for the French automobile firm Renault. In 1939 he joined the staff of the Madrid newspaper *Arriba,* eventually becoming editor-in-chief, and then assistant director. In 1946 he was appointed editor of *Revista de las Artes los Oficios.*

Sánchez-Silva began to travel widely after World War II, journeying to Italy on assignment for *Arriba* in 1946, and to England in 1948 to cover the winter Olympic games. In 1949 he went on what was termed in the *Third Book of Junior Authors* as a "round-the-world pilgrimage (commemorating the four hundredth anniversary of St. Francis Xavier's arrival in Japan)." The next year he covered the World Cup soccer tournament in Brazil, and he went to France, Holland, Belgium, and Sweden as a sports reporter in 1951.

Sánchez-Silva began producing more children's books in the mid-1950s, when he left journalism for a short time. *Marcelino,* published in English in 1955, was among these works; it imaginatively and gently examines the serious topic that German critic Bettina Huerlimann described in *Three Centuries of Children's Books in Europe* as "the glad acceptance of death." The story features a nine-year-old orphan boy, Marcelino, raised by monks, who enjoys killing his pets through elaborate means (characterized by Huerlimann as "an expression of the juvenile preliminaries to a passion for bullfighting"). In an attic the monks forbid him to enter is a figure of Christ carved out of wood. Marcelino persistently steals food to offer to the Christ figure, which comes to life in the boy's presence and finally persuades

him to accept death—what Huerlimann terms as actually being "the door to true life."

The Boy and the Whale, published in English in 1964, concerns an imaginary whale who is named Josefina by her keeper, Santiago. The boy keeps Josefina in a glass of water when he goes to bed at night and sends her off to visit relatives when he goes on holiday. At the end of the story, as Santiago stands at the school gates ready to begin his first day in class, Josefina volunteers to die. Laurence Adkins, writing in *School Librarian and School Library Review,* explained that "at the end [Santiago] can say good-bye with ease because he is grown up."

In *Ladis and the Ant,* published in English in 1969, Sánchez-Silva tells the story of a poor boy, Ladis, who is sent to live in the country with a forester. In the forest Ladis can speak with the ants, and he learns to love the insect world. The queen ant, Mufra, reduces Ladis in size so he can visit her subjects. Frances M. Postell related in *School Library Journal* that Sánchez-Silva imparts interesting information about the living habits of ants, "but the purpose of the contrived fantastical episodes is to provide a bridge for the chasm between the initially lonely, frightened, self-centered boy who returns home stronger, happier, and wiser." In *Second Summer with Ladis,* the sequel to *Ladis and the Ant,* Ladis's ant friends engage in war with more powerful rivals. Under oath not to disturb the course of nature, Ladis must witness the defeat of his friends. At the end, however, Ladis takes Mufra and a few of her friends home in a matchbox, where they begin the colony anew.

Sánchez-Silva consistently manages to reveal something divine or magical about the everyday struggles of his child subjects. He claimed in *Bookbird* to have found "no more dignified task than the occupation of education, upbringing and poetic development of children. I believe that the famous concept of 'Cherchez la femme' [look for the woman] is no longer a possible road for understanding the human predicament. From now on it must be 'Cherchez l'enfant' [look for the child]."

Biographical and Critical Sources

BOOKS

Contemporary Literary Criticism, Volume 12, Gale (Detroit, MI), 1980.

De Montreville, Doris, and Donna Hill, editors, *Third Book of Junior Authors,* H. W. Wilson (New York, NY), 1972.

Huerlimann, Bettina, *Three Centuries of Children's Books in Europe,* edited and translated by Brian W. Alderson, Oxford University Press (London, England), 1967, pp. 76-92.

Twentieth-Century Children's Writers, 3rd edition, St. James Press (Detroit, MI), 1989.

PERIODICALS

Bookbird, December 15, 1968, "José Maria Sánchez-Silva," pp. 18-19.

Kirkus Reviews, April 15, 1969, p. 442.

Library Journal, May 15, 1969, p. 1207.

New York Times Book Review, July 13, 1969, p. 26.

School Librarian and School Library Review, July, 1964, Laurence Adkins, review of *The Boy and the Whale,* p. 214.

School Library Journal, May, 1969, Frances M. Postell, review of *Ladis and the Ant,* pp. 93-94.*

*   *   *

SOBOL, Donald J. 1924-

Personal

Born October 4, 1924, in New York, NY; son of Ira J. and Ida (Gelula) Sobol; married Rose Tiplitz (an engineer and author), August 14, 1955; children: Diane, Glenn (deceased, 1983), Eric, John. *Education:* Oberlin College, B.A., 1948; attended New School for Social Research, 1949-51. *Avocational interests:* Gardening, travel reading, theater.

Addresses

Agent—McIntosh & Otis, 353 Lexington Ave., New York, NY 10016.

Career

Author of fiction and nonfiction for children. *New York Sun,* New York, NY, reporter, 1948-49; *Long Island Daily Press,* New York, NY, reporter, 1949-50; R. H. Macy, New York, NY, buyer, 1953-55; freelance writer, 1954—. *Military service:* U.S. Army, Corps of Combat Engineers, 1943-46; served in Pacific Theater.

Member

Authors Guild, Authors League of America.

Awards, Honors

Young Readers Choice Award, Pacific Northwest Library Association, 1972, for *Encyclopedia Brown Keeps the Peace;* Edgar Allan Poe Award, Mystery Writers of America, 1974, for entire body of work; Garden State Children's Book Award, 1977, for *Encyclopedia Brown Lends a Hand;* Aiken County Children's Book Award, 1977, for *Encyclopedia Brown Takes the Case;* Buckeye honor citation (grades 4-8 category), 1982, for *Encyclopedia Brown and the Case of the Midnight Visitor.* Several of Sobol's books were Junior Literary Guild selections.

Writings

FOR YOUNG ADULTS

The Double Quest, illustrated by Lili Rethi, Watts (New York, NY), 1957.

The Lost Dispatch, illustrated by Anthony Palombo, Watts (New York, NY), 1958.

First Book of Medieval Man (nonfiction), illustrated by Rethi, Watts (New York, NY), 1959, revised edition

Donald J. Sobol

published in England as *The First Book of Medieval Britain,* Mayflower, 1960.

Two Flags Flying (biographies of Civil War leaders), illustrated by Jerry Robinson, Platt, 1960.

A Civil War Sampler, illustrated by Henry S. Gilette, Watts (New York, NY), 1961.

The Wright Brothers at Kitty Hawk (nonfiction), illustrated by Stuart Mackenzie, T. Nelson (Nashville, TN), 1961.

(Editor, with wife, Rose Sobol) *The First Book of the Barbarian Invaders, A.D. 375-511* (nonfiction), illustrated by W. Kirtman Plummer, Watts (New York, NY), 1962.

(With Rose Sobol) *The First Book of Stocks and Bonds* (nonfiction), Watts (New York, NY), 1963.

(Editor) *An American Revolutionary War Reader,* Watts (New York, NY), 1964.

Lock, Stock, and Barrel (biographies of American Revolutionary War leaders), illustrated by Edward J. Smith, Westminster (Louisville, KY), 1965.

Secret Agents Four, illustrated by Leonard Shortall, Four Winds (New York, NY), 1967.

(Editor) *The Strongest Man in the World,* illustrated by Cliff Schule, Westminster (Louisville, KY), 1967.

Two-Minute Mysteries, Dutton (New York, NY), 1967.

Greta the Strong, illustrated by Trina Schart Hyman, Follett, 1970.

Milton, the Model A, illustrated by J. Drescher, Harvey House, 1970.

More Two-Minute Mysteries, Dutton (New York, NY), 1971.

The Amazons of Greek Mythology, A. S. Barnes, 1972.

Great Sea Stories, Dutton (New York, NY), 1975.

Still More Two-Minute Mysteries, Dutton (New York, NY), 1975.

True Sea Adventures, T. Nelson (Nashville, TN), 1975.

(Editor) *The Best Animal Stories of Science Fiction and Fantasy,* Warne, 1979.

Disasters, Archway, 1979.

Angie's First Case, illustrated by Gail Owens, Four Winds (New York, NY), 1981.

The Amazing Power of Ashur Fine: A Fine Mystery, Macmillan Children's Book Group (New York, NY), 1986.

My Name Is Amelia, Macmillan (New York, NY), 1994.

"ENCYCLOPEDIA BROWN" SERIES

Encyclopedia Brown: Boy Detective (also see below), illustrated by Leonard Shortall, T. Nelson (Nashville, TN), 1963.

Encyclopedia Brown and the Case of the Secret Pitch, illustrated by Shortall, T. Nelson (Nashville, TN), 1965.

Encyclopedia Brown Finds the Clues, illustrated by Shortall, T. Nelson (Nashville, TN), 1966.

Encyclopedia Brown Gets His Man, illustrated by Shortall, T. Nelson (Nashville, TN), 1967.

Encyclopedia Brown Solves Them All, illustrated by Shortall, T. Nelson (Nashville, TN), 1968.

Encyclopedia Brown Keeps the Peace, illustrated by Shortall, T. Nelson (Nashville, TN), 1969.

Encyclopedia Brown Saves the Day, illustrated by Shortall, T. Nelson (Nashville, TN), 1970.

Encyclopedia Brown Tracks Them Down, illustrated by Shortall, T. Nelson (Nashville, TN), 1971.

Encyclopedia Brown Shows the Way, illustrated by Shortall, T. Nelson (Nashville, TN), 1972.

Encyclopedia Brown Takes the Case, illustrated by Shortall, T. Nelson (Nashville, TN), 1973.

Encyclopedia Brown Lends a Hand, illustrated by Shortall, T. Nelson (Nashville, TN), 1974.

Encyclopedia Brown and the Case of the Dead Eagles, illustrated by Shortall, T. Nelson (Nashville, TN), 1975.

Encyclopedia Brown and the Eleven: Case of the Exploding Plumbing and Other Mysteries, illustrated by Shortall, Dutton (New York, NY), 1976.

Encyclopedia Brown and the Case of the Midnight Visitor, illustrated by Lillian Brandi, T. Nelson (Nashville, TN), 1977, Bantam (New York, NY), 1982.

Encyclopedia Brown's Record Book of Weird and Wonderful Facts, illustrated by Sal Murdocca, Delacorte (New York, NY), 1979, illustrated by Bruce Degen, Dell (New York, NY), 1981.

Encyclopedia Brown Carries On, illustrated by Ib Ohlsson, Four Winds (New York, NY), 1980.

Encyclopedia Brown Sets the Pace, illustrated by Ohlsson, Dutton (New York, NY), 1982.

Encyclopedia Brown's Second Record Book of Weird and Wonderful Facts, illustrated by Degen, Delacorte (New York, NY), 1981.

Encyclopedia Brown's Third Record Book of Weird and Wonderful Facts, illustrated by Murdocca, Delacorte (New York, NY), 1981.

Encyclopedia Brown's Book of Wacky Crimes, illustrated by Shortall, Dutton (New York, NY), 1982.

Encyclopedia Brown (omnibus), illustrated by Shortall, Angus & Robertson (London, England), 1983.

Encyclopedia Brown's Book of Wacky Spies, illustrated by Ted Enik, Morrow (New York, NY), 1984.

Encyclopedia Brown's Book of Wacky Sports, illustrated by Enik, Morrow (New York, NY), 1984.

(With Glenn Andrews) *Encyclopedia Brown Takes the Cake!: A Cook and Case Book,* illustrated by Ohlsson, Scholastic (New York, NY), 1983.

Encyclopedia Brown and the Case of the Mysterious Handprints, illustrated by Owens, Morrow (New York, NY), 1985.

Encyclopedia Brown's Book of Wacky Animals, illustrated by Enik, Morrow (New York, NY), 1985.

Encyclopedia Brown's Book of the Wacky Outdoors, illustrated by Enik, Morrow (New York, NY), 1987.

Encyclopedia Brown's Book of Wacky Cars, illustrated by Enik, Morrow (New York, NY), 1987.

Encyclopedia Brown and the Case of the Treasure Hunt, illustrated by Owens, Morrow (New York, NY), 1988.

Encyclopedia Brown and the Case of the Disgusting Sneakers, illustrated by Owens, Morrow (New York, NY), 1990.

(With Rose Sobol) *Encyclopedia Brown's Book of Strange but True Crimes,* illustrated by John Zielinski, Scholastic (New York, NY), 1991.

Encyclopedia Brown and the Case of the Two Spies, illustrated by Eric Velasquez, Delacorte (New York, NY), 1994.

Encyclopedia Brown and the Case of Pablo's Nose, illustrated by Velasquez, Delacorte (New York, NY), 1996.

Encyclopedia Brown and the Case of the Sleeping Dog, Delacorte (New York, NY), 1998.

Encyclopedia Brown and the Case of the Slippery Salamander, Delacorte (New York, NY), 1999.

The Best of Encyclopedia Brown, illustrated by Ohlsson, Scholastic (New York, NY), in press.

Books from the "Encyclopedia Brown" series have been translated into thirteen languages and Braille.

OTHER

Author of syndicated column, "Two Minute Mysteries," 1959-68. Contributor of more than 150 stories and articles to national magazines under a variety of pen names. Work appears in more than fifty-five readers and anthologies. Sobol's manuscripts are kept in the Kerlan Collection, University of Minnesota, Minneapolis, MN.

Adaptations

The Best of Encyclopedia Brown (includes "The Case of the Natty Nut," "The Case of the Scattered Cards," "The Case of the Hungry Hitchhiker," and "The Case of the Whistling Ghost"), with cassette, Miller-Brody, 1977. Books from the "Encyclopedia Brown" series have also been made into comic strips.

Sidelights

American children's mystery author Donald J. Sobol has kept schoolchildren investigating since 1963, with the publication of the original Encyclopedia Brown book. *Encyclopedia Brown: Boy Detective* began the popular series, which has continued for more than three decades. Over the years, Leroy "Encyclopedia" Brown, Sobol's young sleuth, has faced intriguing cases involving everything from dead eagles to disgusting sneakers. Solutions to each case are printed in the back of the book, but children are encouraged to try to solve the cases themselves.

The *Encyclopedia Brown* books each contain ten mysteries presented in readable sentences and enhanced with witty puns and other verbal jokes. It takes careful reading and a variety of methods—deductive reasoning, psychology, and careful observation of physical evidence—to solve the mysteries. "Complexity in writing style is not Sobol's intent, nor is it required for the success of these books," wrote Christine McDonnell in *Twentieth Century Children's Writers.* "Although the stories are simply written, they are clever and fresh, and seldom obvious or easy to solve."

Ten-year-old Leroy Brown is called "Encyclopedia" because he is so smart that it seems he must have an entire set of encyclopedias crammed into his head. He is so adept at finding clues that he helps his father, the Chief of Police, solve criminal cases. "Readers constantly ask me if Encyclopedia Brown is a real boy. The answer is no," Sobol once commented. "He is, perhaps, the boy I wanted to be—doing the things I wanted to read about but could not find in any book when I was ten."

Sobol was born in 1924 in New York City, where he attended the Ethical Cultural Schools. During World War II, he served with the combat engineer corps in the Pacific, and after his discharge he earned a B.A. from Oberlin College. It wasn't until he took a short-story writing course in college that Sobol thought of becoming a writer, and even then he waited several years before making writing his profession. Sobol's first job was as a copyboy for the *New York Sun.* Later he became a journalist for the *Sun* and for the *Long Island Daily News.* "At the age of thirty I quit job-holding for good, married Rose Tiplitz, an engineer, and began to write full time," Sobol once noted.

For many years, Sobol has received letters from stumped young readers complaining that his mysteries have no proper explanation. These letters are often written by readers who have missed some significant detail. But in 1990, students in a Philadelphia school detected an actual error in the first *Encyclopedia Brown* book. The story about a trickster who bilks his classmates in an egg-spinning contest fails to explain how the cheater managed to get a boiled egg into the dozen before the contestants bought it at the grocery store. After the students wrote to Sobol asking for the explanation, he re-read the story for the first time in nearly thirty years.

Seventy-nine mysteries are presented to young readers, along with clues and answers, in Sobol's fun puzzle book.

He admitted the solution should be more fully explained. "This is the first time in a couple of decades where it is really my fault," Sobol told Martha Woodall of the *Detroit Free Press.* "They are really smart kids." The teacher of the first- and second-graders who spotted the error said it has taught the students the importance of questioning the accuracy of what they read. She said they also learned that when something that is incorrect appears in print, there is something they can do about it. New editions including "The Case of the Champion Egg-Spinner" will contain the revised version.

The *Encyclopedia Brown* series, now lasting four decades, has becomes something of a classic for young readers. With some two dozen mystery titles, and another dozen related titles, the "Encyclopedia Brown" books continue to attract new readers. Each succeeding generation loves a mystery, it seems. Over the years Leroy Brown has been updated to fit the changing times. *Booklist*'s Ilene Cooper pointed out in a review of the 1998 *Encyclopedia Brown and the Case of Pablo's Nose,* for example, that Encyclopedia Brown is now depicted on the dust jacket "sporting jeans and a work shirt ...." Cooper also noted that his hometown, Idaville, has a deli and a synagogue, other signs of the changing times. "As usual," Cooper concluded, the book is "a good and fun workout for the brain." Leroy the ten-year-old sleuth is back for more adventures in the 1999 *Encyclopedia Brown and the Case of the Slippery Salamander*, "a book that will most likely be as popular as others in the series," according to *Booklist*'s Lauren Peterson. Peterson opined that the success of the series "lies in its format," for, as Peterson noted, "[b]udding detectives love the excitement of trying to solve cases on their own or with a buddy ...."

In addition to the boy-detective series, Sobol has written many nonfiction books that required him to do extensive research on topics as varied as King Arthur's England (*Greta the Strong*) and ancient Greece (*The Amazons of Greek Mythology*). His other nonfiction works include biographies of American military leaders of the Revolutionary and Civil Wars, in *Lock, Stock and Barrel* and *Two Flags Flying*. Sobol has also written an internationally syndicated newspaper feature, "Two-Minute Mystery Series," hundreds of articles and stories for adult magazines, historical books, and biographies. He is the editor of two history collections, *A Civil War Sampler* and *An American Revolutionary War Reader*, and the

Idaville's annual disgusting-sneaker contest provides the backdrop for Sobol's mysteries to be solved by the immensely popular boy-sleuth. (Cover illustration by Eric Velasquez.)

author, with his wife, Rose, of a book on stocks and bonds.

Sobol once said, "Good luck has been a major component in my career. I had a wonderful childhood, a confession that rewards me with looks of disbelief (or disgust) from my contemporaries who are convinced an author must suffer in order to write 'meaningful' books. I had parents who loved me and I them, and I have children who bring me happiness. Best of all I have Rose. She is not my colleague or my best friend. She is infinitely more; she is my wife.

"I never write fiction for children or adults to educate. If I discover a message has crept into a story I have written (a message besides brotherhood) I strike it out in a flash. I write to entertain. Messages I leave to others."

Biographical and Critical Sources

BOOKS

Children's Literature Review, Volume 4, Gale, 1982.
Fourth Book of Junior Authors, H. W. Wilson, 1978.
McDonnell, Christine, "Donald Sobol," *Twentieth Century Children's Writers*, 2nd edition, St. Martin's Press (New York, NY), 1989.
Silvey, Anita, editor, *Children's Books and Their Creators*, Houghton Mifflin (Boston, MA), 1995.
St. James Guide to Children's Writers, 5th edition, St. James Press (Detroit, MI), 1999.
Ward, Martha E., et al, *Authors of Books for Young People*, 3rd edition, Scarecrow Press (Metuchen, NJ), 1990.

PERIODICALS

Booklist, February 1, 1983, p. 27; May 1, 1984, p. 1254; March 1, 1991, p. 1382; January 1, 1995, p. 822; January 1, 1997, Ilene Cooper, review of *Encyclopedia Brown and the Case of Pablo's Nose*, p. 862; September 1, 1999, Lauren Peterson, review of *Encyclopedia Brown and the Case of the Slippery Salamander*, p. 134.
Christian Century, December 13, 1967, p. 1602.
Christian Science Monitor, October 5, 1967, p. 10; April 6, 1984, p. B7.
Detroit Free Press, February 12, 1991, Martha Woodall, "Youngsters Outsmart Encyclopedia Brown."
Fantasy Review, May, 1987, p. 795.
Horn Book Guide, July, 1990, p. 79.
New York Times Book Review, November 11, 1979, pp. 56, 69; November 5, 1967, p. 44.
Pacific Northwest Library Association Quarterly, winter, 1973, pp. 18-20.
People, March 12, 1990, pp. 17-18.
Publishers Weekly, October 4, 1985, p. 77.
School Library Journal, February, 1982, p. 81; August, 1982, p. 107; April, 1984, p. 119; April, 1985, p. 93; December, 1984, p. 103; December, 1985, p. 95; November, 1986, p. 94; April, 1987, p. 104; January, 1988, p. 83; January, 1991, p. 97; March, 1994, p. 224; January, 1995, p. 110; November, 1996, p. 110.
Science Fiction Chronicle, August, 1987, p. 53.

Young Readers' Review, November, 1967; November, 1968.

*   *   *

SPINNER, Stephanie 1943-

Personal

Born November 16, 1943, in Davenport, IA; daughter of Ralph (in business) and Edna (Lowry) Spinner. *Education:* Bennington College, B.A., 1964. *Hobbies and other interests:* Horses, painting, traveling.

Addresses

Home—Hickory Lane, Pawling, NY 12564.

Career

Children's book editor and writer.

Awards, Honors

Texas Bluebonnet Award, 1991, for *Aliens for Breakfast.*

Writings

Water Skiing and Surfboarding, Golden Press (New York, NY), 1968.

First Aid, Golden Press (New York, NY), 1968.

(Adaptor) *Popeye: The Storybook Based on the Movie,* Random House (New York, NY), 1980.

(Adaptor) *Dracula,* illustrated by Jim Spence, Random House (New York, NY), 1982.

Raggedy Ann and Andy and How Raggedy Ann Was Born, Bobbs-Merrill (Indianapolis, IN), 1982.

(Adaptor) Carlo Lorenzini, *The Adventures of Pinocchio,* illustrated by Diane Goode, Random House (New York, NY), 1983.

The Mummy's Tomb, Bantam (New York, NY), 1985.

(With Jonathan Etra) *Aliens for Breakfast,* illustrated by Steve Bjorkman, Random House (New York, NY), 1988.

(With Jonathan Etra) *Aliens for Lunch,* illustrated by Steve Bjorkman, Random House (New York, NY), 1991.

Little Sure Shot: The Story of Annie Oakley, illustrated by Jose Miralles, Random House (New York, NY), 1993.

Aliens for Dinner, Random House (New York, NY), 1994.

(With Ellen Weiss) *Gerbilitis,* illustrated by Steve Bjorkman, HarperCollins (New York, NY), 1996.

(With Ellen Weiss) *Sing, Elvis, Sing,* illustrated by Steve Bjorkman, HarperCollins (New York, NY), 1996.

(With Ellen Weiss) *Born to Be Wild,* HarperCollins (New York, NY), 1997.

(With Ellen Weiss) *Bright Lights, Little Gerbil,* HarperCollins (New York, NY), 1997.

(With Ellen Weiss) *The Bird Is the Word,* HarperCollins (New York, NY), 1997.

(With Ellen Weiss) *We're Off to See the Lizard,* illustrated by Steve Bjorkman, HarperCollins (New York, NY), 1998.

In Stephanie Spinner's fantasy, cowritten with Terry Bisson, twins Tod and Tessa discover a shop in the mall run by an alien who sells them fascinating gadgets and helps them bring about a change in their mean-spirited classmates. (Cover illustration by Eric Brace.)

Snake Hair: The Story of Medusa, illustrated by Susan Swan, Grosset & Dunlap (New York, NY), 1999.

The Magic of Merlin, illustrated by Valerie Sokolova, Golden Books (New York, NY), 2000.

(With Terry Bisson) *Be First in the Universe,* Delacorte (New York, NY), 2000.

(Adaptor) Margaret Landon, *Anna and the King,* illustrated by Margaret Ayer, HarperTrophy (New York, NY), 2000.

Monster in the Maze: The Story of the Minotaur, illustrated by Susan Swan, Grosset & Dunlap (New York, NY), 2000.

(With Terry Bisson) *Expiration Date: Never,* Delacorte (New York, NY), 2001.

King Arthur's Courage, illustrated by Valerie Sokolova, Golden Books (New York, NY), 2002.

Who Was Annie Oakley?, Penguin Putnam (New York, NY), 2002.

Quiver, Knopf (New York, NY), 2002.

It's a Miracle: A Hanukkah Storybook, illustrated by Jill McElmurry, Atheneum (New York, NY), 2003.

EDITOR

Rock Is Beautiful: An Anthology of American Lyrics, 1953-1968, Dell (New York, NY), 1969.

Feminine Plural: Stories by Women about Growing Up, Macmillan (New York, NY), 1972.

Live and Learn: Stories about Students and Their Teachers, Macmillan (New York, NY), 1973.

Motherlove: Stories by Women about Motherhood, Dell (New York, NY), 1978.

Sidelights

Stephanie Spinner's success with the "Aliens" series in the early 1990s led to a collaborative project with Ellen Weiss about a clever gerbil, Weebie. The "Weebie Zone" books began in 1996 with *Gerbilitis* and followed the travails of Weebie, the third-grade classroom pet who is taken home for the summer by a boy named Garth. Angered when he feels that Garth is neglecting him, Weebie bites him one day on the hand, and the injury gives Garth the ability to communicate with Weebie. Even Garth's cat, who wants to eat Weebie, joins in on their conversations. During that summer,

Tod and Tessa and their alien friend, Gemini Jack, try to use Jack's extraordinary resources to solve some problems, only to create new ones in the process. (Cover illustration by Eric Brace.)

Garth's family goes camping, and Garth is able to talk to a friendly bear he meets in the woods. Stressed because of his parents' squabbles, Garth acquiesces to Weebie's idea: the bear will "attack" the campsite, which works in reconciling the parents.

Garth's ability to talk with animals continues in the next "Weebie Zone" book, *Sing, Elvis, Sing.* This story involves a dog named Elvis, owned by Garth's aunt, and his dreams of achieving stardom for his ability to "sing" the national anthem. "Readers will delight in the light-hearted humor in this entry," noted *Booklist*'s Shelley Townsend-Hudson in a review. The series continued through several titles, including *Born to Be Wild,* in which Spinner and Weiss present Weebie along for another family vacation, this one in Maine, where he and Garth must rescue Ding Dong, a rabbit who has run away from its adoring owner. *School Library Journal*'s Jody McCoy called it "an entertaining, quick read."

Spinner is also the author of *Snake Hair: The Story of Medusa,* published in 1999. The book retells the Greek myth about a woman who was utterly frightening in appearance because of her tresses, which were made of serpents. "Spinner does an excellent job," noted *Booklist*'s Ilene Cooper, in translating the tale and "keeping all its exciting moments." Next, Spinner teamed with author Terry Bisson for *Be First in the Universe,* a comic science-fiction tale about the adventures of twins Tessa and Todd. One day, they visit their local mall on an errand and by walking backwards find a mysterious new store. "Gemini Jack's U Rent All" sells fascinating gadgets, such as the Fib Muncher, which beeps when someone tells a lie. Readers learn that Jack is really an alien and has set up shop on Earth in order to steal a DNA sample from a pair of twins. Tessa and Todd, however, are not ruthless enough for his needs, but when the twins take Jack's electronic pet to school, it is stolen. Their sleuthing leads them to the Gneiss twins, who are suitably unsound enough for Jack's purpose. They deliver the necessary DNA and in turn are injected with something that makes them nicer. A *Kirkus Reviews* contributor termed it "an amusing, satisfying caper."

Spinner and Bisson reunited to write a sequel, *Expiration Date: Never,* which finds Tessa and Todd again working with Jack. Now, his planet Gemini is threatened by Voron invasion. Meanwhile, at the mall they meet Nigel Throbber, a famous rock drummer, and take him to Jack when he says he is desperate for some peace from his fans. Jack sprays "Fame Ban" on Nigel, which indeed makes him anonymous, but Nigel then becomes depressed. A secondary plot involves the mysterious behavior of some goats belonging to Tessa and Todd's hippie grandparents. Critiquing the book for *Booklist,* GraceAnne A. DeCandido stated that "a daft and deft mixture of mall culture, [science-fiction] tropes, and flower-child references bedazzle" in *Expiration Date.* "The characters are zany, yet believable; real, yet surreal," wrote *School Library Journal* critic Kay Bowes.

Biographical and Critical Sources

PERIODICALS

Booklist, February 1, 1994, Ilene Cooper, review of *Little Sure Shot: The Story of Annie Oakley,* p. 1013; January 1, 1997, Shelley Townsend-Hudson, reviews of *Gerbilitis* and *Sing, Elvis, Sing!,* p. 862; December 1, 1999, Ilene Cooper, review of *Snake Hair: The Story of Medusa,* p. 716; August, 2001, GraceAnne A. DeCandido, review of *Expiration Date: Never,* p. 2122.

Kirkus Reviews, January 1, 1997, review of *Born to Be Wild,* p. 68; December 1, 1999, review of *Be First in the Universe,* p. 1891.

New Yorker, December 5, 1983, Faith McNulty, review of *The Adventures of Pinocchio,* p. 204.

Publishers Weekly, November 25, 1988, review of *Aliens for Breakfast,* pp. 66-67; July 29, 1996, review of *Gerbilitis,* p. 89; May 12, 1997, "Spinner Leaves HC Children's in Reorganization," p. 17; January 31, 2000, review of *Be First in the Universe,* p. 107.

School Library Journal, April, 1985, Drew Stevenson, review of *The Mummy's Tomb,* p. 103; March, 1989, Sharron McElmeel, review of *Aliens for Breakfast,* p. 156; December, 1992, Elizabeth C. Fiene, "Step-Up to Classic Chillers," p. 59; February, 1994, Sharron McElmeel, review of *Little Sure Shot,* p. 98; November, 1996, Charlyn Lyons, reviews of *Gerbilitis* and *Sing, Elvis, Sing!,* pp. 110A-110B; February, 1997, Jody McCoy, review of *Born to Be Wild,* pp. 84-85; July, 1997, Elizabeth Trotter, review of *Bright Lights, Little Gerbil,* p. 76; February, 2000, Beth Wright, review of *Be First in the Universe,* p. 104; July, 2001, Kay Bowes, review of *Expiration Date,* p. 89.*

*   *   *

STENEMAN, Shep 1945-

Personal

Born August 8, 1945, in Grangeville, ID; son of George P. (a farmer) and Martha (Veedon) Steneman; married Felicia Moore, June 28, 1965 (divorced, November, 1976). *Education:* University of Idaho, B.S., 1967. *Politics:* "Anti." *Religion:* "The Almighty Dollar."

Addresses

Home—New York, NY. *Agent*—c/o Author Mail, Random House, Inc., 1540 Broadway, New York, NY 10036.

Career

Northern Idaho Growers' Cooperative, Genesee, ID, part-time laborer, 1963-67; *Spud,* Orofino, ID, staff writer, 1967-72, managing editor, 1972-76; freelance writer, 1976—. Waiter. Member of Greer Volunteer Fire Department, Greer, ID, 1967-76.

Writings

The Black Hole Storybook, Random House (New York, NY), 1979.

The Empire Strikes Back Storybook (also see below), Random House (New York, NY), 1980.

Superman's Book of Superhuman Achievements, illustrated by Ross Andru and Joe Orlando, Random House (New York, NY), 1981.

Garfield: The Complete Cat Book, Random House (New York, NY), 1981.

(With others) *Star Wars—The First Ten Years—Storybook Trilogy: The Storybook Based on the Movies* (includes *The Empire Strikes Back Storybook*), Random House (New York, NY), 1987.

Sidelights

Shep Steneman once commented, "I guess the one piece of useful advice I can dig up for another scrivener is 'being a freelance writer is a hard row to hoe.' I give myself that little pearl of wisdom every time I have to serve a hunk of reheated quiche to some salesman from New Jersey in a polyester suit. One other item: don't let your marriage and your magazine go belly up at the same time."

Biographical and Critical Sources

PERIODICALS

Bulletin of the Center for Children's Books, February, 1982, review of *Garfield: The Complete Cat Book,* p. 118.

School Library Journal, April, 1980, Carolyn Caywood, review of *The Black Hole Storybook,* pp. 116-117; September, 1980, Margaret L. Chatham, review of *The Empire Strikes Back Storybook,* p. 63; January, 1982, Margaret L. Chatham, review of *Garfield: The Complete Cat Book,* p. 82.*

*   *   *

STOUT, William 1949-

Personal

Born September 18, 1949, in Salt Lake City, UT; son of William (a farmer) and Joyce (an insurance adjuster; maiden name, Newirth) Stout; married Mary Kent Wilson (an actress), June 21, 1982; children: Andrew William Dragon, James Dylan Wolf. *Education:* Chouinard Art Institute (now California Institute of the Arts), B.A., 1971. *Politics:* "Extreme environmentalist."

Addresses

Home—1468 Loma Vista St., Pasadena, CA 91104. *Office*—812 South La Brea, Los Angeles, CA 90036.

Career

Artist and writer. Art director of *Bomp,* 1976-1977, and Varese-Sarabande Records, beginning 1978. Assisted

Russ Manning on *Tarzan of the Apes* comics, beginning 1971, and Harvey Kurtzman and Will Elder on *Little Annie Fanny* comic strip, beginning 1972. Involved with motion picture production, 1978—, including work on *Buck Rogers, First Blood, The Hitcher, Return of the Living Dead, Masters of the Universe,* and *Men in Black.* Key character designer for Walt Disney animated film *Dinosaurs.* Designer for Walt Disney Imagineering, Lucasfilm/Industrial Light and Magic, "Wonderful World of Oz" theme park, "Michael Jackson Neverland" theme parks, and "Dinotopia" theme park. Senior concept designer, GameWorks, 1995-97. *Exhibitions:* Work featured with others in traveling exhibition "Dinosaurs Past and Present," and one-man shows "The Prehistoric World of William Stout" and "Dinosaurs, Penguins and Whales—The Wildlife of Antarctica."

Member

Comic Art Professional Society (founding member of board of directors, 1977-81; president, 1986-87), American Film Institute, National Geographic Society, Audubon Society, Oceanic Society, Sierra Club, Smithsonian Institution, American Museum of Natural History, California Art Club (member of advisory and executive boards), Greater Los Angeles Zoo Association.

Awards, Honors

Inkpot Award, 1978; Children's Choice Award, 1984, for *The Little Blue Brontosaurus;* Signature Member, California Art Club, 1997.

Writings

(Illustrator, with Don Morgan) Byron Preiss, *The Little Blue Brontosaurus,* Caedman (New York, NY), 1983.
(Illustrator) Ray Bradbury, *Dinosaur Tales,* Bantam (New York, NY), 1983.
Charles R. Knight Sketchbook, illustrated by Charles R. Knight, Terra Nova Press (Pasadena, CA), 2002.
(Illustrator) Richard Matheson, *Aby and the Seven Miracles,* Gauntlet Press (Springfield, PA), 2002.

SELF-ILLUSTRATED

The Dinosaurs: A Fantastic New View of a Lost Era, introduction and scientific commentary by Peter Dodson, Bantam (New York, NY), 1981, revised edition published as *The New Dinosaurs,* ibooks (New York, NY), 2000.
Mickey at Sixty, Terra Nova Press (Pasadena, CA), 1988.
William Stout—Fifty Convention Sketches, Volume One, Terra Nova Press (Pasadena, CA), 1992.
William Stout—Fifty Convention Sketches, Volume Two, Terra Nova Press (Pasadena, CA), 1993.
William Stout—Fifty Convention Sketches, Volume Three, Terra Nova Press (Pasadena, CA), 1994.
William Stout—Fifty Convention Sketches, Volume Four, Terra Nova Press (Pasadena, CA), 1995.
Mickey at Sixty, Volume 2, Terra Nova Press (Pasadena, CA), 1996.
William Stout—The Dinosaurs Sketchbook, Terra Nova Press (Pasadena, CA), 1997.

Monsters Sketchbook, Terra Nova Press (Pasadena, CA), 2000.
William Stout—The Dinosaurs Sketchbook, Volume 3, Terra Nova Press (Pasadena, CA), 2000.
William Stout—Fifty Convention Sketches, Volume Seven, Terra Nova Press (Pasadena, CA), 2000.
William Stout—Fifty Convention Sketches, Volume Eight, Terra Nova Press (Pasadena, CA), 2001.

Contributor to *Heavy Metal* magazine. Contributor of illustrations to *Tainted Treats: A Collection of Horror Tales, Poems, and Drawings,* by R. Payne Cabeen, Streamline Enterprises, 1994; *The Wonderful Wizard of Oz,* by L. Frank Baum, HarperCollins, 2000; and *The Land of Oz,* by L. Frank Baum, ibooks, 2001. Author of screenplays, including *The Warrior and the Sorceress, Conan the Buccaneer, Spawn of the Dead,* and *Natural History Project.* Designer of trading card set "William Stout's Lost Worlds." Illustrator of record album covers and movie posters.

Adaptations

The Little Blue Brontosaurus was adapted into a movie titled *The Land before Time,* Universal, 1988.

Sidelights

"My first professional work came in 1968," William Stout recalled, "when I did the cover for the first issue of the pulp magazine *Coven 13.* I continued making illustrations for a variety of clients and contributed to Petersen Publications' *Cycle-Toons.* In 1971 I began to assist Russ Manning on the 'Tarzan' syndicated comic strips. I worked with Harvey Kurtzman and Will Elder on the 'Little Annie Fanny' strip for *Playboy* in 1972. In Paris the following year, I was offered work by the European magazine *Pilote.* From 1973 to 1974 I produced more than thirty-five 'bootleg' record album covers, which earned me international recognition and a . . . retrospective in the French magazine *Metal Hurlant.* I also worked with the Firesign Theatre to create the graphics for their film *Everything You Know Is Wrong* and the cover for their album *In the Next World, You're on Your Own.*

"From 1976 to 1977 I was the art director for the rock magazine *Bomp.* I also made my first movie poster, for *Wizards.* Dozens more followed, including posters for *Monty Python's Life of Brian, More American Graffiti, Allegro non Troppo,* and *Rock 'n' Roll High School.* The same year my first one-man show, *The Prehistoric World of William Stout,* attracted paleontologists and fantasy lovers alike.

"I worked as a production artist for *Buck Rogers* in 1978. This led to more film work, including a large series of paintings and designs for the 'Amber' epic based on the popular science-fantasy series written by Roger Zelazny. This finally culminated with my work with Ron Cobb as the production artist on John Milius's *Conan.* It was also at this time that my work came to the attention of Steven Spielberg. I storyboarded the stunt sequences for *First Blood* and was the coauthor of the film *Kain of Dark Planet.*

"Since then I have designed the monsters on *Monster in the Closet,* then worked for five months in Mexico as the concept artist for *Conan the Destroyer.* While in Mexico, I dubbed the voice of the robot in *Dune.* A series of paintings and drawings for *The Clan of the Cave Bear* and *Red Sonja* followed. Then I worked as the production designer for Steve Miner's *Godzilla, King of the Monsters* and Dan O'Bannon's *Return of the Living Dead.*

"My screenwriting began as a painful, but quick, path to my goal of becoming a film director. The writing eventually became fun and fulfilling in itself. Whether I am working as an artist or writer, I strive for specific standards. I will not relinquish a piece until the problems I have set for myself are completely solved. They may not be solved in the way I imagined at the beginning of the project, but they will be solved in a way that is not ordinary, that is stimulating, positive, and/or funny. I never do less than my best on any given project. I also feel it is crucial to give back to the community that gives to me. Hence, I do community service work and head community groups in an effort to make life better for other people.

"I speak passable Spanish and crummy French, Serbo-Croatian, and Italian due to my film travels. I have traveled extensively through Canada, Czechoslovakia, Belgium, Germany, the Galapagos, Ecuador, Peru, Tanzania, Kenya, Ethiopia, and Colombia. I have lived for extended periods of time in Mexico, Spain, Italy, Yugoslavia, and France."

In 1978, Stout became the art director for Varese-Sarabande Records. He has continued to produce record covers for other companies and recording artists such as Rhino Records and the Beach Boys. His work appears in the form of prints, television commercials, t-shirt designs, comic books, murals, and even toy box covers, and has been published in Australia, England, France, Germany, Italy, Spain, and Japan.

Biographical and Critical Sources

PERIODICALS

Comics Feature, September, 1984.
Life, November, 1981.
Metal Hurlant, January, 1981.
Publishers Weekly, April 15, 2002, review of *Abu and the Seven Marvels,* p. 46.
Starlog, May, 1987.
Starlog (Japan), April, 1982.

OTHER

William Stout Web Site, http://www.williamstout.com (June 2, 2002).*

T

THOMPSON, Lauren (Stevens) 1962-

Personal

Born November 7, 1962, in Eugene, OR; daughter of David A. (a professor of psychology) and Ruth M. (a psychiatric nurse; maiden name, Flynn) Stevens; married Robert E. Thompson (a college English teacher), May 21, 1994; children: Owen R. *Education:* Mount Holyoke College, B.A. (math), 1984; Clark University, M.A. (English), 1991. *Religion:* Unitarian Universalist. *Hobbies and other interests:* Nature, religion.

Addresses

Home—Brooklyn, NY. *Agent*—c/o Author Mail, Simon and Schuster, 1230 Avenue of the Americas, New York, NY 10020.

Career

Author and editor, 1988—. Senior editor at a New York children's book publishing company.

Member

Society of Children's Book Writers and Illustrators.

Awards, Honors

Children's Choice selection, International Reading Association, for *One Riddle, One Answer.*

Writings

Mouse's First Christmas, illustrated by Buket Erdogan, Simon & Schuster (New York, NY), 1999.
(Reteller) *Love One Another: The Last Days of Jesus,* illustrated by Elizabeth Uyehara, Scholastic Press (New York, NY), 2000.
Mouse's First Halloween, illustrated by Buket Erdogan, Simon & Schuster (New York, NY), 2000.

Lauren Thompson

One Riddle, One Answer, illustrated by Linda S. Wingerter, Scholastic Press (New York, NY), 2001.
Mouse's First Valentine, illustrated by Buket Erdogan, Simon & Schuster (New York, NY), 2002.

Work in Progress

Little Quack, illustrated by Derek Anderson, and *Mouse's First Day of School,* illustrated by Buket Erdogan, both for Simon & Schuster (New York, NY); *A*

Offering an interesting segue into math concepts, Thompson's picture book is the tale of a Persian princess who creates a mathematical riddle to be solved by the man destined to be her husband. (From One Riddle, One Answer, *illustrated by Linda S. Wingerter.)*

Christmas Gift for Mama, illustrated by Jim Burke, for Scholastic Press (New York, NY).

Sidelights

"When I was in grade school my family spent two years in the Netherlands, where I attended school, made friends, and became fluent in Dutch," Lauren Thompson told *SATA.* "Unfortunately, I can now barely count in Dutch, but I suspect that the experience of living in two different cultures when I was so young still influences the way I see the world. In the same way, loving two very different subjects, literature and math, continues to shape my work.

"I was interested in almost every subject when I was young, but especially reading and writing my own stories—and math. I focused on the latter up through college. Yet when it came time to imagine life in the real world, I changed my course away from numbers toward my other love, words. But it seems inevitable that eventually I would write about math.

"In *One Riddle, One Answer,* I set out quite intentionally to create a story that played with words while playing with math—a riddle story about numbers. I struggled

with the riddle until I saw I needed to begin with the solution. I tried five, two, zero . . . but once I hit on one, I knew that one was the one! I knew then that finding the right 'one' to love would be the theme of the story, too.

"The place of the story was intentional as well. I chose Persia, where many important math concepts were first developed, including our 'Arabic' numeral system. But the source for the main character, Aziza, who loves words and numbers, is purely personal—myself.

"My fourteen years' experience as a children's book editor has taught me a lot about structure and pacing in stories, about the importance of concision, and in picture books, leaving something of the tale for the illustrations. But I draw on my childhood rather than adult experiences when I am plumbing for book ideas. In my books for very young children, such as *Mouse's First Christmas* or *Mouse's First Halloween,* I try to put in words for them that sense of wonder and excitement they bring to everything, for everything is still new to them. I try to celebrate that sense of wonder and foster it. In my picture books for older children, such as *Love One Another: The Last Days of Jesus* and others still upcoming, my aim is to honor the deep feelings that the bonds of love invoke. In every case, on some level, I am really writing for the child I was."

Thompson has garnered praise for her "Mouse" books, which take off from very simple ideas and, with the help of illustrator Buket Erdogan, become something truly memorable, according to reviewers. In her first book, *Mouse's First Christmas,* Thompson plays with the rhythms and borrows some of the language of the famous poem "'Twas the Night before Christmas," but turns Mouse's first experiences of the sights, sounds, textures, and tastes of the holiday into a celebration of the senses. The overall experience of sharing Mouse's first Christmas with Thompson's character is cozy, familiar, and gently humorous, reviewers noted. A contributor to *Publishers Weekly* noted how well the author's text, illustrator's paintings, and designer's design interact, claiming that together they "make much from a simple premise." A contributor to the *Children's Book Review Service* called *Mouse's First Christmas* "a perfect read-aloud for classrooms and libraries."

Mouse's First Christmas was followed by *Mouse's First Halloween,* a gentle, rhyming rendition of Mouse's first experience with the daunting aspects of this holiday. As Mouse steps outside to join the after-dark Halloween festivities, he is overcome by fear. With effective use of page turns and repetition, *Mouse's First Halloween* becomes a reassuring litany of things that may seem frightening but turn out not to be. *Booklist* reviewer Carolyn Phelan remarked: "This is a fine Halloween read-aloud for young children who like the idea of a scary book, but need plenty of reassurance along the way." Again, text and illustrations were found to work well together. "This author and illustrator make a superb team," enthused Karen Land in *School Library Journal,* who recommended *Mouse's First Halloween* for children who enjoyed the earlier Mouse book.

Mouse sets out to explore another popular American holiday in *Mouse's First Valentine*. Here, Mouse spies on big sister Minka as she secretively gathers such mysterious items as red paper, ribbon, lace, and paste from around the house, and then assembles them into a valentine for Mouse. Reviewers had come to expect a heartwarming story and richly colored illustrations from the pair, and the publication of *Mouse's First Valentine* was greeted by a contributor to *Kirkus Reviews* with the statement: "Thompson and Erdogan pair up yet again for a delightful dose of holiday cheer." Readers and reviewers may anticipate further adventures with Mouse, including *Mouse's First Day of School*.

Thompson is also the author of *One Riddle, One Answer*, a book for early readers in which a Persian girl is granted permission to choose her own husband from among those who correctly answer a riddle of her own devising. The riddle is a mathematical one, and reviewers noted that, along with the Persian motif, which is echoed in Linda S. Wingerter's fanciful illustrations, this folktale-like story provides an interesting segue into math units. "Thompson chooses her riddle wisely, since it presents a challenge for her audience, yet perspicacious readers can solve it by themselves," remarked a contributor to *Publishers Weekly*. *Booklist* reviewer Carolyn Phelan similarly praised Thompson's effort, concluding, "This story joins a growing number of enjoyable picture-book tales with mathematical themes."

Biographical and Critical Sources

PERIODICALS

Booklist, September 1, 1999, Carolyn Phelan, review of *Mouse's First Christmas,* p. 151; February 1, 2000, Shelley Townsend-Hudson, review of *Love One Another,* p. 1027; September 1, 2000, Carolyn Phelan, review of *Mouse's First Halloween,* p. 135; February 1, 2001, Carolyn Phelan, review of *One Riddle, One Answer,* p. 1058.

Children's Book Review Service, November, 1999, review of *Mouse's First Christmas,* p. 28.

Instructor, November-December, 2001, Judy Freeman, review of *One Riddle, One Answer,* p. 16.

Kirkus Reviews, December 15, 2001, review of *Mouse's First Valentine,* p. 1763.

Publishers Weekly, September 27, 1999, review of *Mouse's First Christmas,* p. 55; February 21, 2000, Elizabeth Devereaux, review of *Love One Another,* p. 55; February 19, 2001, review of *One Riddle, One Answer,* p. 91.

School Library Journal, October, 1999, Maureen Wade, review of *Mouse's First Christmas,* p. 71; March, 2000, Patricia Pearl Dole, review of *Love One Another,* p. 232; August, 2000, Karen Land, review of *Mouse's First Halloween,* p. 166; April, 2001, Barbara Scotto, review of *One Riddle, One Answer,* p. 123.

THON, Melanie Rae 1957-

Personal

Born August 23, 1957, in Kalispell, MT; daughter of Raymond Albert (an architect) and Lois Ann (a homemaker; maiden name, Lockwood) Thon. *Education:* University of Michigan, B.A., 1980; Boston University, M.A., 1982. *Religion:* "Believer."

Addresses

Office—Department of English, 255 South Central Campus Dr., Rm. 3500, University of Utah, Salt Lake City, UT 84112. *Agent*—Irene Skolnick, 22 West 23rd St., Ste. 5, New York, NY 10010.

Career

Emerson College, Boston, MA, instructor, 1987-93; Syracuse University, Syracuse, NY, assistant professor of English, 1993-96; Ohio State University, Columbus, OH, associate professor of English, 1996-99; University of Utah, Salt Lake City, UT, professor of English and creative writing, 1999—. Also taught at Harvard University, University of Massachusetts, and Boston University. Consulting editor, *Mid-American Review.*

Melanie Rae Thon

Awards, Honors

Massachusetts Artists Foundation fellow, 1988; National Endowment for the Arts fellow, 1992; New York Foundation for the Arts fellow, 1996; named one of "Best Young American Novelists," *Granta,* 1996; Whiting Writers award, 1997; Ohio Arts Council fellow, 2000.

Writings

Meteors in August: A Novel, Random House (New York, NY), 1990.

Girls in the Grass: Stories, Random House (New York, NY), 1991.

Iona Moon (novel), Poseidon (New York, NY), 1993.

First, Body: Stories, Houghton (Boston, MA), 1997.

Sweet Hearts (novel), Houghton (Boston, MA), 2000

Thon's stories have been selected for inclusion in *Best American Short Stories.*

Work in Progress

A collection of short stories; researching Native American history, Christian and biblical history, and gender transformation.

Sidelights

Melanie Rae Thon was named one of the Best Young American Novelists by the English literary magazine *Granta* in the mid-1990s for her wrenching tales of the socially and emotionally dispossessed. "Thon is clearly a writer to watch," declared a reviewer in *Publishers Weekly.* After three novels and two collections of short stories, Thon is earning strong critical accolades for her fiction; critics liked the pitch-perfect narrative voices she was able to create as well as the daring structural style. Thon, noted Leslie Haynsworth in another *Publishers Weekly* article, "often abandons traditional narrative trajectories to plunge readers into the landscapes of her characters' minds."

Thon was born and raised in Montana. "I wasn't much of a reader when I was young," she admitted in an interview with Haynsworth. "But I was physically active. My life was very experientially based." Thon then spent several years away from the American West and its landscapes that would come to serve as the setting for much of her fiction: she attended the University of Michigan, where she first decided to write, and then earned a graduate degree in creative writing from Boston University in 1982. For several years, she worked at various jobs, including waiting tables, while teaching English courses at Emerson College.

Thon's debut novel was published in 1990. *Meteors in August: A Novel* centers around a young woman named Lizzie, who lives in a small town in northern Montana. Her older sister ran away because she was pregnant, and Lizzie fears that a catastrophe will befall her if she is not careful. She lets herself be led by a pair of religious

fanatics but in the end must learn for herself that sin is something to be forgiven, not avoided. Sybil Steinberg, writing in *Publishers Weekly,* stated that Thon's "steely-eyed, sharpshooting prose brings both urgency and spontaneity" to Lizzie and the other characters who populate *Meteors in August.*

Girls in the Grass: Stories was the title of Thon's first collection of short stories and appeared in 1991. The title story tracks the first stirrings of adolescence in a young woman, but a second, "Punishment," is far bleaker. That tale is set in 1858 and recounts the story of a slave hanged after being accused of murdering her master's infant son. Throughout the rest of the collection, Thon writes of other cultures and places, and ably captures America's diversity across history. Donna Seaman, writing in *Booklist,* noted that "while the exteriors vary, the internal ache is the same," and singled out one of the stories, "Chances of Survival," as "perfect, lyrical, funny, and sad."

Thon's second novel, *Iona Moon,* is set in the 1960s in a rural Western setting. The title teenager lives near the small town of White Falls, Idaho; her family farm is located in the potato fields of Kila Flats. The novel opens with the suicide of a local Vietnam veteran, which leads the man's brother to drive the family car into the river. Disowned, Matt makes his home in a shed, where Iona visits him. Already promiscuous after having been abused by her own brothers for several years, Iona is tough and wary of the fact that little else save for tragedy will befall her if she stays in the area. She drops out of school after her mother is diagnosed with cancer in order to care for her and sees that friends her own age all bear similar burdens—whether from pregnancy, abuse, or injury.

When Iona's mother dies, she flees the farm and White Falls for Seattle, where she works in a convenience store. There she makes friends with a Native American man, Eddie Birdheart, and eventually returns home to discover more about herself and her past. A *Publishers Weekly* contributor praised *Iona Moon,* comparing it to the work of Larry McMurtry and Dorothy Allison, but noting that "the prose strikes a tone of pained detachment that is singularly Thon's." *People Weekly* writer Louisa Ermelino commended the work and Thon's writing as "a rare glimpse of a young girl's triumphant coming of age in a landscape that offers no sympathy."

By this point in her career, Thon was teaching at Syracuse University. In 1996, she began an associate professorship at Ohio State University, was named one of *Granta*'s "Best Young American Novelists," and published her second collection of short stories, *First, Body: Stories.* Many of the works had appeared elsewhere, and *Ploughshares* critic Christopher Tilghman asserted in his review, "the effect of reading all of them together after seeing many of them when originally published is simply to encounter genius." The degradation of the physical self, by various means, is a strong theme across the stories; characters destroy what seems to be their only possession with drugs or alcohol. A white woman and her drug habit leads to a prison term for a Native American man in "Little White Sister," while "Father, Lover, Deadman, Dreamer" recounts one teen's accidental killing of an inebriated Native American. "Nobody's Daughters" centers on a homeless teenage girl, Nadine, who believes that her dead sister talks to her and cajoles her to commit the crimes she does. The title story revolves around an alcoholic Vietnam veteran who tries to lift the corpse of 326-pound woman in a morgue for his job, but she falls on him and leaves him trapped. "Thon has a dark, fierce imagination expressed in a torrential sweep of words," stated a *Publishers Weekly* reviewer, who also noted that while the collection as a whole was bleak, "the stories nonetheless leave an indelible impression of heartbreaking truth." "What is finally most distinctive about this work is the author's willingness to become each one of her characters," wrote Tilghman in *Ploughshares.* "Character, narrator, and author are the same person here."

Reviewers of Thon's works often commented upon the non-linear narrative structures of her novels and stories, but like Tilghman, praised the creation of memorable characters. As the writer told Haynsworth in the *Publishers Weekly* interview, "I'm not trying to represent characters' external voices so much as I'm trying to understand the most intimate associations these people have, through memory, desire and sensation."

In her third novel, *Sweet Hearts,* Thon creates her first male protagonist for a lengthier work. He is sixteen-year-old Flint Zimmer, but his story is recounted in all its tragic detail by his aunt, Marie, who is deaf. Marie knows that the dangerous northwestern Montana landscape in which she and Flint have grown up is a collision of cultures, a place with a history of violence and bloodshed dating back several generations, when the Crow nation fought U.S. soldiers. "We are the place where enemies meet," Marie asserts. "We are the place where everything happens."

Sweet Hearts opens when Flint has left a Montana juvenile detention facility after five years in custody. He hitchhikes to his old house and lives underneath the porch for several days. Eventually he goes inside, but his alcoholic mother Frances lets him stay just one night; during that time he convinces his ten-year-old half-sister, Cecile, into running away with him. They begin a crime spree by assaulting a local pediatrician. Marie recounts these events as if speaking to Frances and interweaves the family's tragic history into the story. Flint is part Crow, and Frances's neglect of him was an inherited one. As Marie discusses the Crow genocide, she observes that tragedies endure up to several generations into the future. "Episodic, intensely imagined and darkly portentous, the novel's suspense accrues to the ultraliterary drumbeat of metaphor," asserted a *Publishers Weekly* reviewer. "Thon has created a shattering yet deeply spiritual novel that fuses personal loss with cultural devastation in searing remembrances" of such low points in American history, wrote Seaman in *Booklist.* Thon discussed Flint and his life in the interview with Haynsworth for *Publishers Weekly.* "If we exile people, put them away from us and refuse to acknowledge our part in what happened to them, we can feel safe.... We don't heal ourselves as a society by ostracizing people or locking them in distant institutions."

Since 1999 Thon has been a professor of English and creative writing at the University of Utah, and says that she enjoys teaching, feeling that, as she told Haynsworth, it taps into what she called a "shared desire to understand experience and render it truthfully and compassionately, and to figure out what we as people really believe."

Thon told *SATA:* "I love doing research. I've climbed the Black Hills and the Absaroka Mountains, wandered alone through the Badlands in December. I toured Montana State Prison, where I encountered boys as vulnerable and violent as the children in my stories, and where I saw inmates—kidnappers, killers, rapists—planting columbines and poppies. I've witnessed an autopsy, been charged by a buffalo bull, chased by mountain goats, and besieged by swallows.

"Research is food for the imagination! But for every hour spent catching lizards whose tails regenerate or seeking buffalo that once traveled in herds twenty-five miles wide and fifty miles long, for every night spent walking the streets of Boston's Combat Zone, I may spend ten hours—or a hundred—in secluded contemplation. I need to learn and then forget, to recover memories and images in the voices of particular people, to describe the killing of a weasel as the potato farmer who wields the shovel sees it, to live through the blizzard as if I have been thrown away by my mother, as if I were a child again, already a criminal, forever homeless.

"During the fall of 1998, I lived alone in a cabin at the edge of a lake in Montana. One morning, hours before daybreak, I heard someone knocking hard on my window. I looked out but met only my own reflection. The visitor tried the doors, front and back, rattling the handles, then banged again at another window. I was living without a phone, half a mile from my closest neighbors. There was no one to hear me scream at this hour. Except perhaps the one outside, the one circling and hammering.

"When I turned off the lights, I saw the long nose and furred back of an auburn bear. The huckleberry crop had been unusually sparse that year. Now, facing winter without enough fat to keep them alive through the months of hibernation, the bears in Montana had become desperate.

"I had plenty of food in my cabin, a refrigerator stocked with soup and fish and vegetables. We could have shared. We might have eaten together. But I am no saint. I am not one of those monks in the desert who befriends beasts and tames their wild spirits. I had enough food but not enough faith to feed us. And I saw that the bear had come to teach me about the boy in my story, about his hunger and my fear, about my willingness to let children like him starve in body and spirit, about my need to make him an exile so that I might live with the illusion of safety. I saw the limits of my compassion and the failure of my courage."

Biographical and Critical Sources

PERIODICALS

Belles Lettres, spring, 1994, Gale Harris, review of *Iona Moon,* pp. 40-41.

Booklist, June 1, 1991, Donna Seaman, review of *Girls in the Grass: Stories,* p. 1860; May 15, 1993, Donna Seaman, review of *Iona Moon,* p. 1676; December 1, 1996, Donna Seaman, review of *First, Body: Stories,* p. 642; December 15, 2000, Donna Seaman, review of *Sweet Hearts,* p. 786.

Kirkus Reviews, April 1, 1993, review of *Iona Moon,* p. 407.

Library Journal, August, 1990, Jessica Grim, review of *Meteors in August: A Novel,* p. 146; April 15, 1991, Marcia Tager, review of *Girls in the Grass,* p. 128; May 15, 1993, Joanna M. Burkhardt, review of *Iona Moon,* p. 98; December, 1996, Reba Leiding, review of *First, Body,* p. 150.

New York Times Book Review, October 4, 1998, Scott Veale, review of *Girls in the Grass,* p. 36.

People Weekly, July 12, 1993, Louisa Ermelino, review of *Iona Moon,* p. 29.

Ploughshares, winter, 1990, Don Lee, review of *Meteors in August,* pp. 284-285; spring, 1997, Christopher Tilghman, review of *First, Body,* pp. 208-209.

Publishers Weekly, July 6, 1990, Sybil Steinberg, review of *Meteors in August,* p. 59; April 26, 1993, review of *Iona Moon,* p. 58; November 4, 1996, review of *First, Body,* p. 62; November 27, 2000, review of *Sweet Hearts,* p. 52; January 29, 2001, Leslie Haynsworth, "Fighting for Solace," p. 60.

School Library Journal, May, 2001, Francisca Goldsmith, review of *Sweet Hearts,* p. 176.

Times Literary Supplement, July 23, 1993, Claire Messud, review of *Iona Moon,* p. 19; September 28, 2001, Lucy Beresford, review of *Sweet Hearts,* p. 25.

*　　　*　　　*

TOWNSEND, John Rowe 1922-

Personal

Born May 10, 1922, in Leeds, England; son of George Edmund Rowe and Gladys (Page) Townsend; married Vera Lancaster, July 3, 1948 (died May 9, 1973); children: Alethea Mary, Nicholas John, Penelope Anne. *Education:* Emmanuel College, Cambridge, England, B.A., 1949, M.A., 1954.

Addresses

Home—4 Banhams Close, Cambridge CB4 1HX, England.

Career

Writer and lecturer, 1969—. *Yorkshire Post,* 1946 and *Evening Standard,* 1949, journalist; *Guardian,* Manchester, England, sub-editor, 1949-54, art editor, 1954-55, editor of weekly international edition, 1955-69, part-time children's books editor, 1968-79, columnist, 1968-81. Simmons College Center for the Study of Children's Literature, visiting lecturer, 1978-86; Children's Literature New England, visiting lecturer, 1987—, adjunct board member, 1990—; Society of Authors (UK), chairman of children's writers and illustrators group, 1977-78, 1990-91, member of management committee, 1982-85. Member of Harvard International Seminar, 1956; visiting lecturer, University of Pennsylvania, 1965, and University of Washington, 1969 and 1971; May Hill Arbuthnot Honor Lecturer, Atlanta, GA, 1971; Anne Carroll Moore Lecturer, New York Public Library, 1971; Whittall Lecturer, Library of Congress (Washington, D. C.), 1976. *Military service:* Royal Air Force, 1942-46; became flight sergeant.

Member

Society of Authors.

Awards, Honors

Carnegie Medal honors list, 1963, for *Hell's Edge;* Carnegie Medal honors list, 1969, Silver Pen award, English Centre of International PEN, 1970, *Boston Globe-Horn Book* Award, 1970, and Edgar Allan Poe Award from Mystery Writers of America, all for *The Intruder;* Christopher Award, 1981, for *The Islanders;* American Library Association notable books list, *Trouble in the Jungle, Good-bye to the Jungle, Pirate's Island, The Intruder, The Summer People, Noah's Castle,* and *Good-night, Prof, Dear; Horn Book* Honor List, *Trouble in the Jungle, The Intruder, The Islanders,* and *A Sense of Story.*

Writings

FOR CHILDREN

Gumble's Yard, illustrated by Dick Hart, Hutchinson (London, England), 1961, published as *Trouble in the Jungle,* illustrated by W. T. Mars, Lippincott (Philadelphia, PA), 1969.

Widdershins Crescent, Hutchinson (London, England), 1965, published as *Good-bye to the Jungle,* Lippincott (Philadelphia, PA), 1967.

Pirate's Island, illustrated by Douglas Hall, Lippincott (Philadelphia, PA), 1968.

Top of the World, illustrated by Nikki Jones, Oxford University Press (Oxford, England), 1976, pictures by John Wallner, Lippincott (Philadelphia, PA), 1977.

Dan Alone, Lippincott (Philadelphia, PA), 1983.

Tom Tiddler's Ground, Lippincott (Philadelphia, PA), 1986, published as *The Hidden Treasure,* Scholastic, Inc. (New York, NY), 1988.

The Persuading Stick, Lothrop (New York, NY), 1986.

Rob's Place, Viking/Kestrel (London, England), 1987, Lothrop (New York, NY), 1988.

FOR YOUNG ADULTS

Hell's Edge, Hutchinson (London, England), 1963, Lothrop (New York, NY), 1969.

The Hallersage Sound, Hutchinson (London, England), 1966.

The Intruder, illustrated by Graham Humphreys, Oxford University Press (Oxford, England), 1969, illustrated by Joseph A. Phelan, Lippincott (Philadelphia, PA), 1970.

Good-night, Prof, Love, illustrated by Peter Farmer, Oxford University Press (Oxford, England)), 1970, published as *Good-night, Prof, Dear,* Lippincott (Philadelphia, PA), 1971, published as *The Runaways,* edited by David Fickling, Oxford University Press (New York, NY), 1979.

The Summer People, illustrated by Robert Micklewright, Lippincott (Philadelphia, PA), 1972.

Forest of the Night, illustrated by Peter Farmer, Oxford University Press (Oxford, England), 1974, illustrated by Beverly Brodsky McDermott, Lippincott (Philadelphia, PA), 1975.

Noah's Castle, Oxford University Press (Oxford, England), 1975, Lippincott (Philadelphia, PA), 1976.

The Xanadu Manuscript, illustrated by Paul Ritchie, Oxford University Press (Oxford, England), 1977, published as *The Visitors,* Lippincott (Philadelphia, PA), 1977.

King Creature, Come, Oxford University Press (Oxford, England), 1980, published as *The Creatures,* Lippincott (Philadelphia, PA), 1980.

The Islanders, Lippincott (Philadelphia, PA), 1981.

A Foreign Affair, Kestrel Books (London, England), 1982, published as *Kate and the Revolution,* Lippincott (Philadelphia, PA), 1982.

Cloudy-bright, Lippincott (Philadelphia, PA), 1984.

Downstream, Lippincott (Philadelphia, PA), 1987.

The Golden Journey, Viking/Kestrel (London, England), 1989, published as *The Fortunate Isles,* Lippincott (Philadelphia, PA), 1989.

The Invaders, Oxford University Press (New York, NY), 1992.

OTHER

Written for Children: An Outline of English Children's Literature, J. Garnet Miller, 1965, Lothrop (New York, NY), 1967, 6th edition, Bodley Head (London, England), 1995, 6th American edition, Scarecrow Press (Lanham, MD), 1996.

A Sense of Story: Essays on Contemporary Writers for Children, Longman/Lippincott (Philadelphia, PA and New York, NY), 1971.

(Editor) *Modern Poetry: A Selection for Young People,* Oxford University Press (Oxford, England), 1971, with photographs by Barbara Pfeffer, Lippincott (Philadelphia, PA), 1974.

(Editor) *Twenty-five Years of British Children's Books,* National Book League, 1977.

A Sounding of Storytellers, Lippincott (Philadelphia, PA and New York, NY), 1979.

(Contributor) Virginia Haviland, editor, *The Openhearted Audience: Ten Authors Talk about Writing for Children,* Library of Congress (Washington, D.C.), 1980.

Cranford Revisited (adult fiction), Green Bay Publications (Cambridge, England), 1990.

John Newbery and His Books: Trade and Plumb-Cake for Ever, Huzza!, Scarecrow Press (Metuchen, NJ), 1994.

Contributor to several other books, as well as contributor of articles and reviews to *Guardian, Times Literary Supplement,* and numerous other publications.

Adaptations

Gumble's Yard was adapted for television; ITV television series were produced for *The Intruder,* 1972, and *Noah's Castle,* 1980.

Sidelights

John Rowe Townsend is an author of children's and young adult fiction whose works have received high praise in his native England, the United States, and many other countries. Originally a journalist for the Manchester *Guardian,* Townsend did not begin his career as a children's book writer until he was in his late thirties. Townsend, however, has always had a passion for writing, and he found that—once he started—he enjoyed writing for young people, an audience he considers just as important and demanding as adult readers. As he stated in one *Horn Book Magazine* article, Townsend believes children's authors "should approach children with humble affection—conscious of our errors and not deluding ourselves that we know all the answers." The author makes no pretense of trying to teach or influence his readers in any way, for, he attested, "I know of no evidence ... that children's recreational reading is a decisive factor in their attitudes.... I suspect that the best to be hoped for is that you might, incidentally, make them think and feel." Townsend once told *SATA:* "I'd rather write for children than anyone else. They're a responsive audience: eager, unsated, ready to live the story. They won't put up with longwindedness or pomposity, they won't go on reading if they're not enjoying the book, but that's a healthy discipline."

One of the concerns that prompted his first novel, *Gumble's Yard,* was Townsend's belief that there was a need for books that depicted children facing such realities of life as economic and family hardships. In conjunction with research he was currently undertaking for the British Society for the Prevention of Cruelty to Children, Townsend found himself spending a good deal of his time in the industrialized areas of Manchester, a major British commercial center. It was against that urban backdrop, supplemented with memories of his own upbringing in the nearby city of Leeds, that his imagination went to work creating the characters and plot of *Gumble's Yard.* Townsend fictionalized a story he read in the newspaper, writing of a father and his girlfriend, Walter and Doris, who leave Walter's niece, nephew, and two children to their own wits for their survival. Critics responded to the publication of the book with praise and respect, citing the vividness of the story line and the strong cast of characters. A *Times Literary Supplement* contributor wrote that "the end of the book is perfect: undramatic, perhaps saddening, but perfectly and poetically right." Townsend used the inner-city landscape of *Gumble's Yard* in other books as well, including *Pirate's Island* and *Dan Alone.*

In addition to what he saw as a dearth of books for and about children from lower-class families, Townsend also perceived a need for more books for teenage readers. In *Written for Children: An Outline of English-Language Children's Literature,* which he published in 1965, Townsend stated what he then saw as the status quo: "Young people who read at all ... will be reading adult books before they are far into their teens. So they will and so they should. But I do not think we can safely assume that adult books will meet all their needs, any more than adult recreations meet all their needs. There are matters ... that are of the utmost interest to adolescents but that are not often dealt with in adult fiction, or at least not often looked at from a 'young' point of view." In his young adult novels, Townsend deals with things of specific interest to adolescent readers: first loves, relationships between parents and children, leaving school to start work. In many of his books for teenagers he takes the approach characteristic of his work for younger readers, focusing on young protagonists who find themselves victims of financial deprivation and social class discrimination.

With these thoughts about needing books for teenage readers, as well as the feeling that the kind of young adult book that was being written in the United States was being sorely missed in England and that the characterization of girls in children's fiction was shallow and therefore inaccurate, Townsend wrote *Hell's Edge.* Set in Yorkshire, not far from Townsend's own Leeds, the book examines the tenuous relationship that develops between Norman, who has grown up in town, and his cousin Amaryllis, who has relocated from southern England. In the *New York Times Book Review,* Jane Manthorne called *Hell's Edge* "a thoroughly rousing adventure story."

After *Hell's Edge* was published, Townsend's job at the Guardian began to take a backseat to his writing, and his ambition to be a writer was being fulfilled. His third book, *Widdershins Crescent* (published in the United States as *Good-bye to the Jungle*), was a sequel to his first, *Gumble's Yard.* Taking Walter and Doris's "family" and placing them in a new housing site, Townsend's book examines their plight in realistic terms. Critics praised the well-drawn, rounded characters who behave believably in situations that genuinely echo contemporary life and also acknowledged Townsend's refusal to condescend to his readers. A Times Literary Supplement reviewer found Townsend's style "always a pleasure to read" and complimented him on his "beautiful sense of timing."

The Intruder, published in the same year Townsend left his job at the *Guardian,* received both critical acclaim and several honors, including the Silver Pen award and the Edgar Allan Poe Award. "*The Intruder* remains Townsend's most considerable achievement to date,"

wrote Ron Barnes in *Children's Literature in Education.* "It has a fascinating setting, tells an absorbing and exciting story that rises to a tremendous climax, and deals with an interestingly varied group of characters." The imaginary setting of the book is quite a different one than that evoked in Townsend's earlier works: choked streets and urban grime are replaced by sand, wind, and the tides of the Irish Sea. The protagonist, Arnold Haithwaite, is a sixteen year old who works on the estuary sands as a guide and lives in an old house with Ernest Haithwaite, the man Arnold has assumed is his father but who seems more probably his grandfather. Arnold's contentment with his life is disrupted by the arrival of a stranger, Sonny, a grim character whose beret and glass eye are enough to intimidate Arnold but who further frightens him by asserting that he is Arnold Haithwaite. Barnes lauded Townsend's depiction of Sonny, noting, "This character is one of the most original creations to be found in children's fiction." Sonny's presence threatens Arnold's own sense of self, and he sets out to try to determine who he could be if this mysterious stranger's claim is correct. As Arnold looks for clues to the real truth of his past, Sonny turns murderous, and chases Arnold across the sands on the night of a tempest. Sonny dies in the ensuing storm, and Arnold's guilt at having caused another's death overcomes him. Finally, however, he accepts that his identity is determined not by what his name happens to be or who his father is, but instead by who he makes himself to be through his actions.

"Over the whole novel," Barnes wrote, "there hangs a sense of the transience of mortal things in comparison with the permanence of the natural world." Neil Millar described *The Intruder* in the Christian Science Monitor as "unsentimental, unsweetened, [and] uncompromisingly honest." In *The Nesbit Tradition: The Children's Novel in England, 1945-1970,* Marcus Crouch called the novel "one of the outstanding books of its decade." Reviewing the book in 2000, thirty years after its original publication, Martha V. Parravano wrote in a *Horn Book Magazine,* "John Rowe Townsend broke barriers in the 1960s with books about working-class kids that ... began the tradition of social realism in British children's literature." Parravano continued that *The Intruder* "reads less like a respected but musty forefather of today's risk-taking YA fiction and more like a fresh and daring contemporary," and further pointed to a "lack of solid ground on which to plant one's feet" that made *The Intruder* "as unsettling and disturbing today as it was thirty years ago."

For his 1982 book *A Foreign Affair* (published in the United States as *Kate and the Revolution*), Townsend built on a game he and his friends had played while at Leeds Grammar School; they had secretly created a complex game in which each of the players was the ruler of a Ruritanian state. They conducted the affairs of state with notes passed between them when the teacher was distracted. Later, the game gave Townsend the idea for a book, and *A Foreign Affair* was the result. Written to provide fun and enjoyment, the book pairs Kate, a sixteen-year-old Londoner, with Rudi, a prince from a tiny kingdom in the middle of Europe, Essenheim. Kate is suspicious of Rudi's advances at a party, his handsomeness making her skeptical that he could be genuinely attracted to a plain girl like herself. Her suspicions are well-founded: Rudi uses Kate, the type of woman respected and found desirable in Essenheim, to get his great uncle, the Prince Laureate, to make him his successor. The ensuing escapades are filled with comedy and satire. A *Growing Point* contributor praised "the sheer professional technique which lies behind the smooth, rapid, easy narrative style," and maintained: "The sentence rhythms and syntax suit perfectly an adventure story illuminated with verbal wit and a most disarming sense of the ridiculous. Indeed, this is a book to enjoy." In the *Times Literary Supplement,* Alan Brownjohn wrote that *A Foreign Affair* "is salted with more than a little wry intelligence and nicely-placed wisdom."

In *The Persuading Stick,* Townsend again moved to new ground, this time touching on the realm of magic. Sarah Casson, routinely overlooked by both her family members and schoolmates, finds a stick beside the canal. Suddenly, she realizes that the stick allows her to make people do the things she wishes them to. At first, those actions are minor and innocent: her family spends more time together and gives her more attention, her teacher dismisses the class early, and her mother makes her special dishes. Sarah soon worries that she shouldn't be using this newfound power, however, because it doesn't seem right to manipulate people. But when Sarah's distressed older brother threatens to kill himself, she manages to change his mind without the benefit of the stick, leaving it up to the reader to decide whether the stick is truly magical or if Sarah herself has been doing the persuading. A *Kirkus Reviews* contributor called *The Persuading Stick* "a thoughtful exploration of the discovery of constructive assertiveness by a naturally nondominant child," and Gerald Mangan identified the novel in the *Times Literary Supplement* as "a very absorbing little parable."

Rob's Place, which was published in 1987, also deals with the plight of a troubled child. After eleven-year-old Rob's parents divorce, his best friend moves away, leaving him to deal with the new home situation alone. Then his mother and new stepfather have a baby, and the child's crying keeps all of them up during the night. To escape the situation, Rob turns to fantasy: he envisions an island that he peoples with characters he has read about in books. He daydreams of the island when his environment is too much for him to handle, but the innocent psychological game becomes more serious as he becomes more depressed and the island begins to invade both his waking and sleeping hours. Eventually, Rob does manage to get help from a new friend. A *School Library Journal* contributor praised the scenes that take place on the island for being "especially vivid," and a *Publishers Weekly* reviewer called *Rob's Place* "an imaginative and thought-provoking depiction of a boy's struggle to adjust."

Further stepping away from the social realism which marked his early novels, Townsend writes of a purely fantastical setting in 1989's *The Golden Journey* (published in the United States as *The Fortunate Isles*). On a group of islands inspired by the Greek philosopher Plato's descriptions of the legendary city Atlantis, Townsend creates a nation of people consisting of two classes: nobles, who are identified by their blond hair and blue eyes, and plebeians, who all have black hair and dark eyes. Against this backdrop, the poor Eleni stands out: her unique combination of dark hair and blue eyes assigns her the prophesied role of Messenger, to whom legend has given the duty to travel to the Holy Mountain and see the Living God in order to free her people from their unjust king. Though Eleni herself doesn't uphold these religious beliefs, she sets out on a challenging, peril-filled journey with two companions. The setting of *The Golden Journey* was called "believable" by a *Kirkus Reviews* contributor, and a *Horn Book* reviewer praised Townsend's ability to build "some of the scenes into an extravaganza constructed of myth, legend, and fantasy."

Townsend is almost as well known among teachers and librarians for his books *about* children's literature as for his works of original fiction. His *Written for Children* is in its 6th edition, and in 1994 he published a biography of the pioneering eighteenth-century publisher of children's books, John Newbery, whose very name has been preserved by the America Library Association for its most prestigious annual award in the field of children's literature. Newbery led a varied professional life, with business ventures in patent medicine and publishing, and was a friend of literary stars of his day, including Oliver Goldsmith. Townsend "has examined the resources available and selected the more significant," wrote Mary M. Burns in a *Horn Book Magazine* review of *John Newbery and His Books: Trade and Plumb-Cake for Ever, Huzza!* Burns went on to conclude that Townsend's is a "notable study of Newbery's life and works."

Overall, the novels of Townsend have found increasing popularity among both critics and young readers. That he possesses "an uncanny sensitivity to the deepest yearnings of children who have inadequate parents or are orphaned," is an aspect of his prose noted by Bryna J. Fireside in the *New York Times Book Review.* Describing the author's "heroes" as young people who "live on the edge of poverty, but are not themselves impoverished," Fireside explains: "Rather, they are endowed with a tenaciousness that helps them survive situations that would crush those more protected." Whether writing a novel for young adult readers, a story for younger children, or an article discussing the craft of children's fiction, Townsend's enthusiasm for his work is apparent. "I like writing for adults about children's books and trying to get them interested in the books for their own sake," he told *SATA:* "That way we can all share with children, and maybe recapture a little of childhood's excitement."

Biographical and Critical Sources

BOOKS

Blishen, Edward, editor, *The Thorny Paradise,* Kestrel (London, England), 1975.

Children's Literature Review, Volume 2, Gale (Detroit, MI), 1976.

Crouch, Marcus, *The Nesbit Tradition: The Children's Novel in England, 1945-1970,* Ernest Benn, 1972, p. 208.

Montreville, Doris, and Elizabeth D. Crawford, *Fourth Book of Junior Authors and Illustrators,* H. W. Wilson (New York, NY), 1978.

St. James Guide to Young Adult Writers, 2nd edition, St. James Press (Detroit, MI), 1999.

Townsend, John Rowe, *Written for Children: An Outline of English Children's Literature,* revised edition, Lippincott (Philadelphia, PA), 1975.

PERIODICALS

Best Sellers, May 1, 1967; June 1, 1969.

Book Report, November-December, 1996, p. 53.

Books and Bookmen, July, 1968.

Book World, December 3, 1967; May 5, 1968; May 17, 1970; May 9, 1971.

Canadian Children's Literature, Volume 48, 1987, John Rowe Townsend, "Border Country," pp. 29-41.

Children's Literature in Education, winter, 1975, Ron Barnes, "John Rowe Townsend's Novels of Adolescence," pp. 178-190.

Christian Science Monitor, May 4, 1967; May 7, 1970, Neil Miller, review of *The Intruder,* p. B6.

Cricket, September, 1983.

English Journal, February, 1988, pp. 82-83.

Growing Point, September, 1982, review of *A Foreign Affair,* p. 3942.

Horn Book Magazine, April, 1967; June, 1967; August, 1968; August, 1970; June, 1971; August, 1971; October, 1971; April, 1973; June, 1973, John Rowe Townsend, "The Now Child," pp. 241-247; April, 1975; October, 1975; August, 1977; December, 1977; October, 1982; January, 1985; January, 1987; July, 1987; March-April, 1988, p. 205; March-April, 1990, review of *The Fortunate Isles,* pp. 211-212, 231; May-June, 1996, Mary M. Burns, review of *John Newbery and His Books,* p. 356; September-October, 2000, Martha V. Parravano, review of *The Intruder,* pp. 605-610.

Journal of Reading, May, 1995, p. 693.

Kirkus Reviews, September 15, 1987, review of *The Persuading Stick,* p. 1398; September 15, 1989, review of *The Fortunate Isles,* p. 1410.

New Society (London), December 7, 1967.

New Yorker, December 16, 1967; December 14, 1968.

New York Times Book Review, May 7, 1967; November 5, 1967; May 26, 1968; August 31, 1969, Jane Manthorne, review of *Hell's Edge,* p. 16; April 26, 1970; May 2, 1971; November 5, 1972; November 19, 1972; December 29, 1974; April 11, 1976; April 3, 1977; November 6, 1977; February 19, 1984.

Publishers Weekly, October 30, 1987, p. 72; April 29, 1988, review of *Rob's Place,* p. 78.

School Library Journal, March, 1988, review of *Rob's Place,* p. 201; October, 1989, p. 138.

Times Educational Supplement, December 7, 1990, p. 30; October 16, 1992, p. R11; July 15, 1994, p. 28.

Times Literary Supplement, December 1, 1961, review of *Gumble's Yard;* December 9, 1965, review of *Widdershins Crescent,* p. 1142; November 24, 1966; May 25, 1967; March 14, 1968; October 16, 1969; October 30, 1970; October 22, 1971; December 3, 1971; November 3, 1972; December 6, 1974; April 4, 1975; December 5, 1975; December 10, 1976; July 15, 1977; July 18, 1980; September 18, 1981; September 17, 1982, Alan Brownjohn, review of *A Foreign Affair,* p. 1001; July 27, 1984; October 11, 1985; November 28, 1986.

Washington Post Book World, May 2, 1976.

Young Reader's Review, May, 1967; April, 1968.

OTHER

Green Bay Publications Author Page, http://www.greenbay.co.uk/jrt.html (June 12, 2002).

* * *

John Rowe Townsend

I wrote my first novel when I was eight and my second when I was thirty-eight. The second was published, and has sold about half a million copies. The manuscript of the first, unfortunately, has long been lost. If I could put my hands on it now, I would have high hopes of finding a publisher for it. It was good gripping stuff, though I say so myself.

It filled five red-backed penny notebooks. (In England, in those far-off days, you could buy a notebook for a penny.) It was written in pencil and illustrated in colored crayon. It had two readers, my mother and myself, and we both thought it was terrific. I resolved to write several more novels, and listed about a dozen forthcoming titles. But I must have run out of pennies, or pencils, or patience—or found something more fascinating to do—for the subsequent books were never written.

The book that was completed had more than two hundred pages. It was called *The Crew's Boat,* and was about the adventures of a family of twelve children, six boys and six girls. This family was more remarkable than I realized, for all the children were aged between nine and twelve, and none of them were twins. The eldest boy was called John, like me, and was brave, strong, and endlessly resourceful. The others did as John told them.

There was a big tree growing in the back yard, and one day, under John's direction, the children took an axe to it, hollowed it out to make a boat, carried it down to the ocean, and launched it. So far as I can recall, the book didn't say how long this took. It was probably all of twenty minutes. The Crew then rowed around the world, having adventures all the way.

One episode recurred, with variations, several times. The Crew would arrive, in their hollowed-out tree, at a faraway island in the Caribbean, the Pacific, or some other convenient ocean. The island would be inhabited by fierce, painted savages, seven feet high, armed with sticks, stones, spears, clubs, bows-and-arrows, and any other weapons I could think of. But John and his siblings were undaunted. They would row ashore through a hail of flying arrows, all of which would, fortunately, miss. John would knock the savage chief flat with a straight left to the jaw, whereupon the savages would instantly surrender. What chance, after all, has a tribe of fierce, painted savages against a family of English children? Our heroes would then hoist the Union Jack on the nearest palm tree and proclaim the island part of the British Empire. (On second thoughts, even if I did

John Rowe Townsend, 2001

find this masterpiece, it might be better not to publish it. It would be justly condemned as imperialist and racist.)

John would then give instructions to the savages on how to run a democracy, British-style, and how eating people was wrong. He would teach them to sing "God Save the King." The savages would promise to behave themselves in future. Our heroes would then reembark in their hollowed-out tree and row on to the next island, though delayed perhaps by an encounter with pirates, whom they would compel to walk their own plank, or with a shark, whose jaws they would wedge apart with a stout stick. They returned home at the end of Volume Five, laden with

Four generations: infant John with mother Gladys, grandfather Hedley Page, and great-grandfather Reuben Page

presents for their parents, who were proud of them all, especially John.

I wrote *The Crew's Boat* with great speed and confidence. It was, I may say, the most purely literary work I have ever produced, for the adventures of the Crew were based entirely on stories I had read. My actual experience of life had been about as different as it could be. I was born in an inner district of Leeds, an industrial city in Yorkshire, in the North of England.

The real world I knew as a child would seem to many people to be a grim one. It was a small, urban world—a maze of narrow streets and alleyways, a world of little cramped dwellings and corner shops. It was a sloping world, for our district was built on what had once been a living hillside, though it was buried now under bricks and mortar. Through the middle of it ran a main road, and along the main road journeyed the tall, two-deck streetcar, known as the Tram. The Tram groaned painfully uphill toward the higher, and superior, suburbs; then came wailing and clanging back down its tracks into town at twice the speed.

Though the world was a brick world, there were living things in it. There were grimy grasses and riotous dandelions on empty sites where houses had been pulled down. There were cats and dogs around the garbage-bins, and budgerigars in cages that hung in windows. Children played, and in summer almost lived, on the street. On a sunny summer day the pavement was hot to your bare feet and the doorstep hot to your bottom. On freezing winter mornings, men slipped and skidded in their booted, before-dawn descent to the clothing factory or engineering works. There was laughter and singing, shouting and swearing and quarreling outside the pubs on a Saturday night, and on fine Mondays the clotheslines were hung across the streets and blossomed with washing. (Anyone who has read my novel *Dan Alone*, published in 1983, will recognize some of this description.)

I wrote a great deal as a child and as a teenager, but I never dreamed of setting a story in such a district. I preferred distant oceans and exotic islands. I didn't realize that a writer's inspiration lies around and within him. I recognize now that at the deepest roots I am, and shall be until I die, a child from Leeds. The seas of humble rooftops that used to stretch in great waves around the city are to me

as the "blue remembered hills" of Shropshire were to the poet A. E. Housman.

We lived in Lucas Place, and my Grandpa Page—my mother's father—was round the corner in Hartley Avenue. These streets were at the upper, more desirable end of the district. My mother, who had herself been left motherless when in her teens, had been married young; and she and Grandpa Page were child and parent still. When I was small, Mother went round to Grandpa's every day, leading me by the hand and pushing my baby sister in her trolley. She told Grandpa her problems, and Grandpa told her what to do about them. And Grandpa always had something for me, if I'd behaved myself.

"Has he been a good boy, Gladys?" Grandpa would ask. Usually Mother would say "Yes," although sometimes she'd squeeze my fingers as she said it, meaning that I hadn't been as good as I might have been but she wasn't going to give me away. Then Grandpa would give me something: an orange or a handful of dates or a biscuit; never money. Occasionally, but very rarely, I was in disgrace when we arrived at Grandpa's, and Mother told him I hadn't been good. Then I got nothing.

Grandpa Page was severe in moral and religious matters, but in everything else he was a mild, kind, helpful man. He was round-faced with a fringe of white hair, and I think of his appearance as saintly, though this may be because my idea of saintliness is derived from Grandpa Page. A neighbor once told me, "Your Grandpa's a saint." I didn't doubt the truth of this, but was not altogether delighted by it. Saintliness took a lot of living up to.

Like Grandpa Purvis in *Dan Alone*, Grandpa Page had on his sitting-room wall a Lord's Prayer, cut out of satinwood with a fine saw, mounted on dark blue plush, and framed like a picture. It was two feet wide and three feet deep, and had taken the leisure time of three years to make. It was in elaborate Gothic lettering, surrounded by marvelously convoluted scrolls and flourishes. But as he neared the end of his task, Grandpa's saw had slipped and taken the middle out of the final "e" of "for ever and ever." He was not dismayed, and often pointed to this flaw as demonstrating the imperfection of all human achievement. "Only that which God does is perfect," he used to say.

Grandpa Page's father, Great-Grandpa Page, died when I was very small. I have only one memory of him—a large old man with a bushy gray moustache who was propped up on a brass-railed bed and had a moustache-cup at his bedside. I was fascinated by the moustache-cup, which had a little shelf to keep his whiskers out of the water.

There was once a Great-Grandma Page, but I don't remember her at all. She had been a bonneted Salvation Army lass and had kept up her connection with the Army; and when she was dying at over eighty, my mother told me, she sang hymns at all hours of the day and night in a voice that was still strong and confident. The Army gave her a slap-up funeral, and a brass band led the procession and played the Dead March all the way down Woodhouse Lane.

Grandpa Page's first wife—my mother's mother—was born Ada Pinder, and was a volunteer nurse in a hospital for wounded soldiers in World War I. She died soon after it ended. Great-Grandpa Pinder was a tanner, and I have a magnificent sepia photograph, taken in Leeds about 1890, of him with his handsome, bombazine-dressed wife and their family of five children, of whom Ada was the youngest.

The Pages and Pinders and their numerous kin were solid, rooted Leeds folk of the lower middle or upper working class. They were not "the poor," of whom there were plenty in the Leeds of the 1920s when I was born, but they were far from well-to-do. They saved from modest earnings so that in their old age they would not be a burden on their children or the public purse. They went to Chapel on Sundays. "Respectable" was a key word in their vocabulary. They were honest, truthful, plain-spoken, down-to-earth, and totally unimaginative. None of them had the slightest interest in the arts, or would have encouraged writing aspirations in their children. It was not through any expectations of theirs that, from the age of five or perhaps before, I was always sure I was going to be a writer.

In childhood, I didn't see much of my father's family. The Townsends had their roots in Dorset, an agricultural county almost at the other end of England. Though England is a small country, its regions and the people who live in them are very different. Dorset and Yorkshire people in my childhood were as far apart as Californians and New Englanders now are.

My father, George Townsend, born in 1886, was the eldest of eight children. He was the son of another George Townsend, said to have been "a great man with horses." Grandad Townsend had been a coachman and a head stableman, but in his later years, when I knew him, he had become a small farmer who kept a few cows and had a milk round. Grandfather and Grandmother Townsend were referred to by my parents, when speaking to my sister or me, as Grandad and Granny, to distinguish them from Grandfather and Step-Grandmother Page, who were Grandpa and Grandma. As a small boy, on my rare visits to the farm, I would often drive around with Grandad in his high horse-drawn trap, in which stood a couple of galvanized milk-churns. He sold his milk by the pint or half-pint, measured out in long-handled ladles to customers who brought their own jugs.

"You're a stubborn lot, you Townsends," my mother used to complain to my father from time to time, and she was quite right. Three hundred years of closeness to the soil had bred an earthy peasant rigidity in them. Grandad and Granny were a match for each other in stubbornness. Granny would not let Grandad into the main part of the farmhouse, which had gaslight, unless he first took off his heavy boots. Grandad refused to take off his boots, and sat reading his newspaper by candlelight in the lean-to kitchen until bedtime, when he would at last remove the boots and pad in his stockinged feet to bed.

Granny tried several times to persuade him to wear slippers, but he would have no truck with such effeminacy. He had worn boots all his life, as a man should, and had no intention of wearing anything else on his feet. He had a refuge in the shape of a room above the cowshed, perilously heated by a coke stove, to which he would retire at lunchtime and in any period of leisure during the day. Granny visited him there once, and was distressed to find

him brewing tea over the stove in a rusty old tin can. She bought him a kettle, a china teapot, and a matching cup and saucer. Grandad hid them under the eaves, and went on using his old tin can.

The Townsends had come down in the world. They were kinsfolk of a former Bishop of Salisbury and Chaplain to the King. But their heyday was a long time ago. For three centuries they had been ordinary villagers at Upwey, near Dorchester. I know a lot about them now, because of some genealogical research I once did at the request of an American cousin.

But as a child I knew nothing of the ups and downs of the Townsend family. Apart from Grandad and Granny, I hardly knew the Townsends existed. Leeds, my mother's city, was my home and my horizon. My parents met in Leeds, were married in Leeds, and lived in or near Leeds for the rest of their lives. My father came to the city as chief clerk with an outfit called the Yorkshire Copper Works; my mother was a secretary there. He was thirty-four and she was just twenty-one when they married, and I was born a week before my mother's twenty-second birthday.

Of my earliest memories, the most vivid is of the day when my step-grandmother, Grandpa Page's second wife, who was not an amiable woman, sat on a piece of purple Glitterwax which I had left in an armchair. Glitterwax was an easily melted material which, when warm, could be molded by a child into any desired shape. Overheated by Grandma's posterior, it spread itself greasily over a large area of her dress, causing allegedly irreparable damage.

John with Granny Townsend, about 1924

George Townsend and Gladys Page, about the time of their wedding, 1921

After more than half a century, I can still quake at the recollection of her fury and my disgrace.

I have an equally vivid memory which must unfortunately be rejected as spurious. This is of the arrival of the family doctor, Dr. North, who told me, "I have a lovely surprise for you, John. I've brought you a little sister." Whereupon he opened his gladstone bag and produced my only sibling, Lois, who is four years younger than I am. I recall perfectly his appearance, the size and shape of the bag, and his putting it on the sitting-room table, which was covered with a dark green plush cloth. Even now, I can hardly believe that this didn't happen.

I was an early reader; and my earliest reading seems, in retrospect, to have been done on Sunday afternoons at Grandpa Page's house. It was the gathering-place of perhaps a dozen relatives, who would sit around and talk in immense detail of everything that had happened in the past week to themselves and their friends, relations, neighbors, friends of neighbors, neighbors of relations, friends of neighbors of relations, and so on in an endless network. I would not be allowed to go out and play, since Grandpa Page was a strict sabbatarian, and I would lie on the carpet, as the hours of adult small-talk droned over my head, reading a children's book from Grandpa's shelves.

The books all dated from Grandpa's own, Victorian, childhood. They were unbelievably moral and pious. Wicked children—that is, children who did almost any of the things that children would normally want to do—were duly punished and warned where their sins would ultimately lead them. Goody-goodies were praised and rewarded. It was all rather alarming.

I never went into a bookstore in my childhood, but when I started at elementary school I soon began borrowing from the school library. The books were battered in condition and mostly not very good, but they were a great deal more enjoyable than Grandpa's. I was ahead of my age in reading skills, though not in judgment, and at seven and eight I read numbers of school and adventure stories. By the time I wrote *The Crew's Boat,* I had certainly read

Treasure Island and *The Coral Island,* as well as a great deal of inferior stuff in the same mode.

My father was a handsome man, bright and promising, and his job was quite a good one. For a while we were modestly prosperous. We even had a maidservant, a young girl called Mabel. But two or three years after my sister was born, my father was afflicted with Parkinson's disease, the "shaking palsy." The rest of his life, to borrow a phrase from Arnold Bennett, was a tragedy in ten thousand acts. His illness killed him in the end, but took thirty years to do it.

His condition deteriorated very slowly over the decades. Gradually his hands trembled more and more; his strange, skating gait degenerated to a perilous totter; he had ever greater difficulty in eating and in washing and dressing himself. He was a constantly increasing burden on my mother. For some years he managed to go to work, in successively humbler capacities, but this became too difficult for him and he retired early on a very small pension. After that we were desperately hard up.

My later childhood and adolescence were, in fact, heavily shadowed by my father's illness. At elementary school, where the competition was not very strong, I was something of a star pupil, and when I was eleven I won a scholarship to Leeds Grammar School, an academically orientated high school. My six years there coincided with the years of deepest difficulty at home.

The school was an ancient foundation, dating from 1552, at which most of the pupils were fee-paying. It was assumed that students came from fairly well-to-do homes. A good deal of expenditure was required on books, school uniform, sports kit, and outings of one sort or another.

My scholarship paid for my books but didn't cover the other expenses. Though not particularly sensitive, I could see that every demand for the purchase or replacement of some item of school or sportswear presented my parents with a crisis. I would go to considerable pains to avoid telling them of such needs. I destroyed the notifications of school or class outings, and never went on any of them. My friendships were heavily restricted by a fear of becoming involved with freespending families from the plushy suburbs which were the habitat of most of my fellow students.

I fell, I think, between two stools. I was gradually being separated by education from those around me. The Page and Pinder relations and their friends were awed by my learning and at the same time slightly contemptuous of it, because it came from books. If I'd been outstanding at a major sport I might, for better or worse, have moved upward socially in spite of my parents' lack of money, since at our school as elsewhere everyone wanted the friendship of the brilliant sportsmen. But the only sport at which I excelled was cross-country running—I had a certain dogged determination that kept me going when the rest had got bored with the whole thing—and this was not highly regarded.

At Leeds Grammar School, I was no longer the star pupil, for the competition was now much fiercer, but I was still among the little cluster at the top of the class. It didn't do me much good at the time. I was unaware of any such concept as the love of learning. So far as I was concerned, education was a matter of passing examinations at the right level and obtaining the right certificates. I saw this as a duty I owed to my parents, who were making great sacrifices to keep me at school. Oddly, I was still a would-be writer. How it was possible to wish to write and yet have no interest in English literature, except as examination fodder, I do not know. I would not have dreamed of reading for pleasure the books I had to read to fulfil my class assignments. For enjoyment I turned to such popular writers as P. G. Wodehouse and Agatha Christie.

The one thing I did in school hours that was creative was something I'd have been punished for if the school authorities had known. This was to construct, together with half a dozen of my contemporaries, an elaborate system of Ruritanian states. Its moving spirit was Richard Beck—still a friend today—and it was based for some unknown reason on the old Germany before the unification of that country, when it consisted of a large number of little principalities and Grand Duchies. Dick Beck was the ruler of Mecklenburg; I was the Grand-Duke of Thurn-Taxis; others of our contemporaries reigned over Brandenburg, Württemberg,

Alsace-Lorraine, and Lausitz-Altenburg. We had our (bizarre) political and legal systems, our imaginary statesmen, our newspapers and popular entertainers; we formed alliances and made war on one another. The affairs of Mecklenburg and Thurn-Taxis were conducted by means of announcements, drawings, and news bulletins, surreptitiously passed around the classroom when the teacher was not looking. They were an escape from what I saw as the necessary drudgery of schoolwork and from the hard times that afflicted my home. Many years later I was able to turn them to advantage, for they gave me the idea of writing my novel *Kate and the Revolution,* set in the imaginary principality of Essenheim. Of all my writings, this book probably gave me the purest and most self-indulgent pleasure.

My parents didn't want me to go to university. Even if I'd won another scholarship, they couldn't have afforded to have me dependent on them in any way. I had to earn. They took me from school and put me, at the age of just seventeen, into the lowest ranks of the civil service. All my Page and Pinder relatives approved of that. As people who kept with some difficulty above the poverty line and had lived through the Depression, they were profoundly conscious of the benefits of security. The civil service was a Safe Job. I could not be fired for any offense less serious than running amok among my superiors with an axe. I would never be hungry. At sixty—forty-three years hence—I would retire with a pension and be in no danger of ending my life in the workhouse.

Besides, the Second World War was looming. I don't know whether my parents and the relations thought it would really come, and there is no one still alive whom I can ask. But they got me into the Inland Revenue just in time, for no permanent appointments were made during the war.

I stuck at the Inland Revenue (the income-tax department) for three years. Looking back, I think I could have done worse. Contrary to what might be supposed, work in the Revenue gave one remarkable insights into people's histories, ways of life and private secrets, as well as their finances. I used to read the files with eager interest while eating my lunchtime sandwiches. They were an education in the ways of the world.

But the war was on, and Government offices were frustratingly far away from where the action was. We did have a roster for "firewatching," which required us to sleep on camp-beds in the office once a week. If the Luftwaffe had dropped firebombs on the Inland Revenue offices in Leeds, we should have been there with hand-pumps and buckets of sand to put them out. This, however, showed no sign of happening.

At the age of twenty, I left the Revenue for ever and joined the Royal Air Force. I was realistic enough to know I could never be a pilot; my eyesight wasn't good enough; but I thought I might just scrape by as a radio-navigator, a new species of airman required for night-flying bombers. Fortunately for my conscience, which would later have had a hard time of it (if, of course, I had survived), I failed the vision test for that as well, and finished up fairly safe on the ground, among the complexities of codes and cyphers.

Out for a stroll in Leeds, 1925: John with his father, George Townsend

And so to the main turning point of my life. In the spring of 1944, after brief spells in Egypt and Palestine, I arrived in Italy with the Mediterranean Allied Air Force. I was posted to Number One Field Intelligence Unit, one of a number of small maverick units operating on the Italian front. We were supposed to follow the troops into newly captured territory and report on the materials that the enemy would carelessly have left behind in his flight. My personal role was merely to encode the reports. But soon after the unit was formed, the front came to a prolonged halt between Florence and Bologna, and Number One Field Intelligence Unit came to a similar halt, rather elegantly ensconced in requisitioned premises in the heart of Florence. There my education began.

I had left school an ignorant youth with a heap of certificates. I had carried my ignorance intact through the Inland Revenue and two years of the RAF. Now I suddenly found myself aware of art and architecture, and, arising rapidly out of this awareness, literature. It was the Enlightenment; it was the Brave New World.

During the long days and weeks in which there were no enemy materials to report on, and consequently no

John with a cricket bat, 1935

cypher messages to be sent, I wandered around Florence until I felt I knew every street and square and statue; I made Italian friends and learned rather good Italian; I studied French and Italian language and literature. My bewildered parents found themselves mailing art books and books of poetry out to me.

It was a voyage of discovery. I found that certain poems and paintings did more for me, or less for me, than others; I wondered why. I found that one thing led me on to another, and that to another. I found that people had written about poems that I read and paintings that I looked at; I wanted to know what they had said and how their experience compared with mine. I wanted to go to university to extend my discoveries.

Back in England in 1946, I took a train from Leeds to Cambridge, and a bus from Cambridge station to the city center. I knew that the University of Cambridge was divided into about twenty colleges; that was all I did know about it. From the bus I saw on my right a building that looked as if it might be a college. I got off the bus. The building was indeed a college. I walked in and said I wanted to become a student. Somebody from the college office took me to see the Senior Tutor. He talked to me for three hours, at the end of which he offered me a place. I thanked him politely, and took a train back to Leeds.

I didn't know that by luck rather than judgment I had achieved the almost-impossible. Cambridge colleges were beset at that time by thousands of bright, highly qualified young people competing for admission. Colleges didn't admit provincial nobodies who just walked in off the street. But I had had the good fortune to encounter Edward Welbourne, Senior Tutor and afterward Master of Emmanuel College, a remarkable and unorthodox figure. I was one of his minor unorthodoxies. The following year, at the age of twenty-five, I became a student. And soon after becoming a student I got married.

I haven't said anything so far about affairs of the heart. Actually I'd been in love throughout my childhood and adolescence with a succession first of little girls, then of young girls, then of young women older than myself. These love affairs were conducted almost entirely inside my head, and only the earliest of my passions were declared. (I proposed to a little girl at the age of five, and was promptly rejected.) In later adolescence there were more serious connections.

I met my wife, born Vera Lancaster, at a time in my Inland Revenue days when we were both members of a walking club that rambled the Yorkshire hills and dales. We were married for a quarter of a century and had three children; she died in 1973 after a long illness. As I write, her death was nearly twelve years ago. I have never quite come out from its shadow, and I think I never shall; but the worst times do pass, and I am now able to look back and be thankful for the good years we had together.

Postwar Cambridge, in spite of some lingering austerity, was an idyll. There were a great many veterans, ranging from ex-privates to ex-colonels, among the undergraduates, and Vera and I were among some hundreds of married couples. We didn't need anything for happiness beyond the modest grant made by His Majesty's Government, a pair of bicycles to get around on, time out for an occasional visit to the Arts Theatre or afternoon on the river, some friends, and of course each other. We lived in Cambridge all year, and could welcome the rush of activity with the start of each new term and the pleasant peace that descended when term was over.

My major was in English. The English faculty was dominated by the austere, impressive figure of Dr. F. R. Leavis, whose stringent critical methods were not to everybody's taste but served to concentrate all minds. My tutor gave me two pieces of advice at the outset of my career as a student: "Read books, not books about books" and "Don't spend time discussing Dr. Leavis." The former of these two pieces of advice holds good, I believe, today. Dr. Leavis has died, but when Cambridge English graduates who are old enough to remember him get together they still discuss him. He was one of those teachers who leave a deep and lasting mark on all who encounter them.

While at Cambridge, I developed, for better or worse, an infatuation with journalism. There was an excellent student newspaper in those days, printed on the presses of the local daily, and selling over 5,000 copies of each issue, though the student population was only about 7,000. I joined it. Promotion in student organizations is rapid, and from a reporter I soon became news editor and then chief editor. The cost to my academic work was high, and I paid it gladly.

We had enormous fun with the paper. We wrote slashing editorials, telling the authorities how a university should be run. (They'd been doing it for about 600 years, but we all felt we could teach them a thing or two.) We turned out features, columns, "profiles," diary paragraphs, the lot. We had photographers, who included the young man later to be Lord Snowdon and husband of Princess Margaret; he was fired from the student newspaper by the picture editor. We had sports writers and we had would-be political correspondents who wrote about the university's would-be politicians. We designed elaborate layouts, and each week we saw our paper through the press, learning and nonchalantly using as many of the technical terms of printing as we could absorb. I never enjoyed journalism so much again.

It was still my ambition to be an author, but when the time came for me to leave the university I was under the powerful spell of journalism. My immediate aim, I decided, was to be a newspaperman on a serious paper; then, in the fullness of time, the ultimate objective would be achieved and I would modulate from journalism to authorship. The paper for which, above all others, I wanted to work was the *Manchester Guardian,* whose editor was then the late A. P. Wadsworth—a brilliant, infuriating, and lovable man. I wrote to him, offering my services. He didn't reply. I wrote to him again, two weeks later, reminding him of my offer. He still didn't reply.

Then came the day when I, a married student, was threatened with court proceedings by the local Gas Board for nonpayment of a bill which in fact had, with much effort, been paid. I sat at the typewriter, rolled up my sleeves, and wrote a scorching letter to the chairman of the Gas Board. By the time I'd finished it, I was thoroughly warmed up, and in the mood to compose more scorchers. I

Townsend as a recruit in the Royal Air Force, 1942

remembered the editor of the *Manchester Guardian,* and wrote him an angry letter which concluded, as nearly as I can remember: "Kindly regard my application as cancelled. I would prefer to work for an editor who has the courtesy to answer his correspondence." Back by return of post came a letter from Wadsworth inviting me to Manchester for an interview, after which he offered me a job.

Once again, as had been the case when I got into Cambridge, I didn't realize how lucky I was. Wadsworth received scores of applications from bright young people just leaving Oxford or Cambridge who wanted to work for the *Manchester Guardian.* He hardly ever accepted any of them. But he liked outspoken and cussed people; and in the succeeding years I sometimes thought I disappointed him— not, I hope, professionally, but by being, as a rule, fairly even-tempered and amenable. I think he'd have liked a bit more devilment.

I believe that Wadsworth was influenced in deciding to hire me by my interest in newspaper design and production. These matters had little appeal for most of the bright young people who wanted to work for the *Guardian.* He set me to work as a sub-editor, headlining other people's copy and specifying column widths and type sizes; and he kept me at it for the next three years. From time to time I would tell him that (like all the rest) I wanted to be a reporter or editorial-writer, to which he would invariably reply that

John and Vera Townsend on their honeymoon in Alassio, Italy, 1945

reporters and editorial-writers were ten a penny and that the best prospects in journalism lay with the backroom people who put the paper together.

After three years of this, he made me picture editor of the *Guardian.* I had to arrange for pictures, mostly of news or sporting events, to be taken by our own photographers, and I also had to choose from among the photographs sent in by freelancers and picture agencies. And, having got the pictures I wanted, I had to bargain for space in the paper to display them, and I had to cut them to the right sizes and shapes. Many years later I made use of this experience in my novel *Cloudy-Bright,* whose hero is trying to get a job as a photographer on the local evening paper.

From being picture editor I graduated to the editorship of the *Guardian*'s weekly international edition. This was, and is, mainly but not entirely a selection of the best material from a week's issues of the daily paper. It circulates largely overseas, and in my day it sold far more copies in North America than any other British publication.

I liked this job of selection, and it allowed me to make up my own paper just as I wished, with the satisfying feeling when the week's work was over that there was something to show for it: a brand new crisp clean issue. It also brought me my first trip to the United States, in 1956. I was invited by a certain Dr. Henry Kissinger to take part in the Harvard International Seminar. This seminar, which was Dr. Kissinger's brainchild, brought together each year some forty young or youngish people from a variety of countries, offered them a program of lectures, seminars, and visits, and exposed them for six weeks to the American way of life, or at any rate the American way of life as seen from Harvard. The program was excellent, but I would say without disrespect to Dr. Kissinger that the main benefit to me lay in getting around and meeting people off campus.

Editing the *Guardian Weekly,* in spite of its advantages, was out of the mainstream and didn't involve much writing. I used to think I could do any job on a newspaper except that of music critic or sports reporter, and that if really pushed I'd have had a good shot at those. Wadsworth, I believe, would have brought me back to the main paper; but a year or two after I took over the weekly edition he died, and I stayed where I was.

A year or two later came another turning-point. One day the book review editor came to me and suggested that I might like to write about children's books for the daily paper. My only apparent qualifications were my own two small children, and I had no special knowledge of children's literature. The Victorian books on Grandpa Page's shelves and the adventure stories I had so indiscriminately gobbled were the whole of my own childhood reading. I accepted the suggestion mainly because I was glad to contribute to the daily *Guardian.* I had no inkling that within a very short time I would be deeply interested and excited; that I would see children's books as a new field of discovery, a new and unique stimulus.

Inside myself, down at the deepest roots, I was still the boy from industrial northern England. My blue remembered hills were still in Leeds. And whereas my experience of the arts, of higher education, of journalism with the *Guardian,* had taken me back no farther than to my own awakening at the age of twenty, here was something that led me back into the profound depths of childhood. My involvement in books for children, my attempts to read as a child would read, brought my two selves together in what turned out to be a complicated creative tangle. Before long, either the Leeds child in John Townsend was writing a book, or John Townsend was writing a book for the Leeds child alive in himself.

This was *Gumble's Yard* (American title *Trouble in the Jungle):* a story about poor children in a district not unlike the one I'd lived in, fending for themselves after they'd been abandoned by the grown-ups who were supposed to be looking after them.

I had four immediate reasons for writing *Gumble's Yard.* As a reviewer of books for children I'd come to the conclusion, rightly or wrongly, that British children's books of that time were altogether too harmless, hygienic, and middle class, with little in them of the flavor of life as it was known to a large part of the population. I had been writing some articles for a magazine on the work of the National Society for the Prevention of Cruelty to Children, and for this purpose had had to go out on the beat with some of the NSPCC inspectors in poor districts of London and Manchester. This had brought it sharply home to me that many children were poorer than I had thought possible, and that the most desperate form of poverty was not financial but was the lack of loving care.

About this time there was a report in our evening paper, the *Manchester Evening News,* about a family of children whose mother had walked out on them, and who had attempted to look after themselves because they were afraid of being "taken into care" and split up among different homes. And finally, I started going to work in Manchester on the train; and the train seemed to stop every day on top of a viaduct overlooking a canal basin. This basin was part of an industrial landscape which at first one would dismiss as ugly and dismal, but which, seeing it every day, I eventually perceived to be extraordinarily beautiful in its own strange way. I wandered around it in my lunch-hour; I found myself putting people into it, especially the four abandoned children as I imagined them to look; and from this it all grew. At long last, thirty years after my childhood epic, I was writing a book.

I didn't think it would be published, and referred to it in conversation as Townsend's Folly. But newspapermen hate to write anything and not see it in print. I thought I would at least try to find a publisher, and sent it to three leading houses. Two of them turned it down. The first liked the characters and background but not the story; the second liked the story but not the characters and background.

The third was the London firm of Hutchinson, whose adviser on books for children in those days was the poet James Reeves. He recommended publication, and they published it. It ran into a certain amount of flak. A young lady who interviewed me accused me of writing a sordid book for children. I can't remember exactly what I replied; I hope I said I didn't see it as a sordid book but in its way as an inspiring one, since it showed children winning through in very adverse circumstances, and if they'd won through once they could win through again.

While I was working on *Gumble's Yard,* I thought I was trying to write a book that would say something to, and about, and on behalf of, ordinary poor city children. It was years before I realized that this was not the heart of the matter. I wrote *Gumble's Yard* because it was there inside me, wanting to come out; and it was there inside me because of the child I had once been.

Writing and publishing *Gumble's Yard* changed my life, though I didn't at first realize that it would do so. In its first year after publication it earned a little over two hundred pounds. One couldn't support a young family on that kind of money. I saw it as an interesting and worthwhile venture, but not one that I could afford to repeat very often. Essentially I was still a journalist with a full-time job to hold down.

In the long run, *Gumble's Yard* did well. It was broadcast and televised; it was published in hard and softcovers in half a dozen countries; it is still in print after twenty-three years. But at the time I didn't foresee any of this.

A side effect of publication which I also underestimated at the time was in changing the name I was known by. I had always been plain John Townsend. Soon after the book was accepted, my editor called to tell me there was another John Townsend already writing. He had published a book called *The Young Devils,* about his experiences as a teacher

in a tough inner-city school. He had also written two children's novels. If I started publishing under the same name, my editor said, there would be hopeless confusion.

"Do you have a middle name?" she went on.

"Yes," I said. "It's Rowe."

"That's fine. We'll use that. You can be John Rowe Townsend, okay?"

I'd never before given the name Rowe a moment's thought. It was the maiden name of Grandad Townsend's mother, who died before I was born. I didn't give it a moment's thought now.

"Okay," I said. "After all, it's my name." And that was that. For twenty-three years now I've been John Rowe Townsend. What happened to the other John Townsend I don't know. I've never heard of him since. Occasionally I curse him. Having three names instead of two is a great nuisance.

Americans don't get me wrong. They take it for granted that my surname is Townsend, and they index me correctly under T. But the British are hopelessly at sea. I am frequently given a hyphen; I am introduced, as often as not, as "Mr. Rowe-Townsend"; I am as likely to be indexed under R as under T. People who look under the wrong letter think that I'm not on the telephone or my books are not in print.

Townsend, 1962

Maybe that's only a minor nuisance; and the extra time taken to sign a three-name autograph is also not important, although there are occasions when, signing my name 100 times at a school, I wish it were Bill Hill. A more important drawback, for a person who like myself has written about poor people in poor city districts, is that to have three names is considered in Britain to be upper or at any rate upper middle class. Nobody with three names, it's thought, could possibly know what it is to be poor or to live in an industrial city. So, for instance, a British commentator has accused me of writing "outside-looking-in" books, based on "observation rather than experience." He hadn't bothered to find out the facts.

The involvement with children's books took over my professional life by stealth. *Gumble's Yard* was some fifteen months in the press, and by the time it came out, in 1961, I had found I was again with book. As with *Gumble's Yard,* I had a sense of what wasn't being produced in Britain, though it was already common in the U.S.A. This was the teenage, or "young-adult," novel. In Britain, it seemed to be assumed that young people suddenly grew up overnight at around the age of thirteen, and moved straight from children's to adult fiction.

It was plain to me—but was not then a commonplace in my own country—that there were subjects which were of special interest to adolescents but which were not being written about for young people: such matters as leaving school and starting work, or not leaving school and not starting work when all your friends are doing so; arriving at new relationships with parents and authority and the other sex; and above all finding out who you are and what you have it in you to be and to do. It also seemed to me, as a convinced feminist since long before the women's movement took off, that there was a fictional dearth of spirited, enterprising girls who were not merely "tomboys"; since there are after all real and valuable differences between the sexes other than the obvious physical ones.

Hence my second book, *Hell's Edge,* in which a girl from a superior private school in the South of England is thrown together with a rough, tough, gruff boy from the North, and they strike quite a few sparks from each other before they can come to terms. This book is set in the hill country of western industrial Yorkshire, a few miles from Leeds—a land that, as somebody says in the book, is ugly on the surface but beautiful in the bone. *Hell's Edge* is not as well-known a book as *Gumble's Yard,* and not a particularly good one, but in Britain it has stayed in print for twenty-one years so far, and I have a soft spot for it myself.

Meanwhile Irene Slade, my editor at Hutchinson, had left to take charge of the list of a small publisher, Garnet Miller; and it was her suggestion that I should write a brief historical outline of English children's literature. There was one accredited history, written in 1932 by F. J. Harvey Darton, and taking the story only up to about the year 1900. Irene thought it was time for another. In between doing my job as editor of the *Manchester Guardian Weekly* and writing a third novel, I managed somehow to fit in the reading and research required for this project.

The first edition of *Written for Children* came out in 1965 and, along with the reviewing I'd been doing in the

Townsend at the tiller of a 60-foot canalboat, jointly owned with Jill Paton Walsh, 1975

daily *Guardian,* helped to establish me as a writer about children's books as well as a writer of them. It was this new reputation that took me on my second trip to the United States, and was to take me on most of the subsequent thirteen. It was this second trip also that found me an American publisher.

America has been of great and increasing importance to me. I am immensely pro-American, and one of my favorite and most firmly held beliefs is that there is nobody in the world as nice as nice Americans. I seem to have met a great many of them.

In 1965, I was invited to teach for a semester at the University of Pennsylvania, in Philadelphia. I had a dual appointment—to run a seminar at the Annenberg School of Communications on the comparative merits and demerits of American and British newspapers, and to teach a course in the Graduate School of Education on children's literature. In the four months I was there I grew fond of Philadelphia and made good friends. The key encounter, professionally, was with Hugh Johnson, then a vice president of the fine old publishing house of Lippincott.

Hugh and I met for the first time in the house of friends, and talked the sun down the sky on the subjects, naturally, of people and books. My own third novel, a sequel to *Gumble's Yard,* was just out in the U.K. Hugh showed great interest, and had me send a copy to Lippincott's children's editor, who was then Jeanne Vestal. She accepted it. Its British title was *Widdershins Crescent.*

Joseph Lippincott, Jr. declared—correctly, I am sure—that such a title would never do for the American market, and it was changed for the United States to *Good-bye to the Jungle*, the "Jungle" being the slummy area in which my fictional family lived.

The timing was right. It was the era of the Great Society and of Title II. *Good-bye to the Jungle* got excellent notices; it sold, and went on selling. Lippincott published my next book, *Pirate's Island*, which in spite of its exotic title had the same industrial-city setting. Among other reviews was a long, favorable one in the *New Yorker*. Lippincott then went back and picked up *Gumble's Yard*, soon to be retitled *Trouble in the Jungle*. The three books were A.L.A. notables, and together became known as the Jungle Trilogy.

It was the beginning of the end of my career as a journalist. In 1969, *Gumble's Yard* was published in Britain as a Puffin paperback. This, combined with American publication of all three books and the sale of subsidiary rights, pushed my earnings as a book writer to a higher figure than my salary. There was of course no certainty that this situation would last. Writing is a notoriously chancy business. But I was in deep time trouble. To do my job properly, write my books, and see anything like enough of my wife and children was clearly impossible, failing the introduction of the fifty-hour day, the ten-day week, and the hundred-week year.

Meanwhile, my old Government department, the Inland Revenue, was taking large bites out of my earnings. For a long time I complained bitterly to all who would listen that the Revenue made financial nonsense of my efforts as a fiction writer. Then one day the simple, beautiful, and liberating thought occurred to me that I could put this complaint the other way round. What if I were to regard my writing income as basic? In that case, the Revenue was making nonsense of my salary and I was working for peanuts. I should leave the *Guardian*.

In spite of the financial logic, it wasn't an easy decision to make. I was giving up an appointment of some standing. I had three children, all in school, and a large mortgage. I suffered a good deal from financial cold feet. But it was now or never. Naturally, I talked it over with my wife.

"If it's what you want to do," she said, "do it." In June 1969, I handed over the reins of the *Guardian Weekly* to John Perkin, and left next day for Seattle to teach summer school in the University of Washington. Knowing that ex-editors always disapprove of the direction taken by their successors, I never again opened a copy of the paper. I did however retain for the next nine years a small part-time connection with the daily *Guardian* as children's book review editor.

As these words are written, I've been a full-time professional writer for sixteen years, and I do not expect or wish to be anything else. America has continued to be important to me. The visit I make this year will be my fifteenth. After the semester at Penn and the summer school at Seattle, I taught a second time at Washington and made three lecture tours, incorporating the May Hill Arbuthnot lecture, the Whittall lecture at the Library of Congress, and the Anne Carroll Moore lecture in the New York Public Library. Since 1978 I have been, with Jill Paton Walsh, a visiting faculty member at the Center for Children's Literature in Simmons College, Boston. I have also spent a month on tour in Australia and a few—too few—days in Japan. When my wife died in 1973, I didn't want to go on living in the home we had built together at Knutsford, near Manchester, and I moved back to Cambridge, which I had always loved. Here I have stayed, through twelve years and as many books. My children have grown up and my first grandchild has been born.

Professionally, I'm one of the world's lucky ones. I am what I always wanted to be, a writer. People ask me often if I don't want to write for adults. Actually *Written for Children* is a book for adults, and I have written a great deal of journalism for adults; but they mean fiction, of course. I have always said that if I were captivated by an idea which could only be realized in an adult novel, then I would write an adult novel. In the meantime I am very happy to write for children and young people, who seem to me to be an ideal audience, receptive, and constantly renewed.

The writing of each successive book is a new and different enterprise. It never becomes a routine. Yet there are stages to be gone through every time. There's the initial fascination with an idea, the excitement of planning and starting work, the first fine careless rapture of writing. Then come the problems: the tendency of every narrative to go its own way and of every character to do what he or she is not supposed to do; the falling apart of plots, the wrong directions taken, the dead ends arrived at, the despair.

There's a period of sheer, dogged slog, when only willpower keeps me going. Then, with luck, comes the recovery—the realization that it can be made to work out after all, the returning enthusiasm, the completion of the first rough draft. That first draft is the hardest part, accomplished by what Arnold Bennett called "brute force of brain." Then there's a second, and sometimes a third draft; the book must be shaped and reshaped, improved and polished. It's hard, craftsman's work, and it takes a lot of time. For me, completing the final revision is like coming into port at the end of a long voyage. But somehow the book is never *quite* as good as I'd hoped when setting out. Perhaps next time will be different. At least it will be a different voyage. I don't ever want to make the same one twice.

Looking back, I can see that certain themes have recurred in my work, although it was never a deliberate intention that they should do so. One is a theme that a great many writers for children and young people have explored in different ways—the theme of youngsters taking on responsibility for their own and other lives when the adults cannot or will not do so. Other themes are more individual to myself. I am endlessly fascinated by human relationships which have to grow and flower in a brief period of time, like those (in my own books) of Graham and Lynn in *Goodnight, Prof Dear;* of Philip and Ann in *The Summer People;* of Ben and Katherine in *The Visitors*.

I am intrigued by moral problems to which there is no easy answer, as in *Noah's Castle*, set in a future time when millions are starving. The central character is a father who saw what was going to happen and stocked the basement of his big old Victorian house with everything needed to withstand a siege—which is what he has to do in the end. He doesn't care what happens to anyone else, so long as his own family survives. Is he a terrible man, or is he only doing what a father ought to do, namely protect his own young at all costs? I don't know the answer; if I'd known it, I probably wouldn't have wanted to write the book. I am interested in asking moral questions; I'm not interested in laying down a moral line.

Places inspire me—in particular strange, remote places that in some sense are the end of the world, whether it be the row of derelict cottages on the canal bank in *Gumble's Yard* or the village that is crumbling into the sea in *The Summer People.* I love dens and refuges of all kinds; and I love, especially, islands. Islands seem as if they were specially made for adventure; and for a writer they have the advantage that you can concentrate a great deal of human passion and conflict into a small space.

The mystery of time intrigues me, too, and I have a feeling that I may well explore it further. I like to show events in the distant past still working themselves out today, as in my recent book *Tom Tiddler's Ground;* and there's the impossible but ever-appealing notion of time travel, which I have handled only once. This was in *The Visitors.* In contrast to fairly numerous books in which people from the present have traveled into the past or the future, *The Visitors* has people from the future arriving in the present. It's a situation which allows the writer to take a look from outside at our own society.

And then there have been the books that were sheer fun: the Ruritanian extravaganza of *Kate and the Revolution,* and two which are published only in England and probably wouldn't travel to the States—*Clever Dick,* the diary of a thoroughly obnoxious child, and *Gone to the Dogs,* in which a family of dogs keep two children. as pets.

My sustained critical writings have been *Written for Children* and two books of essays on contemporary children's writers, *A Sense of Story* and *A Sounding of Storytellers.* The criticism of children's literature has been something of a minefield in recent years; one is under heavy pressure to judge books from nonliterary points of view, in terms of social, psychological, or educational desirability.

I have always declined to do this, though I wouldn't deny the right of others to do it. I have never understood why it should be supposed that there is only one correct critical stance and all others must be wrong. There is room, in my view, for different kinds of critics. For myself, I have no wish to construct abstract critical theories or to engage in the kind of criticism that lays works of art out on the slab and dissects them. That way, it is all too easy to finish up with the dead remnants rather than with the living body, the thing that breathes and moves.

My personal leaning is toward appreciative criticism. I try to approach every new book in a spirit of hope and excitement, though not without discrimination. One thing I believe most passionately is that a good book for young people must be a good book, period.

My present way of life is quiet, and pleasant enough. I still live in Cambridge, and have no thought at present of moving. I have a half-share in a country cottage in the riverside village of Hemingford Grey with Jill Paton Walsh, and we work there together for three days in every week. Thanks to our yearly visit to Simmons, we've discovered the joys not only of Boston itself but of Maine and New Hampshire and Vermont; of Cape Cod and the islands. It's been a good life.

And Leeds? Oddly enough, my younger daughter, Penny, went of her own choice to Leeds University, lived and started work there, and married a young man from Pudsey (a township between Leeds and the neighboring city of Bradford). She is now teaching in that part of the world, and shows every sign of staying. So a connection is maintained.

I find as I grow older that my heroes in the arts are those who continue working with undiminished powers in ripe old age. In an eightieth birthday interview a year or two ago, the famous novelist Graham Greene was asked whether he had any remaining ambitions.

"Yes," said Greene. "To write a good book."

We can't all be Graham Greene, but, while ever we have the health and strength to push a pen or pound a typewriter, we can all keep trying to fulfil that aim as far as our talents allow. That is what writers are for.

POSTSCRIPT

John Rowe Townsend contributed the following update to *SATA* in 2002:

That account of my life and books was written in 1985—seventeen years ago. It mentioned briefly the country cottage in the English riverside village of Hemingford Grey, in which I had a half-share with my fellow-writer, Jill Paton Walsh. Looking back now, with a touch of nostalgia, I can see that this was a wonderfully tranquil and happy part of our lives. It was, we used to tell people, not a weekend cottage but a midweek one, to which we escaped for the inside days of each week from our duties and distractions at our respective home bases, in order to be together and get some work done. We had converted the attic-space into a large joint study, with big windows back and front, through which, when the leaves were off the trees, you could see the spires of five village churches. Hemingford Grey was in a small, idyllic enclave in deep countryside, through which flowed the lovely and usually (but not always) peaceful River Ouse.

Beside the river, not far from us, was Hemingford Grey's manor-house, the original of the famous Green Knowe books and home of their author L.M. Boston, who became our friend. She was already an old lady, softly spoken and yet formidable; she didn't suffer fools gladly. I was always a little in awe of her, and it was a long time before I dared to call her Lucy. The manor-house is said, perhaps with truth, to be the oldest continually inhabited house in England; its known history stretches back over eight hundred years. Lucy had devoted her life to it, and had written about it in six Green Knowe books and two more about the house itself, so it is hardly to be described in a sentence. But you could stand in the central hall which was its heart and feel the centuries all around you; it was easy to imagine you heard the voices of those long-ago Children of Green Knowe. Lucy died in her own house—as

"Do-it-yourself publishing": Townsend and Jill Paton Walsh at work on the first Green Bay publication, 1986

everyone knew she would, if Death ever dared to claim her—at the age of ninety-eight.

The river at Hemingford Grey was the setting, and in large part the inspiration, for my young adult novel *Downstream,* which appeared in the United States in 1987. It was about a boy, a high school student, whose father comes into a modest windfall and spends it on acquiring a patch of remote river-bank on which stands a wooden shack. Father soon appears to lose interest, but the boy spends some time doing it up. He falls in love with the attractive young woman, some years older than himself, who is employed by his parents to give him home tuition, only to find, on an unexpected visit to the shack, that his father and his tutor are making love there. The boy's shock at this discovery leads to an emotionally explosive ending.

Downstream did quite well in the United States, but was turned down by my regular British publishers, probably because they found it too explicit. Eventually it was published in Britain by Walker Books, both in hard and soft covers, but was not a great success. I think it fell through the gap between children's (which in organizational terms includes young adult) and adult fiction. It could and perhaps should have been written as an adult novel.

Jill and I gave up the Hemingford cottage with regret, but for a reason which was in itself a happy one. In the year in which I was writing *Downstream,* new circumstances made it possible for us to amalgamate our households and live together full-time. We have been together ever since, and for me it has been by far the best change in the past

quarter-century. But the cottage was far too small to hold us, our personal possessions, our domestic and business equipment, our children and friends if they came to visit us, and above all our two sizeable collections of books. We had to go househunting, and we finished up in Histon, a village just outside Cambridge and within that city's field of gravity.

We told a real-estate agent that we wanted an old house with some character, and a few days later he called and said, "There's a house I want you to look at." We said, "How old?" He said, "Twelve years." We said, "But we told you we wanted an *old* house." He said, "I know, I know. But I want you to see this one. You'll either love it or hate it." Reluctantly we went along, more inclined to hate than to love. And in fact it was love at first sight. It was a modern house designed by an architect with imagination: basically a simple barn structure but arranged to have one large main room the full height and width of the house and all the other rooms—kitchen, bathrooms, bedrooms, study—tacked on to it. The principal bedroom projected forward at upper-floor level into the big main room; we could have placed a small orchestra there, or used it as the balcony in a performance of *Romeo and Juliet.* We bought the house, and were there for fourteen years.

Jill and I are extremely compatible. By and large we like the same things, but there are enough differences in our tastes and opinions to add spice to our conversations. We have worked in the same room ever since the Hemingford days. We have some complementary skills. Jill is mildly dyslexic and has trouble with spelling, while I always say that if I can't do anything else at least I can spell. She is a whiz at the computer, whereas I am barely computer-literate and am always having problems at the keyboard. She asks me things like "How do you spell 'unparalleled'?" I ask her things like "How do you make this horrible machine give you a circumflex accent?" Between us, we get by pretty well. Our principle in housekeeping is that we share the work as equally as we can. Cooking is probably the real test. One week, Jill shops and cooks while I clear away and put the dishes to wash; the following week it's the other way round. We are firmly agreed that it is impossible to cook with somebody else's shopping. The same person must do both. I must say in honesty that while I aspire to be a good plain cook it is Jill who is the artist. If it's for a dinner party, she takes over.

Though we settled comfortably into the new house, we missed having a retreat to which we could go, either for a break or to get on with some steady writing, in a place where there would be fewer interruptions and fewer business matters cluttering our desks, and where our telephone number would be known only to people we actually wanted to call us. Jill had spent much of her early childhood at St. Ives, in Cornwall, and has always been deeply attached to it. It's a small, pretty town, traditionally a fishing village. Though fishing has long been in decline, there are still boats in the harbour, which is surrounded by narrow, crowded streets and relics of former days such as fish-cellars and sail lofts. It also has a serious long-established colony of artists and an outpost of London's Tate Gallery. We managed to acquire for our retreat half a Victorian stone house, quite close to Jill's childhood home, on a hillside overlooking the town and also overlooking the vast expanse of St. Ives Bay. The sea here is an ever-changing pattern of colors: silver, reflected sky-blue, eau-de-nil, ultramarine, turquoise, indigo, all in a thousand different shades. Add the great wide cloudscapes and the white flecks of wavecrest, and you can understand why, twenty times a day, we call to one another, "Just look at it now!" Looking out from our window, as I am doing at the moment, you see the island lighthouse of Godrevy, a pencil of white on a distant rock. This was the original lighthouse in Virginia Woolf's novel *To the Lighthouse.*

Many friends have stayed with us here. Among those from America have been Charles and Ursula Le Guin, Jane Langton, and Gregory Maguire. I recall with particular affection, sharply tinged with the sense of loss, the visit of Paul and Ethel Heins, both of whom were to die quite soon afterwards. I remember Ethel trudging, raincoated but joyful, through the little town in a downpour, exclaiming with surprise and delight at each successive picturesque but rainsoaked sight that met her eyes. And I remember when we took Paul and Ethel to St. Michael's Mount, a few miles away. This looks for all the world like a fairytale castle, standing out at sea and reached by a causeway that can be crossed on foot, but only at low water. On our way back an exceptionally high tide, driven in early by a following wind, overtook us on the causeway and rose rapidly around our knees; there was real danger that we could be swept away. But Ethel and Paul, linked arm-in-arm between us, were serene, with a touching faith that no harm could come in our company. We got safely to shore. Afterwards, Ethel exclaimed happily that it had been just like an adventure in a children's book.

Some years earlier Jill had written a sequence of four short stories, set on the Cornish coast and published in an anthology long out of print. I thought they should be back in print and persuaded her to write a fifth story which, with the others, would add up to a book. This we would call *Five Tides* and would design, typeset, and publish ourselves. I had always, from early days, loved type and typographical design, so for me there was an element of self-indulgence in the project, though my wish to see the stories in print again was real enough. We worked together on the production and were pleased with the result, although it now looks somewhat primitive. Our edition sold out quite quickly.

This was the beginning of our venture into small-scale publishing. We called our imprint Green Bay Publications, putting our faith in a supposed prediction from the Bible that "the wicked shall grow and flourish like the green bay tree." (Actually, we hadn't got it quite right; the correct quotation, from Psalm 37, verses 35-40, shows that the wicked had it coming to them and were severely punished. But then, we were not really all that wicked.)

In the late 1980s, I wrote a novel which was an act of homage to Elizabeth Gaskell, a Victorian writer whose work I had always admired. Mrs. Gaskell's best known (though not her best) book was *Cranford,* a portrait of small-town life based on Knutsford, in Cheshire, where I had formerly lived. *Cranford* was in large part a celebration of the old-fashioned, indomitable English spinster. I felt the time had come to celebrate the equally indomitable married woman of today, who manages a house, a husband, children, and a career, and copes with everything a busy modern life throws at her. The result was *Cranford Revisited,* and although I acquired a collection of compli-

mentary letters from publishers, they all concluded with expressions of regret: this was not the kind of thing the market wanted today. One publisher wrote: "I enjoyed it from beginning to end. So did X" (a fellow-director.) "But we agree with our colleagues in Sales and Publicity that without a very expensive promotion campaign it would almost certainly fail in commercial terms.... None of us understands how books which we *know* many readers would like and would be pleased to come across in the library sell in hundreds, not thousands."

Here was another job for Green Bay. We brought out *Cranford Revisited* in hardback, with witty drawings by our dear friend the American artist-novelist Jane Langton, in an attractive production. (We had learned quite a lot from *Five Tides.*) But the publisher I have just quoted was right about selling in hundreds rather than thousands. *Cranford Revisited* just managed to top 700. As we had virtually no overheads, this was a sufficient sale to give us a modest profit. The most interesting thing about *Cranford Revisited* is that we registered it for Public Lending Right, the system under which British authors receive a small payment for every library loan, and the PLR returns show it to have had 13,600 issues by 2001. As we think that not more than half the 700 copies can have gone into libraries, this figure suggests that on average each copy has had thirty-eight borrowings, a remarkable number. It seems the publisher was right about what people would like to see in the library. Unfortunately, a book brought out by a very small publisher is unlikely to get into many libraries, and most of the public don't get the chance of seeing it.

The big success of Green Bay was still to come. Jill's novel *Knowledge of Angels,* about a wild child found on a theocratically-ruled island in the Middle Ages, was published in the States to considerable acclaim, but was refused by nineteen British publishers (mainly, it seems, on the mistaken view that it was not relevant to the present day.) The American editor called us to say that it had sold out there and was reprinting before publication. Would we like a few copies for our friends? We thought rapidly, asked if we could have a thousand, and swiftaired a Green Bay title page and logo to Boston. These were substituted for the American ones in our thousand copies, which the publishers (Houghton Mifflin, to whom high praise) printed and shipped to us without any fuss. The book then did spectacularly well in Britain and was short-listed for the Booker, the premier literary prize. By that time, it had sold large numbers and had been taken over, with our willing agreement, by a firm run by friends in the trade, Robert and Linda Yeatman, who were better equipped to handle it.

Green Bay has now brought out eight titles. We were particularly pleased to publish, in conjunction with Children's Literature New England, *Earthsea Revisioned,* a lecture by Ursula Le Guin on her famous "Earthsea" quartet of novels. The most recent production has been a soft-cover edition of my own *Noah's Castle,* which, alas, had fallen out of print in both the U.S.A. and Britain. But we are not now very active as publishers. A lesson we have learned is that producing a book is not all that difficult if you have the skills; and if you haven't the skills you can purchase them. The really difficult trick is to sell the books you produce. It is hard, and has grown harder, to do so without a sales organization. Our advice to the many people who have consulted us is always to get a professional

Townsend with partner Jill Paton Walsh, February 2002

publisher if you can; go in for self-publishing only as a last resort, and don't risk money you can't afford to lose.

Jill and I have been associated with Children's Literature New England (CLNE), just mentioned, since it began in 1987. It had its origin in the Center for Children's Literature, which was established at Simmons College, Boston, a decade earlier. Among the moving spirits at that time were the first Director, Barbara Harrison, and Paul and Ethel Heins. The faculty of the Centre, including these three and also the Deputy Director and author Gregory Maguire and author Betty Levin, parted company with Simmons in 1987 and set up CLNE, a nonprofit educational foundation which has run institutes (intensive study courses) yearly ever since, built around themes in children's literature: among them *Robinson Crusoe and His Heirs, Travelers in Time, Swords into Ploughshares,* and *Pathfinders.* Jill and I are adjunct board members for the U.K.

This has given us insights into the complexities of running large conferences. We have held our institutes in different venues year by year, having been at Harvard (three times), Radcliffe, Oxford, Cambridge (twice), Toronto, and elsewhere. For Jill and myself, the first Cambridge institute in 1989 was the most demanding, because we were here on the spot and our colleagues were in America. We had to make advance arrangements, get help from the Arts Council and from publishers and booksellers, and find British speakers and participants. The great majority of our participants were, then as now, American, but we have had sizeable contingents from Canada, the U.K., Ireland, Japan, and other countries.

At Cambridge, when not in lecture hall or seminar room, our American colleagues quickly acquired the traditional art of punting. A punt is a shallow, flat-bottomed vessel in which the passengers are expected to lounge gracefully on cushions while some hero or heroine stands dangerously poised on a little platform at the back and provides the motive power by way of a long pole. My most vivid single memory of that institute, in fact, is of punting on the River Cam. One of our speakers was the distinguished historical novelist Rosemary Sutcliff, who had a serious lifelong disability and has since died. She had long had the ambition to travel by punt along the Cam, past the architectural glories of the ancient colleges; and it fell to us, with Jane Langton, to bring this about.

A disabled elderly lady in a wheelchair balanced in a punt is a precious and perilous cargo, especially when the river is busy with carefree holidaymakers who may barge their vessel into yours if you don't get out of the way quickly enough. Luckily Rosemary, sitting happily with her back to me, could not see the anguished expressions that, I am told, followed each other rapidly across my face when I took the pole. We were as delighted as she was, though for different reasons, when eventually the strong arms of landing-stage attendants got her safely ashore.

We have had successful institutes both in Oxford and Cambridge since then, but later ones have not asked so much of us. Our American friends were quick to learn the British ropes and have been both able and blessedly willing to take most of the work upon themselves.

Travel abroad is good for writers, both in broadening their outlook on life and in giving them ideas. It was a journey to Majorca that triggered Jill's *Knowledge of Angels,* though the idea behind it had been in her mind for a long time, waiting for the right setting to spark it into life. For me, a walking holiday in Greece and stays on two Greek islands were the inspiration for *The Fortunate Isles,* a quest story set in the realm of Atlantis, the fabled lost island of antiquity. A rough country girl called Eleni has to fulfill a prophecy that she will make her way to the summit of the Holy Mountain and, as the long-awaited Messenger to the Living God, will save the Fortunate Isles from war and destruction. A challenge that intrigued me was that of trying to write a fantasy that would have no magic swords, flying horses, witches, wizards, monsters, or other such standard trappings, but would rely on naturalistic character-isation and action.

This was not my first book to have an island setting. In 1981, I had written *The Islanders,* set maybe 100 years ago on an island in the midst of a great ocean, "a speck of land as remote and lonely as a planet in space." My island was rather similar to Tristan da Cunha, in the South Atlantic; I called it Halcyon, and in 1992 I wrote another book set on it two generations later, with the young people in the new book being the grandchildren of those in the earlier one. The title of the later one, published in 1992, is *The Invaders,* and there are several kinds of invasion: an invasion of new ideas, an invasion by the island's faraway Mother Country, now taking an interest for security reasons, and finally invasion by a hostile foreign power. The islanders survive. Survival is what they are good at.

I think myself that *The Invaders* is as good as any of my earlier books, but it didn't sell well. Though I felt, and still feel, able and willing to write, I now had a strong sense that the wheel had turned; a new generation of writers had arrived, and in the short-term world that is modern publishing, old writers are old hat. I knew of too many who had gone on too long; maybe it was time to retire from the fray. So I haven't written any fiction since *The Invaders.* Fortunately, I haven't quite disappeared from the scene. In the last two or three years, two of my early books, *Gumble's Yard* and *The Intruder,* have been reissued by Oxford University Press as "children's modern classics." *Tom Tiddler's Ground* has been issued by Cambridge University Press in a series called Cambridge Reading, and *The Islanders* by Random House under their Red Fox imprint in a series called Definitions.

Some day I may be seized by an irresistible idea and may suddenly find myself hard at work; but until that happens I am resting my case so far as fiction is concerned. Jill has completed, at the request of the trustees of Dorothy L. Sayers, a Lord Peter Wimsey novel which Dorothy Sayers had left unfinished. It was highly praised, and as I write she is working on a further Wimsey novel, which will be almost entirely her own invention. After that I expect she will do something quite different and will go on writing for a long time.

We have now moved to a small house on the river bank in Cambridge, opposite a spacious common and in walking distance of the city centre. We have many friends within reach. Rowing crews, canal boats, swans and other water-fowl go past our window on the river; beyond it, people cycle, walk their dogs or play with their children on the common. We are one of a little group of nine interestingly varied households; I hope the others find us as congenial as we find them. On the wider scale, Cambridge has several interlocking communities: the academic one, a scientific one based in the Science Park, known locally as Silicon Fen, and a sizeable publishing base. It is also still the market town for a wide area. It's full of interesting people, the university library is world class, and you could go to a play or concert almost any evening of the year.

I know I've been one of life's lucky ones. My three grown children have given me seven grandchildren, all bright and healthy. Jill has two (so far), so we have nine in all and love them dearly. We enjoy walking, travel, reading, writing, listening to music, and, perhaps above all, conversation. I always used to say, having worked hard all my life, that somewhere inside myself there was a lazy man signalling to get out. Now he is having his day, although somehow, like most of the supposedly retired people I know, I don't actually seem to be less busy, I just tend not to get paid for what I do. But that's all right. Better wear out than rust out, they say.

TRUEMAN, Terry 1947-

Personal

Born December 15, 1947, in Birmingham, AL; married and divorced three times; children: Sheehan and Jesse. *Education:* University of Washington, B.A., 1971; Eastern Washington University, M.S. (developmental psychology), 1975; Eastern Washington University, M.F.A. (creative writing), 1985; attended Washington State University. *Religion:* Roman Catholic.

Addresses

Home—Spokane, WA. *Agent*—c/o Author Mail, Harper-Collins, 10 East 53rd St., New York, NY 10022. *E-mail*—tet@quest.net.

Career

White Hills Technical School, Bendigo, Australia, English and social studies teacher, 1972-74; Spokane Community Health Center, Spokane, WA, therapist, 1975-80; Escuela International Sanpedrana, San Pedro Sula, Honduras, school counselor, 1981-82; Eastern Washington University, Cheney, WA, teaching fellow, 1983-85; Spokane Falls Community College, Spokane, WA, instructor, 1985-91, 1993—; Spokane Public Schools, Spokane, WA, substance abuse intervention specialist, 1991-93. KPBX-FM, Spokane, WA, critic, community producer, reviewer, and commentator, 1992-95.

Awards, Honors

Grants from Louisa Kern Fund, 1970 and 1971; Exceptional Faculty Award, Spokane Falls Community College, 1996, for teaching excellence; Editors Choice Awards, *Booklist,* 2000, Best Teen Reads for Summer, *Seattle Post Intelligencer,* 2000, Michael L. Printz Honor Book, 2001, NASEN Highly Recommended Award, Publishers Association, 2001, Best Reads for Teens List, New York Public Library, 2001, and Best Book for Young Adults and Quick Pick for Reluctant Young Adult Readers, American Library Association, all for *Stuck in Neutral.*

Writings

The Chinese Painting Poems, Rednblack Press (Spokane, WA), 1990.

Black Lipstick (poem), Siobhan Press (Spokane, WA), 1991.

Sheehan (poem), Siobhan Press (Spokane, WA), 1992.

Love on the Rack, Rednblack Press (Spokane, WA), 1995.

(With Michael Gurian) *What Stories Does My Son Need: A Guide to Books and Movies That Build Character in Boys,* Jeremy P. Tarcher/Putnam (New York, NY), 2000.

Stuck in Neutral, HarperCollins (New York, NY), 2000.

(With Michael Gurian and Patricia Henley) *Boys and Girls Learn Differently: A Guide for Teachers and Parents,* Jossey-Bass (San Francisco, CA), 2001.

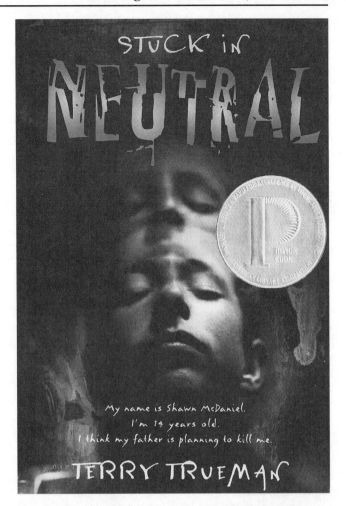

In his suspenseful novel, Terry Trueman portrays Shawn McDaniel, a fourteen-year-old boy with crippling cerebral palsy who fears his father may have plans to end his suffering by killing him. (Cover illustration by Cliff Nielsen.)

Also author, with Craig T. Nelson, of a screenplay version of *Stuck in Neutral,* which has been optioned for a feature film by Nelson's Family Tree Productions in Los Angeles, CA. Contributor of poems, stories, and articles to magazines and newspapers, including *Choice, Measure, Poetry Australia, Parachute, Wisconsin Review, Idiom, Puget Soundings, Small Press Review,* and *Northwest Artpaper.*

Work in Progress

Two novels for HarperCollins, including *Crazy Boy,* about a schizophrenic teenager.

Sidelights

In 2000 Terry Trueman burst onto the literary scene with the young adult novel *Stuck in Neutral,* which earned popular and critical acclaim. In this novel, he portrayed the interior life of Shawn, a boy with cerebral palsy who appears outwardly to be severely impaired, yet has a rich mental existence. Prior to writing this novel, Trueman had worked as a poet and book and film reviewer. "At the age of forty-eight, I decided it's now or never if I'm ever going to write anything that has the possibility of commercial success," he recalled in an online interview for ACHUKA. His method involved "getting up at six in the morning every day and working as long as I could." He added, "A miracle happened while I was doing it. I found I loved writing more than any other human activity, really loved the process of being so selfish, so self-indulgent, so centered in my own place, which is what writing allows you to do."

Trueman's literary models include Charles Bukowski and Raymond Carver, who write very direct prose. Trueman emulated them in the telling of *Stuck in Neutral.* He also found inspiration in the life of his own son Sheehan, who was injured at birth and suffers from severe cerebral palsy. "I have no way in the world of knowing if my son Sheehan has any of the abilities or personality and spirt of Shawn, and I don't think he does," Trueman told ACHUKA. "But it's also possible, and that's where the story came from—that things are very different inside that person than you can ever imagine." The thread of plot that holds together the novel is Shawn's dawning awareness that his father believes that he is suffering and is thinking of killing him. The ending is such that the reader must decide what happens when father and son are left alone in the house together.

Although Trueman did not intend *Stuck in Neutral* to be a young adult novel, it was accepted for publication as one. In 2000 and 2001 the novel won a handful of awards and earned qualified praise from critics. Although a *Publishers Weekly* contributor found the "book's concepts are more compelling than the story line itself," *Booklist* reviewer Ilene Cooper declared, "This short novel packs a punch that transcends its length." Writing in *School Library Journal,* Tim Rausch praised the "compassionately drawn" character of Shawn, which Trueman "vividly captured" and which will challenge readers "to look beyond people's surfaces." A controversy evolved around a negative British review of *Stuck in Neutral,* which Trueman believed was motivated by the critic's misunderstanding of his position on euthanasia. "My feelings on euthanasia are that I have a right to end my life whenever I want to.... But ... the book itself is such a strong argument against euthanising someone else," Trueman told ACHUKA. "The whole theme of the story is that his father thinks he understands his son's life and experiences but really he doesn't. The father's response might be out of love to end the child's pain when in fact the child isn't in pain. So you can't have a more show-me-rather-than-tell-me demonstration against making a decision for euthanising someone else."

Biographical and Critical Sources

PERIODICALS

Booklist, July, 2000, Ilene Cooper, review of *Stuck in Neutral,* p. 2034; November 15, 2000, Hazel Rochman, review of *Stuck in Neutral,* p. 631; December 1, 2000, Stephanie Zvirin, review of *Stuck in Neutral,* p. 693.

Horn Book, May, 2000, review of *Stuck in Neutral,* p. 322.

Library Journal, July, 2000, Kay Brodie, review of *What Stories Does My Son Need?: A Guide to Books and Movies That Build Character in Boys,* p. 121.

Publishers Weekly, July 10, 2000, review of *Stuck in Neutral,* p. 64; March 12, 2001, review of *Boys and Girls Learn Differently: A Guide for Teachers and Parents,* p. 83.

School Library Journal, July, 2000, Tim Rausch, review of *Stuck in Neutral,* p. 111.

Times Educational Supplement, May 25, 2001, Nicola Robinson, review of *Stuck in Neutral,* p. SS20.

OTHER

ACHUKA, http://www.achuka.com.uk/ (December 7, 2001), interview with Terry Trueman.

Terry Trueman, http://www.terrytruemannews.com/ (December 7, 2001).

Terry Trueman Web Site, http://www.terrytrueman.com/ (December 7, 2001).*

V

van FRANKENHUYZEN, Gijsbert
1951-

Personal

Born July 6, 1951, in Goes, The Netherlands; son of André (an entomologist) and Gijsbertha van Frankenhuyzen; immigrated to the United States, 1976; married Robbyn Smith (an animal technician), August 8, 1981; children: Heather, Kelly. *Education:* Royal Academy of Arts, The Netherlands, 1973. *Hobbies and other interests:* Birdwatching, "working around our farm—turning it into a nature preserve (forty acres)."

Addresses

Home and office—7409 Clark Rd., Bath, MI 48808. *E-mail*—robbyn@voyager.net.

Career

Michigan Natural Resources magazine, art director and illustrator 1976-93; freelance artist and illustrator, 1993—. *Exhibitions:* Van Frankenhuyzen's work appears in the Mazza Collection, University of Findlay, and has been selected to appear in the Leigh Yawkey Woodson "Birds in Art" exhibition, Wausau, WI.

Awards, Honors

Wildlife Artist of the Year Award, 1980; winner, Michigan Duck Stamp Competition, Michigan Duck Hunters Association, 1982; Great Lakes Award, 1999, for *The Legend of Mackinac Island;* Children's Choice Award, 2001, for *The Legend of the Teddy Bear* and *Legend of the Loon;* National Arbor Day Award, 2001, for *The Blue Spruce;* Read Michigan Award, 2001, for *A Place Called Home,* and 2002, for *Adopted by an Owl.*

Illustrator

"LEGENDS" SERIES

Kathy-Jo Wargin, *The Legend of the Sleeping Bear,* Sleeping Bear Press (Chelsea, MI), 1998.

Gijsbert van Frankenhuyzen

Kathy-Jo Wargin, *The Legend of Mackinac Island,* Sleeping Bear Press (Chelsea, MI), 1999.

Frank Murphy, *The Legend of the Teddy Bear,* Sleeping Bear Press (Chelsea, MI), 2000.

Kathy-Jo Wargin, *The Legend of the Loon,* Sleeping Bear Press (Chelsea, MI), 2000.

Kathy-Jo Wargin, *The Legend of the Lady's Slipper,* Sleeping Bear Press (Chelsea, MI), 2001.

OTHER

Mario Matthew Cuomo, *The Blue Spruce,* Sleeping Bear Press (Chelsea, MI), 1999.

Kathy-Jo Wargin, *L Is for Lincoln: An Illinois Alphabet,* Sleeping Bear Press (Chelsea, MI), 2000.

Janie Lynn Panagopoulos, *A Place Called Home: The Story of Michigan's Mill Creek,* Sleeping Bear Press (Chelsea, MI), 2001.

Robbyn Smith van Frankenhuyzen, *Adopted by an Owl: The True Story of Jackson, the Owl,* Sleeping Bear Press (Chelsea, MI), 2001.

Also illustrator of Margot Theis Raven's *Mercedes and the Chocolate Pilot,* Sleeping Bear Press (Chelsea, MI).

Sidelights

While vacationing in Michigan, Netherlands native Gijsbert van Frankenhuyzen fell in love with the state and with its critically acclaimed magazine *Michigan Natural Resources.* After nearly a year of contact via mail with the magazine's editor in chief, van Frankenhuyzen was hired as the art director and head illustrator. He enjoyed this position for seventeen years, producing illustrations for the magazine and a series of posters for the state. When the governor of Michigan decided to let the state-supported publication go into private hands, van Frankenhuyzen lost his job. Yet he turned a heartfelt disappointment into the chance of a lifetime by striking out on his own, creating original artworks, museum murals, and illustrations for children's books in an impressionistic style. "Now I see it as the best thing that ever happened to me," he told Kym Reinstadler of the *Grand Rapids Press.* "I had wanted to be a painter and book illustrator since I was ten years old. I love painting a story."

Many of van Frankenhuyzen's books focus on Michigan, such as the "Legends" series, which have become standard fair in many of the state's elementary schools. In addition to legends about Sleeping Bear Sand Dunes and the beautiful and mysterious loon, the "Legends" series includes *The Legend of the Teddy Bear.* Author Frank Murphy told the story of the creation of the first Teddy bears in honor of Theodore "Teddy" Roosevelt's refusal to shoot a captive bear. *Gazette* writer Linda DuVal praised both text and artwork: "Rich illustrations make this book a delight to look at, as well as read."

From 1985 to 1998 van Frankenhuyzen and his wife, Robbyn, became the special friends of a wild owl, which they named Jackson, who would go so far as to protectively fly the van Frankenhuyzen children to their school bus stop. Such close contact with Jackson gave

van Frankenhuyzen plenty of time to study and draw the beautiful bird. Although Robbyn originally wrote a chapter book about the various hurt animals they had rehabilitated on their farm, Sleeping Bear Press wanted a picture book about the owl. *Adopted by an Owl: The True Story of Jackson, the Owl* was the result.

Van Frankenhuyzen told *SATA:* "I love illustrating children's books—knowing that your paintings are being enjoyed by thousands of kids is a very good feeling. I hope I do this for years to come. Every new story I work on is a new challenge."

Biographical and Critical Sources

PERIODICALS

Gazette (Colorado Springs, CO), Linda DuVal, December 24, 2000, review of *The Legend of the Teddy Bear,* p. T&B5.

Grand Rapids Press (Grand Rapids, MI), April 18, 2001, Kym Reinstadler, "Picture This: Artist Loses Coveted Job, The Result Is a Storied Career," p. L1.

OTHER

Gijsbert van Frankenhuyzen Web Site, http://www.my.voyager.net/~robbyn/pages/ (December 11, 2001).

*   *   *

Van LEEUWEN, Jean 1937-

Personal

Surname pronounced "Van *Loo*-en"; born December 26, 1937, in Glen Ridge, NJ; daughter of Cornelius (a clergyman) and Dorothy (a teacher; maiden name, Charlton) Van Leeuwen; married Bruce David Gavril (a digital computer systems designer), July 7, 1968; children: David Andrew, Elizabeth Eva. *Education:* Syracuse University, B.A., 1959. *Hobbies and other interests:* Gardening, reading, antiques, music.

Addresses

Home—7 Colony Row, Chappaqua, NY 10514.

Career

Began career working for *TV Guide;* Random House, Inc., New York, NY, began as assistant editor, became associate editor of juvenile books, 1963-68; Viking Press, Inc., New York, NY, associate editor of juvenile books, 1968-70; Dial Press, New York, NY, senior editor of juvenile books, 1971-73; currently full-time writer.

Awards, Honors

New Jersey Institute of Technology award, 1972, for *I Was a 98-Pound Duckling;* Art Books for Children award, 1974, for adaptation of Hans Christian Andersen's *The Emperor's New Clothes;* New Jersey Institute of Technology award, 1975 and 1976, for *Too Hot for*

Ice Cream; Ethical Culture School award, 1975, William Allen White award, 1978, and South Carolina Children's Book award, 1979, all for *The Great Christmas Kidnapping Caper; Seems Like This Road Goes on Forever* was named one of the best books of 1979, American Library Association (ALA), Young Adult Services Division; Massachusetts Honor Book Award, 1981, for *The Great Cheese Conspiracy;* Pick of the Lists selection, American Booksellers Association, and Parents' Choice Remarkable Books for Literature selection, both for *The Great Rescue Operation;* International Reading Association Teachers' Choice selection, Pick of the Lists selection, American Booksellers Association, and Best in Kids' Entertainment selection, *Parents'* magazine, all for *Going West.*

More Tales of Oliver Pig, Amanda Pig and Her Big Brother Oliver, Tales of Amanda Pig, and *More Tales of Amanda Pig* all won the *Booklist* Children's Editors' Choice award; *More Tales of Oliver Pig, Amanda Pig and Her Big Brother Oliver,* and *More Tales of Amanda Pig* were noted on the American Booksellers Association Pick of the Lists; *Amanda Pig and Her Big Brother Oliver, Benjy and the Power of Zingies,* and *Benjy in Business* were all listed as Child Study Association Children's Books of the Year; *Oliver, Amanda, and Grandmother Pig* and *Going West* were listed in New York Public Library: 100 Titles for Reading and Sharing; *Oliver, Amanda, and Grandmother Pig* and *Tales of Amanda Pig* received the Library of Congress Books of the Year award; *More Tales of Oliver Pig, Amanda Pig and Her Big Brother Oliver,* and *Tales of Amanda Pig* have all been named ALA Notable Books.

Writings

(Editor) *A Time of Growing,* Random House (New York, NY), 1967.

Timothy's Flower, illustrated by Moneta Barnett, Random House (New York, NY), 1967.

One Day in Summer, illustrated by Richard Fish, Random House (New York, NY), 1969.

The Great Cheese Conspiracy, Random House (New York, NY), 1969.

(Adaptor) Hans Christian Andersen, *The Emperor's New Clothes,* illustrated by Jack Delano and Irene Delano, Random House (New York, NY), 1971.

I Was a 98-Pound Duckling, Dial (New York, NY), 1972.

Too Hot for Ice Cream, illustrated by Martha Alexander, Dial (New York, NY), 1974.

The Great Christmas Kidnapping Caper, illustrated by Steven Kellogg, Dial (New York, NY), 1975.

Seems Like This Road Goes on Forever, Dial (New York, NY), 1979.

Tales of Oliver Pig, illustrated by Arnold Lobel, Dial (New York, NY), 1979.

More Tales of Oliver Pig, illustrated by Arnold Lobel, Dial (New York, NY), 1981.

The Great Rescue Operation, illustrated by Margot Apple, Dial (New York, NY), 1982.

Amanda Pig and Her Big Brother Oliver, illustrated by Ann Schweninger, Dial (New York, NY), 1982.

Jean Van Leeuwen

Benjy and the Power of Zingies, illustrated by Margot Apple, Dial (New York, NY), 1982.

Benjy in Business, illustrated by Margot Apple, Dial (New York, NY), 1983.

Tales of Amanda Pig, illustrated by Ann Schweninger, Dial (New York, NY), 1983.

Benjy the Football Hero, illustrated by Gail Owens, Dial (New York, NY), 1985.

More Tales of Amanda Pig, illustrated by Ann Schweninger, Dial (New York, NY), 1985.

Oliver, Amanda, and Grandmother Pig, illustrated by Ann Schweninger, Dial (New York, NY), 1987.

Dear Mom, You're Ruining My Life, Dial (New York, NY), 1989.

Oliver and Amanda's Christmas, illustrated by Ann Schweninger, Dial (New York, NY), 1989.

Oliver Pig at School, illustrated by Ann Schweninger, Dial (New York, NY), 1990.

Amanda Pig on Her Own, illustrated by Ann Schweninger, Dial (New York, NY), 1991.

Going West, illustrated by Thomas B. Allen, Dial (New York, NY), 1991.

The Great Summer Camp Catastrophe, illustrated by Diane deGroat, Dial (New York, NY), 1992.

Oliver and Amanda's Halloween, illustrated by Ann Schweninger, Dial (New York, NY), 1992.

Emma Bean, illustrated by Juan Wijngaard, Dial (New York, NY), 1993.

Two Girls in Sister Dresses, illustrated by Linda Benson, Dial (New York, NY), 1994.

Bound for Oregon, Dial (New York, NY), 1994.

Across the Wide Dark Sea, illustrated by Thomas B. Allen, Dial (New York, NY), 1995.

Oliver and Amanda and the Big Snow, illustrated by Ann Schweninger, Dial (New York, NY), 1995.

Blue Sky, Butterfly, Dial (New York, NY), 1996.

Amanda Pig, School Girl, Dial (New York, NY), 1997.

A Fourth of July on the Plains, illustrated by Henri Sorensen, Dial (New York, NY), 1997.

Touch the Sky Summer, illustrated by Dan Andreasen, Dial (New York, NY), 1997.

Nothing Here But Trees, illustrated by Phil Boatwright, Dial (New York, NY), 1998.

Growing Ideas (biography), photographs by David Gavril, Richard C. Owen (Katonah, NY), 1998.

The Tickle Stories, illustrated by Mary Whyte, Dial (New York, NY), 1998.

Amanda Pig and Her Best Friend Lollipop, illustrated by Ann Schweninger, Penguin Putnam (New York, NY), 1998.

Hannah of Fairfield, illustrated by Donna Diamond, Dial (New York, NY), 1999.

Hannah's Helping Hands, illustrated by Donna Diamond, Phyllis Fogelman Books (New York, NY), 1999.

The Strange Adventures of Blue Dog, illustrated by Marco Ventura, Dial (New York, NY), 1999.

Hannah's Winter of Hope, illustrated by Donna Diamond, Phyllis Fogelman Books (New York, NY), 2000.

Oliver and Albert, Friends Forever, illustrated by Ann Schweninger, Phyllis Fogelman Books (New York, NY), 2000.

Sorry, illustrated by Brad Sneed, Phyllis Fogelman Books (New York, NY), 2001.

"Wait for Me!" Said Maggie McGee, illustrated by Jacqueline Rogers, Phyllis Fogelman Books (New York, NY), 2001.

Lucy Was There. . . , Phyllis Fogelman Books (New York, NY), 2002.

The Amazing Air Balloon, illustrated by Marco Ventura, Phyllis Fogelman Books (New York, NY), 2003.

When the White Man Came to Our Shores, illustrated by James Bernardin, Phyllis Fogelman Books (New York, NY), 2003.

Amanda Pig and the Awful, Scary Monster, illustrated by Ann Schweninger, Phyllis Fogelman Books (New York, NY), 2003.

The Great Googlestein Museum Mystery, illustrated by R. W. Alley, Phyllis Fogelman Books (New York, NY), 2003.

Sidelights

Jean Van Leeuwen is the award-winning author of over fifty books for young readers. Equally adept and entertaining in picture books as she is in chapter books and novels for middle graders and young adults, Van Leeuwen has charmed young readers for over three decades. Her stories about the jovial pig siblings, Oliver and Amanda, number in the double digits and have drawn praise from fans and critics alike. Other books that have survived over time include *The Great Cheese Conspiracy,* featuring a trio of meddlesome mice, and its several sequels. But Van Leeuwen does not entertain only with animal protagonists. Characters in the "Benjy" stories, and in *I Was a 98-Pound Duckling, Too Hot for Ice Cream, Dear Mom, You're Ruining My Life,* and *Blue Sky, Butterfly* are only too real and deal with contemporary issues in both humorous and heart-wrenching ways. This prolific and versatile writer has also mined a historical vein in her fiction, with books such as *Going West* and *Bound for Oregon,* both set during pioneering days in America. And with the "Pioneer Daughters" series of novels, Van Leeuwen takes audiences back to the Revolutionary War in a trio of novels that explores life in the eighteenth-century through the adventures of young Hannah.

Van Leeuwen had a long and close relationship with the printed word before she became a writer. "I had a book-filled childhood," Van Leeuwen wrote in *Something about the Author Autobiography Series (SAAS).* "It was not that my family was a particularly literary one. I was just irresistibly attracted to books. Any time, anywhere, I was likely to be found with a book in my hand. I read riding in the car, even though it made me dizzy. I read when the family went visiting, even though my mother said it was rude. I read late at night under the covers, by flashlight, when I was supposed to be asleep. And I would read almost anything, just as long as it had a story. What I liked best of all was to stretch out on my bed with a book, so far lost inside some other world that when I heard my mother's voice, summoning me to dinner, I would look around and blink, wondering where I was."

Van Leeuwen recalled her earliest childhood "as a secure, carefree time." The oldest of three children, she was raised in Rutherford, New Jersey, where her father was the minister of the Congregational church. The author noted the main sources of any early unhappiness as stemming from her own shyness, especially when compared to her younger sister, "who not only had an outgoing personality, but was also pretty and annoyingly good all the time," and from the high expectations placed on her as a minister's daughter. These themes have appeared in Van Leeuwen's books for children. The feelings associated with competing with a younger sibling are treated in a lighthearted fashion in Van Leeuwen's book *Two Girls in Sister Dresses,* and she addresses an adolescent girl's extreme reaction to repressive parenting by a minister-father in the somber young adult novel, *Seems Like This Road Goes on Forever.*

After a tomboyish childhood and an adolescence spent "trying to be popular," Van Leeuwen entered Syracuse University, graduating with a bachelor's degree in journalism. A first job at *TV Guide,* while not the glamorous career she had envisioned at a women's magazine, inspired a move to New York City and gave her a start in publishing that eventually led to work as a children's book editor. Van Leeuwen rediscovered her childhood ambition to write while working as an editor and in 1967 joyfully saw the publication of her first book, *Timothy's Flower.*

Timothy's Flower, "based on a small boy whom I had observed in my New York City neighborhood," Van Leeuwen recalled in her *SAAS* essay, was warmly received by critics. A reviewer for the *Bulletin of the Center for Children's Books* credited the "simple, unpretentious style" of the prose for the book's successful rendering of how a flower improves the life of a poor boy. Van Leeuwen's early works also include *A Time of Growing,* an anthology of fictional reminiscences of adolescence by established authors, which she edited, and the picture book *One Day in Summer,* described by a *Bulletin of the Center for Children's Books* critic as a "quiet" story with possibly limited appeal due to the "static quality" of the plot.

During this time Van Leeuwen married Bruce Gavril, a computer systems designer who became her "technical consultant, a role which he has continued to play admirably through the years," as she said in her *SAAS* essay. Her husband was also the inspiration for the character Raymond in *The Great Cheese Conspiracy* and its sequels. Van Leeuwen describes Raymond as the one "with brains": "a thinker, problem solver, and saver of seemingly useless objects—just like Bruce." *The Great Cheese Conspiracy* features three mice—Raymond, Marvin, the brave but foolhardy leader of the gang, and Fats, whose laziness and passion for food often land him and his friends in trouble—in a story about the trio's efforts to rob a cheese store. Van Leeuwen's mouse books have typically received praise from critics. For example, one *Bulletin of the Center for Children's Books* reviewer, writing about *The Great Rescue Operation,* noted that "[Marvin, Raymond, and Fats] are distinct—if exaggerated—personalities, the style is colorful and breezy, the plot—deliberately unrestrained—is nicely structured and paced."

In the first sequel to *The Great Cheese Conspiracy, The Great Christmas Kidnapping Caper,* the three mice move into a dollhouse in Macy's department store, where they are befriended by Mr. Dunderhoff, who annually plays Santa Claus. When Mr. Dunderhoff is abducted by the store's greedy competitor, the mice use all their ingenuity to rescue him. A critic described the result as "zestful and surprising" in *Publishers Weekly;* a *Bulletin of the Center for Children's Books* reviewer commented that the "story has a happy blend of humor in dialogue, Christmas setting, local color, and silly situations." The trio are put to the test again in *The Great Rescue Operation,* in which Marvin and Raymond wake up one day to find that Fats has disappeared along with the doll carriage in which he likes to nap. The friends' attempts to rescue Fats from what they fear is a horrible fate at the hands of a scientist lead to "slapstick humor and nonstop action," according to Caroline S. Parr in the *School Library Journal.* Doris Orgel similarly described the story in her *New York Times Book Review* article as a "funny, lively and appealing book." The three mice again leave Macy's in *The Great Summer*

Camp Catastrophe, in which they are inadvertently packed off with a box of cookies to summer camp in Vermont. "What will grab readers," observed Jacqueline Rose in the *School Library Journal,* "is the action-packed plot, with its series of near disasters." And in *The Great Googlestein Museum Mystery,* the trio of mice once again depart their home at Macy's department store and spend a fine time at the Guggenheim Museum.

In the early years of her marriage to Gavril, Van Leeuwen published her first young adult novel, *I Was a 98-Pound Duckling,* a comical account of a girl's thirteenth summer, when she and her best friend are consumed with thoughts of boys and dates and following the beauty regimen outlined in a teen magazine. Although several reviewers noted the lack of originality in the story's plot, a *Bulletin of the Center for Children's Books* contributor remarked: "Kathy tells her story ... with such wry humor and candor that it gives a fresh vitality to a familiar pattern." In a *Publishers Weekly* review, a contributor declared: "This is a witty and charming book."

In the early 1970s Van Leeuwen left publishing to care for her two small children but was determined to continue to write. Her first effort, *Too Hot for Ice Cream,* dubbed by a *Publishers Weekly* critic as "a curiously charming book," tells the story of the everyday adventures of two sisters who spend a hot day in a city park when their father cannot take them to the beach. A more far-reaching consequence of Van Leeuwen's decision to stay home to raise her children is the series of first-reader books filled with stories about Oliver and Amanda Pig, based on her experiences with her own children.

Tales of Oliver Pig, and the subsequent books in this series, fifteen strong and growing, have been warmly received for their gentle humor and loving portrayal of the everyday trials and joys of living with small children. Mary Gordon described the relationship between Amanda and Oliver Pig, which is at the center of each of the books in this series, in the *New York Times Book Review:* "The younger Pigs are occasionally perfectly dreadful to each other. But remember, they are siblings, and one of the great values of these books is their ability to dramatize the ridiculous and trivial and sickeningly frequent fights that siblings engage in every day of their lives, and yet suggest the siblings' essential fondness for each other, their dependency, their mutual good will."

More Tales of Oliver Pig, the first sequel to Van Leeuwen's successful *Tales of Oliver Pig,* features stories about Oliver's first efforts at gardening, how he adjusts to being cared for by his grandmother, and his attempts to stall at bed-time. A *Bulletin of the Center for Children's Books* critic singled out the "gentle humor in the simple, fluent writing style" for praise in its review of this work. In response to her daughter's request, Van Leeuwen's next work in this series shifted the focus away from Oliver toward his younger sister, Amanda. The stories in *Amanda Pig and Her Big Brother Oliver* highlight Amanda's frustrations at being unable to do some of the things her big brother can do and her parents' sympathetic responses. "Never cloying, the humor is genuine, the incidents right on the younger-sibling mark," remarked a *School Library Journal* reviewer.

Critics noted that Amanda is more than an envious younger sister in *Tales of Amanda Pig,* the next work in this series. The stories in this volume find her refusing to eat a fried egg, scaring the clock-monster in the front hall with the help of her father, and switching roles with her sleepy mother at bed-time. Though a reviewer in *School Library Journal* found "the domestic drama . . . a bit dull this time out," a contributor to *Kirkus Reviews* praised "the same irreproachable, unforced child psychology, and if anything more sly by-play" in this installment. Amanda "maintains her pluck, imagination and vulnerability," according to a *School Library Journal* critic, in *More Tales of Amanda Pig,* in which she plays house with her brother, becomes jealous of visiting cousins, and gives her father her favorite toy for his birthday. *Horn Book* reviewer Karen Jameyson found the story to be as "comfortable as an easy chair, as warm and filling as a cup of cocoa."

In *Oliver, Amanda, and Grandmother Pig,* the Pig family enjoys a week-long visit by Grandmother Pig, who cannot do everything younger adults can but can tell stories and give good hugs. This was followed by *Oliver and Amanda's Christmas,* in which the two young pigs learn to keep Christmas secrets, bake cookies, and select the perfect Christmas tree. Reviewers compared this work favorably with earlier books in the series; Betsy Hearne, writing in *Bulletin of the Center for Children's Books,* described it to be "as comfortable as tradition."

Oliver and Amanda are starting to grow up in the next two works in this series. In *Oliver Pig at School,* Oliver experiences his first day of kindergarten, befriending a scary classmate and making and eating a necklace in art class. Martha V. Parravano praised "the author's understanding of childhood experiences" in her review in *Horn Book.* In *Amanda Pig on Her Own,* Amanda learns to enjoy the adventures she can have when her big brother is away at school. Reviewing the work in *Bulletin of the Center for Children's Books,* Ruth Ann Smith particularly enjoyed Van Leeuwen's ability to "combine gentle humor with ingenuous dialogue."

Van Leeuwen has continued her easy-reader series with seasonal tales such as *Oliver and Amanda's Halloween* and *Oliver and Amanda and the Big Snow.* In the former title, the little pigs make a jack-o'-lantern and help prepare doughnuts as they get ready for Halloween. Brother and sister have to learn to compromise over the pumpkin's expression in "this warmhearted installment," as a critic described the book in *Publishers Weekly.* In *Oliver and Amanda and the Big Snow,* the porcine siblings go out to play after a snow storm and Amanda proves herself adept at snow games. "The warm interactions among family members continue to make

these gentle stories a delight for early readers," wrote Hanna B. Zeiger in a *Horn Book* review. *Booklist*'s Carolyn Phelan also noted the "gentle humor" in this tale. Susan Dove Lempke, reviewing the same title in *Bulletin of the Center for Children's Books,* noted that though the series had, at the time, been going strong for sixteen years, the "family adventures are as fresh and funny as ever." Lempke concluded that "young readers will wish they could bundle up and join Oliver and Amanda outside." And Gale W. Sherman minced no words in her *School Library Journal* review: "An outstanding selection for beginning-to-read collections."

Oliver got his first day in school and so does Amanda in *Amanda Pig, Schoolgirl,* and it is every bit as fantastic as she always hoped it would be. Amanda even meets a new friend whom she dubs Lollipop. *Horn Book*'s Parravano praised this title for its "thorough understanding of the emotions and situations of childhood," while *School Library Journal*'s Virginia Opocensky felt that fans of the series "will applaud this addition to the tales of Oliver and Amanda." Friendship is celebrated in two further titles in the series, *Amanda Pig and Her Best Friend Lollipop* and *Oliver and Albert, Friends Forever.* In the former title, Amanda continues her progress out into a wider world than family. She and her new friend have good times together at each other's houses and also have their first sleepover. "Amanda is as engaging a character as ever," noted *Horn Book*'s Parravano, and *Booklist*'s Carolyn Phelan noted that this "pleasant entry" in the series is written with "simplicity and affection." Oliver makes friends with the new boy in school in *Oliver and Albert, Friends Forever,* playing kickball and collecting bugs. Albert is not an easy friend at first, bookish and ignorant of the rules of the easiest games, but Oliver finds he is willing to learn and takes him under his wing. Leslie S. Hilverding, reviewing the title in *School Library Journal,* felt that the tale provides a "sweet and simple beginning chapter book about friendship." Shelle Rosenfeld, writing in *Booklist,* also noted the theme of friendship, writing that this tale "illustrates the importance of appreciating and respecting differences." Rosenfeld concluded that *Oliver and Albert, Friends Forever* is an "entertaining story."

Van Leeuwen has also written several chapter books for slightly older readers, featuring Benjy, a third-grade boy critics have described as a lovable academic and athletic underachiever. A reviewer commented in *Horn Book,* "Like Henry Huggins, Ellen Tebbits, and Ramona, Benjy is an engaging personality—one not quickly forgotten." In *Benjy and the Power of Zingies,* Benjy decides his only chance against the school bully who picks on him is to build up his body by eating Zingies breakfast cereal. A *Bulletin of the Center for Children's Books* critic praised the book's "light-hearted" and "often funny" treatment of life in the third grade. This was followed by *Benjy in Business,* in which Benjy attempts to earn enough money to buy a special baseball mitt he hopes will improve his game. "Benjy displays a sturdy tenacity that makes his extended effort credible and enjoyable," commented Carolyn Noah in the *School Library Journal.* Ilene Cooper remarked in *Booklist* that some of the action in the third work in this series, *Benjy the Football Hero,* may be lost on readers not familiar with the rules of the game at the book's center, but the critic added "this has the same good humor and engaging characters of the other Benjy books." About the series as a whole, Robert E. Unsworth remarked in *School Library Journal* that "Van Leeuwen has a fine ability to see the humor in the tribulations of nine year olds and she writes about them with understanding."

Although she is best known for her picture books and simple stories for first readers, Van Leeuwen noted in her *SAAS* essay that she has always enjoyed writing for older children and adolescents. One of her first attempts for this age group, *Seems Like This Road Goes on Forever,* draws on the author's understanding of the kinds of expectations and pressures put on children of members of the clergy. Mary Alice, the daughter of an overly strict minister, retraces with the help of a psychologist the steps that brought her to a hospital bed with a broken leg, unable to communicate or think clearly about her recent past. Although a reviewer in *Bulletin of the Center for Children's Books* found this a "slow-paced" if "convincing account of an emotional breakdown," a *New York Times Book Review* contributor concluded that it "is finely written, though cheerless— which it must be, I suppose, in order to be told properly." In a more lighthearted vein, *Dear Mom, You're Ruining My Life* is a novel for upper elementary school grades inspired by Van Leeuwen's daughter, Elizabeth. "As a sixth grader," the author wrote in her *SAAS* essay, "she was acutely embarrassed by everything about her family: our rusty old car, her father who actually insisted on *talking* to her friends, and especially me." A critic in *Kirkus Reviews* called the resulting portrait of life in the sixth grade "a genuinely funny look at a roller-coaster year."

Writing for middle graders, Van Leeuwen tells the story of an eleven-year-old trying to cope with her parents' separation in her 1996 novel, *Blue Sky, Butterfly.* Young Twig feels isolated from both her mom and her older brother after her father leaves, and they all try and cope with the changed circumstances in their lives. Finally, through the intervention of a grandmother and the healing influences of a garden, she is able to deal with her life. Reviewing the novel in *Horn Book Guide,* Patricia Riley called attention to Van Leeuwen's "well-drawn, interesting characters," and *Booklist*'s Susan Dove Lempke noted that Van Leeuwen "evokes the desolate period immediately following parental breakup" with "aching sharpness."

Returning to the picture book format, Van Leeuwen continues to provide warm, wholesome stories for young readers, dealing with family relations and friendship, among other themes. *Touch the Sky Summer* is narrated by Luke and tells of a special vacation taken with his family by the lake. "Children who have visited lakeside cabins will enjoy the vicarious experience, related in a natural-sounding text," wrote Phelan in a *Booklist* review. *School Library Journal*'s Opocensky also praised this story of a "happy family and an idyllic

setting," calling it a "warm, wonderful read." A grandfather puts his three grandchildren to bed with tall tales from his childhood on the farm in *The Tickle Stories,* a book "perfect for bedtime stalling," commented Linda Perkins in a *Booklist* review. In *The Strange Adventures of Blue Dog,* a small wooden toy dog comes to life for a time and lives some very dog-like adventures.

Family relations are the subject of two further picture book titles from 2001. In *Sorry,* two brothers who cannot apologize to each other over a bowl of oatmeal manage to turn this into a feud that lasts generations. Finally, through the intercession of two great-grandchildren, the chasm between families is bridged with the word "sorry" when these children are on the verge of fighting over an apple. "Familiar themes of feuding families and the power of a simple apology dominate this story," wrote Susan L. Rogers in a *School Library Journal* review. Rogers went on to note that this "folkloric comic satire with overtones of universal truths should appeal to a wide range of readers and listeners." Further positive remarks came from a *Publishers Weekly* reviewer who commented that "regret permeates this unforgiving story of a needless feud, rendered in poignant detail." And combining these two sentiments, *Booklist*'s Rosenfeld concluded, "Humorous yet poignant, the story shows how a single word can make all the difference."

Family dynamics of a less serious sort are at the center of *"Wait for Me!" Said Maggie McGee,* in which the youngest of eight children is left out of the games of her older siblings. Too young to ride a tricycle or even get to the cookie jar, Maggie longs for the day when she can go to school. Once she does, she manages to help her older brother remember his lines in the school play and as a result becomes one of the gang. "Maggie McGee is a spunky, appealing role model for the youngest among us," remarked Rosalyn Pierini in a *School Library Journal* review. And *Booklist*'s Gillian Engberg had more laudatory words for the book, noting that with "gentle, poignant humor, Van Leeuwen tells a charming, straightforward story most younger siblings can relate to."

Van Leeuwen credits her advancing age with her increased interest in the past. In her *SAAS* essay she states: "In my writing . . . I find that I am starting to look backward. I have always been fascinated by history, not the history of big events and dates that I was taught in school, but of people and how they lived. I have written recently about my own childhood. I have ideas of writing about my family history, and perhaps, if I can find the right way to do it, about our country's history." Van Leeuwen's reminiscence of her childhood, *Two Girls in Sister Dresses,* evokes the author's feelings about her younger sister. The book was highly praised for its realistic yet sensitive portrayal of the relationship between sisters. Phelan noted in her review in *Booklist* that *Two Girls in Sister Dresses* is written with Van Leeuwen's "accustomed simplicity and finesse." Also memorable for its nostalgic atmosphere is *Emma Bean,* which details the life of a homemade stuffed rabbit, a gift to Molly at birth from her grandmother. Critics noted similarities between *Emma Bean* and the children's classic, *The Velveteen Rabbit,* but Annie Ayres argued in her *Booklist* review that Van Leeuwen's "warmly sentimental book" is for those children not yet ready for the "more sophisticated and emotionally weighty themes" of the latter title.

Van Leeuwen has also produced historical books for young readers: *Going West,* a fictional journal of seven-year-old Hannah as she and her family travel west by wagon in the days of the pioneers, and *Bound for Oregon,* based on the real-life journey of Mary Ellen Todd and her family on the Oregon trail in the 1850s. Although more serious than many of the works for which she is best known, these books have been praised for the author's signature emphasis on a warm and supportive family atmosphere. A *Publishers Weekly* critic called *Going West* a "haunting evocation of times past," and further remarked, "Into a gentle text brimming with family warmth and love, Van Leeuwen ... packs a wealth of emotional moments." In *Bound for Oregon,* Van Leeuwen presents another pioneer tale, narrated by nine-year-old Mary Ellen. A description primarily of life on the trail, the "concrete details ... will draw readers," noted *Booklist*'s Phelan, who also felt that the book was a "fine introduction" to such a life. A reviewer for *Publishers Weekly* thought that the "contrast between the tenderness of Mary Ellen's perceptions and the hardships of the frontier is deeply moving," while *Horn Book*'s Ellen Fader praised the "especially vivid and well-rounded" characters and dubbed the book "inspiring reading."

More novel-length historical fiction is served up in the trilogy of books about Hannah Perley and her family during the Revolutionary War in Fairfield, Connecticut. In the initial volume, *Hannah of Fairfield,* the nine-year-old protagonist faces the approach of war, and Hannah's older brother Ben is eager to join General Washington's army. But the focus in this first novel is more on the domestic side of life than on the battlefield, and Hannah rails against having to do "girl's" work all the time when she would rather be working with the animals. *Booklist*'s Hazel Rochman felt that this "simply written docu-novel will give middle-grade readers a strong sense of what it was like to be a young girl then." Similarly, a critic for *Kirkus Reviews* wrote that Hannah's story "will entertain and inspire anyone who is interested in the past." In *Hannah's Helping Hands,* the young girl and her family try to keep a sense of normalcy as the war goes on all around them. Details of farming life are interspersed in the narrative as are bits of war history, supplied by brother Ben. Hannah is instrumental in saving her family's farm animals when the British attack, though their home and many others are burned to the ground. "Van Leeuwen has provided a refreshing approach to the period that is accessible to reluctant readers," noted Cheryl Cufari in a *School Library Journal* review of this second novel in the series. And with *Hannah's Winter of Hope,* the family is living in the father's clock shop until their home can be rebuilt. The long cold winter of 1799-80 comes to life in this novel, with Ben captured by the English. However, toward the end of the winter he is finally released and returns home. "Van Leeuwen is brilliant at showing the effects of war through the prism of one family's life," wrote Connie Fletcher in a *Booklist* review of the final novel in the trilogy.

History for a younger audience also finds its way into Van Leeuwen's picture books. *Across the Wide Dark Sea* tells of life on the *Mayflower* as it makes its way across the Atlantic to the New World. Storms and suffering make the nine-week trip harrowing, and upon arrival there is a harsh winter and Indians to contend with. *Booklist*'s Phelan praised Van Leeuwen for "telling a particular story that reflects the broader immigrant experience." *A Fourth of July on the Plains* is another of Van Leeuwen's historical tales based on real accounts, this one from a diary account of a celebration on the Oregon Trail in 1852. Jesse is too young to go hunting with the men and the women do not need his help sewing a flag for the Fourth of July, so he and other young boys scrape together whistles and bells and make a parade for the adults as a surprise. Rochman, writing in *Booklist,* observed that this story "combines a child's voice and viewpoint with handsome paintings that capture the pioneer experience." A reviewer for *Publishers Weekly* voiced similar opinions, noting that Van Leeuwen's tale provides "a likeably informal child's view of pioneer life, as well as an enthusiastic appreciation for the rituals, both solemn and boisterous, of the Fourth." *Nothing Here But Trees* once again gives insight to the pioneer experience through the eyes of a young narrator. The setting is Ohio in the early nineteenth century and a boy and his brother help Pa clear the land, build fences, plant corn, and harvest their crop. "This is close to Laura Ingalls Wilder country," commented *Booklist*'s Rochman, and a contributor for *Kirkus Reviews* called the picture book "Engaging, entertaining, unsentimental."

That same three-word description could be used to describe much of Van Leeuwen's work for young readers. Reviewers have consistently praised the warm yet realistic celebrations of family life found in her books, emphasizing her gentle humor and insightful portrayal of common childhood experiences. For example, in a review of *Oliver, Amanda, and Grandmother Pig,* Karen Jameyson concluded in *Horn Book:* "With perceptiveness and gentle humor Jean Van Leeuwen shapes even the most mundane subjects into pleasing, warm tales." Such warm tales are Van Leeuwen's staple product; they are what readers have come to expect when they pick up one of her numerous titles.

Biographical and Critical Sources

BOOKS

Van Leeuwen, Jean, essay in *Something about the Author Autobiography Series,* Volume 8, Gale (Detroit, MI), 1989, pp. 317-330.
Ward, Martha E., et al, *Authors of Books for Young People,* 3rd edition, Scarecrow Press (Metuchen, NJ), 1990.

PERIODICALS

Booklist, September 1, 1985, Ilene Cooper, review of *Benjy the Football Hero,* p. 72; July, 1993, Annie Ayres, review of *Emma Bean,* p. 1977; May 1, 1992, p. 1603; April 1, 1994, Carolyn Phelan, review of *Two Girls in Sister Dresses,* p. 1453; October 1, 1994, Carolyn Phelan, review of *Bound for Oregon,* p. 329; September 15, 1995, Carolyn Phelan, review of *Across the Wide Sea,* p. 161; January 1, 1996, Carolyn Phelan, review of *Oliver and Amanda and the Big Snow,* p. 850; June 1, 1996, Susan Dove Lempke, review of *Blue Sky, Butterfly,* p. 1724; May 15, 1997, Hazel Rochman, review of *A Fourth of July on the Plains,* p. 1582; June 1, 1997, Carolyn Phelan, review of *Touch the Sky Summer,* p. 1723; May 1, 1998, Linda Perkins, review of *The Tickle Stories,* p. 1524; July, 1998, Carolyn Phelan, review of *Amanda Pig and Her Best Friend Lollipop,* p. 1892; September 1, 1998, Hazel Rochman, review of *Nothing Here but Trees,* p. 129; March 1, 1999, Hazel Rochman, review of *Hannah of Fairfield,* p. 1215; August, 2000, Connie Fletcher, review of *Hannah's Winter of Hope,* p. 2142; December 1, 2000, Shelle Rosenfeld, review of *Oliver and Albert, Friends Forever,* p. 727; May 15, 2001, Gillian Engberg, review of *"Wait for Me!" Said Maggie McGee,* p. 1761; June 1, 2001, Shelle Rosenfeld, review of *Sorry,* p. 1896.

Bulletin of the Center for Children's Books, February, 1968, p. 103; June, 1968, review of *Timothy's Flower,* p. 166; July, 1969, review of *One Day in Summer,* p. 184; September, 1973, review of *I Was a 98-Pound Duckling,* p. 19; February, 1975, p. 100; November, 1975, review of *The Great Christmas Kidnapping Caper;* October, 1979, review of *Seems Like This Road Goes on Forever;* July, 1981, review of *More Tales of Oliver Pig,* p. 221; July-August, 1982; review of *The Great Rescue Operation;* March, 1983, review of *Benjy and the Power of Zingies;* January, 1986, p. 98; May, 1989, pp. 238-239; October, 1989, Betsy Hearne, review of *Oliver and Amanda's Christmas,* p. 47; September, 1990, p. 18; March, 1991, Ruth Ann Smith, review of *Amanda Pig on Her Own,* pp. 180-181; November, 1994, p. 107; December, 1995, Susan Dove Lempke, review of *Oliver and Amanda and the Big Snow,* p. 143.

Horn Book, February, 1975; December, 1979, p. 660; August, 1981, p. 419; June, 1982, p. 294; December, 1982, pp. 646-647; April, 1983, review of *Benjy and the Power of Zingies,* pp. 168-169; December, 1983, p. 713; February, 1984, pp. 48-49; March-April, 1986, Karen Jameyson, review of *More Tales of Amanda Pig,* pp. 199-200; September, 1987, Karen Jameyson, review of *Oliver, Amanda, and Grandmother Pig,* pp. 606-607; November, 1989, p. 754; September-October, 1990, Martha V. Parravano, review of *Oliver Pig at School,* p. 599; March-April, 1992, p. 199; July-August, 1994, pp. 447-448; March-April, 1995, Ellen Fader, review of *Bound for Oregon,* p. 197; September-October, 1995, Hanna B. Zeiger, review of *Oliver and Amanda and the Big Snow,* p. 628; May-June, 1997, Martha V. Parravano, review of *Amanda Pig, Schoolgirl,* p. 329; July-August, 1998, Martha V.

Parravano, review of *Amanda Pig and Her Best Friend Lollipop,* pp. 499-500; September-October, 2000, p. 584.

Horn Book Guide, spring, 1995, p. 85; fall, 1996, Patricia Riley, review of *Blue Sky, Butterfly,* p. 298; fall, 1996, p. 283; fall, 1998, p. 309; spring, 1999, p. 60; fall, 1999, p. 270.

Kirkus Reviews, October 1, 1967, p. 1202; April 15, 1969, p. 436; October 1, 1972, p. 1155; September 1, 1982, p. 997; December 1, 1982, p. 1293; September 1, 1983, review of *Tales of Amanda Pig;* May 15, 1989, review of *Dear Mom, You're Ruining My Life,* p. 772; June 1, 1992, p. 724; August 1, 1993, p. 1008; April 15, 1996, pp. 608-609; April 15, 1998, p. 588; September 1, 1998, review of *Nothing Here But Trees,* p. 1294; January 1, 1999, review of *Hannah of Fairfield,* p. 73; May 1, 1999, p. 729.

New York Times Book Review, November 5, 1967; November 30, 1975, p. 26; June 24, 1979; November 11, 1979, review of *Seems Like This Road Goes on Forever;* May 3, 1981; April 25, 1982, Doris Orgel, "Mice in Macy's"; November 13, 1983; May 19, 1985; November 10, 1985, Mary Gordon, "Pig Tales"; January 10, 1988, p. 36.

Publishers Weekly, December 4, 1967, p. 44; September 25, 1972, review of *I Was a 98-Pound Duckling;* October 7, 1974, review of *Too Hot for Ice Cream,* p. 63; September 8, 1975, review of *The Great Christmas Kidnapping Caper;* August 14, 1987, p. 107; December 13, 1991, review of *Going West,* p. 55; September 2, 1992, review of *Oliver and Amanda's Halloween,* p. 59; August 2, 1993, p. 79; April 25, 1994, p. 78; September 5, 1994, review of *Bound for Oregon,* p. 112; May 19, 1997, review of *A Fourth of July on the Plains,* pp. 75-76; June 7, 1999, p. 82; July 27, 1999, p. 93; May 21, 2001, review of *Sorry,* p. 107.

School Library Journal, October, 1975, p. 78; May, 1979, p. 76; December, 1979, p. 93; May, 1981, p. 80; August, 1982, Caroline S. Parr, review of *The Great Rescue Operation,* p. 123; December, 1982, review of *Amanda Pig and Her Big Brother Oliver,* p. 75; January, 1983, p. 80; December, 1983, Carolyn Noah, review of *Benjy in Business,* p. 70; December, 1983, review of *Tales of Amanda Pig,* p. 80; May, 1985, Robert E. Unsworth, review of *Benjy the Football Hero,* p. 111; December, 1985, review of *More Tales of Amanda Pig,* p. 110; March, 1988, p. 177; June, 1989, pp. 109-110; October, 1989, p. 45; May, 1991, p. 85; March, 1992, p. 225; April, 1992, Jacqueline Rose, review of *The Great Summer Camp Catastrophe,* p. 126; June, 1994; October, 1994, p. 128; September, 1995, pp. 187-188; December, 1995, Gale W. Sherman, review of *Oliver and Amanda and the Big Snow,* p. 92; June, 1996, p. 126; May, 1997, p. 116; July, 1997, Virginia Opocensky, review of *Touch the Sky Summer* and *Amanda Pig, School Girl,* p. 77; July, 1998, p. 84; November, 1998, p. 99; May, 1999, pp. 99-100; July, 1999, p. 82; November, 1999, Cheryl Cufari, review of *Hannah's Helping Hands,* pp. 131-132; July, 2000, p. 89; November, 2000, Leslie S. Hilverding, review of *Oliver and Albert, Friends Forever,* p. 136; May, 2001, Susan L. Rogers,

review of *Sorry,* p. 138; July, 2001, Rosalyn Pierini, review of *"Wait for Me!" Said Maggie McGee,* p. 90.
Time, December 3, 1979, p. 100.
Times Educational Supplement, June 8, 1984.

Wilson Library Bulletin, April, 1995, p. 112

OTHER

Meet Jean Van Leeuwen, http://www.eduplace.com/ (February 24, 2002).

W

WAHL, Jan (Boyer) 1933-

Personal

Born April 1, 1933, in Columbus, OH; son of Russell Rothenburger (a physician/surgeon) and Nina Marie (an artist; maiden name, Boyer) Wahl. *Education:* Cornell University, B.A., 1953; University of Copenhagen, graduate study, 1954-55; University of Michigan, M.A., 1958. *Avocational interests:* Collecting old films, particularly animated films by Lotte Reiniger, Ladislas Starevitch, Max Fleischer, Walt Disney, Hugh Harman, and Rudolph Ising; collecting old toys, comic strip and animation art; traveling from the Sahara Desert to Lapland to the Yucatan, and best of all, "journeys of the imagine."

Addresses

Home—6766 Carrietowne Ln., Toledo, OH 43617.

Career

Worked with Danish film director Carl Theodor Dreyer during the making of Dreyer's prize-winning *Ordet,* 1954-55; returned to Denmark as secretary to writer Isak Dinesen, 1957-58; later worked with illustrator Garth Williams in Mexico, and with Erik Blegvad in England, 1966-67; writer for young people. Served as correspondent from Copehagen for *Dance* magazine during the 1950s, and worked as a translator of French communiques for two Danish newspapers.

Awards, Honors

Fulbright scholar in Copenhagen, 1953-54; Avery Hopwood Award in fiction, University of Michigan, 1955, for a group of short stories collectively entitled *Seven Old Maids* (the stories appeared in various magazines); Young Critics' award at International Children's Book Fair, Bologna, Italy, 1969, for *Pocahontas in London;* Ohioana Book Award winner, 1970, for *The Norman Rockwell Storybook;* American Library Association (ALA) Notable Book citation, 1974, for *The Woman with the Eggs;* Bowling Green State University, Ohio, declared May 1, 1980, as "Jan Wahl Day"; Parents' Choice literary award, 1982, for *Tiger Watch; Redbook* award, 1987, Christopher Medal, 1987, both for *Humphrey's Bear;* Honorary Doctorate in Arts & Letters, Bowling Green State University, 1996.

Jan Wahl

Writings

CHILDREN'S FICTION

Pleasant Fieldmouse, illustrated by Maurice Sendak, Harper (New York, NY), 1964.

The Howards Go Sledding, illustrated by John E. Johnson, Holt (New York, NY), 1964.

Hello, Elephant, illustrated by Edward Ardizzone, Holt (New York, NY), 1964.

Cabbage Moon, illustrated by Adrienne Adams, Holt (New York, NY), 1965, new edition, illustrated by Arden Johnson-Petrov, Boyds Mills Press (Honesdale, PA), 1998.

The Muffletumps: A Story of Four Dolls, illustrated by E. Ardizzone, Holt (New York, NY), 1966.

Christmas in the Forest, illustrated by Eleanor Schick, Macmillan (New York, NY), 1967.

Pocahontas in London, illustrated by John Alcorn, Delacorte (New York, NY), 1967.

Cobweb Castle, illustrated by Edward Gorey, Holt (New York, NY), 1968.

The Furious Flycycle, illustrated by Fernando Krahn, Delacorte (New York, NY), 1968.

Push Kitty, illustrated by Garth Williams, Harper (New York, NY), 1968.

Rickety Rackety Rooster, illustrated by J. E. Johnson, Simon & Schuster (New York, NY), 1968.

Runaway Jonah, and Other Tales (adapted from Biblical stories), illustrated by Uri Shulevitz, Macmillan (New York, NY), 1968, illustrated by Jane Conteh-Morgan, Caedmon (New York, NY), 1985.

The Fisherman, illustrated by Emily Arnold McCully, Norton (New York, NY), 1969.

How the Children Stopped the Wars (fable), illustrated by Mitchell Miller, Farrar, Straus, 1969, illustrated by Gerald Rose, Abelard Schuman, 1975, new edition, illustrated by Maureen O'Keefe, Tricycle Press (Berkeley, CA), 1993.

May Horses, illustrated by Blair Lent, Delacorte (New York, NY), 1969.

The Norman Rockwell Storybook, illustrated by Norman Rockwell, Windmill (New York, NY), 1969.

A Wolf of My Own, illustrated by Lilian Hoban, Macmillan (New York, NY), 1969.

The Animals' Peace Day, illustrated by Victoria Chess, Crown (New York, NY), 1970.

Doctor Rabbit, illustrated by Peter Parnall, Delacorte (New York, NY), 1970.

The Mulberry Tree, illustrated by Feodor Rojankovsky, Grosset, 1970.

The Prince Who Was a Fish, illustrated by Robin Jacques, Simon & Schuster (New York, NY), 1970.

Abe Lincoln's Beard, illustrated by F. Krahn, Delacorte (New York, NY), 1971.

Anna Help Ginger, illustrated by Lawrence Di Fiori, Putnam (New York, NY), 1971.

Crabapple Night, illustrated by Steven Kellogg, Holt (New York, NY), 1971.

Lorenzo Bear and Company, illustrated by F. Krahn, Putnam (New York, NY), 1971.

Margaret's Birthday, illustrated by Mercer Mayer, Four Winds Press (New York, NY), 1971.

The Six Voyages of Pleasant Fieldmouse, illustrated by P. Parnall, Delacorte (New York, NY), 1971.

The Wonderful Kite, illustrated by U. Shulevitz, Delacorte (New York, NY), 1971.

Cristobal and the Witch, illustrated by Janet McCaffery, Putnam (New York, NY), 1972.

Grandmother Told Me, illustrated by M. Mayer, Little, Brown (Boston, MA), 1972.

Magic Heart, illustrated by Trina Schart Hyman, Seabury (New York, NY), 1972.

The Very Peculiar Tunnel, illustrated by S. Kellogg, Putnam (New York, NY), 1972.

Crazy Brobobalou (adapted from *Le Prince spirituel,* by Countess Prince de Beaumont), illustrated by Paula Winter, Putnam (New York, NY), 1973.

S.O.S. Bobomobile! or, The Future Adventures of Melvin Spitznagle and Professor Mickimecki, illustrated by F. Krahn, Delacorte (New York, NY), 1973.

Jeremiah Knucklebones, illustrated by Jane Breskin Zalben, Holt (New York, NY), 1974.

(With Dolores Janes Garcia) *Juan Diego and the Lady/La dama y Juan Diego* (bilingual edition), illustrated by Leonard Everett Fisher, Putnam (New York, NY), 1974.

Mooga Mega Mekki, illustrated by F. Krahn, O'Hara (Chicago, IL), 1974.

Pleasant Fieldmouse's Halloween Party, illustrated by Wallace Tripp, Putnam (New York, NY), 1974.

The Five in the Forest, illustrated by Erik Blegvad, Follett (Chicago, IL), 1974.

The Woman with the Eggs (adapted from the poem by Hans Christian Andersen), illustrated by Ray Cruz, Crown (New York, NY), 1974.

Bear, Wolf, and Mouse, illustrated by Kinuko Craft, Follett (Chicago, IL), 1975.

The Clumpets Go Sailing, illustrated by Cyndy Szekeres, Parents' Magazine Press (New York, NY), 1975.

The Muffletumps' Christmas Party, illustrated by C. Szekeres, Follett (Chicago, IL), 1975.

The Muffletump Storybook, illustrated by C. Szekeres, Follett (Chicago, IL), 1975.

The Screeching Door; or, What Happened at the Elephant Hotel, illustrated by J. Winslow Higginbottom, Four Winds Press (New York, NY), 1975.

Follow Me, Cried Bee, illustrated by John Wallner, Crown (New York, NY), 1976.

Grandpa's Indian Summer, illustrated by Joanne Scribner, Prentice-Hall (Englewood Cliffs, NJ), 1976.

Great-Grandmother Cat Tales, illustrated by C. Szekeres, Pantheon (New York, NY), 1976.

Doctor Rabbit's Foundling, illustrated by C. Szekeres, Pantheon (New York, NY), 1977.

Frankenstein's Dog (also see below), illustrated by Kay Chorao, Prentice-Hall (Englewood Cliffs, NJ), 1977.

The Muffletumps' Halloween Scare, illustrated by C. Szekeres, Follett (Chicago, IL), 1977.

The Pleasant Fieldmouse Storybook, illustrated by E. Blegvad, Prentice-Hall (Englewood Cliffs, NJ), 1977.

Pleasant Fieldmouse's Valentine Trick, illustrated by Marc Brown, Windmill (New York, NY), 1977.

Carrot Nose, illustrated by James Marshall, Farrar, Straus (New York, NY), 1977.

Dracula's Cat (also see below), illustrated by K. Chorao, Prentice-Hall (Englewood Cliffs, NJ), 1977.

Drakestail (adapted from English folktales), illustrated by Byron Barton, Greenwillow (New York, NY), 1978.

Jamie's Tiger, illustrated by Tomie dePaola, Harcourt (New York, NY), 1978.

Who Will Believe Tim Kitten?, illustrated by C. Szekeres, Pantheon (New York, NY), 1978.

Doctor Rabbit's Lost Scout, illustrated by C. Szekeres, Pantheon (New York, NY), 1979.

Needle Noodle, and Other Silly Stories (English folktales), illustrated by Stan Mack, Pantheon (New York, NY), 1979.

Sylvester Bear Overslept, illustrated by Lee Lorenz, Parents' Magazine Press (New York, NY), 1979.

The Teeny Tiny Witches, illustrated by Margot Tomes, Putnam (New York, NY), 1979.

Button Eye's Orange, illustrated by Wendy Watson, Warne (New York, NY), 1980.

Old Hippo's Easter Egg, illustrated by Lorinda Bryan-Cauley, Harcourt (San Diego, CA), 1980.

The Cucumber Princess, illustrated by Caren Caraway, Stemmer House (Owings Mills, MD), 1981.

Grandpa Gus's Birthday Cake, illustrated by J. Wallner, Prentice-Hall (Englewood Cliffs, NJ), 1981.

The Little Blind Goat, illustrated by Antonio Frasconi, Stemmer House (Owings Mills, MD), 1981.

The Pipkins Go Camping, illustrated by J. Wallner, Prentice-Hall (Englewood Cliffs, NJ), 1982.

Tiger Watch, illustrated by Charles Mikolaycak, Harcourt (San Diego, CA), 1982.

More Room for the Pipkins, illustrated by J. Wallner, Prentice-Hall (Englewood Cliffs, NJ), 1983.

Small One, illustrated by Beth Wiener, Hastings House (Norwalk, CT), 1983.

Peter and the Troll Baby, illustrated by E. Blegvad, Golden Press (New York, NY), 1984.

Cheltenham's Party, illustrated by Lucinda McQueen, Golden Press (New York, NY), 1985.

So Many Raccoons, illustrated by Beth Lee Weiner, Caedmon (New York, NY), 1985.

Rabbits on Roller Skates!, illustrated by David Allender, Crown (New York, NY), 1986.

The Toy Circus, illustrated by Tim Bowers, Gulliver Books/Harcourt (San Diego, CA), 1986.

Let's Go Fishing, illustrated by Bruce Lemorise, Golden Press (New York, NY), 1987.

Humphrey's Bear, illustrated by William Joyce, Holt (New York, NY), 1987.

Timothy Tiger's Terrible Toothache, illustrated by Lisa McCue, Golden Press (New York, NY), 1988.

Little Dragon's Grandmother, illustrated by L. McQueen, Golden Press (New York, NY), 1988.

Tim Kitten and the Red Cupboard, illustrated by Bruce Degen, Simon & Schuster (New York, NY), 1988.

The Golden Christmas Tree, illustrated by Leonard Weisgard, Golden Press (New York, NY), 1988.

Tales of Fuzzy Mouse: Six Cozy Stories for Bedtime, illustrated by L. Hoban, Golden Press (New York, NY), 1988.

The Adventures of Underwater Dog, illustrated by Tim Bowers, Grosset (New York, NY), 1989.

Through the eyes of a field mouse, Wahl tells of the excavation of the largest tyrannosaurus, reassembled for exhibition at Chicago's Field Museum. (From The Field Mouse and the Dinosaur Named Sue, *illustrated by Bob Doucet.)*

The Wizard of Oz Movie Storybook, Golden Press (New York, NY), 1989.

Dracula's Cat [and] *Frankenstein's Dog,* illustrated by K. Chorao, Simon & Schuster (New York, NY), 1990.

A Gift for Miss Milo, illustrated by Jeff Grove, Ten Speed Press (Berkeley, CA), 1990.

The Rabbit Club, Harcourt (San Diego, CA), 1990.

Mrs. Owl and Mr. Pig, illustrated by Eileen Christelow, Lodestar/Dutton (New York, NY), 1991.

Tailypo!, illustrated by Wil Clay, Holt (New York, NY), 1991.

The Sleepytime Book, illustrated by Arden Johnson, Tambourine Books (New York, NY), 1992.

Little Eight John, illustrated by W. Clay, Lodestar/Dutton (New York, NY), 1992.

My Cat Ginger, illustrated by Naava, Tambourine Books (New York, NY), 1992.

Suzy and the Mouse King, illustrated by Katie Macaro, Monroe County Library System, 1992.

Little Gray One, illustrated by Frane Lessac, Tambourine Books (New York, NY), 1993.

I Remember, Cried Grandma Pinky, illustrated by Arden Johnson, Bridgewater Books (Mahwah, NJ), 1994.

Emily and the Snowflake, illustrated by Carolyn Ewing, Whistlestop/Troll Associates (Mahwah, NJ), 1995.

Cats and Robbers, pictures by Dolores Avendano, Tambourine Books (New York, NY), 1995.

Once When the World was Green, illustrated, Fabricio Vandenbroeck, Tricycle Press (Berkeley, CA), 1996.

I Met a Dinosaur, illustrated by Chris Sheban, Creative Edition/Harcourt Brace (San Diego, CA), 1997.

Cabbage Moon, illustrated by Arden Johnson-Petrov, Boyds Mills Press (Honesdale, PA), 1998.

The Singing Geese, illustrated by Sterling Brown, Lodestar Books (New York, NY), 1998.

Little Johnny Buttermilk: After an Old English Folktale, illustrated by Jennifer Mazzucco, August House Little-Folk (Little Rock, AR), 1999.

Christmas Present, illustrated by Michael McCurdy, Creative Editions (Mankato, MN), 1999.

Rosa's Parrot, illustrated by Kim Howard, Whispering Coyote Press (Dallas, TX), 1999.

Three Pandas, illustrated by Naava, Boyds Mills Press (Honesdale, PA), 1999.

The Field Mouse and the Dinosaur Named Sue, illustrated by Bob Doucet, Scholastic (New York, NY), 2000.

Mabel Ran Away with the Toys, illustrated by Liza Woodruff, Whispering Coyote (Watertown, MA), 2000.

Elf Night, illustrated by Peter Weevers, Carolrhoda Books (Minneapolis, MN), 2002.

OTHER

Paradiso! Paradiso! (play), first produced at Cornell University, 1954.

The Beast Book (children's verse), illustrated by E. W. Eichel, Harper (New York, NY), 1964.

Youth's Magic Horn: Seven Stories (young adult), Thomas Nelson (Nashville, TN), 1978.

Also author of *Seven Old Maids,* a collection of previously published short stories. Contributor of short stories and essays to a number of magazines, such as

When her pleasant life is disrupted by a new, constantly crying baby, young Mabel decides to move into her playhouse with her stuffed-animal companions. (Cover illustration by Liza Woodruff.)

Transatlantic Review, Prairie Schooner, Epoch, Films in Review, Kosmorama, and *Montage.* Poetry and articles on films have appeared in periodicals in America and abroad. Wahl's manuscripts are housed in a Jan Wahl Collection at the University of Wyoming, Laramie, at Bowling Green State University, Bowling Green, Ohio, and at the Kerlan Collection at the University of Minnesota, Minneapolis.

Adaptations

An animated film entitled *Why We Need Each Other: The Animals' Picnic Day,* adapted from *The Animals' Peace Day,* was produced by Bosustow/Learning Corporation, 1973; a filmstrip with cassette was produced of *The Clumpets Go Sailing* by Listening Library, 1979; an animated film based on *The Furious Flycycle* was produced by Bosustow/Churchill and was later presented on CBS-TV, 1980; an opera based on *How the Children Stopped the Wars* was produced by Northwestern University in 1986, and at Fairfield University in 1991.

Work in Progress

A new edition of *How the Children Stopped the Wars* for Ten Speed Press; *Rabbits On Mars,* illustrated by Kimberly Schamber, for Carolrhoda Books, 2003; *Knock! Knock!,* illustrated by Mary Newall De Palma, for Henry Holt (New York, NY), 2003; *Candy Shop,* for Charlesbridge Publishing.

Sidelights

Jan Wahl is an imaginative and prolific writer of children's books, many of which are graced by the work of the most notable of illustrators. When he was born in Columbus, Ohio, in 1933, his father was a pre-medical student at Ohio State University and his mother an art student; therefore, Wahl spent a good portion of the Great Depression years with both sets of grandparents in northwest Ohio improvising stories for his own amusement and later for the amusement of his five other brothers. One of his first literary efforts involved trying to improve upon the story of "Jack and the Beanstalk." At the age of three, though, he remembers being enthralled as his great-grandmother sketched a chicken on what had previously been a blank sheet of paper. "And I believe at that moment I became 'hooked' on art in general," said Wahl in an autobiographical essay in *Something about the Author Autobiography Series.* "Virtually the whole of my adult life has been spent in writing and scribbling so that some artist might make nifty pictures. Much of my life, too, has been spent recalling the freshness of that morning on an Ohio farm where I spent much of my childhood."

As the Great Depression was ending, the family settled in Toledo, Ohio, where Wahl's father had established his medical practice. Since one of his mother's cousins happened to be the music director for a local broadcasting company, Wahl was invited to play on a Saturday morning radio program and described his life at the time. "I did puppet shows, magic shows; I pretended to be

Danny Kaye and lip-synched his records," recalled Wahl. "I performed before church groups, traveled to other schools, made a buffoon of myself in front of Parent-Teacher groups. And on Saturday mornings did 'The Kiddies' Karnival.'" Wahl also fell in love with the movies, a passion retained in his collection of old films, particularly animated films by Lotte Reiniger, Ladislas Starevitch, Max Fleischer, Walt Disney, Hugh Harman, and Rudolph Ising. Although Wahl, with an early training in piano, wanted to write music for film, he believes that movies have helped him in his career as a writer, enabling him to think visually.

After high school graduation, Wahl entered Cornell University where he began to study creative writing and published stories in a few small magazines. After finishing his bachelor's degree, he won a Fulbright scholarship to Denmark, the land of his ancestors. While studying there, he met several influential people, including writer Isak Dinesen. Also, a fortuitous invitation allowed him to work on director Carl Theodor Dreyer's classic film, *Ordet.* Upon his return to the United States, Wahl accepted a scholarship to earn a master's degree at the University of Michigan and continued his efforts to become a writer, winning the Avery Hopwood Award in fiction for a group of short stories collectively entitled *Seven Old Maids.* Then came an unexpected cable from an ailing Isak Dinesen in Denmark requesting Wahl to join her there so that she could dictate her last tales. Although he was neither a stenographer nor a professional typist, he was eager to assist the writer; however, the arrangement proved unsatisfactory to her and he was soon dismissed. While in Denmark, Wahl also did research for the Danish Film Museum and became correspondent from Copenhagen for *Dance* magazine and worked briefly for Danish newspapers.

Upon his return to the United States, Wahl began work on a novel as well as a few little animal stories for children. "This was a lot more fun. I had found what I could do. I MUST write for children. In a way, I was writing the films I wished I could see. A picture book is related to an animated cartoon." Although his first efforts to publish children's books were unsuccessful, Wahl once commented: "When my first children's book, *Pleasant Fieldmouse,* won reviews such as 'belongs on the same high shelf as Beatrix Potter' and 'not since *Wind in the Willows*' and 'if you buy only one book this year, make it this one,' all my own childhood dreams seemed to come true."

Wahl's output has been prodigious, with more than 20 books since 1990. In *I Met a Dinosaur,* Wahl tells the tale of a girl whose vivid imagination causes her to start seeing dinosaurs after a trip to a museum. A *Publishers Weekly* reviewer called the book "a bewitching blend of fantasy and realism." In *The Singing Geese,* Wahl retells an African American tall tale he first heard from an elderly man sitting on his porch. Hazel Rochman, in a review for *Booklist,* said the tale was "retold with verve," and a *Publishers Weekly* reviewer noted that Wahl and illustrator Sterling Brown recapture "the homespun magic of both the tale and the telling." In one

of his most recent books, *The Field Mouse and the Dinosaur Named Sue,* Wahl delights readers with a story of a mouse from South Dakota that finds itself in Chicago's Field Museum of Natural History. Lauralyn Persson, writing a review in the *School Library Journal,* said "both story and artwork keep child appeal uppermost in mind." In his autobiographical essay, Wahl also said: "My promise to myself was to write in a positive way. To connect with children and their parents through fables and animal stories. To know that truth can be reached via fantasy."

Jan Wahl told *SATA:* "I am very pleased that in Spring 2002, my very first book, *Pleasant Fieldmouse,* which Maurice Sendak so charmingly illustrated, will be back in print with HarperCollins; it does not seem like thirty-seven years since I had the joy of opening my first box of author's copies. What a memorable moment! A dream come true. It was Tasha Tudor who first encouraged me, not by having read any of my little stories but rather by looking directly into my eyes and then seeing that, apparently, I had a 'spark' and the determination! 'You will be published—I'm sure of it,' she promised me; and I knew that she was telling the truth. Could Tasha Tudor ever lie? When I meet children, or grown-ups now too, who tell me that such-and-such is their favorite book among all books they have read, it is the best payment possible.

"I am grateful to the many editors through the years who helped bring my stories to life. When I am asked, 'What is *your* favorite books of the books you have written?' I must answer truthfully, *Pleasant Fieldmouse,* since it is my first-born; and *How the Children Stopped the Wars,* since its message is still (alas) pertinent not only in the grim days of the Vietnam conflict, but today as well. And my next favorite of course is a book in progress; but indeed I love them every one—these are my children and I'm proud of them and wish them a long life. There is nothing nicer than holding a book of your own in your hand! Honest. My advice to young aspiring writers: believe in yourself!"

Biographical and Critical Sources

BOOKS

Something about the Author Autobiography Series, Volume 3, Gale (Detroit, MI), 1986, pp. 293-311.

Pendergast, Sara, and Tom Pendergast, *St. James Guide to Children's Writers,* 5th edition, St. James Press (Detroit, MI), 1999.

Twentieth-Century Children's Writers, 3rd edition, St. James Press, 1989.

Ward, Martha E., and Dorothy A. Marquardt, editors, *Authors of Books for Young People,* Scarecrow, 1971.

PERIODICALS

Booklist, February 15, 1998, Hazel Rochman, review of *The Singing Geese,* p. 101; December 15, 1999, Ilene Cooper, review of *Little Johnny Buttermilk,* p. 788; February 15, 2000, Shelley Townsend-Hudson, review of *Three Pandas,* p. 1122; May 15, 2000, Ellen

Mandel, review of *The Field Mouse and the Dinosaur Named Sue,* p. 1750.

Book World, December 10, 1967.

Kirkus Reviews, October 15, 1971, p. 1117; March 15, 1986, p. 474; April 15, 1991, p. 540.

National Observer, December 11, 1967.

Newsweek, December 6, 1982.

New York Times Book Review, December 3, 1967; November 7, 1971, p. 46; November 11, 1984, p. 48; August 9, 1987, p. 29.

Ohioana Quarterly, autumn, 1980.

Publishers Weekly, December 14, 1970, p. 39; February 8, 1971, p. 81; November 11, 1974, p. 48; December 5, 1980, p. 53; January 17, 1986, p. 69; April 25, 1986, p. 72; October 31, 1986, p. 66; April 24, 1987, p. 69; October 13, 1989, p. 56; June 8, 1990, p. 54; May 10, 1991, p. 283; September 22, 1997, review of *I Met a Dinosaur,* p. 80; December 1, 1997, review of *The Singing Geese,* p. 53; February 1, 1999, review of *Rosa's Parrot,* p. 85.

School Library Journal, January, 1985, p. 48; May, 1986, p. 114; February, 1987, p. 75; August, 1987, p. 76; January, 1990, p. 92; August, 1990, p. 135; September, 1990, p. 232; August, 2000, Lauralyn Persson, review of *The Field Mouse and the Dinosaur Named Sue,* p. 167.

School Library Media Activities Monthly, February, 1990, pp. 33-35.

*   *   *

WHYBROW, Ian

Personal

Male. *Hobbies and other interests:* Walking, swimming, digging, reading, theatre-going, cycling.

Addresses

Home—Harrow and Herefordshire, England. *Agent*—c/o Author Mail, Carolrhoda Books, Inc., Lerner Publishing Group, 241 First Ave. N., Minneapolis, MN 55401. *E-mail*—littlewolf@lineone.net.

Career

Author. Former teacher of English and drama. Worked variously as a deck chair attendant, ice cream salesman, brewery worker, teacher of foreign students, travel guide, waiter, builder, gardener, and washer.

Awards, Honors

Mother Goose Award, runner-up, 1992, for *Quacky Quack-Quack!*

Writings

The Sniff Stories, Bodley Head (London, England), 1989, republished as *Sniff,* illustrated by Tony Ross, Hodder (London, England), 1999.

Sniff Bounces Back, illustrated by Toni Goffe, Bodley Head (London, England), 1990, republished with illustrations by Tony Ross, Hodder (London, England), 1999.

Sniff and the Secret of Spalderton Hall, illustrated by Toni Goffe, Bodley Head (London, England), 1991, republished as *Sniff the Wonderdog,* illustrated by Tony Ross, Hodder (London, England), 1999.

Quacky Quack-Quack!, illustrated by Russell Ayto, Walker (London, England), Four Winds Press (New York, NY), 1991.

Holly and the Skyboard, illustrated by Mike Gordon, Walker (London, England), 1993.

The Time Sailors, illustrated by Anthony Lewis, Walker (London, England), 1994.

Can I Stand on Your Head?, illustrated by Tim Archbold, Orchard Books (London, England), 1994.

Nice One, Sniff, illustrated by Toni Goffe, Bodley Head (London, England), 1994, republished with illustrations by Tony Ross, Hodder (London, England), 1999.

Sing Boogie Boogie, illustrated by Tim Archbold, Orchard Books (London, England), 1995.

Fix It with Bubblegum, illustrated by Tim Archbold, Orchard Books (London, England), 1995.

Red's Wish Day, illustrated by Tim Archbold, Orchard Books (London, England), 1995.

Little Wolf's Book of Badness, illustrated by Tony Ross, Collins (London, England), 1995, Carolrhoda Books (Minneapolis, MN), 1999.

Miss Wire and the Three Kind Mice, illustrated by Emma Chichester-Clark, Kingfisher (London, England), 1996.

The Bedtime Bear, illustrated by Axel Scheffler, Macmillan, 1996.

Little Wolf's Diary of Daring Deeds, illustrated by Tony Ross, Collins (London, England), 1996, Carolrhoda Books (Minneapolis, MN), 2000.

Harry and the Snow King, illustrated by Adrian Reynolds, Levinson Books (London, England), 1997.

Parcel for Stanley, illustrated by Sally Hobson, Levinson Books (London, England), 1997.

A Baby for Grace, illustrated by Christian Birmingham, Kingfisher (London, England and New York, NY), 1998.

Goo Goo Gorilla, illustrated by Tony Blundell, Viking (London, England), 1998.

The Christmas Bear, illustrated by Axel Scheffler, Macmillan (London, England), 1998.

Little Wolf's Haunted Hall for Small Horrors, illustrated by Tony Ross, Collins (London, England), 1998, Carolrhoda Books (Minneapolis, MN), 2000.

Jump In!, illustrated by David Melling, Barron's (Hauppauge, NY), 1999.

Harry and the Bucketful of Dinosaurs, illustrated by Adrian Reynolds, David and Charles (London, England), 1999, published as *Sammy and the Dinosaurs,* Orchard Books (New York, NY), 1999.

Whiff, or, How the Beautiful Big Fat Smelly Baby Found a Friend, illustrated by Russell Ayto, Doubleday (London, England), 1999.

Where's Tim's Ted?, illustrated by Russell Ayto, Collins (London, England), 1999, Barron's (Hauppauge, NY), 2000.

Little Wonder, illustrated by Emily Bolam, Hodder (London, England), 1999.

The Tickle Book, illustrated by Axel Scheffler, Macmillan (London, England), 2000.

Little Wolf's Postbag, illustrated by Tony Ross, Collins (London, England), 2000, published as *Dear Little Wolf,* Carolrhoda Books (Minneapolis, MN), 2002.

Jungly Japes, illustrated by Ross Collins, David and Charles (London, England), 2000.

Harry and the Robots, illustrated by Adrian Reynolds, David and Charles (London, England), 2000, published as *Sammy and the Robots,* Orchard Books (New York, NY), 2001.

Little Wolf: Forest Detective, illustrated by Tony Ross, Collins (London, England), 2000, Carolrhoda Books (Minneapolis, MN), 2001.

The Houseminders, illustrated by Julie Monks, Hodder (London, England), 2000.

Little Farmer Joe, illustrated by Christian Birmingham, Kingfisher (New York, NY), 2001.

All Change!, illustrated by David Melling, Hodder (London, England), Barron's (Hauppauge, NY), 2001.

Where's Bitesize?, illustrated by Penny Dann, Dorling Kindersley (London, England and New York, NY), 2001.

I'm Not Scared!, illustrated by Christian Birmingham, Kingfisher (New York, NY), 2001.

Harry and the Dinosaurs Say 'Raahh!', illustrated by Adrian Reynolds, Gullane (London, England), 2001, published as *Sammy and the Dinosaurs Say "Ahhh!,"* Orchard Books (New York, NY), 2002.

Wish, Change, Friend, illustrated by Tiphanie Beeke, Margaret K. McElderry Books (New York, NY), 2002.

Little Wolf, Scout Leader, illustrated by Tony Ross, Carolrhoda Books (Minneapolis, MN), 2002.

Little Wolf's Handy Book of Poems, illustrated by Tony Ross, Carolrhoda Books (Minneapolis, MN), 2002.

Good Night, Monster, illustrated by Ken Wilson-Max, Knopf (New York, NY), 2002.

Sissy Buttons Takes Charge!, illustrated by Olivia Villet, Chicken House (Frome, England), 2002.

Whybrow's books have been translated into French, German, Spanish, Japanese, Korean, Finnish, Norwegian, Swedish, Dutch, Italian, and Polish. Also author of *Sniff on Holiday* and *Whizz the Fleabag* ("Books for Boys" series), both illustrated by Tony Ross, Hodder.

"BOOKS FOR BOYS" SERIES

Young Robin's Hood, illustrated by Tony Ross, Hodder (London, England), 2000.

A Footballer Called Flip, illustrated by Tony Ross, Hodder (London, England), 2000.

The Magic Sneeze, illustrated by Tony Ross, Hodder (London, England), 2000.

Boy Racer, illustrated by Tony Ross, Hodder (London, England), 2000.

Aliens Stole My Dog, illustrated by Tony Ross, Hodder (London, England), 2000.

Little Wolf, who does not meet his parents' standard for proper ferociousness, is packed off to Uncle Bigbad's Cunning College in Ian Whybrow's book for young readers. (Cover illustration by Tony Ross.)

Adaptations

The Sniff Stories was adapted for audio cassette, narrated by Tony Robinson, Chivers Press Audio, 1990; *Little Wolf's Book of Badness* was adapted for audio cassette, narrated by Griff Rhys Jones, HarperCollins Audio, 1999.

Sidelights

Ian Whybrow writes humorous books for children that range from the whimsical and poignant to the raucous and slightly naughty. His early books, including several for toddlers, such as *Quacky Quack-Quack!* and *Sammy and the Dinosaurs,* garnered praise for capturing realistic moments and emotions that young children can identify with and cleverly placing them in simple stories with satisfying conclusions. In *Quacky Quack-Quack!,* for example, a baby with bread to feed the ducks at the park begins to eat the bread himself, setting off a cacophony of protests from the ducks, geese, and all the other animals (and even a nearby marching band!) in the area. But when big brother gives baby some ice-cream and offers the bread to the birds, everyone quiets down and is happy. The repetition of the animal noises invites children to join in the story, reviewers remarked; a contributor to *Kirkus Reviews* dubbed this "a winning interactive tale." Likewise, Nancy Seiner, who reviewed *Quacky Quack-Quack!* for *School Library Journal,* concluded: "this book may become a favorite with the toddler story-time set."

Whybrow has written several books for preschoolers that explore feelings such as the desire for friendship, handling disappointments, and the mixture of feelings that arise when a new sibling comes home. In *Harry and the Snow King,* a little boy works hard to turn a scanty snowfall into a snowman and produces only a miniature snow king that melts away by the next day. But, encouraged by a neighbor to believe that the snow king has only gone away to get more snow, Harry is rewarded the next morning by the sight of a yard full of snow—and of snow people. This mysterious occurrence "perfectly captures the wonder and delight generated by winter's first major snow," asserted Kathy Piehl in *School Library Journal.* In *Parcel for Stanley,* Whybrow tells the story of a group of friends all busily preparing for a visit by the queen (depicted as a little girl in dress-up clothes), except for Stanley, who never does much until the day he receives a package in the mail with equipment for a magic show inside. *School Library Journal* contributor Judith Constantinides described this as a "simple story that celebrates individuality." In *A Baby for Grace,* a little girl is deeply disappointed when everything she tries to do to welcome home the new baby is greeted by a negative response from the adults in the house. Then her father helps her pick flowers for the baby and everyone praises her. "Children with younger siblings will recognize ... the frustrating feelings the text revives," remarked Lauren Peterson of *Booklist.* And in *Wish, Change, Friend,* a bookish pig sets off to

discover the meaning of the words of the title and ends up with new friends and a shop where anyone with a wish for change can come to meet new friends. According to a *Kirkus Reviews* critic, "Few readers will be able to resist this gentle invitation to gather ... the words that are most important to them."

Another reassuring story for the preschool set is *Harry and the Bucketful of Dinosaurs,* published in the United States as *Sammy and the Dinosaurs,* in which a little boy discovers a box of toy dinosaurs in his grandmother's attic. After cleaning and fixing them up, he gives them a proper bucket to live in. Then he goes off to the library to learn their names, a gesture for which they are very grateful. When the youth accidentally leaves the bucket on a train however, it is because he can call them by name that the conductor believes they truly belong to him. "This is a beautiful, cheering story full of offbeat charm," proclaimed a contributor to *Kirkus Reviews.* Other reviewers similarly relished the story's gentle humor, element of fantasy (the dinosaurs are only animated around the boy), and portrayal of true friendship. "The story, alternately humorous and poignant, is beautifully written and always right on target," concluded Lolly Robinson in the *Horn Book.* JoAnn Jonas, writing in the *School Library Journal,* called *Sammy and the Dinosaurs* "a delight from endpaper to endpaper." A sequel, *Harry and the Robots,* published in the United States as *Sammy and the Robots,* tells the story of a time when the youngster's favorite robot goes to the robot hospital just when his beloved grandmother must go to the hospital too. So the child builds an army of robots to help Grandma recover and just as she returns home, so does his favorite robot. "Sammy is a winsome winner," wrote DeAnn Tabuchi in a review of *Sammy and the Robots* for *School Library Journal.*

Everything little Grace tries to do to welcome home the new baby is dismissed by the adults, until her father comes up with the perfect solution. (From A Baby for Grace, *written by Whybrow and illustrated by Christian Birmingham.)*

Whybrow has also written several books for early readers, some of which feature a broad, boisterous humor that critics compare to Dav Pilkey's "Captain Underpants" series. In *Little Wolf's Book of Badness,* Whybrow introduced one of his most winning characters, a young wolf who does not meet his parents' standard for properly ferocious behavior. When Little Wolf is packed off to his Uncle Bigbad's school, Cunning College, the uncle is quickly exposed as a has-been and eventually explodes while standing close to the fire after eating too many baked beans. Little Wolf is forced to continue his education on his own and quickly takes up with a group of Cub Scouts and earns a badge. The story is narrated by Little Wolf, in letters written home to his parents, and the text features ink blots, words scratched out, and doodles in the margins, as well as a host of corrupt English words, providing much of the book's humor. "This is a delicious, laugh-out-loud revisionist view of the fairy-tale cad as reported by his nephew," remarked a reviewer in the *Horn Book.* A reviewer for the *Observer* predicted, "With more plot than you'd get in many an adult novel, wonderfully funny cartoons by Tony Ross and great comic writing, this is going to be a favourite for all ages."

In *Little Wolf's Diary of Daring Deeds,* Little Wolf's letters home recount his exciting adventures once he decides to take the money Uncle Bigbad left behind and start his own school with the help of his cousin, Yeller, and Mister Marvo, who signs on as a teacher. But Mister Marvo is revealed to be Mister Twister the Fox, an old cohort of Uncle Bigbad, who steals the money and kidnaps Little Wolf's younger brother, Smellybreff. "This is bound to be a favorite with the beginning chapter-book set," predicted Wendy S. Carroll in *School Library Journal.* Another sequel, *Little Wolf's Haunted Hall for Small Horrors,* features the same cast involved in opening another school, this one called The Best School for Brute Beasts. Little Wolf enlists the ghost of Uncle Bigbad to give the school some spirit and is dared by his nasty uncle to find a student he cannot frighten off. Mister Twister the Fox returns to upset Little Wolf's plans again, but in the end, the friends decide to close the school and open a detective agency instead. "Fans of the series will enjoy the further adventures of these characters, and newcomers will have no trouble following the story," concluded Marilyn Ackerman in her review in *School Library Journal.*

Whybrow told *SATA,* "I'm best known for writing humorous books that other people style as whacky or original, but I like to think of myself as a truthful observer of people's language and behavior; I always write with adult readers as well as youngsters in mind. I have a good ear for the music of voices and I'm very proud of the fact that people say that my work reads aloud very well. I loved being read to as a child, and I loved the sense that my mother and father were enjoying themselves too. For me, that's the acid test for any good book—that there's something in it for everyone to enjoy.

Biographical and Critical Sources

PERIODICALS

Booklist, October 1, 1998, Lauren Peterson, review of *A Baby for Grace,* p. 337; July, 1999, Carolyn Phelan, review of *Harry and the Snow King,* p. 1956; February 15, 2002, Ilene Cooper, review of *Wish, Change, Friend,* p. 1023.

Books for Keeps, July, 1993, Moira Small, review of *Quacky Quack-Quack!,* p. 10.

Horn Book, September, 1999, Lolly Robinson, review of *Sammy and the Dinosaurs,* p. 602; January, 2000, review of *Little Wolf's Book of Badness,* p. 86.

Junior Bookshelf, December, 1991, review of *Quacky Quack-Quack!,* p. 246.

Kirkus Reviews, July 1, 1999, review of *Sammy and the Dinosaurs,* p. 1061; September 1, 1999, review of *Quacky Quack-Quack!,* p. 1170; October 1, 1999, review of *Little Wolf's Book of Badness,* p. 1585; November 15, 2001, review of *Wish, Change, Friend,* p. 1616.

Language Arts, September, 1992, Miriam Martinez and Marcia F. Nash, review of *Quacky Quack-Quack!,* p. 375.

Magpies, March, 1999, Moira Robinson, review of *A Baby for Grace,* p. 26.

Observer (London, England), October 24, 1999, review of *Little Wolf's Book of Badness,* p. 13.

Publishers Weekly, October 26, 1998, review of *A Baby for Grace,* p. 64; December 7, 1998, review of *Parcel for Stanley,* p. 59; November 15, 1999, review of *Little Wolf's Book of Badness,* p. 67; February 5, 2001, review of *Little Wolf's Book of Badness,* p. 90; February 19, 2001, review of *Little Wolf, Forest Detective,* p. 70; November 26, 2001, review of *Wish, Change, Friend,* p. 61; November 26, 2001, review of review of *Wish, Change, Friend,* p. 61.

School Librarian, May, 1995, review of *The Time Sailors,* p. 66; May, 1996, review of *Sing Boogie Boogie* and *Can I Stand on Your Head?,* p. 65; autumn, 1999, Rebecca Taylor, review of *Whiff,* p. 132.

School Library Journal, January, 1992, Nancy Seiner, review of *Quacky Quack-Quack!,* p. 100; January, 1999, Martha Topol, review of *A Baby for Grace,* p. 108; March, 1999, Judith Constantinides, review of *Parcel for Stanley,* p. 188; July, 1999, Kathy Piehl, review of *Harry and the Snow King,* p. 83; September, 1999, JoAnn Jonas, review of *Sammy and the Dinosaurs,* p. 209; November, 1999, Beth Wright, review of *Little Wolf's Book of Badness,* p. 132; June, 2000, Wendy S. Carroll, review of *Little Wolf's Diary of Daring Deeds,* p. 127; September, 2000, Marilyn Ackerman, review of *Little Wolf's Haunted Hall for Small Horrors,* p. 211; July, 2001, DeAnn Tabuchi, review of *Sammy and the Robots,* p. 91; November, 2001, Lee Bock, review of *Little Farmer Joe,* p. 138; January, 2002, Shawn Brommer, review of *Wish, Change, Friend,* p. 112.

Times Educational Supplement, March 10, 1989, Andrew Davies, review of *The Sniff Stories,* p. B11; August 3, 1990, Nicholas Tucker, review of *Sniff Bounces Back,* p. 17.

OTHER

Little Wolf's Website, http://www.littlewolf.co.uk (January 23, 2002).

*   *   *

WOOD, Douglas (Eric) 1951-

Personal

Born December 10, 1951, in New York, NY; son of James H. (a college professor) and Joyce (a college professor; maiden name, Wilton) Wood; married Kathryn Sokolowski (a teacher and singer), May 26, 1973; children: Eric, Bryan. *Education:* Morningside College (Iowa), B.Ed., 1973; attended St. Cloud State University, 1984. *Hobbies and other interests:* Canoeing and wilderness trips, tennis, fishing, reading.

Addresses

Home and office—3835 Pine Point Rd., Sartell, MN 56377. *E-mail*—doug@douglaswood.com.

Career

Writer, musician, and recording artist. Music teacher in Iowa and Minnesota, 1973-77; naturalist and wilderness guide in northern Minnesota, 1977—; host of a weekly radio show, "Wood's Lore," in St. Cloud, MN, 1984-91.

Awards, Honors

Named one of Ten Outstanding Young Minnesotans by Minnesota Jaycees, 1991; Minnesota Book Award for younger children, 1992, and American Booksellers Book of the Year (ABBY) Award (children's division), American Booksellers Association, Children's Book Award (younger division), International Reading Association Children's Book Award, and Midwest Publishers Award, all 1993, all for *Old Turtle; Minnesota: The Spirit of the Land* was nominated for the Minnesota Book Award and the North East Minnesota Book Award, 1995; *Grandad's Prayers of the Earth* received the Christopher Medal, 1999.

Writings

FOR CHILDREN

Old Turtle, illustrated by Cheng-Khee Chee, Pfeifer-Hamilton (Duluth, MN), 1992.

Northwoods Cradle Song: From a Menominee Lullaby, illustrated by Lisa Desimini, Simon & Schuster (New York, NY), 1996.

The Windigo's Return: A North Woods Story, illustrated by Greg Couch, Simon & Schuster (New York, NY), 1996.

Rabbit and the Moon, illustrated by Leslie Baker, Simon & Schuster (New York, NY), 1998.

Making the World, illustrated by Yoshi and Hibiki Miyazaki, Simon & Schuster (New York, NY), 1998.

Grandad's Prayers of the Earth, illustrated by P. J. Lynch, Candlewick Press (Cambridge, MA), 1999.

What Dads Can't Do, illustrated by Doug Cushman, Simon & Schuster (New York, NY), 2000.

What Moms Can't Do, illustrated by Doug Cushman, Simon & Schuster (New York, NY), 2001.

A Quiet Place, illustrated by Dan Andreasen, Simon & Schuster (New York, NY), 2001.

What Teachers Can't Do, illustrated by Doug Cushman, Simon & Schuster (New York, NY), 2002.

OTHER

(And illustrator) *Paddle Whispers* (adult nonfiction), Pfeifer-Hamilton (Duluth, MN), 1993.

Minnesota, Naturally (adult nonfiction), Voyageur Press (Stillwater, MN), 1995.

Minnesota: The Spirit of the Land, Voyageur Press (Stillwater, MN), 1995.

(And illustrator) *Fawn Island,* University of Minnesota Press (Minneapolis, MN), 2001.

Has also recorded albums, including *Solitary Shores,* EarthSong, 1980; *EarthSong,* NorthWord Press, 1985; *Northwoods Nights,* EarthSong, 1986; and *Wilderness Daydreams,* Pfeifer-Hamilton, 1988. Contributor to *NorthWriters,* University of Minnesota Press, 1991, a book of naturalist essays; contributor of numerous articles on wilderness and naturalist topics to magazines.

Sidelights

Douglas Wood became an overnight sensation in the world of children's books with the 1992 publication of *Old Turtle,* "a New Age fable," as Shirley Wilton described it in *School Library Journal.* A first-time author published by a small regional house, Wood broke all the publishing rules with this gently didactic book that reminds readers of the unity of all living things: from a modest first printing of seven thousand copies that sold out in a few weeks in Minnesota, the book continued to have strong local sales. Finally, Wood—a folk singer, wilderness guide, and naturalist—set out on a forty-two-city, nationwide promotional tour. The book has since sold over three hundred thousand copies and has received prestigious awards, including the American Booksellers Association Book of the Year.

Nobody was more surprised by this success than Wood himself. "I never set out to write a children's book," Wood told *SATA* in an interview. "And I sure never thought that it would touch so many people across the nation and the world. Clearly there is a resonance at work—it reaches both adults and children." Part of that resonance comes from the text itself, which is deceptively simple, like good song lyrics. Wood, who has been writing and performing music for years, is no amateur in this area. "My whole family is involved in music," he said. "My parents were both music instructors at the college level, and my two brothers are professional musicians. [In my family,] music was kind of like breathing." Trained in the piano and violin, Wood did not start playing guitar until he graduated from high school. "My father got me my first guitar," Wood recalled. "For him, loving classical music as he does, it was a symbolic act—giving me my freedom." Wood went on to play violin and to major in music at college, but more and more he was drawn to the simple yet eloquent themes of folk music. At the same time, he was plagued by a tension between two loves. "I was always frustrated with music as a kid," Wood said, "because I didn't like to practice. I liked to be outdoors."

Music and nature are the twin themes of Wood's life. Growing up in Sioux City, Iowa, the summers he spent in the north woods of Minnesota became synonymous with the outdoors. "There were some wild places near Sioux City," Wood recalled in his interview. "There was fishing and hunting, but it was Minnesota that really held me. I knew from age seven that I would live there some day." That day came in 1975 when, fresh out of college and after a stint as a music teacher in Iowa, Wood and his wife moved north. Another couple of years of teaching convinced Wood that he wanted to do something else with his life.

At age twenty-five, while teaching in Minnesota, Wood was introduced to the naturalist writings of the Minnesotan Sigurd Olson. "A student of mine saw all the outdoor pictures I had on the walls of my office and said that I must like to read Olson. I'd never heard of him, so I checked some [books] out of the library and then forgot about them. But soon after I came down with a really horrible case of the flu, so bad I couldn't even read, so I had my wife read to me from Olson's books, and it changed my life. I heard a voice that had been inside me all the time; there was somebody else out there who felt the way I did about nature and could put it down in words. I wrote to Olson and told him how much his books meant to me, and he actually wrote back and commended me on my own writing. I had never looked at myself as a writer before that point."

It was a turning point in Wood's life. He saw how he might blend his twin loves of nature and music, writing songs about nature. He began reading all the greats of nature writing—Henry David Thoreau, John Muir, Rachel Carson, Ralph Waldo Emerson—and putting his own thoughts to music. He also became involved in wilderness guiding, taking workshops at the Northwoods Audubon Center near his home in St. Cloud and eventually graduating to wilderness guide himself. Meanwhile, there was still a living to be earned, though he decided that he could make enough money performing his music instead of teaching. "But it wasn't all that easy," he recalled for *SATA*. "The first seven years were pretty awful, but my wife was very supportive, and we persevered together. I had this vision of making wilderness music, and here I was performing covers in smoky bars. I remember one night walking out of a bar after a gig, and I told myself that would be the last bar I ever played in."

Wood began playing more concerts, performing his own folk music, a soft and gentle blend of guitar and baritone voice. He also began publishing cassettes and albums, on both his own EarthSong label and for others: inspirational reminders of how connected humans are to the natural world and how it is the responsibility of all people—not just the younger generation—to turn the environment around. More and more the twin aspects of Wood's creative life were fusing. He began writing reflective nature essays for outdoor magazines, initiated a nature program, "Wood's Lore," on a local radio station, and also participated in artist-in-residence programs in the Minnesota public schools.

It was during one such public school stint that Wood was inspired to write *Old Turtle*. "I'd been working all day with these kids, with their energy and love for creativity, and I was driving back to my parents' home, where I was visiting. Suddenly the idea for *Old Turtle* popped into my mind all of a piece. I knew exactly what I wanted to say, exactly where the story would take me. I got to my parents' house, said 'Hi,' and went upstairs and set to work. In a half an hour I had the basic text of what became *Old Turtle*. It took another couple of months to keep polishing and polishing, to turn every word into glass so that meaning could shine through clearly." Wood still didn't know what to do with the piece and showed it to his publishers at Pfeifer-Hamilton, who had been working on inspirational tapes with Wood. "They saw that it was a children's book," Wood

In Douglas Wood's retelling of a Cree legend, the trickster-hero Rabbit convinces the crane to fly him up to the sky in an attempt to reach the moon. (From Rabbit and the Moon, *illustrated by Leslie Baker.*)

said in his interview, "and then they got hold of Cheng-Khee Chee to do the art work. *Old Turtle* was born. The rest is history."

Essentially a teaching book in the manner of Sufi or other religious texts, *Old Turtle* blends Wood's subtle word play with Chee's lush watercolors to create a message of love for one another and for the natural world. The very image of a turtle is resonant of mythic symbols for wisdom and nature: from Aesop's wise tortoise to Turtle Island, the Native American name for the North American continent. Publication of the book soon drew national attention. "Its message of saving the Earth is told in lyrical prose and pictures that delight the eye," Wilton wrote in her *School Library Journal* review. A *Publishers Weekly* critic commented on the "lilting cadence of the poetic text" that helped produce an "enchanting book." And Merry Mattson, writing in *Wilson Library Bulletin*, called *Old Turtle* a "marvelous fable," that deals with the concept of God, our planet Earth, and the "interconnectedness" of all creatures.

Set in a time when all living and inanimate things could communicate, *Old Turtle* tells of the discord caused by an argument over the forms that God takes—over knowing who or what God is. A cacophony ensues, which Old Turtle stops with sage words: "God is indeed deep. . . ./He is swift and free as the wind. . . ./She is the life of the world. . . ./God is all that we dream of. . . ./God is." To remind the world of God's presence, humans are sent to Earth, but they soon forget the message of love that they themselves are meant to convey and begin to destroy the Earth. Old Turtle once again has to remind all creatures "to see God in one another and in the beauty of all the Earth."

Wood was careful to balance the gender of God, sometimes referring to God as "He" and other times as "She." This was a factor noted by more than one reviewer, as well as the non-sectarian aspect of this God. "It's a surprise to me," Wood commented to *SATA,* "that the book is used in so many schools, mentioning God as it does. But this is a God for many people. Not Catholic or Protestant or Buddhist. This is not something I find myself doing much, talking about God. I even say it of Old Turtle in the book: 'Old Turtle hardly ever said anything, and certainly never argued about God.' But the message of love for one another and for the Earth grows out of this argument over what and where God is." In an interview with Lynne Heffley published in the *Los Angeles Times,* Wood expanded on this idea of the universality of God: Whether the life force is called God or "Yahweh or Allah or Gitche Manito, Wakan Tanka or Tao, it's the concept that matters, in trying to understand what it means to be human and how we live on the Earth." And most important, as Wood told *SATA,* "I

A young boy loses his ability to pray after his beloved grandfather's death, but he rediscovers his faith when he visits the forest where Grandad first explained the meaning of prayer. (From Grandad's Prayers of the Earth, *written by Wood and illustrated by P. J. Lynch.)*

tried not to be preachy or heavy-handed in the message. I think if you present people with a gentle reminder, they'll take it from there." Julie Corsaro, writing in *Booklist,* similarly felt that Wood's environmental message was "delivered with a light, graceful touch."

The success of *Old Turtle* has allowed Wood to focus more on his writing, though he has not given up his other varied activities. "Actually," Wood said in his *SATA* interview, "I'm still juggling the different aspects of my life: guiding, performing, doing school programs and speaking engagements, touring the bookshops. Part of me would like to have the genteel author's life, but I'm also restless enough to like the ebb and flow of all aspects of my life." Wood followed up his first book with *Paddle Whispers,* an adult book of reflections on nature and humanity's part in it. Written and illustrated by Wood, the book records a metaphoric canoe voyage that mirrors one's own journey through life.

Since the success of *Old Turtle,* Wood has established himself as a unique voice in children's literature, particularly in his adaptations of Native American folktales. In *The Windigo Returns* an Ojibwe tribe notices that some of their people are missing, and the terrifying Windigo is blamed. A pit is dug, and when the Windigo is tricked into falling in it, the monster is set on fire, where his dying threat of coming back to eat the tribe and all succeeding generations is considered to come true the next summer in the stinging bite of the mosquito. "The changing seasons flow through this story like a slow river, linking the plot to nature's calendar," remarked a contributor to *Kirkus Reviews.* Karen Morgan, writing in *Booklist,* considered Wood's attempt to blend horror and humor utterly successful as the ashes of the monster are transformed into the ubiquitous and annoying mosquito. Wood offers "a blending of humor and spookiness that children will surely love," Morgan concluded.

Northwoods Cradle Song is an adaptation of a Menominee lullaby and features a Native American woman rocking her child and pointing out the ways in which the creatures of the natural world are preparing to go to sleep too. "The tender tone and quiet, respectful references to nature beautifully convey the timeless sense of night and lullaby," remarked Margaret A. Bush in *Horn Book.* Others highlighted the lyricism of Wood's adaptation. "Wood has crafted an image-rich, eminently musical lullaby," concluded a contributor to *Publishers Weekly.* The author's next book, *Rabbit and the Moon,* is another Native American folktale which, like *The Windigo Returns,* contains a *pourquoi* element. Rabbit wishes he could ride on the moon and convinces the crane to fly him up to the sky, holding onto the bird's legs so tightly that they bleed, and patting the bird in thanks upon his arrival, thus giving the crane its distinctive red legs and crown.

Like *Old Turtle,* the message of Wood's *Making the World* drives the story, as artist and author journey from continent to continent, observing how the world is continually altered by its interactions with wind and sun, animals and humans. "This ambitious, philosophical picture book, with its lyrical, simple prose, attempts to show how everything and everyone has a significant effect upon life and the landscape," Shelle Rosenfeld observed in *Booklist*. For Diane Nunn, writing in *School Library Journal*, the collaboration between illustration and text in *Making the World* "broadens a young child's awareness of our planet, its beauty, and everyone's ability to affect change."

Wood tests the capacity of the picture book genre yet again in *Grandad's Prayers of the Earth*, in which a young boy asks his father about prayer and receives an answer that encompasses all the creatures on earth. When the grandfather dies, the boy loses his ability to pray for a long time, until one day, when he returns to the forest where Grandad had first explained it to him. "This is a depiction of the spiritual that is without reference to a particular faith or tradition, and that doesn't lapse into greeting-card platitudes," observed a contributor to *Kirkus Reviews*. By centering the story on the loving relationship between a grandson and his grandfather, and through extensive use of tangible metaphors, Wood makes "a difficult religious concept somewhat more concrete for children," remarked a contributor to *Publishers Weekly*. Likewise, Shelley Townsend-Hudson, writing in *Booklist*, concluded that "Wood presents the subjects of prayer and death in a way that stirs the imagination and offers hope."

Wood is also the author of two well-loved, humorous picture books featuring dinosaurs as main characters. In *What Dads Can't Do* and *What Moms Can't Do*, a young dinosaur narrator recounts the many things his parents cannot seem to get right without his help, from picking out clothes to sleeping in on Saturday morning. At the end of each book, however, the young dinosaur allows that one thing parents always know how to do is love their children. "This amusing picture book will tickle youngsters' funny bones and make every parent and child smile with recognition," predicted Wanda Meyers-Hines in a review of *What Dads Can't Do* for *School Library Journal*.

"I love writing for children," Wood once told *SATA*. "It is clearly different than writing for adults, which is not to say that one is less important. It's the focus I take that is different. I write for children in a pure way. It's idea-oriented, and my number one priority is to find one good and meaningful idea. In that way, it's not so different than writing a good song. All my years spent song writing prepared me very well for writing children's books. That experience enabled me to hear and listen for the rhythm of a sentence. I'll spend two hours on a sentence getting the rhythm right. I'm always using my ear when I write."

As for the effect he hopes his work makes on his readers, Wood is very clear. "I came to a decision long ago that I was not going to be topical or political in my work. And I am not a scientist. What I am is a poet. I want to try to capture in my words and music the meanings of nature. And if by those words and that music I can help

someone else fall in love with the Earth, then I've done my job, because they will find a way to become connected in it and to help re-establish a connectedness with others. To me, the natural world is inside us all as well as outside. We're all a part of one big thing called nature, and when we forget that, that's when bad things happen."

Biographical and Critical Sources

BOOKS

Wood, Douglas, *Old Turtle*, illustrated by Cheng-Khee Chee, Pfeifer-Hamilton (Duluth, MN), 1992.

PERIODICALS

Audubon, November-December, 2001, Christopher Camuto, review of *Grandad's Prayers of the Earth*, p. 86.
Bloomsbury Review, December, 1991, p. 19.
Booklist, August, 1992, Julie Corsaro, review of *Old Turtle*, p. 2016; September 15, 1996, Karen Morgan, review of *The Windigo's Return*, p. 235; February 15, 1998, Elizabeth Drennan, review of *Rabbit and the Moon*, p. 1016; July, 1998, Shelle Rosenfeld, review of *Making the World*, p. 1892; December 1, 1999, Shelley Townsend-Hudson, review of *Grandad's Prayers of the Earth*, p. 715; April 15, 2001, Amy Brandt, review of *What Moms Can't Do*, p. 1567; February 15, 2002, Hazel Rochman, review of *A Quiet Place*, p. 1023.
Bulletin of the Center for Children's Books, November, 1996, Betsy Hearne, review of *The Windigo's Return*, p. 112.
Horn Book, May-June, 1996, Margaret A. Bush, review of *Northwood's Cradle Song*, p. 331.
Horn Book Guide, fall, 1998, Debbie A. Reese, review of *Rabbit and the Moon*, p. 368; spring, 1999, Martha Sibert, review of *Making the World*, p. 49.
Kirkus Reviews, December 1, 1991, p. 1541; July 15, 1996, review of *The Windigo's Return*, pp. 1057-1058; January 15, 1998, review of *Rabbit and the Moon*, p. 120; November 1, 1999, review of *Grandad's Prayers of the Earth*, p. 1750.
Los Angeles Times, August 29, 1992, Lynne Heffley, "Naturalist Sings, Writes of Love of Earth," pp. F5, F7.
Publishers Weekly, January 1, 1992, review of *Old Turtle*, p. 55; February 26, 1996, review of *Old Turtle* (audio cassette), p. 43; April 15, 1996, review of *North Woods Cradle Song*, p. 67; September 16, 1996, review of *The Windigo's Return*, p. 82; February 23, 1998, review of *Rabbit and the Moon*, p. 75; August 10, 1998, review of *Making the World*, p. 386; September 27, 1999, review of *Grandad's Prayers of the Earth*, p. 97; May 15, 2000, review of *What Dads Can't Do*, p. 115; July 2, 2001, review of *Rabbit and the Moon*, p. 78; February 4, 2002, review of *A Quiet Place*, p. 75.
School Library Journal, June, 1992, Shirley Wilton, review of *Old Turtle*, p. 105; May, 1996, Ruth K. MacDonald, review of *Northwoods Cradle Song*, p. 109; November, 1996, Ellen Fader, review of *The Windigo's Return*, p. 102; April, 1997, review of *Old Turtle* (audio cassette), p. 41; July, 1998, Adele Greenlee,

review of *Rabbit and the Moon,* p. 91; August, 1998, Diane Nunn, review of *Making the World,* pp. 147-148; January, 2000, Patricia Pearl Dole, review of *Grandad's Prayers of the Earth,* p. 114; May, 2000, Wanda Meyers-Hines, review of *What Dads Can't Do,* p. 159; March, 2001, Sally R. Dow, review of *What Moms Can't Do,* p. 224.

Voice of Youth Advocates, April, 1992, p. 38.

Wilson Library Bulletin, December, 1993, Merry Mattson, review of *Old Turtle,* p. 31.

OTHER

Douglas Wood Web Site, http://www.douglaswood.com (June 8, 2002).

Wood, Douglas, telephone interview with J. Sydney Jones for *Something about the Author,* conducted September 6, 1994.*

Y

YOUNG, Jeff C. 1948-

Personal

Born March 24, 1948, in Orangeburg, South Carolina; son of Clair (an industrial engineer) and Charlotte (a secretary; maiden name, Hanna) Young; *Ethnicity:* "German." *Education:* Ball State University, B.S., 1971; University of South Florida, M.A., 1989. *Politics:* Democrat. *Religion:* Protestant. *Hobbies and other interests:* Sports, traveling, U.S. history.

Addresses

Home—P.O. Box 176, Lake Hamilton, FL 33851. *E-mail*—jcyauth@mindspring.com.

Career

The Ledger, Lakeland, FL, news clerk/sports correspondent, 1985-86; *Avon Park Sun,* Avon Park, FL, sports editor, 1986-87; Department of Corrections, Tallahassee, FL, prison librarian, 1989-91, 1993; Enid Baa Library, St. Thomas, U.S. Virgin Islands, librarian, 1991-92; Montverde Academy, Montverde, FL, media specialist, 1993-95; Polk County School Board, Bartow, FL, media specialist, 1995-2001; Keiser College, Lakeland, FL, librarian, 2001—.

Member

Society of Children's Book Writers and Illustrators.

Writings

The Fathers of American Presidents: From Augustine Washington to William Blythe and Roger Clinton, McFarland (Jefferson, NC), 1997.
Top 10 Basketball Shot-Blockers, Enslow Publishers (Springfield, NJ), 2000.
Top 10 World Series MVPs, Enslow Publishers (Berkeley Heights, NJ), 2001.

Jeff C. Young

Dwight D. Eisenhower: Soldier and President, Morgan Reynolds (Greensboro, NC), 2001.
Benjamin Harrison, MyReportLinks.com Books (Berkeley Heights, NJ), 2002.
Chester A. Arthur, MyReportLinks.com Books (Berkeley Heights, NJ), 2002.
Franklin Pierce, MyReportLinks.com Books (Berkeley Heights, NJ), 2002.
James Buchanan, MyReportLinks.com Books (Berkeley Heights, NJ), 2003.
James Garfield, MyReportLinks.com Books (Berkeley Heights, NJ), 2003.

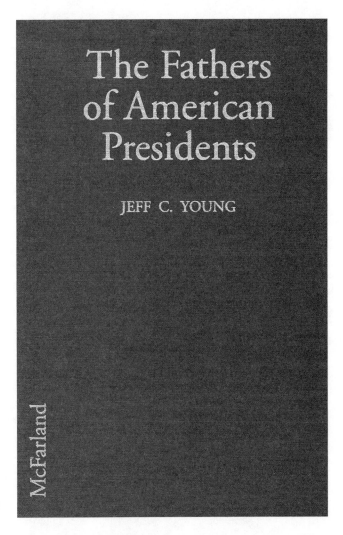

In his study of the Presidents and their fathers, Young discusses the ways in which the fathers and sons had similar personalities and how the father's views influenced the son.

Contributor of sports articles to Florida newspapers, including *St. Petersburg Times, Tampa Tribune,* and *Citrus County Chronicle.* Contributor to magazines, including *Black Collegian, Vegetarian Times,* and *Southern RV.*

Work in Progress

Juvenile biographies of Ronald Reagan and Grover Cleveland; "a book of baseball scandals and tragedies in the twentieth century."

Sidelights

"As a child," Jeff C. Young told *SATA,* "my favorite books were biographies, sports books, and books about U.S. history." Therefore it is not surprising that Young should grow up to write sports stories and books as well as biographies of American presidents. In fact, his first book was about some of the most important people in the presidents' lives: their fathers. "My first book, *The Fathers of American Presidents,* started out as an idea for a magazine article. I planned to write an article on George Washington's father, Augustine," Young recalled. "Later, I checked *Books in Print* and found that no book had ever been written on the subject of presidential fathers. I began researching all the father's lives and sent three sample chapters to McFarland, which resulted in a book contract." In *The Fathers of American Presidents: From Augustine Washington to William Blythe and Roger Clinton,* Young discussed the ways in which the fathers and sons had similar personalities, the role of the father's personality on the development of his son, and the ways the father's views influenced the son.

Young's advice to aspiring writers is to "simply persevere." "Be prepared to face a lot of rejection, but don't let it discourage you," he told *SATA.* "It's something every writer goes through while learning the craft. Read as much as you can and write something every day."

Biographical and Critical Sources

PERIODICALS

Booklist, November 15, 2001, Roger Leslie, review of *Dwight D. Eisenhower: Soldier and President,* p. 564.
Children's Bookwatch, January, 2002, review of *Dwight D. Eisenhower,* p. 7.
Reference and Research Book News, May, 1997, review of *The Fathers of American Presidents: From Augustine Washington to William Blythe and Roger Clinton,* p. 33.
School Library Journal, February, 2002, Marilyn Heath, review of *Dwight D. Eisenhower,* p. 152.